Evidence Problems and Materials
Fifth Edition

Evidence Problems and Materials

Fifth Edition

Steven I. Friedland
Professor of Law and Senior Scholar
Elon University School of Law

John P. Sahl
Professor of Law, Faculty Director of The Joseph G. Miller and William C. Becker
Center for Professional Responsibility
The University of Akron School of Law

ISBN: 978–1–6328–3392–1

Library of Congress Cataloging-in-Publication Data

Names: Friedland, Steven I., author. I Saul, John P., author.
Title: Evidence Problems and Materials / Steven I. Freidland, John P. Sahl
Description: Fifth Edition I New Providence, NJ: LexisNexis, 2015
Identifiers: LCCN 2015041427 (print) I LCCN 2015041599 (ebook) I ISBN 9781632833921 (softbound) I ISBN 9781632833938 (epub)
Subjects: Evidence (Law)--United States. I LCGFT: Casebooks
Classification: LCC KF8935.F754 2015 (print) I LCC KF8935 (ebook) I DDC 345.73/06--dc23
LC record available at http://lccn.loc.gov/2015041427

NOTE TO USERS

To ensure that you are using the latest materials available in this area, please be sure to periodically check the LexisNexis Law School web site for downloadable updates and supplements at www.lexisnexis.com/lawschool.

Editorial Offices
630 Central Ave., New Providence, NJ 07974 (908) 464-6800
201 Mission St., San Francisco, CA 94105-1831 (415) 908-3200
www.lexisnexis.com

MATTHEW◆BENDER

Dedication

In loving memory of my uncle, Bernard Friedland.

For my parents, Geraldine and George, my wife, Joann, and our children, Mandakini and Anish — for making every day special!

Preface

Assigning a label to this book is difficult primarily because it is not a traditional law school text. To call it a "casebook," one that revolves around evidence decisions, would be in error. In fact, appellate case reports comprise only a small fraction of the book's contents. Yet, the book is not a "problem" book either. While the "problem" label is certainly more accurate, such a label usually indicates a status as a course supplement. This book, however, is intended to serve as more than a supplemental source of problems; it also can be used in conjunction with the pertinent federal or state rules of evidence and their associated legislative history as an all-purpose guide to the law of evidence.

The conceptualization of the book as an evidence text is derived from one of the book's premises: understanding the rules of evidence can occur effectively and directly through applied learning methods such as problem-solving. The book is predicated on the belief that an understanding of evidence law will be promoted if the reader actively participates in the learning process. The delivery of information to the learner is only a part of that process.

Thus, in light of the book's premises, case reports are not the "text" of this textbook. Rather than presenting an orderly recitation of cases followed by questions, this book inverts, and then expands on, a traditional casebook ordering. The book is structured so that each section commences with brief explanatory comments about a particular area of evidence law, including an illustration of the subject matter. It then proceeds with a wide variety of problems intended to test the reader's understanding of the evidentiary rules and their intended meaning. (The problems are primarily designed to be answered using the Federal Rules of Evidence and the associated Advisory Committee's Notes. The text is sufficiently generic, however, to allow the use of applicable state evidentiary rules as well.) Immediately prior to the conclusion of each section, cases and other statutes are presented for comparative purposes. Since "muscle memory" requires that knowledge be imprinted, each section concludes with a summary and review.

To further promote the learning process, an attempt is made to "thicken" the problems with real world contexts that often confront trial lawyers. These contexts include: (1) the courtroom (some problems are presented in transcript form); (2) lawyering skills (some areas of the book include a discussion of skills, such as qualifying an expert, distinguishing and comparing statutes, and conducting a cross-examination of a witness); and (3) the inclusion of identifying characteristics that may significantly affect evidentiary rulings, such as race, gender, sexual preference, and ethnicity (some problems seek to discern the relevance of these characteristics by probing the values and ideology underlying the evidentiary analysis).

The inclusion of these contexts is intended not only to make the book more useful to integrating the rules with lawyering skills, but also to place legal analysis where many commentators argue that it belongs — within the social sciences. By recognizing the significance of social science contexts, readers may observe a closer connection between the application of the evidence rules and the experiences of everyday life.

We also broke with tradition by melding Evidence and Ethics — adding the ethical implications of evidentiary issues that often arise in every chapter. While the legal education agenda is stocked with concerns about incorporating skills into the curriculum in addition to

Preface

legal analysis, the discussion of professionalism is still an important and primary topic. By weaving evidence and ethics together, we offer a more realistic approach — the two often arise together in the real world, after all — and allow students to better understand the larger picture of practice, where legal issues are often a mosaic. This approach reflects some of the recommendations contained in two major reports examining legal education — Educating Lawyers by the Carnegie Foundation and Best Practices for Legal Education by the Clinical Legal Education Association.

Of course, the ethics components are such that they can be treated as supplemental issues or bypassed completely, if desired. The primary focal points of this book remain evidence law and its application, and we took care not to let the ethics problems overshadow or obscure the evidence questions.

This edition also includes new "practical tips" and "background boxes" material that help students apply the rules. Another feature is the outline at the beginning of each chapter to help students organize and synthesize the rules and related material.

If the primary learning mechanism used in the book is problem solving, the primary context within which the problem solving occurs is the courtroom. A courtroom orientation offers several pedagogical advantages. The courtroom setting facilitates role playing and encourages simulations and active participation. Role playing, in turn, allows students to consider different perspectives and to focus on how to persuade others to adopt those perspectives. In reenacting the courtroom "drama," the students also engage in a narrative discourse. Studies have found that the narrative is an effective learning tool. Additionally, the courtroom context elevates the significance of issues relating to fact determination. The determination of fact, so important to the resolution of trials and cases, is all too often minimized in the legal education process. By using the courtroom setting, fact determination issues can be studied directly.

In addition, the courtroom backdrop allows lawyering skills to be woven into the basic fabric of the evidence course. The inclusion of lawyering skills provides a view of the "big picture" of evidence law as it is applied. Skills training also permits instructors to provide a broader critique of students, including feedback on courtroom performance as well as on the students' understanding of the evidence rules.

By incorporating identifying characteristics in the problems such as race, ethnicity, gender, religion, sexual preference, and other socio-economic factors, the book seeks to highlight the relevance of these factors to evidentiary determinations. In particular, these factors suggest that evidentiary determinations often depend on interpretive theories of human behavior. These theories may be sufficiently important to consider and discuss in class.

The book breaks with tradition in one other way. There are occasional illustrations accompanying the problems. The reason for this inclusion is simple — people learn differently, and visual imagery can be as important as a multiplicity of words. As many trial attorneys who regularly use photographs, charts, and diagrams will attest, a single picture can greatly promote and enhance the audience's attention.

We hope that you have as much fun in puzzling over the problems and in sorting out the values and ideology upon which the conclusions rest as we have had in putting the book together. We further hope you find that the book facilitates an understanding of the evidence rules and their constitutive framework, as well as synthesizes a broader perspective of how

Preface

the rules relate to lawyering, legal theory, and human nature.

As with most books, this one was the product of the diligent work of people too numerous to mention. We would, however, like to acknowledge and thank our families and close friends for their unconditional support and Kevin Day, Ragan Riddle, Talia Nowicki, and Marian Kousaie for their research assistance.

Steven I. Friedland
Elon University School of Law
August 2015

Jack Sahl
University of Akron School of Law
August 2015

Table of Contents

Table of Contents

Table of Contents

Table of Contents

Table of Contents

Table of Contents

Table of Contents

Table of Contents

Table of Contents

Table of Contents

Chapter 1

INTRODUCTION TO EVIDENCE

CHAPTER FRAMEWORK: Evidence generally is associated with the litigation process. This process includes preliminary stages prior to the formal filing of suit, the pre-trial process, trial, and then post-trial issues and appeal. While the actual use of evidence most often occurs at trial, it is important to understand the place of evidence within the entire process. Within the trial process, there are distinct stages as well, from *voir dire*, or jury selection, to opening statements, to the offering of evidence, to closing arguments. Evidence can be offered in each party's case-in-chief or in the parties' rebuttal cases. There are certain formats and accepted methods for offering evidence, such as witness testimony or the offer of real or representative evidence.

WHY ARE THE CONCEPTS IN THIS CHAPTER IMPORTANT? Evidence is used to prove the elements of a claim, cause of action, or defense. Evidence is the backbone of our system, which relies on proof (proper evidence) for convictions and verdicts in a party's favor. Thus, evidence determines who wins and loses lawsuits. Evidence generally is the currency used to prove the elements of a case. If a party has the burden of production or the burden of persuasion, it must offer some evidence. If a party does not have any burden, it will win if no evidence is offered, even in the event of a "tie."

In addition to understanding the role of evidence in the larger context of the legal system, understanding what the word *evidence* means is an important predicate to tackling the rules relating to the use of evidence. The word "evidence" is essentially a term of art (having special significance in the law) with different meanings. When the different meanings of the term are laid out, that becomes the first step in understanding what the Federal Rules of Evidence (FRE) and associated state codes are attempting to accomplish in creating their evidentiary frameworks.

CONNECTIONS: Evidence has a close relationship with trial advocacy, since the available *evidence* shapes trial strategy and, conversely, evidentiary issues generally occur within the vessel of a trial or hearing. Evidence also relates to business law, since all attorneys should keep one eye on what might happen if litigation should arise.

CHAPTER OUTLINE:

    I. What Are the Meanings of the Term "Evidence?"

        A. Proof

        B. Only proof properly admitted for consideration by the trier of fact

        C. The rules governing the admission of evidence

    II. What Is the Lawsuit Process?

A.Filing and charging — starting the action
    1.Criminal
        a.Indictments (by grand juries)
        b.Informations (by prosecutors)
    2.Civil
        a.Well-pleaded complaints
        b.Answers
B.Pre-trial
    1.Motions
        a.To dismiss
        b.For extensions of time
        c.For summary judgment
        d.For change of venue
        e.For recusal of the judge
    2.Discovery
    3.Negotiating
        a.Plea bargaining
        b.Settlements
C.Trial
    1.Voir Dire ("to tell the truth")
    2.Opening statements
    3.Case-in-chief
    4.Rebuttal cases
    5.Closing arguments
D.Post-trial
    1.Motions
    2.Release (criminal)
E.An Illustrative Lawsuit: *United States v. Wayne Gillis*
III.Types of Evidence
A.Real, representative, or testimonial
B.Direct or circumstantial

RELEVANT EVIDENCE RULES

FRE 101. Scope; Definitions

(a) **Scope.** These rules apply to proceedings in United States courts. The specific courts and proceedings, to which the rules apply, along with exceptions, are set out in FRE 1011.

(b) **Definitions.** In these rules:

(1) "civil case" means a civil action or proceeding;

(2) "criminal case" includes a criminal proceeding;

(3) "public office" includes a public agency;

(4) "record" includes a memorandum, report, or data compilation;

(5) a "rule prescribed by the Supreme Court" means a rule adopted by the Supreme Court under statutory authority

(6) a reference to any kind of written material or any other medium includes electronically stored information.

FRE 102. Purpose

These rules should be construed so as to administer every proceeding fairly, eliminate unjustifiable expense and delay, and promote the development of evidence law, to the end of ascertaining the truth and securing a just determination.

§ 1.01   THE MEANINGS AND USES OF EVIDENCE

The term *evidence* is given special meaning by the Federal Rules of Evidence (FRE) and associated state codes. Instead of just meaning "the proof" or "the stuff" relating to an incident or event, it takes on greater significance to mean "the admissible proof" or "the proof that can be properly considered by the trier of fact." The FRE provide a structure for deciding what qualifies as admissible evidence and what does not.

Evidence is generally offered at trial to prove a party's case, meaning the elements of that party's claim, cause of action, or defense. For example, in an armed robbery case, the prosecution will offer evidence that a robbery took place in that particular jurisdiction, that the perpetrator was armed, and that the defendant was the perpetrator. Evidence can be offered for other purposes as well, particularly the credibility of witnesses. When offered for this purpose, the evidence generally is offered to attack a witness's truthfulness or accuracy. Some evidence has the dual function of attacking a witness's truthfulness and proving an element of the case.

Simply because a party offers evidence relating to an element does not mean that party will prevail. The trier of fact — often a jury — must have confidence in the reliability and accuracy of the evidence and weigh its value. In this broader sense, the evidence is used to paint a picture of a prior event, person, or thing and to persuade the trier of fact that the picture is an accurate one. Evidence offered to impeach a witness illustrates an attempt to colorize how the trier of fact views and weighs that witness's testimony.

Not all evidence a party might offer will be admitted for consideration by the trier of fact. Some evidence, deemed irrelevant, is not useful to the jury's determination of the issues in the case. Other evidence may be useful, but countervailing considerations, such as unfair prejudice, warrant its exclusion. Still other evidence may be useful and not harmful, but might still be excluded for independent policy reasons. For example, these policies sometimes create privileges that exclude confidential communications between attorney and client, clergy and penitent, or spouses.

§ 1.02 THE RULES OF EVIDENCE

[A] History

The Federal Rules of Evidence (FRE) did not take effect until 1975, after President Gerald Ford signed them into law. Prior to that time, the federal common law supplied the rules governing the admissibility of evidence in federal cases. While earlier efforts had been made to codify the law of evidence, the impetus necessary to adopt such significant legislation was lacking.

States have adopted their own codes of evidence, some in special free-standing statutes and others with rules integrated into various areas of substantive law. Many of the state codes have been patterned after the FRE.

The federal rules have not remained static since their adoption. In the 1990s and early 2000s, several modifications were made to the existing rules, such as the addition of a notice requirement to FRE 404(b) (the provision permitting evidence of other crimes, wrongs or acts), the extension of the applicability of FRE 407, Subsequent Remedial Measures, to cases involving strict products liability, clarification of the uses of convictions to impeach in FRE 609(a), and the expansion of FRE 412 (dealing with the sexual history of a sex crime victim) to civil cases. New rules were added, including FRE 413–415, which concern the use of other offenses in cases involving sexual assault or molestation. Some changes were procedural or intended to provide greater clarity, such as the substitution in 2006 in FRE 608(b) of the term "character for truthfulness" for the word "credibility." Other changes were substantive, such as the December 2000 addition to FRE 404, "If evidence of a trait of character of the crime is offered by an accused and admitted under FRE 404(a)(2), evidence of the same trait of character of the accused [may be] offered by the prosecution." In a major undertaking that became effective December 1, 2011, the FRE were restyled to be more "easily understood and to make style and terminology consistent throughout." *See* FRE 101 Restyled Rules Committee Note. Significantly, these were only stylistic changes and not intended to change any ruling on evidence admissibility. *Id.*

The adoption of the original FRE was neither sudden nor simple. In 1965, Chief Justice Earl Warren appointed an Advisory Committee to draw up evidence rules for the federal courts. The Committee's proposal was considered by the Supreme Court and in 1972 sent to Congress for its approval. It was intended to go into effect in July of 1973. Instead, Congress further shaped and refined the rules, and adopted them in this modified form. They became effective July 1, 1975.

Various sources of legislative history assist users in understanding the FRE. The Advisory Committee, for example, created Notes to each provision to explain and support the rule. When the House Committee on the Judiciary and the Senate Committee on the Judiciary made their own changes to the proposed rules, they also created explanatory notes. Further, when the modifications of the House and Senate committees conflicted, a Conference Report reflected the Conference Committee's resolution. The legislative history of a given rule is instructive both to the novice reader and courts assigned the difficult job of interpreting a subtlety in the law.

[B]   The Objectives of the Rules

The FRE can be understood to promote several goals, including uniformity, fairness, and efficiency. In light of these policies, not all evidence is admissible. The FRE limit what may be admitted and what a jury may consider during its deliberations. The FRE promote fairness by providing an equal playing field for the parties in the courtroom. If an accused introduces character evidence under FRE 404(a), the prosecution is allowed to rebut it; if a party introduces part of writing, the opponent is permitted to introduce its remainder. *See* FRE 106. Some of the Federal Rules seek greater efficiency in the trial process. Efficiency is promoted by excluding evidence that is irrelevant, evidence that might cause unfair prejudice, and evidence such as subsequent remedial measures, offers to compromise, offers to pay medical expenses, plea bargaining, liability insurance, and, in proceedings involving alleged sexual misconduct, the victim's past sexual behavior or sexual predisposition. The FRE advance uniformity by telling judges what types of convictions can be used to impeach a witness (FRE 609) and when character evidence is permissible (FRE 404 and 405).

The various policies that inform the evidence rules can sometimes clash. Should a privilege be applied to exclude important relevant evidence? Does "other acts" evidence unfairly prejudice the jury? Do limiting jury instructions really limit prejudice? These questions can only be answered based on logic and experience. Ironically, the clashes reveal what experienced observers of the judicial system have known for a long time — there are often no absolutely correct answers as to whether evidence is admissible; it depends on the context of the offer. Important factors may include other evidence in the case, the nature of the case, and the people involved in the offer and decision. That is why viewing evidence law as an exact science, with "rights and wrongs," often fundamentally misconceives the subject matter; the rules give the judge considerable discretion in many admissibility decisions.

§ 1.03   EVIDENCE IN ACTION

The law of evidence does not occur in a vacuum. More than any other subject, evidence depends on context. The initial context is in anticipation of litigation. The second context is litigation and pre-trial, which then only occasionally stretches to an actual trial. Lastly, some evidentiary rulings are challenged on appeal.

Appellate courts rule on a wide variety of evidentiary issues. Even so, the primary locus for evidentiary questions lies in the trial courts. Evidentiary issues arise throughout trial, and the numerous evidentiary rulings by trial courts are seldom appealed, let alone reversed on appeal. For example, an improper leading question would rarely be considered by a court on appeal or constitute a ground for reversal, if only because of its limited impact on the case. Thus, competent trial lawyers must know how to negotiate the rules to successfully bring their cases before a jury.

Transactional lawyers, who may never set foot in a courtroom (as per their desire), still must have great familiarity with the rules. While transactional attorneys provide advice to businesses on how to avoid legal problems, the attorneys also must help to prepare clients for the possibility of a lawsuit. Transactional attorneys must know how to maintain records, must preserve the evidentiary significance of documents and other business-related materials, and must know how to otherwise protect clients under the evidence rules if litigation should arise.

One way to better understand how the rules work is to situate them in the broader environment of a lawsuit. A lawsuit includes far more than the evidentiary rules; it also involves: (1) the pleadings that initiate the case and propel it forward, either to trial or to an alternative disposition such as a plea or settlement; (2) lawyering strategies and arguments; and (3) jury selection and deliberation.

An excerpt from a hypothetical case file is reprinted below to better provide a view of the "big picture" of a lawsuit — a view of evidence "in action." Consider the questions that follow the file when reviewing it.

A CRIMINAL CASE: *UNITED STATES v. WAYNE GILLIS*

The following excerpt from a narcotics prosecution is based on a real case that occurred in Washington, D.C. Many similar cases are brought on a daily basis throughout the United States. The inclusion of this case is intended to provide useful background information; it offers an opportunity to observe how evidence exists within the context of a lawsuit.

A. The Facts of the Case

The facts of the case are in dispute. The facts according to the prosecutor and defense follow.

1. The Facts According to the Prosecutor

On August 24, at approximately 2:15 p.m., Officer Friday (W-1), a Park Police officer, was traveling north on Rock Creek Parkway in Washington, D.C. As he passed by Parking Lot # 6, he observed a 1995 Green Volvo without a front tag. The officer drove up to the car, approached the driver's window, and motioned for the driver to open it. The driver, later identified as the defendant, rolled down the window several inches. W-1 smelled marijuana. W-1 then asked the defendant to get out of the car.

The defendant showed W-1 his license and registration. Defendant's license and registration were from the State of Alabama. W-1 asked the defendant whether there was any marijuana inside the car. Defendant went back into the car, pulled out the front ashtray, and brought it outside to W-1. W-1 then asked a male who was sitting in the front passenger seat (co-defendant), to get out of the car. W-1 discovered rolling papers and a package of white powder under the right front mat on the passenger side.

W-1 then conducted a complete search of the car. When W-1 took the thick seat mats off of the front seat, he observed a .22 caliber Smith & Wesson pistol wedged in the crack separating the back of the driver's seat and the driver's seat itself.

W-1 then searched defendant and co-defendant. W-1 did not find any contraband on the person of the defendant. A large quantity of a brown weed and sticks substance in a plastic bag was found on the passenger. W-1 seized all of the evidence and field-tested the powder and substance in the bag. The contents of the bag, discovered on the co-defendant, tested positive for marijuana. The package of white powder tested positive for cocaine. Defendant did not appear to be under the influence of narcotics, but the co-defendant did. Both persons were extremely cooperative. The defendant and co-defendant were read their rights. During the reading, the defendant spontaneously said, "That stuff you found in the car was not mine, but a friend's! I'm not going to say anything more without a lawyer, I can tell you that."

2. *The Facts According to the Defense*

The defendant, Wayne Gillis, is 34 years old. Wayne is not married, but resides part of the time with his girlfriend, with whom he has two children, Samantha (age three) and Chase (age five). He is employed as a long-distance trucker by Amalgamated Trucking, Inc., and is consequently out-of-town for long periods of time. On August 24th, Wayne had driven to Rock Creek Park to relax after a five-day trip to Nebraska for Amalgamated. He was accompanied by his good friend, Bob, who was sitting in the passenger's seat. Wayne routinely lets friends borrow the car while he is out-of-town, and had let his friend Jim use it during this past trip. At the park, Wayne and Bob were chatting in the car, minding their own business, when a police officer approached Wayne and tapped loudly on the window. The officer rudely asked Wayne what he was doing and then ordered him out of the car. The officer searched them and the car without permission. When the officer confronted Wayne, claiming to have found a gun and drugs in the car, Wayne told the officer that he (Wayne) knew nothing about it. Later, Wayne informed me (his attorney) that the stuff was either planted by the police or left there by his friend, Jim, who borrowed the car a couple of times before Wayne was arrested in it. Wayne did not have Jim's address or last name; Jim was a friend from the neighborhood. Wayne said that there were others in the neighborhood who could verify that Jim lived and hung out there, although Jim had not been seen lately. Wayne also stated that he had been convicted of the possession of marijuana eight years ago and disorderly conduct seven years ago. Five years ago, he was charged with conspiracy to distribute cocaine and weapons possession, but all of the charges were dropped. Wayne also thought he should mention that fifteen years ago, when he was in middle school, he had been caught taking a teacher's car for a joyride with a classmate. As a result, the boys were sent to a juvenile home for a few months.

B. The Criminal Case File

Excerpts from the defendant's criminal case file follow. When reviewing these excerpts: (1) identify the possible evidence in the case; and (2) arrange the evidence in a persuasive manner, first for the prosecution and then for the defense.

UNITED STATES v. WAYNE GILLIS
Misdemeanor # 468459-98
Washington, D.C.

1. The Information

The following is the prosecutor's charging document, called the "information." Did the prosecutor properly charge the defendant? What does the prosecutor have to prove at trial to overcome a motion for judgment of acquittal, the criminal equivalent of a directed verdict? What evidence would the prosecutor use to prove each element of the crimes?

In some criminal cases, a defendant might be guilty, just not guilty of the crimes with which he has been charged. In this sense, the defendant has been mischarged. Mischarging happens enough in criminal cases to warrant close attention from criminal defense attorneys.

CRIMINAL DIVISION

The United States Attorney for the District of Columbia informs the Court that within the District of Columbia:

DEFENDANT'S NAME	Wayne	Gillis	
	(FIRST)	(LAST)	PDID

DEFENDANT'S ADDRESS	1204 P Street N.W., Washington, D.C.

did on or about <u>August 24, 1998</u> commits the crime or crimes indicated herein and identified by an X-mark or X-marks.

POSSESSION OF A CONTROLLED SUBSTANCE — in that he unlawfully, knowingly, and intentionally had in his possession a controlled substance consisting of <u>Cocaine</u> in violation of 33 District of Columbia Code, Section 541(c).

POSSESSION OF A CONTROLLED SUBSTANCE — in that he unlawfully, knowingly, and intentionally had in his possession a controlled substance consisting of <u>Cannabis,</u> in violation of 33 District of Columbia Code, Section 541(c).

DISTRIBUTION OF A SCHEDULE V CONTROLLED SUBSTANCE — in that he unlawfully, knowingly, and intentionally did distribute a quantity of X, a Schedule V controlled substance, in violation of 33 District of Columbia Code, Section 541(a)(1).

POSSESSION WITH INTENT TO DISTRIBUTE A SCHEDULE V CON-TROLLED SUBSTANCE — in that he unlawfully, knowingly, and intentionally did possess with intent to distribute a quantity of X, a Schedule V controlled substance, in violation of 33 District of Columbia Code, Section 541(a)(1).

CARRYING PISTOL WITHOUT A LICENSE — in that he carried openly and concealed on and about his person, a Pistol without a license therefore issued as provided by Section 22-3206, District of Columbia Code, in violation of Section 22-3204, District of Columbia.

UNITED STATES ATTORNEY FOR THE DISTRICT OF
COLUMBIA
BY ASSISTANT UNITED STATES ATTORNEY
FOR THE DISTRICT OF COLUMBIA

BY: Janet Parker
DATE: 9/3/98
OFFICER: Friday
DISTRICT: Rock Creek Park, Washington, D.C.

2. The Prosecutor's Notes
Summary of Case

8/24/98-2:15 p.m.

6th Parking Lot, Rock Creek Park, N.W.

Charges: Possession of Cocaine, Possession of Marijuana, Carrying a Pistol Without a License

Witnesses

Witness #1	Arresting Officer/Chain of custody
Witness #2	Assisting Officer
Witness #3	Crime Scene Search Officer — Took fingerprints
Witness #4	Transporting Officer

Evidence	Who and Where Found
1 .22 Caliber Pistol	Witness # 1: wedged in the front seat.
1 Bag of Marijuana	Witness # 1: in possession of passenger.
3 Marijuana Cigarettes	Witness # 1: front ashtray.
2 Packets of Cocaine	Witness # 1: under front passenger's mat.
1 Package of Rolling Paper	Witness # 1: under front passenger's mat.
1 Hemostat	Witness # 1: under front driver's mat.

3. Transcript of Deposition of Eyewitness, Ronald Samoa

[taken on September 14, in the office of the defense counsel]

DEFENSE COUNSEL: Would you please state your name for the record?

A: Ronald T. Samoa

DEFENSE COUNSEL: Where do you live, Mr. Samoa?

A: I live at 1405 Cleveland Park Circle, N.W., Washington, D.C.

DEFENSE COUNSEL: Where were you on August 24, at approximately 2:15 p.m.?

A: I was in Rock Creek Park, taking a walk.

DEFENSE COUNSEL: What did you see at that time, if anything?

A: I saw a police officer go over to a parked car and animatedly say something through a rolled-up window. The driver rolled down the window a crack and I saw what looked like smoke come out of it.

DEFENSE COUNSEL: Then what happened?

A: The driver got out of the car, put his hands up in front of him, and seemed to tell the officer to take it easy. The passenger got out at the same time. Then the officer practically dove into the car and emerged with some stuff in his hands.

DEFENSE COUNSEL: Where did the stuff in his hands come from?

A: I could not see.

DEFENSE COUNSEL: When the officer went into the car, can you describe what he was doing with his hands?

A: The officer's right hand was balled up, like a fist, but I couldn't see if he was holding anything in it; I just am not sure.

DEFENSE COUNSEL: Thank you.

How would you approach the case as the prosecutor? As the defense counsel? Explain your strategy for each side. What would you include in an opening statement to the jury in this case? Note that the opening statements by counsel are not evidence. Instead, they can be thought of as the "road maps" of what the evidence will show. They offer a peek at all of the pieces in the puzzle, presented in its entirety before the evidentiary component of the trial begins, much like the table of contents for a book. The opening statement is not an opening argument about the other side's evidence. While attorneys construct their openings subject to personal preference, common features include: (1) a one-line theme for the case, much like the title of a book or film; (2) a story about what happened (that is, what the evidence will show); and (3) a request for a favorable verdict based on the evidence.

PRE-TRIAL

1. *Motions.* Suppose the accused has moved to dismiss one of the charges above. Which charge is least likely to be proven at trial? What if the judge turns out to be a former prosecutor who is known as "Maximum Maxine," for her propensity to sentence defendants to the maximum time within the sentencing guidelines of the jurisdiction? Would a motion to recuse the judge be proper? Would it likely succeed?

2. *Discovery.* If the accused wants to take a deposition of the investigating police officer, what should be asked? Draw out a list of questions.

3. *Defense Witnesses.* Who should the defendant prepare as possible witnesses at trial? Why? Should the accused testify? What are the arguments pro and con for such an eventuality?

TRIAL

1. *Voir Dire.* During *voir dire*, the attorney is permitted to question the members of the jury panel in this jurisdiction. What questions should the attorney ask? Should the attorney ask about the panel members' attitudes toward drugs? Police officers? Whether jury panel members could be fair in this case? Do you expect panel members to tell the truth?

2. *The Case-in-Chief.* What should be the order of evidence for the prosecution? When should the defense rest without offering evidence? What should be the order for the defense, if any?

3. *Rebuttal Case.* If the accused offers a family member as a character witness, should the prosecution rebut? How?

POST-TRIAL

1. *Motions.* What motions should the accused make if convicted?

2. *Release.* If convicted, should the defendant be released during an appeal?

§ 1.04 ELABORATING ON THE MEANINGS OF THE TERM "EVIDENCE"

There are at least three different commonly used definitions of the term "evidence." These definitions indicate how the word "evidence" is applied, especially at trial. The definitions include: (1) *proof* of a cause of action, claim, or defense; (2) *the rules* governing the admissibility and exclusion of proof at trial; and (3) the things that jurors can take back with them to the jury room for the process of deliberations that have been admitted *in evidence.*

(1) *Proof* refers to the "stuff" offered by the parties at trial to prove the elements of a claim, cause of action, or defense. In the American system of justice, lawsuits are generally won — or lost — through the proof offered by the parties. Proof is offered through marked tangible material called "exhibits" and oral testimony by witnesses.

Special prerequisites must be met by the offering party before a jury will be permitted to observe and consider any evidence.

(2) *The rules* governing the admissibility of proof not only provide the focus of a law school course but also guide how a judge conducts a trial. These rules can be found in the federal or state codification, as well as in the common law. Significantly, the rules contain numerous evidentiary "foundations" — procedures and judicial findings that are prerequisites to the admissibility of evidence at trial. Lawyers and law students struggle to understand and apply these foundations, which are crucial to the introduction of evidence. Those who can best negotiate these foundations have better chances for success at trial. (One pointed example to the contrary can be found in the film, "The Verdict," starring Paul Newman as a plaintiff's attorney. In the film, the court excluded evidence by a nurse about the medical negligence of several defendant physicians. Despite the exclusion, the jury obviously considered the evidence in finding for the plaintiff, giving Mr. Newman an unexpected victory.)

(3) *In evidence*, the third common use of the term "evidence," overlaps with the first use, proof, but is intended to refer to the special proof the jury can take into the jury room during deliberations. This type of evidence, which includes a large portion of tangible proof under meaning (1) above, is distinguished from mere demonstrative evidence, which is used only to illustrate a witness's point in court. Demonstrative evidence is generally not subject to the same rigorous admissions requirements as other evidence and often is not permitted to be taken by the jury into the jury room. Once proposed exhibits are admitted "in evidence," they no longer are controlled by the parties, but become a part of the official case file and are under the control of the court.

Illustration: The Term "Evidence" and Its Uses

Dr. Amy Millsap, a surgeon, is sued by her patient, Lenny Ferona, for medical malpractice. Dr. Millsap allegedly performed an important operating procedure with the incorrect scalpel. At trial, the plaintiff introduced the scalpel that Dr. Millsap used during the operation. Is the scalpel admissible in evidence?

Answer: The scalpel used by Dr. Millsap touches on all three uses of the term "evidence." It may be relevant to proving malpractice and thus might be admitted as the "stuff" offered by a party at trial. The "stuff" must satisfy the rules governing admissibility, including the evidentiary foundation — the party must first properly authenticate the scalpel and show that it is relevant to the case. If it was not the scalpel in question, but rather a different scalpel, it may not be admitted. If the scalpel is admitted as an exhibit and not merely as a demonstrative aid to illustrate the testimony of a witness, the scalpel is considered "in evidence," and may be physically brought to the jury room by the jury for its deliberations.

Problems on Using Evidence as Proof

Problem #1-1: Go Ahead and Prove It

Mr. Rick Turkish, owner and president of Turkish Advertising, Inc., created an advertising campaign for Bill's Furniture Store. Rick had negotiated the deal with one of Bill's employees, Sarina, who agreed to a fee of $40,000 for Rick's services. Sarina told Rick to send her the bill. After completing the work, Rick dropped the finished product off at Bill's, along with an invoice for $40,000, which was the only written confirmation of the job. Eleven months later, Rick still had not been paid by Bill's Furniture, so he filed suit to collect his fee.

What are the legal grounds for recovery? What should Rick allege in his complaint? Why?

Suppose Rick testified at trial on his own behalf as follows:

Illustration: Direct Examination

PLAINTIFF'S ATTORNEY: Rick, would you please state your name for the record and spell it for the court reporter.

A: Rick Turkish, that's R-i-c-k T-u-r-k-i-s-h.

PLAINTIFF'S ATTORNEY: What do you do for a living, Mr. Turkish?

A: I own a small advertising firm.

PLAINTIFF'S ATTORNEY: What is your family status?

A: I have been married for 17 years and have three children and a dog.

PLAINTIFF'S ATTORNEY: Please describe what happened on the afternoon of October 1st.

A: I spoke to Sarina Johnson, of Bill's Furniture Store, about doing an advertising campaign for the store. I agreed during the conversation to design and implement several advertisements in the local newspapers for Bill's Fall Sale.

PLAINTIFF'S ATTORNEY: What happened after you agreed to do the work?

A: I created and designed the advertising campaign. Then I dropped the campaign off at Bill's with one of his employees, Jimmy, along with an invoice for the work.

PLAINTIFF'S ATTORNEY: Who is Jimmy?

A: He used to work for Bill's Furniture. I gave it to him because Sarina and Bill were not in the office that day.

PLAINTIFF'S ATTORNEY: What happened after that?

A: Nothing. I didn't hear from Bill's. And I would like to get paid for the work I did for them.

What additional questions would you want to ask Rick, keeping in mind that proof is required to win this contract action and all other actions at trial? What are your goals in asking these questions?

If you represented Bill's, how would you cross-examine Rick? What would be your objectives?

Problem #1-2: Evidently, My Dear Watson

Inspector Watson investigates the scene of a gruesome murder. He finds, among other things:

1. A blueprint of the building in which the murder occurred.

2. One of the victim's earrings lying on the ground near the victim's body.

3. A paint brush spattered with blood.

4. A photograph of the scene without the body in it.

5. A "Saturday Night Special" handgun, lying under a bed nearby.

The Inspector then interviews three people who are standing at the scene. One of the three, a neighbor, Bill, knew the murder victim. The neighbor tells Watson that the victim was Jane Duplane and that she was having a torrid affair with Bill's best friend, Harley. During the interview, Watson observes the maid furtively placing an object in her pocket, and a young man running away with what appeared to be an earring in his hand.

Which of Watson's findings or interviews constitutes proof of the crime? What rules of evidence might apply to that proof? What proof might the jury be allowed to take back with them to the jury room? Why?

§ 1.05 TYPES OF EVIDENCE

[A] Real, Representative, or Testimonial Evidence

One useful way to classify evidence is to categorize it as (a) real, (b) representative, or (c) testimonial. "Real" evidence is physical, tangible evidence — the thing itself. It is the gun used in an armed robbery, the fender from a car in an auto accident, or the original contract in a breach of contract action. Representative evidence, on the other hand, is evidence that represents another thing — a diagram, chart, photograph, X-ray, etc. Testimonial evidence comes from witness's *viva voce*, meaning by voice. These three forms of evidence have differing requirements for admissibility, particularly in the area of authentication.

Problem #1-3: Watson Again

In Problem #1-2, above, what evidence would qualify as real evidence? Representative evidence? Testimonial evidence? Explain.

Background Box: Depositions

A deposition is a written record of a witness's out-of-court testimony for subsequent use in trial or for discovery purposes such as uncovering additional tangible evidence (e.g., documents) or witnesses. Black's Law Dictionary 534 (10th ed. 2014). Depositions are an important part of the formal discovery process during litigation and occur weeks or months before the trial. Lawyers may use depositions to: confirm what they have learned though informal investigation, obtain admissions, and evaluate a witness's testimony and demeanor. *See* James W. McElhaney, McElhaney's Litigation 36 (1995). Parties sometimes videotape depositions and show clips during their opening statements at trial. Lawyers can be sanctioned for abusive conduct during the discovery process. *Security Nat'l Bank Labs of Sioux City v. Abbot Laboratories*, 2014 U.S. Dist. LEXIS 102228 (N.D. Iowa July 28, 2015) (sanctioning a lawyer for "obstructionist" deposition conduct, including repeated use of "objections to [the] form" of the question without offering any grounds for the objections (e.g., leading), making it "difficult . . . for a reviewing court to determine whether the objection was proper or frivolous.").

[B] Direct and Circumstantial Evidence

Evidence also can be categorized as either direct or circumstantial in nature. Circumstantial evidence does not itself address a fact in issue; such evidence is relevant if an inference to be drawn from it bears in some way on a fact in issue. Thus, circumstantial evidence is used indirectly. Direct evidence, on the other hand, proves a fact — often an important fact — without requiring any inferences. For example, an eyewitness to a murder who testifies, "I saw the defendant fire the gun, killing the victim," provides direct evidence of the killer's identity. A bloody knife found at the scene of the crime, on the other hand, provides indirect or circumstantial evidence of the murder, as does the fact that a suspect fled the scene after the killing. The bloody knife and running suspect both require inferences to prove the material fact that a murder occurred.

Julie Janson, a school teacher of modest means, is charged with the larceny of her neighbor's priceless Picasso. She was arrested three weeks after the theft, following her purchase of a $2,000,000 yacht. Is the purchase of the yacht direct or circumstantial evidence of the larceny?

Illustration: Direct and Circumstantial Evidence

Answer: The newly purchased yacht would be circumstantial evidence of the larceny. It can be inferred from Julie's recent purchase of the yacht that she suddenly obtained a significant amount of money, and that the amount of the windfall was consistent with the theft and sale of a priceless Picasso. Direct evidence of the larceny would be an eyewitness who actually observed Julie take the painting.

Distinction Between Direct and Circumstantial Evidence

Problem #1-4: Direct v. Circumstantial

Which of the following are examples of circumstantial evidence? Which examples are best classified as direct evidence? Explain.

Cir 1. To show that a letter was received, evidence is offered that the letter was properly postmarked, addressed, and mailed.

dir 2. On the issue of whether it was raining on March 14th, Ellie testified, "I looked out my window and saw rain falling."

Circ 3. On the issue of whether it was raining on March 14th, Paul testified, "when people came into the office on that day, they were wearing raincoats and shaking water from their umbrellas."

Circ 4. On the issue of whether the elephant that escaped from the circus had crossed Alexandra's backyard, Alexandra testified, "I looked into my backyard and saw huge elephant footprints."

circ 5. On the issue of whether Betty robbed the bank, an employee of the police department testified that the handgun dropped at the bank by the perpetrator was registered in Betty's name.

dir 6. On the issue of whether Larry robbed Sandra, a bystander testified, "I saw Larry rob Sandra."

Circ 7. On the issue of whether Larry robbed Sandra, another bystander testified, "I saw Larry running away from the scene."

Circ 8. On the issue of whether Barney attended the hockey game, Sheila's statement, "Ed told me he 'saw Barney walking toward the arena where the hockey game was played.'"

§ 1.06 MIXED PROBLEM

Problem #1-5: The Pirate

Bob was accused of breaking into a neighbor's apartment carrying an old-fashioned but very sharp sword. Bob admitted he entered the neighbor's apartment, but claimed he thought a woman was in distress in the apartment, based on what he had heard through the wall. In rebuttal, the neighbor was called to testify that he was watching a television movie including a woman crying. Is the neighbor's testimony admissible? Could the prosecution offer the published television schedule, including a description of the film as a real "tear-jerker?" [Note: This problem is based on a true incident.]

§ 1.07 SUMMARY AND REVIEW

1. What are the main stages of civil and criminal cases?

2. What are the different meanings of the term "evidence?"

3. Is direct evidence better than indirect evidence? Explain.

4. Why is some evidence excluded from consideration by the trier of fact?

5. What are some of the differences between direct and cross-examinations?

RELEVANT ETHICS RULES:

Professionalism Guidelines

Professionalism Dos & Don'ts: Depositions,
The Supreme Court of Ohio Commission on Professionalism (2014)
http://www.supremecourt.ohio.gov/Publications/AttySvcs/Depositions.pdf

[T]hese guidelines — which are consistent with . . . the Supreme Court's State-ments on Professionalism — [will enable] lawyers . . . to use depositions to advance the legitimate interests of their clients, while, at the same time, treating all participants in the process, including deponents and opposing counsel, with courtesy, civility, and respect.

Therefore, as a lawyer who is scheduling, conducting or attending a deposition:

DO:

*   Review the local rules of the jurisdiction where you are practicing before you begin.

*   [C]all opposing counsel first and cooperate on the selection of the date, time, and place.

*   Then send out a notice reflecting the agreed upon date.

*   If, after a deposition has been scheduled, a postponement is requested by the other side, cooperate in the rescheduling unless the requested postponement would be one of those rare instances that would adversely affect your client's rights.

*   Arrive on time.

*   Be prepared, including having multiple copies of all pertinent documents available in the deposition room, so that the deposition can proceed efficiently and expeditiously.

*   Turn off all electronic devices for receiving calls and messages while the deposition is in progress.

*   Attempt to agree, either before or during the deposition, to a reasonable time limit for the deposition.

*   Treat other counsel and the deponent with courtesy and civility.

*   Go "off record" and confer with opposing counsel, privately and outside the deposition room, if you are having problems with respect to objections, the tone of the questions being asked or the form of the questions.

*   Recess the deposition and call the court for guidance if your off-the-record conversations with opposing counsel are not successful in resolving the "problem."

- If a witness is shown a document, make sure that you have ample copies to distribute simultaneously to all counsel who are present.

- If a deponent asks to see a document upon which questions are being asked, provide a copy to the deponent.

- Inform your client in advance of the deposition (if the client plans to attend) that you will be conducting yourself at the deposition in accordance with these "dos and don'ts."

DON'T:

- Attempt to "beat your opponent to the punch" by scheduling a deposition for a date earlier than the date requested by your opponent for deposition(s) that he or she wants to take.

- Coach the deponent during the deposition when he or she is being questioned by the other side.

- Make speaking objections to questions or make statements that are intended to coach the deponent. Simply say "object" or "objection."

- Make rude and degrading comments to, or ad hominen attacks on, deponent or opposing counsel, either when asking questions or objecting to questions.

- Instruct a witness to refuse to answer a question unless the testimony sought is deemed by you to be privileged, work product, or self-incriminating, or if you believe the examination is being conducted in a manner as to unreasonably annoy or embarrass the deponent.

- Overtly or covertly provide answers to questions asked of the witness.

- Demand conferences or breaks while a question is pending, unless the purpose is to determine whether a privilege should be asserted.

Chapter 2

THE FUNCTIONS OF JUDGE, JURY, AND ATTORNEYS AT TRIAL

CHAPTER FRAMEWORK: The judge, jury, and attorneys create the basic framework of the adversary trial system in the United States. The roles of judge, jury, and attorneys can vary, depending on the nature and purpose of the hearing. The judge and jury are supposed to be objectively neutral. The attorneys are supposed to argue zealously — and ethically — on their clients' behalf. Thus, the attorneys are responsible for managing their cases, in part, by seeking to admit (or exclude) evidence, the judge serves as the umpire or referee, and the jury decides whether the burden of persuasion has been reached.

Ethics codes for judges and attorneys, sometimes called rules for professional conduct, also shape the roles of judge and attorney. Jury duty can be seen as a branch of democratic governance, because jurors represent the community in reaching a surrogate for the truth.

WHY ARE THE CONCEPTS IN THIS CHAPTER IMPORTANT? The roles of judge, jury, and attorney dictate how a dispute will be resolved under the relevant rules of evidence. To understand each individual role, it is helpful to know by comparison what the other positions entail.

CONNECTIONS: The functions of the participants connect to all aspects of evidence law — how and when the attorneys offer evidence, how judges utilize the FRE to determine whether to admit or exclude proof and what evidence is properly considered by the trier of fact.

CHAPTER OUTLINE:

    I. Judge

        A. Ruling on evidence

            1. Overrule

            2. Sustained

        B. Burden of production — Initial burden of going forward. Establishes *prima face* case of elements. Judge decides if the burden is met. If burden is met it generally moves case to the jury. If not met, upon proper motion, the case is not moved to jury.

        C. Appellate

            1. De novo — generally for questions of law

   2.   Abuse of discretion — for most evidentiary rulings involving law and fact

II.   Jury

   A.   Determines whether burden of persuasion has been met

III.   Attorneys Jury Selection — *voir dire*

   A.   Opening statements

   B.   Offering proof: case-in-chief

   C.   Objections to evidence

      1.   Timely

      2.   Specific grounds

   D.   Ethics

      1.   How relevant to acceptable attorney or judge conduct?

      2.   The rules of professional conduct

      3.   Professionalism generally

* * * * *

RELEVANT EVIDENCE RULES

FRE 103. Rulings on Evidence

(a) Preserving a Claim of Error. A party may claim error in a ruling to admit or exclude evidence only if the error affects a substantial right of the party and:

(1)   if the ruling admits evidence, a party, on the record:

   (A)   timely objects or moves to strike; and

   (B)   states the specific ground, unless it was apparent from the context; or

(2)   if the ruling excludes evidence, a party informs the court of its substance by an offer of proof, unless the substance was apparent from the context.

(b) Not Needing to Renew an Objection or Offer of Proof. Once the court rules definitively on the record — either before or at trial — a party need not renew an objection or offer of proof to preserve a claim of error for appeal.

(c) Court's Statement About the Ruling; Directing an Offer of Proof. The Court may make any statement about the character or form of the evidence, the objection made, and the ruling. The court may direct that an offer of proof be made in question-and-answer form.

(d) Preventing the Jury from hearing Inadmissible Evidence. To the extent practicable, the court must conduct a jury trial so that inadmissible evidence is not suggested to the jury by any means.

(e) Taking Notice of Plain Error. A court may take notice of plain error affecting a substantial right, even if the claim of error was not properly preserved.

FRE 104. Preliminary Questions

(a) In General. The court must decide preliminary questions about whether a witness is qualified, a privilege exists, or evidence is admissible. In so deciding, the court is not bound by evidence rules, except those on privilege.

(b) Relevance that Depends on Fact. When the relevancy of evidence depends upon whether a fact exists, proof must be introduced sufficient to support a finding that the fact does exist. The court may admit the proposed evidence on the condition that the proof is introduced later.

(c) Conducting a Hearing So That the Jury Cannot Hear It. The court must conduct any hearing on a preliminary question so that the jury cannot hear it if:

(1) the hearing involves the admissibility of a confession;

(2) a defendant in a criminal case is a witness and so requests; or

(3) justice so requires.

(d) Cross-Examining a Defendant in a Criminal Case. By testifying on a preliminary question, a defendant in a criminal case does not become subject to cross-examination on other issues in the case.

(e) Evidence Relevant to Weight and Credibility. This rule does not limit a party's right to introduce before the jury evidence that is relevant to the weight or credibility of other evidence.

FRE 105. Limiting Evidence That Is Not Admissible Against Other Parties or for Other Purposes

If the court admits evidence that is admissible against a party or for a purpose — but not against another party or for another purpose — the court on timely request, must restrict the evidence to its proper scope and instruct the jury accordingly.

FRE 106. Remainder of or Related Writings or Recorded Statements

If a party introduces all or part of a writing or recorded statement, an adverse party may require the introduction, at that time, of any other part — or any other writing or recorded statement — that in fairness ought to be considered at the same time.

§ 2.01 INTRODUCTION

The judge, jury, and attorneys have different responsibilities at trial. Prominent among those responsibilities are the gathering, offering, objecting to, and admission of evidence. The evidence rules play a significant role in the division of those duties, although general rules of trial procedure and standards of professional conduct have a large impact as well.

It is the responsibility of the judge to manage the trial. As the trial's "chief operating officer," the judge is both an umpire of disputes and an air traffic controller. It is the judge's duty to ensure that the case progresses procedurally in an orderly and predictable fashion. *See* FRE 611. As part of this general responsibility, it is the judge's job to rule on evidentiary objections and on the admissibility of evidence. The judge is given some discretion in making evidentiary rulings, but is constrained by the dictates of the rules. For example, while judges can call witnesses, see FRE 614, and may even comment on the evidence, they must exclude both irrelevant evidence, see FRE 402, and improper lay opinion testimony. *See* FRE 701.

A judge's admissibility determinations include decisions such as whether evidence is hearsay, whether a witness is properly qualified to testify, whether a sufficient foundation was laid for an exhibit, and whether a privilege applies to certain evidence. In making these and other admissibility determinations, a judge has wide latitude to consider many types of evidence. The judge can even take into account inadmissible evidence, such as hearsay. There is one form of evidence, however, that the rules officially prohibit the judge from considering in making admissibility determinations, and that is privileged evidence. Privileged evidence is thus unique, in that it is excluded both from trial and from the judge's consideration in making determinations of admissibility. *See* FRE 104(a).

The jury's role differs from that of the judge. While the judge oversees the trial process, the jury comprises the basic trial machinery, deciding on the facts as they relate to guilt, liability, and aspects of dispute resolution. The jury's role is both crucial to and larger than the individual case. In a jury-based legal system, the jury is an integral part of democratic governance; the United States Constitution demands the selection of jurors from a cross-section of society. *See* United States Constitution, Sixth Amendment. Yet, jurors are not the only persons given the power to decide facts and thus resolve legal disputes. Some cases are resolved by judges, who add the role of fact finder to their usual repertoire. This occurs in cases where the parties either are not entitled to a jury or waive their right to one. Other cases are resolved by arbitrators as part of a growing trend toward alternative methods of dispute resolution.

Background Box: Juries and Jurors:

It is the judge's job to decide what evidence is admissible, pursuant to the rules of evidence. The judge controls the direction of the trial by admitting or excluding evidence, in effect deciding what evidence the trier of fact, often a jury, will ultimately consider. While many trial observers might evaluate guilt or innocence with unfiltered observations, the jury is tasked with deciding only based on what it is permitted to consider through the judicial filter.

For example, in the trial of former governor Rod Blagojevich, the judge limited the number of undercover tapes that the defense could play for the jury. (*See* Jeff Coen, *No head-butting in court, judge tells Blagojevich*, Chicago Breaking News Center, Apr. 21, 2010).

When a jury serves as the "judge" of the facts at trial, it is the jury's responsibility to evaluate the admitted evidence, to apply the law as given by the judge to that evidence, and, if possible, to reach a verdict. While the jury generally observes the trial passively, in some courts jurors are permitted to take notes. Some judges even allow jurors to ask questions of the witnesses, if the jurors submit the questions to the judge in writing so the judge and attorneys can ensure that they comply with the evidentiary rules. Especially in criminal cases, the jury is treated as the conscience of the community. As the community's moral conscience, a jury has considerable powers, most notably the power to "nullify" the evidence and return a verdict of "not guilty" if it sees fit, no matter how rationally compelling the prosecutor's evidence.

Significantly, juries do not have plenary control over deciding all of the facts at trial. FRE 104(b), describing "conditional relevance," really concerns the division of fact-finding between the judge and the jury. Specifically, FRE 104(b) instructs the judge to make an initial determination about the existence of preliminary questions of fact pertaining to rulings on admissibility. Such predicate fact-finding covers a wide range of facts, such as whether other crimes, wrongs, or acts, offered pursuant to FRE 404(b), actually occurred. *See Huddleston v. United States*, 485 U.S. 681 (1988). If a judge concludes that a reasonable jury could find that a predicate fact exists by a preponderance of the evidence, that fact is given to the jury to find — or not find — as it sees fit.

Illustration

At 2:00 a.m. on January 6th, two cars collided on Interstate 95. One of the cars was going the wrong way. After the crash, the cars were turned and entangled in such a manner that it was difficult to determine which driver was at fault. At a civil trial between the drivers of the two cars, both of whom survived with serious injuries, the plaintiff offered in evidence a piece of metal that was found approximately 40 feet away from the crash, claiming that it was part of the defendant's car. The metal was offered because its location supported the theory that the defendant's car was the one traveling in the wrong direction. At an earlier part of the trial, an expert from the Ford Motor Company had testified that this piece of metal "looked like" the kind that came from a 1994 Ford Galaxy, the defendant's car. An eyewitness had testified that he had seen the accident and that the impact had spewed pieces of metal everywhere, even as much as 60 feet away. From the judge's perspective, the eyewitness was not very credible, and it appeared that the expert witness had made several mistakes in the past. Further, an affidavit from a passenger of another car, who attempted to describe the accident, was filled with hearsay statements made by other people. However, it generally supported the plaintiff's claim about the piece of metal. Despite all of these deficiencies, the judge admitted the piece of metal, on the basis that a reasonable juror could decide, by a preponderance of the evidence, that the piece was indeed a part of the defendant's car.

The judge also believed the jury could reasonably discredit the evidence of the eyewitness and the expert, and find that the metal was not part of the defendant's car. However, that belief was not a reason under the rules to exclude the metal. The basic fact-finding function belongs to the jury, not the court. It was simply the court's job to screen out "bad" evidence, meaning evidence whose relevance was not supported by evidence sufficient to support a finding of fact pursuant to FRE 104(b).

Attorneys have multiple obligations at trial. The lawyers are officers of the court. As such, they have a duty to act ethically to maintain the integrity of the judicial system. The lawyers also serve as representatives of their clients. In this capacity, the attorneys must act competently and zealously on their clients' behalf. Sometimes these roles conflict, such as when a client intends to testify falsely.

The duty to act zealously on behalf of clients operates on two different levels: in the present, to secure the most favorable outcome for the client at trial; and in the future, to create a record for any potential appeal. In carrying out this dual role, the attorney must be able to understand and apply the rules of evidence, including laying foundations for the admissibility of evidence, while at the same time making a sufficiently clear record in the event of an appeal.

Laying "foundations" for evidence is an important lawyering skill. It means to be able to demonstrate the prerequisites to admissibility required by the rules of evidence. These evidentiary prerequisites are better thought of as affirmative building blocks to admissibility rather than as negative prohibitions. The rules do not often sound like punishing authority figures, saying "you cannot do this; you cannot do that." If the right foundational ingredients are shown, the evidence is admitted. With the notable exception of irrelevant evidence, most evidence can be admitted for some purpose, such as to prove an element of the case or to impeach a witness.

Judges' rulings and lawyers' arguments typically focus on the sufficiency of foundations, not on "what the rules ought to be." Foundations thus can be viewed as the organizational center of evidence law; they serve as the primary intersection between evidence law in the classroom and evidence law in the courtroom. That is why this textbook focuses on the proof and sufficiency of foundations.

When the judge has ruled on the admissibility of evidence, the attorneys have an additional responsibility specifically triggered by an adverse ruling or outcome, namely to create a sufficient record for an appeal. The duty to create an appellate record translates into several requirements for the competent attorney. These include objecting to evidence and making a proffer for the record:

1. If improper evidence is admitted, the lawyer must object, setting forth the specific basis of each objection. A general objection of "irrelevant, incompetent and immaterial" is rarely sufficient.

2. If proper evidence is excluded, the lawyer must make an offer of proof, called a proffer, stating what the excluded evidence would have shown if it had been admitted. *See* FRE 103(a)(2).

If the attorney fails to object or make a proffer, the point is generally foreclosed on appeal. However, there is one major exception to this rule. An appellate court can consider "plain error" even though there was no objection or proffer. *See* FRE 103(d). Attorneys should not rely on the "plain error" rule to save them from objection omissions, but rather use it only as a last resort.

§ 2.02 THE JUDGE'S ROLE

"Judges rule on the basis of law, not public opinion, and they should be totally indifferent to pressures of the times." — Warren Burger, former Chief Justice, United States Supreme Court.

[A] Questions of Admissibility

Perhaps the best-known job of the judge is the duty to rule on questions of admissibility. Judges must decide whether to sustain (uphold) or overrule (deny) a party's objections to evidence or actions by the court. If the attorneys fail to object to evidence or make a proffer, judges generally bite their tongues and remain silent, since it is the prerogative of the attorneys to try their own cases. When judges are asked to rule on questions of relevancy, they base the ruling on reason and experience. *See, e.g.*, Advisory Committee Note to FRE 401. When judges are asked to rule on other areas, such as hearsay or privilege, the judges also may need to apply legal rules and principles. Since admissibility rulings often involve the particular facts of a case, each ruling may pose new and challenging considerations. (Some questions, like those involving judicial notice, are not intended to vary much from case to case. *See* FRE 201, which is discussed in Chapter 14.)

Judges must make essentially two different kinds of admissibility decisions: (1) whether an attorney has offered enough evidence to meet the requisites of a rule (104(a)) and (2) whether under FRE 104(b) an attorney has offered sufficient evidence for a jury to believe a fact relevant to the case exists. The 104(a) ruling is about whether foundations have been met; the 104(b) ruling is about whether counsel has enough support to argue that certain facts exist. Thus, an attorney claiming that an out-of-court assertion is an excited utterance must show by a preponderance of the evidence that the assertion was made under the stress of excitement and relates to the stress-creating event. *See* FRE 803(2)(2). The judge is unencumbered by the rules of evidence, save privileged evidence, which remains out-of-bounds. *See* FRE 104(a). Even if the excited utterance is admissible, what allegedly happened must still be proven by competent evidence.

Illustration

In a breach of contract action between a company that makes gates and fences and its primary supplier, the plaintiff company offers the testimony of a witness to the agreement. The testimony includes the following:

PLAINTIFF'S ATTORNEY: Now, Sheila, tell us about what happened immediately prior to the agreement.

A: Well, before they signed the paper in front of them, the defendant's brother stated . . .

DEFENDANT'S ATTORNEY: Objection, Your Honor, the answer is riddled with inadmissible hearsay. May we approach the bench?

JUDGE: (at sidebar) Yes. Please proffer, plaintiff's counsel, what Sheila would have said had she been allowed to answer the question.

PLAINTIFF'S ATTORNEY: Certainly, Your Honor. She would have testified that she heard the defendant's brother say to the defendant, "You realize that the agreement does not allow us to supply the gate company with materials from our usual supplier in Maine and that it's going to cost us a heap more to get supplies elsewhere?" and that the defendant just stared silently back at his brother prior to signing the agreement.

JUDGE: Why is this objectionable, counsel?

DEFENDANT'S ATTORNEY: It is inadmissible hearsay, Your Honor.

JUDGE: I rule that the evidence is admissible under Rule 104(a), constituting an admission by a party opponent by silence. The defendant acquiesced in the statement and it is offered against him, as Rule 801(d)(2) provides. I am satisfied, based on the entire record in this case, that the evidence is relevant to the breach issue and is not hearsay because it qualifies as an admission by a party opponent.

Thus, the judge not only rules on questions of admissibility to determine whether the rules of evidence have been met under FRE 104(a), but also acts as a screener of the facts under FRE 104(b). In this capacity as screener, the judge shares the role of "fact finder" with the jury, although it is the jury's responsibility to ultimately determine whether admitted facts exist.

Problems on the Judge's Role in Ruling on Evidence

Problem #2-1: Until Death Do Us Part

Mrs. Holly Ramone brought suit against the Alliant Insurance Company to recover on her husband Bill's life insurance policy. The insurance company claims that although Bill has been missing for one year, he is not dead. At trial, Mrs. Ramone offers a death certificate, showing her husband died on a skiing trip in the Lake Tahoe area, which he took with some friends several months before. The trial judge excluded the certificate because he did not find it persuasive of death. Mrs. Ramone appealed. How should the appellate court rule?

Problem #2-2: "Objection! I think."

At trial, plaintiff's attorney Locke Jones objected to the opinion testimony of a defense witness. The witness had stated, "While I didn't see what happened, anyone would agree that it would have been appropriate for plaintiff to react differently than he did, that's for sure." Attorney Jones argued, "The testimony is irrelevant under FRE 401 and unfairly prejudicial under FRE 403, Your Honor." On appeal, can the court consider whether the testimony was an improper lay opinion under FRE 701?

Problem on What a Trial Judge Can Consider in Ruling on Evidence

Problem #2-3: Alan and Anne

Alan sued his ex-wife Anne for increased alimony payments. Anne seeks to introduce at trial a journal that Alan regularly kept of his expenses. Alan objects, claiming the book is a fake. Alan submits a letter from a person who claims to have secretly written the journal in exchange for a $4,000 payment from Anne.

1. Can the judge consider the letter from the purported author of the journal in determining whether to admit the book? Why?

2. Anne calls Alan's new wife, Kristine, to the witness stand. Alan objects, relying on the marital communications privilege. What standard of admissibility applies in determining whether the privilege exists? How does the standard compare to general relevancy determinations?

3. Ethics Consideration. You are Alan's attorney and you told him that you would represent him in the suit on a contingency fee basis. Is this fee agreement, in which payment occurs only if Alan prevails, permissible? South Dakota Rules of Prof'l Conduct R. 1.5. *See* Model Rules of Prof'l Conduct (MRPC) 1.5.

[B]   The Standard of Review on Appeal

An appellate judge usually does not retry a case on appeal. This means that the judge must take the record made below "as is," including the facts. The standard of review, meaning the test the appellate judges apply in considering the issues on appeal, can vary, depending on the nature of the issue. Variables include the type of error alleged (e.g., did it involve a constitutional right?) and whether the error occurred in a criminal or civil case. Standards of review include review for "abuse of discretion," review "de novo," and review for "plain error." Reversible error cannot generally be found in an evidentiary ruling unless the error caused harm that rendered the trial proceedings unfair. In the words of the FRE, the error must affect a "substantial right" of the aggrieved party. *See* FRE 103(a).

Problem on the Standard of Review on Appeal

Problem #2-4: "Justice was done, so appeal immediately"

Rebecca is tried on charges of robbing a grocery store. In her defense, Rebecca offers to testify that she had a fist fight with the grocery store's manager more than one year prior to the alleged robbery and had not been in the store since that time. The prosecution objects, claiming the evidence is irrelevant. The trial judge improperly sustains the objection, ruling that no mention of the fist fight would be allowed. Rebecca is convicted. She appeals the conviction, claiming the exclusion was in error.

1. What is the appropriate standard of review by the appellate court?

2. Ethics Consideration. You are Rebecca's attorney. Assume that following the conviction you do not file an appeal and the time to appeal elapses. Rebecca has called you numerous times following the conviction but you never called her back. Does Rebecca have a claim for ineffective assistance of counsel? *See Roe v. Flores-Ortega*, 528 U.S. 470 (2000). *See also* Colorado Rules of Prof'l Conduct R. 1.4; MRPC 1.4; *Maples v. Thomas*, 520 U.S. 470

(2011) (where two attorneys in a large New York law firm representing a death row inmate on an appeal pro bono took another job and the time for appeal expired because notice was not forwarded by the law firm but returned to sender).

Practical Tip:

Generally, any time there is a judgment against an attorney's client the client will be interested in a possible appeal. Therefore, an attorney should consult with his or her client about appellate opportunities any time the client receives an adverse judgment.

---

§ 2.03 THE JURY'S ROLE

"I'm no idealist to believe firmly in the integrity of our courts and in the jury system — that is no ideal to me, it is a living, working reality. Gentlemen, a court is no better than each man of you sitting before me on this jury. A court is only as sound as its jury, and a jury is only as sound as the men who make it up." — Atticus Finch in Harper Lee's, *To Kill a Mockingbird* at 51–52 (1960).

The determination of the facts is perhaps the jury's most important responsibility. It is the jury's job to weigh the evidence, reach a decision about what the facts are, and decide how the law applies to those facts. Of course, it is still the responsibility of the attorneys to offer competent evidence for consideration by the trier of fact. How the attorney organizes the evidence in support of a party's theory of the case may greatly affect how the jury does its job and the eventual outcome of the case.

Fact determination is complex. This is attributable in large part to the nature of human behavior. Studies have shown that even though a juror's "common sense" may indeed be common, it does not always make sense. To illustrate, studies indicate that people tend to forget information much more rapidly immediately after an event than later on (a phenomenon called "the forgetting curve"), and that the confidence eyewitnesses have in their identifications often does not correlate with the accuracy of those identifications. The difficulty of fact determination supports the privacy of jury deliberations.

The rules of evidence intrude on the jury's fact-finding role when there are special kinds of proof problems. In rare occasions in civil cases, for example, when facts are beyond dispute, the court will instruct juries to accept certain facts as true. This judicial declaration of fact is called judicial notice. *See* FRE 201. Also, on certain occasions there is the opposite problem, a lack of proof that threatens to deny justice. In this situation, the rules of evidence permit the creation of a presumption, which shifts at least some of the burden of proving the case to the opposing party in order to flush out evidence. *See* FRE 301. Judicial notice and presumptions are discussed in Chapter 14.

§ 2.04   THE ATTORNEY'S ROLE

At trial, an attorney must juggle two different roles. Counsel must keep one eye on trial strategy and the other on creating a record for a potential appeal. If counsel fails to create an accurate and specific record of objections — unless the error is evident and satisfies the "plain error" rule — or does not make a proffer about what excluded evidence would have shown had it been admitted, the appellate court may properly refuse to hear the issue on appeal.

Practical Tip:

Develop two or three simple core trial themes to provide a conceptual framework for understanding evidence. Master the record and develop narratives — storytelling is an effective communication method, especially with juries. Pay attention to the jury; juror expressions can inform the lawyer about her effectiveness. Arnold Schwartz, *Litigation Boutiques Hot List*, NAT. L.J. 10–15 (2/2/15) (reporting lawyers' trial tips).

Problems on the Attorney's Role at Trial

Problem #2-5: My Cousin, the Lawyer, Vinnie

Vinnie, a new member of the bar, was conducting his first trial, a murder defense of his friend in a small, conservative southern town. In its case-in-chief, the prosecution offered evidence that the defendant had committed adultery on several occasions and had made contributions to animal rights groups. Vinnie objected to the evidence, saying, "No way, those things are admissible, judge! The evidence is incompetent, immaterial, and irrelevant, and I object." The defendant was convicted and Vinnie appealed.

Should the appellate court consider Vinnie's objections? Why?

Problem #2-6: "Objection. Leading Question!"

At trial, the accused's attorney, Pemburton Burke, failed to object to a line of questioning in a case in which his client had been charged with fraud. The questioning included several leading questions. On appeal, the accused claimed the leading questions were "plain error" pursuant to Rule 103. Should the court consider the propriety of the leading questions on appeal?

§ 2.05 CASE SUPPLEMENT

[A] Ohler v. United States

United States Supreme Court
529 U.S. 753 (2000)

CHIEF JUSTICE REHNQUIST delivered the opinion of the Court:

Petitioner, Maria Ohler, was arrested and charged with importation of marijuana and possession of marijuana with the intent to distribute. The District Court granted the Government's motion in limine seeking to admit evidence of her prior felony conviction as impeachment evidence under Federal Rule of Evidence 609(a)(1). Ohler testified at trial and admitted on direct examination that she had been convicted of possession of methamphetamine in 1993. The jury convicted her of both counts, and the Court of Appeals for the Ninth Circuit affirmed. We agree with the Court of Appeals that Ohler may not challenge the *in limine* ruling of the District Court on appeal.

We granted certiorari to resolve a conflict among the Circuits regarding whether appellate review of an in limine ruling is available in this situation. *See United States v. Fisher*, 106 F.3d 622 (CA5 1997) (allowing review); *United States v. Smiley*, 997 F.2d 475 (CA8 1993) (holding objection waived). We affirm.

Generally, a party introducing evidence cannot complain on appeal that the evidence was erroneously admitted. Ohler seeks to avoid the consequences of this well-established commonsense principle by invoking Rules 103 and 609 of the Federal Rules of Evidence. But neither of these Rules addresses the question at issue here. Rule 103 sets forth the unremarkable propositions that a party must make a timely objection to a ruling admitting evidence and that a party cannot challenge an evidentiary ruling unless it affects a substantial right. The Rule does not purport to determine when a party waives a prior objection, and it is silent with respect to the effect of introducing evidence on direct examination, and later assigning its admission as error on appeal.

Rule 609(a) is equally unavailing for Ohler; it merely identifies the situations in which a witness' prior conviction may be admitted for impeachment purposes. The Rule originally provided that admissible prior conviction evidence could be elicited from the defendant or established by public record during cross-examination, but it was amended in 1990 to clarify that the evidence could also be introduced on direct examination. According to Ohler, it follows from this amendment that a party does not waive her objection to the *in limine* ruling by introducing the evidence herself. However, like Rule 103, Rule 609(a) simply does not address this issue.

Next, Ohler argues that it would be unfair to apply such a waiver rule in this situation because it compels a defendant to forgo the tactical advantage of preemptively introducing the conviction in order to appeal the *in limine* ruling. She argues that if a defendant is forced to wait for evidence of the conviction to be introduced on cross-examination, the jury will believe that the defendant is less credible because she was trying to conceal the conviction. The Government disputes that the defendant is unduly disadvantaged by waiting for the prosecution to introduce the conviction on cross-examination. First, the Government argues that it is debatable whether jurors actually perceive a defendant to be more credible if she introduces a conviction herself. Second, even if jurors do consider the defendant more credible, the Government suggests that it is an unwarranted advantage because the jury does not realize that the defendant disclosed the conviction only after failing to persuade the court to exclude it.

Whatever the merits of these contentions, they tend to obscure the fact that both the Government and the defendant in a criminal trial must make choices as the trial progresses. For example, the defendant must decide whether or not to take the stand in her own behalf. But once the defendant testifies, she is subject to cross-examination, including impeachment by prior convictions, and the decision to take the stand may prove damaging instead of helpful. A defendant has a further choice to make if she decides to testify, notwithstanding a prior conviction. The defendant must choose whether to introduce the conviction on direct examination and remove the sting or to take her chances with the prosecutor's possible elicitation of the conviction on cross-examination.

The Government, too, in a case such as this, must make a choice. If the defendant testifies, it must choose whether or not to impeach her by use of her prior conviction. Here the trial judge had indicated he would allow its use, but the Government still had to consider whether its use might be deemed reversible error on appeal. This choice is often based on the Government's appraisal of the apparent effect of the defendant's testimony. If she has offered a plausible, innocent explanation of the evidence against her, it will be inclined to use the prior conviction; if not, it may decide not to risk possible reversal on appeal from its use.

Due to the structure of trial, the Government has one inherent advantage in these competing trial strategies. Cross-examination comes after direct examination, and therefore the Government need not make its choice until the defendant has elected whether or not to take the stand in her own behalf and after the Government has heard the defendant testify.

Ohler's submission would deny to the Government its usual right to decide, after she testifies, whether or not to use her prior conviction against her. She seeks to short-circuit that decisional process by offering the conviction herself (and thereby removing the sting) and still preserve its admission as a claim of error on appeal. But here petitioner runs into the position taken by the Court in a similar, but not identical, situation in *Luce v. United States*, 469 U.S. 38 (1984), that "any possible harm flowing from a district court's *in limine* ruling permitting impeachment by a prior conviction is wholly speculative." Only when the government exercises its option to elicit the testimony is an appellate court confronted with a case where, under the normal rules of trial, the defendant can claim the denial of a substantial right if in fact the district court's *in limine* ruling proved to be erroneous. In our view, there is nothing "unfair," as petitioner puts it, about putting petitioner to her choice in accordance with the normal rules of trial.

Finally, Ohler argues that applying this rule to her situation unconstitutionally burdens her right to testify. She relies on *Rock v. Arkansas*, 483 U.S. 44 (1987), where we held that a prohibition of hypnotically refreshed testimony interfered with the defendant's right to testify. But here the rule in question does not prevent Ohler from taking the stand and presenting any admissible testimony which she chooses.

For these reasons, we conclude that a defendant who preemptively introduces evidence of a prior conviction on direct examination may not on appeal claim that the admission of such evidence was error.

The judgment of the Court of Appeals for the Ninth Circuit is therefore affirmed.

It is so ordered.

JUSTICE SOUTER, with whom JUSTICE STEVENS, JUSTICE GINSBURG, and JUSTICE BREYER join, dissenting.

The majority holds that a testifying defendant perforce waives the right to appeal an adverse in limine ruling admitting prior convictions for impeachment. The holding is without support in precedent, the rules of evidence, or the reasonable objectives of trial, and I respectfully dissent.

The only case of this Court that the majority claims as even tangential support for its waiver rule is *Luce v. United States*, 469 U.S. 38 (1984). We held there that a criminal defendant who remained off the stand could not appeal an in limine ruling to admit prior convictions as impeachment evidence under Federal Rule of Evidence 609(a). Since the defendant had not testified, he had never suffered the impeachment, and the question was whether he should be allowed to appeal the in limine ruling anyway, on the rationale that the threatened impeachment had discouraged the exercise of his right to defend by his own testimony. The answer turned on the practical realities of appellate review.

This case is different, there being a factual record on which Ohler's claim can be reviewed. She testified, and there is no question that the in limine ruling controlled her counsel's decision to enquire about the earlier conviction; defense lawyers do not set out to impeach their own witnesses, much less their clients.

In fact, the majority's principal reliance is not on precedent but on the "common-sense" rule that "a party introducing evidence cannot complain on appeal that the evidence was erroneously admitted." But this is no more support for today's holding than Luce is, for the common sense that approves the rule also limits its reach to a point well short of this case. The general rule makes sense, first, when a party who has freely chosen to introduce evidence of a particular fact later sees his opponent's evidence of the same fact erroneously admitted. He suffers no prejudice. The rule makes sense, second, when the objecting party takes inconsistent positions, first requesting admission and then assigning error to the admission of precisely the same evidence at his opponent's behest. "The party should not be permitted 'to blow hot and cold' in this way" (citation omitted). Neither of these reasons applies when (as here) the defendant has opposed admission of the evidence and introduced it herself only to mitigate its effect in the hands of her adversary. Such a case falls beyond the scope of the general principle, and the scholarship almost uniformly treats it as exceptional.

With neither precedent nor principle to support its chosen rule, the majority is reduced to saying that "there is nothing 'unfair' . . . about putting petitioner to her choice in accordance with the normal rules of trial." Any claim of a new rule's fairness under normal trial conditions will have to stand or fall on how well the rule would serve the objects that trials in general, and the Rules of Evidence in particular, are designed to achieve.

*   *   *

Allowing the defendant to introduce the convictions on direct examination thus tends to promote fairness of trial without depriving the Government of anything to which it is entitled. There is no reason to discourage the defendant from introducing the conviction herself, as the majority's waiver rule necessarily does.

[B]   United States v. White

United States Court of Appeals for the Tenth Circuit
302 Fed. Appx. 813 (2008)

DAVID M. EBEL, CIRCUIT JUDGE:

Defendant-Appellant Joseph N. White requests leave to appeal the district court's denial of his petition for habeas corpus. White contends that he received ineffective assistance of trial counsel because his counsel failed to object to the sentencing court's significant upward departure from the guidelines range. For substantially the same reasons stated by the district court, this court denies White's request for a certificate of appealability and dismisses this appeal.

I. Background

White pled guilty to one of the sixteen counts initially brought against him. In exchange for his plea, the prosecutor dropped the other fifteen counts and agreed to recommend a 60-month sentence and not to request any upward departures. . . . The sentencing judge subsequently notified the parties that he was contemplating an upward departure *sua sponte*. White's counsel submitted a memorandum challenging any upward departures. Nonetheless, the judge sentenced White to 147 months, 87 months above the guideline sentence. On direct appeal, this court affirmed White's sentence under a plain error standard of review because White's counsel "failed to object following imposition of sentence." (citation omitted)

II. Discussion

Under 28 U.S.C. § 2253(c)(1), a defendant seeking to appeal a denial of habeas relief under 28 U.S.C. § 2255 must first obtain a certificate of appealability ("COA"). "A COA may be issued 'only if the applicant has made a substantial showing of the denial of a constitutional right.' 28 U.S.C. § 2253(c)(2). This requires [Mr. White] to show 'that reasonable jurists could debate whether (or, for that matter, agree that) the petition should have been resolved in a different manner or that the issues presented were adequate to deserve encouragement to proceed further.'" *Fleming v. Evans*, 481F.3d 1249, 1254 (10th Cir. 2007) (quoting *Slack v. Evans*, 481 F.3d 1249, 1254 (10th Cir. 2007) (quoting Slack v. McDaniel, 529 U.S. 473, 484 ((2000)).

White argues that he was denied effective assistance of counsel when his counsel failed to object to the court's decision to depart from the guideline sentence based on the dropped charges. White argues that the departure was unreasonable because the plea agreement created the false impression that he would not be sentenced to more than 60 months.

As the district court stated, "[t]his argument is completely bogus." (Dist. Ct. Order at 1.) The plea agreement merely stated that the prosecutor would not recommend a sentence above 60 months; the government made no promise that the court would follow its recommendation. Further, White was fully aware of the court's ability to ignore the prosecution's recommendation. During the plea colloquy, he acknowledged that the "government's recommendation of a five-year sentence was not binding on the court." *White*, 265 Fed. Appx. at 723. Similarly, this court has repeatedly found that a sentencing judge is not bound by the terms of a plea agreement, and may consider counts dismissed as a result of the plea bargain.

For the first time in this request for COA, White argues that he was denied effective assistance of counsel because his attorney's failure to object to the reasonableness of his sentence reduced White's likelihood of success on appeal. White's failure to raise this issue to the district court absolves this court of any duty to address this argument. Even in the context of *pro se* litigants, whose pleadings receive a "liberal construction," this court does not generally "address arguments presented for the first time on appeal." U.S. v. Mora, 293 F.3d 1213, 1216 (10th Cir. 2002).

Were we to consider this additional argument, we would still deny White's request for a COA because White cannot point to any prejudice resulting from his counsel's failure to object. To demonstrate the existence of prejudice under *Strickland*, White must show that "there is a reasonable probability that but for" his counsel's failure to object to the sentencing judge's upward departure, "the result of the proceeding would have been different." *U.S. v. Hemsley*, 287 Fed. Appx. 649, 650 (10th Cir. 2008) (quoting *Strickland v. Washington*, 466 U.S. 668, 687 (1984). This court's Order and Judgment on direct appeal stated that White's sentence was procedurally reasonable because "the judge not only stated, but relied principally upon, appropriate reasons, *under any standard of review.*" *White*, 265 Fed. Appx. at 728 (emphasis added). Further, our review in the direct appeal of this case of the issue of the substantive reasonableness of the sentences was for "abuse of discretion," which is the same standard of review used in cases where a defendant's attorney has objected at the sentencing hearing. *See, e.g., U.S. v. Verdin-Garcia*, 516 F.3d 884, 898 (10th Cir. 2008) (reviewing the substantive reasonableness of defendant's sentence for an abuse of discretion). White cannot, therefore, demonstrate that "there is a reasonable probability that" the outcome of his appeal would have been different had his counsel objected at the sentencing hearing. *Strickland*, 466 U.S. at 687. Absent such a showing, defense counsel's failure to object does not rise to the level of ineffective assistance of counsel under *Strickland*.

§ 2.06   MIXED PROBLEMS

Problem #2-7: Judge, Jury, and Attorney

Defendant was charged with conspiring with members of the KKK to commit kidnapping. Defendant was tried by a jury and was convicted. He appealed and argued that the judge abused his discretion by admitting certain evidence. First, he claimed that the admission of a certain journal into evidence was improper, as the contents were irrelevant and highly prejudicial because it referenced defendant's involvement in the KKK. Defendant also objected to the testimony of a witness that had been given immunity by the prosecution and who claimed to have first-hand knowledge of defendant's involvement in the conspiracy, contrary to the witness's earlier story.

1. What result on appeal? *See United States v. Seale*, 600 F.3d 473 (2010).

2. What if Defendant's attorney did not object to this evidence at trial?

Problem #2-8: Evidence and Ethics

Defendant was on trial for child molestation. Defense counsel introduced the testimony of psychologist regarding whether Defendant was a good candidate for probation. The psychologist stated that she had evaluated Defendant to determine whether he would be a good candidate. Defense counsel began to ask his next question but was not able to say more than a few words when the prosecutor objected. The judge sustained the objection. The trial continued without the psychologist ever stating how she would have answered the question of whether Defendant would be a good candidate for probation. Defendant was convicted and he appealed. Both defense counsel and the prosecutor file appellate briefs. In the prosecutor's brief, he cites a case that is controlling in that jurisdiction that held that evidence as to whether a defendant is a proper candidate for probation is generally inadmissible. However, there was another more recent case from the same jurisdiction with the opposite holding.

1. Will Defendant be allowed to appeal the exclusion of the psychologist's testimony? *See Alberts v. State*, 302 S.W.3d 495 (Tex. App. 2009).

2. May the prosecutor be subject to professional discipline for failing to cite the more recent case law that was adverse to his position? Ohio Rules of Prof'l Conduct R. 3.3 (a)(2); 3.5(a)(3)(i). *See* MRPC 3.3(a)(2); 3.5(a)(3)(i).

Ethics Problem

Problem #2-9: "Reckless Accusations Against the Judge!"

Plaintiff instructs her attorney to "do whatever you have to do" to avoid having the judge assigned to the case, Judge Esker, hear her case. Attorney files a motion for reassignment, alleging that Judge Esker had improper (ex parte) communications with defendant's counsel about the scheduling of a hearing date and that Judge Esker gives preferential treatment to the defendant's law firm. The Judge notifies the state bar association and it files a grievance with the state disciplinary board. You are the

Chairman of the Statewide Disciplinary Panel reviewing the plaintiff's allegations. What is your conclusion? *See* South Carolina Rules of Prof'l Conduct R. 8.2 (a); MRPC 8.2; N.Y. Admin. Rules of the Unified Court System & Uniform Rules of the Trial Courts § 100.3 (B) (6) (a), (d) & (e); ABA Model Code of Judicial Conduct R. 2.9 (A), (1), (4) & (5).

§ 2.07 RELEVANT ETHICS RULES

Rule 1.5. Fees

(c) A fee may be contingent on the outcome of the matter for which the service is rendered, except in a matter in which a contingent fee is prohibited by paragraph (d) or other law. A contingent fee agreement shall be in writing signed by the client and shall state the method by which the fee is to be determined, including the percentage or percentages that shall accrue to the lawyer in the event of settlement, trial or appeal; litigation and other expenses to be deducted from recovery; and whether such expenses are to be deducted before or after the contingent fee is calculated. The agreement must clearly notify the client of potential expenses for which the client will be liable whether or not the client is the prevailing party. Upon conclusion of a contingent fee matter, the lawyer shall provide the client with a written statement stating the outcome of the matter and, if there is recovery, showing the remittance to the client and the method of its determination. S. Dakota Rules of Prof'l Conduct R. 1.5(c). *See* MRPC 1.5(c).

Rule 1.4. Communications

(a) A lawyer shall:

(1) promptly inform the client of any decision or circumstance with respect to which the client's informed consent, as defined in Rule 1.0(e), is required by these rules;

(2) reasonably consult with the client about the means by which the client's objectives are to be accomplished;

(3) keep the client reasonably informed about the status of the matter;

(4) promptly comply with reasonable requests for information; and

(5) consult with the client about any relevant limitation on the lawyer's conduct when the lawyer knows that the client expects assistance not permitted by the Rules of Professional Conduct or other law. S. Dakota Rules of Prof'l Conduct R. 1.4. *See* MRPC 1.4.

Rule 3.3. Candor Toward the Tribunal

(a) A lawyer shall not knowingly do any of the following:

(2) fail to disclose to the tribunal legal authority in the controlling jurisdiction known to the lawyer to be directly adverse to the position of the client and not disclosed by opposing counsel. Ohio Rules of Prof'l Conduct R. 3.3 (a)(2). *See* MRPC R.3.3 (a)(2).

Rule 3.5. Impartiality and Decorum of the Tribunal

(a) A lawyer shall not do any of the following:

    (3)   communicate ex parte with either of the following:

        (i) a judicial officer or other official as to the merits of the case during the proceeding unless authorized by law or court order. Ohio Rules of Prof'l Conduct R. 3.5 (a)(3)(i). See MRPC 3.5 (a)(3)(i).

Rule 8.2. Judicial and Legal Officials

(a) A lawyer shall not make a statement that the lawyer knows to be false with reckless disregard as to its truth or falsity concerning the qualifications or integrity of a judge, adjudicatory officer or public legal officer, or of a candidate for election or appointment to judge of legal office. S. Carolina Rules of Prof'l Conduct R. 8.2(a). *See* MRPC 8.2.

Section 100.3. A Judge Shall Perform the Duties of Judicial Office Impartially and Diligently.

(B) Adjudicative Responsibilities.

(6) A judge shall accord to every person who has a legal interest in a proceeding, or that person's lawyer, the right to be heard according to law. A judge shall not initiate, permit, or consider ex parte communications, or consider other communications made to the judge outside the presence of the parties or their lawyers concerning a pending or impending proceeding, except:

    (a) Ex parte communications that are made for scheduling or administrative purposes and that do not affect a substantial right of any party are authorized, provided the judge reasonably believes that no party will gain a procedural or tactical advantage as a result of the ex parrte communication, and the judge, insofar as practical and appropriate, makes provision for prompt notification of other parties or their lawyers of the substance of the ex parte communication and allows an opportunity to respond.

    (d) A judge, with the consent of the parties, may confer separately with the parities and their lawyers on agreed-upon matters.

    (e) A judge may intimated or consider any ex parte communications when authorized by law to do so. N.Y. Admin. Rules of the Unified Court System & Uniform Rules of the Trial Courts § 100.3. *See* ABA Model Code of Judicial Conduct R. 2.9 (A), (1), (4) & (5). Ex Parte Communications.

§ 2.08 SUMMARY AND REVIEW

1. Can the judge, *sua sponte* (i.e., on his or her own motion), offer strategy suggestions to a party?

2. What are the ethical limitations on attorneys at trial?

3. Why should attorneys state the specific grounds for an objection?

4. Who decides how much weight to give to evidence?

5. What are evidentiary foundations?

6. What is an offer of proof, also known as a proffer?

Chapter 3

RELEVANCE [FRE 401, 402]

CHAPTER FRAMEWORK: The initial inquiry in most evidentiary questions is tied to relevance, namely, "What is the evidence offered to prove?" A synonymous question is, "Relevant to what?" The answers to these questions flow logically from inferences that link evidence to an issue in the case, the impeachment of a witness, or both. The answers also reveal that the evidence "highway" has a major "fork in the road," leading to widely disparate analyses of impeachment and issues in the case.

WHY ARE THE CONCEPTS IN THIS CHAPTER IMPORTANT? Relevance serves as the gatekeeper of admissible evidence, meaning that it serves as the initial exclusion of unhelpful evidence at trial.

CONNECTIONS: Relevance frames the analysis in many other evidentiary areas, including hearsay, authentication, extrinsic impeachment and the *best evidence* rule. All of these areas, among others, ask how evidence is relevant to a case.

CHAPTER OUTLINE:

   I. Importance of Relevance

      A. First hurdle of admissibility

         1. Evidence must be relevant to be admissible

         2. Irrelevant evidence is inadmissible

  II. Defining Relevance

      A. Evidence relevant if:

         1. Probative of (i.e., making something more or less likely)

         2. A fact of consequence to the determination of the case

      B. Facts of consequence — three kinds

         1. Elements of claim or defense

         2. Credibility (impeachment) of witness

         3. Background information (e.g., witness's age or employment)

 III. Defining Conditional Relevance

      A. Relevance of evidence (e.g., X's testimony) depends on missing evidence (e.g., Y's testimony)

      B. Counsel promises to supply missing evidence (Y's testimony) later.

* * * * *

RELEVANT EVIDENCE RULES

FRE 401. Test for Relevant Evidence

Evidence is relevant if:

(a) it has any tendency to make a fact more or less probable than it would be without the evidence; and

(b) the fact is of consequence in determining the action

FRE 402. General Admissibility of Relevant Evidence

Relevant evidence is admissible unless any of the following provides otherwise:

* the United States Constitution;

* a federal statute;

* these rules; or

* other rules prescribed by the Supreme Court.

Irrelevant evidence is not admissible.

§ 3.01 THE IMPORTANCE OF RELEVANCE

Why is relevance an important concept? The answer lies partly in its primacy — it is the first hurdle to admissibility. Just as the judge is the gatekeeper of admissibility determinations, relevance is the threshold through which all evidence must pass. All evidence, without exception, must be relevant to be admissible. *See* FRE 401. Being the first in the line of evidentiary requirements is significant enough, but relevance also plays a recurring role on the "evidence highway." Relevance is considered in the assessment of the admissibility of hearsay, impeachment, and other forms of evidence, as well.

Even though an assessment of relevance is fact-oriented and dependent on everyday human experience, the relevance rules offer some bright lines. For example, only relevant evidence is eligible for admission. *See* FRE 401. Conversely, all irrelevant evidence, which suffers from a variety of defects, is inadmissible. For example, irrelevant evidence is distracting, unhelpful, and counterproductive to judicial economy. *See* FRE 402.

Of course, the fact that evidence is relevant does not mean that it will be admitted. (If that was the case, a course in Evidence Law might be extraordinarily compact.) Not all relevant evidence is admissible. Relevant evidence still must comply with other exclusionary rules, such as those concerning character, hearsay, privilege, and improper impeachment, among others, to qualify for admission. Thus, rather than acting as the sole hurdle to admissibility, relevancy only serves as one of many prerequisites.

§ 3.02   DEFINING RELEVANCE

The legal test of relevance is often divided into two parts. Evidence is relevant if it is (1) **probative** of (2) a **fact of consequence** to the determination of the action. *See* FRE 401. If evidence is irrelevant, there is no need to consider whether other prerequisites or rules of admissibility would lead to the exclusion of the evidence.

[A]   "Probative"

The term "probative" essentially means to make something more or less likely. Evidence is probative of a fact at issue in the case if it has any tendency to make the fact more or less likely. Alternatively, this means that a "chain of inferences" can be constructed that connects the evidence to issues in the case. The fact that the evidence also yields inference chains that do not relate to the case is of no significance; all that is needed is one inference chain that bears on the case at hand. Further, evidence satisfies this standard even if it only makes the pertinent fact a tiny bit more or less likely. Thus, the probative part of the relevancy standard is not a difficult obstacle to overcome in seeking to admit evidence. As the Advisory Committee observed, "[a]ny more stringent requirement is unworkable and unreasonable." Advisory Committee Note, FRE 401.

It is important to appreciate that the probative standard of FRE 401 does not require that evidence make a fact of consequence probable or not probable. The standard requires much less than probability; as noted above it only requires that evidence *tends* to make a fact a little more or less likely — but not necessarily probable.

To further illustrate this important distinction of probative value from higher standards such as probable cause or clear and convincing evidence, imagine a probative value scale where ten represents evidence that has the highest probative value — the evidence conclusively establishes a fact of consequence. Zero on the scale reflects evidence that has no probative value — the evidence does not even make a fact of consequence slightly more or less likely — and is subject to exclusion under FRE 401. If the FRE 401 relevancy standard required that evidence make a fact of consequence probable (instead of just a little more or less likely), then evidence should have a probative value greater than 5.0 (e.g., 5.1) on the scale — making it probable that a fact did or did not occur. However, the drafters of FRE 401's relevancy standard did not adopt a probability standard for finding that evidence is probative. Instead, they adopted a standard that permits judges to admit evidence with a 2 or 1 value on the probative scale. The evidence only has to make a fact of consequence slightly more or less likely.

It is important not to confuse FRE 401's liberal probative standard with a more restrictive probability standard. The 401 standard results in more, rather than less, evidence being found probative and admitted. In theory, having more evidence admitted at a trial should help the judge and jury to reach a more efficient and fair result.

Illustration: Visiting the Crime Scene

The accused, Joey, was charged with the robbery of a clothing store, The Gyp. At trial, the prosecutor, Jenna, offers evidence that Joey was in the store the day before the robbery, and that he walked around the aisles without purchasing anything before he left. Is this evidence probative of whether Joey robbed the store?

Answer: On the one hand, inferences may be drawn from Joey's presence in the store that are not probative of whether he committed the crime, such as: (1) Joey likes that Gyp store; (2) Joey likes to shop for clothes; (3) Joey does not buy clothes often; or (4) Joey knows what kind of merchandise is sold at Gyp stores. On the other hand, the fact that Joey was in the store the day before the robbery is probative in two different ways. If Joey was in the store the day before and was just looking around, it makes it more likely he was the robber because it appears that he was "casing the store" in preparation for the robbery. From the defense perspective, if Joey was in the store the day before the robbery, it makes it less likely that he was the robber because a prudent person would not visit a store he was going to rob the very next day.

[B] "Fact of Consequence"

A "fact of consequence to the determination of the action" is a fact that is "properly provable" in a case. This term describes facts that relate to: (i) the elements of a legal claim or defense, (ii) the credibility of a witness, or (iii) helpful background information. The Advisory Committee abandoned "material fact," a term that had been commonly used instead of "fact of consequence." As the Advisory Committee noted, the word "material" was "loosely used and ambiguous." Advisory Committee Note, FRE 401.

Illustration: Parties' Prior Agreement

Balou sued Rodriguez for breach of contract regarding a deck that Rodriguez had agreed to build in Balou's backyard. Balou claimed that the deck was incomplete, in that Rodriguez had left woodwork unfinished and excess garbage everywhere. Rodriguez responded by claiming that the deck was finished and the contract completed. At trial, Balou testified that a similar agreement between the same parties for a deck on the side of Balou's house included the purchase and application of a wood sealer and the removal of garbage. Rodriguez objected to this evidence, claiming it was irrelevant. On cross-examination, Balou was asked whether he had been convicted of grand theft auto, a felony, five years earlier. Balou objected to this evidence. How should the judge rule on these objections?

Answer: Both objections should be overruled. The prior agreement clarifies a fact of consequence in the case, namely the intent of the parties as it relates to their current agreement, and makes it more likely that Balou's claim will succeed. The impeachment of Balou with a felony conviction makes a fact of consequence, Balou's believability, less likely, and therefore makes it less likely that Balou's claim will succeed. While the facts of consequence differ, both the intent of the parties and the believability or credibility of the witnesses are important to resolving the suit.

The key to relevance is understanding that it describes how one thing *relates to* another thing, if at all. The Advisory Committee Note to FRE 401 puts it this way:

> Relevancy is not an inherent characteristic of any item of evidence but exists only as a <u>relation</u> between an item of evidence and a matter properly provable in the case.

A relationship indicates that there is some *connection* between the two things, based on inferences. A piece of evidence gives rise to an inference if the existence of the evidence logically makes the existence of another thing or fact more or less likely. For example, if a person is holding a pen in her right hand, it may be inferred that she writes with her right hand, uses her right hand as the dominant hand generally, writes with a pen, has written or is about to write something, or knows how to write.

Because there is usually some uncertainty about what may be inferred from particular evidence, relevance is oriented around probabilities. For example, "If someone is wearing a raincoat, then it is more probable than not that it is raining out." For that matter, the reconstruction of prior events, which is what fact-finding really constitutes at trial, is hardly ever based on certainty. Instead, most facts are really probabilities — no matter how sure we are of their existence. Even scientific evidence, which some say is "certain," is subject to differing opinions, exceptions, revisions, and new discoveries. (*See*, for example, the debates about the origins of the universe, "nature versus nurture," and other continuing scientific disagreements.)

The drawing of inferences in the relevance enterprise differs from general forms of logic. One judge has noted that it is unlike the process of deduction, where major and minor premises are supplied. Instead, "[i]inferential processes . . . generally proceed from one proven premise to a conclusion. The one drawing the inference supplies the missing premise, typically from a reservoir of experience." *United States v. Hannigan*, 27 F.3d 890, 898 n.3 (3d Cir. 1994) (Becker, J., concurring). Thus, relevance determinations are rooted in both science and experience. *See* Advisory Committee Note, FRE 401.

Judge Becker offered an illustration of relevance in *Hannigan*, stating that an eyewitness who hears a gun fire can only assume that the gunshot hit the victim who was standing nearby. If a bullet in fact was fired from the gun and struck a victim, it was traveling much too fast for the witness to actually see it go by. Yet, logic and experience dictate that if a person is observed aiming a gun at another person, the trigger is pulled (making a loud sound), and the person in the line of fire falls down covered with blood, then a bullet must have been fired from the gun and must have struck the victim. This kind of probabilistic reasoning occurs routinely, and generally unconsciously. In relevance analysis, however, a more conscious approach is favored. *See United States v. Hannigan*, 27 F.3d 890, 898 n.3 (3d Cir. 1994) (Becker, J., concurring).

In relevance analysis, numerous inferences (or probabilities) may be drawn from a single premise. To illustrate further, in a case involving the attempted robbery of a person in a mall parking lot, eyeglasses found on the ground at the scene of the crime could relate to various pertinent facts. For example, the presence of the glasses could indicate the alleged victim struggled to prevent the robbery (if it is shown the glasses belonged to the alleged victim); or that the victim wore glasses and needed them to perceive the alleged perpetrator (which relates to the witness's credibility); or that the alleged perpetrator wore glasses (which constitutes a fact relating to identification). On the other hand, the pair of eyeglasses found at the scene may relate to a variety of irrelevant facts as well. The glasses might belong to a person not involved in the incident. Even if they did belong to a participant, they could show irrelevancies such as which brand of eyeglasses the wearer prefers, whether the glasses are designed for athletic usage, or whether the glasses are made with special shock-resistant glass.

This "eyeglasses" example illustrates how a single piece of evidence can relate to a wide variety of facts. The example also demonstrates that relevancy is not an inherent characteristic of a piece of evidence, but depends on the facts of the case. *See, e.g.,* Advisory Committee Note, FRE 401. For example, if a banana peel is found on the floorboard beneath the passenger seat of an automobile, it may be probative of many facts, including: the driver eats in the car; the driver is messy; the driver carries groceries in the car; the driver has a pet monkey; there was a passenger in the car; the passenger eats in the car; the passenger is messy, and so on. The relevance of the banana peel depends on the specific issues in the case and those issues are largely determined by the legal theory underlying the case. Thus, it is extremely important for a lawyer to understand the legal concepts involved in a complaint or defense.

With such a wide variety of inferences associated with a single piece of evidence, the task for an attorney is to find a connection between the evidence and either an issue at trial, the credibility of a witness, a background fact, or a combination of these things. Attorneys must be prepared to persuade the court that such a connection exists if opposing counsel objects to evidence on relevancy grounds — i.e., that evidence is irrelevant. Whether the evidence can be linked to the case requires an answer to the question: "Relevant to what?" or "What is the evidence being offered to prove?"

In arguing the relevancy of evidence it is important to recall FRE 105. It recognizes that evidence can be relevant for one purpose or party while irrelevant for other purposes or parties. The combination of FRE 105 and 401 — with its broad and liberal relevancy standard (i.e., admitting facts that have any tendency to make a fact of consequence more or less probable) — means generally that more rather than less evidence will be admitted into the trial record. Although there will be occasions when evidence is irrelevant, lawyers are well advised to keep in mind the combination's permissive standard of admissibility when raising an irrelevancy objection.

Illustration: Connecting Sadness to Suicide

One evening, Bruce was killed in a one-car accident. The only issue in a subsequent lawsuit was whether Bruce's death was an accident or a suicide. Bruce's close friend, Natasha, said that on the day of the crash, Bruce appeared to be "very sad." Is this evidence relevant?

Answer: The evidence that Bruce appeared to be very sad prior to the accident is relevant to something, but to what? This fact may be relevant to the case if Bruce's sadness is probative of (i.e., makes more likely) a fact in issue (e.g., the reason Bruce died). The sadness is probative of suicide because sadness tends to make it more likely Bruce was depressed, which in turn could provide a motive for suicide. While there may be many other explanations for Bruce's sadness, the alternative inference chains probably would be irrelevant to the case. As long as one inference chain can be connected to the case, making it even a little bit more (or less) likely that Bruce died as a result of a suicide, the evidence will be considered relevant. Remember, the evidence does not have to make it probable that Bruce died as a result of suicide. The relevancy standard is much less stringent; the evidence need only make it slightly more likely he died as a result of suicide.

Practical Tip:

Facts of consequence can provide keywords, phrases, or concepts for electronic discovery. There are two broad categories of e-discovery technologies: linguistic and sociological. *See* John Markoff, *Armies of Expensive Lawyers Replaced by Cheaper Software*, N.Y. Times, Mar. 5, 2011, at A1. For example, in the context of the illustration, "Connecting Sadness to Suicide," one might conduct a linguistic search of all of Bruce's emails or other documents for the keywords: sadness (and related terms, i.e., depression); suicide; and accident in hope of better understanding the cause of Bruce's death. Of course, opposing counsel might request that Bruce's lawyer undertake the same search. Facts of consequence also help with a sociological e-discovery approach. This approach adds an inferential analysis to the search "by mimicking the deductive powers of a human Sherlock Holmes." *Id.* A sociological approach does not rely on keywords but rather attempts to visualize a chain of events. For example, to uncover securities fraud, a sociological approach may look at the number of times an S.E.C. document was edited and the roles of the person involved in the editing. In a different context concerning corporate insider information being leaked to the press, a sociological approach to e-discovery might involve a search of executive communications with "call me" around the time the information was leaked. Someone with something to hide — leaking information — would want to talk directly with persons or the press.

[C] Identifying Relevant Evidence

[1] Constructing Inference Chains

The following problems provide the opportunity to apply the relevance rules by constructing inference chains to link various types of evidence to the case. In drawing these inference chains, it becomes clear that the application of the doctrine of relevance can be quite complex.

Relevance Analysis Problems

Problem #3-1: Solomon's Parable

Judge Judy was asked to decide a most difficult question: which of two women claiming to be the mother of an infant child was indeed the biological mother? Each woman claimed that the child was hers. Judge Judy told the women that there was an easy solution: she was going to cut the child in half. At this pronouncement, one of the women began to cry. She shouted, "No! I can't stand it; don't do it!" The other woman was ashen-faced, but silent.

1. Are the women's reactions to Judge Judy's decision relevant? To what issue are their reactions relevant?

2. What assistance do the Advisory Committee Notes provide in resolving the relevancy issues in this problem?

3. If the parable instead involved two men, who both claimed to be the father of the child, would their reactions be similarly relevant or irrelevant? Compare the relevancy of the reactions of the alleged mothers with the reactions of the alleged fathers.

4. Ethics Consideration. You are the attorney for one of the women. She testified that she is the biological mother. Before the conclusion of the trial, she told you that she is not the biological mother. What should you do? Illinois Rules of Prof'l Conduct R. 3.3(a) (3). *See* MRPC 3.3 (a)(3).

Practical Tip:

The lawyer may wish to consult the judge about how best to proceed when a client has refused to correct false testimony.

Problem #3-2: With Love, Freddy

Freddy Krueger is accused of killing his friend Jason with a single blow to the head. At trial, the prosecution wishes to introduce love letters written by Freddy to Jason's wife only months before Jason's death. The defense objects to the introduction of the letters.

If Freddy did write the letters, are the letters probative? To what are they probative? Write out the chain of inferences that makes the letters relevant.

Problem #3-3: Missing

Joan accidentally left her purse on the snack bar after purchasing popcorn at the local movie theater. Joan remembers seeing other patrons in the area, but cannot describe any of the people, even in the most general of terms; she was in a hurry to catch the beginning of the feature film. In her purse were four new $50 bills. The purse was recovered in a bathroom after the movie, but all of the money was missing.

Which of the following evidence is relevant in determining who took the money? Explain your answers by describing the inferences you drew from the evidence.

1. Bob, another patron, paid for popcorn right before the movie started with a new $50 bill. *rel . to* _____

2. Patrons Susan and Jamie left the movie theater halfway through the film.

3. Harvey, another patron, was convicted of the possession of marijuana in 1999. · *rel. , but excl. b/c unf. prej.*

4. The purse was found in the restroom. (Does it matter whether the purse was recovered in the women's room or the men's room? Why? If the purse was recovered in the women's room, what impact, if any, is there on the relevancy of the evidence in numbers 1, 2, and 3 of this problem, above?)

Problem #3-4: Eddie from Boston

Eddie from Boston was accused of robbing the First City Bank of Massachusetts. Eddie is alleged to have used a "Saturday Night Special" revolver during the robbery.

Which of the following items of evidence would be relevant to the prosecution's case? Explain, using inference chains.

1. Eddie withdrew money at the same bank the day prior to the robbery after having a friendly ten-minute conversation with the teller (no one else was in line).

2. Eddie had an eight-year-old bank robbery conviction in a different state, Maryland.

3. Eddie was fired from his previous job as a clerk in a convenience store as a result of an unproven allegation that he stole money from the cash register.

rel 4. Eddie had participated in two barroom brawls the week before the bank robbery.

rel 5. Eddie was divorced and delinquent in his payments of $400 per month in child support.

rel 6. Eddie was virtually broke. His only asset was a $49 savings account at a different bank.

irr 7. Eddie owned a rifle.

irrel 8. Eddie has two children, ages two and seven. *T backg*

irrel 9. Eddie has been convicted of marijuana possession on two separate occasions in the past four years.

irrel 10. Eddie prefers "rock" to Bach and gin without tonic.

Problem #3-5: The Reel Thing

Wanda brought suit against three insurance companies, all of which had insured the life of her husband, Harry. She claimed that the body recently found in Pond Apple

Creek was Harry's and that, as the beneficiary, she should be paid the million dollars from the insurance policies on Harry's life. Wanda offers in evidence an authenticated letter from Harry's fishing buddy, Al. Al wrote to Harry saying, "I look forward to fishing with you at the Pond Apple Creek at the end of September." Harry has been missing since September 30th.

Is this letter relevant? If it is relevant, relevant to what? Write out the inference chain that justifies your conclusion.

[2]   Identifying the Line Between Relevance and Irrelevance

Problem #3-6: "Beam Me Up . . ."

Scotty was a driver for the Letrek Company. While driving a Letrek truck, Scotty collided with a car driven by Kirk. Kirk sued the Letrek Company for damages in tort based on the theory of "respondeat superior." The parties reached a written stipulation on most of the facts. The only issue at trial was whether Scotty was acting within the scope of his employment at the time of the accident or whether he was on a "fun and frolic" detour. Plaintiff Kirk offers evidence that "at the time of the accident, Scotty was not looking where he was going. In fact, he was falling asleep."

Is this evidence relevant? If so, relevant to what?

Problem #3-7: Fire! (a.k.a. Burning Down the House)

Hal was driving in his car when he turned on the radio and heard that his own house had burst into flames. Hal was subsequently charged with burning down the house to obtain the insurance proceeds. At trial, the prosecutor intended to offer evidence that Hal took out additional fire insurance seven months before the fire. In its case-in-chief, the prosecution calls Wanda, an employee of the insurance company, as a witness. The following exchange occurred at trial:

> PROSECUTOR: Wanda, as the insurance agent for the defendant, Hal, could you please describe the insurance that Hal had on the house, especially within the past year of its destruction?
>
> DEFENSE COUNSEL: Objection, Your Honor. Irrelevant.
>
> JUDGE: Counsel, please approach the bench.
>
> 1. How would you argue this objection if you were the prosecutor? How would you argue the objection if you were the defense counsel? What ruling would you make if you were the judge?
>
> 2. Ethics Consideration. The prosecutor hands Wanda a check for $200 after the trial to cover the time she missed from work, parking expenses, and mileage. Is this permissible? Arizona Rules of Prof'l Conduct R. 3.4 (b). *See* MRPC 3.4 (b).

Problem #3-8: I Wuz Robbed!

John and Johanna are being prosecuted for robbing a bank on June 4th at 9:00 a.m. Their defense is mistaken identity. At trial, Tommy, the bank teller who was robbed, testified about the robbery.

PROSECUTOR: Tommy, directing your attention to 8:55 a.m. on June 4th, where were you?

DEFENSE ATTORNEY: Objection! Where the teller was at that particular time is irrelevant.

1. Is the question necessarily irrelevant? What answer would make the question relevant?

PROSECUTOR: How did you feel, Tommy, as the robbers handed you the note that stated, "Your money or your life"?

A: I felt—

DEFENSE ATTORNEY: Objection! Irrelevant. How the teller felt is irrelevant to whether a robbery occurred.

2. You are the prosecutor; how would you respond?

3. How should the judge rule and why?

Problem #3-9: Benny and the Jets

The defendant, Benny, is charged with the *distribution* of cocaine. The prosecution calls Benny's friend, Jets, to the witness stand to testify that he, Jets, had *used* cocaine with the defendant three months prior to the defendant's arrest.

PROSECUTOR: Jets, please tell the ladies and gentlemen of the jury where you were on March 6th, at approximately 3:00 p.m.?

A: I was at the Giants football game with my friend, Benny.

PROSECUTOR: Describe what happened between you and Benny at the game.

DEFENSE COUNSEL: Objection. Irrelevant.

Is this evidence relevant? Explain.

Problem #3-10: Ahnald

The defendant, Franz, is prosecuted for assault and battery on Ahnald. Franz claims self-defense. Franz testified that, immediately before the altercation with Ahnald, Franz was told by a third party that Ahnald was out to get him.

1. Is this testimony relevant? Relevant to what?

2. Does it matter whether Ahnald was in fact "out to get" Franz?

3. If Franz cannot recall who told him that Ahnald was out to get him, is the evidence still relevant?

Problem #3-11: Sexual Battery

Joe is charged with sexual battery. To prove Joe's age, which is relevant to the elements of the offense, the government offers evidence that Joe generally dates women between the ages of 17 and 20.

If you were the judge, would you find that this evidence is relevant? Why?

Problem #3-12: The Commuter

Sean was approached by four youths while riding on a nearly empty commuter train one weekend morning. The youths stood on both sides of Sean, two to a side. One of them said, "Give me five dollars." Sean, fearing an attack that would result in serious bodily harm, took out a revolver and shot the four youths, injuring each of them seriously. In a subsequent prosecution for attempted murder, which of the following facts is relevant?

1. Sean (or any of the four youths) is female or male.

2. Sean (or any of the four youths) is of color or Caucasian.

3. Sean (or any of the four youths) is younger or older than 21.

4. Sean (or any of the four youths) is of high, average, or low socioeconomic status.

5. Sean (or any of the four youths) is gay or lesbian.

6. Any of the four youths has a prior criminal record.

7. The train is in a subway or above ground.

8. The train is located in a rural area, the suburbs of a city, or an inner city.

9. The incident occurred at night or during the day. Or during the summer or the winter.

10. Sean had been mugged once before, but not on a train.

Explain your conclusions.

"The Commuter" is based on the so-called "subway vigilante" case. *People v. Goetz*, 73 N.Y.2d 751, 532 N.E.2d 1273 (1988). The defendant, Bernhard Goetz, was found not guilty by a jury on charges of attempted murder. Goetz shot and injured four youths on December 22, 1984, in a New York City subway train after the youths flanked him and one of the youths asked Goetz to give him five dollars. Goetz successfully claimed that he acted in self-defense.

The following is an excerpt from the jury instructions given by Justice Stephen Crane of the Supreme Court of New York (the trial court) in *People v. Goetz:*[1]

> Please note that before he can be justified in using deadly physical force in defense of the person, the defendant must have reasonably

---

[1] Charge to Jury, Justice Stephen Crane, Supreme Court of the State of New York, County of New York, Criminal Term: Part 81. *The People of the State of New York v. Bernhard H. Goetz.*

believed that he was being threatened with deadly physical force.

What then is a reasonable belief? A determination of reasonableness must be based upon the circumstances facing the defendant or his situation in terms encompassing more than the physical movements of the potential assailant or assailants. These terms include any relevant knowledge the defendant had about that person or persons; they also necessarily bring in the physical attributes of a person's involvement, including the defendant.

Furthermore, the defendant's circumstances encompass any prior experiences he had, which would provide a reasonable basis for belief that another person's intentions were to injure him or that the use of deadly force was necessary under the circumstances.

A person may be said to reasonably believe that deadly physical force is about to be used against him, if a reasonable person in his shoes, that is, in the same circumstances and situation that he faced, would so believe. In other words, in this case you must scrutinize the reasonableness of any belief the defendant claims to have had by reference to a hypothetical reasonable person who was transported into the subway car on December 22, 1984, and who face the exact situation which confronted the defendant.

1. How is the *Goetz* jury asked to deal with the particular circumstances of the shooting?

2. How does the jury instruction define the scope of relevant evidence in the case?

3. In light of the jury instructions, how broad is the permissible scope of relevant evidence?

4. How is the scope of relevant evidence affected by whether the self-defense instruction is "objective" or "subjective"?

Problem #3-13: A Bottle of Red

Billy was observed purchasing a bottle of red wine at a liquor store at 2:00 p.m. on Tuesday. At 7:00 p.m. on the same day, he was arrested for driving while intoxicated on the local highway. The prosecution offers evidence about Billy's wine purchase in Billy's subsequent trial for driving while intoxicated. The defense objects.

1. Should the judge admit the evidence? Why?

2. Would it be relevant if Billy was seen carrying an empty, rather than a full, bottle of wine at 2:00 p.m.?

3. Would it be relevant if Billy was observed carrying a half-empty wine bottle at 2:00 p.m.?

4. Would the 2:00 p.m. purchase of wine be relevant, if, at the time Billy was arrested, he smelled of beer? Explain.

Problem #3-14: "Name Your Price"

The defendant offers the testimony of Price in a workers' compensation action. Price states that, "The plaintiff tried to bribe me to testify in his favor."

Is this testimony relevant? If so, relevant to what? Explain.

Problem #3-15: Rough Justice

In the days of yore, Judge S. Martin presided over the judicial system. The primary test used at that time to determine guilt or innocence in criminal cases was the "jump" test. An accused was told to jump off of a 50-foot cliff into the trees and jagged rocks below. It was widely believed that an innocent person would survive the fall without serious injury.

Haynes is charged with battery for biting his former friend, Jockey. Judge Martin tells Haynes, "Jump thou, Sirrah!" Haynes refuses, saying, "Hearest thou me well, thou dost not appreciate my situation if thou thinkest I would go over yon cliff."

1. Is Haynes's refusal to jump relevant? To what?

2. Is it relevant if Haynes, prior to being told to jump, attempted to escape while in custody? Why?

Problem #3-16: "Lions and Tigers and . . ."

The defendant, Bear, is charged with extortion. Bear allegedly threatened to shoot the local butcher if the butcher did not pay for "protection." At trial, the government offers evidence that the defendant kept several guns in his bedroom.

Is this evidence relevant? Explain. *See United States v. Gilley*, 836 F.2d 1206 (9th Cir. 1988).

Problem #3-17: Drugs 4 Sale

Arnie is charged with leading a very profitable cocaine distribution ring for more than two years, mainly in the boardrooms of Wall Street. Arnie denies the charges. The prosecutor seeks to offer the following evidence. *Is any of the evidence relevant?*

1. Arnie's bank deposits in the past two years surpassed his declared wages and income by a considerable amount, even though he had earned a significant income from his job as a stock-broker.

2. Arnie regularly kept a loaded gun in his possession.

3. A Drug Enforcement Agency field agent, Annie Lapidus, would testify that no fingerprints were found on any of the drugs recovered because of the way drug traffickers structured their handling of the product. Ms. Lapidus would further testify about how these large drug trafficking organizations worked, removing fingerprints and other identifying marks. The accused does not plan on raising the question of fingerprints.

4. Arnie's recent ex-wife, Polly, had threatened the accuser's associate, Al, about cooperating with the police against the accused. Al still was the target

of an investigation and was expected to incriminate the accused at trial. The prosecution also wanted Al to testify about Polly's threat.

5. When Arnie was initially stopped by the police, he was asked to produce identification. Arnie offered fake identification, although he later called it "just a misunderstanding."

Problem #3-18: The Lousy Ladder

Louis fell off a ladder manufactured by the XYZ Ladder Company while working at Midas College. Louis filed a products-liability suit against XYZ in district court based on diversity jurisdiction under 28 U.S.C. § 1352. Before trial, the court granted XYZ's motion in limine precluding evidence of other accidents and injuries involving XYZ ladders because there was no showing that those accidents occurred under "substantially similar" circumstances. The jury returned a verdict for XYZ. Louis appealed claiming the trial court erred in excluding the evidence of prior accidents and injuries.

Is the evidence of prior accidents and injuries relevant? Why? How should the appellate court rule?

Problem #3-19: Drugs 4 Sale II

Arnie, from problem #3-17, also was charged with the possession with the intent to distribute methamphetamine ("speed"). The prosecution offers the fact that Arnie purchased significant quantities of iodine, which is used in the production of methamphetamine. Is this evidence admissible?

§ 3.03 CONDITIONAL RELEVANCE

When the relevance of evidence depends on the existence of a separate fact, the evidence is considered to be "conditionally relevant." FRE 104(b). This type of evidence generally relates to what happened in the lawsuit — whether the gun was part of the robbery, a person was present at a meeting, or another person left a party at a certain time. These fact questions are ultimately for the trier of fact, usually the jury, but the judge plays a role as screener, making sure there is enough evidence of fact so as not to mislead the jury or waste its time. Such conditional evidence will be admitted by the judge if there is sufficient evidence for a reasonable jury to find by a preponderance of the evidence that the fact in question exists.

As noted in the previous chapter on the roles of judge, jury, and attorneys at trial, conditional relevance is more about the division of fact-finding responsibilities at trial than about relevance. In this sense, it is misplaced in the relevance rules. FRE 104(b) attempts to limit the judge's fact-finding role in this area to screening out allegations that clearly could not rise to the level of acceptable facts (i.e., rumor and innuendo are insufficient), thus delineating the judge's prefatory fact-finding function from the jury's primary responsibility.

Conditional relevance also can be viewed as a question of procedure, a first-step foundation toward admissibility. Other types of foundations include authenticating exhibits, setting up hearsay exceptions, establishing claims of privilege, and so on. In another sense, conditional relevance poses a type of "competency" requirement, because it demands that evidence have a minimum level of connection to the facts in the case. Without a sufficient showing of a connection, the evidence is incompetent and ineligible for consideration by a jury.

From yet another perspective, conditionally relevant evidence is like a chain with one or more of its links missing. The missing link signifies the omitted but necessary separate fact. When evidence is conditionally admitted, this means that counsel promises to supply the missing fact or facts at a later time in the party's case-in-chief. For example, in a breach of contract action, the plaintiff may be permitted to connect up the defendant's signature on the contract as the last remaining fact about the contract. If the missing link is not provided, the evidence will be subject to exclusion by the judge.

Conditional relevance situations arise for a variety of reasons. A single witness may not be able to lay the entire foundation required for a piece of evidence, in which case the party must use additional evidence or witnesses. Further, even if a party is able to offer its evidence chronologically, so as to avoid gaps, the party may choose to rearrange its order of presentation for strategic purposes. Thus, a party may rely on several witnesses to lay the foundation for a single piece of evidence, such as a gun or a computer printout, even though a fragmented approach is not necessary.

The admissibility of conditionally relevant evidence provides needed flexibility to attorneys in presenting their case. It allows the attorneys to control what evidence to present and in what order. While a counsel's ordering of witnesses may be confusing to the jury, the opening statement and closing arguments can offer clarity and guidance.

FRE 104(b) codifies conditional relevance. FRE 104(b) gives judges discretion to conditionally admit evidence so long as the evidence will be "connected up" at a later time by proof of the missing fact.

Illustration: Connecting the Gun to the Crime

Jorge was charged with the shooting death of his girlfriend, Lourdes. A gun was found outside of the house where Lourdes was killed. Is the gun relevant evidence?

Answer. The gun may be conditionally relevant to the shooting death of Lourdes if additional evidence shows that it was the particular gun used in the shooting (and not a gun unconnected to the incident). The gun may be admitted in evidence pending a later showing, through ballistics tests or otherwise, that this was the gun in question.

Conditional Relevance Problems

 ### Problem #3-20: Hedge Cutter

With wispy white clouds drifting lazily overhead one hot and sunny May day, Gilligan was severely injured while cutting the hedges. Gilligan claimed that he was injured when the rotary hedge cutter he was using suddenly exploded. At trial, Gilligan offers a piece of steel blade found ten yards away from the accident site.

relevance

1. The defendant objects to this evidence. What is the basis for this objection?

2. How is this evidence conditionally relevant?

3. Does adding visual language to the problem, such as "[w]ith wispy white clouds drifting lazily overhead one hot and sunny May day," affect the way this problem is considered? How would this visual language be received by a jury?

Problem #3-21: Stoneys

Alice is accused of breaking into Jim's Stone Crab Restaurant through a rear window and stealing 80 stone crab claws and two tins of mustard sauce. No fingerprints were discovered. At trial, the prosecution offers in evidence a pair of thin black kitchen gloves found near the perpetrator's point of entry. The defendant objects to this evidence.

1. Are these gloves conditionally relevant? Why?

2. What must be shown for the gloves to be admitted?

Problem #3-22: "Conditionally Yours . . ."

Leandra was brutally knifed and killed at approximately 11 p.m. as she was opening the door to her apartment. Her boyfriend, Bob Jones, is charged with murdering Leandra. At the crime scene, police found the following evidence. What facts must exist for each piece of evidence to be relevant? Explain.

1. A serrated knife purchased at the local Sweig & Halmut knife store was found in the bushes near the front door to the condominium.

2. Tire prints were discovered on the gravel approximately 15 feet away from the front door.

3. A love letter by a spurned suitor that did not reference anyone's name was found in Leandra's purse and signed "Conditionally yours, Ray."

§ 3.04   MIXED PROBLEMS

Problem #3-23: The Swallower

The defendant, Alan Onano, is charged with knowingly possessing heroin, with the intent to distribute it, in violation of 21 U.S.C. § 841(a). On March 14th, Onano was a passenger on Nigerian Airlines Flight 859, traveling from Nigeria to Kennedy Airport in New York. He was arrested at the airport after acting suspiciously. Several days later, following a bowel movement, he was found to have swallowed 83 condoms containing heroin. At trial, the defendant did not deny swallowing the condoms, but claimed that he believed he was swallowing diamonds, not drugs. The defendant offered an expert witness, Dr. Elliot Berns, a gemologist and a professor at the Fashion Institute of Technology. Dr. Berns was expected to testify on two points: the feasibility of smuggling diamonds by ingesting condoms, and the value of the smuggling venture if diamonds had been placed in the 83 condoms.

1. Is Dr. Berns' testimony relevant? Explain.

2. If Dr. Berns is allowed to testify, is his testimony conditionally relevant? Why?

3. How would you question Dr. Berns on direct examination? How would you question him on cross-examination? Prepare both examinations.

Problem #3-24: "Friends Don't Let Friends . . ."

After working all day at the airport as a mechanic, Ulysses spent from 6:30 to 9:30 p.m. at a local bar, Aundra's Place. While driving home, Ulysses was stopped by a police officer for speeding and charged with driving under the influence of alcohol. Which of the following items of evidence are relevant to the case?

1. Ulysses was seen in a different bar, Tony's Place, earlier on the same day of the incident.

2. Ulysses collects beer cans.

3. Ulysses is married with two young children, Monique and Les.

4. Ulysses was convicted of driving under the influence of alcohol in 1993.

5. Ulysses also was convicted of reckless driving in 1992.

6. Ulysses was a high-level executive of a Fortune 500 company at the time of the arrest.

7. Ulysses keeps a six-pack of beer in his refrigerator.

8. Ulysses likes psychedelic rock music such as the songs of Jimi Hendrix.

9. Ulysses runs an extremely important meeting every Friday morning at 7:30 a.m.

10. Ulysses is out of shape and has a protruding stomach, also sometimes called a "beer belly."

Problem #3-25: "The Smoking Gun"

Ivy is charged with the unregistered possession of a firearm. The firearm, a pistol, was found in the unlocked closet of a motel room (a "Motel 7"). Which of the following items of evidence are relevant to the case? Explain.

1. Ivy was found with a key to the motel room in her purse.

2. Three other people, Sam, Woody, and Rebecca, were found with keys to the same motel room on their persons.

3. Ivy was observed in the motel lobby earlier on the day the gun was found.

4. Ivy's birth certificate was found in the same closet as the gun.

5. Ivy has been convicted of disorderly conduct and battery.

6. Ivy is a recovering alcoholic.

7. A housekeeping employee at the motel, Carla, entered the room to clean it on the day the gun was discovered.

8. The pistol apparently had been purchased in Kansas (the identity of the purchaser was unknown); the motel room and Ivy's residence are in New York.

Problem #3-26: Rodney Runner

Rodney Runner brought suit against the Wily Coyote Corporation for disabling injuries. The only issue in this workers' compensation action was whether Rodney was injured on the job. Which of the following items of evidence are relevant? Explain.

1. The Wily Coyote Corp. shows that Rodney was a poor worker.

2. The Wily Coyote Corp. offers evidence that Rodney was reprimanded on three occasions for drinking alcoholic beverages during company time.

3. The Wily Coyote Corp. offers evidence that Rodney often ran to work over uneven terrain.

4. The Wily Coyote Corp. offers evidence that Rodney attempted to bribe the central defense witness not to testify.

Problem #3-27: Gary, Baseball & Steroids

The defendant, Gary Yikes, is an outstanding baseball player. He is known for his hitting and is a perennial top fielder, despite nearing the end of a distinguished career. Gary is charged with using illegal steroids to improve his baseball performance. The prosecution offers Gary's prior conviction for marijuana use and the defendant objects, arguing that the evidence is irrelevant.

1. Is testimony about the prior conviction relevant? Explain.

2. Gary's former girlfriend then testifies about changes in his sexual performance, hair growth, anger, violence and baldness at or near the time of his alleged steroid use. Is this testimony relevant? More specifically, is it conditionally relevant?

3. The prosecution offers a neighbor of Gary's who lived across the street from him and who will testify that he saw Gary injecting himself one evening on his front door steps with another known steroid user. The defendant objects to neighbor's testimony as irrelevant because the neighbor has very poor eyesight. Is the evidence admissible under Fed. R. Evid. 104(b)'s conditional relevance standard?

4. The prosecution offers as evidence several needles found next to Gary's front door steps. Is this evidence conditionally relevant? Why?

Problem #3-28: 10 of 1700 Treated

After various cancer treatments proved to be ineffective, Beth receives experimental cancer treatment. She files a claim for the payment of these medical expenses with her insurance company. The insurance company refused to pay for the expenses because the procedures had not gained acceptance as being medically "necessary" for cancer treatment. In a subsequent trial, Beth offered the deposition testimony of two doctors concerning 10 successful cases of patients who had been similarly treated at the same facility to prove that the treatment is "necessary." The insurance company objects, claiming the testimony is irrelevant and misleading.

1. Is the testimony admissible?

2. If the trial court admits the deposition testimony, the appellate court will apply what standard of review in assessing the trial court's decision to admit? *See Dallis v. Aetna Life Ins. Co.*, 768 F.2d 1303 (11th Cir. 1985).

§ 3.05   CASES AND RULES

[A]   Dortch v. Fowler

United States Court of Appeals for the Sixth Circuit
588 F.3d 396 (6th Cir. 2009)

RONALD LEE GILMAN, CIRCUIT JUDGE.

This case arises out of a traffic accident involving a vehicle driven by Angela Dortch and a Con-Way Transportation Services, Inc. tractor-trailer driven by Loren Fowler. The accident left Fowler unhurt, but Dortch suffered permanently disabling injuries that caused her to lose all memory of the collision. . . . The trial boiled down to whether the accident occurred in Dortch's or Fowler's lane of travel. Central to that inquiry is whether either of the two gouges (one in each lane) was caused by the underlying accident. Con-Way presented persuasive evidence that the first gouge in Fowler's lane of travel was caused by the accident, and therefore Dortch was at fault for crossing over the dividing line and causing the accident. Dortch countered with her own expert who testified that the second gouge (in her lane) was caused by the underlying accident. In an effort to discredit Dortch's expert, Con-Way undertook an extensive search of past accident records in the hopes of finding some evidence of a past accident that might have caused the second gouge. It failed to find any such evidence to corroborate its theory.

Dortch now challenges the district court's evidentiary ruling precluding her from cross-examining Con-Way's witnesses about the absence of record evidence corroborating its theory that a previous accident caused the second gouge. We conclude that the district court abused its discretion in preventing Dortch from pursuing this line of questioning because it was relevant to a central issue at trial. Nonetheless, we find that the error was harmless.

The standard for relevancy is "extremely liberal" under the Federal Rules of Evidence. *See United States v. Whittington*, 455 F.3d 736, 738 (6th Cir. 2006). Evidence is relevant if it has "any tendency to make the existence of any fact that is of consequence to the determination of the action more probable or less probable than it would be without the evidence." Fed. R. Evid. 401. Just as positive evidence of a past accident that could have created the second gouge would have been admissible as tending to support Con-Way (had such evidence been found), the absence of any such evidence in the accident records makes it less likely that the second gouge predated the underlying accident in this case. Put another way, the absence of any past accident record is exactly what you would expect to find if Dortch's theory that the gouge was caused by this accident is correct. Although it may not be very strong evidence, it is certainly some evidence in Dortch's favor. She therefore should have been permitted to inquire about it under Rule 401.

Con-Way counters that "[e]vidence of this type could hardly establish that it was more probable than not that the [second] gouge preexisted the Dortch accident or who crossed the center line first." This argument, however, mistakenly conflates the standard for evidentiary sufficiency with the Rule 401 standard for relevance. There is no doubt that Con-Way's fruitless records search, standing alone, does not make it more probable than not that either party crossed the center line first. But a piece of evidence does not need to carry a party's evidentiary burden in order to be relevant; it simply has to advance the ball. As one leading commentator has explained:

> It is enough if the item could reasonably show that a fact is slightly more probable than it would appear without that evidence. Even after the probative force of the evidence is spent, the proposition for which it is offered still can seem quite improbable. Thus, the common objection that the inference for which the fact is offered "does not necessarily follow" is untenable. It poses a standard of conclusiveness that very few single items of circumstantial evidence could ever meet. A brick is not a wall.

Edward W. Cleary et al., McCormick on Evidence § 185, at 542–43.

. . . We note the importance of distinguishing the present case-where Con-Way searched the accident records and found nothing to corroborate its preexisting second-gouge theory-from a hypothetical case where nobody searched the accident records. If there had been no investigation and we knew nothing about the records of past accidents, then that fact would support neither party. It would be irrelevant under Rule 401. Here, we do know something about the accident records. We know they are extensive and document numerous past accidents on the roadway in question, yet reveal no evidence of a past accident that caused the second gouge. Because they do not corroborate Con-Way's theory that the gouge was preexisting, the records provide some evidence for Dortch's conclusion that the gouge was not preexisting.

Although we conclude that the trial court abused its discretion in precluding Dortch from inquiring about the absence of record evidence supporting Con-Way's theory by ruling that the evidence was irrelevant, we find that the error was harmless.

. . . In the present case, the fact that Con-Way could find no record of an incident creating the second gouge is of little probative value. The part of the highway where the accident occurred runs through the City of Louisville, a major metropolitan area, and is undoubtedly used by hundreds of thousands of vehicles a year, including large vehicles like tractor-trailers, snow plows, and construction equipment. Many, if not most, incidents that damage such well-used roadways likely go unreported.

Also, there was absolutely nothing preventing Dortch from presenting her own witness to speak to the record evidence. If the record evidence was really all that probative, Dortch could have put her own investigator on the stand to explain the lack of records supporting Con-Way's theory that the gouge was preexisting. That Dortch did not feel compelled or even think to take this approach speaks volumes about how unimportant she really believed this evidence to be. This was a multi-day trial with numerous experts and extensive testimony regarding the physical evidence. The absence of a record documenting a previous accident, while marginally relevant, has too little weight to raise any likelihood that it would have affected the jury's verdict. We therefore will not reverse the district court on this basis.

QUESTIONS:

1.   Do you agree with the court's conclusion that the research on the origin of the second gouge is relevant? Why?

2.   What standard of review did the court use in this case? What does the appellate court's use of the standard tell you about relevance?

[B]   Rules Comparison

Compare Federal Rule of Evidence 401 with a different approach, formerly used in Texas:

Test of Relevancy

(a) "Materiality" inquires whether there is any rational relationship or pertinence of the offered evidence to any provable or controlling fact issue in dispute.

(b) "Relevancy" inquires whether the offered evidence has probative value tending to establish the presence or absence, truth or falsity, of a fact.

(c) Test: Is it material? If not, exclude. If yes, and only in that event, is it relevant? If not, exclude. If yes, admit.

Which is the clearer rule, the Texas rule or the Federal Rule of Evidence? Why?

§ 3.06   RELEVANT ETHICS RULES

Rule 3.3: Candor Toward The Tribunal

A lawyer shall not knowingly:

(3) offer evidence that the lawyer knows to be false. If a lawyer, the lawyer's client, or a witness called by the lawyer, has offered material evidence and the lawyer comes to know of its falsity, the lawyer shall take reasonable remedial measures, including, if necessary, disclosure to the tribunal. A lawyer may refuse to offer evidence, other than the testimony of a defendant in a criminal matter, that the lawyer reasonably believes is false. Illinois Rules of Prof'l Conduct R. 3.3(a)(3). *See* MRPC 3.3(a)(3).

Rule 3.4 Fairness to Opposing Party and Counsel

A lawyer shall not:

(a) unlawfully obstruct another party's access to evidence or unlawfully alter, destroy or conceal a document or other material having potential evidentiary value. A lawyer shall not counsel or assist another to any such act;

(b) falsify evidence, counsel or assist a witness to testify falsely, or offer an inducement to a witness that is prohibited by law . . . . Arizona Rules of Prof'l Conduct R. 3.4. *See* MRPC 3.4.

§ 3.07 SUMMARY AND REVIEW

1. Why is the concept of relevance dependent on the particular case?

2. What is the definition of relevance under the FRE?

3. Compare the concept of "probativeness" with the concept of "fact of consequence."

4. Define conditional relevance.

5. Specify whether each of the following statements is true or false.

   a. Only certain select forms of irrelevant evidence are admissible at trial.

   b. If evidence is relevant, it will be admitted at trial.

   c. Evidence that requires more than fifteen links to connect it with the issues in the case will be excluded.

   d. Circumstantial evidence is more likely to be relevant than direct evidence.

   e. Conditionally admitted evidence is admitted for a limited purpose.

   f. Relevance objections are almost always sustained.

Chapter 4

UNFAIRLY PREJUDICIAL EVIDENCE [FRE 403]

CHAPTER FRAMEWORK: Unfair prejudice is an exclusion that covers a wide variety of evidence. The test for this type of evidence is weighted in favor of admissibility. Unfair prejudice can be considered an umbrella for several recurring types of misleading or distracting evidence, such as similar occurrences and novel scientific evidence.

WHY ARE THE CONCEPTS IN THIS CHAPTER IMPORTANT? Unfair prejudice begins the litany of exceptions where even helpful evidence, on balance, is excluded because of its potential for harm. The exclusion of this evidence indicates that fairness and accuracy are important concerns at trial.

CONNECTIONS: The exclusion of unfairly prejudicial evidence can be viewed as a predicate for more specific exclusions, such as character evidence, subsequent remedial measures, settlement offers, plea offers, liability insurance, and the prior history of sexual assault victims.

CHAPTER OUTLINE:

I. Exclusion of Relevant but Unfairly Prejudicial Evidence [FRE 403]

    A. Judges may exclude relevant evidence that is substantially more prejudicial than probative if it:

        1. Is unfairly prejudicial

        2. Confuses the issues

        3. Misleads the fact finder

        4. Causes undue delay

        5. Wastes time

        6. Needlessly presents cumulative evidence, or

        7. Constitutes other unfair prejudice (1–7 is a non-exclusive list)

II. FRE 403 Balancing Test for Excluding Relevant Evidence:

    A. Weighted in favor of admissibility

        1. Excludes only evidence that is "substantially" more prejudicial than probative

        2. Need for relevant evidence typically greater than potential harm

        3. Judge must consider a limiting instruction (FRE 105) before excluding evidence under FRE 403

III.   Common Exclusions Under FRE 403

    A.   Probability evidence of guilt in a criminal case

    B.   Evidence of excessive violence

    C.   Scientific evidence

    D.   Similar occurrences, happenings, and events

* * * * *

RELEVANT EVIDENCE RULES

FRE 403. Excluding Relevant Evidence for Prejudice, Confusion, Waste of Time, or Other Reasons

The court may exclude relevant evidence if its probative value is substantially outweighed by a danger of one or more of the following: unfair prejudice, confusing the issues, misleading the jury, undue delay, wasting time, or needlessly presenting cumulative evidence.

§ 4.01   INTRODUCTION

Not all relevant evidence is admissible. As FRE 402 provides, relevant evidence may be made inadmissible by "the United States Constitution; a federal statute; these rules; or by other rules prescribed by the Supreme Court." The reasons for excluding relevant evidence range from causing a violation of a criminal defendant's constitutional rights to a violation of the hearsay rule.

Pursuant to FRE 403, as well as many equivalent state rules, trial courts have the authority to exclude relevant evidence if that evidence poses a significant risk of unfair prejudice, misleads the fact finder, confuses the issues, or simply wastes time. *See* FRE 403. Under FRE 403, the Court must administer a weighted balancing test (favoring admissibility) and decide whether the probative value of the evidence is substantially outweighed by one or more of these forms of prejudice.

The Advisory Committee Note to FRE 403 states:

> These circumstances [in which relevant evidence is excluded] entail risks which range all the way from inducing decision on a purely emotional basis, at one extreme, to nothing more harmful than merely wasting time, at the other extreme.

"Unfair prejudice" does not mean simply that the evidence strongly influences the jury. Evidence is offered by a party for the very purpose of influencing and persuading jurors to decide in that party's favor. Most evidence in fact will cause jurors to form immediate initial impressions or judgments — effectively triggering some prejudging — based on the jurors' own experiences and natures. According to the Advisory Committee Note to FRE 403, evidence creates "unfair prejudice" when it has "an undue tendency to suggest [a] decision on an improper basis, commonly, though not necessarily, an emotional one." Thus, the risk of "unfair prejudice" is that the jury may not be able to properly assess or evaluate the evidence. This risk arises when admission of the evidence would be perceived as unfair, or when the evidence would adversely affect the fairness of the trial process.

Not all evidence that poses a danger of unfair prejudice is excluded under this rule. Some evidence that is highly prejudicial is also highly probative of a fact in issue. Prior bad acts of a party offered to show a party's propensity to act in a certain manner, for example, can be both highly probative and highly prejudicial at the same time (Chapter 5 discusses the problems with propensity evidence). Thus, in a robbery trial, the fact that the defendant stole a car the day before to use in the robbery makes it more likely that the defendant was indeed the robber but also carries the inference that the defendant has a propensity toward criminal behavior (i.e., he is a one-man crime gang). Similarly, evidence of the horrible nature of a crime, such as a murder, is part of the basic fabric of a case and is important to understanding the crime story.

Under the FRE, the need for relevant evidence often is considered greater than the potential harm that could result from the admission of such evidence. Thus, evidence that poses a danger of unfair prejudice is excluded only if the danger of unfair prejudice "substantially outweighs" the probative value of the evidence. This weighted balancing test exhibits a preference for relevant evidence, even if the relevant evidence presents a risk of harm. However, the application of the unfair prejudice balancing test is firmly committed to the judge's sound discretion, and determinations under FRE 403 are rarely reversed on appeal.

As the Advisory Committee Note to FRE 403 points out, excluding evidence because it is unfairly prejudicial should be a last resort, occurring only after the judge has determined that a limiting instruction to the jury would be insufficient to offset any prejudice. *See* FRE 105. A limiting instruction is a directive by the judge to the jury to use the evidence only for a legitimate purpose and to disregard impermissible purposes. For example, the judge who admits evidence in the robbery trial that the defendant stole a car on the day preceding the robbery might be asked to instruct the jury to use the evidence only as it pertains to the robber's identity and not as it relates to the defendant's propensity to violate the law.

> Limited instructions are double-edged swords. The instructions admit evidence for a particular purpose. But, like rubbernecking at a car accident, they make people more curious about the impermissible purposes.

One case that traces the intricacies of the unfair prejudice balancing test is *Old Chief v. United States*, 519 U.S. 172 (1997). In *Old Chief*, the accused was charged with possessing a firearm as a previously convicted felon. The accused offered to stipulate to the fact that he was a prior felon, but the prosecution refused to accept the stipulation. Instead, the prosecution wished to offer evidence at trial of the prior crime, which was one of violence. The district court and the court of appeals both sided with the prosecution, allowing the government to prove its own case. The Supreme Court, in an opinion by Justice Souter, reversed.

While the Court found that the type of conviction was relevant to the current charge, and observed that the prosecution usually has the option of proving its own case as it sees fit (even on matters that are not in dispute), the Court still found that the evidence should have been excluded as unfairly prejudicial. In defining "unfair prejudice," the Court turned to the Advisory Committee Note to FRE 403, which defined "unfair prejudice" as "an undue tendency to suggest decision on an improper basis, commonly, though not necessarily, an emotional one." Justice Souter concluded that unfair prejudice of this sort had occurred in the case of Johnny Lynn Old Chief. Said Justice Souter:[1]

> Such improper grounds certainly include the one that Old Chief points to here: generalizing a defendant's earlier bad act into bad character and taking that as raising the odds that he did the later bad act now charged (or, worse, as calling for preventive conviction even if he should happen to be innocent momentarily).

Justice Souter went on to discuss the analytical method that courts should employ in balancing probative value against risk of unfair prejudice under FRE 403. He observed that a court's decision on admissibility might require a review of evidentiary alternatives as well as the evidence in question: "What counts as the FRE 403 'probative value' of an item of evidence, as distinct from its FRE 401 'relevance,' may be calculated by comparing evidentiary alternatives." *Id.* at 184. These alternatives might include revealing only the general nature of the offense to the jury or some other evidentiary manner of minimizing prejudice. (For additional information about the case, see the case excerpt at § 4.07).

Illustration: Unfair Prejudice

Susan alleges that she was raped by an acquaintance, John. At trial, John introduces a photograph of Susan dancing with him one year prior to the alleged rape. The photograph shows Susan wearing a strapless gown. Does the photograph present a risk of unfair prejudice?

Answer: If Susan's manner of dress on an earlier occasion would lead some jurors to consider punishing her through their verdict, the jury may be influenced to decide the issue based on emotion and not on the requirements of the law. Thus, the photograph may obfuscate the relevant facts and hinder the jury in fulfilling its duty to find the truth. The photograph of Susan dancing with John may be probative in several ways. If it was offered on the issue of whether Susan knew John, it probably would be excluded because of its danger of unfair prejudice. If, however, Susan claimed she did not know John, and the photograph is the only evidence that the two were acquainted, then the photograph would have strong probative value, yielding a much greater chance of admissibility.

Unfair Prejudice Problems: Applying the Balancing Test

Problem #4-1: "One Drink Too Many"

On a dark, moonless night in late November, a truck and passenger car collided on a remote section of the interstate. The driver of the car, Albert, was killed. Albert's estate filed a negligence suit against the driver of the truck, Tina, and her company,

---

[1] 519 U.S. at 180–181.

Studio 53, Inc. At trial, the defendants called Dr. Robert Orsky, a hematologist at the Regional Crime Laboratory, to discuss the blood tests performed on Albert. The plaintiff objected and called for a sidebar, at which time the following discussion occurred.

JUDGE: What is the basis for your objection, counsel?

PLAINTIFF'S ATTORNEY: The blood test done by Dr. Orsky is not credible, Your Honor, and should be excluded on grounds of unfair prejudice. We proffer the testimony of Nurse Wilma Jones, who, only minutes before the horrible accident, had assisted in taking the stitches out of Albert's hand at the nearby medical office. Nurse Jones will testify that she came within eighteen inches of Albert's face and that Albert in no way, shape, or form smelled of alcohol.

JUDGE: Defense counsel, any reply?

1. How should the defense counsel reply to the plaintiff's assertions?

JUDGE: In this case, I find that admitting the results of the blood test would be too harmful to the plaintiff's case. In addition, the test performed by Dr. Orsky lacks credibility to me in light of Nurse Jones' proposed testimony. The blood test evidence will be excluded.

2. Did the judge rule correctly? Explain. *See Ballou v. Henri Studios, Inc.*, 656 F.2d 1147 (5th Cir. 1981).

3. Suppose the prosecution offers a videotape at trial that contains inadmissible evidence improperly bolstering testimony by a prosecution's witness who has not yet testified. What should the court do? Would it make a difference if the court previously had ruled that the evidence in the video was inadmissible in response to a motion *in limine*?

Problem #4-2: Sign for a package?

The defendant, Donny, was accused of possessing cocaine received in a package sent through the U.S. mail. The defendant claimed the package was mailed by a complete stranger who must have mistakenly put the defendant's name and address on it. The defendant further claimed he had no idea what was in the package. At trial, the prosecution offered evidence that the return address on the package was the same address as a cousin of the defendant, suggesting that the package was not mailed to the accused accidentally by someone he did not know.

1. Is this evidence from the prosecution unfairly prejudicial? Explain.

2. *90210 Drug Place.* Suppose a police officer testified for the prosecution in the same case that, "I often saw the defendant, Donny, hanging out at 'Drug Place,' a location near the defendant's home that was commonly used as a place where people sold drugs." Admissible?

3. Ethics Consideration. Donny wants his cousin to testify that he does not live at the address listed as the return address on the package. However, as his attorney you have done your due diligence and had your detective do some

digging. It turns out that Donny's cousin is listed as the owner of the property. Do you allow Donny to go on the stand and testify that his cousin does not live at or have any connection to the address listed as the return address on the package? Ohio Rules of Prof'l Conduct R. 3.3(a)(3). *See* MRPC 3.3 (a)(3).

Problem #4-3: Malpractice Monsoon

James Monsoon brought a medical malpractice suit against the M. Cohan Hospital, claiming the physicians did not provide standard treatment for a blood clot in his legs. The hospital, in its defense, offered evidence that the plaintiff did not disclose at any time during his treatment that he was regularly smoking marijuana and taking cocaine, thus interfering with the proper treatment protocols set up by the physicians at the hospital.

1. Is the evidence of the plaintiff's drug use unfairly prejudicial?

Problem #4-4: Discrimination, Inc.

Dan Doniwitz, the Chief Operating Officer of Dash Energy, Inc., was accused of gender discrimination after firing a senior employee, Susan Spikes. Spikes filed a claim before the Civil Rights Commission and, at the hearing, offered the fact that a different employee had submitted a gender discrimination claim as well. The other employee's claim was about the marketing department's conduct, however, not Doniwitz's. Should the Commission consider the other claim in light of an unfair prejudice objection?

Problem #4-5: "A Lot Is Riding on Your Tires . . ."

Kate is charged with cocaine conspiracy. She testifies at trial and mentions she has a five-year-old daughter, named Becca. In rebuttal, the prosecution offers a photograph of Becca playing with large sums of money while sitting inside an empty tire in what looks like Becca's room. Admissible? Why?

Common Types of Exclusion Under FRE 403

A plethora of evidence may be labeled "unfairly prejudicial," but certain kinds of evidence are particularly susceptible to exclusion on this basis. Consequently, most of this chapter will focus on various types of evidence often believed to present a special danger of unfair prejudice: (1) probability evidence of guilt (specifically, the likelihood of another person with the same characteristics committing the crime charged); (2) evidence depicting violence in a manner that is physically revolting; (3) novel scientific evidence; and (4) similar events, happenings, or occurrences.

§ 4.02 PROBABILITY EVIDENCE OF GUILT IN A CRIMINAL CASE

Statistical evidence is routinely admitted at trial to assist the trier of fact. However, one type of statistical evidence is particularly misleading and generally excluded. This type of evidence, denoted here as "probability evidence of guilt," is specifically offered in a criminal case to show the unlikelihood that another person with the same characteristics as the accused committed the crime charged. Such evidence suffers from a variety of defects, not the least of which is its power to exert extreme influence over a jury.

A red flag should go up when probability of guilt evidence is offered. It is important to investigate the reliability of the data "sample" used to calculate the probability. For example, was the data sample reasonable in size and content — was it under inclusive or over inclusive? An arbitrarily drawn sample may skew the probability results and render the evidence misleading, unfairly prejudicial, and ultimately inadmissible under FRE 403.

If the probability of guilt testimony concerns individuals' traits (e.g., hair color, beards, or moustaches), it is important to know whether the traits are dependent or independent, meaning related to and influencing each other or not. Treating dependent traits as independent will undermine the validity of probability results and warrant their exclusion as misleading and unfairly prejudicial. (*See People v. Collins* in the Cases and Rules section of this chapter that discusses the reliability problems of conflating dependent and independent traits in probability testimony; and Daniel L. Faigman, David H. Kaye, Michael J. Saks & Joseph Sanders, *Science in the Law: Standards, Statistics and Research Issues; Science in the Law: Social and Behavioral Science Issues; Science in the Law: Forensic Science Issues*, 215–17 (2002).

Problem #4-6: It Had to Be You . . .

The defendant, Lester, is charged with first-degree murder in Walhalla, South Carolina, a rural town of 4,000 people. At trial, the prosecution introduced evidence showing that the defendant had the same general description, the same nickname, and the same address as the person linked to the crime by independent evidence. The defendant claims mistaken identity. In rebuttal, the prosecution offers a mathematical professor, Egbert Einstein. Professor Einstein intends to testify that there is an extreme improbability, one in twelve million, of these characteristics belonging to a second person in Walhalla.

What flaws, if any, can you find in Professor Einstein's evidence? Should his testimony be admitted? Why? *See e.g., Branion v. Gramly*, 855 F.2d 1256 (7th. Cir. 1988); *People v. Collins*, 68 Cal. 2d 319, 438 P.2d 33 (1968).

Practical Tip:

Consultants (e.g., statisticians) are often helpful in assessing the validity of the underlying data and sample for calculating a probability rate. Consultants also help lawyers develop trial strategies and questions for witnesses, especially expert witnesses. Lawyers sometimes inform consultants at the time of retention that they may be asked later to serve as expert witnesses — in effect, these consultants are really expert witnesses on call.

§ 4.03   EVIDENCE OF EXCESSIVE VIOLENCE

Evidence showing the results of violence is a routine part of many different cases, particularly violent crimes. In a murder case, for example, the prosecutor must prove that a person died. The death may have been horrific. While evidence of the death is permitted to prove the case, Rule 403 imposes some limitations. Specifically, it is improper to offer evidence that so blinds a jury to the facts of the case that the jury makes an emotional determination. A shorthand description of this limit is that the evidence cannot be so violent in appearance that a reasonable jury will "lose its lunch" as a result of viewing it. Excessively violent evidence that fails the "lose your lunch" test is unfairly prejudicial.

Excessive Violence Problems

Problem #4-7: Lose Your Lunch

Ernest and Samantha, the leaders of a radical political party, were found shot to death in their living room. The scene was gruesome and the stench of death was everywhere. Franklyn, a known contract killer, was charged with the murders. At trial, the government offers testimony of a crime scene search officer, Jan, who testified that she visited the scene immediately following the murders and took color photographs of the bodies. The prosecutor then attempted to introduce in evidence the glossy 8 x 10 photographs taken by Jan. Franklyn's attorney objects.

1. What ruling and why?

2. Should the prosecutor agree to stipulate to the fact that Ernest and Samantha were killed by gunshots?

3. Should the judge approve the stipulation if both parties agree to it?

Practical Tip:

Although photographs of excessively violent crimes are routinely admitted to prove elements of a case (e.g., location and condition of the body), defense counsel may limit the total number of photographic exhibits by objecting to some photographic evidence as cumulative and therefore unfairly prejudicial under FRE 403.

Violent Videos & Limiting Instructions

Problem #4-8: More Lose Your Lunch — Terrorism

Defendant was charged with disclosing classified information regarding Navy ships to individuals who support jihad terrorism. At trial, the prosecution showed excerpts from several pro-jihadist videos that included an execution and a suicide bombing. The court only allowed the prosecution to show a minute of a video scene showing bloody bodies and also required the prosecution to delete a scene with a headless body. In addition, the court instructed the jury to view the videos "dispassionately" and to only consider them for the purpose of determining whether defendant acted with knowledge and intent in disclosing the classified information. Did the court abuse its discretion in permitting the state to play excerpts from the videos? *See United States v. Abu-Jihaad*, 630 F.3d 102 (2d Cir. 2010).

Emotionally Difficult Demonstrations & Depictions

Evidence involving emotionally difficult demonstrations and depictions, while different than evidence of violent behavior, can have a similar prejudicial impact on the trier of fact. Yet, this kind of evidence also might be integral to the case and one or more of its elements and consequently admitted. The following problems illustrate this point.

Problem #4-9: Legs

Ned Carlyle lost both of his legs to amputation after an automobile accident. After being fitted with prosthetics, he learned to walk again. Ned sued the driver of the other car on a negligence theory and sought damages. At trial, Ned testified about the accident.

> PLAINTIFF'S ATTORNEY: Ned, please describe the injuries you received from the accident.

> A: My legs were crushed from the knees down. The "jaws of life" were used to extract me from the car. Here's what happened —

> DEFENDANT'S ATTORNEY: Objection. This evidence is unnecessary.

1. What ruling and why?

> PLAINTIFF'S ATTORNEY: Can you show the ladies and gentlemen of the jury what your legs look like today?

> A: Certainly. (Ned begins to remove his prosthetics to show the jury his stumps, intending to point to where his legs once were).

> DEFENDANT'S ATTORNEY: Objection, Your Honor. The witness's actions are unfairly prejudicial.

2. How should the judge rule?

3. If the judge rules in favor of the defendant, but the plaintiff already has engaged in the forbidden behavior, does the defense counsel have any recourse? What can be done?

Problem #4-10: A Day in the Life

Susan White, a crane operator at a major road construction site, was severely injured in a crane accident. Susan sued the crane manufacturer based on a theory of strict products liability. To show damages, Susan offered a film depicting an average day in her life subsequent to the accident, including how she eats, gets out of bed, bathes, and travels on the city streets with other pedestrians.

1. Is such a film admissible? Explain.

2. Ethics Consideration. Suppose that Susan cannot afford to pay to have someone film her for a day. Can Susan's attorney cover the filming costs for her so that they may use the film at trial? Colorado Rules of Prof'l Conduct R. 1.8(e)(1). *See* MRPC 1.8 (e)(1).

Evidence of Stereotypes

It might be assumed that evidence of stereotypes would be unfairly prejudicial and excluded. What if, however, the stereotyping was part of the event in question? The following problem illustrates this issue.

Problem #4-11: Johnny Got His Gun

[The following problem is based on an actual incident that occurred in New York City in the fall of 1992. The facts apply not only to the groups mentioned, but to all stereotypes that can enter into jurors' interpretive assumptions relating to an event.]

Dora and Bart, a white female and white male, respectively, were transit police officers in New York City. One day, while on an anti-crime detail, they came upon two black males in the subway who they believed to be robbing a woman subway rider. The black males were holding handguns. Dora and Bart quickly opened fire, wounding one of the apparent assailants. It turned out that the apparent assailants, Johnny Patton and George Diamond, were undercover police officers from a different district in the process of arresting a suspect.

Assume for the purposes of this problem that Dora and Bart are charged with aggravated assault for the injuries caused to Officer Patton. Dora and Bart wish to argue that their conduct was not culpable.

1. What is the relevance, if any, of perceptions, stereotypes, and statistical data about race?

2. What is the relevance of the fact that the apparent assailants were male and relatively youthful in appearance?

3. Are generalizations about a group always an improper use of stereotypes and, therefore, unfairly prejudicial?

§ 4.04   SCIENTIFIC EVIDENCE

Scientific experiments that seek to replicate or simulate the events on which a lawsuit is based have the potential to be both highly credible and highly misleading. Unlike real evidence that is intrinsic to the case, lawyers generate scientific experiments or simulations in hope of advancing their clients' cases. A simulation can illuminate key factual points of a lawsuit that otherwise might be overshadowed by other evidence or the actual event underlying the lawsuit (e.g., the horrific Air France Jet crash off the coast of Brazil in 2009). Yet, the same simulation can just as likely misrepresent what occurred through misplaced emphasis or inaccurate distortion.

Consequently, experimental scientific evidence is constrained by FRE 403 and may be excluded as unfairly prejudicial if it is not "substantially similar" to what it intends to recreate.

Any form of novel scientific evidence — information based on innovative or cutting-edge processes not yet recognized by the scientific community at large — whether based on experiment, observation, or other formulation, can be unfairly prejudicial. *See* Steven Lubet, Modern Trial Advocacy 172 (1993); David H. Kaye, David E. Bernstein & Jennifer L. Mnookin, The New Wigmore: A Treatise on Evidence, Expert Evidence 434 (Richard D. Friedman ed., Austin: Wolters Kluwer Publishers, 2d ed. 2011). Heightened reliability concerns often attend the use of novel scientific evidence as well as the usual FRE 403 concerns about scientific evidence being misleading and confusing. Courts have placed the analysis of most scientific evidence questions squarely within the expert testimony rules, FRE 702 et seq. The convergence of unfair prejudice and scientific evidence is illustrated by the following example.

Illustration: Polygraph

Al Wiley is prosecuted for white-collar fraud after allegedly bilking several large health care companies out of millions of dollars. At trial, the prosecutors offer the testimony of Dr. Ziggy Topstein, an expert in polygraphy. Dr. Topstein intends to testify that he has administered "lie detector" tests for 20 years and has an advanced degree specializing in interpreting the physiological data from such tests. He administered a "lie detector" test to the defendant, Wiley, immediately after the allegations against him. The test occurred at Wiley's request, but the results indicated that Wiley was evasive and likely untruthful about the events in question.

The defendant objected to the testimony. How should the judge rule?

Answer: Despite claims about the accuracy of polygraph tests, the judge should exclude the evidence as unfairly prejudicial, as well as insufficiently reliable to meet the requisite standard for expert testimony under FRE 702. Jurors may tend to overvalue such evidence, and may forsake their own independent review of the defendant's credibility. Moreover, polygraph testimony does not yet have a sufficiently reliable scientific basis. Many experts find that the human interpretation of the polygraph test is subjective, to the extent that the results are in the "eye of the beholder." Further, there may be disputes about replicating such tests in a laboratory setting.

A brief overview of how courts have approached novel scientific evidence follows. The judicial approach described below also applies today to non-scientific and technical expert evidence.

Courts have been struggling with the admissibility of novel scientific evidence for decades. From 1923 until fairly recently, the federal courts mostly applied the singular test of whether the evidence was "sufficiently established to have gained general acceptance in the particular field in which it belongs." *Frye v. United States*, 293 F. 1013, 1014 (D.C. Cir. 1923). In *Frye*, the District of Columbia Circuit Court of Appeals considered the standard for admitting evidence about the precursor to the polygraph, a "deception test." This "deception test" measured changes in a person's systolic blood pressure. The court held that such evidence must be "sufficiently established to have gained general acceptance in the particular field in which it belongs" to be admitted. Without such scientific recognition, the evidence would be considered merely experimental and insufficiently trustworthy. The court's approach to this evidence was eventually adopted by many jurisdictions as the test for the admissibility of all kinds of novel scientific evidence.

In 1993, however, the Supreme Court held that the *Frye* test had been superseded by the adoption of the FRE. Under the FRE, the appropriate test allows trial courts to consider multiple factors. These factors include the following: (1) whether the subject matter was "scientific knowledge"; (2) whether the theory or technique can be or has been tested; (3) whether the theory or technique has been subjected to peer review and publication; (4) whether the technique has a known or potential rate of error; (5) whether standards controlling the technique's operation exist and are maintained; and (6) finally, but not exclusively, the *Frye* test of general acceptance in the particular field. *See Daubert v. Merrell Dow Pharmaceuticals, Inc.*, 509 U.S. 579, 593–594 (1993). Justice Blackmun stated:[2]

> Faced with a proffer of expert scientific testimony, then, the trial judge must determine at the outset, pursuant to Rule 104(a), whether the expert is proposing to testify to (1) scientific knowledge that (2) will assist the trier of fact to understand or determine a fact in issue. This entails a preliminary assessment of whether the reasoning or methodology underlying the testimony is scientifically valid and whether that reasoning or methodology properly can be applied to the facts in issue.

The meaning of the multiple-factor test of *Daubert* is still unfolding. Courts are being asked to admit novel scientific evidence in a wide variety of lawsuits, many dealing with illness and injury allegedly caused by faulty products or pharmaceuticals. The Supreme Court has decided subsequent cases in an effort to clarify the meaning of *Daubert*.

In *Kumho Tire Co., Ltd. v. Carmichael*, 526 U.S. 137 (1999), a suit resulting from an automobile accident allegedly caused by a defective tire, the Supreme Court attempted to further delineate the scope of the *Daubert* test. The Court considered whether the *Daubert* reliability test should be used for a non-scientific expert, in this case an expert in tire failure analysis. The Court held that the *Daubert* test must also be applied to the testimony of "technical" or other non-scientific experts, such as engineers, but emphasized that the *Daubert* test is a flexible one. The Court referred to its prior decision in *General Electric Co. v. Joiner*, 522 U.S. 136 (1997), where it held that courts of appeals must use an "abuse of discretion" standard when reviewing reliability findings by the district courts. *Id.* at 143. (In *Joiner*, the Supreme Court reviewed the exclusion of an expert witness's opinion on whether a chemical, PCB, caused the plaintiff's cancer). Chapter 9 on expert testimony delves into these cases and the rules governing experts in great detail. The problem that follows illustrates the role FRE 403 still plays with some scientific evidence.

---

[2]   509 U.S. at 592–593.

Reenactment Test Problem

Problem #4-12: Instant Replay *OBJ → U.P. → Mislead Jury*

A tractor-trailer truck collided with a Buick Reatta automobile. The driver of the Buick sued the tractor-trailer driver and his insurance company. At the time of the accident, 1:00 p.m., the pavement was dry and the weather was clear.

At trial, the plaintiff offered in evidence the results of an experimental crash between a tractor-trailer truck similar to the one involved in the accident and an identical Buick automobile. The plaintiff could not obtain the actual truck that collided with the car because it had been too badly damaged in the crash. The only differences between the experiment and the actual crash were that the experimental truck was approximately 115 pounds heavier than the truck involved in the accident and the experiment occurred on a slight incline, not on flat land like the actual accident.

1. Are the results of the experiment admissible?

2. Would it be reversible error if the experiment results were improperly admitted? Why?

Background Box: Visual Demonstrations:

When a party introduces a visual demonstration purporting to recreate an accident or other event, the proponent must establish that the demonstration shares substantial similarity with the conditions of the accident or event. "But when demonstrative evidence is offered only to illustrate general scientific principles, rather than a reenactment of events, it need not pass the substantial similarity test." *Withrow v. Spears*, 967 F. Supp. 2d 982, 998 n. 10 (D. DE 2013) (quoting *Altman v. Bobcat Co.*, 349 Fed. Appx. 758, 763 (3rd Cir. 2009) (permitting a computer animation depicting a backhoe and attachment and alternative designs for eliminating the risk of inadvertent activation). "The test is 'not one of labels,' but 'whether the demonstration is sufficiently close in appearance to the original accident to create the risk of misunderstanding by the jury, for it is that risk that gives rise to the special requirement to show similar conditions.'" *Altman*, 349 Fed. Appx. at 763 (quoting *Fusco v. Gen. Motors Corp.*, 11 F.3d 259, 264 (1st Cir. 1993). A judge's cautionary instruction reminding the jury that the illustration is not a recreation reduces the risk for juror misunderstanding.

Chemical Tests & Hypnosis Problem

Problem #4-13: DNA DNA DNA

After a series of rapes committed by a masked rapist, the police apprehended a suspect. There was no positive eyewitness identification of the defendant as the perpetrator of the crimes. Instead, the prosecution relied on: (a) DNA testing, which revealed that the semen found on the clothes of two of the victims was that of the defendant; and (b) a witness, who claimed after hypnosis that she remembered observing the defendant at the scene of two of the rapes immediately prior to their occurrence.

1. Is either the DNA or hypnosis evidence relevant? Why?

2. Is either the DNA or hypnosis evidence unfairly prejudicial? Why?

3. What is the relevance of *Daubert v. Dow Pharmaceuticals, Inc.*, *Kumho Tire Co., Ltd. v. Carmichael*, and *Frye v. United States*?

4. Which of the following types of evidence would most likely be excluded: (a) polygraph evidence; (b) handwriting analysis (graphology) evidence; (c) voice spectrography identification evidence; or (d) blood alcohol testing? Why?

§ 4.05 SIMILAR OCCURRENCES, HAPPENINGS, AND EVENTS

Evidence of similar occurrences, happenings, or events is generally offered to corroborate or bolster a party's theory of the case. Often, there is an insufficient quantity of direct evidence about an incident or event to adequately explain it. For example, there may be inadequate information about the cause of a person's slip and fall on a dimly lit sidewalk. When there is a lack of information, comparisons to other events or occurrences are especially useful. In a broad sense, the history of an event may be instructive as to its cause, its significance, or its meaning. Yet, because the similar events are still other events — meaning at other times and places — these events are likely unfairly prejudicial when placed before the fact finder.

Similar events evidence is commonly offered concerning the following occurrences: (1) accidents (to show causation or the dangerousness of the instrumentality); (2) dangerous conditions (e.g., a pothole or curve in a road); (3) sales of property or services (to show value); (4) prior course of dealing between the parties (to show the meaning of a contract provision); and (5) prior custom or usage in the industry (to show the meaning of an action or document).

In addition, a lack of similar occurrences, events, or happenings is sometimes offered to show an absence of culpability or fault. The lawyer offering the "absence of similar events" evidence must show that the circumstances that produced the absence were similar to the circumstances that produced the instant event. Reaching back in time to demonstrate similar circumstances can be costly and difficult. For example, it may be impossible to locate key witnesses. The lawyer offering the absence of similar events evidence must also show that there was a reporting mechanism in place to ensure that there really was an absence of similar events and not simply a situation where there was no reporting process in place to record earlier similar events. For example, a plaintiff-employee sues a defendant-employer for personal injuries allegedly caused by the employer's negligent maintenance of machinery. The employer offers the absence of any prior accidents (i.e., the absence of similar events evidence) to show that it was the plaintiff's own negligence that caused her injuries. The employer must show (1) there was a substantial similarity of circumstances concerning the machinery and the workplace before the plaintiff's injury and (2) that the employer would have known of any prior injuries because of the company's reporting mechanism.

Similar events evidence has great potential for unfair prejudice. Prior events, happenings, or occurrences often occur under widely disparate circumstances. Dissimilarities in the circumstances between the other events and the event in question diminish the value of the evidence. Lawyers offering similar event evidence must be prepared to argue the similarities between prior similar events and the event that is the subject of litigation. Lawyers objecting to such evidence must highlight the dissimilarities between prior events and the event at issue, arguing that the evidence is misleading, unfairly prejudicial, and inadmissible under FRE 403.

In addition, jurors may be so misled or distracted by the other events that they are led to focus on the nuances of the other events instead of the event at issue. Further, no matter how similar or helpful to the jury the other occurrences are, the prior events are nevertheless collateral to the specific facts to be decided. For all of these reasons, the evidence of similar occurrences, happenings, and events is often excluded at trial.

Illustration: Similar Sale Prices

Josephine's house was condemned by the state after a new highway was scheduled for construction almost directly through her kitchen. The only issue at trial was what constituted just compensation for her house. Josephine introduced the sale price of other homes in her neighborhood. Are the prices of these other house sales admissible?

Answer: The other sale prices are relevant and not unfairly prejudicial, provided that the other houses being used for comparison are comparable to Josephine's. If the other houses are not sufficiently similar, and can be distinguished based on differences in size, features, location, etc., the admission of the sale prices of other homes probably would be unfairly prejudicial.

Similar Events Problems

 Problem #4-14: Puddles

Wally Witness testifies for the plaintiff in a "slip and fall" personal injury case. The plaintiff contends that the defendant negligently allowed puddles of water to accumulate on the defendant's walkway where the plaintiff fell.

Can Wally testify that he had observed puddles regularly form on the walkway during the three weeks prior to the plaintiff's fall? Can he testify that he had seen three people other than the plaintiff fall on the same walkway earlier that week? Why?

Practical Tip:

Lawyers should be prepared to object to "similar events" evidence and require the proponent to demonstrate the similarity between the prior events and the instant event in the case. The lawyer should also consider asking the judge for a cautionary instruction — reminding the jury that prior similar events evidence is not dispositive of some fact or issue in the case. It is only some circumstantial evidence of the fact or issue.

 Problem #4-15: Seafood Chowder

Memphis Frozen Foods, Inc., shipped three tons of frozen shrimp with Benner Shipping. The shrimp spoiled en route and Memphis Frozen Foods brought suit against Benner Shipping for damages. The key issue was how to interpret the requirements of the contract. Benner Shipping attempted to introduce in evidence prior contracts between the parties concerning the sale of scallops and clams. Memphis Frozen Foods objected, claiming that the prior contracts were irrelevant because they did not deal with shrimp.

What ruling? Why?

Problem #4-16: How Sweet It Isn't

Polly, an employee in an artificial sweetener factory, was severely injured when a "No-Sweet" machine exploded. Polly sued the manufacturer of the machine. At trial, Polly attempted to introduce evidence concerning other "No-Sweet" machines that exploded.

Should such evidence be admitted? Why? *See generally Ponder v. Warren Tool Corp.*, 834 F.2d 1553 (10th Cir. 1987).

Problem #4-17: Harassment

The plaintiff, Janet Fife, brought suit in 1995 against her former employer, Ace Barnes of Ace Hardware, Inc., claiming sexual harassment and unlawful retaliation. The plaintiff testified at trial.

PLAINTIFF'S COUNSEL: Do you know if you are the only person to make allegations of this kind against the defendant?

DEFENDANT'S COUNSEL: Objection. This question calls for an irrelevant and unfairly prejudicial answer.

1. How should the judge rule on this objection?

PLAINTIFF: Actually there were three other complaints that I know of — one by Barnes's former secretary in 1988, one by his store clerk in 1997, and one by his truck driver in 1999.

PLAINTIFF'S COUNSEL: What were the outcomes of those other complaints?

DEFENDANT'S COUNSEL: Objection, Your Honor. This question calls for an irrelevant and unfairly prejudicial response.

JUDGE: Counsel, please approach the bench.

2. How should the judge rule on this objection if the answer to the question would have been as follows?

PLAINTIFF: One of the complaints, the one by the truck driver, was dismissed. The other two complaints were found to have merit by the administrative body that reviewed the complaints, and damages were awarded.

Problem #4-18: Prior Shoplifters

Carl Customer sued Bull's-eye Corporation after he was stabbed by a shoplifter at one of the Bull's-eye stores. Sid the Security Guard was attempting to apprehend the shoplifter when an altercation ensued. Carl stepped in to help Sid and the shoplifter stabbed him. At trial, other incidents at the Bull's-eye store were admitted into evidence. These incidents included other shoplifters who had been carrying weapons and another incident where a customer helped a security guard, just like Carl did. Bull's-eye objected to the admission of this evidence under FRE 403. How should a judge rule on this objection? *Therrien v. Target Corp.*, 617 F.3d 1242, 1255 (10th Cir. 2010).

The Lack of Similar Events

Sometimes, defense attorneys offer evidence of the lack of similar events for the inference that if no other similar events occurred, the defendant or defendant's control over an instrumentality was not the cause of harm. This type of evidence has its own drawbacks.

Problem #4-19: Double Decker

Suzanne was injured when she was thrown from a ride at the State Fair called the "Double Decker." Suzanne sued the ride's owner and its manufacturer. At trial, the defendants attempted to introduce evidence that no one had been injured in 5,000 previous rides on the Double Decker.

1. How is this problem different from other offers of similar acts, occurrences, or happenings evidence? Is this evidence admissible?

2. Ethics Consideration. Before being retained by Suzanne, the attorney had read about her accident in the newspaper. He immediately sent a condolence letter and explained that she should consider coming into his office for a free consultation. She followed his advice and after the meeting retained him as her attorney. Is his solicitation permissible? Alaska Rules of Prof'l Conduct R. 7.3 (b) & (c). *See* MRPC 7.3 (b) & (c).

§ 4.06 MIXED PROBLEMS

Problem #4-20: Pre-Owned Clothes

Jack is arrested and charged with burglary ("the breaking and entering of the dwelling house of another at night with the intent to commit a felony therein"). He is accused of stealing five expensive men's suits. At trial the prosecution offers the following evidence:

1. The closets and dresser drawers in Jack's apartment contained 200 pairs of men's socks and 300 towels (many of which had hotel monograms on them). Is this evidence admissible? Why?

2. Jack had 40 suits in his apartment closet. Is this evidence admissible? Why?

3. Jack had stolen 20 pairs of underwear the year before. Why would such evidence be offered? Is the evidence admissible? Why?

4. Ethical Consideration: Jack is acquitted. At Christmas, he gives his attorney an antique watch worth $75. May his attorney keep the watch? Colorado Rules of Prof'l Conduct R. 1.8 (c). *See* MRPC 1.8(c).

Problem #4-21: Heads Up

Cars driven by Stanley Rodriguez and Frances DeLarue collide on Peachtree Street. An injured Frances sued Stanley for damages based on negligence. At trial, she offers a video of Dr. Gupta suturing her scalp wound. The video highlights the bloody area of the wound.

1. What is the basis for an objection to this evidence? Why?

2. What is the proponent of the evidence's best response to the objection? Why?

3. What ruling and why?

Problem #4-22: "Wax On, Wax Off"

Amy slips and falls in the lobby of the Armitron Corp. She sues the company for damages resulting from the negligent maintenance and repair of the floor.

1. At trial, Amy offers evidence that in the past two weeks at least nine other people slipped and fell in the same general area of the lobby. (Three of the people slipped and fell subsequent to Amy's fall.) Is this evidence admissible to show negligence or culpability? For a different purpose? Why?

2. Amy offers the testimony of a professional floor cleaner, Carl, as an expert on "waxology and the general slipperiness of floors." The expert will testify that he performed an experiment in the lobby of another building on a similar floor that was two years older than the one in question — the original floor on which Amy fell had been destroyed and then remodeled in good faith. The expert found the floor to be highly slippery, much more so than the average floor. Are the expert's findings admissible? Why?

3. Amy also offers the maintenance and repair records of the Armitron Corp. on the lobby floors of other buildings it owns. Are the records admissible? Why?

4. Armitron Corp. offers evidence that Amy slipped and fell twice before during the same week, once in the supermarket and once while getting into her car. Is the evidence of the prior falls admissible? Why?

5. Armitron Corp. also offered evidence that its records reflected that no one had fallen on the floor in the three months preceding Amy's fall. Is the lack of apparent falls evidence admissible? Why?

Problem #4-23: Little Red Corvette

1. On a dark and foggy stretch of a remote two-lane highway, Carlos' Astro Van collided with LeShawn's Corvette. There were no eyewitnesses to the crash and neither Carlos nor LeShawn remembered how the crash had occurred. Carlos later sued LeShawn for damages. At trial, Carlos called a statistics expert, Dr. Lenny Leonardo, to testify that "Corvette drivers are nine times more likely to cause an accident than other drivers, and are fourteen times more likely to cause an accident than Astro Van drivers." Admissible? Why?

2. Carlos is also prosecuted for holding up a Bloomingdale's Department Store earlier that same day. Several eyewitnesses swear they saw a person looking exactly like Carlos, dressed in the same polar-arctic sweater and with a beard and mustache, escape in an Astro Van after robbing the store. Carlos denies the charge. Dr. Leonardo is called to testify by the prosecution. Leonardo states that "the odds of another person fitting Carlos' description, wearing a similar sweater and driving an Astro Van in the same county are one in six million." Admissible? Why?

Problem #4-24: Lobster Bill of Lading

In a breach of contract action between Noah's Lobsters, Inc., and The Olde Edward Inn restaurant, the only issue at trial was the meaning of a term in the bill of lading guaranteeing "Maine lobsters for delivery." Noah's insisted that the term permitted the substitution of South African lobsters on a necessity basis. Noah's offered prior bills of lading for the sale of Maine lobsters to The Olde Edward Inn, and bills of lading for lobster sales involving Noah's and other restaurants.

1. Is the evidence of the prior bills of lading admissible? Explain.

Problem #4-25: Murder He Wrote

Jorge is charged with murder. At trial, the prosecution calls an expert to the witness stand, Dr. Denise Dart, who will testify that bite marks found on the victim were made by Jorge. Is the bite mark evidence admissible? Why?

Problem #4-26: The Horrible Boyfriend

Heidi and her boyfriend Ken were indicted for participating in a scheme to secure mortgages on properties using false information in loan and other documents. They were indicted for wire fraud and conspiracy to commit wire fraud. Heidi testified that she deferred to her boyfriend who filled out all the documents. Heidi's lawyer raised a *mens rea* defense — that she lacked the necessary knowledge and intent to commit wire fraud and sought to offer evidence of domestic abuse, including Ken's refusal to take her to a doctor for her broken leg until she signed loan documents. The trial judge excluded the evidence of abuse under FRE 403 because it possessed no probative value and was "highly prejudicial." Heidi appeals claiming the exclusion of the domestic violence evidence deprived her of a fair trial because it precluded her from showing good faith, lack of knowledge and intent to defraud. How should the appeals court rule? *See United States v. Haischer*, 780 F.3d 1277 (9th Cir. 2015).

Problem #4-27: The Demonstration — "Shaken Baby Syndrome"

Kurt Andrews is charged with the second-degree murder of Kristen, his six-month-old infant daughter, which was caused by "Shaken Baby Syndrome (SBS)." The prosecutor conducts an in-court demonstration before the jury with Dr. Barbara Craig, an expert in pediatrics and child abuse. The demonstration is intended to show the force necessary to cause SBS using a cardiopulmonary resuscitation (CPR) doll. Before the demonstration the following colloquy occurred in front of the jury.

"Q [PROSECUTOR]: Now we have used this doll, State's exhibit 6, for purposes of talking about CPR. And I want to ask you first of all — and this is compared to babies in general and then compared to Kristin Andrews — can you tell us what the similarities and differences are by the way of weight and flexibility of this doll compared to an actual baby in the condition of Kristin Andrews?

A: [Dr. CRAIG]: The doll is much lighter than 11½ pounds.

Q: Okay.

A: This feels like [it] probably weighs about 3 or 4 pounds. So this doll is lighter, and it does not feel as heavy as a baby that would weigh 11½ [pounds] which is [what] Kristin weighed when she died.

Q: What about the neck?

A: And this baby's neck does not really move when you — when you gently move it back and forth. Babies' necks are very weak, and their heads are very heavy.

So if I did this to a baby that was a few months old, their heads would naturally fall all the way back so that the back of the head would almost touch [the] scapula, the shoulder blades on either side.

And if I tip them forward, the baby's head would fall down, and the chin would touch the chest if this were a real baby.

Q: Is it fair to say that aside from being roughly a third the weight of Kristin Andrews, that the rigidity of the neck will make a demonstration incomplete in terms of the exact arc movement and rotational forces at work within the head?

A: That is true.

Q: [PROSECUTOR]: Is that correct? Now when you describe this as violent shaking, and keeping in mind that obviously this doll is lighter, and most significantly that the neck does not have the same consistency, can you demonstrate to the jury the type of movement that an adult would have to do to cause the injuries that caused Kristin's death?

(Witness demonstrates)

Immediately after the demonstration the witness gratuitously added, "[a]lmost more energy than you can do, [unless] your adrenalin [is already] flowing."

Defense counsel requested a cautionary instruction. Granting the request, the trial judge told the jury: [THE COURT]: Well, I will tell the jury this was not an accurate re-enactment, but I think [the prosecutor] made this clear to you. This is Dr. Craig's opinion about the amount of force."

> 1. The defense objects to the demonstration arguing that it will have a particularly potent effect on jurors' minds and that: (a) it is irrelevant and (b) the prosecution has not laid a proper foundation to show sufficient similarity between the doll and Kristen? What result?

> 2. Should the ability of defense counsel to cross-examine Dr. Craig change the result?

> 3. What preliminary evidentiary standard must the lawyer satisfy before the judge will permit the in-court demonstration?

> 4. Ethics Consideration. Suppose Kurt is convicted. He is upset with the outcome of the trial and brings a malpractice claim against his attorney. May his attorney disclose confidential information in his malpractice defense? Ohio Rules of Prof'l Conduct R. 1.6(b)(5). *See* MRPC 1.6 (b)(5).

§ 4.07   CASES AND RULES

[A]   People v. Collins

Supreme Court of California
438 P.2d 33 (Cal. 1968)

SULLIVAN, JUSTICE:

We deal here with the novel question whether evidence of mathematical probability has been properly introduced and used by the prosecution in a criminal case. While we discern no inherent incompatibility between the disciplines of law and mathematics and intend no general disapproval or disparagement of the latter as an auxiliary of the fact-finding processes of the former, we cannot uphold the technique employed in the instant case. As we explain in detail, *infra*, the testimony as to mathematical probability infected the case with fatal error and distorted the jury's traditional role of determining guilt or innocence according to long-settled rules. Mathematics, a veritable sorcerer in our computerized society, while assisting the trier of fact in the search for truth, must not cast a spell over him. We conclude that on the record before us defendant should not have had his guilt determined by the odds and that he is entitled to a new trial. We reverse the judgment. . . .

On June 18th, 1964, at about 11:30 a.m., Mrs. Juanita Brooks, who had been shopping, was walking home along an alley in the San Pedro area of the City of Los Angeles. . . . As she stooped down to pick up an empty carton, she was suddenly pushed to the ground by a person whom she neither saw nor heard approach. . . . She managed to look up and saw a young woman running from the scene. According to Mrs. Brooks the latter appeared to weigh about 145 pounds, was wearing "something dark," and had hair "between a dark blond and a light blond," but lighter than the color of the defendant Janet Collins' hair as it appeared at trial. Immediately after the incident, Mrs. Brooks discovered that her purse, containing between $35 and $40 was missing.

About the same time as the robbery, John Bass, who lived on the street at the end of the alley, was in front of his house watering his lawn. . . . [H]e saw a woman run out of the alley and enter a yellow automobile parked across the street from him. . . . The latter then saw that it was being driven by a male Negro, wearing a mustache and beard. At the trial Bass identified defendant as the driver of the yellow automobile. . . .

. . . At the seven-day trial the prosecution experienced difficulty in establishing the identities of the perpetrator of the crime. The victim could not identify Janet and had never seen the defendant. The identification by the witness Bass, who observed the girl run out of the alley and get into the automobile, was incomplete as to Janet and may have been weakened as to the defendant. . . .

In an apparent attempt to bolster the identifications, the prosecutor called an instructor of mathematics at a state college. Through this witness he sought to establish that, assuming the robbery was committed by a Caucasian woman with a blond ponytail who left the scene accompanied by a Negro with a beard and mustache, there was an overwhelming probability that the crime was committed by any couple answering such distinctive characteristics. The witness testified, in substance, to the "product rule," which states that the probability of the joint occurrence of a number of mutually independent events is equal to the product of the individual probabilities that each of the events will occur. Without presenting any statistical evidence whatsoever in support of the probabilities for the factors selected, the prosecutor then proceeded to have the witness assume probability factors for the various characteristics which he deemed to be shared by the guilty couple and all other couples answering to such distinctive characteristics.[3]

---

[3] (Court's original footnote 10) Although the prosecutor insisted that the factors he used were only for illustrative purposes — to demonstrate how the probability of the occurrence of mutually independent factors affected the probability that they would occur together — he nevertheless attempted to use factors which he personally related to the distinctive characteristics of the defendants. In his argument to the jury he invited the jurors to apply their own factors, and asked defense counsel to suggest what the latter would deem reasonable. The prosecutor himself proposed the individual probabilities set out in the table below. Although the transcript of the examination of the mathematics instructor and the information volunteered by the prosecutor at that time create some uncertainty as to precisely which of the characteristics the prosecutor assigned to the individual probabilities, he restated in his argument to the jury that they should be as follows:

Applying the product rule to his own factors the prosecutor arrived at a probability that there was but one chance in 12 million that any couple possessed the distinctive characteristics of the defendants. Accordingly, under this theory, it was to be inferred that there could be but one chance in 12 million that defendants were innocent and that another equally distinctive couple actually committed the robbery. Expanding on what he had thus purported to suggest as a hypothesis, the prosecutor offered the completely unfounded and improper testimonial assertion that, in his opinion, the factors he had assigned were "conservative estimates" and that, in reality "the chances of anyone else besides these defendants being there, . . . having every similarity, . . . is somewhat like one in a billion." Objections were timely made to the mathematician's testimony on the grounds that it was immaterial, that it invaded the province of the jury, and that it was based on unfounded assumptions. The objections were "temporarily overruled" and the evidence admitted subject to a motion to strike. When that motion was made at the conclusion of the direct examination, the court denied it, stating that the testimony had been received only for the "purpose of illustrating the mathematical probabilities of various matters, the possibilities for them occurring or re-occurring."

As we shall explain, the prosecution's introduction and use of mathematical probability statistics injected two fundamental prejudicial errors into the case: (1) The testimony itself lacked an adequate foundation both in evidence and in statistical theory; and (2) the testimony and the manner in which the prosecution used it distracted the jury from its proper and requisite function of weighing the evidence on the issue of guilt, encouraged the jurors to rely upon an engaging but logically irrelevant expert demonstration, foreclosed the possibility of an effective defense by an attorney apparently unschooled in mathematical refinements, and placed the jurors and defense counsel at a disadvantage in sifting relevant fact from inapplicable theory.

We initially consider the defects in the testimony itself. As we have indicated, the specific technique presented through the mathematician's testimony and advanced by the prosecutor to measure the probabilities in question suffered from two basic and pervasive defects — an inadequate evidentiary foundation and an inadequate proof of statistical independence. First, as to the foundation requirement, we find the record devoid of any evidence relating to any of the six individual probability factors used by the prosecutor and ascribed by him to the six characteristics as we have set them out in footnote 10, *ante*. To put it another way, the prosecution produced no evidence whatsoever showing, or from which it could be in any way inferred, that only one out

Characteristic	Individual Probability
A. Partly yellow automobile	1/10
B. Man with mustache	1/4
C. Girl with ponytail	1/10
D. Girl with blond hair	1/3
E. Negro man with beard	1/10
F. Interracial couple in car	1/1000

In his brief on appeal the defendant agrees that the foregoing appeared on a table presented in the trial court.

of every ten cars which might have been at the scene of the robbery was partly yellow, that only one out of every four men who might have been there wore a mustache, that only one out of every ten girls who might have been there wore a ponytail, or that any of the other individual probability factors listed were even roughly accurate. . . .

We can hardly conceive of a more fatal gap in the prosecution's scheme of proof. A foundation for the admissibility of the witness' testimony was never even attempted to be laid, let alone established. His testimony was neither made to rest on his own testimonial knowledge nor presented by proper hypothetical questions based upon valid data in the record. . . .

But, as we have indicated, there was another glaring defect in the prosecution's technique, namely an inadequate proof of the statistical independence of the six factors. No proof was presented that the characteristics selected were mutually independent, even though the witness himself acknowledged that such condition was essential to the proper application of the "product rule" or "multiplication rule." . . . To the extent that the traits or characteristics were not mutually independent (e.g., Negroes with beards and men with mustaches obviously represent overlapping categories . . .), the "product rule" would inevitably yield a wholly erroneous and exaggerated result even if all of the individual components had been determined with precision. . . .

. . . In the instant case, therefore, because of the aforementioned two defects — the inadequate evidentiary foundations and the inadequate proof of statistical independence — the technique employed by the prosecutor could only lead to wild conjecture without demonstrated relevancy to the issues presented. It acquired no redeeming quality from the prosecutor's statement that it was being used only "for illustrative purposes" since, as we shall point out, the prosecutor's subsequent utilization of the mathematical testimony was not confined within such limits.

We now turn to the second fundamental error caused by the probability testimony. Quite apart from our foregoing objections to the specific technique employed by the prosecution to estimate the probability in question, we think that the entire enterprise upon which the prosecution embarked, and which was directed to the objective of measuring the likelihood of a random couple possessing the characteristics allegedly distinguishing the robbers, was gravely misguided. At best, it might yield an estimate as to how infrequently bearded Negroes drive yellow cars in the company of blonde females with ponytails.

The prosecution's approach, however, could furnish the jury with absolutely no guidance on the crucial issue: *Of the admittedly few such couples, which one, if any, was guilty of committing this robbery?* Probability theory necessarily remains silent on that question, since no mathematical equation can prove beyond a reasonable doubt (1) that the guilty couple *in fact* possessed the characteristics described by the People's witnesses, or even (2) that only *one* couple possessing those distinctive characteristics could be found in the entire Los Angeles area.

As to the first inherent failing we observe that the prosecution's theory of probability rested on the assumption that the witnesses called by the People had conclusively established that the guilty couple possessed the precise characteristics relied upon by the prosecution. But no mathematical formula could ever establish beyond a reasonable doubt that the prosecution's witnesses correctly observed and accurately described the distinctive features which were employed to link defendants to the crime. . . .

The foregoing risks of error permeate the prosecution's circumstantial case. Traditionally, the jury weighs such risks in evaluating the credibility and probative value of trial testimony, but the likelihood of human error or of falsification obviously cannot be quantified; that likelihood must therefore be excluded from any effort to assign a *number* to the probability of guilt or innocence. Confronted with an equation which purports to yield a numerical index of probable guilt, few juries could resist the temptation to accord disproportionate weight to that index; only an exceptional juror, and indeed only a defense attorney schooled in mathematics, could successfully keep in mind the fact that the probability computed by the prosecution can represent, *at best*, the likelihood that a random couple would share the characteristics testified to by the People's witnesses — *not necessarily the characteristics of the actually guilty couple.*

As to the second inherent failing in the prosecution's approach, even assuming that the first failing could be discounted, the most a mathematical computation could *ever* yield would be a measure of the probability that a random couple would possess the distinctive features in question. In the present case, for example, the prosecution attempted to compute the probability that a random couple would include a bearded Negro, a blonde girl with a ponytail, and a partly yellow car; the prosecution urged that this probability was no more than one in 12 million. Even accepting this conclusion as arithmetically accurate, however, one still could not conclude that the Collinses were probably *the* guilty couple. On the contrary, as we explain in the Appendix, the prosecution's figures actually imply a likelihood of over 40 percent that the Collinses could be "duplicated" by at least *one other couple who might equally have committed the San Pedro robbery.* Urging that the Collinses be convicted on the basis of evidence which logically establishes no more than this seems as indefensible as arguing for the conviction of X on the ground that a witness saw either X or X's twin commit the crime.

Again, few defense attorneys, and certainly few jurors, could be expected to comprehend this basic flaw in the prosecution's analysis.

In essence this argument of the prosecutor was calculated to persuade the jury to convict defendants whether or not they were convinced of their guilt to a moral certainty and beyond a reasonable doubt. . . . Undoubtedly the jurors were unduly impressed by the mystique of the mathematical demonstration but were unable to assess its relevancy or value. Although we make no appraisal of the proper applications of mathematical techniques in the proof of facts, we have strong feelings that such applications, particularly in a criminal case, must be critically examined in view of the substantial unfairness to a defendant which may result from ill-conceived techniques with which the trier of fact is not technically equipped to cope. . . . We feel that the technique employed in the case before us falls into the latter category.

We conclude that the court erred in admitting over defendant's objection the evidence pertaining to the mathematical theory of probability and in denying defendant's motion to strike such evidence. . . . The judgment against defendant must therefore be reversed. . . .

Appendix

. . . Hence, even if we should accept the prosecution's figures without question, we would derive a probability of over 40 percent that the couple observed by the witnesses could be "duplicated" by at least one other equally distinctive interracial couple in the area, including a Negro with a beard and mustache, driving a partly yellow car in the company of a blonde with a ponytail. Thus the prosecution's computations, far from establishing beyond a reasonable doubt that the Collinses were the couple described by the prosecution's witnesses, imply a very substantial likelihood that the area contained *more than one* such couple, and that a couple *other* than the Collinses was the one observed at the scene of the robbery. . . .

[B]   Old Chief v. United States

United States Supreme Court
519 U.S. 172 (1997)

SOUTER, J., delivered the opinion of the Court, in which STEVENS, KENNEDY, GINSBURG, and BREYER, J.J., joined. O' CONNOR, J. filed a dissenting opinion, in which REHNQUIST, C.J., and SCALIA and THOMAS, J.J., joined.

Subject to certain limitations, 18 U.S.C. Section 922(g)(1) prohibits possession of a firearm by anyone with a prior felony conviction, which the Government can prove by introducing a record of judgment or similar evidence identifying the previous offense. Fearing prejudice if the jury learns the nature of the earlier crime, defendants sometimes seek to avoid such an informative disclosure by offering to concede the fact of the prior conviction. The issue here is whether a district court abuses its discretion if it spurns such an offer and admits the full record of a prior judgment, when the name or nature of the prior offense raises the risk of a verdict tainted by improper considerations, and when the purpose of the evidence is solely to prove the element of prior conviction. We hold that it does.

In 1993, petitioner, Old Chief, was arrested after a fracas involving at least one gunshot. The ensuing federal charges included [possession of a firearm by a convicted felon.]. . . . The earlier crime charged in the indictment against Old Chief was assault causing serious bodily injury. Before trial, he moved for an order requiring the Government "to refrain from mentioning . . . the prior criminal convictions of the Defendant, except to state that the Defendant has been convicted of a crime punishable by imprisonment exceeding one (1) year." The Assistant United States Attorney refused to join in a stipulation, insisting on his right to prove his case his own way, and the District Court agreed. . . .

We granted Old Chief's petition for writ of certiorari . . . because the Courts of Appeals have divided sharply. . . . As a threshold matter, [the nature of the prior conviction is relevant.] A documentary record of the conviction for that named offense was thus relevant evidence in making Old Chief's Section 922(g)(1) status more probable than it would have been without the evidence. . . . .

The principal issue is the scope of a trial judge's discretion under Rule 403, ... The term "unfair prejudice," as to a criminal defendant, speaks to . . . "an undue tendency to suggest decisions on an improper basis. . . . Advisory Committee's Notes on Fed. Rule Evid. 403.

Such improper grounds certainly include the one that Old Chief points to here: generalizing a defendant's earlier bad act into bad character and taking that as raising the odds that he did the later bad act now charged. . . . There is, accordingly, no question that propensity would be an "improper basis" for conviction. . . . [W]hen a court considers "whether to exclude on grounds of unfair prejudice," the "availability of other means of proof may . . . be an appropriate factor." Advisory Committee's Notes on Fed. Rule Evid. 403. . . .

. . . Where a prior conviction was for a gun crime or one similar to other charges in a pending case, the risk of unfair prejudice would be especially obvious, and Old Chief sensibly worried that the prejudicial effect of his prior assault conviction, significant enough with respect to the current gun charges alone, would take on added weight from the related assault charge against him. . . .

. . . In arguing that the stipulation or admission would not have carried equivalent value, the Government invokes the familiar, standard rule that the prosecution is entitled to prove its case by evidence of its own choice, or, more exactly, that a criminal defendant may not stipulate or admit his way out of the full evidentiary force of the case as the government chooses to present it. . . .

This is unquestionably true as a general matter. The "fair and legitimate weight" of conventional evidence showing individual thoughts and acts amounting to a crime reflect the fact that making a case with testimony and tangible things not only satisfies the formal definition of an offense, but tells a colorful story with descriptive richness . . .

. . . This recognition that the prosecution with its burden of persuasion needs evidentiary depth to tell a continuous story has, however, virtually no application when the point at issue is a defendant's legal status, dependent on some judgment rendered wholly independently of the concrete events of later criminal behavior charged against him . . .

. . . .

. . . In this case, . . . the only reasonable conclusion was that the risk of unfair prejudice did substantially outweigh the discounted probative value of the record of conviction, and it was an abuse of discretion to admit the record when an admission was available. . . . .

The judgment is reversed, and the case is remanded to the Ninth Circuit for further proceedings consistent with this opinion.

[C]   Sprint/United Mgmt. Co. v. Mendelsohn

United States Supreme Court
552 U.S. 379 (2008)

JUSTICE THOMAS delivered the opinion of the Court.

In this age discrimination case, the District Court excluded testimony by nonparties alleging discrimination at the hands of supervisors of the defendant company who played no role in the adverse employment decision challenged by the plaintiff. The Court of Appeals, having concluded that the District Court improperly applied a *per se* rule excluding the evidence, engaged in its own analysis of the relevant factors under Federal Rules of Evidence 401 and 403, and remanded with instructions to admit the challenged testimony. We granted certiorari on the question whether the Federal Rules of Evidence required admission of the testimony. We conclude that such evidence is neither *per se* admissible nor *per se* inadmissible. Because it is not entirely clear whether the District Court applied a *per se* rule, we vacate the judgment of the Court of Appeals and remand for the District Court to conduct the relevant inquiry under the appropriate standard.

I

Respondent Ellen Mendelsohn was employed in the Business Development Strategy Group of petitioner Sprint/United Management Company (Sprint) from 1989 until 2002, when Sprint terminated her as a part of an ongoing company-wide reduction in force. She sued Sprint under the Age Discrimination in Employment Act of 1967 (ADEA), 81 Stat. 602, as amended, 29 U.S.C. § 621 *et seq.*, alleging disparate treatment based on her age.

In support of her claim, Mendelsohn sought to introduce testimony by five other former Sprint employees who claimed that their supervisors had discriminated against them because of age. . . .

None of the five witnesses worked in the Business Development Strategy Group with Mendelsohn, nor had any of them worked under the supervisors in her chain of command, which included James Fee, Mendelsohn's direct supervisor; Paul Reddick, Fee's direct manager and the decision maker in Mendelsohn's termination; and Bill Blessing, Reddick's supervisor and head of the Business Development Strategy Group. Neither did any of the proffered witnesses report hearing discriminatory remarks by Fee, Reddick, or Blessing.

Sprint moved *in limine* to exclude the testimony, arguing that it was irrelevant to the central issue in the case: whether Reddick terminated Mendelsohn because of her age. See Fed. Rules Evid. 401, 402. Sprint claimed that the testimony would be relevant only if it came from employees who were "similarly situated" to Mendelsohn in that they had the same supervisors. App. 156a. Sprint also argued that, under Rule 403, the probative value of the evidence would be substantially outweighed by the danger of unfair prejudice, confusion of the issues, misleading of the jury, and undue delay.

In a minute order, the District Court granted the motion, excluding, in relevant part, evidence of "discrimination against employees not similarly situated to plaintiff." App. to Pet. for Cert. 24a. In clarifying that Mendelsohn could only "offer evidence of discrimination against Sprint employees who are similarly situated to her," the court defined " '[s]imilarly situated employees,' for the purpose of this ruling, [as] requir[ing] proof that (1) Paul Ruddick *[sic]* was the decision-maker in any adverse employment action; and (2) temporal proximity." *Ibid.* Beyond that, the District Court provided no explanation of the basis for its ruling. As the trial proceeded, the judge orally clarified that the minute order was meant to exclude only testimony "that Sprint treated other people unfairly on the basis of age," and would not bar testimony going to the "totally different" question "whether the [reduction in force], which is [Sprint's] stated nondiscriminatory reason, is a pretext for age discrimination." App. 295a–296a.

The Court of Appeals for the Tenth Circuit treated the minute order as the application of a *per se* rule that evidence from employees with other supervisors is irrelevant to proving discrimination in an ADEA case. Specifically, it concluded that the District Court abused its discretion by relying on *Aramburu v. Boeing Co.*, 112 F.3d 1398 (C.A.10 1997). 466 F.3d 1223, 1227–1228 (C.A.10 2006). *Aramburu* held that "[s]imilarly situated employees," for the purpose of showing disparate treatment in employee discipline, "are those who deal with the same supervisor and are subject to the same standards governing performance evaluation and discipline." 112 F.3d, at 1404 (internal quotation marks omitted). The Court of Appeals viewed that case as inapposite because it addressed discriminatory discipline, not a company-wide policy of discrimination. The Court of Appeals then determined that the evidence was relevant and not unduly prejudicial, and reversed and remanded for a new trial. We granted certiorari, Byrd v. United States, 551 U.S. 1116, 127 S. Ct. 2937, 168 L. Ed. 2d 261 (2007), to determine whether, in an employment discrimination action, the Federal Rules of Evidence require admission of testimony by nonparties alleging discrimination at the hands of persons who played no role in the adverse employment decision challenged by the plaintiff.

II

The parties focus their dispute on whether the Court of Appeals correctly held that the evidence was relevant and not unduly prejudicial under Rules 401 and 403. We conclude, however, that the Court of Appeals should not have engaged in that inquiry. Rather, as explained below, we hold that the Court of Appeals erred in concluding that the District Court applied a *per se* rule. Given the circumstances of this case and the unclear basis of the District Court's decision, the Court of Appeals should have remanded the case to the District Court for clarification.

A

In deference to a district court's familiarity with the details of the case and its greater experience in evidentiary matters, courts of appeals afford broad discretion to a district court's evidentiary rulings.

. . . .

Here, however, the Court of Appeals did not accord the District Court the deference we have described as the "hallmark of abuse-of-discretion review." *General Elec. Co. v. Joiner*, 522 U.S. 136, 143, 118 S. Ct. 512, 139 L. Ed. 2d 508 (1997). Instead, it reasoned that the District Court had "erroneous[ly] concluded that *Aramburu* controlled the fate of the evidence in this case." 466 F.3d at 1230, n. 4.

To be sure, Sprint in its motion *in limine* argued, with a citation to *Aramburu*'s categorical bar, that "[e]mployees may be similarly situated only if they had the same supervisor," App. 163a, and the District Court's minute order mirrors that blanket language.

But the District Court's discussion of the evidence neither cited *Aramburu* nor gave any other indication that its decision relied on that case. The minute order included only two sentences discussing the admissibility of the evidence:

> "Plaintiff may offer evidence of discrimination against Sprint employees who are similarly situated to her. 'Similarly situated employees,' for the purpose of this ruling, requires proof that (1) Paul Ruddick *[sic]* was the decision-maker in any adverse employment action; and (2) temporal proximity." App. to Pet. for Cert. 24a.

Contrary to the Court of Appeals' conclusion, these sentences include no analysis suggesting that the District Court applied a *per se* rule excluding this type of evidence.

. . . .

Mendelsohn additionally argued that the District Court must have meant to apply such a rule because that was the nature of the argument in Sprint's *in limine* motion. But the *in limine* motion did not suggest that the evidence is never admissible; it simply argued that such evidence lacked sufficient probative value "in this case" to be relevant or outweigh prejudice and delay. App. 156a.

When a district court's language is ambiguous, as it was here, it is improper for the court of appeals to presume that the lower court reached an incorrect legal conclusion. A remand directing the district court to clarify its order is generally permissible and would have been the better approach in this case.

B

In the Court of Appeals' view, the District Court excluded the evidence as *per se* irrelevant, and so had no occasion to reach the question whether such evidence, if relevant, should be excluded under Rule 403. The Court of Appeals, upon concluding that such evidence was not *per se* irrelevant, decided that it was relevant in the circumstances of this case and undertook its own balancing under Rule 403. But questions of relevance and prejudice are for the District Court to determine in the first instance. . . . Rather than assess the relevance of the evidence itself and conduct its own balancing of its probative value and potential prejudicial effect, the Court of Appeals should have allowed the District Court to make these determinations in the first instance, explicitly and on the record.

We note that, had the District Court applied a *per se* rule excluding the evidence, the Court of Appeals would have been correct to conclude that it had abused its discretion. Relevance and prejudice under Rules 401 and 403 are determined in the context of the facts and arguments in a particular case, and thus are generally not amenable to broad *per se* rules. *See* Advisory Committee's Notes on Fed. Rule Evid. 401, 28 U.S.C. App., p. 864 ("Relevancy is not an inherent characteristic of any item of evidence but exists only as a relation between an item of evidence and a matter properly provable in the case"). But, as we have discussed, there is no basis in the record for concluding that the District Court applied a blanket rule.

III

The question whether evidence of discrimination by other supervisors is relevant in an individual ADEA case is fact based and depends on many factors, including how closely related the evidence is to the plaintiff's circumstances and theory of the case. Applying Rule 403 to determine if evidence is prejudicial also requires a fact-intensive, context-specific inquiry. Because Rules 401 and 403 do not make such evidence *per se* admissible or *per se* inadmissible, and because the inquiry required by those Rules is within the province of the District Court in the first instance, we vacate the judgment of the Court of Appeals and remand the case with instructions to have the District Court clarify the basis for its evidentiary ruling under the applicable Rules.

It is so ordered.

[D]   Rules Comparison

Compare FRE 403 with an earlier draft of the same rule. Which version is preferable?

FRE 403. Exclusion of Relevant Evidence on Grounds of Prejudice, Confusion, or Waste of Time

(a) Exclusion Mandatory. Although relevant, evidence is not admissible if its probative value is substantially outweighed by the danger of unfair prejudice, of confusion of the issues, or of misleading the jury.

(b) Exclusion Discretionary. Although relevant, evidence may be excluded if its probative value is substantially outweighed by considerations of undue delay, waste of time, or needless presentation of cumulative evidence. (March 1969 and March 1971 drafts).

§ 4.08   RELEVANT ETHICS RULES

Rule 3.3: Candor Toward the Tribunal

(a) A lawyer shall not *knowingly*: . . . . (3) offer evidence that the lawyer *knows* to be false. If a lawyer, the lawyer's client, or a witness called by the lawyer has offered material evidence and the lawyer comes to *know* of its falsity, the lawyer shall take *reasonable* measures to remedy the situation, including, if necessary, disclosure to the *tribunal*. A lawyer may refuse to offer evidence, other than the testimony of a defendant in a criminal matter, that the lawyer *reasonably believes* is false." Ohio Rules of Prof. Conduct R. 3.3(a)(3) (emphasis in original). *See* MRPC 3.3 (a)(3).

Rule 1.8 Conflict of Interest: Current Clients: Specific Rules

(e) A lawyer shall not provide financial assistance to a client in connection with pending or contemplated litigation, except that:

(1) a lawyer may advance court costs and expenses of litigation, the repayment of which may be contingent on the outcome of the matter; and

(2) a lawyer representing an indigent client may pay court costs and expenses of litigation on behalf of the client. Colo. Rules of Prof'l Conduct R. 1.8(e). *See* MRPC 1.8 (e).

Rule 7.3 Direct Contact with Prospective Clients

(b) A lawyer shall not solicit professional employment from a prospective client by written, recorded or electronic communication or by in-person, telephone or real-time electronic contact even when not otherwise prohibited by paragraph (a) if:

(1) the prospective clients has made known to the lawyer a desire not to be solicited by the lawyer; or

(2) the solicitation involves coercion, duress or harassment.

(c) Every written, recorded, or electronic communication from a lawyer soliciting professional employment from a prospective client known to be in need of legal services in a particular mater shall include the words "Advertising Material" on the outside envelope, if any, and at the beginning and ending of an recorded or electronic communication, unless the recipient of the communication is a person specified in paragraphs (a)(1) or (a)(2) lawyer.

Alaska Rules of Prof'l Conduct R. 7.3 (b) & (c). *See* MRPC 7.3(b) & (c).

Rule 1.6: Confidentiality of Information

(b) A lawyer may reveal information relating to the representation of a client, including information protected by the attorney-client privilege under applicable law, to the extent the lawyer *reasonably believes* necessary for any of the following purposes:

. . .

(5) to establish a claim or defense on behalf of the lawyer in a controversy between the lawyer and the client, to establish a defense to a criminal charge or civil claim against the lawyer based upon conduct in

which the client was involved, or to respond to allegations in any
proceeding, including any disciplinary matter, concerning the lawyer's
representation of the client;

Ohio Rules of Prof. Conduct R. 1.6(b)(5). *See* MRPC 1.6(b)(5).

§ 4.09   SUMMARY AND REVIEW

1. Should a judge exclude evidence that is more prejudicial than probative upon
    a proper objection?

2. What is the difference between unfairly prejudicial evidence and prejudicial
    evidence?

3. Why use a weighted balancing test for unfair prejudice?

4. Why is most statistical evidence allowed even though courts usually exclude
    probability evidence about the likelihood of a person other than the accused
    committing the alleged crime?

5. What are the dangers of other similar acts evidence?

6. Why admit gruesome evidence of a murder scene?

Chapter 5

CHARACTER AND HABIT EVIDENCE [FRE 404–406]

CHAPTER FRAMEWORK: Character and habit evidence are often useful forms of evidence about a party or victim, particularly when direct evidence of action at a particular date and time is unavailable. Character evidence is often perceived as highly probative, meaning that a person who is grumpy, mean-spirited, violent, peaceful, happy etc., will act in a consistent manner with that character trait on any given day. The real problem with character evidence is that it is highly prejudicial as well, because it is a generalization that does not account for people changing. Thus, the overall rule excludes character evidence, with certain well-accepted exceptions. These exceptions include: (i) the accused offering it first in a criminal case, (ii) when character is an element to be proven in the case, such as in defamation cases, or (iii) when it is used in specific act form for a non-character purpose, such as to show motive, intent, or common scheme or plan. Habit evidence offers a specialized exception to the general exclusion of other specific acts, since it has greater relevance and is more reliable than mere haphazard other acts.

WHY ARE THE CONCEPTS IN THIS CHAPTER IMPORTANT? Character is a special type of recurring evidence that has to be dealt with in both civil and criminal cases, and when offered to prove an element or, in a special narrow context of truthfulness, when used to impeach or rehabilitate a witness. Habit evidence is a special exception to the general exclusion of other specific acts.

CONNECTIONS: Character exclusions can be viewed as a more individualized exclusion within the umbrella of unfair prejudice, since character likely would be excluded under FRE 403 if there were no special attention accorded it in FRE 404. Character evidence also connects to the impeachment rules, since impeachment is a specialized application of the character of a witness for truthfulness.

CHAPTER OUTLINE:

    I. Character Evidence

        A. Consists of personality traits (e.g., peaceful, violent, honest) of a party or victim

        B. Three forms: opinion, reputation, and specific acts [FRE 405(a) & (b)]

    II. General Rule: prohibited when offered to show propensity (e.g., once a thief always a thief)

        A. Rationale: distracts fact finder from specific facts of case — unfairly prejudicial [FRE 404(a)]

    III. Exceptions (when character evidence is admissible)

A. Character is element of case [FRE 405(a) & (b)]

   1. E.g., defamation case or entrapment defense, must prove character to win. Plaintiff or Prosecution and Defendant can offer all three kinds of character evidence regarding plaintiff's pertinent trait.

B. Accused offers character evidence first to show not guilty [FRE 404(a)(1) & (2)]

   1. Only reputation or opinion evidence

   2. Prosecution responses — cross-exam; and rebuttal character witness

C. Offered to impeach a witness — to show witness's truthfulness or untruthfulness (but not to show propensity) [FRE 404(a)(3)] [*see* 600 series]

D. To prove a relevant issue other than propensity, such as motive, opportunity, intent, or common scheme or plan. [FRE 404(b)]

IV. Habit [FRE 406] — Admissible

A. Requires regular responses to a repeated, specific stimulus. Means invariable conduct in reaction to specific circumstances (i) E.g., Defendant stops each morning for espresso at the same deli store on the way to work.

* * * * *

RELEVANT EVIDENCE RULES

FRE 404. Character Evidence; Crimes or Other Acts

(a) Character Evidence. *exclusion*

(1) Prohibited Uses. Evidence of a person's character or character trait is not admissible to prove that on a particular occasion the person acted in accordance with the character or trait.

(2) Exceptions for a Defendant or Victim in a Criminal Case. The following exceptions apply in a criminal case:

(A) A defendant may offer evidence of the defendant's pertinent trait, and if the evidence is admitted, the prosecutor may offer evidence to rebut it;

(B) Subject to the limitations in FRE 412, a defendant may offer evidence of an alleged victim's pertinent trait, and if the evidence is admitted, the prosecutor may:

(i) Offer evidence to rebut it; and

(ii) Offer evidence of the defendant's same trait; and

(C) In a homicide case, the prosecutor may offer evidence of the alleged victim's trait of peacefulness to rebut evidence that the victim was the first aggressor.

(3) Exceptions for a Witness. Evidence of a witness's character may be admitted under FREs 607, 608, and 609.

(b) Crimes, Wrongs, or Other Acts.

(1) Prohibited Uses. Evidence of a crime, wrong, or other act is not admissible to prove a person's character in order to show that on a particular occasion the person acted in accordance with the character.

(2) Permitted Uses; Notice in a Criminal Case. This evidence may be admissible for another purpose, such as proving motive, opportunity, intent, preparation, plan, knowledge, identity, absence of mistake, or lack of accident. On request by a defendant in a criminal case, the prosecutor must:

(A) Provide reasonable notice of the general nature of any such evidence that the prosecutor intends to offer at trial; and

(B) Do so before trial or during trial if the court, for good cause, excuses lack of pretrial notice.

FRE 405. Methods of Proving Character

(a) By Reputation or Opinion. When evidence of a person's character or character trait is admissible, it may be proved by testimony about the person's reputation or by testimony in the form of an opinion. On cross-examination of the character witness, the court may allow an inquiry into relevant specific instances of the person's conduct.

(b) By specific Instances of Conduct. When a person's character or character trait is an essential element of a charge, claim, or defense, the character or trait may also be proved by relevant specific instances of the person's conduct.

FRE 406. Habit; Routine Practice   inclusion

Evidence of a person's habit or an organization's routine practice may be admitted to prove that on a particular occasion the person or organization acted in accordance with the habit or routine practice. The court may admit this evidence regardless of whether it is corroborated or whether there was an eyewitness.

§ 5.01 INTRODUCTION

[A] What Is Character Evidence?

The Advisory Committee Note to FRE 406 defines character by quoting Professor McCormick, *Evidence*:

"Character is a generalized description of one's disposition, or of one's disposition in respect to a general trait, such as honesty, temperance, or peacefulness."

One key to understanding character evidence under FREs 404 and 405 is that it concerns certain persons — parties, witnesses, and victims. Character evidence relating to the truthfulness of witnesses is treated in a different area of the rules, the 600 series (FRE 607 et seq.).

Trait or disposition evidence often is offered when there is a lack of direct evidence about an event, such as who started a bar fight, who committed theft, or who drove carelessly. While character evidence is not bad in and of itself, its admissibility is carefully scrutinized because it is often highly prejudicial. Character evidence is predicated on a sometimes faulty inference — that people act consistently with their traits. Because people change and do not act consistently with their character traits all of the time, this evidence is suspect.

Within the evidence vernacular, character evidence is generally excluded because it is unfairly prejudicial, especially when offered to show the propensity of a party or victim to act in a certain manner. This exclusion is subject to significant counter-weights, however, because character is commonly used to describe people and is firmly embedded in the fabric of our society.

A special form of character evidence is often labeled credibility evidence, meaning impeaching the truthfulness or accuracy of a witness. This character cousin, credibility evidence, solely concerns witnesses and is offered so the trier of fact can more accurately evaluate the weight or value of testimony. Rules governing credibility evidence can be found beginning at FRE 607 et seq.

Several exceptions exist for civil and criminal cases: (1) character evidence is admissible if the character of a party, victim, or third person is an element of a crime or civil wrong — or a defense to either; (2) character evidence is admissible in criminal cases if it is first offered by the accused to show his lack of propensity to commit the crime or the alleged victim's propensity to have been the aggressor; and (3) character evidence is permissible in either civil or criminal cases if it is not offered for its character inference, but for an unrelated relevant purpose, such as motive, intent, absence of mistake or common scheme or plan. Habit evidence can be considered an exception to the general exclusion of character evidence or, with its requirements of automaticity and frequency, simply a distant cousin.

Consequently, as a general proposition, FRE 404 excludes character evidence. *See* FRE 404(a). The general inadmissibility of character evidence about a party or victim to prove an issue in the case is balanced by several major exceptions. These exceptions depend on whether the evidence is offered to show character or for a different purpose and whether character is in issue. *See* FRE 405.

Background Box: Real World Example

Often, character evidence emerges in daily life in news about celebrities and their activities, usually activities that implicate ethics or the criminal law. In one highly publicized case in 2010, the actress, Lindsey Lohan, violated the terms of her probation for drunk driving convictions and was sentenced to jail time, causing endless speculation and commentary in the press.

Thus, it is useful to categorize the purposes for which character is offered. Character evidence is offered: (1) to indirectly show that because a person has a propensity to act in a particular manner, that person more likely acted in conformity with the propensity on a specific occasion; (2) to directly prove a person's character trait when it is an element of a cause of action, claim, or defense; or (3) for purposes other than to show a person's character trait, such as to prove motive, intent, plan, common scheme, absence of mistake, or identity.

Because of its different forms and the diversity of purposes for which it may be offered, an understanding of character evidence often is elusive. Unraveling the mystery of character evidence usually depends on the answers to three questions: (1) Is the evidence being offered to show character? (Or is it offered for non-character purposes?); (2) If it is offered to show character, for what specific purpose is it being offered? (i.e., is it being offered to show a person's propensity, to show a relevant person's character directly, or to attack a witness's credibility for truthfulness or veracity?); and (3) Is the *form* of the character evidence (reputation, opinion, or specific acts) proper? These three questions will be discussed in greater detail below.

[B]   The Three Forms of Character Evidence

Character evidence can take several distinct forms: (1) reputation, (2) opinion, or (3) specific acts. Specific acts often are viewed as the most probative form of character evidence because they create the most direct picture of a person's character. At the same time, specific acts are generally disfavored because they also have the greatest potential to unduly influence the jury. Thus, reputation and opinion evidence are the preferred forms of character evidence under the FRE.

[C]   Character vs. Credibility Evidence

"Credibility" evidence is a special type of character evidence. It is offered to show a witness's character for truthfulness or veracity and is used to accredit or discredit the witness's testimony. When character evidence is offered to show the credibility of a witness, either to impeach or to rehabilitate, it is governed by a separate set of rules. (*See* FRE 404(a)(3), which directs the reader to FRE 607–609.) By comparison, when character evidence is offered as substantive evidence to prove a fact in issue, it is governed by FRE 404 and 405.

§ 5.02   PROPENSITY CHARACTER EVIDENCE

[A]   Propensity Evidence Defined

"Propensity" evidence is a type of character evidence. It is offered to show that a person with a particular trait or disposition has a propensity to act in a certain way, meaning the person is more likely to have acted in conformity with that character trait on a particular occasion. In essence, propensity evidence is offered as indirect or circumstantial proof. For example, "If he or she acted that way before, then he or she would be more likely to act that way again" (e.g., "once a thief, always a thief"). A person who is characterized as a "thief" is more likely to have stolen an item on a particular day than an honest person. Similarly, a violent person is more likely to have started a fight on a particular day than a peaceful person.

The three forms of character evidence (reputation evidence, opinion evidence, and specific acts) all have the potential of showing propensity. To illustrate, a witness can claim that the defendant has a reputation in the community for being a thief. A witness also can state that in her opinion, the defendant is a thief. Finally, a prior specific act of theft can be used to infer that the defendant is a thief and that once a thief, the defendant is always a thief.

Practical Tip:

Nicknames often reflect a person's character trait. This is especially true in the world of sports. From "Hulk" Hogan, to "Speedy" Gonzalez, to Lenny "Nails" Dykstra, nicknames are used to reflect dominant traits.

[B]   Why Offer Propensity Evidence?

Propensity character evidence is offered to supplement direct evidence about an event or occurrence. When Anita Hill and Clarence Thomas testified in the now-famous Senate confirmation hearings for Supreme Court Justice about the sexual harassment allegations she levied against him, their character traits were offered to show which person was testifying truthfully. The character evidence was offered to show the likelihood of that *type* of person acting in a particular way. Their character traits thus helped to determine which person and which version of the facts was the most believable.

[C]   Why Exclude Propensity Evidence?

 While propensity evidence often satisfies the test of relevance, it is generally inadmissible. Propensity evidence poses a risk of unfair prejudice for several reasons:

1. Character traits are not always accurate representations of people. In essence, even if the description of a person's character is accurate, people sometimes act in a manner inconsistent with their general disposition. Thus, propensity character evidence tends to distort the facts of a case by rewarding the good person and

punishing the bad. Criminal defendants, for example, should not be convicted for who they are, but rather for having committed the charged offense.

2. People and their character traits can change over time. Thus, a purported character trait may become outdated. Even if incremental changes in character traits are observable, jurors may not sufficiently take these changes into account.

3. Character evidence requires looking backward or forward from the event in question and likely distracts the trier of fact from the event at issue. Such distractions can be misleading and a waste of the jury's time. After all, the litigants generally are trying to prove what happened, not a person's character.

For all of the above reasons, propensity evidence presents a risk of unfair prejudice. Consequently, it is generally excluded from evidence.

[D] Exceptions: Admissible Propensity Evidence

[1] For a person accused of a crime

There are two exceptions to the general exclusion of propensity evidence. The first exception benefits criminal defendants. Since the risk of stigma, incarceration, and even death from a conviction is significant, an accused is given a special dispensation to use propensity evidence. The propensity evidence may concern either the defendant or the alleged victim. If the accused offers propensity evidence, however, the rules adopt an "equal time" fairness provision which permits the government to rebut the character evidence offered by the accused.

[2] To attack a witness's veracity

The second major exception permits the use of character evidence to impeach the veracity or accuracy of a witness. Impeachment character evidence can be offered in either civil or criminal cases and by either party. The use of character evidence to impeach a witness is covered in Article VI of the FRE, particularly FRE 607, 608, 609, and 613. These rules will be discussed in greater detail in Chapter 7, The Examination and Impeachment of Witnesses.

[E] Forms of Admissible Propensity Evidence

If propensity evidence is permitted, either on behalf of a criminal defendant or in the government's rebuttal of that evidence, only evidence in the form of reputation or opinion is allowed. *See* FRE 405(a). Specific acts are not permitted because of their potential for unfair prejudice.

Illustration: Propensity Evidence

As a result of an undercover police operation known as "Operation Court Sale," Judge Harris is charged with accepting a bribe. When he served as a public defender and during his fifteen years on the bench, Judge Harris had a reputation in the legal community for unimpeachable honesty. Once, in fact, the judge found a person's lost wallet containing $1,000 in cash and he returned the wallet and its contents to the rightful owner. The judge's best friend, the Attorney General of the United States, will vouch for his honesty. Which of this evidence is propensity evidence? What evidence is admissible?

Answer: The judge's reputation in the legal community, his conduct in returning the wallet, and the Attorney General's opinion of the judge are all examples of propensity evidence. Each shows that the judge is an honest person. The collective inference to be drawn from such evidence is that the judge is less likely to have committed the crime charged, the receipt of a bribe, which is predicated on dishonesty.

At trial, the judge would be permitted to offer the reputation evidence and the Attorney General's opinion, but not the evidence that he returned the wallet. Under the exception carved out by FRE 404(a) for criminal defendants, an accused can offer propensity evidence of a pertinent trait to the crime charged. In this case, the pertinent trait is honesty. FRE 405(a) allows either reputation or opinion evidence, but not specific acts, so the incident involving the return of the wallet would be excluded.

[F] Problems

[1] Identifying Propensity Character Evidence: Problems Involving the Elements

 Problem #5-1: "What a Character"

Identify the instances of character evidence in the following transcript. The testimony occurs in a personal injury action arising out of an automobile accident during a rainy afternoon near a school while parents were driving to the school to pick-up their children. The plaintiff, Mrs. Musial, suffered various injuries in the collision, slipping, and falling after the accident and suffering the most significant injury, a broken leg.

Plaintiff's Attorney: Now Mrs. Musial, how long had you been licensed to drive at the time of the accident?

Plaintiff: Oh, about 20 years. And in that time, I have not had a single automobile collision, until this one with Mrs. Parnell, the defendant.

Plaintiff's Attorney: What do you know about Mrs. Parnell?

Plaintiff: I worked with her briefly on a school matter. She was very distracted during our committee meetings, always checking her messages on her phone and all that.

Plaintiff's Attorney: Describe the drive to the school on April 14th, the day in question.

Plaintiff: It was raining. When it rains, I generally drive extra-carefully and give an extra couple of yards between my car and the car in front of me. Just to be safe, you know? She aggressively cut in front of me. It was not cool.

Problem #5-2: Rambo II

[This problem explores some critical character distinctions, such as whether the evidence is offered in a civil or criminal case and, if criminal, who offered the evidence first, the defense or the prosecution.]

Houston Rambo II collects exotic weapons as a hobby, participates in bodybuilding competitions, loves the film *Natural Born Killers* (which is about several serial killers), and was a professional wrestler for several years. At approximately 3 a.m. on Saturday, July 14th, Rambo was involved in a brawl outside of a local bar named The Varsity.

1. If Rambo is sued for assault and battery by Betty, a person injured in the fight, can Betty introduce evidence of Rambo's hobby, bodybuilding activities, or prior employment? Why?

2. If Rambo is prosecuted for assault as a result of the same brawl, can the prosecution introduce evidence of Rambo's hobby, bodybuilding, or prior employment? Explain. Δ must offer 1st ✗

3. In the assault prosecution, can Rambo's business partner, Manny, testify for the defense if he states that for the past five years Rambo has been a responsible attorney and that Rambo has a very meek personality? ✓

4. In the same prosecution, can Rambo's mother testify that Rambo has a reputation in the community for being a very peaceful person, so peaceful that he refused to fight others on at least eight separate occasions when challenged?

5. If Rambo's mother testifies, can the prosecution ask her on cross-examination whether she has heard that Rambo was arrested for attempted murder six years ago? Can she still be questioned about the arrest if the attempted murder charges were eventually dropped?

6. If Rambo's mother testifies, can the prosecution call Rambo's former music teacher, Martha, in rebuttal to testify that Rambo has a reputation in the community as a very violent individual?

 Problem #5-3: The Wanderlust of Cows and Other True Stories does not apply

[This problem explores the treatment of non-human character evidence.]

Farmer Stephanie brought suit against Jesse for running over and killing one of her cows. Jesse counterclaimed, alleging that Stephanie inadequately supervised her cows, to the extent that her lack of supervision permitted the cows to escape. At trial, Stephanie called another farmer, John, to testify. John stated that in his expert opinion, based on 30 years of experience in raising and herding cows, cows have a propensity to wander. Can cows have character traits? Is farmer John's opinion on this issue inadmissible character evidence? Why? admiss.

Problem #5-4: Crash Johnson

[This problem explores the existence or lack of prior conduct.]

Cars driven by Johnny "Crash" Johnson and Buford Gump collided at the intersection of Haight and Ashbury. Crash was charged with reckless driving.

1. Can the prosecution offer evidence that Crash had been in an alcohol treatment program the previous year?

2. Can Crash testify, "I am a terrific driver, better than Stewart, Earnhardt, Elliott, or the rest?"✓ trait

3. Can Crash testify, "Just look at my driving record; no blemishes whatsoever!"? ✗ prior acts

Problem #5-5: Heavyweight Champ

The heavyweight champion of the world, the Champ, sued the contender, Charley Challenger, for assault and battery. The Champ claimed that Charley Challenger accosted him outside of a nightclub at 4:00 a.m. one morning. Which of the following evidence is admissible?

1. The Champ offers to testify that Charley Challenger started two other bar fights earlier that week.

2. The Champ wishes to testify that Charley Challenger has a reputation for being a very violent individual, particularly when drinking.

3. Charley Challenger intends to testify that he has never been in a fight outside the ring prior to this occasion.

4. Charley Challenger offers to testify that the Champ has been involved in numerous other fights outside of the ring and has, in Charley's opinion, a bad temper.

Problem #5-6: Conspiracy!

[This problem illuminates the different types of character evidence.]

Eeny, Meany, and Miny Moe are prosecuted for conspiracy to obstruct justice in a probe of the trucking industry. At trial, the prosecutor asks the undercover officer who infiltrated the conspiracy the following questions. Identify the form of the character evidence presented.

PROSECUTOR: So, Officer Krupke, what is your opinion of Meany?

A: He is the kind of person who would obstruct justice in a moment's notice.

DEFENSE COUNSEL: Objection!

Why?

PROSECUTOR: Officer, what do you know about Meany?

A: He was charged with conspiracy the year before, sold marijuana three years earlier, and snitched on his brother to save himself about 15 or so years ago.

DEFENSE COUNSEL: Objection!

Why?

§ 5.03   CHARACTER EVIDENCE EXCEPTION: THE ACCUSED OFFERS EVIDENCE FIRST

Problem #5-7: Heavyweight Champ

The heavyweight champion of the world, the Champ, claimed that Charley Challenger accosted him outside of a nightclub at 4:00 a.m. one morning. The government has criminally prosecuted Charley Challenger for assault and battery of the Champ. Which of the following evidence is admissible?

1. The Champ offers to testify that Charley Challenger started two other bar fights earlier that week. ✗ △ 1st

2. The Champ wishes to testify that Charley Challenger has a reputation for being a very violent individual, particularly when drinking. ✗ disc

3. Charley Challenger intends to testify that he has never been in a fight outside of the ring prior to this occasion. ✗ rep or opinion

4. Charley Challenger offers to testify that the Champ has been involved in numerous other fights outside of the ring and has, in Charley's opinion, a bad temper. ✓

5. Ethics Consideration. Charley Challenger informs you that his friend, Joe Fracas, will testify that in his opinion the Champ has a bad temper. Charley informs you that Fracas' testimony is false. Charley persuaded Fracas to offer a false opinion, in part, to repay a debt that Fracas owes to Charley. As Charley's lawyer, can you offer Fracas' opinion testimony that the Champ has a bad temper? Illinois Rules of Prof'l Conduct R. 3.3(a)(3). *See* MRPC 3.3(a)(3).

Problem #5-8: Horse? Heroin! Smack

Defendant Tara is charged with possession with intent to distribute heroin. In the defendant's case-in-chief, the defendant's mother will testify that the defendant has a fine reputation in the community for truthfulness. Is the defendant's mother's testimony admissible? Why?

Problem #5-9: BWS

Fawcett is charged with killing her husband, Harry, while he slept. Fawcett asserts the defense of battered woman's syndrome (BWS), claiming she reasonably believed she had no other alternative but to kill him. Fawcett perceived serious bodily harm was imminent.

At trial, Fawcett's sister, Pam, testifies on Fawcett's behalf. Pam makes the following statements: (1) "I observed Harry beat up his first wife, the one before

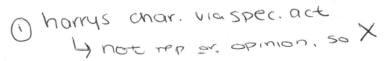

① harrys char. via spec. act
↳ not rep or. opinion, so ✗

Fawcett, so badly she was taken to the hospital." (2) "Based on what I saw of him, I firmly believe Harry was a violent man." ② *opinion.* ✓

Are Pam's two statements, (1) and (2) above, admissible? Why?

Problem #5-10: Honestly, No Lie

The defendant, Plato, is charged with bribery. In the defendant's case-in-chief, his college ethics teacher, Professor Stotle, testifies that, in his opinion, Plato has a high moral character for honesty.   *party*

1. Is this testimony admissible? Why? ✓   *crim D*
                                                pro

2. In the same bribery case, the prosecution offers in rebuttal a witness who will testify that (1) Plato's reputation in the community is one of dishonesty, and that (2) Plato had stolen three hubcaps from a car the year before. Is this testimony admissible? Why? ✗

Problem #5-11: Godzilla

In a homicide prosecution, the defendant, Pee Wee, offers evidence indicating that the victim, Godzilla, began the scuffle that led to Godzilla's death by gunshot. In rebuttal, the prosecution offers a reputation witness to testify that Godzilla was known in the community as a peaceful person. Is this testimony admissible? Why?

Problem #5-12: Six to Ten

Shortly after a "Six to Ten" convenience store opened for business one chilly winter morning, it was robbed by a white male. The description of the perpetrator indicated that he was 5 feet, 10 inches tall, weighed approximately 180 pounds, wore a beard, blue denim jacket, blue jeans, and sneakers, and held what looked like a hunting knife.

1. The prosecution attempts to introduce evidence that the defendant has robbed two other convenience stores within the past year. Is this evidence admissible? Why?

2. Can the prosecution introduce evidence that a man answering the defendant's description was seen robbing a nearby Wal-Mart store two hours later on that same day? Why?

§ 5.04   CHARACTER EVIDENCE ON AN ESSENTIAL ELEMENT

A person's character sometimes will be directly provable as an element of a cause of action, claim, or defense. Character "in issue" means character is directly relevant to a case, not merely helpful. In these cases, a party has to prove a person's character trait to win. Character is directly in issue, for example: (1) in a criminal seduction action (showing that the victim was of chaste character); (2) to prove entrapment (but only if a subjective entrapment standard applies; an element of that standard is that the defendant was not predisposed to committing the crime); (3) in a negligent entrustment or negligent hiring action (showing that the defendant was negligent in loaning an instrumentality to someone he or she knew or should have known was dangerous, or in hiring someone he or she knew or should have known was dangerous); and (4) in a defamation case (determining whether the plaintiff's reputation was defamed).

What these four examples show is that character can be an issue in both criminal (entrapment) and civil cases (negligent entrustment and hiring) and pertain to an element of a claim (seduction) or a defense (entrapment). The legislature, in determining the elements of a claim or defense, can readily add to the list of when character is truly at issue in a case.

If character is in issue, all forms of evidence may be used as proof, including reputation, and opinion evidence, as well as specific acts. *See* FRE 405. When character comprises an element, it is more important to the case than when it is offered circumstantially to prove conduct.

Illustration: Character Evidence as an Essential Element

One dark night, Dad loaned his car to his oldest child, Sonny, so Sonny could go on a date with Barbara. Sonny had been in eleven accidents in the preceding year, had received fourteen moving vehicle violations, and had his license suspended three times. Dad thought "Maybe this time will be different." Sonny drove Barbara home and parked the car in Barbara's driveway. Unbeknownst to Sonny, the car was still in "drive" and the car ended up in Barbara's living room. Dad is sued for negligent entrustment of the automobile to Sonny. Is Sonny's prior driving record admissible?

Answer: Sonny's prior driving record, including all of his specific instances of misconduct behind the wheel, is admissible character evidence. Sonny's character as a reckless driver is directly in issue in this negligent entrustment action. One of the elements of the tort of negligent entrustment is that Dad knew or should have known of Sonny's propensity for reckless driving and consequently should not have loaned him the car. When character is directly provable as it is here, all forms of character evidence (reputation, opinion, and specific acts) are permitted.

[A] Problems Involving Character as an Essential Element of a Case

The problems that follow identify and provide illustrations of the types of problems that might fall within the exception to the general rule excluding character evidence, character as an essential element. This exception is sometimes labeled, "character in issue" evidence, but it is more precisely seen as evidence that must be offered to prove an element of the claim, cause of action, or defense, not evidence that is merely helpful, in an indirect way, to proving a case.

Problem #5-13: Rambo III

Jim Rambo, Houston Rambo's cousin, was known around town as a "one-man terrorist gang." He had burned down the town hall, shot three different people in the leg, and participated in twenty-four different bar fights. One hot and dusty June day, Perry, the owner of Perry's Grocery, hired Rambo to serve as the security guard for the store. Perry gave Rambo a low-caliber pistol to carry while on duty. During his fifth day on the job, Rambo got into a fight with one of the customers and shot the customer in the leg. The customer brought suit against Perry, claiming negligent hiring. Plaintiff's first witness is the mayor of the town. The mayor will testify that in his opinion, Rambo is extremely dangerous, if not lethal. He will also recount all of the prior incidents involving Rambo's harmful behavior. Which parts of the mayor's testimony, if any, are admissible?

Problem #5-14: Blue v. Jones

In this slander action, Jones, a Portland businesswoman, allegedly called the commissioner of baseball, Vincent T. Blue, a "lazy nerd" after Portland was denied a major league baseball franchise. Which of the following evidence is admissible at trial? Why?

1. Blue offers testimony that he worked past midnight on eighteen previous occasions.

2. Blue offers testimony that he has a reputation in baseball for being very industrious.

3. Blue offers evidence that he is a peaceful, non-violent person.

4. Jones offers the testimony of Peter Potamkin, a former commissioner, who states that in his opinion, Blue was "lazy."

5. Jones offers evidence that Blue has a reputation among major league baseball owners for being a nerd.

Problem #5-15: United States v. Lorean

The defendant, Lorean, is charged with possession with intent to distribute cocaine after a government "sting" operation. Lorean admits to possessing the cocaine, but claims he was entrapped by an undercover police officer. The jurisdiction uses a subjective test of entrapment, which asks (1) whether the police induced or created the crime, and (2) whether the defendant was predisposed to committing the crime charged. Which, if any, of the following items of evidence offered by Lorean are admissible?

1. Testimony by Lorean's father stating that his son would never violate any criminal laws whatsoever. To the father's knowledge, his son had violated the law only once, when as a child he stole a ball from the local five and dime store. Admissible?

2. Lorean's brother testifies that, in his opinion, Lorean is an extremely honest person. Admissible?

3. Can the prosecution offer evidence that Lorean was arrested for the possession of marijuana fifteen years prior to trial?

§ 5.05   MIXED CHARACTER EVIDENCE PROBLEMS

Problem #5-16: Bad Cop, Good Cop

Austin was prosecuted for resisting arrest and assault on a police officer after being stopped and frisked while leaving a bar. Austin claimed he acted in self-defense. At trial, Austin offered Cheryl, a former friend of the officer, as a character witness to state the officer had a reputation in the community for exhibiting "excessively aggressive and violent tendencies."

    1. Is Cheryl's testimony admissible? Why?

    2. Suppose the prosecution offers evidence that the accused, Austin, had committed four prior assaults on police officers. Admissible?

Problem #5-17: Murray Christmas

The defendant, Murray Christmas, is prosecuted for check forgery. The prosecution's first witness, Alec, recounts the events in question. He then exclaims, "That Christmas fellow has a reputation in this community for being a liar."

    1. Is this testimony admissible? Explain.

    2. Murray's good friend, Magritte, is the first witness for the defense. He testifies that Murray's reputation in the community is one of peacefulness and truthfulness. Is this testimony admissible? Why?

    3. On cross-examination, Magritte is asked whether he has heard that Murray had been arrested for attempted embezzlement from the American Express Company the previous year. Is this question permissible?

    4. Can the prosecution cross-examine Magritte about Murray's purported embezzlement if the prosecution has no concrete knowledge about the embezzlement, but instead bases its question on rumors?

    5. In rebuttal, the government offers a new witness, Sgt. MacKnife, to testify that defendant, Murray, had been arrested for embezzlement three years earlier, and that the witness, Magritte, had been indicted for perjury only two months before the trial. Is this testimony admissible? Why?

§ 5.06   OTHER ACTS EVIDENCE: OFFERED FOR NON-CHARACTER PURPOSES [FRE 404(B)]

Sometimes, acts occurring prior or subsequent to the incident in question are admissible at trial for a limited purpose, one other than to show a person's propensity. Admissible non-character purposes include, but are not restricted to, (1) motive, (2) intent, (3) identity, (4) absence of mistake, (5) knowledge, (6) opportunity, (7) common scheme or plan, and (8) guilty conscience. "Motive" evidence indicates why someone behaved the way he or she did on a later occasion. "Intent" evidence suggests what was in the person's mind — the mental state — at the exact time of the incident. (Thus, motive is different from intent. Motive can precede an incident by a considerable amount of time, while intent is measured only at the precise time of the incident. Motive can help create and give rise to intent. For example, a love triangle may be the motive for a violent crime, while the intent of the actor is the desire to kill.) "Absence of mistake" evidence negates an opponent's suggestion that the bad result, for example, a house burning down, was an accident or mere mistake. "Knowledge" evidence indicates that a person knew or at least should have known something, often negating a claim of ignorance. The knowledge issue arises, for example, when drugs are imported in the hull of a boat or trunk of a car and the transporter claims no knowledge of the contents. "Opportunity" evidence generally negates a claim of lack of opportunity to act. "Common scheme or plan" evidence indicates several crimes or improper acts are linked together to achieve a common objective. In conspiracies for example, some crimes are committed as a predicate to the ultimate objective of the conspiracy, such as stealing ammunition for a subsequent armed robbery. Finally, "guilty conscience" evidence, such as bribing a witness or running away, derives from acts of a party that create an inference of a person's guilt.

The use of other acts evidence remains problematic. Such acts may be highly probative of an issue, but may be highly prejudicial as well. For example, while other acts of evidence can be offered for non-character purposes such as those listed above, other acts also readily suggest that the actor has a propensity to act in a certain manner (i.e., "once a crook, always a . . .").

To ensure that the jury considers the other acts evidence only for its non-propensity purpose, counsel can ask the court for a jury instruction limiting the evidence's admissibility. The paradox of such a request, however, is that a limiting instruction may simply call additional attention to the forbidden propensity inference.

Illustration: Other Acts Evidence

Lil is charged with stealing a co-worker's wallet from a desk drawer. The thief left a photograph of a wallet in place of the stolen wallet. At trial, the prosecution offers evidence that Lil previously stole a blouse from a local department store, leaving a photograph of the blouse in its place. Is this other acts evidence admissible?

Answer: The evidence that Lil stole a blouse on a previous occasion and then left a photograph of the blouse in its place is admissible for the non-character purpose of showing identity, but not to show that Lil has the propensity to be a thief. The evidence is admissible to show identity because the theft of the blouse has a unique or "signature" quality about it that indicates Lil's modus operandi. The theft of the blouse is not admissible for propensity purposes; i.e., it is not admissible to show that, because Lil stole on a prior occasion, she is a thief, and therefore, is more likely to have acted as a thief on this occasion and stolen the wallet as well.

Problems Involving Evidence Offered for a Non-Propensity Purpose

When engaging with these problems, first identify whether the evidence has a character inference — and could qualify as character evidence — and then identify how the same evidence still could be relevant if offered for a different, non-propensity purpose.

Problem #5-18: Big Al

The defendant, Capone, is charged with the distribution of cocaine and phencyclidine (PCP). The prosecution offers evidence in its case-in-chief of baggies, scales, and other narcotics paraphernalia found in the defendant's home four days after his arrest. What argument should Capone's defense attorney make to exclude the evidence? Will that argument be successful? *drugy → other acts → com. scheme or plan ✓*

Problem #5-19: Frozen Dinners

The defendant, Chaos, was charged with extortion. Four days after the charges were filed, the defendant attempted to kill the alleged victim of the extortion scheme, Max Schmaat, by poisoning his frozen dinner (chicken a la king). Schmaat survived to testify. Is the attempt to poison the victim relevant? Is it admissible? *killer ✓ other → guilty consc.*

Problem #5-20: Lester the Child Molester

4/18

Lester is charged with molesting a ten-year-old girl. Lester allegedly molested the girl in his car after promising to take her to see a black and white bunny rabbit. At trial, the government offers evidence of two prior allegations of child abuse against Lester. Both allegations involved Lester molesting young girls after inviting the girls into his car to see black and white bunny rabbits. Are Lester's prior acts admissible?

Problem #5-21: Stress, Duress, and Redress

The defendant, Roberto, was prosecuted for robbery. He asserted the defense of duress. Roberto claimed that his brother-in-law coerced him into participating in the robbery by threatening to kill Roberto's sister if Roberto did not stand look-out. Roberto claimed, "My brother-in-law made me do it!" In rebuttal, the prosecution offers evidence that Roberto had committed several other prior robberies without his brother-in-law's participation.

  1. Are these other acts admissible?

  2. Ethics Consideration. Assume that Roberto was convicted of the robbery. The prosecutor later learns (post conviction) that its key witness had perjured himself on the witness stand. What are the prosecutor's ethical responsibilities after learning of the perjury? Idaho Rules of Prof'l Conduct R. 3.8(g). *See* MRPC 3.8(g).

Problem #5-22: More Duress

The defendant, Shinoy, is charged with bank robbery. She asserted the defense of duress, claiming that other participants in the robbery, William and Emily, coerced her into committing the crime. The prosecution offers evidence at trial of other criminal activity in which the defendant had participated:

  1. During one event, which took place within a month of the bank robbery, William was apprehended for alleged shoplifting. Shinoy then fired a rifle which permitted William to escape.

2. In the second event, William and Emily kidnapped a third party. Shinoy did not attempt to assist the victim or to escape herself, even though she had an apparent opportunity to do so.

The court's law clerk researched the question of duress. The clerk found that duress exists when "[a] defendant who, without opportunity to escape, has a well grounded fear of imminent death or serious injury unless he complies with his captor's wrongful commands." *United States v. Hearst*, 563 F.2d 1331 (9th Cir. 1977).

Should these two other acts described above be admitted at trial? *See United States v. Hearst*, 563 F.2d 1331 (9th Cir. 1977).

Problem #5-23: Attempted Murder, She Wrote

The defendant, Agnes, has AIDS. After biting an FBI agent, she is charged with attempted murder. The prosecution wants to offer evidence that the FBI agent had arrested the defendant on three prior occasions. Should these prior acts be allowed in evidence?

Problem #5-24: Oregano?

Vern Parrish, a college student, was charged with the possession of marijuana. Vern testified at trial that he did not know what marijuana looked like. He claimed that he was surprised when the police, who were conducting a search pursuant to a valid warrant, found the substance in the back of his refrigerator. In rebuttal, the prosecutor, Anne Bluestone, offers evidence that the defendant had been charged with the possession of marijuana on two prior occasions. (Both of those prosecutions were dropped for insufficient evidence.) Admit? Why? Is the fact that the defendant was a young college student relevant to the admissibility of this other acts evidence? Would the analysis change if the defendant attended middle school? Was a senior citizen?

Problem #5-25: Psychobubbles

Mickey's wife, Sarah, died in their Jacuzzi hot tub one evening in January. Mickey later was charged with her murder. Mickey claims at trial that the death was the result of a terrible accident. In rebuttal, the prosecution offers evidence that two of the defendant's three previous wives died of unknown and allegedly accidental causes in their Jacuzzi hot tubs as well.

1. Is this evidence admissible? If so, is the evidence admissible to show the defendant's propensity to kill? Y   *absence of mistake*

2. Can the other acts evidence be admitted on a non-character theory, called the "doctrine of chances"? (Pursuant to this theory, the evidence is offered to show that the occurrence of other events diminishes the probability that the event in question occurred by chance.) Does it matter which justification for admissibility is advanced?

3. If Mickey is charged only with the death of his first wife, who also died in a hot tub, are the *subsequent* deaths of his other wives in hot tubs relevant and

admissible? Does it make a difference whether the "other acts" occurred before or after the event in question?

Problem #5-26: Procrastinate Now!

Four people from a group known as "Procrastinate Now!" are accused of blowing up a McDonald's with dynamite. An anonymous announcement claimed that the act was intended to be a symbolic gesture against one of the spear-carriers of American capitalism, and warned that Dairy Queen was next. At trial, the prosecution introduced evidence that the defendants had been observed stealing ten sticks of dynamite and several blasting caps one week prior to the explosion from a display case at the "Club Dyn-o-mite" Weaponry Store. The trial court admitted the evidence over objection.

Was it error for the court to admit the evidence? Explain.

Problem #5-27: Child Abuse

Sally brings suit against her former husband, Gary, seeking damages for the sexual abuse of their daughter, Megan. At trial, Sally offers an expert to testify that Gary's child from another marriage was sexually abused by him. Is the expert's testimony admissible?

Problem #5-28: Going in Stiles

The defendant, Joshua, is charged with selling cocaine to an undercover police officer, Officer Stiles. At trial, the prosecution offers the testimony of Officer Stiles.

PROSECUTOR: Now Officer Stiles, what happened exactly nine months to the day after the cocaine sale at issue in this case?

A: Well, nine months after the defendant sold me cocaine, I observed him selling cocaine to another officer, Officer Burnes.

1. Admissible? *propensity*

2. Would it be significant if the alleged sale to Officer Burnes was still a pending felony case? Would it be relevant if there had been a conviction in the sale to Officer Burnes?

3. If the "other act" sale to Officer Burnes is admitted at trial pursuant to FRE 404(b), would it be proper for the trial judge to explain the purpose of such evidence to the jury by simply repeating FRE 404(b)? Would such an instruction constitute reversible error? *See United States v. Cortijo-Diaz*, 875 F.2d 13 (1st Cir. 1989).   *must be explained*

Problem #5-29: Muddy for the Defense

Mark Muddy, attorney at law, was prosecuted for filing a false statement with the Securities and Exchange Commission on behalf of a local bank. He defends the suit by claiming that he mistakenly filed the erroneous statements.

1. In rebuttal, can the prosecutor introduce other false statements filed by Muddy for other clients?

2. Can the prosecutor show that Muddy is a greedy person by offering evidence of shady transactions in which Muddy took financial advantage of his siblings?

3. Can the prosecutor offer Muddy's sudden preference for untraceable financial transactions to show Muddy's intent regarding the statements he filed with the Securities and Exchange Commission?

Problem #5-30: I. M. Rich

Cindy Ford was charged with passing a bad check, which she signed "I. M. Rich." Can the prosecution introduce the fact that on three prior occasions, Cindy also wrote checks signed "I. M. Rich"? Explain. *other acts → signature quality*

Problem #5-31: Napa Valley Prison

Riesling was an inmate serving 25 years to life on an aggravated battery conviction. He subsequently was charged while serving his sentence in prison with assaulting a correctional officer. At the assault trial, the prosecutor offered evidence that the defendant Riesling made wine in prison and distributed it to other inmates. The officer the defendant was charged with assaulting had routinely shut down Riesling's business. Is this evidence offered by the prosecution permitted?

Problem #5-32: A Propensity to Burn

The defendant was accused of intentionally burning down his own restaurant, The Atlantic Cove, to recover the insurance on it. At trial, the prosecutor offered a former friend of the defendant as a witness, who said, "Yeah, a little while back, Stick, the defendant, also burned a car he had leased." Is this evidence admissible?

Problem #5-33: No Union?!

The defendant employer, Southwestern Technical University, was sued by a worker, Alva, who was fired after trying to organize a union. The employer's president, Ed, claimed the firing was solely based on job performance and that there was no problem with union organization at the employer's company. At trial, Alva offered evidence that the employer company had discriminated against other workers who had participated in union activity. Is Alva's evidence admissible?

§ 5.07 RES GESTAE: COMPLETING THE STORY

Some other acts evidence is so closely connected to the act in issue that to exclude the other acts would impede the trier's ability to determine the facts. These closely connected other acts are admitted under the "res gestae" principle, which essentially means to complete the story.

Illustration: Res Gestae Evidence

Manfred agreed to sell Barfeld some cocaine. When Barfeld checked out the substance prior to payment, he exclaimed, "This stuff is cut, you cheat!" Barfeld then knifed Manfred, severely injuring him. Barfeld is charged with attempted murder. Is Manfred's attempt to sell Barfeld cocaine admissible in the attempted murder trial?

Answer: In the prosecution of Barfeld for attempted murder, the prosecution likely will be able to offer evidence of the attempted cocaine sale as part of its case-in-chief. The evidence will be admitted to complete the story of the attempted murder. Specifically, the aborted cocaine sale provides the motive for the knifing. There is a sufficiently close nexus between the attempted cocaine sale and the knifing for the cocaine evidence to be considered a part of the same act or transaction as the knifing, and not as a separate "other act" falling under FRE 404(b). (Alternatively, the attempted cocaine sale could be offered under Rule 404(b) to show motive.)

Res Gestae Problems

Problem #5-34: Tango and Cash

Tango was short on money one Wednesday evening after losing big in a card game. Consequently, he decided to rob the local gas station to obtain some "fast cash." Tango successfully robbed the gas station attendant and fled on foot. As Tango danced quickly around a corner, he knocked over and severely injured an elderly woman. Tango was tried separately for the robbery of the gas station and the battery of the elderly woman. At the battery trial, the prosecution wishes to introduce evidence of the robbery to show why Tango was running so quickly at the time. Should the judge permit evidence of the robbery?

Problem #5-35: Outlaw Turtles

Raphael, Donatello, and Michelangelo are charged with conspiracy to import an illegal substance, green slime. The prosecution offers the testimony of a man named Roger the Rat. Roger will state that he purchased green slime from Donatello. The trials of the co-defendants are severed and this testimony is offered in Michaelangelo's trial. Is the testimony admissible? *See United States v. Troop*, 890 F.2d 1393 (7th Cir. 1989).

Mixed Other Acts Problems

Problem #5-36: More Questions

1. *The Brakeman.* The plaintiff, Jones, survived a crash as a passenger in a pick-up truck that was hit by a freight train. The plaintiff sued the railroad company, claiming that the train's brakeman was negligent. Plaintiff offered testimony indicating that the train's brakeman had received citations on nine separate occasions for failing to brake adequately, speeding, and for similar improprieties. Should the court admit this evidence? *See Jones v. Southern Pacific Railroad*, 962 F.2d 447 (5th Cir. 1992).

2. *Huddler.* Jimmy Huddler was charged with robbing a convenience store just before it closed at midnight after bringing a can of sweet tea to the register and trying to pay for it with pennies. Huddler had been charged with a similar crime three years before in another jurisdiction, where he had brought a large can of sweet tea to the register just before closing and tried to pay with pennies, but was acquitted in that

case by a jury at trial. Can the prior case be offered as evidence by the prosecution in its case-in-chief? If yes, how can it be offered?

3. *Beeched.* The defendant, Jim Beech, a substitute mail carrier, was prosecuted for allegedly possessing an 1890 silver dollar that he knew to be stolen from the mail. The defendant conceded possessing the silver dollar; the only issue in the case was whether he intended to return the coin.

The defendant claimed that he intended to return the silver dollar. The prosecution rebutted this claim at trial by offering evidence that the defendant also possessed two Sears credit cards at the time of his arrest. These cards had been mailed ten months earlier to customers on the defendant's route, but had never been delivered. If you were the judge, would you admit the prosecution's rebuttal evidence? Why? *See United States v. Beechum*, 582 F.2d 898, 912 (5th Cir. 1978).

§ 5.08   CASES AND RULES

[A]   People v. Zackowitz

Court of Appeals of New York
254 N.Y. 192, 172 N.E. 466 (1930)

CARDOZO, C.J.:

On November 10, 1929, shortly after midnight, the defendant in Kings county shot Frank Coppola and killed him without justification or excuse. A crime is admitted. What is doubtful is the degree only.

Four young men, of whom Coppola was one, were at work repairing an automobile in a Brooklyn street. A woman, the defendant's wife, walked by on the opposite side. One of the men spoke to her insultingly, or so at least she understood him. The defendant, who had dropped behind to buy a newspaper, came up to find his wife in tears. He was told she had been insulted, though she did not then repeat the words. Enraged, he stepped across the street and upbraided the offenders with words of coarse profanity. He informed them, so the survivors testify, that "if they did not get out of there in five minutes, he would come back and bump them all off." Rejoining his wife, he walked with her to their apartment house located close at hand. He was heated with liquor which he had been drinking at a dance. Within the apartment he induced her to tell him what the insulting words had been. A youth had asked her to lie with him, and had offered her $2. With rage aroused again, the defendant went back to the scene of the insult and found the four young men still working at the car. In a statement to the police, he said that he had armed himself at the apartment with a .25-caliber automatic pistol. In his testimony at the trial he said that this pistol had been in his pocket all the evening. Words and blows followed, and then a shot. . . . The pistol came from the pocket, and from the pistol a single shot, which did its deadly work. The defendant walked away and at the corner met his wife who had followed him from the home. The two took a taxicab to Manhattan, where they spent the rest of the night at the dwelling of a friend. On the way the defendant threw his pistol into the river. He was arrested on January 7, 1930, about two months following the crime.

At the trial the vital question was the defendant's state of mind at the moment of the homicide. Did he shoot with a deliberate and premeditated design to kill? Was he so inflamed by drink or by anger or by both combined that, though he knew the nature of his act, he was the prey to sudden impulse, the fury of the fleeting moment? *People v. Caruso*, 246 N.Y. 437, 446, 159 N.E. 390 (1927). If he went forth from his apartment with a preconceived design to kill, how is it that he failed to shoot at once? How reconcile such a design with the drawing of the pistol later in the heat and rage of an affray? These and like questions the jurors were to ask themselves and answer before measuring the defendant's guilt. . . . There must be no blurring of the issues by evidence illegally admitted and carrying with it in its admission an appeal to prejudice and passion.

Evidence charged with that appeal was, we think, admitted here. Not only was it admitted, and this under objection and exception, but the changes were rung upon it by prosecutor and judge. Almost at the opening of the trial the people began the endeavor to load the defendant down with the burden of an evil character. He was to be put before the jury as a man of murderous disposition. To that end they were allowed to prove that at the time of the encounter and at that of his arrest he had in his apartment, kept there in a radio box, three pistols and a tear-gas gun. There was no claim that he had brought these weapons out at the time of the affray, no claim that with any of them he had discharged the fatal shot. He could not have done so, for they were all of different caliber. The end to be served by laying the weapons before the jury was something very different. The end was to bring persuasion that here was a man of vicious and dangerous propensities, who because of those propensities was more likely to kill with deliberate and premeditated design than a man of irreproach-able life and amiable manners. Indeed, this is the very ground on which the introduction of the evidence is now explained and defended. The district attorney tells us in his brief that the possession of the weapons characterized the defendant as "a desperate type of criminal," a "person criminally inclined." The dissenting opinion, if it puts the argument less bluntly, leaves the substance of the thought unchanged. "Defendant was presented to the jury as a man having dangerous weapons in his possession, making a selection therefrom and going forth to put into execution his threats to kill." The weapons were not brought by the defendant to the scene of the encounter. They were left in his apartment where they were incapable of harm. In such circumstances, ownership of the weapons, if it has any relevance at all, has relevance only as indicating a general disposition to make use of them thereafter, and a general disposition to make use of them thereafter is without relevance except as indicating a "desperate type of criminal," a criminal affected with a murderous propensity.

We are asked to extenuate the error by calling it an incident; what was proved may have an air of innocence if it is styled the history of the crime. The virus of the ruling is not so easily extracted. There was no passing reference to something casually brought out in the narrative of the killing, as if an admission had been proved against the defendant that he had picked one weapon out of several. Here in the forefront of the trial, immediately following the statement of the medical examiner, testimony was admitted that weapons, not the instruments of the killing, had been discovered by the police in the apartment of the killer; and the weapons with great display were laid before the jury, marked as exhibits, and thereafter made the subject of animated argument. Room for doubt there is none that in the thought of the jury, as in that of the district attorney, the tendency of the whole performance was to characterize the defendant as a man murderously inclined. The purpose was not disguised. From the opening to the verdict, it was flaunted and avowed.

If a murderous propensity may be proved against a defendant as one of the tokens of his guilt, a rule of criminal evidence, long believed to be of fundamental importance for the protection of the innocent, must be first declared away. Fundamental hitherto has been the rule that character is never an issue in a criminal prosecution unless the defendant chooses to make it one. . . . In a very real sense a defendant starts his life afresh when he stands before a jury, a prisoner at the bar. There has been a homicide in a public place. The killer admits the killing, but urges self-defense and sudden impulse. Inflexibly the law has set its face against the endeavor to fasten guilt upon him by proof of character or experience predisposing to an act of crime. . . . The endeavor has been often made, but always it has failed. At times, when the issue has been self-defense, testimony has been admitted as to the murderous propensity of the deceased, the victim of the homicide, . . . but never of such a propensity on the part of the killer. The principle back of the exclusion is one, not of logic, but of policy. . . . There may be cogency in the argument that a quarrelsome defendant is more likely to start a quarrel than one of milder type, a man of dangerous mode of life more likely than a shy recluse. The law is not blind to this, but equally it is not blind to the peril to the innocent if character is accepted as probative of crime. "The natural and inevitable tendency of the tribunal — whether judge or jury — is to give excessive weight to the vicious record of crime thus exhibited, and either to allow it to bear too strongly on the present charge, or to take the proof of it as justifying a condemnation irrespective of guilt of the present charge." (Citations omitted.) A different question would be here if the pistols had been bought in expectation of this particular encounter. They would then have been admissible as evidence of preparation and design. . . .

A different question would be here if they were so connected with the crime as to identify the perpetrator, if he had dropped them, for example, at the scene of the affray. *People v. Hill*, 198 N.Y. 64, 91 N.E. 272 (1910). They would then have been admissible as tending to implicate the possessor (if identity was disputed), no matter what the opprobrium attached to his possession. Different, also, would be the question if the defendant had been shown to have gone forth from the apartment with all the weapons on his person. To be armed from head to foot at the very moment of an encounter may be a circumstance worthy to be considered, like acts of preparation generally, as a proof of preconceived design. There can be no such implication from the ownership of weapons which one leaves behind at home.

The endeavor was to generate an atmosphere of professional criminality. It was an endeavor the more unfair in that, apart from the suspicion attaching to the possession of these weapons, there is nothing to mark the defendant as a man of evil life. He was not in crime as a business. He did not shoot as a bandit shoots in the hope of wrongful gain. He was engaged in a decent calling, an optician regularly employed, without criminal record, or criminal associates. If his own testimony be true, he had gathered these weapons together as curios, a collection that interested and amused him.

Perhaps his explanation of their ownership is false. There is nothing stronger than mere suspicion to guide us to an answer. Whether the explanation be false or true, he should not have been driven by the people to the necessity of offering it. Brought to answer a specific charge, and to defend himself against it, he was placed in a position where he had to defend himself against another, more general and sweeping. He was made to answer to the charge, pervasive and poisonous even if insidious and covert, that he was a man of murderous heart, of criminal disposition.

. . . .

The judgment of conviction should be reversed, and a new trial ordered.

LEHMAN, KELLOGG, and O'BRIEN, JJ., concur with CARDOZO, C. J.

POUND, J., dissents in opinion in which CRANE and HUBBS, JJ., concur.

POUND, J. (dissenting).

The indictment herein accuses defendant of the crime of murder in the first degree committed in Kings county on November 10, 1929, by shooting Frank Coppola with a revolver. That defendant did shoot and kill Coppola is admitted. The jury was justified on the evidence in finding that he did so from a deliberate and premeditated design to effect death. The proofs tend to establish that defendant, aged twenty-four, and his seventeen year old wife, 'Fluff,' had attended a dance at a dance hall; . . . that he made a confession in which he sought to defend the act of killing by saying that Coppola threatened him with a monkey wrench and that he did not realize that he had shot him; that he got the gun at his home and went back to ask them to apologize; that he took the gun to protect himself 'because they were four guys'; that he had been drinking, was a little excited, but not drunk; that he knew what he was doing.

The case would have been quite different if the weapons came into defendant's possession after the killing. The proof would then be of separate crimes unconnected with the killing and its admission reversible error under the Molineux Case, supra.

It is urged that defendant may have been half-drunk, infuriated, frightened, impulsive, and measurably irresponsible; that he should not have been convicted of murder in the first degree; that the proof of possession of the weapons prejudiced the jury against him. If, as we have held, the proof was competent the jury was free to give it such weight as it deserved. On the other hand, if it was incompetent, was the error substantial enough to call for the reversal of his conviction? Defendant presented his side of the case to the jury. He gave his account of the weapons and how he came by them, which was consistent with innocent purpose on his part. Admittedly he did have an argument with Coppola and his fellows, did go home, did return armed, and did quarrel and kill. His answer is that the killing was accidental. How can we say with confidence in the circumstances of this case that the evidence, even if technically objectionable, so tended to influence the jury against him that 'justice requires a new trial'? Code Cr. Proc. § 528. While it is not inconceivable that the result might have been otherwise without this evidence *People v. Slover*, 232 N. Y. 264, 267, 133 N.E. 633, it is unlikely that it turned the minds of the jury from a lesser degree of crime to the disadvantage of accused. In the circumstances of this case, whether he had one weapon or a dozen would not materially change the nature of his offense. The proof merely darkened that which was black enough when painted by his own brush.

The judgment of conviction should be affirmed.

[B]   Michelson v. United States

United States Supreme Court
335 U.S. 469, 69 S. Ct. 213, 93 L. Ed. 168 (1948)

Mr. Justice Jackson delivered the opinion of the Court

In 1947 petitioner Michelson was convicted of bribing a federal revenue agent. The Government proved a large payment by the accused to the agent for the purpose of influencing his official action. The defendant, as a witness on his own behalf, admitted passing the money but claimed it was done in response to the agent's demands, threats, solicitations, and inducements that amounted to entrapment. It is enough for our purposes to say that determination of the issue turned on whether the jury should believe the agent or the accused.

On direct examination of defendant, his own counsel brought out that, in 1927, he had been convicted of a misdemeanor having to do with trading in counterfeit watch dials. On cross-examination it appeared that in 1930, in executing an application for a license to deal in second-hand jewelry, he answered 'No' to the question whether he had theretofore been arrested or summoned for any offense.

Defendant called five witnesses to prove that he enjoyed a good reputation. Two of them testified that their acquaintance with him extended over a period of about thirty years and the others said they had known him at least half that long. A typical examination in chief was as follows:

"Q. Do you know the defendant Michelson?

"A. Yes

"Q. How long did you know Mr. Michelson?

"A. About 30 years.

"Q. Do you know other people who know him?

"A. Yes.

"Q. Have you had occasion to discuss his reputation for honesty and truthfulness and for being a law-abiding citizen?

"A. It is very good.

"Q. You have talked to others?

"A. Yes.

"Q. And what is his reputation.

"A. Very good." "

These are representative of answers by three witnesses; two others replied, in substance, that they never had heard anything against Michelson.

On cross-examination, four of the witnesses were asked in substance, this question: "Did you ever hear that Mr. Michelson on March 4, 1927, was convicted of a violation of the trademark law in New York City in regard to watches?" This referred to the twenty-year-old conviction about which defendant himself had testified on direct examination. Two of them had heard of it and two had not.

To four of these witnesses the prosecution also addressed the question the allowance of which, over defendant's objection, is claimed to be reversible error."

Did you ever hear that on October 11th, 1920, the defendant, Solomon Michelson, was arrested for receiving stolen goods?"

None of the witnesses appears to have heard of this.

The trial court asked counsel for the prosecution, out of presence of the jury, "Is it a fact according to the best information in your possession that Michelson was arrested for receiving stolen goods?" Counsel replied that it was, and to support his good faith exhibited a paper record which defendant's counsel did not challenge.

The judge also on three occasions warned the jury, in terms that are not criticized, of the limited purpose for which this evidence was received.

. . . .

Courts that follow the common-law tradition almost unanimously have come to disallow resort by the prosecution to any kind of evidence or a defendant's evil character to establish a probability of his guilt. Not that the law invests the defendant with a presumption of good character, *Greer v. United States*, 245 U.S. 559, 38 S. Ct. 209, 62 L. Ed. 469, but it simply closes the whole matter of character, disposition and reputation on the prosecution's case-in-chief. The State may not show defendant's prior trouble with the law, specific criminal acts, or ill name among his neighbors, even though such facts might logically be persuasive that he is by propensity a probable perpetrator of the crime. The inquiry is not rejected because character is irrelevant; on the contrary, it is said to weigh too much with the jury and to so over persuade them as to prejudge one with a bad general record and deny him a fair opportunity to defend against a particular charge. The overriding policy of excluding such evidence, despite its admitted probative value, is the practical experience that its disallowance tends to prevent confusion of issues, unfair surprise and undue prejudice.

But this line of inquiry firmly denied to the State is opened to the defendant because character is relevant in resolving probabilities of guilt. He may introduce affirmative testimony that the general estimate of his character is so favorable that the jury may infer that he would not be likely to commit the offense charged. This privilege is sometimes valuable to a defendant for this Court has held that such testimony alone, in some circumstances, may be enough to raise a reasonable doubt of guilt and that in the federal courts a jury in a proper case should be so instructed.

When the defendant elects to initiate a character inquiry, another anomalous rule comes into play. Not only is he permitted to call witnesses to testify from hearsay, but indeed such a witness is not allowed to base his testimony on anything but hearsay. What commonly is called "character evidence" is only such when "character" is employed as a synonym for "reputation." The witness may not testify about defendant's specific acts or courses of conduct or his possession of a particular disposition, or of benign mental and moral traits; nor can he testify that his own acquaintance, observation, and knowledge of defendant leads to his own independent opinion that defendant possesses a good general or specific character inconsistent with commission of acts charged. The witness is, however, allowed to summarize what he has heard in the community, although much of it may have been said by persons less qualified to judge than himself. The evidence which the law permits is not as to the personality of defendant but only as to the shadow his daily life has cast in his neighborhood . . . .

[out of order in opinion].

. . . The price a defendant must pay for attempting to prove his good name is to throw open the entire subject which the law has kept closed for his benefit and to make himself vulnerable where the law otherwise shields him. The prosecution may pursue the inquiry with contradictory witnesses to show that damaging rumors, whether or not well-grounded, were afloat — for it is not the man that he is, but the name that he has which is put in issue. Another hazard is that his own witness is subject to cross-examination as to the contents and extent of the hearsay on which he bases his conclusions, and he may be required to disclose rumors and reports that are current even if they do not affect his own conclusion. It may test the sufficiency of his knowledge by asking what stories were circulating concerning events, such as one's arrest, about which people normally comment and speculate . . . .

A character witness may be cross-examined as to an arrest whether or not it culminated in a conviction, according to the overwhelming weight of authority. This rule is sometimes confused with that which prohibits cross-examination to credibility by asking a witness whether he himself has been arrested.

Arrest without more does not, in law any more than in reason, impeach the integrity or impair the credibility of a witness. It happens to the innocent as well as the guilty. Only a conviction, therefore, may be inquired to undermine the trustworthiness of a witness. Arrest without more may nevertheless impair or cloud one's reputation. False arrest may do that. Even to be acquitted may damage one's good name if the community receives the verdict with a wink and chooses to remember defendant as one who ought to have been convicted. A conviction, on the other hand, may be accepted as a misfortune or an injustice, and even enhance the standing of one who mends his ways and lives it down. Reputation is the net balance of so many debits and credits that the law does not attach the finality to a conviction, when the issue is reputation, that is given to it when the issue is the credibility of the convict. The inquiry as to an arrest is permissible also because the prosecution has a right to test the qualifications of the witness to bespeak the community opinion. If one never heard the speculations and rumors in which even one's friends indulge upon his arrest, the jury may doubt whether he is capable of giving any very reliable conclusions as to his reputation.

In this case the crime inquired about was receiving stolen goods; the trial was for bribery. The Court of Appeals thought this dissimilarity of offenses too great to sustain the inquiry in logic, though conceding that it is authorized by preponderance of authority. It asks us to substitute the Illinois rule which allows inquiry about arrest, but only for very closely similar if not identical charges, in place of the rule more generally adhered to in this country and in England. We think the facts of this case show the proposal to be inexpedient.

. . . However, limiting instructions on this subject are no more difficult to comprehend or apply than those upon various other subjects; for example, instructions that admissions of a co-defendant are to be limited to the question of his guilt and are not to be considered as evidence against other defendants, and instructions as to other problems in the trial of conspiracy charges. A defendant in such a case is powerless to prevent his cause from being irretrievably obscured and confused; but, in cases such as the one before us, the law foreclosed this whole confounding line of inquiry, unless defendant thought the net advantage from opening it up would be with him. Given this option we think defendants in general and this defendant in particular have no valid complaint at the latitude which existing law allows to the prosecution to meet by cross examination an issue voluntarily tendered by the defense.

The law of evidence of evidence relating to proof of reputation in criminal cases has developed almost entirely at the hands of state courts of last resort, which have such questions frequently before them. This Court, on the other hand, has contributed little to this or to any phase of the law of evidence, for the reason, among others, that it has had extremely rare occasion to decide such issues, as the paucity of citations in this opinion to our own writings attests. It is obvious that a court which can make only infrequent sallies into the field cannot recast the body of case law on this subject in many, many years, even if it were clear what the rules should be.

We concur in the general opinion of courts, text writers and the profession that much of this law is archaic, paradoxical and full of compromises and compensations by which an irrational advantage to one side is offset by a poorly reasoned counter-privilege to the other. But somehow it has proved a workable even if clumsy system when moderated by discretionary controls in the hands of a wise and strong trial court. To pull one misshapen stone out of the grotesque structure is more likely simply to upset its present balance between adverse interests than to establish a rational edifice.

The present suggestion is that we adopt for all federal courts a new rule as to cross-examination about prior arrest, adhered to by the courts of only one state and rejected elsewhere. The confusion and error it would engender would seem too heavy a price to pay for an almost imperceptible logical improvement, if any, in a system which is justified, if at all, by accumulated judicial experience rather than abstract logic.

The judgment is

Affirmed.

MR. JUSTICE RUTLEDGE, with whom MR. JUSTICE MURPHY joins, dissenting.

The Court's opinion candidly and interestingly points out the anomalous features characterizing the exclusion and admission of so-called character evidence in criminal cases. It also for the first time puts the stamp of the Court's approval upon the most anomalous and, what is more important, the most unfair stage in this evidentiary sequence.

There are three stages. The first denies the prosecution the right to attack the defendant's reputation as part of its case in chief, either by proof of bad general reputation or by proof of specific derogatory incidents disconnected from the one charged as the crime. The second permits the defendant, at his option, to prove by qualified witnesses that he bears a good general reputation or at least one not tarnished by ill repute. The witness is forbidden, however, to go into particular incidents or details of the defendant's life and conduct. The witness, once qualified, can state only the general conclusions of the community concerning the defendant's character as the witness knows that reputation. The third stage comprehends the prosecution's rebuttal, and particularly the latitude of cross-examination to be allowed.

Moreover, I do not think the mere question of knowledge of a prior arrest is one proper to be asked, even if inquiry as to clearly derogatory acts is to be permitted. Of course men take such an inquiry as reflecting upon the person arrested. But, for use in a criminal prosecution, I do not think they should be allowed to do so. The mere fact of a single arrest twenty-seven years before trial, without further showing of criminal proceedings or their outcome, whether acquittal or conviction, seldom could have substantial bearing upon one's present general reputation; indeed it is not per se a derogatory fact. But it is put in generally, and I think was put in evidence in this case, not to call in question the witness' standard of opinion but, by the very question, to give room for play of the jury's unguarded conjecture and prejudice. This is neither fair play nor due process. It is a perversion of the criminal process as we know it. For it permits what the rule applied in the first stage forbids, trial of the accused not only for general bad conduct or reputation but also for conjecture, gossip, innuendo and insinuation.

Accordingly, I think this judgment should be reversed. I also think the prevailing practice should be changed. One judge of the Court of Appeals has suggested we do this by adopting the Illinois rule, namely, by limiting inquiry concerning specific incidents to questions relating to prior offenses similar to that for which the defendant is on trial. Logically that rule is subject to the same objections as the generally prevailing one. But it has the practical merit of greatly reducing the scope and volume of allowable questions concerning specific acts, rumors, etc., with comparable reduction of innuendo, insinuation and gossip. My own preference and, I think, the only fair rule would be to foreclose the entire line of inquiry concerning specific incidents in the defendant's past, both on cross-examination and on new evidence in rebuttal. This would leave room for proper rebuttal without turning the defendant's trial for a specific offense into one for all his previous misconduct, criminal or other, and would put the prosecution on the same plane with the defendant in relation to the use of character evidence. This, it seems to me, is the only fair way to handle the matter.

[C]   Rex v. Smith

Court of Criminal Appeal
11 Cr. App. R. 229, 84 L.J.K.B. 2153 (1915)

THE LORD CHIEF JUSTICE:

The appellant was charged with the murder of Bessie Munday; evidence was admitted to show that he murdered two other women at a later date. The first question raised is that the judge was wrong in admitting evidence of the deaths of Alice Burnham and Margaret Lofty. Whether the evidence was admissible or not depends on principles of law which have been considered by this Court many times, and which depend in the main on the statement of the law by Lord Herschell in Makin v. Attorney-General for New South Wales. The Lord Chancellor there points out: "It is undoubtedly not competent for the prosecution to adduce evidence tending to show that the accused has been guilty of criminal acts other than those covered by the indictment, for the purpose of leading to the conclusion that the accused is a person likely, from his criminal conduct or character, to have committed the offence for which he is being tried. On the other hand, the mere fact that the evidence adduced tends to show the commission of other crimes does not render it inadmissible if it be relevant to an issue before the jury, and it may be so relevant if it bears upon the question whether the acts alleged to constitute the crime charged in the indictment were designed or accidental, or to rebut a defense which would otherwise be open to the accused." Now in this case the prosecution tendered the evidence, and it was admitted by the judge on the ground that it tended to show that the act charged had been committed, that is, had been designed. A question has been raised on which we have heard valuable arguments, but it is a matter which we need not, and do not intend to decide in this case. It is undesirable that we should decide the point unless it has been fully argued. It is sufficient to say that it is not disputed, and could not be disputed, that if as a matter of law there was Primâ facie evidence that the appellant committed the act charged, evidence of similar acts became admissible, and the other point does not arise for the reason that we have come to the conclusion that there was undoubtedly, as a matter of law, Primâ facie evidence that the appellant committed the act charged apart altogether from the other cases. Viewing the case put forward with regard to Bessie Munday only, we are of opinion that there was a case which the judge was bound in strict law to put to the jury. The case was reinforced by the evidence admitted with reference to the other two cases for the purpose of showing the design of the appellant. We think that that evidence was properly admitted, and the judge was very careful to point out to the jury the use they could properly make of the evidence. He directed them more than once that they must not allow their minds to be confused and think that they were deciding whether the murders of Burnham and Lofty had been committed, they were trying the appellant for the murder of Munday. We are of opinion therefore that the first point fails.

The second point taken is that even assuming that evidence of the death of the other two women was admissible, the prosecution ought only to have been allowed to prove that the women were found dead in their baths. For the reasons already given in dealing with the first point, it is apparent that to cut short the evidence there would have been of no assistance to the case. In our opinion it was open to the prosecution to give, and the judge was right in admitting, evidence of the facts surrounding the deaths of the two women.

Appeal Dismissed.

[D]   Dowling v. United States

United States Supreme Court
493 U.S. 342, 110 S. Ct. 668, 107 L. Ed. 2d 708 (1990)

JUSTICE WHITE delivered the opinion of the Court:

At petitioner's trial for various offenses arising out of a bank robbery, testimony was admitted under Rule 404(b) of the Federal Rules of Evidence, relating to an alleged crime that the defendant had previously been acquitted of committing. We conclude that neither the Double Jeopardy nor the Due Process Clause barred the use of this testimony.

I

On the afternoon of July 8, 1985, a man wearing a ski mask and armed with a small pistol robbed the First Pennsylvania Bank in Frederiksted, St. Croix, Virgin Islands, taking over $7,000 in cash from a bank teller, approximately $5,000 in cash from a customer, and various personal and travelers' checks. The culprit ran from the bank, scurried around in the street momentarily, and then commandeered a passing taxi van. While driving away from the scene, the robber pulled off his ski mask. An eyewitness, who had slipped out of the bank while the robbery was taking place, saw the mask less man and at trial identified him as petitioner, Rueben Dowling. Other witnesses testified that they had seen Dowling driving the hijacked taxi van outside of Frederiksted shortly after the bank robbery.

Following his arrest, Dowling was charged with the federal crimes of bank robbery, 18 U.S.C. § 2113(a), and armed robbery, § 2113(d), and with various crimes under Virgin Islands law. Dowling pleaded not guilty to all charges. Dowling's first trial ended with a hung jury. He was tried again and convicted, but the Third Circuit reversed this conviction on appeal. *Government of Virgin Islands v. Dowling*, 814 F.2d 134 (1987). After a third trial, Dowling was convicted on most of the counts; the trial judge sentenced him to 70 years' imprisonment.

During petitioner's third trial, the Government, over petitioner's objection, called a woman named Vena Henry to the stand. Ms. Henry testified that a man wearing a knitted mask with cutout eyes and carrying a small handgun had, together with a man named Delroy Christian, entered her home in Frederiksted approximately two weeks after the First Pennsylvania Bank robbery. Ms. Henry testified that a struggle ensued and that she unmasked the intruder, whom she identified as Dowling. Based on this incident, Dowling had been charged, under Virgin Islands law with burglary, attempted robbery, assault, and weapons offenses, but had been acquitted after a trial held before his third trial in the bank robbery case.

We granted certiorari to consider Dowling's contention that Henry's testimony was inadmissible under both the Double Jeopardy and the Due Process Clause of the Fifth Amendment.

II

There is no claim here that the acquittal in the case involving Ms. Henry barred further prosecution in the present case. The issue is the inadmissibility of Henry's testimony.

In *Ashe v. Swenson*, 397 U.S. 436, 90 S. Ct. 1189, 25 L. Ed. 2d 469 (1970), we recognized that the Double Jeopardy Clause incorporates the doctrine of collateral estoppels. In that case, a group of masked men had robbed six men playing poker in the basement of a home. The State unsuccessfully prosecuted Ashe for robbing one of the men. Six weeks later, however, the defendant was convicted for the robbery of one of the other players. Applying the doctrine of collateral estoppels which we found implicit in the Double Jeopardy Clause, we reversed Ashe's conviction, holding that his acquittal in the first trial precluded the State from charging him for the second offense. *Id.*, at 445–446, 90 S. Ct., at 1195. We defined the collateral-estoppels doctrine as providing that "when an issue of ultimate fact has once been determined by a valid and final judgment, that issue cannot again be litigated between the same parties in any future lawsuit." *Id.*, at 443, 90 S. Ct., at 1194. Ashe's acquittal in the first trial foreclosed the second trial because, in the circumstances of that case, the acquittal verdict could only have meant that the jury was unable to conclude beyond a reasonable doubt that the defendant was one of the bandits. A second prosecution was impermissible because, to have convicted the defendant in the second trial, the second jury had to have reached a directly contrary conclusion. See *id.*, at 445, 90 S. Ct., at 1195.

Dowling contends that, by the same principle, his prior acquittal precluded the Government from introducing into evidence Henry's testimony at the third trial in the bank robbery case. We disagree because, unlike the situation in *Ashe v. Swenson*, the prior acquittal did not determine an ultimate issue in the present case.

For present purposes, we assume for the sake of argument that Dowling's acquittal established that there was a reasonable doubt as to whether Dowling was the masked man who entered Vena Henry's home with Delroy Christian two weeks after the First Pennsylvania Bank robbery trial. But to introduce evidence on this point at the bank robbery trial, the Government did not have to demonstrate that Dowling was the man who entered the home beyond a reasonable doubt; the Government sought to introduce Henry's testimony under Rule 404(b), and, as mentioned earlier, in *Huddleston v. United States*, 485 U.S., at 681, we held that "[i]n the Rule 404(b) context, similar act evidence is relevant only if the jury can reasonably conclude that the act occurred and that the defendant was the actor."

Even if we agreed with petitioner that the lower burden of proof at the second proceeding does not serve to avoid the collateral-estoppels component of the Double Jeopardy Clause, we agree with the Government that the challenged evidence was nevertheless admissible because Dowling did not demonstrate that his acquittal in his first trial represented a jury determination that he was not one of the men who entered Ms. Henry's home.

There are any number of possible explanations for the jury's acquittal verdict at Dowling's first trial. As the record stands, there is nothing at all that persuasively indicates that the question of identity was at issue and was determined in Dowling's favor at the prior trial; at oral argument, Dowling conceded as much. As a result, even if we were to apply the Double Jeopardy Clause to this case, we would conclude that petitioner has failed to satisfy his burden of demonstrating that the first jury concluded that he was not one of the intruders in Ms. Henry's home.

III

Besides arguing that the introduction of Henry's testimony violated the Double Jeopardy Clause, petitioner also contends that the introduction of this evidence was unconstitutional because it failed the due process test of "fundamental fairness." . . . The question . . . is whether it is acceptable to deal with the potential for abuse through no constitutional sources like the Federal Rules of Evidence (footnote omitted), or whether the introduction of this type of evidence is so extremely unfair that its admission violates "fundamental conceptions of justice."

Especially in the light of limiting instructions provided by the trial judge, we cannot hold that the introduction of Henry's testimony merits this kind of condemnation. Plainly Henry's testimony was at least circumstantially valuable in providing petitioner's guilt.

Petitioner lists four reasons why, according to him, admission of Henry's testimony was fundamentally unfair. First, petitioner suggests that evidence relating to acquitted conduct is inherently unreliable. We disagree: the jury in this case, for example, remained free to assess the truthfulness and the significance of Henry's testimony, and petitioner had the opportunity to refute it. Second, Dowling contends that the use of this type of evidence creates a constitutionally unacceptable risk that the jury will convict the defendant on the basis of inferences drawn from the acquitted conduct; we believe that the trial court's authority to exclude potentially prejudicial evidence adequately addresses this possibility.

Third, petitioner claims that the exclusion of acquitted conduct evidence furthers the desirable goal of consistent jury verdicts. [I]inconsistent verdicts are constitutionally tolerable. See *Standefer v. United States*, 447 U.S. 10, 25, 100 S. Ct. 1999, 2008, 64 L. Ed. 2d 689 (1980).

Fourth, petitioner argues that the introduction of Henry's testimony in this case contravenes a tradition that the government may not force a person acquitted in one trial to defend against the same accusation in a subsequent proceeding. We acknowledge the tradition, but find it amply protected by the Double Jeopardy Clause. We decline to use the Due Process Clause as a device for extending the double jeopardy protection to cases where it otherwise would not extend.

IV

Because we conclude that the admission of Ms. Henry's testimony was constitutional and the Court of Appeals therefore applied that correct harmless-error standard, we affirm the judgment of the Court of Appeals.

JUSTICE BRENNAN, with whom JUSTICE MARSHALL and JUSTICE STEVENS join, dissenting

The Court today adds a powerful new weapon to the Government's arsenal. The ability to relitigate the facts relating to an offense for which the defendant has been acquitted benefits the Government because there are many situations in which the defendant will not be able to present a second defense because of the passage of time, the expense, or some other factor. Indeed there is no discernible limit to the Court's rule; the defendant could be forced to relitigate these facts in trial after trial. Moreover, the Court's reasoning appears to extend even further than the facts of this case and seems to allow a prosecutor to rely on a prior criminal offense (despite an acquittal) as evidence in a trial for an offense which is part of the *same transaction* as the prior offense. For example, a prosecutor could introduce facts relating to a substantive offense as evidence in a trial for conspiracy, *even though* the defendant had been acquitted of the substantive offense. Cf. *Ashe*, 397 U.S., at 445, n. 10, 90 S. Ct., at 1195, n. 10 (the question whether collateral estoppels was a constitutional requirement was of little concern until modern statutes gave prosecutors the ability to "spin out a startlingly numerous series of offenses from a single alleged criminal transaction"). Indeed, the Court's reasoning could apply even more broadly to justify the introduction of evidence of a prior offense for which the defendant had been acquitted in order to enhance a defendant's sentence under a sentencing scheme that requires proof by less than a reasonable doubt. See, *e.g.*, *McMillan v. Pennsylvania*, 477 U.S. 79, 91–93, 106 S. Ct. 2411, 2418–2419, 91 L. Ed. 2d 67 (1986) (upholding constitutionality of sentencing scheme requiring proof of additional facts by preponderance of evidence). Only by ignoring the principles upon which the collateral-estoppels doctrine is based is it possible for the Court to tip the scales this far in the prosecution's favor.

II

The Court's holding today deprives an acquitted defendant of his rightful end to the "blight and suspicious aura which surround an accusation that he is guilty of a specific crime." *Wingate v. Wainwright*, 464 F.2d 209, 215 (CA5 1972). Because the Court's holding is based on a hyper technical view of an acquittal and reflects a naive view of the defendant's burden in a criminal trial, I respectfully dissent.

[E]   Huddleston v. United States

United States Supreme Court
485 U.S. 681, 108 S. Ct. 1496, 99 L. Ed. 2d 771 (1988)

CHIEF JUSTICE REHNQUIST delivered the opinion of the Court: Federal Rule of Evidence 404(b) provides:

> " 'Other crimes, wrongs, or acts. — Evidence of other crimes, wrongs, or acts is not admissible to prove the character of a person in order to show action in conformity therewith. It may, however, be admissible for other purposes, such as proof of motive, opportunity, intent, preparation, plan, knowledge, identity, or absence of mistake or accident.' "

This case presents the question whether the district court must itself make a preliminary finding that the Government has proved the "other act" by a preponderance of the evidence before it submits the evidence to the jury. We hold that it need not do so.

Petitioner, Guy Rufus Huddleston, was charged with one count of selling stolen goods in interstate commerce, 18 U.S.C. § 2315, and one count of possessing stolen property in interstate commerce, 18 U.S.C. § 659. The two counts related to two portions of a shipment of stolen Memorex videocassette tapes that petitioner was alleged to have possessed and sold, knowing that they were stolen.

The evidence at trial showed that a trailer containing over 32,000 blank Memorex videocassette tapes with a manufacturing cost of $4.53 per tape was stolen from the Overnight Express yard in South Holland, Illinois, sometime between April 11 and 15, 1985. On April 17, 1985, petitioner contacted Karen Curry, the manager of the Magic Rent-to-Own in Ypsilanti, Michigan, seeking her assistance in selling a large number of blank Memorex videocassette tapes. After assuring Curry that the tapes were not stolen, he told her he wished to sell them in lots of at least 500 at $2.75 to $3 per tape. Curry subsequently arranged for the sale of a total of 5,000 tapes, which petitioner delivered to the various purchasers — who apparently believed the sales were legitimate.

. . .The first piece of similar act evidence offered by the Government was the testimony of Paul Toney, a record store owner. He testified that . . . petitioner offered to sell new 12? black and white televisions for $28 a piece.

The second piece of similar act evidence was the testimony of Robert Nelson, an undercover FBI agent posing as a buyer for an appliance store. Nelson testified that in May 1985, petitioner offered to sell him a large quantity of Amana appliances. . . .

Petitioner testified that the Memorex tapes, the televisions, and the appliances had all been provided by Leroy Wesby, who had represented that all of the merchandise was obtained legitimately. Petitioner maintained that . . . he had no knowledge that any of the goods were stolen. . . .

A divided panel of the United States Court of Appeals for the Sixth Circuit initially reversed the conviction, concluding that because the Government had failed to prove by clear and convincing evidence that the televisions were stolen, the District Court erred in admitting the testimony concerning the televisions. The panel subsequently granted rehearing to address the decision in *United States v. Ebens*, 800 F.2d 1422 (6th Cir. 1986), which held: "Courts may admit evidence of prior bad acts if the proof shows by a preponderance of the evidence that the defendant did in fact commit the act." On rehearing the court affirmed the conviction. . . .

We granted certiorari, 484 U.S. 894 (1987), to resolve a conflict among the Courts of Appeals as to whether the trial court must make a preliminary finding before "similar act" and other Rule 404(b) evidence is submitted to the jury. We conclude that such evidence should be admitted if there is sufficient evidence to support a finding by the jury that the defendant committed the similar act. . . .

Federal Rule of Evidence 404(b) — which applies in both civil and criminal cases — generally prohibits the introduction of evidence of extrinsic acts that might adversely reflect on the actor's character, unless that evidence bears upon a relevant issue in the case such as motive, opportunity, or knowledge. Extrinsic acts evidence may be critical to the establishment of the truth as to a disputed issue, especially when that issue involves the actor's state of mind and the only means of ascertaining that mental state is by drawing inferences from conduct. The actor in the instant case was a criminal defendant, and the act in question was "similar" to the one with which he was charged. Our use of these terms is not meant to suggest that our analysis is limited to such circumstances.

. . . .

Petitioner argues from the premise that evidence of similar acts has a grave potential for causing improper prejudice. For instance, the jury may choose to punish the defendant for the similar rather than the charged act, or the jury may infer that the defendant is an evil person inclined to violate the law. Because of this danger, petitioner maintains, the jury ought not to be exposed to similar act evidence until the trial court has heard the evidence and made a determination under Federal Rules of Evidence 104(a) that the defendant committed the similar act.

We reject petitioner's position, for it is inconsistent with the structure of the Rules of Evidence and with the plain language of Rule 404(b). Article IV of the Rules of Evidence deals with the relevancy of evidence. Rules 401 and 402 establish the broad principle that relevant evidence — evidence that makes the existence of any fact at issue more or less probable — is admissible unless the Rules provide otherwise. Rule 403 allows the trial judge to exclude relevant evidence if, among other things, "its probative value is substantially outweighed by the danger of unfair prejudice." Rules 404 through 412 address specific types of evidence that have generated problems. Generally, these latter Rules do not flatly prohibit the introduction of such evidence but instead limit the purpose for which it may be introduced. Rule 404(b), for example, protects against the introduction of extrinsic act evidence when that evidence is offered solely to prove character. The text contains no intimation, however, that any preliminary showing is necessary before such evidence may be introduced for a proper purpose. If offered for such a proper purpose, the evidence is subject only to general strictures limiting admissibility such as Rules 402 and 403.

Petitioner's reading of Rule 404(b) as mandating a preliminary finding by the trial court that the act in question occurred not only superimposes a level of judicial oversight that is nowhere apparent from the language of that provision, but it is simply inconsistent with the legislative history behind Rule 404(b). The Advisory Committee specifically declined to offer any "mechanical solution" to the admission of evidence under 404(b). Advisory Committee's Notes on Fed. Rule Evid. 404(b), 28 U.S.C. App., p. 691. Rather, the Committee indicated that the trial court should assess such evidence under the usual rules for admissibility: "The determination must be made whether the danger of undue prejudice outweighs the probative value of the evidence in view of the availability of other means of proof and other facts appropriate for making decisions of this kind under Rule 403." (Citation omitted.)

Such questions of relevance conditioned on a fact are dealt with under Federal Rule of Evidence 104(b). . . . Rule 104(b) provides:

"When the relevance of evidence depends upon the fulfillment of a condition of fact, the court shall admit it upon, or subject to, the introduction of evidence sufficient to support a find of the fulfillment of the condition."

In determining whether the Government has introduced sufficient evidence to meet Rule 104(b), the trial court neither weighs credibility nor makes a finding that the government has proved the conditional fact by a preponderance of the evidence. The court simply examines all the evidence in the case and decides whether the jury could reasonably find the conditional fact — here, that the televisions were stolen — by a preponderance of the evidence. . . . The trial court has traditionally exercised the broadest sort of discretion in controlling the order of proof at trial, and we see nothing in the Rules of Evidence that would change this practice. Often the trial court may decide to allow the proponent to introduce evidence concerning a similar act, and at a later point in the trial assess whether sufficient evidence has been offered to permit the jury to make the requisite finding.[1] If the proponent has failed to meet this minimal standard of proof, the trial court must instruct the jury to disregard the evidence.

We emphasize that in assessing the sufficiency of the evidence under Rule 104(b), the trial court must consider all evidence presented to the jury. "[I]ndividual pieces of evidence, insufficient in themselves to prove a point, may in cumulation prove it. The sum of an evidentiary presentation may well be greater than its constituent parts." *Bourjaily v. United States*, 483 U.S. 171, 179–180 (1987). In assessing whether the evidence was sufficient to support a finding that the televisions were stolen, the court here was required to consider not only the direct evidence on that point — the low price of the televisions, the large quantity offered for sale, and petitioner's inability to produce a bill of sale — but also the evidence concerning petitioner's involvement in the

---

[1] (Court's original footnote 7) "When an item of evidence is conditionally relevant, it is often not possible for the offeror to prove the fact upon which relevance is conditioned at the time the evidence is offered. In such cases it is customary to permit him to introduce the evidence and 'connect it up' later. Rule 104(b) continues this practice, specifically authorizing the judge to admit the evidence 'subject to' proof of the preliminary fact. It is, of course, not the responsibility of the judge sua sponte to insure that the foundation evidence is offered; the objector must move to strike the evidence if at the close of the trial the offeror has failed to satisfy the condition." 21 C. Wright & K. Graham, Federal Practice and Procedure § 5054, pp. 269–270 (1977) (Footnotes omitted.)

sales of other stolen merchandise obtained from Wesby, such as the Memorex tapes and the Amana appliances. Given this evidence, the jury reasonably could have concluded that the televisions were stolen, and the trial court therefore properly allowed the evidence to go to the jury. Affirmed.

[F]   People v. Chambers

The following transcript is an excerpt from the so-called "preppy murder" case, *People v. Chambers*, 512 N.Y.S.2d 631 (N.Y. Ct. App. 1987). The defendant, Robert Chambers, was charged with the strangulation death of a woman named Jennifer Levin. He claimed that the death was accidental, that it occurred during consensual "rough sex." At trial, Chambers was found guilty. This excerpt reveals how other acts issues apply in the context of an actual murder case.

SUPREME COURT OF THE STATE OF NEW YORK
COUNTY OF NEW YORK

THE PEOPLE OF
THE STATE OF NEW YORK
against
ROBERT M. CHAMBERS,
Defendant

Ind. No.
6394/86
Charge: Murder
2nd Degree

AFTERNOON SESSION

(Whereupon the following was taken in the jury room outside the presence of the general public:)

MR. KENDRIS [the prosecutor]:

Judge, so we can illuminate what we are talking about for the Court, for the record, there is evidence that money, that Jennifer was in possession of some money on the night she was at Dorian's Bar. I think the Court is aware there will be testimony from people perhaps on both sides of this case who were at Dorian's with the defendant and Jennifer Levin that night.

There is also evidence that Jennifer Levin was wearing earrings, very specifically earrings that looked like diamond earrings.

As to the earrings, the state of the evidence I think is that there will be some testimonial evidence that she had earrings on and there are also photographs taken at the bar that evening. I don't know whether the Court has seen them at any stage in this case so far and there are several photographs of Jennifer Levin and at least one, maybe more, I don't recall very clear shots of the earrings, that she is wearing at the bar, sometime after midnight that night, maybe even later than that, or earlier in the morning than that.

At the crime scene, Judge, no money is found on her person, only a torn dollar bill and at the crime scene, no earrings are found either at the scene around her body, anywhere in Central Park, no earrings are recovered and there are no earrings in her ears. These are diamond stud earrings. They are not actually diamond that will be probably also be part of the proof, but the fact is they were missing.

THE COURT:

What type of earrings, ones that screw?

MR. KENDRIS:

Screw on, studs.

She leaves with the defendant and as she leaves she sees a good friend and she doesn't give the earrings to that friend.

Now, we have the video tape which your Honor has also seen in addition to the two photographs.

The defendant says he leaves with her, walks to Central Park with her, kills her accident tally as he described. He says he watches the scene until the police arrive.

Mentions nothing about anyone else taking earrings or her money.

He mentions nothing about Jennifer Levin taking her earrings off at anytime.

When Jennifer Levin's body is found while the defendant is watching, no earrings are found on her and no earrings are found in the surrounding area, not the backs, not the jewel itself.

Judge, the conclusion is inescapably that the defendant took those earrings.

It's circumstantial evidence, but it's compelling.

It goes directly to what this defendant's defense is as he puts it out on a video tape, whether or not he's being truthful on that video tape.

THE COURT:

I am concerned right now and you probably answered part of it as to what value is this to your case, that is the elements that you have to prove, that's what I'm concerned with.

You see, if it's not necessary with respect to the elements and you have to prove the elements of the case before you even get to the jury —

MR. KENDRIS:

I'll address it.

THE COURT:

That's it.

If it's not necessary, that's a different story.

MR. KENDRIS:

Judge, we think this evidence is very probative in this case.

This defendant's state of mind before and after the crime, the murder or the accident, whichever the jury is going to decide this was, is what's this case is about.

That's what we have to prove. Whether he intended to kill her; whether he acted intentionally at all that night or whether he acted with depraved indifference to human life and there might be lesser included charges like recklessness involved or intent to cause physical injury.

The defendant in his videotaped statement claims that a certain fact transpired before the incident and then he claims after the incident he was in shock, he was in a daze, he couldn't believe he wasn't moving. He walked over and sat on a wall and was in a daze.

If this jury finds, Judge, that he took those earrings and her money and the conclusion is inescapable that he did, there's no one else who could have taken them and there's no other reasonable argument as to what happened to them.

If this jury concludes that he took them, that goes to whether or not he's in a daze, goes to his state of mind.

It goes to whether or not he tried to help her after she was accidentally killed, and that goes to whether or not he showed a depraved indifference to human life.

It goes to whether or not this is an accident or intentional act, whether or not he was thinking clearly or whether or not he was in a daze and didn't know what was going on.

It goes to motive, because if he did take the earrings and the money pursuant to this crime, then he might have a motive to kill her or to hurt her in the course of that.

So those are the reasons why it's highly probative, Judge.

Now, I'm — I'll get back to that in a second.

I would like to discuss some other things that I think are important.

Very briefly, Judge, if the jury doesn't draw the inference that the defendant took the earrings and money, if they say, "Hey, I don't buy that — this, I don't think he did, maybe she did take them off on the walk to Central Park and tossed them into the street," that's what they think, then it is evidence — this evidence is not prejudicial.

This isn't a case where the jury will hear evidence about a prior distinct crime with different victims who were traumatized, where a juror can say, "I don't think they proved to me that he committed that prior crime," but because they heard the evidence about the prior crime they are now themselves inflamed, their passions are aroused because they heard about prior rape — they don't think the defendant did it, but they heard about another rape and now they want to convict him for this rape because they heard about the other one, even though they have not decided that the defendant committed that other one.

This isn't the case.

This isn't, Judge, a prior distinct crime.

Therefore, there is no possibility of that type of prejudice occurring here.

Either it's probative or it's not.

That's all I have to say about it, Judge.

THE COURT:

All right.

You want to be heard? Mr. Litman?

MR. LITMAN [defense counsel]:

Your Honor, I deny what the prosecutor says about what he claims the facts are, other than at a time very close to 12:00 o'clock midnight, this photograph was taken (indicating), which shows at sometime around midnight or 12:15 or so in the morning, there is an earring in Jennifer Levin's right ear. That's what this photograph shows in terms of the earring.

And when this photograph was taken (indicating), your Honor, which was at approximately 9:00 o'clock or 8:30 in the morning, some eight hours or eight-and-a-half hours later, from a view of this photograph, there is no earring in the right ear.

I will admit that this photograph was taken at around 12:30 in the morning and that there was an earring in the right ear, and some eight hours later this photograph was taken and there is no earring in the right ear (indicating).

There is no credible witness who would testify at a hearing, and you have heard none of their supposed offer of proof, that they claim they saw Jennifer Levin leave the bar with an earring.

Nobody says that.

He tried to draw that conclusion by saying that she didn't give them to anybody else.

I don't have to tell you that there are — I won't even speculate — that there are plenty of other ways that the earrings could have been gotten rid of other than handing them to someone.

She could have taken them off. People take off jewelry. Kids take off jewelry. I have the — a kid . . . who takes them on and off faster than you can whistle it.

Again, your Honor, remember some other facts.

Please remember that the person that they claim stole this on this quote offer of proof, was sitting on the wall in the full view of the police while the police came to the scene.

So they want to believe, and they call this speculation what I am about to say, that he took the stuff and sat on the wall in full view of the police, with scratches all over his face, with this quote incriminating stuff on him.

They ask you to buy that.

He is sitting on a wall with this stuff, according to them, while the police are all over the place.

It's not irrational to say that she could have taken it off or that it came off during the struggle, someone looked at it. There is a whole variety of possibilities.

Your Honor asked what this has to do with the case. They don't even know what it has to do with the case.

They say it proves that it happened beforehand, but then say that it happened after hand.

You can't allow a prosecutor, Judge, in a case like this to get up before a jury and say he had candidly admitted yesterday, and today, "I don't really know if it happened before or after, but either way, Ladies and Gentlemen, it ain't good for the defendant."

That's not the way you should do things in producing proof of prior crimes.

And what probative value does it have here?

But I will get to what I think is the determinative issue, which is the prejudice, which is so overwhelming.

MR. STAVIS:

Can I have one minute? I am usually a man of few words.

THE COURT:

Yes.

MR. STAVIS:

If your Honor had a case before you where a defendant is charged with a robbery or larceny by the D.A.'s office, and at twelve o'clock somebody has a piece of property and six-and-a-half hours later they don't have the piece of property, and within the six-and-a-half hours the defendant is with the victim, would that case go to a jury, your Honor? I don't think that it would.

I don't think in this case that there is any proof that Robert Chambers took the earrings. That's number one.

Then number two, Mr. Kendris said if the jury finds that he took the earrings, it would go to whether or not he had depraved indifference or intent to kill, it would go to whether or not he murdered her. To have said that and to then say that there is no possibility of prejudice here, is just to ignore the realities.

If this robbery business comes in, it would blow the case out of the water.

The defendant is on trial for murder, your Honor. Let him be tried for murder.

1. How would you have ruled on this other acts evidence if you were the judge?

2. How should the Court in *People v. Chambers* instruct the jury about other acts evidence?

3. Is the following jury instruction appropriate? Would the prosecutor request this instruction? Would the defense counsel request it?

Ninth Circuit Pattern Jury Instruction: 4.04 — Similar Acts of Defendant

You have heard evidence that the defendant committed acts similar to the crime charged here. You may consider such evidence, not to prove that the defendant did the acts charged here, but only to prove defendant's state of mind, that is, that the defendant acted with the necessary intent and not through accident or mistake.

Therefore, if you find:

1. that the government has proved beyond a reasonable doubt that defendant committed the acts charged in the indictment, and

2. that the defendant committed similar acts at other times, then you may consider these similar acts as evidence that the defendant committed the acts here deliberately and not through accident or mistake.

[G] Rules Comparison

Contrast Federal Rule of Evidence 404(a) with the following California rule. Which is the preferable rule?

California Evidence Code § 1103. Evidence of character of victim of crime.

(a) In a criminal action, evidence of the character or a trait of character (in the form of an opinion, evidence of reputation, or evidence of specific instances of conduct) of the victim of the crime for which the defendant is being prosecuted is not made inadmissible by Section 1101 if the evidence is:

(1) Offered by the defendant to prove conduct of the victim in conformity with the character or trait of character.

(2) Offered by the prosecution to rebut evidence adduced by the defendant under paragraph (1).

§ 5.09   CHARACTER EVIDENCE REVIEW

[A]   Mixed Character Evidence Problems

Problem #5-37: "No Coke, Pepsi"

Sherri is prosecuted for the distribution of cocaine after she allegedly sold one gram of the substance to an undercover police officer.

1. The prosecution offers evidence in its case-in-chief that Sherri had sold cocaine on four prior occasions. Sherri objects. What is the basis for her objection? What ruling and why?

2. What if Sherri had been acquitted after a jury trial about two of the alleged sales? Admissible? Explain.

3. If the prior sales are otherwise admissible, what is the quantum of proof required before a court appropriately admits the evidence?

Problem #5-38: "A Streetcar Named Desire"

Debbie, a cabbie, gave Eldridge a ride across town, from 7th Street to Piedmont. While Debbie was telling Eldridge that she would one day be famous because of her great desire to succeed, she forgot to pay attention to the road and crashed. In the ensuing lawsuit brought by Eldridge, Eldridge offers evidence that Debbie had received twelve citations for reckless driving in the past two years. Is this evidence admissible to show Debbie's propensity to drive carelessly? Why?

Problem #5-39: Defamaaaaaaaaation!

Television news reporter Alain Prather is sued for defamation by the State Water Commissioner, Carol Young, after Prather called her "an incompetent thief." At trial, the plaintiff offers the following evidence. Which items of evidence, if any, are admissible?

1. Plaintiff was given an award for excellence in her position as Water Commissioner by the Boy Scouts of America six years ago.

2. The plaintiff is known in the community for her honesty.

3. In 1992, the plaintiff voluntarily returned an erroneous bank draft that gave her a windfall of thirty thousand dollars.

The defendant then offers evidence in its case-in-chief. Which items of evidence, if any, are admissible?

4. The plaintiff was charged with disorderly conduct after attending an R.E.M. concert two years ago.

5. The plaintiff shoplifted a dress from a Bloomingdale's five years earlier.

6. The water supply decreased by 35 percent during the plaintiff's tenure as commissioner.

Problem #5-40: "But Mom!"

Wayne is charged with assaulting his estranged brother Michael. At trial, Wayne testifies on his own behalf. He concedes punching Michael and breaking his nose, but claims "I only did so after he swung a chain saw at me!"

1. If Michael swung the chain saw almost simultaneously with Wayne's punch, would the evidence about the chain saw be admissible? Why?

2. If Michael swung the chain saw at Wayne several hours earlier that same day, would the evidence about the chain saw be admissible? Why?

[B]   Character Evidence Summary and Review

1. What is "propensity" character evidence?

2. What is the difference between character evidence and credibility evidence?

3. Distinguish character evidence offered to show propensity and character evidence offered for a purpose other than to show propensity.

4. When is character "in issue"?

5. Distinguish situations in which the character of a person is in issue because character is an element, claim, or defense, and those in which the accused places it in issue.

6. Create three examples of propensity evidence.

7. (true or false) In a perjury prosecution, the government can offer in its case-in-chief evidence that the defendant has a reputation in the community for being a chronic liar.

8. (true or false) In an action in tort for the conversion of property, the defendant can offer testimony that she has a reputation in the community for being honest.

9. (true or false) In an action for libel in which the defendant allegedly called the plaintiff "a giraffe-faced liar," the defendant can offer evidence that the plaintiff, a law student, has cheated on three of her driver's license examinations.

10. (true or false) If a witness testifies for the accused in a criminal assault and battery action and states that the defendant has a reputation in the community for peacefulness, the witness may be asked on cross-examination if she had heard that the defendant had been indicted for aggravated battery two years earlier.

§ 5.10   HABIT EVIDENCE [FRE 406]

Habit is "a regular response to a repeated, specific stimulus." FRE 406, Advisory Committee's Note.

Unlike rules that provide for the exclusion of certain types of relevant evidence (such as subsequent remedial measures, offers to compromise, or offers to plead guilty), the rule on habit evidence is a rule of inclusion. FRE 406 is a special relevancy rule that states the qualifications necessary for evidence to be admissible as "habit."

In contrast to the generalized traits and dispositions that comprise character evidence, habit evidence is quite specific. Habit denotes a special kind of semi-reflexive or automatic behavior that occurs only in response to a specific stimulus. Thus, habit is defined by predictable causes and effects.

Habit evidence is distinguishable from character evidence rhetorically as well. Habit often can be identified by linguistic devices indicating that the conduct is routine and reliable. This includes words such as "always," "semi-consciously," "reflexively," "automatically," and "invariably."

But don't be fooled that just because a person "always" or "reflexively" acts in a particular manner as a result of a specific stimulus, it is a habit. FRE 406 requires a certain frequency as well as invariability in order to attain habit status. Thus, "always" signaling when turning left in a car is not a habit if it is the second time the person has made a left turn. While there is no specific number of occurrences recognized, generally an action must occur ten or more times before it will be considered a habit.

Illustration: Habit Evidence

The president of Wing Air, a commuter airline, was killed in a crash of one of the company's small planes. The only issue in a trial brought by the president's estate was whether the person flying the plane at the time of the crash was the president (himself a licensed pilot) or one of the regular pilots. Evidence is offered to show that the president piloted the plane on all ten of the prior occasions in which he flew on company aircraft. Is this evidence admissible?

Answer: This evidence of the president's prior conduct is admissible as habit. It is sufficiently repetitious and responsive to a particular stimulus, namely the president flying on company aircraft, to qualify as habit. Even if the president's prior conduct was a result of a business decision and not a personal preference, it still would be admissible as habit. FRE 406 permits evidence of a business custom or practice as well as the habit of a person.

HABIT EVIDENCE PROBLEMS: BASIC ELEMENTS OF HABIT

Problem Involving Business Habits

Problem #5-41: Stolen Sneakers

The defendant was accused of stealing sneakers from My Left Foot, a sporting goods store. The defendant claimed at trial that he purchased the goods but was not given a sales receipt. The prosecution then attempted to introduce evidence showing that it was the custom of the store to give sales receipts with every purchase.

1. Is the evidence admissible? Why?

2. Must specific examples of the store's practice regarding receipts be provided prior to the admission of evidence showing the habit of a person or a routine business practice?

Problem Involving the Elements of Specificity and Frequency

Another way of describing the requirements of habit evidence is that it must be specific — a response to a particular stimulus — and frequent, occurring regularly. The next problem illustrates these elements.

Problem #5-42: "The Hurrieder I Go, The Behinder I Get"

A fiery crash occurred between cars driven by plaintiff and defendant. Plaintiff claimed that defendant negligently caused the accident.

    1. At trial, plaintiff attempted to introduce evidence that defendant "is always in a rush." Admissible? Why?

    2. Plaintiff testifies that she "regularly uses turn signals." Is this permissible habit evidence? Why?

    3. Plaintiff was asked on cross-examination how many times she had used her turn signals and she responded, "After getting my license 3 months ago, I have used my signals about seven times; I just don't drive that much, you know?"

Problem Illustrating the Difference Between Evidentiary Habit and Cultural Habit

Problem #5-43: Chivas

The defendant, Rob, is prosecuted for driving while intoxicated at 1:00 p.m. on a Tuesday. The state introduced evidence at trial that the defendant always drank a shot of Chivas Regal liquor promptly at noon every day.

    1. Is the evidence admissible? Why?

    2. Would it be admissible habit evidence if the state offered to show that Rob was in the habit of getting drunk every day around noon?

Problem #5-44: Don't Do Me Like That

The plaintiff claims he was fired from the police force because he exercised his First Amendment right to freedom of speech. The plaintiff offers evidence at trial that the police department habitually fired individuals who exercised their First Amendment rights, letting go several different people for speaking out. Is this evidence admissible? *See McWhorter v. City of Birmingham*, 906 F.2d 674 (11th Cir. 1990).

Problem #5-45: Ms. Shark

A former client of famous criminal defense counsel, Sally Shark, claimed that Sally had failed to tell the client about the plea offer from the prosecutor. Had the accused known about the plea offer, he would have taken it instead of going to trial and getting convicted. At a hearing on the convicted defendant's motion for a new trial, Sally Shark testified that she "always relayed plea offers to clients." Is this testimony permitted? *See also* Rules of the Supreme Court of Kentucky 3.130. (1.4) Communication; MRPC 1.2.

§ 5.11 RELEVANT ETHICS RULES

SCR 3.130 (1.4) Communication

A lawyer shall:

(1) Promptly inform the client of any decision or circumstance with the respect to which the clients informed consent, as defined in rule 1.0 (e) is required by these rules

(2) reasonably consult with the client about the means by which the client's objectives are to be accomplished.

(3) keep the clients reasonably informed about the status of the matter; Rules of the Supreme Court of Kentucky.

Com't (2) If these Rules require that a particular decision about the representation be made by the client, paragraph (a)(1) requires that the lawyer promptly consult with and secure the client's consent prior to taking action unless prior discussions with the client have resolved what action the client wants the lawyer to take. For example, a lawyer who receives . . . an offer of settlement in a civil controversy or a proffered plea bargain in a criminal case must promptly inform the client . . . unless the client has previously communicated to the lawyer that the proposal will be acceptable or unacceptable or has authorized the lawyer to accept or to reject the offer. Rules of the Supreme Court of Kentucky. *See* MRPC 1.2(a) (noting, in part, that the client decides whether to accept an offer for a plea or to testify).

Rule 3.3: Candor Toward The Tribunal

(a) A lawyer shall not knowingly:

(3) offer evidence that the lawyer knows to be false. If a lawyer, the lawyer's client, or a witness called by the lawyer, has offered material evidence and the lawyer comes to know of its falsity, the lawyer shall take reasonable remedial measures, including, if necessary, disclosure to the tribunal. A lawyer may refuse to offer evidence, other than the testimony of a defendant in a criminal matter, that the lawyer reasonably believes is false. Illinois Rules of Prof'l Conduct R. 3.3(a)(3). *See* MRPC 3.3(a)(3).

Rule 3.8 Special Responsibilities of a Prosecutor

The prosecutor in a criminal case shall:

*(g) when a prosecutor knows of new, credible material evidence creating a reasonable likelihood that a convicted defendant did not commit an offense of which the defendant was convicted, the prosecutor shall:

(1) promptly disclose that evidence to an appropriate court or authority, and

(2) if the conviction was obtained in the prosecutor's jurisdiction,

(A) promptly disclose that evidence to the defendant unless a court authorizes delay, and

(B) undertake further investigation, or make reasonable efforts to cause an investigation, to determine whether the defendant was convicted of an offense that the defendant did not commit.

[](h) when a prosecutor knows of clear and convincing evidence establishing that a defendant in the prosecutor's jurisdiction was convicted of an offense that the defendant did not commit, the prosecutor shall seek to remedy the conviction." Idaho Rules of Prof'l Conduct R. 3.8. *See* MRPC 3.8 & Com't [9] (finding no ethical violation when a prosecutor's concludes in good faith, albeit subsequently determined to be erroneous, that evidence does not trigger the obligations of subsections (g) and (h)).

§ 5.12 HABIT EVIDENCE SUMMARY AND REVIEW

1. Why is habit evidence generally permitted when character evidence is generally excluded?

2. How does habit evidence compare to character evidence?

3. How does the habit of an individual compare to the habit of a business?

4. What do the two requirements of habit evidence, specificity and frequency, mean?

Chapter 6

OTHER EXCLUSIONS OF RELEVANT EVIDENCE
[FRE 407–415]

CHAPTER FRAMEWORK: Some otherwise relevant evidence is inadmissible because of public policy as well as unfair prejudice. This evidence, from subsequent remedial measures to settlement and plea negotiations, to a sexual assault victim's history, is only excluded for certain purposes. The evidence may be admitted for other purposes, often to rebut a claim asserted by the opposing side on fairness grounds.

WHY ARE THE CONCEPTS IN THIS CHAPTER IMPORTANT? These concepts further illustrate the breadth of reasons why relevant evidence is excluded. The partial exclusions suggest that the purposes for which evidence is offered and the trial context, particularly whether the evidence is used to rebut an opposing claim, create a more refined and nuanced analysis than mere wholesale exclusions.

CONNECTIONS: These exclusions can be viewed as a subset of the *unfair prejudice* exclusions of Rule FRE. Yet the rules also have a policy component for excluding evidence that makes these exclusions seem like *quasi-privileges*.

CHAPTER OUTLINE:

I. Relevant Evidence Excluded for Two Reasons

    A. Likely to mislead jury if offered for culpability or guilt

    B. Exclusion promotes extrinsic public policy ("policy") (e.g., repairs)

II. Exclusions

    A. Subsequent remedial measures [FRE 407]

        1. Excludes remediation evidence to show fault

        2. Exceptions — for non-fault purposes (e.g., control)

        3. Policy — promotes remediation, public safety

    B. Compromise offers & negotiations [FRE 408]

        1. Requires dispute re liability for, validity of, or amount of claim

        2. Excludes evidence if promoting settlement

            a. Caveat: Evidence of settling civil claim with public agency admissible in criminal case

        3. Exceptions — for purposes other than showing liability, validity, or amount o of claim (e.g., prove witness's bias)

    4. Policy — promotes judicial economy (facilitating out-of-court resolutions)

C. Offers to pay medical & similar expenses [FRE 409]

    1. Excludes evidence of offering or giving assistance

    2. Exceptions — for non-liability purposes (e.g., control)

    3. Policy — encourages assistance to the injured

D. Pleas, plea discussions & related statements [FRE 410]

    1. Excludes following evidence against defendant in civil and criminal cases

        a. Withdrawn guilty pleas

        b. Nolo contendere pleas

        c. Statements during F. R. Crim. Proc. 11 or comparable state proceedings

        d. Statements during plea negotiations with prosecutor if no guilty plea or plea withdrawn

    2. Exceptions — when fairness requires statement because another statement during same plea discussions already admitted or statements admissible in criminal perjury proceeding

    3. Policy — promotes judicial economy

E. Liability insurance [FRE 411]

    1. Excludes evidence of having (or not) liability insurance to show fault

    2. Exceptions — for non-fault purposes (e.g., ownership, bias)

    3. Policy — supports acquisition of insurance

F. Sex offense cases: victim's sexual behavior & predispositions [FRE 412]

    1. Excludes victim's other sexual behavior and victim's sexual predisposition

    2. Exceptions in *criminal* cases — specific conduct evidence of sexual behavior or predisposition admissible

        a. to show defendant not source of semen, injury, or other physical evidence

        b. conduct evidence involving victim and accused offered by accused or prosecutor to show victim's consent and

        c. evidence that if excluded would violate defendant's constitutional rights

    3. Exception *civil* cases — conduct evidence of victim's sexual behavior or predisposition if probative value substantially outweighs harm to victim or unfair prejudice to any party

        a. Evidence of victim's reputation admitted if victim places it in controversy

    4. Foundational requirements for admission of sex evidence (e.g., notification, in camera hearing)

    5. Policy — promotes reporting of sex offenses and protects victim

G. Similar crimes in sexual assault [FRE 413] & child-molestation cases [FRE 414]

    1. Permits only similar acts evidence (not reputation or opinion)

    2. Foundational requirements for admission of similar sex crimes (e.g., notification, including witnesses' statements or summary of expected testimony)

    3. Policy — promotes reporting and the prosecution of certain sex crimes

H. Similar acts in *civil* cases re Sexual Assault or Child Molestation [FRE 415]

    1. Permits only similar acts evidence of crimes provided for in FRE 413 & FRE 414

    2. Foundational requirements for admission of similar sex crimes (e.g., notification, including witnesses' statements or summary of expected testimony)

    3. Policy — promotes reporting and prosecution of certain sex crimes

* * * * *

RELEVANT EVIDENCE RULES

Rule 407. Subsequent Remedial Measures

When measures are taken that would have made an earlier injury or harm less likely to occur, evidence of the subsequent measures is not admissible to prove:

- negligence;
- culpable conduct;
- a defect in a product or its design; or
- a need for a warning or instruction.

But the court may admit this evidence for another purpose, such as impeachment or — if disputed — proving ownership, control, or the feasibility of precautionary measures.

Rule 408. Compromise Offers and Negotiations

(a) Prohibited Uses. Evidence of the following is not admissible — on behalf of any party — either to prove or disprove the validity or amount of a disputed claim or to impeach by a prior inconsistent statement or a contradiction:

(1) furnishing, promising, or offering — or accepting, promising to accept, or offering to accept — a valuable consideration in compromising or attempting to compromise the claim; and

(2) conduct or a statement made during compromise negotiations about the claim except when offered in a criminal case and when the negotiations related to a claim by a public office in the exercise of its regulatory, investigative, or enforcement authority.

(b) Exceptions. The court may admit this evidence for another purpose, such as proving a witness's bias or prejudice, negating a contention of undue delay, or proving an effort to obstruct a criminal investigation or prosecution.

Rule 409. Offers to Pay Medical and Similar Expenses

Evidence of furnishing, promising to pay, or offering to pay medical, hospital, or similar expenses resulting from an injury is not admissible to prove liability for the injury.

Rule 410. Pleas, Plea Discussions, and Related Statements

(a) Prohibited Uses. In a civil or criminal case, evidence of the following is not admissible against the defendant who made the plea or participated in the plea discussions:

(1) a guilty plea that was later withdrawn;

(2) a nolo contendere plea;

(3) a statement made during a proceeding on either of those pleas under Federal Rule of Criminal Procedure 11 or a comparable state procedure; or

(4) a statement made during plea discussions with an attorney for the prosecuting authority if the discussions did not result in a guilty plea or they resulted in a later-withdrawn guilty plea.

(b) Exceptions. The court may admit a statement described in Rule 410(a)(3) or (4):

(1) in any proceeding in which another statement made during the same plea or plea discussions has been introduced, if in fairness the statements ought to be considered together; or

(2) in a criminal proceeding for perjury or false statement, if the defendant made the statement under oath, on the record, and with counsel present.

Rule 411. Liability Insurance

Evidence that a person was or was not insured against liability is not admissible to prove whether the person acted negligently or otherwise wrongfully. But the court may admit this evidence for another purpose, such as proving a witness's bias or prejudice or proving agency, ownership, or control.

Rule 412. Sex-Offense Cases: The Victim's Sexual Behavior or Predisposition

(a) Prohibited Uses. The following evidence is not admissible in a civil or criminal proceeding involving alleged sexual misconduct:

(1) evidence offered to prove that a victim engaged in other sexual behavior; or

(2) evidence offered to prove a victim's sexual predisposition.

(b) Exceptions.

(1) *Criminal Cases.* The court may admit the following evidence in a criminal case:

(A) evidence of specific instances of a victim's sexual behavior, if offered to prove that someone other than the defendant was the source of semen, injury, or other physical evidence;

(B) evidence of specific instances of a victim's sexual behavior with respect to the person accused of the sexual misconduct, if offered by the defendant to prove consent or if offered by the prosecutor; and

(C) evidence whose exclusion would violate the defendant's constitutional rights.

(2) *Civil Cases.* In a civil case, the court may admit evidence offered to prove a victim's sexual behavior or sexual predisposition if its probative value substantially outweighs the danger of harm to any victim and of unfair prejudice to any party. The court may admit evidence of a victim's reputation only if the victim has placed it in controversy.

(c) Procedure to Determine Admissibility.

(1) *Motion.* If a party intends to offer evidence under Rule 412(b), the party must:

(A) file a motion that specifically describes the evidence and states the purpose for which it is to be offered;

(B) do so at least 14 days before trial unless the court, for good cause, sets a different time;

(C) serve the motion on all parties; and

(D) notify the victim or, when appropriate, the victim's guardian or representative.

(2) *Hearing.* Before admitting evidence under this rule, the court must conduct an in camera hearing and give the victim and parties a right to attend and be heard. Unless the court orders otherwise, the motion, related materials, and the record of the hearing must be and remain sealed.

(d) Definition of "Victim." In this rule, "victim" includes an alleged victim.

Rule 413. Similar Crimes in Sexual-Assault Cases

(a) Permitted Uses. In a criminal case in which a defendant is accused of a sexual assault, the court may admit evidence that the defendant committed any other sexual assault. The evidence may be considered on any matter to which it is relevant.

(b) Disclosure to the Defendant. If the prosecutor intends to offer this evidence, the prosecutor must disclose it to the defendant, including witnesses' statements or a summary of the expected testimony. The prosecutor must do so at least 15 days before trial or at a later time that the court allows for good cause.

(c) Effect on Other Rules. This rule does not limit the admission or consideration of evidence under any other rule.

(d) Definition of "Sexual Assault." In this rule and Rule 415, "sexual assault" means a crime under federal law or under state law (as "state" is defined in 18 U.S.C. § 513) involving:

(1) any conduct prohibited by 18 U.S.C. chapter 109A;

(2) contact, without consent, between any part of the defendant's body — or an object — and another person's genitals or anus;

(3) contact, without consent, between the defendant's genitals or anus and any part of another person's body;

(4) deriving sexual pleasure or gratification from inflicting death, bodily injury, or physical pain on another person; or

(5) an attempt or conspiracy to engage in conduct described in subparagraphs (1)–(4).

Rule 414. Similar Crimes in Child-Molestation Cases

(a) Permitted Uses. In a criminal case in which a defendant is accused of child molestation, the court may admit evidence that the defendant committed any other child molestation. The evidence may be considered on any matter to which it is relevant.

(b) Disclosure to the Defendant. If the prosecutor intends to offer this evidence, the prosecutor must disclose it to the defendant, including witnesses' statements or a summary of the expected testimony. The prosecutor must do so at least 15 days before trial or at a later time that the court allows for good cause.

(c) Effect on Other Rules. This rule does not limit the admission or consideration of evidence under any other rule.

(d) Definition of "Child" and "Child Molestation."

In this rule and Rule 415:

(1) "child" means a person below the age of 14; and

(2) "child molestation" means a crime under federal law or under state law (as "state" is defined in 18 U.S.C. § 513) involving:

(A) any conduct prohibited by 18 U.S.C. chapter 109A and committed with a child;

(B) any conduct prohibited by 18 U.S.C. chapter 110;

(C) contact between any part of the defendant's body — or an object — and a child's genitals or anus;

(D) contact between the defendant's genitals or anus and any part of a child's body;

(E) deriving sexual pleasure or gratification from inflicting death, bodily injury, or physical pain on a child; or

(F) an attempt or conspiracy to engage in conduct described in subparagraphs (A)–(E).

Rule 415. Similar Acts in Civil Cases Involving Sexual Assault or Child Molestation

(a) **Permitted Uses.** In a civil case involving a claim for relief based on a party's alleged sexual assault or child molestation, the court may admit evidence that the party committed any other sexual assault or child molestation. The evidence may be considered as provided in Rules 413 and 414.

(b) **Disclosure to the Opponent.** If a party intends to offer this evidence, the party must disclose it to the party against whom it will be offered, including witnesses' statements or a summary of the expected testimony. The party must do so at least 15 days before trial or at a later time that the court allows for good cause.

(c) **Effect on Other Rules.** This rule does not limit the admission or consideration of evidence under any other rule.

§ 6.01 INTRODUCTION

reasons to exclude

The dangers of unfair prejudice, misleading the trier of fact, and wasting time are not the only bases for excluding relevant evidence. Other relevant evidence that may be excluded under the FRE includes subsequent remedial measures, compromises and offers to compromise, offers to pay medical expenses, offers to plead guilty, the existence or lack of liability insurance, and the complainant's prior sexual history in rape cases. *See* FRE 407–412.

Despite its relevance, such evidence is excluded for one or both of the following reasons: (1) the evidence likely will mislead the jury if it is offered to show culpability or guilt; and (2) its exclusion promotes various public policies. These policies include the promotion of safety (subsequent remedial measures), the encouragement of full disclosure in the attempt to settle cases (compromises and offers to compromise and offers to plead guilty), and the recognition of humanitarian gestures (furnishing or offering to pay medical expenses).

Thus, evidence subject to these rules (e.g., liability insurance coverage) is excluded partly because jurors tend to misuse it, especially by over-valuing it. Particular evidence may be excluded under FRE 403, as well as under one of the specific prohibitions of FRE 407 through 412. The adoption of specific exclusionary rules such as FRE 407–412, however, indicates a strong preference for the exclusion of this type of evidence, subject only to narrowly framed exceptions.

Illustration: Relevant but Inadmissible Evidence

Skates tripped on a piece of protruding cement while entering Bauer's Pizza Restaurant, suffering a sprained ankle. After Skates limped into the restaurant, a waiter carelessly spilled hot soup all over Skates, burning him severely. The next day, Bauer's owner covered up the offending cement and fired the careless waiter. Skates sued Bauer's for damages. Can Skates introduce evidence at trial about the owner's conduct in covering up the cement and firing the waiter?

Answer: Skates would not be permitted to offer the evidence. Bauer's actions after the event are intended to minimize the likelihood that such events would reoccur. Therefore, both acts by the owner constitute subsequent remedial measures and are inadmissible pursuant to FRE 407. The owner's actions are excluded to encourage Bauer's and others to take remedial measures without fearing that their conduct would be used against them as a tacit admission of fault or culpability. The exclusion of the evidence is further justified by its potential for misuse by the jury — remedial measures may be motivated by humanitarian concerns instead of a guilty conscience.

§ 6.02   SUBSEQUENT REMEDIAL MEASURES [FRE 407]

As explained in the Advisory Committee's Note to FRE 407:

> [E]vidence of subsequent remedial measures [is excluded] as proof of an admission of fault. The rule rests on two grounds. (1) The conduct is not in fact an admission. . . . (2) The other, and more impressive, ground for exclusion rests on a social policy of encouraging people to take, or at least not discouraging them from taking, steps in furtherance of added safety.

Measures taken after an event occurs are considered subsequent remedial measures if they would have decreased the likelihood of the event occurring had they been taken previously. Parties may not introduce evidence of such measures to show culpability or negligence. A wide variety of actions constitute subsequent remedial measures, ranging from the hiring or firing of employees, to the posting of warning signs or notices. Other examples include the redesign of products (e.g., post-accident automobile redesign), the installation of safety precautions (e.g., new lighting near steps), and the revision of a company's operating policy (e.g., discontinuation of disputed policy limiting payment for hospital room and board).

The scope of FRE 407's prohibition was clarified by an amendment in 1997 extending the rule to strict products liability actions. Specifically, the rule prohibits the introduction of subsequent remedial measures to show strict liability in a products liability case. Subsequent remedial measures, however, are not always excluded from evidence. These measures are admissible if offered for a purpose other than to show culpability, liability, or negligence. The other purposes include proving ownership, control, or feasibility of precautionary measures, if controverted. Thus, the party who undertook the remedial measure must initiate some question or dispute about one of these "other purposes" before the opposing party is permitted to offer evidence of subsequent remedial measures regarding the controverted purpose.

In addition, FRE 407 expressly permits a party to impeach a witness with subsequent remedial measures. Judges carefully exercise their discretion however in permitting evidence of subsequent remedial measures for impeachment because of the potential to undermine FRE 407's exclusion and its public policy of promoting remediation or public safety. For example, in *Kelly v. Crown Equipment Co.*, 970 F.2d 1273, 1278 (3d Cir. 1992), evidence of subsequent design changes could not be used to impeach a witness who merely testified that the forklift had an "excellent and proper design" — rather than the design was the best, the safest, or the only possible design.

Excluding Subsequent Remedial Measures

Problem #6-1: The Gas Grill

The manufacturer of "Michael J's Gas Grill" had a detailed set of instructions about set-up and use. A purchaser of the grill, Betty Lingsteen, was burned when the grill exploded as Lingsteen was starting it. In a later trial based on products liability, Lingsteen testified she was following the recommendations in the grill instructions. She added that, "Two months after my injuries, I received in the mail from the manufacturer a service bulletin that recommended several other inspections before starting the unit." If there is an objection to this testimony, what ruling and why?

Problem #6-2: Off-Track

An Off-Track Railroad passenger train crashed in Indiana. Subsequently, Off-Track (1) fired its chief engineer and (2) generated a post-accident study, which was its practice after every crash (mostly derailments). This study is offered in evidence in a lawsuit brought by three passengers injured in the crash. Is (1) the firing or (2) the study admissible? *See generally In re Air Crash in Bali, Indonesia*, 871 F.2d 812 (9th Cir. 1989).

Did the trial court err in admitting this evidence? Explain.

Problem #6-3: Billy's Shears

Billy purchased a pair of hedge shears from the local gardening store. He was injured while using the shears to trim the hedges in his backyard. He brought suit, claiming the shears had a design defect that caused the accident.

1. Shortly after he filed suit, the defendant company changed the design of the shears. Is this change in design admissible at trial?

2. Ethics Consideration. During the design defect litigation, in house counsel for the gardening shears company learns that its VP for marketing authorized some false advertising about the shears. She informed the CEO who then completed a cost-benefit analysis and decided not to change the advertising. What actions, if any, should the attorney take? Colorado Rules of Prof'l Conduct R. 1.13. *See* MRPC 1.13.

Problem #6-4: Controvert

Mary sued the Elks Club after falling on wet pavement immediately outside the entrance to the Club. She claimed at trial that the Club negligently maintained the entrance. The Club defended by asserting that the walkway was not slippery that night — Mary's fall was entirely Mary's fault. In rebuttal, Mary offered evidence that, on the day after her fall, the Club put up a sign on the walkway stating, "Careful! Walkway Slippery When Wet!" Mary claimed this evidence shows that the Elks Club owned the property on which she slipped. Is Mary's evidence admissible?

Problem #6-5: The Sign from Next Door

Kevin slipped on a patch of ice immediately outside of Joe's Diner located in Tulsa. Bonnie was the proprietor of Bonnie's Hair and Nails, a store located adjacent to Joe's Diner. She observed Kevin's fall and became concerned that others would trip and fall as well. Consequently, Bonnie put up a sign adjacent to Joe's sidewalk stating, "Beware of Ice!" If Kevin sues Joe's Diner for negligence, can he offer Bonnie's sign as evidence?

Problem #6-6: Gas

A tank of propane gas in the possession of plaintiff exploded, injuring him severely. Plaintiff sued the supplier of the gas on a theory of strict products liability. Plaintiff alleged that the gas contained an insufficient quantity of a special odorizing agent, which resulted in the explosion. At trial, plaintiff offered a brochure prepared by the defendant after the accident. The brochure explained that the odor of petroleum gas may fade with time and that if the odor fades, then the gas should be replaced. Is this brochure a subsequent remedial measure? Is it admissible? *See Donahue v. Phillips Petroleum Co.*, 866 F.2d 1008 (8th Cir. 1989).

Subsequent Remedial Measures for "Another Purpose"

Problem #6-7: A Rose by Any Other Name

A patron in an outdoor restaurant in La Jolla, California, was severely scratched by a rosebush on her way into the restaurant. The patron brought an action against the restaurant for damages resulting from her injuries. She claimed that the restaurant was negligent in failing to maintain a clear walkway. The restaurant claimed the bush was not on the restaurant's property and, consequently, the bush was not its responsibility. At trial, the plaintiff was permitted to show that the defendant had hired workers to clip the branches of the rose bush after the incident occurred.

Did the trial court err in admitting this evidence? Explain.

Problem #6-8: WARNING: Road Narrows Ahead

A construction company had a contract with the state to widen a section of highway. The company warned the highway department that an area of the highway was dangerous and that they had observed several cars going off the side of the road there. Neither placed signs to warn motorists of the dangerous road condition. After an accident occurred at this area, the injured party sued the construction company. At trial, the main issue is who had control of the highway — the state or the construction company? The plaintiff moved to admit into evidence that the construction company put up danger signs and smudge pots after the accident. How should the trial judge rule? *See Powers v. J.B. Michael & Co.*, 329 F.2d 674 (6th Cir. 1964).

§ 6.03 OFFERS TO COMPROMISE, PAY MEDICAL EXPENSES, AND PLEAS OF GUILTY OR NOLO CONTENDERE [FRE 408–10]

The Advisory Committee's Note to FRE 408 explains the Rule as follows:

As a matter of general agreement, evidence of an offer to compromise a claim is not receivable in evidence as an admission of, as the case may be, the validity or invalidity of the claim. . . . The evidence is irrelevant, since the offer may be motivated by a desire for peace rather than from any concession of weakness of position. . . . A more consistently impressive ground is promotion of the public policy favoring the compromise and settlement of disputes.

FRE 409 is described by the following language from the Advisory Committee's Note:

[G]enerally, evidence of payment of medical, hospital, or similar expenses of an injured party by the opposing party, is not admissible, the reason often given being that such payment or offer is usually made from humane impulses and not from an admission of liability, and that to hold otherwise would tend to discourage assistance to the injured person.

The following explanation of FRE 410 appears in the Advisory Committee's Note to the 1980 amendments:

[T]he purpose of Fed. R. Evid. 410 and Fed. R. Crim. P. 11(e)(6) is to permit the unrestrained candor which produces effective plea discussions between the "attorney for the government and the attorney for the defendant or the defendant when acting pro se."

The Advisory Committee's Note to the original FRE 410 noted that "Withdrawn pleas of guilty were held inadmissible in federal prosecutions in *Kercheval v. United States*, 274 U.S. 220, 47 S. Ct. 582, 71 L. Ed. 1009 (1927)."

The FRE exclude completed compromises and offers to compromise, furnishing or offering to pay medical expenses, and offers to plead guilty or nolo contendere (i.e., "no contest"). Compromises and offers to compromise, or furnishing or offering to pay medical expenses, are excluded when offered to show fault or culpability. Offers to plead guilty generally cannot be used against an accused at trial or in subsequent proceedings. The rationales for these exclusions are similar to the rationales for subsequent remedial measures: (1) there exists considerable potential for unfair prejudice, and (2) they promote certain public policies.

The exclusion of compromises, offers to compromise, and offers to plead guilty advance the policy of settling conflicts. To encourage such conduct, they are excluded from evidence. To ensure full and open discussions during negotiations, statements made in connection with plea bargaining or settlement negotiations also are excluded from evidence.

Comparing Offers: To Compromise, Pay Medical Expenses, and Plead Guilty

The FRE treat furnishing or offering to pay medical expenses differently than compromises, offers to compromise, and offers to plead guilty. Under FRE 409, evidence that someone has furnished or offered to pay medical expenses is excluded from evidence, but not any factual statements that may have been made in conjunction with such offer or payment. Unlike compromises and offers to compromise and offers to plead guilty, furnishing or offering to pay medical expenses is viewed generally as a gratuitous act, motivated by humanitarian impulses. There is no policy basis for shielding factual statements made in conjunction with furnishing or offering to pay because there is no associated bargaining process or conflict resolution that would be promoted. In contrast, FRE 408's policy of promoting a frank bargaining process prohibits the use of statements or conduct during settlement negotiations to impeach the credibility of witnesses at trials should negotiations fail. As the Advisory Committee noted:

> "the use of statements in settlement negotiations when offered to impeach by prior inconsistent statement or through contradiction . . . would tend to swallow the exclusionary rule and impair the public policy of promoting settlements." Similarly, a defendant may not be impeached with evidence (e.g., prior inconsistent statements) excluded by FRE 410.

While these exclusions shield evidence from admission, the shield is not impermeable. The exclusion of compromises and offers to compromise under FRE 408, for example, does not extend to otherwise discoverable documents produced during negotiations. Furthermore, the exclusion of compromises and offers to compromise takes effect only when a disputed claim exists. If there is no dispute about the claim or the amount owed, the exclusion is inapplicable.

These exclusionary rules are sometimes interpreted more expansively than their literal meaning. The exclusion of offers to plead guilty or nolo contendere, for example, applies to statements made by prosecutors as well as defendants, even though the language of FRE 410 could be construed to protect only the accused.

Offers to plead guilty are excluded from evidence under FRE 410 only if later withdrawn. If offers to plead guilty are not later withdrawn, they may serve as an admission of culpability or guilt in a later case. If a defendant pleads "nolo contendere" (no contest) in a criminal case, however, the plea is not considered to be an admission of guilt and cannot be used as such in later cases.

Illustration: Offers to Compromise, Pay Medical Expenses, and Plead Guilty

One crisp fall day at the Kommander Condominium Club, Rob Arbuckle was late for his 10:30 a.m. tennis appointment. He left the elevator while looking at his watch and bowled over 86-year-old Alfred Macumber. A distraught Rob exclaimed, "Oh Mac! I hope you're okay. Why don't you go to the Mellon Hospital and I'll pay for the check-up?" Later that night, Mac's attorney called Rob and told him Mac was thinking of bringing suit because of his fairly severe injuries. Rob responded, "Look, I don't want any trouble. I admit I was not looking when I ran into Mac; I was in a hurry. If I gave Mac $1,000, would this whole thing go away?" The attorney refused Rob's proposal. Prior to the civil trial, Rob was prosecuted for the battery of Mr. Macumber. He sought a plea bargain in which he would admit guilt if he received a suspended sentence. The prosecutor rejected Rob's offer. Which, if any, of Rob's statements are admissible against him in the civil trial?

Answer: None of Rob's statements can be offered against him in the civil suit filed by Mac if offered to show culpability or fault. Rob's offer to pay for Mac's trip to the Mellon Hospital is an offer to pay medical expenses and excluded under FRE 409. Rob's offer to Mac's attorney to pay $1,000 "to make this whole thing go away" is an offer to compromise a disputed claim and excluded under FRE 408. The factual admissions by Rob that he was "not looking and . . . in a hurry" also would be excluded under FRE 408. Finally, any admissions by Rob during the unsuccessful plea bargaining in the criminal action are sheltered from admissibility in any later case pursuant to FRE 410.

Problem #6-9: Let's Make a Deal

Barbara owed Alice $500. When Barbara saw Alice hanging out in front of the local convenience store, Barbara asked Alice, "If I give you $350 and a ticket to the Harry Connick Jr. concert, would that be an adequate settlement? I don't have the full $500 I owe you, and I just won't have it by the agreed date. I'm very short on cash at the moment." If Alice does not accept Barbara's offer, can Alice introduce Barbara's statements in a later trial for payment of the $500?

Problem #6-10: Med X

After a frustrating business meeting, Jan hurried away, lost in thought. Jan crashed into Arsenio, knocking him over. As Arsenio writhed in pain on the ground, Jan stated, "I'm really sorry; I was preoccupied and our collision was all my fault. If you don't bring suit, I'll be more than happy to pay for all of your medical expenses. Hey, I'll even pay for your ripped pants and for any embarrassment this incident may have caused you. What do you say?" Arsenio replied by saying "No," and filed suit.

    1.   Are any of Jan's statements admissible at trial?

2. Ethics Consideration. You are Jan's attorney. Someone calls your office and tells you that they know that your client was drinking at the time of the accident. Is the information protected by the ethical obligation of confidentiality? Delaware Rules of Prof'l Conduct R. 1.6. *See* MRPC 1.6. Is it protected by the attorney-client privilege?

Problem #6-11: On the Hook

Bob's Fish and Tackle frequently makes purchase orders from Stan's Fishing Emporium. Bob thinks that he paid all of his invoices, but Stan argues that he is still owed the last invoice. Wanting to continue to have a good working relationship with Stan, Bob tells Stan, "I'll pay half of the last invoice if you let me off the hook." When Stan sues Bob, should this statement be admitted into evidence?

Problem #6-12: Engulf and Devour

Johann is sued by a business partner, Domino. Domino claimed that Johann understated profits by $1 million over a period of five years and clandestinely siphoned off partnership money for personal use. During negotiations with Domino, Johann admitted to taking some money because he needed to pay off some gambling losses. Johann claimed, however, that he did not owe Domino anything because Domino had swindled him at the time they had formed the partnership. Therefore, the money he took was rightfully his.

1. If Johann was incorrect in his belief that the money he took was rightfully his, can Domino offer Johann's statements at trial?

2. If Johann had produced all of the tax forms relating to the years in question and the betting slips verifying his losses during the negotiations, could these documents still be offered at trial?

3. If Johann had agreed that he owed Domino the $1 million as Domino claimed, but offered during negotiations to pay "500 grand" to have the lawsuit dropped, are any factual admissions made in conjunction with Johann's offer to pay admissible?

4. If subsequent criminal proceedings are initiated against Johann for his failure to pay income taxes on the monies in question, would the statements he made during the previous settlement negotiations be admissible in the subsequent criminal case?

Problem #6-13: Did I Say That?

Leslie is sued by her neighbor, Murray, for breaking a very expensive mirror in Murray's house. During settlement negotiations, Leslie admitted she had been smoking marijuana at Murray's at the time the mirror broke. She denied, however, actually breaking the heirloom. The following month, Leslie is prosecuted for the possession of marijuana at her neighbor's house.

1. Can the prosecution offer Leslie's prior admission during settlement negotiations regarding her marijuana use?

2. If Leslie had pled guilty to using marijuana at her neighbor's house, and then was sued in a civil action by her neighbor for breaking the mirror, could the guilty plea be used against her in the later civil trial?

Problem #6-14: The Singing Sparrow

The defendant, Sparrow, is charged with murdering Goodot. During a plea negotiation with the prosecutor, the defendant blurts out, "You guys don't know who you're up against! You think I killed Goodot, but you really should ask me about the unsolved murder of Blaine in the next county. I have personal knowledge about that one and you coppers are way off base in your investigation!"

Sparrow is subsequently charged with Blaine's murder. At that trial, can the prosecutor offer Sparrow's inculpatory statements made during the Goodot plea negotiations?

Problems Concerning Exceptions

Problem #6-15: Battery

Jesse is sued by Cohan for damages resulting from an alleged battery outside of a local nightclub, Crickett Place. Cohan and Jesse engaged in a series of discussions about settling the suit before trial. During one discussion, Cohan stated, "The only reason I hit you from behind was because you were doing a song and dance with my girlfriend inside the club." Negotiations were unsuccessful. At trial, Cohan takes the stand and states, "I was in the club until after Jesse left; I didn't learn about him getting hurt until I heard the sirens and ran outside to see what had happened." Jesse seeks to impeach Cohan with the admissions he made during the settlement negotiations. Is this permissible?

Problem #6-16: Gorky Park

McGillicuddy is charged with two counts of breaking and entering the kitchen of a local restaurant, Sim's Place. A day after the charges were filed, McGillicuddy visited a local police officer, Officer Gorky. McGillicuddy and Gorky were social acquaintances. McGillicuddy proposed to Gorky, "If you ditch these charges against me, I can help you catch some big-time crooks. I admit I broke into Sim's, but I was hungry and wanted some food; you can understand that, right?"

1. At McGillicuddy's trial for breaking and entering, can the prosecution offer McGillicuddy's statements to Officer Gorky?

2. Assume that McGillicuddy's friend, Bobby, also is charged with breaking and entering as an aider and abetter. Bobby agrees to testify against McGillicuddy, provided that the prosecution drops the charges against him. Can statements made by Bobby while entering a plea of guilty be used by McGillicuddy to impeach Bobby on cross-examination?

3. McGillicuddy unsuccessfully attempted to negotiate a plea directly with the prosecutor. At trial, McGillicuddy introduces some of his own statements

made during plea discussions with the prosecutor. What can the prosecutor do in response to McGillicuddy's evidence, if anything?

4. After reading FRE 410, McGillicuddy concluded that the Rule is designed to protect the accused during plea bargaining. Consequently, McGillicuddy offered the statements made by the prosecutor during their unsuccessful plea negotiations. Are the prosecutor's statements admissible?

Problem #6-17: Plea Negotiations & Waiver

Criminal defendant and his attorney were meeting with the prosecutor to discuss a plea. Before the plea discussion began, the prosecutor required that the defendant sign a waiver agreeing that any statements made in the meeting could be used to impeach him at trial. The defendant agreed after discussing the waiver with his counsel. At the subsequent trial, the prosecutor used the statements made in plea discussions to impeach the defendant. Defense counsel objects. What result? (*See United States v. Mezzanatto*, 513 U.S. 196 (1995), which is in the Cases and Rules section, *infra*.)

Practical Tip:

FRE 410 does not bar statements made during plea negotiations from being used at sentencing hearings. *United States v Smith*, 770 F.3d 628 (7th Cir. 2014) (citing FRE 1101(d)(3)).

---

§ 6.04   LIABILITY INSURANCE [FRE 411]

The FRE exclude any mention of the existence of liability insurance, or the lack thereof, to show culpability or wrongful behavior. Like other relevant but inadmissible evidence, however, the existence of liability insurance may be offered for other purposes, such as showing bias.

Illustration: Liability Insurance

Jill owned a motorboat named "Doggone Doug." After crashing into another boat, the "Mystic Lady," Jill is sued for damages. Can the owners of "Mystic Lady," Mary and Rich, offer in evidence Jill's substantial liability insurance policy?

Answer: Mary and Rich would not be permitted to mention Jill's insurance policy to show negligence or fault. Since that appears to be the only reason why the existence of the insurance policy is relevant to the boating accident, it will be excluded under FRE 411.

Problem #6-18: "I Forgot"

Defendant is sued for injuries resulting from an automobile accident. The defendant did not have automobile liability insurance; he "forgot to buy some." At trial, the defendant testified on direct examination.

DEFENDANT'S ATTORNEY: How careful a driver are you?

PLAINTIFF'S ATTORNEY: Objection. This evidence is irrelevant and unfairly prejudicial.

1. What ruling and why?

DEFENDANT'S ATTORNEY: What is your motive to be careful while driving?

PLAINTIFF'S ATTORNEY: Objection.

DEFENDANT'S ATTORNEY: (at the bench) I will proffer, Your Honor, that the defendant will say that "I'm a careful driver in large part because I forgot to take out car insurance; I knew that I could be held personally liable if I was in an automobile accident."

PLAINTIFF'S ATTORNEY: Objection.

2. What ruling and why?

3. Is this evidence admissible if it is offered to rebut the implicit assumption that because many people have automobile insurance, the defendant likely has automobile insurance as well?

Problem #6-19: Go Ahead and Jump

Plaintiff, Laurie, brought suit against a bungee-jumping facility in Michigan. Plaintiff jumped and was injured when the rope broke. Plaintiff offered evidence at trial that the defendant was insured, corroborating her claim that the defendant owner operated the business with the lackadaisical attitude of "Why worry? Be happy," the facility's unofficial motto.

1.   Is this evidence admissible?

2.   Ethics Consideration. Assume that Bobby, an employee of the business, is a witness for the defense. You are the defendant's attorney. The defendant is the corporation. When the suit is originally filed you sit down to talk with Bobby. Are the communications with Bobby? Delaware Rules of Prof'l Conduct R. 1.6; Colorado Rules of Prof'l Conduct R. 1.13. *See* MRPC 1.6 & 1.13.

Problem #6-20: Flood Zone

Allison sold various items for clients on eBay, charging a service fee and a percentage of the sale. She stored all of the items in a small warehouse in a flood zone. When the area flooded, much of what was stored was completely ruined. She was sued by several of her customers. At trial, the plaintiffs wished to introduce a letter from Allison to her insurance company indicating Allison's concern about possible flood damage to the items stored in the warehouse. Are the portions of the letter indicating Allison's concern admissible?

Problem #6-21: Columbo

A defense witness, Samantha, testified about the position of two cars involved in an automobile accident at a busy intersection. On cross-examination, she was asked by an apparently bumbling attorney named Columbo whether she was employed by the defendant's insurer. The defendant objected to the question and the court sustained the objection. Should the lower court's ruling be affirmed on appeal? (*See Charter v. Chleborad*, 551 F.2d 246 (8th Cir.), *cert. denied*, 434 U.S. 856 (1977), which is excerpted in the Cases and Statutes section, *infra*.)

§ 6.05   RAPE CASES [FRE 412]

FRE 412 was added to the Federal Rules of Evidence in the Privacy Protection for Rape Victims Act of 1978. One proponent of the legislation, Representative Mann, gave the following explanation (124 Cong. Rec., H11944 (daily ed. Oct. 10, 1978)):

> The effect of this legislation [Rule 412], therefore, is to preclude the routine use of evidence of specific instances [or reputation or opinion evidence] of a rape victim's prior sexual behavior. Such evidence will be admitted only in clearly and narrowly defined circumstances and only after an in camera hearing.

The subject of rape or sexual assault is controversial. It readily promotes discussions about social policy and the appropriate balance at trial of competing interests, namely the defendant's, the alleged victim's, and society's in general. The problems that follow are intended to create an understanding of the complexity of the issues associated with this subject area. Close scrutiny reveals various subissues, ranging from statutory interpretation to those involving human behavior. These subissues, in turn, raise questions involving the relationship between power, emotions, the social sciences, and legal rules and principles.

One premise of this section is that rape, while a sexual crime, is also a crime of power and violence. Pursuant to this conceptualization, rape cases present a broader array of evidentiary issues than many other areas. Rape law also raises questions about the roles of gender, race, and socioeconomic status in the definition and application of legal rules. Some of these issues are presented in the following article, as well as in the succeeding problems. (All of the problems in this section are based on actual cases.)

DATE RAPE AND THE CULTURE OF ACCEPTANCE
43 U. Fl. L. Rev. 487 (1991)[1]
By Steven I. Friedland

The crime of rape is widely viewed as horrific, violent and exceedingly invasive. Yet not all forms of rape are viewed similarly. Instead, some forms of rape are viewed as more egregious than others.

---

[1] Copyright © 1991 by the University of Florida Law Review. Reprinted with permission. (Footnotes omitted.)

Rape by a stranger, for example, is generally considered to be the most heinous of rape offenses. It has been characterized as "real rape." In marked contrast, rape by a social acquaintance or date is viewed by many as a far less serious offense. To a large segment of American society, date rape does not deserve the same appellation or vigorous moral condemnation as "real rape."

This lax attitude towards date rape exists in a variety of forms. It is an attitude often supported and reinforced by popular culture. The attitude also plays a role in the low incidence of reported date rapes as well as in the marginal success of the few prosecutions brought.

Societal ambivalence towards date rape is based on a special permissiveness regarding male sexual aggression against female social acquaintances. This article labels that permissive attitude "the culture of acceptance."

The culture of acceptance includes two dominant stereotypes. One stereotype is the "aggressive male" — the male who actively pursues sexual relations with a female despite cues to the contrary. The other is the "punished" female — the female who, by her dress or other apparently provocative non-verbal actions, implicitly "deserves" or "asks for" sexual intercourse.

Trials in the criminal justice system offer the most controversial manifestation of the "culture of acceptance," perhaps because so much is at stake. A criminal defendant risks not only a potentially substantial loss of liberty, but the stigma of conviction as well.

A paradigmatic illustration of the influence of the culture of acceptance occurred in Florida state court in State v. Lord. In *Lord*, the defendant was tried and acquitted on a charge of rape. The verdict was not unusual; persons charged with rape face only a small chance of conviction. After the *Lord* verdict, however, the foreperson created a nation-wide controversy by explaining that the acquittal was reached in part because of the manner of dress of the alleged victim. At the time of the alleged incident, the complainant was wearing a lace skirt without underwear. In explaining the verdict, the foreperson stated, "she asked for it." The foreperson added: " 'it' meant sex, not rape. If a woman goes out at 3:00 a.m. in that kind of skirt, she is advertising for sex, and she got what she advertised for."

The thesis of this paper is that the culture of acceptance — and the stereotypes it promotes — generates latent gender-based prejudice that unfairly influences the trial of date rape cases. This influence prejudices the jury's evaluation of evidence bearing on whether the complainant had consented to sexual intercourse, an issue generally dispositive of the case. The prejudicial impact becomes even more virulent when the defendant claims that he was at least reasonably mistaken in believing the complainant's conduct was consensual.

The article argues that the current application of the rape laws merely ignores the prejudice resulting from latent gender-based biases. Consequently, the current law is inadequate. If date rape trials are to be fairly administered within evidentiary rules and constitutional and moral requirements, an active attempt must be made at all stages of a trial to neutralize the culture of acceptance.

Neutralization of the culture of acceptance involves both preventive and educational measures. These techniques are intended either to eliminate tainted jurors from the jury panel or to educate those who are selected to serve. The educational function relies on a phenomenological approach to demystify the non-verbal contextual evidence. For any measure used, the court must be vigilant in not permitting attorneys or jurors to perpetuate latent gender biases.

1. Do you agree with the perspective advanced in the article? Explain.

2. How should juries be instructed about social mores and societal traditions, if at all?

Illustration: Rape Law

Brandi went to a party with her friend, Rhonda. Brandi met Craig at the party and agreed to take a walk with him. During the walk, Craig forced her to have sexual intercourse with him. At trial, Craig wishes to introduce testimony that Brandi had three different sex partners in the previous year. Is this evidence admissible?

Answer: The prior sexual history of Brandi is inadmissible pursuant to FRE 412. Only if Brandi's prior sexual conduct with others is relevant to show the source of the semen or injury would it possibly be admissible.

Problem #6-22: More Than Words

Betty met Bill in a bar. They talked for a while and he then asked her for a ride home. She agreed and drove him to his apartment. Bill invited Betty up, but she said no. Bill then took her car keys, and Betty relented, agreeing to go into the apartment. Upon entering the apartment, Betty was frightened by the look in Bill's eyes. He began to undress her and asked her to continue undressing, which she did. He then had sex with her.

1. At common law, rape was generally defined as the "unlawful carnal knowledge of a woman by force or fear." Which evidence in the above problem is relevant to the issue of "by force or fear"?

2. Is the concept of "by force or fear" different for males and females? Is a "reasonable woman" standard different than a "reasonable man" standard? Are there distinct perspectives?

3. At what time is the "by force or fear" standard measured? Must it be contemporaneous with the sexual act?

4. Did Bill commit rape?

5. Ethics Consideration. You represent the defendant, Bill. Bill tells you that he wants you to make this trial as difficult for the prosecutor as possible. Bill wants you to object to every question the prosecutor asks. You do not believe that this is good trial strategy, as it is likely to annoy the jury and the judge. Bill exclaims, "I'm the client. You have to do what I want." Is this true? Colorado Rules of Prof'l Conduct 1.2. *See* MRPC 1.2.

Problem #6-23: Resistance

Dan and Cindy had a sexual relationship, characterized by his aggressiveness and her passivity. There were several violent sexual acts in their relationship, all initiated by Dan. One night, after they had been dating for more than one year, Dan unexpectedly showed up at Cindy's house. He had alcohol on his breath. Dan demanded to be let inside, and Cindy reluctantly agreed. Once inside the house, Dan began to undress Cindy, who told him she did not want to have sex with him. Dan began to kiss Cindy, and she informed him again that she did not want to have sex with him. Dan began to kiss her again. She did not pull away because she generally feared him. They had sexual intercourse. Dan is subsequently charged with rape.

1. Is the prior sexual relationship between Dan and Cindy relevant? How, if at all, is it relevant? Would prior sexual relationships between Cindy and others be relevant? Would such relationships be admissible?

2. Is it relevant if Cindy did not report the alleged rape until several days, weeks, or months after it occurred? Should such information be admitted?

3. Is it relevant if Dan was silent after being informed of the rape charges against him? Is it relevant if he uttered a denial upon being informed of the charge? Is such evidence admissible?

Problem #6-24: Anger, Violence, and Privacy

Which of the following evidence is admissible in rape cases?

1. The victim's marital status. ⟍

2. The victim had a child out of wedlock. ⟍

3. Reputation evidence of the victim's lack of chastity. *See Doe v. United States*, 666 F.2d 43 (4th Cir. 1981). ⟍

4. The victim made a prior false accusation against another man of rape. *See United States v. Bartlett*, 856 F.2d 1071 (8th Cir. 1988). ⟍ *not about pres. case*

Problem #6-25: Sexual Harassment, Discovery, and Social Networking

Jim sued the defendant-School for sexual harassment claiming that his female co-workers offended him by using sexual innuendo and banter in the workplace. The defendant filed a motion to compel production of electronic communications and records, including copies of photos or videos posted by Jim or any photos in which he has been "tagged" on any social networking website, including but not limited to Twitter, Facebook and/or MYSpace from the time of alleged harassment through the time of trial. The defendant also sought Jim's profile on any social networking site and all messages both sent and received, activity streams, blog entries, and comments. The defendant sought this electronic evidence to discover whether Jim's terminology when interacting with others showed whether he was subjectively offended by his co-workers' statements. Jim objects. How should the trial judge rule on the defendant's motion? *See Ogden v. All-State Career School*, 299 F.R.D. 446 (W. D. Pa. 2014).

§ 6.06   PRIOR ACTS BY SEXUAL BATTERY DEFENDANTS [FRE 413–15]

FRE 413, 414, and 415 were added after the original adoption of the Rules. These rules offer specific guidelines for the admissibility of similar crimes evidence against defendants in the burgeoning and troublesome area of sexual offenses. Thus, instead of excluding evidence, these are rules of inclusion. These rules go beyond FRE 404(b) in providing the admissibility of other specific acts of the defendant in sexual-assault and child molestation cases. The rules reflect a societal trend to clamp down on sex predators.

FRE 413 covers criminal sexual-assault cases, FRE 414 applies to criminal child-molestation cases, and FRE415 concerns civil cases of sexual-assault or child-molestation. Excerpts from these rules are presented below. Compare these rules to FRE 404. Were these rules a good idea? Is it appropriate to modify the rules of evidence to deal with important social issues? Explain.

Rule 413. Similar Crimes in Sexual Assault Cases

(a) In a criminal case in which a defendant is accused of a sexual assault, the court may admit evidence that the defendant committed any other sexual assault. The evidence may be considered on any matter to which it is relevant. . . .

Rule 414. Similar Crimes in Child Molestation Cases

(a) In a criminal case in which a defendant is accused of child molestation, the court may admit evidence that the defendant committed any other child molestation. The evidence may be considered for any matter to which it is relevant. . . .

Rule 415. Similar Acts in Civil Cases Involving Sexual Assault or Child Molestation

(a) In a civil case involving a claim for relief based on a party's alleged sexual assault or child molestation, the court may admit evidence that the party committed any other sexual assault or child molestation. The evidence may be considered as provided in Rule 413 and Rule 414.

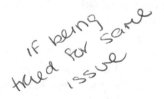

§ 6.07   CASES AND RULES

[A]   Moe v. Avions Marcel Dassault-Breguet Aviation

United States Court of Appeals for the Tenth Circuit
727 F.2d 917 (10th Cir. 1984), cert. denied, *469 U.S. 853 (1984)*

BARRETT, CIRCUIT JUDGE:

The plaintiffs-appellants appeal from a judgment entered on jury verdicts for the defendants-appellees in an action for damages for wrongful deaths, personal injuries and property damages on theories of negligence and strict product liability arising from an airplane crash near Denver, Colorado at 4:52 a.m. on April 3, 1977. Jurisdiction vests by virtue of diversity of citizenship under 28 U.S.C. § 1332. Plaintiffs claimed multiple theories of negligence and defect as the cause of the crash, including defective design of the autopilot system, runaway to the high position of the artificial feel system (Arthur Q), clogging of the suction filters for both of the two independent hydraulic systems, or a combination of the above, together with defect of the power plant system and a failure to warn. . . .

. . . .

At the outset, we observe some basic rules governing our appellate review. . . . In *Miller v. City of Broken Arrow, Okl., (citations omitted), we said, inter alia:*

> . . . In a diversity of citizenship case the federal district court sits as a state trial court and applies the law of the forum state. The federal district court [or jury if tried to jury], as trier of fact, has the responsibility of weighing the credibility of the witnesses. On appeal, the reviewing court must view the evidence in the light most favorable to the prevailing party. A judgment may be affirmed on any ground arising from the record. Findings of a trial court will not be disturbed on appeal unless they are clearly erroneous.

Appellants argue that the trial court erred in applying Rule 407, *supra*, in light of the law of Colorado then controlling as set forth in *Good v. A.B. Chance Co.*, *supra*, which followed the reasoning of *Ault v. International Harvester*, 13 Cal.3d 113, 117 Cal. Rptr. 812, 528 P.2d 1148 (1974). *Ault* held, in a products liability action, that evidence of a manufacturer's post-accident warning had a direct bearing on liability as tending to establish knowledge of the defect, feasibility of giving warnings, duty to warn, and breach of that duty. The *Good v. Chance* court referred to *Hiigel v. General Motors Corp.*, *supra*, for the rule that failure to warn may render a product defective when that failure is a proximate cause of the injury, but it also relied on *Hiigel* for the rule that, "[a] [sic] affirmative defense in a products liability case exists when it can be shown that the injured party knew of the dangerous defect in the product and voluntarily and unreasonably encountered the known danger it presented." (Citation omitted.)

The trial court ruled that Rule 407, *supra*, is not governed by or made applicable by state law. On this predicate, the court did not view the *Good* decision as binding. The trial court stated that Rule 407 should not discourage defendants to take remedial measures following an accident. We respectfully disagree with the trial court's conclusion that the admissibility of evidence in diversity actions is governed exclusively by federal law — that is, the Federal Rules of Evidence. . . .

It is our view that when state courts have interpreted Rule 407 or its equivalent state counterpart, the question whether subsequent remedial measures are excluded from evidence is a matter of state policy. The purpose of Rule 407 is not to seek the truth or to expedite trial proceedings; rather, in our view, it is one designed to promote state policy in a substantive law area. For example, the State of Maine has adopted a rule of evidence which repudiates the rule of exclusion with regard to subsequent remedial repairs. This creates a conflict between Rule 407 and the Maine rule. We hold that when such conflicts arise, because Rule 407 is based primarily on policy considerations rather than relevancy or truth seeking, the state rule controls because (a) there is no federal products liability law, (b) the elements and proof of a products liability action are governed by the law of the state where the injury occurred and these may, and do, for policy reasons, vary from state to state, and (c) an announced state rule in variance with Rule 407 is so closely tied to the substantive law to which it relates (product liability) that it must be applied in a diversity action in order to effect uniformity and to prevent forum shopping. We are not unmindful of the rule laid down in *Hanna v. Plumer*, 380 U.S. 460, 85 S. Ct. 1136, 14 L. Ed. 2d 8 (1965), that where the federal and state rules both govern the issue in dispute and are in direct conflict, the federal rule applies in a diversity based case if the federal rule is arguably procedural in nature. However, we observe that while the sufficiency of the evidence is tested against the federal standard in a diversity case, *Hidalgo Properties, Inc.* v. Wachovia Mortgage Co., 617 F.2d 196, 198 (10th Cir. 1980), the underlying cause of action, with its attendant elements and requirement of proof in a diversity case, is governed by state law. The ground for exclusion of remedial measures under Rule 407 rests on the social policy of encouraging people to take steps in furtherance of safety. The decision is necessarily a state policy matter. Product liability is not a federal cause of action but, rather, a state cause of action with varying degrees of proof and exclusion from state to state. If a state has not announced controlling rules, such as New Mexico (*Herndon, supra*) the federal district court, sitting as a state court in a product liability diversity case, must determine whether Rule 407 applies. Where the state law is expressed in product liability cases, these expressions control the application of Rule 407. If the law of the state supplies the rule of decision, there is no justification for reliance on Rule 407. We recognize that, by its terms, Rule 407, when read in conjunction with Rules 401 and 402, does appear to apply in these cases. However, such a result is an unwarranted incursion into the *Erie* doctrine. The crux of this conclusion is well stated, as follows:

> The constitutional meaning of the *Erie* doctrine seems to be this: The enumerated powers set forth for the Congress in Article II and for the Judiciary in Article III are by implication limited powers, and the notion of limited federal authority is reinforced by the Tenth Amendment. Therefore, the federal judiciary may not "find" or "create" general law to resolve controversies merely because they are litigated in federal court. One difficulty in advancing such an argument against the application of Rule 407 lies in the

fact that the constitutional boundaries of congressional power, where there are competing state rules, have not been clearly defined. . . . Although *Erie* itself holds that there is no federal general common law of torts, nothing in the case suggests Congress could not pass a statute governing the rights of the parties on the very facts of *Erie*. . . . Despite the problems noted . . . there may well be valid constitutional reasons why Rule 407 cannot be applied in cases where state law supplies the rule of decision. Even if Congress *could* constitutionally enact statutes to govern the rights of parties in a given instance, it does not necessarily follow that the Congress, in codifying the law of evidence, may constitutionally enact a narrow statute governing a single substantive issue in a lawsuit which is otherwise to be resolved by reference to state law. . . . It is unlikely that the Congress intended, in enacting Rule 407 along with the other rules, to make any incursion whatsoever in the *Erie* doctrine. (Footnotes omitted.)

Louisell and Mueller, Federal Evidence, Vol. 2, § 166, pp. 261–264.

Notwithstanding our view that the trial court erred in ruling that Fed. Rule of Evid. Rule 407 applies in diversity actions without regard to state law, we hold that no harm resulted therefrom because the trial court's actions were proper and correct on other grounds. . . .

. . . .

[B] Charter v. Chleborad

In *Charter v. Chleborad*, 551 F.2d 246 (8th Cir.), *cert. denied*, 434 U.S. 856 (1977), the plaintiff claimed that the defendant committed medical malpractice. At trial, the plaintiff offered the testimony of an orthopedic surgeon. The defendant countered with its own medical expert. During cross-examination of the defendant's expert, the plaintiff attempted to show the witness had been employed by the same liability insurance company representing the defendant. The district court disallowed that line of questioning. On appeal, the court held that questions about the possible bias of the witness did not violate the exclusion of liability insurance evidence under Federal Rule of Evidence 411. The court of appeals stated that the existence of insurance may not be used to show negligence or fault, but can be offered for other purposes, such as bias.

[C] Rules Comparison

[1] Rule 407

Compare FRE 407 with the following state rules. Which rule is preferable? Why?

Maine Rule of Evidence 407

(a) **Subsequent remedial measures.** When, after an injury or harm allegedly caused by an event, measures are taken that, if taken previously, would have made the injury or harm less likely to occur, evidence of the subsequent measures is not admissible to prove negligence, culpable conduct, a defect in a product, a defect in a product's design, or a need for a warning or instruction. This rule does not require exclusion of evidence of subsequent measures when offered for another purpose such as proving ownership, control or feasibility of precautionary measures, if controverted, or impeachment.

Tennessee Rule of Evidence 407

Subsequent remedial measures. When, after an event, measures are taken which, if taken previously, would have made the event less likely to occur, evidence of the subsequent remedial measures is not admissible to prove strict liability, negligence, or culpable conduct in connection with the event . . . .

[2]   Rule 408

Compare FRE 408 with the following state rule. Are the rules different? If so, how?

Alaska Rule of Evidence 408

This rule also does not require exclusion when the evidence is offered for another purpose, such as proving bias or prejudice of a witness, negativing a contention of undue delay, or proving an effort to obstruct a criminal investigation or prosecution, but exclusion is required where the sole purpose for offering the evidence is to impeach a party by showing a prior inconsistent statement.

[3]   Rule 409

Compare FRE 409 with the following state rule. Which is preferable?

Montana Rule of Evidence 409. Payment of Expense

Evidence of payment of expenses occasioned by an injury or occurrence is not admissible to prove liability.

[4]   Rule 410

Compare the current FRE 410 with earlier drafts of the rule and a proposed American Bar Association Rule. Is the current version an improvement?

Rule 410 (March 1969). Offer to Plead Guilty; Nolo Contendere; Withdrawn Plea of Guilty

Evidence of a plea of guilty, later withdrawn, or a plea of nolo contendere, or of an offer to plead guilty or nolo contendere to the crime charged or any other crime, is not admissible in a civil or criminal proceeding involving the person who made the plea or offer.

Rule 410 (March 1971 revision)

Evidence of a plea of guilty, later withdrawn, or a plea of nolo contendere, or of an offer to plead guilty or nolo contendere to the crime charged or any other crime, is not admissible in any civil or criminal proceeding. Evidence of statements made in connection with any of the foregoing pleas or offers is not admissible.

Rule 410 (ABA proposal)

Except as otherwise provided in this rule, evidence of the following is not, in any civil or criminal proceeding, admissible against the defendant who made the plea or was a participant in the plea discussions: . . . (4) any statement made in the course of plea discussions with an attorney for the prosecuting authority, or with a law enforcement officer who was authorized by such attorney to enter into plea bargaining discussions or who led the defendant to so believe, which do not result in a plea of guilty or which result in a plea of guilty later withdrawn.

[5] Rule 412

Compare the following rape shield statute with FRE 412. Which is preferable? Why?

MCL § 750.520j(1) (Michigan Statutes Annotated § 28.788(10)). Admissibility of Evidence; Victim's Sexual Conduct

(1) Evidence of specific instances of the victim's sexual conduct, opinion evidence of the victim's sexual conduct, and reputation evidence of the victim's sexual conduct shall not be admitted under sections 520b to 520g unless and only to the extent that the judge finds that the following proposed evidence is material to a fact at issue in the case and that its inflammatory or prejudicial nature does not outweigh its probative value:

(a) Evidence of the victim's past sexual conduct with the actor.

(b) Evidence of specific instances of sexual activity showing the source or origin of semen, pregnancy, or disease.

FRE 412, the "rape shield" provision, has been revised to expand its scope to cover all types of sexual misconduct proceedings, including civil as well as criminal cases. The amendment also excludes evidence of a victim's "sexual predisposition," not simply "past sexual behavior" as the former rule provided. Do you support this amendment? Why?

§ 6.08   MIXED PROBLEMS

Problem #6-26: Prior Similar Payment

Patricia had cancer treatment and filed her claim with her insurance company. The insurance company paid the claim. When Mallory had the same cancer treatment she filed a claim with the same insurance company. This time, the insurance company denied her claim even though Mallory and Patricia had substantially similar insurance policies. At trial, Mallory wants to offer into evidence the prior payment to Patricia to show that Mallory's treatment should be covered by the insurance company. The insurance company makes several objections. *See Dallis v. Aetna Life Ins. Co.*, 768 F.2d 1303 (11th Cir. 1985).

1. Should the evidence be excluded as under FRE 408?

2. Should the evidence be excluded as irrelevant and prejudicial under FRE 403?

Problem #6-27: The Not So Good Samaritan — Offers & More

While driving his truck to evidence class, Bob Smith diverted his attention from the road to read a text message. He hit the back of Lou Longo's car preparing to turn. Lou exits his car, grabs his neck and moans in pain as Bob runs to him. Bob exclaimed: "Why did you stop? I know you think this is my fault! I should never text and drive! I can't afford to miss any school time so here's $200 to fix your bumper! Here's another $100 to have your neck examined (Bob hands Lou the business card of a classmate who is a chiropractor). Lou kept the money and sued for negligence.

1. Are Bob's $300 payments and his statements admissible? What are Bob's possible objections?

2. Assume that the FRE exclude any evidence of Bob's conduct and statements. Assume further that Bob took the stand and testified: "I'm a careful driver. I never talk on the cell phone, text or do anything that distracts my attention." On cross-examination, Bob is asked about his prior inconsistent statement to Lou after the accident that he was texting? Bob's counsel objects. What result?

3. Assume further that Bob was intoxicated at the time of impact resulting in Lou's death. The prosecutor charges Bob with vehicular homicide. During discussions with the prosecutor, Bob states: "you will never prove I was drunk — I hid the whiskey bottle under a rock near the accident." The state proceeds with the prosecution and offers a recording of Bob's statement about hiding the bottle. Is Bob's statement admissible? What is the basis for objecting to its admission?

§ 6.09 RELEVANT ETHICS RULES

Rule 1.13 Organization As Client

(a) A lawyer employed or retained by an organization represents the organization acting through its duly authorized constituents.

(b) If a lawyer for an organization knows that an officer, employee or other person associated with the organization is engaged in action, intends to act or refuses to act in a matter related to the representation that is a violation of a legal obligation to the organization, or a violation of law that reasonably might be imputed to the organization, and is likely to result in substantial injury to the organization, the lawyer shall proceed as is reasonably necessary in the best interest of the organization. Unless the lawyer reasonably believes that it is not necessary in the best interest of the organization to do so, the lawyer shall refer the matter to higher authority in the organization, including, if warranted by the circumstances, to the highest authority that can act on behalf of the organization as determined by applicable law.

(c) Except as provided in paragraph (d), if

(1) despite the lawyer's efforts in accordance with paragraph (b) the highest authority that can act on behalf of the organization insists upon or fails to address in a timely and appropriate manner an action, or a refusal to act, that is clearly a violation of law, and

(2) the lawyer reasonably believes that the violation is reasonably certain to result in substantial injury to the organization, then the lawyer may reveal information relating to the representation whether or not Rule 1.6 permits such disclosure, but only if and to the extent the lawyer reasonably believes necessary to prevent substantial injury to the organization.

(d) Paragraph (c) shall not apply with respect to the information relating to a lawyer's representation of an organization to investigate an alleged violation of law, or to defend the organization or an officer, employee or other constituent associated with the organization against a claim arising out of an alleged violation of law.

(e) A lawyer who reasonably believes that he or she has been discharged because of the lawyer's actions taken pursuant to paragraph (b) or (c), or who withdraws under circumstances that require or permit the lawyer to take action under either of those paragraphs, shall proceed as the lawyer reasonably believes necessary to assure that the organization's highest authority is informed of the lawyer's discharge or withdrawal.

(f) In dealing with an organization's directors, officers, employees, members, shareholders or other constituents, a lawyer shall explain the identity of the client when the lawyer knows or reasonably should know that the organization's interests are adverse to those of the constituents with whom the lawyer is dealing.

(g) A lawyer representing an organization may also represent any of its directors, officers, employees, members, shareholders or other constituents, subject to the provisions of Rule 1.7. If the organization's consent to the dual representation is required by Rule 1.7, the consent shall be given by an appropriate official of the organization other than the individual who is to be represented, or by the shareholders. Colorado Rules of Prof'l Conduct R. 1.13. *See* MRPC 1.13.

Rule 1.6 Confidentiality of information

(a) A lawyer shall not reveal information relating to the representation of a client unless the client gives informed consent, the disclosure is impliedly authorized in order to carry out the representation, or the disclosure is permitted by paragraph (b).

(b) A lawyer may reveal information relating to the representation of a client to the extent the lawyer reasonably believes necessary:

(1) to prevent reasonably certain death or substantial bodily harm;

(2) to prevent the client from committing a crime or fraud that is reasonably certain to result in substantial injury to the financial interests or property of another and in furtherance of which the client has used or is using the lawyer's services;

(3) to prevent, mitigate, or rectify substantial injury to the financial interests or property of another that is reasonably certain to result or has resulted from the client's commission of a crime or fraud in furtherance of which the client has used the lawyer's services;

(4) to secure legal advice about the lawyer's compliance with these Rules;

(5) to establish a claim or defense on behalf of the lawyer in a controversy between the lawyer and the client, to establish a defense to a criminal charge or civil claim against the lawyer based upon conduct in which the client was involved, or to respond to allegations in any proceeding concerning the lawyer's representation of the client; or

(6) to comply with other law or a court order. Delaware Rules of Prof'l Conduct R. 1.6. *See* MRPC 1.6.

Rule 1.2 Scope of representation

(a) Subject to paragraphs (c) and (d), a lawyer shall abide by a client's decisions concerning the objectives of representation and, as required by Rule 1.4, shall consult with the client as to the means by which they are to be pursued. A lawyer may take such action on behalf of the client as is impliedly authorized to carry out the representation. A lawyer shall abide by a client's decision whether to settle a matter. In a criminal case, the lawyer shall abide by the client's decision, after consultation with the lawyer, as to a plea to be entered, whether to waive jury trial and whether the client will testify.

(b) A lawyer's representation of a client, including representation by appointment, does not constitute an endorsement of the client's political, economic, social or moral views or activities.

(c) A lawyer may limit the scope of the representation if the limitation is reasonable under the circumstances and the client gives informed consent.

(d) A lawyer shall not counsel a client to engage, or assist a client, in conduct that the lawyer knows is criminal or fraudulent, but a lawyer may discuss the legal consequences of any proposed course of conduct with a client and may counsel or assist a client to make a good faith effort to determine the validity, scope, meaning or application of the law. Delaware Rules of Prof'l Conduct R. 1.2. *See* MRPC 1.2.

Rule 3.3 Candor Toward The Tribunal

(a) A lawyer shall not knowingly:

(1) make a false statement of material fact or law to a tribunal or fail to correct a false statement of material fact or law previously made to the tribunal by the lawyer;

(2) fail to disclose to the tribunal legal authority in the controlling jurisdiction known to the lawyer to be directly adverse to the position of the client and not disclosed by opposing counsel; or

(3) offer evidence that the lawyer knows to be false. If a lawyer, the lawyer's client, or witness called by the lawyer has offered material evidence and the lawyer comes to know of its falsity, the lawyer shall take reasonable remedial measures, including, if necessary, disclosure to the tribunal. A lawyer may refuse to offer evidence, other than the testimony of a defendant in a criminal matter, that the lawyer reasonably believes is false.

(b) A lawyer who represents a client in an adjudicative proceeding and who knows that a person intends to engage, is engaging or has engaged in criminal or fraudulent conduct related to the proceeding shall take reasonable remedial measures, including, if necessary, disclosure to the tribunal.

(c) The duties stated in paragraphs (a) and (b) continue to the conclusion of the proceeding, and apply even if compliance requires disclosure of information otherwise protected by Rule 1.6.

(d) In an ex parte proceeding, a lawyer shall inform the tribunal of all material facts known to the lawyer that will enable the tribunal to make an informed decision, whether or not the facts are adverse. Colorado Rules of Prof'l Conduct R. 3.3. *See* MRPC 3.3.

§ 6.10 SUMMARY AND REVIEW

1. What public policies underlie the exclusions of subsequent remedial measures, compromises and offers to compromise, furnishing or offering to pay medical expenses, offers to plead guilty, and the existence or lack of liability insurance?

2. Should the exclusion of subsequent remedial measures apply in strict products liability cases? Explain.

3. Compare the exclusion of evidence relating to compromises and offers to compromise with the exclusion of furnishing or offering to pay medical expenses.

4. Why is evidence of subsequent remedial measures, compromises and offers to compromise, furnishing or offering to pay medical expenses, and the existence of liability insurance permitted for "other purposes"?

Problem #6-28: Megan's Law

The defendant, Buddy Castleman, was charged with sexual battery. At trial, evidence of his prior sexual misconduct on three separate occasions was offered by the prosecution. The following exchange occurred at trial:

DEFENSE COUNSEL: Your Honor, I object to the proposed evidence and ask to approach the bench.

JUDGE: You may.

DEFENSE COUNSEL: (at sidebar) Your Honor, this evidence is highly and unfairly prejudicial, given its close similarity to the current alleged offense. It should be excluded pursuant to Rule 403 as unfairly prejudicial evidence.

PROSECUTOR: Your Honor, the evidence is very relevant to determining whether the defendant committed the crime in this case, and is admissible pursuant to Rule 414.

You are the judge. Does FRE 403 apply? How does it relate to FRE 414? How would you rule? *See, e.g., United States v. Castillo,* 131 F.3d 767 (10th Cir. 1998).

Problem #6-29: "Spilled Ink"

Darryl Defendant, while sitting in an 8:30 a.m. class, was preoccupied with his plans for spring break. He absentmindedly spilled ink on Patti Plaintiff, a chemist by training. The ink was toxic and caused a serious adverse reaction. Patti sued Darryl and the Drummond Ink Co., the manufacturer of the ink. At trial, Patti testifies.

PLAINTIFF'S ATTORNEY: Patti, can you compare the defendant Drummond's ink formula at the time of the spill with the formula used after the incident in question?

DEFENDANT'S ATTORNEY: Objection.

1. What is the basis for the objection? What ruling and why?

A: Yes. It was changed to reduce its toxicity.

PLAINTIFF'S ATTORNEY: Have you ever known Darryl to spill ink before?

DEFENDANT'S ATTORNEY: Objection.

2. What is the basis for the objection? What ruling and why?

A: Yes, he has spilled ink on at least five different occasions.

PLAINTIFF'S ATTORNEY: Patti, what is defendant Darryl's reputation in the community for carelessness?

DEFENDANT'S ATTORNEY: Objection.

3. What is the basis for the objection? What ruling and why?

A: Darryl is known for always being in a hurry.

PLAINTIFF'S ATTORNEY: What happened immediately after the spill?

DEFENDANT'S ATTORNEY: Objection.

4. What is the basis for the objection? What ruling and why?

A: Darryl said to me that he'd pay for my visit to the doctor.

PLAINTIFF'S ATTORNEY: Did anything else occur after the incident?

DEFENDANT'S ATTORNEY: Objection.

5. What is the basis for the objection? What ruling and why?

A: Yes. Darryl said to me that when he doesn't concentrate on where he is going, he often spills ink or just bumps into people.

PLAINTIFF'S ATTORNEY: Patti, how carefully were you behaving at the time of the incident?

DEFENDANT'S ATTORNEY: Objection.

6. What is the basis for the objection? What ruling and why?

A: Me? I'm always careful.

PLAINTIFF'S ATTORNEY: What occurred immediately preceding the incident?

DEFENDANT'S ATTORNEY: Objection.

7. What is the basis for the objection? What ruling and why?

A: Well, I saw the defendant Darryl running away from some guy, at whom he had just yelled.

PLAINTIFF'S ATTORNEY: How careful have you been in the past?

DEFENDANT'S ATTORNEY: Objection.

8. What is the basis for the objection? What ruling and why?

A: As I said, I'm generally very careful. I've only been careless on two occasions, when I accidentally caused automobile collisions.

Problem #6-30: Acker Rides Again

Acker was being driven by Calvin Cabbie in his cab to a destination in another part of the city. It was a Saturday afternoon and traffic was light.

Cabbie: (looking in the mirror) You look familiar. Are you Gomer Pyle? Robert Goulet? Jim Palmer? Pete Rose?

Acker: No. Have a light?

Cabbie: No, don't smoke.

Acker: No, I mean . . . never mind.

Cabbie: Are ya sure I don't know you?

Crash! The car veered off the road, knocked over a vegetable stand on the sidewalk, and side-swiped a parked car with a person in it.

Calvin Cabbie apologized profusely to Acker, saying, "Don't worry, I'll pay for your medical expenses if you agree not to sue my boss! I must not have been paying attention to what I was doing."

At the trial of *Acker v. Cabbie and Orange Cab Co.*, a suit seeking damages for the personal injuries which resulted from the driver's alleged negligence, Acker testified as follows:

PLAINTIFF'S ATTORNEY: What happened on September 3rd at approximately 4:00 p.m.?

A: I entered the defendant's cab for a ride home from work. From the minute he picked me up on Broadway and 2nd until he ran off the road ten minutes later, knocking over a vegetable stand and a parked car, he drove like a maniac.

DEFENDANT'S ATTORNEY: Objection!

1. What is the basis for the objection? What is the proper ruling?

PLAINTIFF'S ATTORNEY: What do you know about Calvin Cabbie?

A: I know that he was in five previous accidents, all resulting in injuries.

DEFENDANT'S ATTORNEY: Objection!

2. What is the basis for the objection? What is the proper ruling?

PLAINTIFF'S ATTORNEY: What happened after you entered the cab?

A: I told him to drive slowly. I always tell cabbies that. He said, "I always drive slowly." Hah! And I'm Joe Dimaggio!

DEFENDANT'S ATTORNEY: Objection!

3. What is the basis for the objection? What is the proper ruling?

PLAINTIFF'S ATTORNEY: After the crash, what happened?

A: The cabbie and I jumped out of the cab. He saw I was limping and offered to pay my medical expenses. He said he wasn't looking at the road. He also said he had been drinking at Shooters just before he picked me up.

DEFENDANT'S ATTORNEY: Objection!

4. What is the basis for the objection? What is the proper ruling?

PLAINTIFF'S ATTORNEY: What happened at 4:45 p.m.?

A: This was about forty-five minutes after the accident and I had told him I was going to sue. The cabbie, Calvin, came up to me and said, "Look, a lawsuit will be messy; I'd lose my cabbie license because I had several shots of whiskey, and could possibly go to jail as well. Yet, if it went to trial, I might have a decent shot at winning because you were talking to me. So why don't I pay for your lost time and overall suffering, say $2,000, and we'll call it even — no lawsuit?"

DEFENDANT'S ATTORNEY: Objection!

5. What is the basis for the objection? What is the proper ruling?

PLAINTIFF'S ATTORNEY: What else, if anything, happened at that time?

A: I learned that the cabbie and his company were both insured, which tells you why Calvin drove the way he did.

DEFENDANT'S ATTORNEY: Objection!

6. Basis? Ruling?

Chapter 7

THE EXAMINATION AND IMPEACHMENT OF WITNESSES [FRE 607–615]

CHAPTER FRAMEWORK: This chapter really has two distinct parts: the examination of witnesses, which is both a strategic art and an evidentiary component subject to a variety of rules and norms, and the impeachment of witnesses, which is a substantive component of evidence law as well as an integral part of the adversary process. In essence, the impeachment of witnesses, meaning attacks on a witness's truthfulness or accuracy, occurs during witness examination and is like a "mini-trial" about the witness within the overall process. The examination of witnesses has special "form" requirements, just like ballroom dancing. This is particularly true on direct examination, where leading questions are generally prohibited. Impeachment has its own structure and limits. In effect, it is a different "dance," occurring in two stages — intrinsic, when the witness to be impeached is asked questions, and extrinsic, when new evidence, such as documents or witnesses, are offered in evidence instead of just questions. Following the impeachment of a witness is a corollary stage, the rehabilitation of these witnesses, meaning accrediting the witnesses' character for truthfulness.

WHY ARE THE CONCEPTS IN THIS CHAPTER IMPORTANT? The heart of many trials and an important type of proof is witness testimony. Good trial lawyers learn the art of direct, cross, and redirect examinations. It takes much practice and skill. Impeachment rules are often complex and must be understood both in contrast to rules governing the admission of evidence offered to prove issues in the case, such as evidence of a party's character, and compared internally to other types of impeachment.

CONNECTIONS: Witness examination connects to real world cases and to the public's perception of law in action through courtroom dramas, especially those publicized in the media. The intersection of the real world and the media occurs when the public, serving as jurors, create expectations about attorneys and trials based on views formed by watching generations of law shows and films. In addition, witness examination connects to other substantive areas of evidence law through objections. Without understanding the substantive areas of the law, attorneys would not be able to protect and advance their cases through objections.

CHAPTER OUTLINE:

I. The Examination of Witnesses

    A. Who is a witness?

        1. Prerequisite — FRE 601 — ability to understand the truth

      2. General methodology — questioning

      3. Surrogate witness — hearsay declarant

    B. Control over witness examination

      1. Primarily in the hands of the judge — judicial discretion

      2. Some cross-examination by right

      3. Witnesses generally can be excluded from the courtroom when not testifying

    C. Stages of witness examination

      1. Direct examination — proponent of witness questions

        a. General form: non-leading questions

        b. Objections: leading; compound; asked and answered; etc.

        c. Witness forgets: refresh recollection (memory)

      2. Cross-examination — opponent of witness questions

        a. General form: leading questions

        b. Objections: argumentative; compound; vague; etc.

      3. Re-direct examination — second opportunity for direct examination by proponent to clarify and respond to cross-examination

II. The Impeachment of Witnesses

    A. Attacking witness truth or accuracy

    B. Two stages

      1. Intrinsically — from the witness's mouth

        a. Forms: contradiction; bias; convictions; untruthful prior acts; testimonial capacities; prior inconsistent statements (self-contradiction)

        b. Contours

      2. Extrinsically — other evidence

        a. Rule — must be non-collateral or important

        b. Forms

        c. Contours

III. The Rehabilitation of Witnesses

    A. Follows impeachment

    B. Forms of rehabilitation

      1. Prior consistent statements to rebut

      2. New witness testifying about character traits

IV. Other

* * * * *

RELEVANT EVIDENCE RULES

Rule 607. Who May Impeach a Witness

Any party, including the party that called the witness, may attack the witness's credibility.

Rule 608. A Witness's Character for Truthfulness or Untruthfulness

(a) **Reputation or Opinion Evidence.** A witness's credibility may be attacked or supported by testimony about the witness's reputation for having a character for truthfulness or untruthfulness, or by testimony in the form of an opinion about that character. But evidence of truthful character is admissible only after the witness's character for truthfulness has been attacked.

(b) **Specific Instances of Conduct.** Except for a criminal conviction under Rule 609, extrinsic evidence is not admissible to prove specific instances of a witness's conduct in order to attack or support the witness's character for truthfulness. But the court may, on cross-examination, allow them to be inquired into if they are probative of the character for truthfulness or untruthfulness of:

(1) the witness; or

(2) another witness whose character the witness being cross-examined has testified about.

By testifying on another matter, a witness does not waive any privilege against self-incrimination for testimony that relates only to the witness's character for truthfulness.

Rule 609. Impeachment by Evidence of a Criminal Conviction

(a) **In General.** The following rules apply to attacking a witness's character for truthfulness by evidence of a criminal conviction:

(1) for a crime that, in the convicting jurisdiction, was punishable by death or by imprisonment for more than one year, the evidence:

(A) must be admitted, subject to Rule 403, in a civil case or in a criminal case in which the witness is not a defendant; and

(B) must be admitted in a criminal case in which the witness is a defendant, if the probative value of the evidence outweighs its prejudicial effect to that defendant; and

(2) for any crime regardless of the punishment, the evidence must be admitted if the court can readily determine that establishing the elements of the crime required proving — or the witness's admitting — a dishonest act or false statement.

(b) **Limit on Using the Evidence After 10 Years.** This subdivision (b) applies if more than 10 years have passed since the witness's conviction or release from confinement for it, whichever is later. Evidence of the conviction is admissible only if:

    (1) its probative value, supported by specific facts and circumstances, substantially outweighs its prejudicial effect; and

    (2) the proponent gives an adverse party reasonable written notice of the intent to use it so that the party has a fair opportunity to contest its use.

  (c) **Effect of a Pardon, Annulment, or Certificate of Rehabilitation.** Evidence of a conviction is not admissible if:

    (1) the conviction has been the subject of a pardon, annulment, certificate of rehabilitation, or other equivalent procedure based on a finding that the person has been rehabilitated, and the person has not been convicted of a later crime punishable by death or by imprisonment for more than one year; or

    (2) the conviction has been the subject of a pardon, annulment, or other equivalent procedure based on a finding of innocence.

  (d) **Juvenile Adjudications.** Evidence of a juvenile adjudication is admissible under this rule only if:

    (1) it is offered in a criminal case;

    (2) the adjudication was of a witness other than the defendant;

    (3) an adult's conviction for that offense would be admissible to attack the adult's credibility; and

    (4) admitting the evidence is necessary to fairly determine guilt or innocence.

  (e) **Pendency of an Appeal.** A conviction that satisfies this rule is admissible even if an appeal is pending. Evidence of the pendency is also admissible.

Rule 610. Religious Beliefs or Opinions

Evidence of a witness's religious beliefs or opinions is not admissible to attack or support the witness's credibility.

Rule 611. Mode and Order of Examining Witnesses and Presenting Evidence

  (a) **Control by the Court; Purposes.** The court should exercise reasonable control over the mode and order of examining witnesses and presenting evidence so as to:

    (1) make those procedures effective for determining the truth;

    (2) avoid wasting time; and

    (3) protect witnesses from harassment or undue embarrassment.

  (b) **Scope of Cross-Examination.** Cross-examination should not go beyond the subject matter of the direct examination and matters affecting the witness's credibility. The court may allow inquiry into additional matters as if on direct examination.

  (c) **Leading Questions.** Leading questions should not be used on direct examination except as necessary to develop the witness's testimony. Ordinarily, the court should allow leading questions:

(1) on cross-examination; and

(2) when a party calls a hostile witness, an adverse party, or a witness identified with an adverse party.

Rule 612. Writing Used to Refresh a Witness's Memory

(a) **Scope.** This rule gives an adverse party certain options when a witness uses a writing to refresh memory:

(1) while testifying; or

(2) before testifying, if the court decides that justice requires the party to have those options.

(b) **Adverse Party's Options; Deleting Unrelated Matter.** Unless 18 U.S.C. § 3500 provides otherwise in a criminal case, an adverse party is entitled to have the writing produced at the hearing, to inspect it, to cross-examine the witness about it, and to introduce in evidence any portion that relates to the witness's testimony. If the producing party claims that the writing includes unrelated matter, the court must examine the writing in camera, delete any unrelated portion, and order that the rest be delivered to the adverse party. Any portion deleted over objection must be preserved for the record.

(c) **Failure to Produce or Deliver the Writing.** If a writing is not produced or is not delivered as ordered, the court may issue any appropriate order. But if the prosecution does not comply in a criminal case, the court must strike the witness's testimony or — if justice so requires — declare a mistrial.

Rule 613. Witness's Prior Statement

(a) **Showing or Disclosing the Statement During Examination.** When examining a witness about the witness's prior statement, a party need not show it or disclose its contents to the witness. But the party must, on request, show it or disclose its contents to an adverse party's attorney.

(b) **Extrinsic Evidence of a Prior Inconsistent Statement.** Extrinsic evidence of a witness's prior inconsistent statement is admissible only if the witness is given an opportunity to explain or deny the statement and an adverse party is given an opportunity to examine the witness about it, or if justice so requires. This subdivision (b) does not apply to an opposing party's statement under Rule 801(d)(2).

Rule 614. Court's Calling or Examining a Witness

(a) **Calling.** The court may call a witness on its own or at a party's request. Each party is entitled to cross-examine the witness.

(b) **Examining.** The court may examine a witness regardless of who calls the witness.

(c) **Objections.** A party may object to the court's calling or examining a witness either at that time or at the next opportunity when the jury is not present.

Rule 615. Excluding Witnesses

At a party's request, the court must order witnesses excluded so that they cannot hear other witnesses' testimony. Or the court may do so on its own. But this rule does not authorize excluding:

(a) a party who is a natural person;

(b) an officer or employee of a party that is not a natural person, after being designated as the party's representative by its attorney;

(c) a person whose presence a party shows to be essential to presenting the party's claim or defense; or

(d) a person authorized by statute to be present.

§ 7.01 THE EXAMINATION OF WITNESSES [FRE 607–615]

[A] Overview

As explained in the Advisory Committee's Note to FRE 611:

> "Spelling out detailed rules to govern the mode and order of interrogating witnesses and presenting evidence is neither desirable nor feasible. The ultimate responsibility for the effective working of the adversary system rests with the judge."

Witness testimony, sometimes referred to as "viva voce," or "by voice," is one of the most important types of evidence at trial. Witnesses produce potentially powerful evidence and, as a consequence, witness examination sometimes becomes a "trial within a trial," much like the individual battles within a war. Because of the significance of witness testimony, special rules have been adopted to govern it. Many trials are won or lost on the nature and impact of witness testimony and how the attorneys negotiate the rules governing the admissibility of testimony.

The examination of witnesses is placed by the FRE squarely within the control of the judge. Under FRE 611, the judge has the discretion to decide whether to allow witness testimony, and if so, in what form and at what time. For example, the judge has the authority to prohibit the use of leading questions on direct examination, to restrict the length of time for cross-examination and to limit the scope of cross-examination. *See* FRE 611. Of course, the FRE provide the judge with guidance and impose a variety of limits on judicial discretion, such as the exclusion of hearsay.

Background Box: Demeanor

The demeanor of witnesses is important to the weight accorded their testimony. In trial, it is especially important for jurors to see the witnesses' faces and body language as they testify. It is not what the witness says that counts the most, but rather how they say it that matters most. Studies back

> up the importance of nonverbal cues.

The FRE impose several different types of restrictions on witness testimony. These restrictions range from who may testify (i.e., witness competency), to the substance of the testimony, to the form of the questions and answers during witness examination. Competency restrictions, such as those imposed on judge and jurors as witnesses, help to maintain the fundamental fairness of the trial process. Substantive limits are utilized to deter suspect evidence, such as hearsay, propensity character evidence, and settlement offers. Form limitations foster fairness and efficiency in the stylized "dance" that constitutes the dialogue between examiner and witness. Restrictions on attorneys' questions include prohibitions against leading and compound questions, questions that already have been asked and answered, questions that assume facts not in evidence, and argumentative questions. Limitations on witnesses' answers include the barring of narrative and nonresponsive answers.

[B]   General Principles

The impact and value of a witness's testimony stem from the witness's testimonial capacities, i.e., perception, memory, narration, and sincerity (see § 7.02[B][6]). The proponent of a witness will want to show that the witness accurately observed, remembered, and reported the events at issue in good faith; at the same time, the adverse party may choose to challenge one or more of the witness's testimonial capacities.

A novice attorney often wishes to "score points" or "hit a home run," particularly on cross-examination. However, the experienced trial lawyer knows that a cross-examination rarely causes a witness to confess an egregious error, let alone admit to guilt or liability. Thus, the experienced attorney generally looks to make only a few salient points before sitting down.

An attorney may follow various strategies with witness testimony, particularly when it is recognized that evidence "paints a picture," and that there are many ways to paint a single picture. Trial practice strategies may include the tone of voice that attorneys adopt with witnesses, the place where attorneys stand when examining witnesses, in which direction attorneys face or how they frame particular questions. Much of what a jury receives from testimony lies in its nonverbal subtext and not in the words themselves. Consequently, more and more trial lawyers are paying attention to the relationship between substantive evidence and how it is delivered to the jury by witnesses. Some attorneys hire jury consultants, who assist with jury selection or suggest how to approach the witnesses at trial in the most persuasive manner.

One trial strategy followed by most trial lawyers is embodied in FRE 615. This rule permits attorneys (or the judge, *sua sponte*) to request that prospective witnesses be excluded from the courtroom when other witnesses are testifying. This rule is commonly known among trial attorneys as "the rule on witnesses." Attorneys sometimes use verbal shorthand in asking the judge "to invoke the rule." Despite a judge's invoking the rule, certain witnesses must be permitted to remain in the courtroom while other witnesses testify: the parties; certain experts; and persons whose presence is authorized by statute, such as the victims of crimes.

[C] Witnesses — Testimony *Viva Voce*

A witness is generally someone who testifies at trial. The term, viva voce, essentially meaning "by voice," is sometimes used to describe witness testimony. The definition of a witness can be expanded to include witness-surrogates, which is effectively what hearsay declarants are — out-of-court witnesses. These declarants are not technically witnesses, testifying under oath from the witness stand, but they offer viva voce information nonetheless.

Under early common law, there were many exclusions or incompetencies preventing people from testifying as witnesses. These exclusions were based on categorical assessments of truth-telling, such as that of felons, who were thought to be untruthful because of their convictions. In modern times, these disabilities were largely eliminated, moving the disabling factor, such as a felony conviction, to become part of the impeachment of a witness.

FRE 601 provides for essentially one prerequisite to becoming a witness at a trial in federal court — understanding what it means to tell the truth. This allows persons who understand what the truth is, but intentionally or recklessly ignore it, to testify. It does prevent persons from testifying who are too young to know what truth-telling means, or suffering from a form of mental illness or dementia that undermines truth-telling.

While it seems obvious that impeachment is preceded by a person becoming a witness, it is all too easy to overlook who is or has testified. Thus, preemptive attacks on prospective witnesses are impermissible but can occur if the attorney is not on guard.

[D] The Stages of Witness Testimony

1. Direct Examination

Witness examination usually unfolds in a ritualistic ordering. The proponent of the witness first calls the witness to testify on direct examination. After direct examination, the opposing party has the opportunity to conduct a cross-examination. FRE 611(b) provides that cross-examination "should be limited to the subject matter of the direct examination and matters affecting the credibility of the witness."

The function of direct examination is to elicit information that is relevant to the cause of action, claim, or defense. The proponent offers witnesses who are expected to testify about facts that support the proponent's case. Generally, these are friendly witnesses, who are aligned with the proponent's interests. Occasionally, the proponent has no choice but to call a hostile witness, one who is aligned with an opposing party. Such a witness may try to include unfriendly testimony in addition to the answers sought.

The testimony of a witness on direct examination can be viewed as consisting of three parts: background; scene; and action. The "background" component establishes who the witness is. The goal is to portray the witness as a three-dimensional person and not merely a blank conduit of information. Juries and judges can identify more with a whole person than with an empty name with nothing behind it. The background also helps lay a foundation of authenticity (a showing that this witness is who she says she is) and of credibility (that this witness is believable). Simply put, background facts make the story more realistic. Common background questions address the witness's age, employment, education, and family status.

The "scene" component of testimony is usually the locus or place in which the action occurs. If the case is a prosecution for bank robbery, the scene is the bank. If the case is a domestic family dispute, the scene is the family house. If the case involves securities fraud, the scene is where the fraud was committed. The scene component, while very important, is too often given short shrift, especially by novice trial lawyers. Many attorneys jump right into the action part of the testimony instead.

The "action" component is usually the focal point of the testimony and is readily identifiable. In a bank robbery, the action is the robbery itself. In a family dispute, the action is the actual dispute.

The prohibition against leading questions on direct examination has several rationales. One reason is to allow the jury to hear the testimony directly from the witness and not from the attorney's mouth. If leading questions were permitted, an attorney could present the entire factual story through leading questions, with the witness serving as nothing more than a stage prop. A second reason is that witnesses are considered to be aligned with the party who called them to the witness stand, and, consequently, there is no need for the attorney to lead the witness through the testimony. The assumption about witness alignment, however, is not always accurate. As noted earlier in this chapter, a party sometimes must call a witness even though the person has a bias in favor of the opposing side. For example, an eyewitness with important information may be a family member or neighbor of the opposing party. If the witness on direct examination is considered to be hostile to the examiner, the examiner may seek the judge's permission "to lead the witness."

The rule prohibiting the use of leading questions on direct examination is subject to several exceptions, in addition to the one for hostile witnesses. Leading questions may be appropriate for a witness who is aged, infirm, or a child. Thus, FRE 611(c) provides that leading questions are allowed on direct if they are necessary to develop the witness's testimony. Whether to permit the use of leading questions on direct examination is entirely within the discretion of the court.

"Objection, Your Honor. Counsel is leading the witness."

<u>Illustration</u>

PROSECUTOR: (on direct examination) Wally, where do you live?

DEFENSE COUNSEL: Objection! Leading.

JUDGE: Objection overruled.

[The judge most likely ruled in this manner because the question was not leading. Like most "where," "why," "when," or "how" questions, this question does not suggest an answer. Further, the question properly elicits background information.]

A: I live on the corner of 4th and Overland Street.

PROSECUTOR: What happened on July 10th, at 7:00 p.m.?

A: I saw Johnny B. Badd shoot and kill Louie Ratatooie.

PROSECUTOR: Did Johnny shoot Louie with a revolver?

DEFENSE COUNSEL: Objection. Leading.

JUDGE: Objection sustained.

[The judge probably noted that the question suggests an answer: that Johnny shot Louie with a revolver. There is no reason under FRE 611 to lead the witness during this portion of the direct examination.]

PROSECUTOR: So Johnny shot Louie dead? And after the shooting, in which direction did Johnny drive away and where did he hide the gun?

DEFENSE COUNSEL: Objection on three grounds, Your Honor — asked and answered, compound question, and assuming facts not in evidence.

[If the judge permits an explanation, probably at a sidebar, the defense counsel might elaborate as follows. "First, the question of whether Johnny shot Louie dead has been asked and answered. Second, the question asked by the prosecutor about the events after the shooting is objectionable because it is really two separate questions posed in compound form. The witness was asked where did Johnny drive and where did Johnny hide the gun? Finally, the question is objectionable because it assumes facts not in evidence — that Johnny drove away (he may have walked, taken a boat, or even remained at the scene) and that he hid the gun (he may not have hidden it at all)."]

2. Cross-Examination

Unlike its media portrayals, cross-examination is not always used as a vehicle for attempting to destroy the witness's credibility. While that is one purpose of cross-examination, other purposes exist. These purposes include: (1) testing the witness's testimonial capacities (perception, memory, narration, and sincerity); (2) filling gaps in the testimony or evidence; and (3) corroborating parts of the cross-examiner's case. It cannot be overemphasized that a good cross-examination does not always include a saber-rattling, earth-shattering denunciation of the witness. To the contrary, a cross-examination may be quiet and even supportive, particularly if the witness on cross-examination may be able to affirmatively assist the cross-examiner's case by corroborating facts or filling in missing details.

Cross-examinations are properly stocked with leading questions. It is an oft-stated maxim that examiners should not ask a question to which they do not know the answer. A question such as, "Why did you do that?" or "How can you testify that . . . ?" invites a new and possibly harmful response by the witness, one that could surprise the examiner and greatly damage the case. In addition, such a non-leading question loses the advantage of leading by permitting the witness to explain, bolster, or augment the testimony previously given on direct examination.

Arguing with witnesses about major points of the witness's testimony is usually a vain attempt to get the witness to recant what the witness stated on direct examination. It is more useful to make smaller points about which the attorney already knows the answer. The attorney can argue the salient central questions (such as guilt or liability), using inferences and logic, in the closing argument to the jury. It is the rare case, indeed (except in films or on television), in which a witness collapses on the stand with bowed head, saying "Yes, you're right. I will finally, after all of these years, admit I did it. I am the culprit who committed the evil deed!"

Illustration

An eyewitness to an automobile accident, Lucy Lubner, testified on direct examination about how the accident occurred. Lucy is now on cross-examination.

DEFENDANT'S ATTORNEY: Now, Lucy, you say the accident occurred at approximately 5:00 p.m.?

A: Yes, about that time.

DEFENDANT'S ATTORNEY: You were on your way home after working a six-hour shift in the town mill?

A: Yes, I work from 10:00 a.m. to 5:00 p.m. on Fridays.

DEFENDANT'S ATTORNEY: Is it fair to say that your work requires you to stand over a moving machine for most of the day?

A: Yes, that's right.

DEFENDANT'S ATTORNEY: While you are standing over that machine, you are also operating it, right?

A: Yes.

DEFENDANT'S ATTORNEY: Now this accident occurred on December 18th, true?

A: Yes.

DEFENDANT'S ATTORNEY: The sun was setting at that time, right?

A: Yes.

DEFENDANT'S ATTORNEY: Some of the cars around you had their lights on.

A: Yes.

> [This cross-examination offers inferences that can be argued and aggregated for the jury during the closing argument.]

3. Redirect Examination

Following the cross-examination, the proponent may conduct a redirect examination. As its name implies, a "redirect" examination is a variant of direct and is governed by rules similar to the initial direct examination, particularly with respect to the rule prohibiting leading questions. Redirect examination is not an opportunity for the mere reiteration of points raised on direct. Instead, its purpose is to allow a rebuttal or exploration of points raised on cross-examination. If a party starts to repeat questions asked on direct examination, the opponent should object, stating that the questions have been "asked and answered." After the redirect examination, judges sometimes permit a re-cross-examination. A re-cross-examination must relate to the issues raised on redirect; it may not simply reiterate the initial cross-exam.

Background Box: Trial Tactics — Witness Examination

Attorneys use a variety of tactics when examining witnesses. On direct examination, it is usually the witness who is the star and who the attorney makes sure commands the spotlight. On cross-examination, it is generally the opposite — it is the attorney who is really testifying, through leading questions. On cross-examination, there is a tendency for new attorneys to constantly try to attack a witness, even when the witness could provide helpful information by corroborating some points of the examiner's case. Also, new attorneys go for the ultimate grand slam — witness recantation or the like — which rarely occurs. Instead, the new attorney should try to end each examination on an up note, and then do the toughest thing — sit down.

[E]   Testimonial Objections

A wide variety of objections can be raised concerning a witness's testimony, particularly objections to the form of the examiners' questions. Some of the more common objections, and brief definitions of those objections, are offered below:

1. *Leading questions:* questions that suggest an answer. Questions that call for a "yes" or "no" response are often leading (e.g., questions that begin with "Was," "Were," "Did," "Does," "Have," or "Had" are often leading).

2. *Asked and answered questions:* questions that have already been asked of the witness and answered.

3. *Compound questions:* questions that actually incorporate two or more questions, generally, in a single sentence.

4. *Questions assuming facts not in evidence:* questions that assume the existence of facts not yet testified to by a witness or otherwise introduced into evidence.

5. *Argumentative questions:* questions that are phrased in such a way they merely engage the witness in improper argument.

6. *Questions calling for speculation:* questions asking for information beyond the witness's personal knowledge or for an inadmissible opinion. *See* FRE 701 and 702.

7. *Non-responsive answers:* answers by witnesses that do not respond to the examiner's question.

8. *Narrative answers:* answers by witnesses that exceed the scope of the questions put to them. A party may object to a question that would result in an objectionable answer; in that case, the objection would be phrased as "Calls for a Narrative Answer."

Background Box: Objection Leading!

The leading question objection is one of the most common as well as one of the most confounding. While questions calling for "yes or no" responses are usually leading, this category embraces all questions that suggest an answer.

Direct Examination Problems

Problem #7-1: Form is Everything

Plaintiff sues defendant for breach of contract. Plaintiff is questioned at trial on direct examination. Use the testimonial objections in acting as a lawyer in this problem.

PLAINTIFF'S ATTORNEY: Would you state your name for the record?

A: Alfreida Cohen.

PLAINTIFF'S ATTORNEY: You live in San Francisco, right?

DEFENDANT'S ATTORNEY: Objection!

1. Basis? Ruling?

PLAINTIFF'S ATTORNEY: Do you live in San Francisco, or somewhere else?

DEFENDANT'S ATTORNEY: Objection!

2. Basis? Ruling?

PLAINTIFF'S ATTORNEY: Where were you on the night of June 1, 1992, at 9:00 p.m.?

DEFENDANT'S ATTORNEY: Objection!

3. Basis? Ruling?

A: I was at the Burger King, having a candlelight dinner.

PLAINTIFF'S ATTORNEY: What did you see and hear at that time?

DEFENDANT'S ATTORNEY: Objection!

4. Basis? Ruling?

A: I saw the defendant selling goods to my competitor.

PLAINTIFF'S ATTORNEY: So you saw the defendant selling goods to someone else?

DEFENDANT'S ATTORNEY: Objection!

5. Basis? Ruling?

PLAINTIFF'S ATTORNEY: After you saw the defendant with your competitor, what happened next?

A: They left and I went to my office. Later that week I saw the defendant's sister. Now she's in business with defendant and —

DEFENDANT'S ATTORNEY: Objection!

6. Basis? Ruling? *narrative*

Problem #7-2: More Form

At trial in a civil conversion case, the plaintiff testifies on direct examination:

PLAINTIFF'S ATTORNEY: When you saw the defendant walk by your house at 3:30 p.m., on July 5, what did you do?

DEFENDANT'S ATTORNEY: Objection!

1. Basis? Ruling? *assume fact*

A: I watched him.

PLAINTIFF'S ATTORNEY: What happened at 3:30 p.m. on July 5th?

DEFENDANT'S ATTORNEY: Objection!

2. Basis? Ruling? *ask & answer*

Plaintiff: I saw the defendant walk by my house.

PLAINTIFF'S ATTORNEY: Did the defendant, who you say walked by your house at 3:30 p.m., have anything in his hands?

DEFENDANT'S ATTORNEY: Objection!

3. Basis? Ruling? *leading / ask & answer / assuming fact*

A: Yes, what appeared to be a glass statue.

PLAINTIFF'S ATTORNEY: Do you think the defendant looked suspicious or shifty?

DEFENDANT'S ATTORNEY: Objection!

4. Basis? Ruling? *leading / improp- opinion => 602 violation*

A: Yes, definitely.

PLAINTIFF'S ATTORNEY: Where exactly were you when you observed the defendant?

DEFENDANT'S ATTORNEY: Objection!

5. Basis? Ruling? ask & answer

A: I was on my front porch.

PLAINTIFF'S ATTORNEY: So where were you when you saw the defendant?

A: At first I was still in front of my house. Then I went inside to telephone the police. I was steaming! By 4:00 p.m., the police came and I had calmed down some. It took until 5:00 p.m. before I was fully relaxed. I did drink a beer at 4:50 p.m., but then I was itching to . . .

DEFENDANT'S ATTORNEY: Objection!

6. Basis? Ruling? narrative

Cross-Examination Problems

Problem #7-3: Scope

Bam was employed as a truck driver for a mouthwash company. After detouring during a delivery to visit his friend, Barney, Bam was involved in an accident with a pedestrian, Fred. The only issue at trial was whether Bam was acting outside of the scope of his employment at the time of the accident. At trial, Bam testified for the plaintiff, Fred. Bam was asked only one question — whether he was on duty at the time of the accident. On cross-examination, Bam was asked several questions:

DEFENDANT'S ATTORNEY: Bam, were you distracted at the time of the crash by your friend, Pebbles, yelling at you from the sidewalk?

PLAINTIFF'S ATTORNEY: Objection!

1. Should the question be allowed? leading → overruled b/c ✓ on cross

DEFENDANT'S ATTORNEY: Bam, were you drinking any alcoholic beverages immediately prior to the crash?

PLAINTIFF'S ATTORNEY: Objection! assuming (611) facts

2. Is this question permissible?

DEFENDANT'S ATTORNEY: Describe what you saw immediately after the crash occurred.

PLAINTIFF'S ATTORNEY: Objection!

3. How should the court rule?

Problem #7-4: Succa Mucca Rucca . . .

Arsenic, a prominent local banker, sues Lacey, the mayor of the town, for slander. Lacey called Arsenic a "succa mucca rucca cheat whose business deals are all criminal." At trial, plaintiff Arsenic calls his business partner, Sharon, to testify. Sharon testifies that Arsenic is an honest businessman whose truthfulness, in her opinion, is beyond reproach. Sharon is asked the following question on cross-examination:

> DEFENDANT'S ATTORNEY: Sharon, is it true that you cheated on your civil service examination last year?

> PLAINTIFF'S ATTORNEY: Objection! The question is beyond the scope of the direct examination, your honor.

What is the proper ruling on this objection? Why?

Redirect Examination Problem

Problem #7-5: Wanda Witness

Wanda Witness is asked on cross-examination whether she had taken her employer's car home with her three years earlier without his permission. Wanda answered in the affirmative. If Wanda's attorney stands up to do a redirect examination, which of the following questions would be proper? Explain.

1. Question: Wanda, isn't it true that you returned an overpayment made to you of $500 just last year? X advo. X allowed

2. Question: Wanda, were you convicted of any crime for that incident? X leading + beyond

3. Question: Wanda, had your employer been convicted of any crimes that you know of? X unrelated to cross

4. Question: How often do you attend Church? X 610 cannot inject relig.

5. Question: Can you please explain the circumstances surrounding your taking your employer's car? ✓

[F]   Refreshing the Witness's Memory

Stuck somewhat incongruously in the middle of the impeachment rules, FRE 612 concerns refreshing a witness's memory. Refreshing a witness's memory most often occurs on direct examination. In those circumstances, refreshing memory is entirely distinct from impeachment. In fact, it in effect bolsters the witness's credibility by helping the witness remember events or occurrences more accurately. Sometimes, however, the term is used on cross-examination to attack a witness's purported loss of memory. Thus, counsel may ask a witness who has just testified inconsistently with a prior statement: "Let me refresh your memory. Didn't you say X at your deposition six months ago?" In these circumstances, impeachment is counsel's goal.

Under FRE 612, a witness's memory may be prodded by a wide variety of things, including items that are inadmissible at trial. Thus, the items used for refreshing memory are not subject to the rules of authentication or admissibility. Witnesses may have their memory refreshed by inadmissible hearsay or the equivalent.

Problem on Refreshing a Witness's Memory

Problem #7-6: "Sammy Says"

Sammy testifies for the plaintiff in a complex commercial litigation action. He is asked on direct examination about a particular business meeting the previous year and he answers, "Hmmmm, I really don't remember it." Counsel then shows Sammy the notes Sammy took during the meeting.

1. Can plaintiff's counsel give Sammy his own meeting notes to refresh his memory? What is the proper procedure by which to refresh recollection? Can Sammy read the notes to the jury? 612 refresh memory

2. Do the notes have to be authenticated?

3. Now assume that the notes were not written by Sammy, but by someone else at the meeting. Can Sammy still rely on the notes to refresh his memory about the meeting? Can Sammy read the notes to the jury?

4. If Sammy reviews his notes during the direct examination, can he be questioned about the notes on cross-examination?

5. If Sammy carefully took the notes immediately after the meeting when the events were fresh in his mind, but he has no current recollection about the meeting, can the notes be admitted in evidence at trial? *See* FRE 803(5).

§ 7.02 THE IMPEACHMENT OF WITNESSES [FRE 607–613]

[A] Introduction

To *impeach* a witness means to attack the witness's credibility or believability. A witness's credibility may be undermined by showing that the testimony may be either untrue or inaccurate. Even a well-intentioned witness may have low credibility, such as a person who needs eyeglasses or has a poor memory. Thus, impeachment is not simply about whether a witness is lying or deceitful. An examiner generally impeaches a witness to undermine the weight that will be accorded the witness's testimony by the trier of fact. It bears emphasizing that the impeachment of a witness can be viewed almost as a trial within a trial, since it is distinct from the initial determination of the admissibility of the witness's evidence.

The modern trend is to allow the impeachment of a witness either on direct or cross-examination. *See* FRE 607. Under the common-law "voucher rule," parties were presumed to vouch for the credibility of their own witnesses. Thus, parties were forbidden to impeach their own witnesses unless the witnesses were shown to be hostile or adverse.

The FRE and the evidence codes of many states have abandoned the voucher limitation. These rules recognize that parties often do not have a real choice in selecting their own witnesses. Thus, they should be able to impeach those witnesses when appropriate. Further, parties may seek to impeach their own witness for strategic purposes. For example, the proponent of the witness may wish to "lessen the sting" or "soften the blow" of harmful impeachment evidence by offering the evidence on direct examination. This disclosure makes it appear that the party has made no attempt to hide damaging testimony.

A witness who has been impeached may be rehabilitated. Rehabilitation involves reaffirming or reaccrediting the witness's believability. Time-wise, rehabilitation must follow impeachment. Rehabilitation evidence may not be introduced before impeachment in a preemptive strike. This "rehabilitation-last" rule must be followed even if the judge, jurors, and all of the people in the courtroom know that the witness undoubtedly will be impeached by the party-opponent.

The impeachment of a witness can occur through the use of *intrinsic* evidence or *extrinsic* evidence. The intrinsic-extrinsic distinction is pivotal in understanding what methods are permitted to impeach a witness's credibility. Because of the potential waste of time and distraction created by impeachment with extrinsic evidence, it is subject to greater restrictions than impeachment with intrinsic evidence. Intrinsic impeachment depends on answers given by the witness being impeached. It is impeachment from "the witness' own mouth." A witness may be asked, "Didn't you cheat on your driver's license exam? Didn't you tell a different story last month compared to what you are saying today on the witness stand? Don't you owe the defendant, on behalf of whom you are now testifying, $20,000?" As these questions illustrate, intrinsic impeachment is often elicited through leading questions.

Extrinsic impeachment, on the other hand, depends on either a different witness or the introduction of other evidence, such as a document. Thus, cross-examining a witness about a prior inconsistent statement made in a deposition is intrinsic impeachment, whereas introducing the deposition containing the inconsistent statement in evidence is extrinsic impeachment.

In either event, impeachment evidence is limited to evidence concerning the witness's testimonial capacities and character for veracity. As the Advisory Committee's Note to FRE 608 explains, impeachment by evidence of a witness's character or conduct is "strictly limited" to evidence concerning the witness's character for veracity, rather than allowing evidence as to character generally.

[B]   Intrinsic Impeachment

[1]   Methods of Impeachment

There are six general methods that can be used to impeach a witness intrinsically. Most of these impeachment methods are not expressly described in the FRE, but are implicitly accepted by tradition and case law. They are (1) contradiction, (2) bias, (3) criminal convictions (FRE 609), (4) bad "untruthful" acts (FRE 608(b)), (5) testimonial capacities, and (6) prior inconsistent statements (FRE 613). Contradiction means the facts presented in some part of a witness's testimony are disputed (i.e., "You said X, witness, when it really was Y, right?"). Bias occurs when a witness is not neutral or has an interest in the outcome. Criminal convictions include fraud crimes (dishonesty or false statement) or felonies (convictions punishable by more than a year in prison). Bad "untruthful" acts refer to fraudulent, unconvicted acts by the witness (e.g., lying).

Testimonial capacities concern the witness's perception, memory, and narration and sometimes sincerity (e.g., can the witness see, hear, touch, relate, and communicate accurately?). Finally, prior inconsistent statements require two statements by the witness that are inconsistent with each other (to show the witness is not believable).

Illustration

The witness, Amy Sue, testified on direct examination that she observed the defendant rob the Charley's Chicken restaurant on 9th Street and escape through the side door. The following occurred on cross-examination of Amy Sue.

This is an example of impeachment by contradiction:

DEFENSE COUNSEL: Now, Amy Sue, the Charley's Chicken restaurant that was robbed is actually located at 3200 S.W. 9th Street, not 3400 S.W. 9th Street, as you just testified, right?

A: Actually, you're correct, come to think of it.

This is an example of impeachment by showing bias:

DEFENSE COUNSEL: Amy Sue, you hate people who are charged with violent crime, isn't that right?

A: Well, that's true, but this defendant is the person whom I saw rob Charley's.

This is an example of impeachment by unrelated prior untruthful acts:

DEFENSE COUNSEL: Please just answer the question asked. Last March, you committed mail fraud against the United States Postal Service, did you not?

A: So? What about it?

This is an example of impeachment by prior felony conviction:

DEFENSE COUNSEL: You were convicted nine years ago of attempted murder, right?

A: Yes, but that so-called conviction was a colossal mistake. I was framed!

This is an example of impeachment by showing defects in the witness's testimonial capacities:

DEFENSE COUNSEL: You were not wearing your prescription eyeglasses at the time you say you observed the alleged robber, were you?

A: No, I was not wearing my glasses.

This is an example of impeachment by prior inconsistent statement:

DEFENSE COUNSEL: So it is your testimony here in court that the robber was 5'10? and had brown hair?

A: Yes.

DEFENSE COUNSEL: Didn't you say to your mother after the incident that "the robber was about 6'2? and had blonde hair?"

A: Yes, I did say that to my mother.   ① contr.   ③ convict. ⑤

✱ IMPeach →   ②   bias   ④ prior untruthful ⑥

[handwritten annotations: 609; 608b; amnesia; 613 inconsistent]

Background Box: Note

Most attorneys probably would not be able to squeeze in all six forms of intrinsic impeachment with a single witness unless the witness is thoroughly discreditable. That should not be the goal in any event. The nature of the impeachment — how central it was to the weight of the testimony, and the lasting impression it left on the trier of fact, — are what matter.

Mixed Impeachment Problem

Problem #7-7: Cross My Heart: An Overview

Jim Stone is sued by his neighbor for the conversion of his neighbor's $2,500 bicycle. At trial, Jim testifies on his own behalf, claiming misidentification. Jim offered an alibi. He asserted that he was home watching a movie, *Cinderella*, when the alleged theft occurred. On direct examination, Jim stated, "I didn't leave my house all evening. If someone tried to take that fancy bicycle, I'm sure sorry. But I can tell you this, I was home watching Cinderella and her prince." On cross-examination, Jim is questioned as follows:

PLAINTIFF'S ATTORNEY: Isn't it true that on the day in question, you worked from 1:30 p.m. to 6:00 p.m., and not to 6:45 p.m. as you just testified?

DEFENDANT'S ATTORNEY: Objection! Irrelevant!

1. What ruling and why?   *Rel. to impeach the witness → overruled*

PLAINTIFF'S ATTORNEY: Are you going to lose your job if you are found liable in this case?

DEFENDANT'S ATTORNEY: Objection!   *irrel → bias → overrule*

2. What ruling and why?   *speculation → overruled*

PLAINTIFF'S ATTORNEY: Weren't you convicted of a felony, the distribution of marijuana, three years ago?

DEFENDANT'S ATTORNEY: Objection!

3. What ruling and why?

PLAINTIFF'S ATTORNEY: You cheated on your Law School Admission Test examination last year, didn't you?

DEFENDANT'S ATTORNEY: Objection!   *irrel. → rel.*

4. What ruling and why?

PLAINTIFF'S ATTORNEY: You have intermittent amnesia, Mr. Stone, don't you?

DEFENDANT'S ATTORNEY: Objection!

5. What ruling and why?

PLAINTIFF'S ATTORNEY: Didn't you say in your deposition of June 5th that you saw the movie *Diehard II* on the night in question, not *Cinderella* as you just testified?

DEFENDANT'S ATTORNEY: Objection!

6. What ruling and why?

[2] Contradiction

Contradiction occurs when the examining attorney disputes the witness's testimony about a fact (e.g., "Ms. Witness, you said on direct examination that the house at Greentree Place has no garage, when in fact it has a two-car garage, isn't that right?"). The fact disputed need not be dispositive or even important to the outcome of the case. The theory of contradiction is that if a witness is inaccurate about one of the facts, he or she is more likely to be inaccurate about other facts as well.

Problem #7-8: But Nooooo

Carolyn testified in a commercial litigation action. Which of the following questions are permissible during the cross-examination of Carolyn? Explain.

1. "You attended the March board of directors meeting, and not the May meeting as you testified on direct examination, correct?"

2. "You left your office last Wednesday at 5:30 p.m., not 7:30 p.m. as you testified on direct examination, right?"

3. "Your boss, Ms. Sanders, was wrong when she testified that she deposited the March proceeds on March 4th, wasn't she?"

[3] Bias

Bias is a form of impeachment in which a witness is shown to be influenced, corrupted, prejudiced, or predisposed toward or against a party. A biased witness may be hostile, interested in the outcome, or otherwise non-neutral (e.g., "Mr. Witness, is it true that you owe the plaintiff money? You hate the defendant because he's now married to your ex-wife? You were promised a job by plaintiff's brother if plaintiff wins this case?").

Problem #7-9: The Right Direction

Shawn is prosecuted for allegedly battering Bobbi on a Colorado ski slope. The only eyewitness is Shawn's sister, Tya. The prosecutor calls Tya as a witness. On direct examination, the prosecutor questions Tya.

PROSECUTOR: Tya, you are the sister of the defendant, Shawn?

DEFENSE COUNSEL: Objection. The question is leading and therefore improper.

1. What ruling and why?

2. If this is proper impeachment, can it occur on direct examination? Why?

PROSECUTOR: Tya, are you currently facing a criminal charge of attempted murder?

DEFENSE COUNSEL: Objection. This question is improper impeachment on several grounds.

3. What are the grounds for this objection?

4. What ruling and why?

PROSECUTOR: Have any deals been made in return for your testimony?

DEFENSE COUNSEL: Objection.

5. What ruling and why?

Problem #7-10: Buddies

The defendant, Alexander, is charged with the unlawful possession of a firearm by a felon. At trial, the defendant's friend, Preston, testifies for the defense. Preston states that the gun in question, found on the ground near Alexander, was really Preston's. On cross-examination, the prosecutor asks Preston whether he and Alexander are both members of the same gang, "Red'N Blue Violins."

Admissible? Why?

Problem #7-11: Losing Religion

Shawana is prosecuted for the distribution of cocaine. Father O'Malley testifies for the prosecution as an eyewitness to the crime. On cross-examination he is asked by defense counsel, "Father, isn't it true that Shawana was at one time a member of the church where you are the priest, but that she quit the church after having an argument with you?"

Admissible? Why?

[4] Convictions of Crime [FRE 609]

The underlying theory of impeachment by conviction is that a witness who has been convicted of certain types of crime is less believable. According to FRE 609, two types of crime bear on a witness's credibility and can be used to impeach: (1) crimes of dishonesty or false statement (i.e., those involving deception or fraud), regardless of the potential length of incarceration; and (2) felonies, those crimes punishable by more than one year in prison. Other crimes, such as misdemeanor crimes of violence or drug possession, are not permitted to be used to impeach a witness. Likewise, FRE 609 generally excludes juvenile adjudications and bars "stale" convictions. Convictions are stale if more than ten years have elapsed since the date of conviction or release from incarceration, whichever is later. Under FRE 609, for example, a witness generally could not be impeached with an eleven-year-old felony conviction for which the sentence was probation and a fine.

What qualifies as a crime of "dishonesty or false statement" is not always clear. In *United States v. Brackeen*, 969 F.2d 827 (9th Cir. 1992) (per curiam), for example, the defendant was indicted on one count of aiding and abetting an armed bank robbery and two counts of unarmed robbery. The defendant pled guilty to both counts of unarmed robbery and was tried and convicted of aiding and abetting the armed bank robbery. At the trial of the aiding and abetting charge, the court permitted the defendant to be impeached with the robbery convictions under FRE 609(a)(2) as crimes of dishonesty or false statement. On appeal, the Ninth Circuit, *en banc*, reversed. The Court held that the unarmed robberies were not crimes of dishonesty or false statement for the purposes of FRE 609. The phrase "dishonesty or false statement," could have been intended to refer either to crimes broadly evidencing a lack of integrity or those more narrowly indicating a breach of trust, such as deceit or fraud. The Court chose the narrower construction, stating that Congress, in enacting the rules, intended the narrower view. The phrase is limited to crimes that are "crimen falsi," i.e., crimes that are bad in and of themselves and have some relationship to deceit and lying. It does not include "those crimes which, bad though they are, do not carry with them a tinge of falsification." *Id.* The Court proceeded to cite with approval similar constructions from other circuits.

Prior felony convictions are not automatically permitted for the purpose of impeaching a witness, which makes sense when the conviction is viewed as a proxy for untruthfulness. Some felony convictions, such as those involving violence, appear to have a tenuous connection to truthfulness. FRE 609 was modified in 1990 to provide that the use of felony convictions first must satisfy the unfair prejudice test of FRE 403 for all witnesses other than criminal defendants. (For the situation that preceded the rule change, *see Green v. Bock Laundry Machine Co.*, 490 U.S. 504 (1989). FRE 609 provides testifying criminal defendants with even greater protection against the misuse by the jury of felony convictions admitted for impeachment. Under a special balancing test, felony convictions will be permitted only if their probative value outweighs the prejudicial effect to the accused. This balancing test reverses FRE 403's built-in presumption in favor of admissibility and favors the accused.

Courts may consider a variety of factors in determining whether a defendant's conviction will be unfairly prejudicial. One important factor is the similarity between the impeachment felony and the crime charged. The greater the similarity, the greater the likelihood that the impeaching conviction will be misused by the jurors as evidence that "if the defendant did it before, it is more likely that the defendant did it again" (e.g., "Once a thief, always a thief"). Other factors include the importance of the defendant's credibility to the case, the nature and date of the impeachment crime, and the significance of the defendant's testimony to the case overall. *See, e.g., United States v. Sloman*, 909 F.2d 176 (6th Cir. 1990).

Significantly, the admissibility of a crime offered to impeach a testifying criminal defendant is not tied to the admissibility of that crime as substantive evidence, such as its use as an "other act" under FRE 404. A conviction may be used to impeach even if the underlying crime has been offered — and rejected by the trial court — as an "other act" pursuant to FRE 404. In essence, the fact that evidence is impermissible for one purpose does not mean it is precluded from being offered for another purpose. *See, e.g., United States v. Haslip*, 160 F.3d 649 (10th Cir. 1998). Of course, with evidence admitted for one purpose and not another, a limiting instruction accompanying the evidence might be appropriate. *Id.*

What constitutes a "conviction" for impeachment purposes is not entirely obvious. A conviction can result from a jury or court verdict, or through a guilty plea. Having been indicted, arrested, or otherwise charged with a crime is insufficient to qualify as a conviction under the rules. Further, incarceration is not a necessary antecedent to a conviction. A person who has been given probation and has never set foot in a jail cell can still have multiple felony convictions.

Like other types of impeachment (*see* FRE 607), a witness's criminal convictions may be offered on either direct or cross-examination. While the impeachment of the proponent's own witness at first may seem counterintuitive, it is often done for strategic purposes — to "lessen the sting" or "soften the blow" of the opponent's eventual cross-examination. If a conviction is offered on direct examination, the opponent's use of the conviction is diminished and the trier of fact is left with the inference that the proponent of the witness has nothing to hide.

If a witness denies having been convicted on cross-examination, it may be proved by extrinsic evidence (*see* [C], *below*).

Problem #7-12: Fried Forgery

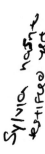

Sylvia is prosecuted for forging signatures on applications for food stamps. The prosecution, in its case-in-chief, offers a witness, Wally, who will testify that Sylvia (1) has been convicted of forgery on three prior occasions, and (2) was charged with embezzlement on a fourth prior occasion.

1. Are these convictions and the criminal charge admissible?

2. If it had been Wally, and not Sylvia, who was convicted of forgery and charged with embezzlement, would the convictions and charge be admissible?

Problem #7-13: Medical Mal

Malerie brought suit against Dr. Sloan for failing to diagnose Mal's carcinoma of the cervix. At trial, the plaintiff's expert, Dr. Inos, testified. On cross-examination, the defendant wished to question the doctor about the doctor's misdemeanor conviction for willfully failing to file a federal income tax return. Is this impeachment permissible? *See Cree v. Hatcher*, 969 F.2d 34 (3d Cir. 1992).

Problem #7-14: One Bad Apple

Johnny Apple was prosecuted for attempted murder. Johnny testified at trial and denied committing the crime charged. On cross-examination, the prosecution attempted to impeach Johnny with the following convictions. Which of the convictions, if any, can be used to impeach Johnny? In addition, what test applies in determining unfair prejudice?

1. A seven-year-old conviction for attempted murder.

2. A two-year-old conviction for assault, punishable by six months in jail and a fine of $1,000.

3. A twelve-year-old juvenile adjudication for murder.

4. An eleven-year-old conviction for aggravated battery, punishable by a maximum of three years in prison, for which the defendant was sentenced to nine months incarceration, sentence suspended.

5. A five-year-old conviction for grand theft, for which the defendant was sentenced to six months incarceration.

[5] Prior Untruthful Acts [FRE 608(b)]

As explained in the Advisory Committee's Note to FRE 608, the rule

"generally bars evidence of specific instances of conduct of a witness for the purpose of attacking or supporting his credibility. There are, however, two exceptions: (1) specific instances are provable when they have been the subject of criminal conviction, and (2) specific instances may be inquired into on cross-examination of the principal witness or of a witness giving an opinion of his character for truthfulness."

Impeachment by prior untruthful acts under FRE 608(b) is limited to specific prior acts of the witness that reflect on the witness's capacity for truthfulness or veracity. This type of impeachment by prior "untruthful" acts is distinguishable from impeachment by conviction because no conviction is required for impeachment by prior acts. In fact, the act may not have been the subject of a criminal charge at all or, might even have been the subject of a criminal charge resulting in an acquittal.

Impeachment under FRE 608(b) is sometimes called "prior bad acts" impeachment. However, the term "bad act" is, in a sense, a misnomer, since there is a limit on the type and nature of the prior acts that fall within this category. The acts that may be used for impeachment are limited to those that involve fraud or deception, such as obtaining property under false pretenses or perjury at a hearing or proceeding. Acts of violence, such as disorderly conduct, battery, or even murder, do not fall within the "bad" acts category and generally cannot be used to impeach.

If impeachment by a prior untruthful act is proper, the witness may only be asked about the underlying bad act itself, and not about an arrest, charge, indictment, suspension, or expulsion relating to the bad act. The witness's credibility does not hinge on the arrest, indictment, impeachment, etc., but rather on the commission of the act itself. Thus, it is permissible to ask, "You defrauded your insurance company, didn't you?," but not, "You were indicted for defrauding your insurance company, weren't you?"

Additionally, permissible untruthful act impeachment may not be proven by extrinsic evidence under the FRE. If the witness denies the act, the questioner must take the witness's answer without any further follow-up. FRE 608(b). Otherwise, a mini-trial would occur and the jury would be distracted and misled. Extrinsic evidence may be allowed under state evidence codes, however.

Problem #7-15: Liar

Janet is prosecuted for committing perjury during her testimony before the grand jury. At trial, she testifies on her own behalf and is asked the following questions on cross-examination:

> PROSECUTOR: You were arrested for lying on your income tax statement last year, weren't you?
>
> DEFENSE COUNSEL: Objection. Improper impeachment.

1. What ruling and why?

> PROSECUTOR: You deceived your boss three weeks ago, didn't you, when you claimed you missed an important meeting because your train was late?
>
> DEFENSE COUNSEL: Objection. Improper impeachment.

2. What ruling and why?

> PROSECUTOR: You bribed an official at a computer company in March of 1989, correct?
>
> DEFENSE COUNSEL: Objection.

3. What is the basis for the objection?

4. Admit or exclude? Why?

[6] Testimonial Capacities

The term "testimonial capacities" refers to aspects of a witness's testimony that are important for accuracy: (1) perception — what the witness saw, heard, smelled, or touched; (2) memory — what the witness recalls from the prior occurrence, happening, or event; (3) narration — how the witness communicates this perception and memory to others; and (4) sincerity (which is sometimes viewed as a combination of the other three capacities), a measurement indicating a lack of prevarication. Sincerity is distinct from accuracy, since a witness can be sincere but still inaccurate.

Attacking a witness's testimonial capacities is accomplished by revealing defects in the witness's memory, perception, or narration, from common deficiencies to physiological defects. Physiological defects are more severe than conditions reflected by statement such as "I forgot," since memory lapses happen to everyone. Instead, they have to do with particular physical or psychological conditions, such as bad eyesight, amnesia, hearing loss, or schizophrenia, that interfere with the witness's ability to be accurate or truthful.

Problem #7-16: Psychotic Chips

In a tort action for false imprisonment, Don Geo is about to testify as an eyewitness for the defense. He yells to the jury as he takes the witness stand, "Would you like some of my psychotic chips?" referring to a bag of potato chips he is carrying. Don adds, "They're mind-altering."

1. On cross-examination, the plaintiff's attorney questions Don about two previous hospital stays for undifferentiated schizophrenia. Are such questions permissible? Why? _Y, interfere_

2. Don also is questioned on cross-examination about whether his psychotic chips contain any mind-altering substances. Is this question permissible? Explain.

3. Can Don be asked on cross-examination whether he was under the influence of alcohol or other drugs at the time he observed the alleged false imprisonment? Can he be asked whether he is currently under the influence of a mind-altering substance at the time of trial? Why?

Problem #7-17: Depression

James Alford was an eyewitness to a bank robbery. After a suspect was apprehended, Alford was asked to testify for the prosecution at trial. On cross-examination, the defense counsel asked Alford if he had been depressed off and on over the past three years and had taken medication for the depression. The prosecutor objected. What ruling and why?

[7] Prior Inconsistent Statements [FRE 613]

Impeachment by a prior inconsistent statement pursuant to FRE 613 is actually a specialized form of impeachment by contradiction, namely "self-contradiction." Two statements are necessary for this type of impeachment, one often occurring during the witness's testimony at trial and a second statement by the witness prior to trial that contradicts the trial testimony. If the witness at trial forgets facts while testifying and says "I don't remember" in response to a question, or fails to make a certain statement at trial, there is no trial statement. If there is only the statement before trial, impeachment with that prior statement alone is generally forbidden. If the witness is acting in bad faith by intentionally "forgetting" the facts at trial, however, an exception is made to this requirement of two statements, and the prior statement may be used to impeach.

FRE 613 drops the common-law requirement of *The Queen's Case*, 2 Br. & B. 284, 129 Eng. Rep. 976 (1820). That case created a "fairness" rule by requiring the examining counsel to first give a witness the opportunity to deny or explain her own prior written statement before being impeached on it. However, FRE 613 imports its own version of fairness by requiring the contents of a prior statement to be shown or disclosed to opposing counsel on request, and by requiring the proponent of the statement to give the witness the opportunity to deny or explain the statement if it is being used as extrinsic impeachment evidence.

Illustration

Jean sues Ted for allegedly breaching a commercial lease extension for Ted's Tender Chicken, a fast-food restaurant located in Jean's shopping center. Ted's defense is that there was no extension to the lease. An important issue at trial concerned a meeting at Ted's restaurant on June 24th. An eyewitness to the meeting, Sophia, testified that, on the day in question at the restaurant, Jean and Ted met, discussed the lease, appeared to agree on an extension, and signed several documents. On cross-examination, Sophia was impeached by a prior inconsistent statement.

DEFENDANT'S ATTORNEY: Now Sophia, you have just testified on direct examination that Jean and Ted signed several documents during the meeting on the day in question?

A: That is correct.

DEFENDANT'S ATTORNEY: You discussed what happened at this meeting with me before, didn't you?

A: Yes, I believe so.

DEFENDANT'S ATTORNEY: It was during your deposition, way back in May, right?

A: Yes, I think it was in May.

DEFENDANT'S ATTORNEY: The meeting occurred only five months or so prior to the deposition, true?

A: Yes.

DEFENDANT'S ATTORNEY: At the deposition, you were under oath?

A: True.

DEFENDANT'S ATTORNEY: You swore to tell the truth?

A: Definitely. Yes.

DEFENDANT'S ATTORNEY: The whole truth and nothing but the truth?

A: Sure.

DEFENDANT'S ATTORNEY: Referring opposing counsel to the witness's deposition, page eight, line nine, I asked you during the deposition: "How many documents did Jean and Ted sign?" and you answered: "They signed only one document." Isn't that correct?

A: Yes, that is what you asked and I answered.

Significantly, the nature of the prior inconsistent statement matters. If a prior inconsistent statement has certain qualifying features (e.g., it was made under oath in a prior proceeding, like a deposition), it will be admitted not only for its impeachment value, but also for the truth of the matter asserted. This means that in the example above, if the witness Sophia's statement in her deposition qualifies under FRE 801, it can be considered by the jury not only for the effect of the apparent inconsistency on Sophia's believability, but also for the truth of what was actually signed at the meeting, and by whom.

Sometimes, a witness confronted with a prior inconsistent statement denies making the statement, even if the statement was taken down by a court reporter as part of a deposition. If this occurs, the witness may be impeached by extrinsic evidence of the statement (such as a writing or a witness) only if the inconsistency is about a matter at issue in the case (see [C], below). If extrinsic impeachment is permitted, a foundation must be laid for the extrinsic evidence. To promote efficiency, it is worth attempting to use the witness to be impeached to help lay the foundation. If a new witness is required, and the witness to be impeached may be needed at a later time, it is important not to excuse the witness, but rather to explain to the court the intended additional use of the witness.

Problem #7-18: Yeah, Right

Ted, the primary witness for the defense in a tort action, states on direct examination that he was not aware that a lawsuit had been filed until four days prior to trial. On cross-examination, Ted is asked whether he told a good friend eight months earlier, right after the suit had been brought, "I heard that good old Plaintiff filed suit this week." Is this question permissible impeachment?

Problem # 7-19: Interregnum I

In a "slip and fall" action, the defendant, Belinda, testified about the fall. Belinda stated that she observed boxes flying all around the plaintiff, Irving, as he fell. On cross-examination, plaintiff's counsel questioned Belinda about her deposition, which was taken one month prior to trial. Specifically, the plaintiff's counsel asked Belinda about her failure to mention flying boxes when she was asked during the deposition to describe the incident. Is this question permissible impeachment?

[8] Mixed Intrinsic Impeachment Problems

Problem #7-20: "You took the tag off of your mattress?!"

Cheryl is prosecuted for shoplifting from the "We R Toys" store. The store clerk, Laurie, testifies for the prosecution. On cross-examination, the clerk is asked the following questions:

DEFENSE COUNSEL: Isn't it true that the "We R Toys" store has only four parking spaces out front and not five, as you testified?

PROSECUTOR: Objection.

1. Is the question permissible? Why?

DEFENSE COUNSEL: You've been arrested for child abuse, haven't you?

PROSECUTOR: Objection.

2. Is the question permissible? Why? *no*

DEFENSE COUNSEL: Laurie, you faked a workers' compensation injury last year to collect benefits, didn't you?

PROSECUTOR: Objection.

3. Is the question permissible? Why? *bad unt. acts*

DEFENSE COUNSEL: You were told by your boss that you'd get an extra vacation day if you testified today, isn't that correct?

PROSECUTOR: Objection.

4. Is the question permissible? Why? *bias*

DEFENSE COUNSEL: Laurie, you were convicted last year of shoplifting at a "Toys R Not U" store, isn't that right?

PROSECUTOR: Objection.

5. Is the question permissible? Why?

DEFENSE COUNSEL: You took the tag that says "do not remove" off of your mattress, didn't you?

PROSECUTOR: Objection.

6. Is the question permissible? Why?

Problem #7-21: Defamation Redux

Sue is called an "inept tabloid-loving dimwit surgeon" in the local newspaper. She sues for libel. At trial, her brother, Bob, also a surgeon, testifies on her behalf as a character witness about Sue's professional competence. Bob is cross-examined by counsel for the defendant newspaper.

DEFENDANT'S ATTORNEY: So, Bob, isn't it true you punched the defendant newspaper editor in the nose outside of Rosie O'Sady's restaurant last week?

PLAINTIFF'S ATTORNEY: Objection! Improper impeachment.

1. What ruling and why?

DEFENDANT'S ATTORNEY: Bob, you are aware that there were two incidents in which your sister was cited by the hospital for cutting into the wrong location, correct?

PLAINTIFF'S ATTORNEY: Objection! Improper impeachment.

2. What ruling and why?

DEFENDANT'S ATTORNEY: You said on direct examination that your sister has participated in at least 800 operations. Yet, in your deposition of

October 5th, at page three, line four, you were asked, "In how many operations did your sister participate?" and you answered, "Oh, I don't know, maybe 400."

PLAINTIFF'S ATTORNEY: Objection! Improper impeachment.

3. What ruling and why?

DEFENDANT'S ATTORNEY: Bob, didn't you misrepresent your college class rank on your medical school application?

PLAINTIFF'S ATTORNEY: Objection! Improper impeachment.

4. What ruling and why?

Problem #7-22: The Young Freud

The young Dr. Von Freud testified about the cause of death in a homicide prosecution.

1. Dr. Von Freud is asked on cross-examination whether his opinion is consistent with *Gray's Anatomy*, which is considered to be an authoritative medical treatise in the field. Is this question admissible? Why?

2. Dr. Von Freud is asked on cross-examination whether he has been convicted of child abuse. Is this question proper?

3. Dr. Von Freud is questioned on cross-examination about whether he had been fired from his previous employment because he had forged medical records. Is this question admissible? Why?

[C] Extrinsic Impeachment

"Extrinsic impeachment" refers to the use of extrinsic evidence to attack a witness's truthfulness or veracity. "Extrinsic" refers to a form of impeachment involving a new witness or evidence offered for consideration by the trier of fact. By comparison, intrinsic impeachment results from responses by the witness to the examiner's questions. Extrinsic impeachment occurs less frequently than intrinsic impeachment, if only because it often follows a failed attempt at intrinsic impeachment, such as with bias.

The rule governing when a witness may be impeached through extrinsic evidence is generally called the "collateral matter" or "collateral issue" rule. It permits impeachment through extrinsic evidence only for non-collateral (i.e., important) matters. If collateral forms of extrinsic impeachment were allowed, the jury would become distracted from the issues at hand and judicial economy would be sacrificed.

The non-collateral matters that are the subject of permissible extrinsic impeachment are: (1) bias, (2) a fact at issue, (3) testimonial capacities, (4) convictions of crime, and (5) reputation or opinion evidence about the truthfulness or veracity of another witness. As compared to intrinsic impeachment, the only type added to the list is (5), a reputation or opinion witness, who has knowledge about another's truthfulness. Some intrinsic forms of impeachment have been dropped from the list, however, including contradiction, prior untruthful acts and prior inconsistent statements — unless these fall within (2), involving a fact at issue in the case.

Extrinsic impeachment is most often used after an attempt to impeach a witness intrinsically has failed. The witness has been asked a question intended to impeach, but denies the impeaching question. Counsel must then either "take the answer" or proceed with extrinsic impeachment.

Illustration

Harold testified for the plaintiff, Maude, in a breach-of-contract action. On cross-examination, Harold was asked if: (1) he was dating Maude; (2) Maude had agreed to enter into the contract without qualification; (3) Harold had been convicted of mayhem ten years earlier; and (4) Harold had lied on his bar application four years earlier. Harold answered "no" to all four questions. On rebuttal, can the defendant offer a new witness to testify that (1) Harold was dating Maude, and (2) Maude had agreed to the contract offer without qualification? Can the defense also offer (1) a certified copy of Harold's prior conviction for mayhem and (2) a copy of his bar application with the allegedly untruthful statement?

Answer: The collateral issue rule permits the defendant to impeach Harold extrinsically in three of the four instances. The new witness can testify about: (1) whether Harold and Maude were dating, because it shows bias, which is never collateral; and (2) the dispute about Maude's responses to the contract offer, because it involves a fact in issue. The certified copy of Harold's conviction for mayhem is admissible, since convictions of crime are considered to be non-collateral matters as well. However, the prior bad act, lying on the bar application, cannot be the subject of extrinsic impeachment, because prior bad acts are considered collateral. Even if Harold is lying anew with respect to the bar application, the questioner must take the witness's answer.

Extrinsic Impeachment Problems

In analyzing these problems, first identify whether there is witness impeachment and then determine whether the impeachment is intrinsic or extrinsic. Sometimes, this distinction is not immediately apparent, such as when counsel is holding a printout of a prior statement of the witness while asking a witness questions. This type of impeachment would be intrinsic if it is still based on the answers supplied by the witness; it only becomes extrinsic if counsel offers the written prior statement for consideration by the trier of fact.

Problem #7-23: Extrinsically Yours

Xavier testifies for the defense in an action involving the sale of real property. Xavier was an eyewitness to the alleged contract to sell the property.

> 1. During cross-examination by the plaintiff, Xavier is asked whether he had been convicted of attempted robbery in 1986. Is this question permissible? Explain.

2. Xavier denied having been convicted of attempted robbery ("preposterous!" he exclaimed). Can the opposing counsel offer in evidence a certified copy of the attempted robbery conviction? Explain.

3. On cross-examination, Xavier is asked whether he was wearing his hearing aid at the time of the alleged sale. Xavier responded by saying that he was indeed using his hearing aid. Can opposing counsel call a different witness, Alec, to testify that Xavier was not wearing a hearing aid at the time of the alleged sale? Explain.

4. On cross-examination, Xavier is asked whether he had worn white sneakers on the day in question, not red ones as he had testified to on direct. Xavier answered the question by denying that he had worn white sneakers. Can opposing counsel call a different witness in rebuttal to testify that Xavier was wearing white sneakers at the meeting? Explain.

5. Xavier is also asked whether he had said in a deposition two months before trial, "I was the first one there for the meeting about the sale," when on direct he testified that he "was only the third or fourth person there." If Xavier claims he made no such prior statement, can a rebuttal witness who was present at the deposition testify that Xavier made the statement? Explain.

6. If Xavier is asked on cross-examination whether he owes the defendant a large sum of money and he denies it, can the plaintiff call a different witness in rebuttal to confirm this fact? Explain.

Problem #7-24: More Perjury

Clark is prosecuted for perjury (*United States v. Clark*). He calls his best friend, Lenny, with whom he went to grade school, to testify on his behalf. Lenny testifies: "Clark's reputation in the community is for complete honesty; he would never lie."

During the cross-examination of Lenny, the prosecutor asks:

PROSECUTOR: Have you heard, Lenny, that Clark was expelled from night school for cheating on an examination two years ago?

1. Is the question permissible? Why?

After Lenny leaves the witness stand, the prosecutor calls Sheila in rebuttal. Sheila testifies: "In my opinion, Lenny is a liar. Everyone in this community says that Clark is about as truthful as that T.V. character, Joe Isuzu; basically, Clark has a reputation for having no veracity at all."

2. Is her testimony admissible? Explain.

Sheila finishes testifying, and Sheila's estranged husband, George, is called to testify on behalf of Clark. On direct examination, George declares: (1) "In my opinion, Sheila is a liar." and (2) "In any event, Lenny's reputation in the community is one of unimpeachable honesty."

3. Are George's statements admissible? Explain.

Problem #7-25: Informant

In a drug prosecution of Willie Williams, the prosecution offered the informant, Peter Parnick, as the first witness. On cross-examination, the accused suggested repeatedly that Parnick was a liar. On rebuttal, the prosecution offered evidence through Officer Joanna Smart that indicated the informant had returned a wallet to the person who had lost it with all of the wallet's cash intact. Is this evidence admissible? Explain.

Problem #7-26: Bigfoot

Bernie is charged with conspiracy to import heroin. At the time of his arrest, which occurred one week after the alleged conspiracy concluded, Bernie was apprehended with alleged heroin in his shoe. At trial, Bernie testified in his own defense and denied being a part of a conspiracy.

   1. On cross-examination, the prosecution asked Bernie if he had heroin in his shoe at the time he was apprehended. Is this question permissible?

   2. If the question is permitted and Bernie denies having had heroin in his shoe, can the prosecutor then call the arresting officer to the witness stand to testify to that fact? Explain.

Problem #7-27: Buddies Revisited

Alexander is prosecuted for a felony. At trial, Alexander's fellow gang member, Preston, testifies on the defendant's behalf. On cross-examination, Preston is asked whether he belongs to the same gang as the defendant. Preston says no. On rebuttal, the prosecution calls a police officer specializing in gangs to testify that both Preston and Alexander belong to the gang, "R U Blud." The officer further testifies that the gang is known for lying to protect fellow members. Alexander is convicted and he appeals, claiming that both the cross-examination of Preston and the police officer's extrinsic testimony should have been excluded. What ruling and why? *See United States v. Martinez*, 962 F.2d 1161 (5th Cir. 1992).

Problem #7-28: Edna to Rachel to Frank

In a civil assault and battery action, the defense calls an eyewitness, Edna. She testifies that the defendant was not the first aggressor, but was merely defending himself.

   1. In rebuttal, the plaintiff calls Rachel, who testifies that, in her opinion, Edna is not a very truthful person. Is this testimony allowed?

   2. On cross-examination of Rachel, the defendant asked her whether she had lied on her college entrance examination. Is this question allowed?

Problem #7-29: Mortgage

The defendant, Rose, was charged with the unlawful possession of a firearm.

1. The central prosecution witness, Rick, testified at trial. On cross-examination, he was asked whether he had made a false statement on his recent mortgage application. Is this question permissible?

2. After Rick denied making any false statements, the judge permitted the prosecutor to offer the mortgage application in evidence. Was this error?

Problem #7-30: Interregnum II

In a "slip and fall" action, the defendant, Belinda, testified about the fall. Belinda stated that she observed boxes flying all around the plaintiff, Irving, as he fell. On cross-examination, plaintiff's counsel asked Belinda whether Irving had ever fired her from a job. Belinda said, "No!" Can plaintiff offer Belinda's former co-worker to testify that Belinda had been fired by Irving? Why?

[D]   After Impeachment: Rehabilitating the Impeached Witness

The proponent of a witness is sometimes given the opportunity to rehabilitate a witness whose credibility has been attacked. Rehabilitation essentially involves accrediting the witness's truthfulness or veracity, but only after it has been challenged. Preemptive accreditation of a witness is not permitted. Rehabilitation can occur either through questions on redirect examination of the witness to be impeached or through a separate reputation or opinion witness testifying about the discredited witness's good character for truthfulness or veracity. If a new character witness is called, the witness may only be asked questions about reputation or opinion. Questions concerning specific acts are not permitted. *See* FRE 608(a)(2).

Rehabilitation Problem

Problem #7-31: Rehab

Maryanne was the star defense witness in a forfeiture action. The government claimed that a considerable amount of marijuana was found in the back seat of the defendant's car, justifying its forfeiture. Anticipating a ferocious cross-examination of Maryanne, the defense first called Maryanne's partner, Marcy, to testify that, in her opinion, Maryanne has an unimpeachable character for truthfulness and veracity.

1. The prosecution objects to Marcy's testimony. What ruling and why?

After Maryanne testified on direct examination, the prosecution zealously cross-examined her, suggesting that Maryanne recently fabricated her testimony to assist the defense case. On re-direct examination, the following occurred:

DEFENSE COUNSEL: When did you first learn of this incident?

A: Almost immediately after the forfeiture occurred.

DEFENSE COUNSEL: What did you do upon hearing about it?

A: I immediately told my friend Jillian the same exact thing that I just testified to on direct, that the hitchhiker had unloaded and then repacked his bag in the back seat before leaving the car.

PROSECUTOR: Objection!

2. What is the basis for the prosecutor's objection? Is Maryanne's prior statement admissible?

3. The defense then calls Samantha, who testifies that her colleague Maryanne has a fantastic reputation for truthfulness at work, Mitchell and Moore, Inc., where both have been employed for 15 years. Is Samantha's testimony admissible?

4. Assume the judge permits Samantha to testify. In response to Samantha's testimony, the prosecution calls Billy, who also has worked at Mitchell and Moore, Inc., for years and will testify that in his opinion, Samantha is a fabricator, who plays fast and loose with the truth. Should Billy's testimony be allowed over a timely objection?

[E] Cases and Rules

[1] Clarett v. Roberts

United States Court of Appeals for the Seventh Circuit
657 F.3d 664 (7th Cir. 2011)

SYKES, CIRCUIT JUDGE.

Police officers went to Patricia Clarett's home in Lansing, Illinois, early one morning to question her sons about a burglary that had occurred overnight in nearby Lynwood, Illinois. A confrontation ensued and escalated quickly. One of the officers Tasered Clarett three times, and the officers arrested her for obstruction and resisting arrest. Those charges were subsequently dropped, and Clarett sued the officers under 42 U.S.C. § 1983 alleging use of excessive force and false arrest in violation of the Fourth Amendment, and various state-law claims. A jury returned a verdict for the officers on all counts. Clarett appealed.

We affirm. Clarett waived her most plausible claim of trial error — the court's decision to admit two of her criminal convictions — when she introduced evidence of the convictions herself, before the officers could do so. Her remaining evidentiary challenges are meritless. We also reject Clarett's claims of instructional error. Finally, the district court properly denied Clarett's motion for judgment as a matter of law as well as her motion for a new trial. The parties told dramatically different stories about the confrontation inside Clarett's home, and the jury was entitled to believe the officers' version of events.

Clarett's appeal focuses primarily on claimed evidentiary and instructional errors. She also argues that the jury's verdict was against the weight of the evidence and asks us to remand for entry of judgment in her favor as a matter of law, or alternatively, a new trial.

A. Evidentiary Challenges

Clarett challenges three evidentiary rulings made by the district court. First, she challenges the court's pretrial decision to admit evidence of two of her criminal convictions, one for retail theft and one for obstructing a police officer. . . . We review the district court's evidentiary decisions for abuse of discretion and will reverse "only where no reasonable person could take the view adopted by the trial court." *United States v. L.E. Myers Co.*, 562 F.3d 845, 855 (7th Cir. 2009).

1. Admission of Clarett's Convictions

The district court entered a ruling in limine that two of Clarett's criminal convictions — for misdemeanor retail theft and obstructing a police officer — could be admitted at trial.[1] The judge held that her retail-theft conviction was admissible under Rule 609(a)(2) of the Federal Rules of Evidence as a crime involving an act of dishonesty. The judge held that her obstruction conviction was also admissible, though he did not specify the grounds. It appears that the judge admitted this conviction — or perhaps both — for purposes of impeachment since Clarett had denied in her deposition that she had ever been convicted of a crime.

These rulings may have been problematic. Admission of a criminal conviction under Rule 609(a)(2) is limited to crimes for which "it readily can be determined that establishing the elements of the crime required proof or admission of an act of dishonesty or false statement by the witness." FED.R.EVID. 609(a)(2). The Advisory Committee Notes explain that this rule is generally limited to "perjury or subornation of perjury, false statement, criminal fraud, embezzlement, or false pretenses," and similar crimes. Retail theft lacks an element of an act of dishonesty that is common to crimes of this type. As such, "[t]his circuit generally does not count retail theft as a crime of dishonesty" for purposes of Rule 609(a)(2). *Kunz v. DeFelice*, 538 F.3d 667, 675 (7th Cir. 2008).

The authority to admit evidence for impeachment purposes is implicit in Rule 607 of the Federal Rules of Evidence. *See* 27 CHARLES ALAN WRIGHT & VICTOR JAMES GOLD, FEDERAL PRACTICE AND PROCEDURE § 6096, at 655 (2d ed. 2007). To the extent that the court gave a green light to the introduction of either of Clarett's convictions to attack her truthfulness, their admission was governed by Rule 608(b), which provides that specific instances of conduct bearing on a witness's character for truthfulness "other than conviction of crime as provided in Rule 609, may not be proved by extrinsic evidence." FED.R.EVID. 608(b). Neither conviction was admissible under Rule 609.[2] So the defendants could not make affirmative use of this evidence or prove it up by way of extrinsic evidence. Moreover, it is generally improper to rely on extrinsic evidence

---

[1] The judge excluded Clarett's third conviction — for forgery — because it was too old.

[2] Under Rule 609(a)(1) evidence of a conviction is admissible for impeachment purposes if the crime is "punishable by death or imprisonment in excess of one year." Clarett's retail theft and obstruction convictions were both misdemeanors; the defendants do not argue that they were admissible under Rule 609(a)(1). As we have already explained, to be admissible for impeachment purposes under Rule 609(a)(2), a conviction must involve an act of dishonesty or false statement as proof of an element of the offense; neither of Clarett's convictions qualifies.

to impeach a witness about a collateral matter. *Young v. James Green Mgmt., Inc.*, 327 F.3d 616, 627 (7th Cir. 2003); *United States v. Bonner*, 302 F.3d 776, 785 (7th Cir. 2002) ("[O]ne may not contradict for the sake of contradiction; the evidence must have an independent purpose and an independent ground for admission." (quotation marks omitted)). "A matter is collateral if it could not have been introduced into evidence for any purpose other than contradiction." *United States v. Williamson*, 202 F.3d 974, 979 (7th Cir. 2000) (quotation marks omitted).

The only remaining evidentiary option available to the officers was inquiry on cross-examination. Under Rule 608(b) specific instances of conduct bearing upon truthfulness "may . . . be inquired into on cross-examination" in the discretion of the court. Perhaps this is what the court and the officers had in mind. As things unfolded at trial, however, and apparently based on the court's pretrial ruling, the first mention of the convictions came during Clarett's case-in-chief, when her counsel questioned her about them on direct examination.

By introducing the convictions herself, Clarett waived the right to challenge their admission on appeal. The Supreme Court has held that criminal defendants who introduce evidence of their own prior convictions in an effort to remove the "sting" forgo the right to appeal the trial court's decision to admit those convictions into evidence. *Ohler v. United States*, 529 U.S. 753, 758, 120 S. Ct. 1851, 146 L. Ed. 2d 826 (2000). The Court held that by introducing the evidence first, the defendant adopts a concerted trial strategy to minimize the prejudicial effect of the evidence and in so doing waives the right to appeal the court's ruling that the evidence may be admitted at trial. *Id.; see also United States v. Saunders*, 359 F.3d 874, 877–78 (7th Cir. 2004).

We have never addressed whether the *Ohler* principle applies in civil cases. Clarett argues against applying *Ohler* in the civil context, noting that criminal defendants have the right not to testify in their defense, while civil plaintiffs generally must do so in order to prove their claim. This distinction is immaterial in light of *Ohler*'s reasoning. The Court noted that even after a criminal defendant chooses to take the stand, she "has a further choice to make. . . . The defendant must choose whether to introduce the conviction on direct examination and remove the sting or to take her chances with the prosecutor's possible elicitation of the conviction on cross-examination." *Ohler.* The same choice is present in civil cases. Similarly, in the criminal context, the government must also make a tactical decision:

If the defendant testifies, [the government] must choose whether or not to impeach her by use of her prior conviction. Here the trial judge had indicated he would allow its use, but the Government still had to consider whether its use might be deemed reversible error on appeal. This choice is often based on the Government's appraisal of the apparent effect of the defendant's testimony. If she has offered a plausible, innocent explanation of the evidence against her, it will be inclined to use the prior conviction; if not, it may decide not to risk possible reversal on appeal from its use.

The Court noted in *Ohler* that when the defendant decides to introduce the conviction evidence herself, she denies the government "its usual right to decide, after she testifies, whether or not to use her prior conviction against her."

The logic of *Ohler* applies with equal force in both criminal and civil cases. The tactical nature of each party's decisions is the same; indeed, the stakes are higher in a criminal case, and still the Supreme Court found waiver. We note that every circuit to have addressed the question has applied *Ohler* in civil cases. *See, e.g., Bowoto v. Chevron Corp.,* 621 F.3d 1116, 1130 (9th Cir. 2010); *Estate of Smith v. City of Wilmington,* 317 Fed. Appx. 237, 239 n. 1 (3d Cir. 2009); *Canny v. Dr. Pepper/Seven — Up Bottling Grp., Inc.,* 439 F.3d 894, 904 (8th Cir. 2006); *Ludwig v. Norfolk So. Ry. Co.,* 50 Fed. Appx. 743, 751 (6th Cir. 2002). In *Canny* the Eighth Circuit observed that a civil litigant should not be allowed to "avoid the consequence of its own trial tactic by arguing it was forced to introduce the evidence . . . to diminish the prejudice." 439 F.3d at 904. We agree. Because Clarett introduced the evidence of her retail theft and obstruction convictions herself, she is precluded from challenging their admissibility on appeal.

Affirmed.

[2] Rules Comparison

Compare the current form of FRE 609(a) with various preliminary draft proposals.

House Subcommittee Draft (1973)

"For the purpose of attacking credibility of a witness, evidence that he has been convicted of a crime is admissible if, but only if (1) the crime involved dishonesty or false statement, or (2) the crime was punishable by death or imprisonment in excess of one year under the law under which he was convicted, unless the judge determines that the danger of unfair prejudice outweighs the probative value of the evidence of conviction."

House Bill H.R. 5463 (February 1974)

"For the purpose of attacking the credibility of a witness, evidence that he has been convicted of a crime is admissible only if the crime involved dishonesty or false statement."

Senate Judiciary Committee (Draft October 1974)

"For the purpose of attacking the credibility of a witness, evidence that he has been convicted of a crime may be elicited from him or established by public record during cross-examination but only if the crime (1) involved dishonesty or false statement or (2) in the case of witnesses other than the accused, was punishable by death or imprisonment in excess of one year under the law under which he was convicted, but only if the court determines that the probative value of admitting this evidence outweighs its prejudicial effect."

Current Version

(a) In General. The following rules apply to attacking a witness's character for truthfulness by evidence of a criminal conviction: (1) for a crime that, in the convicting jurisdiction, was punishable by death or by imprisonment for more than one year, the evidence: (A) must be admitted, subject to Rule 403, in a civil case or in a criminal case in which the witness is not a defendant; and (B) must be admitted in a criminal case in which the witness is a defendant, if the probative value of the evidence outweighs its prejudicial effect to that defendant; and (2) for any crime regardless of the punishment, the evidence must be admitted if the court can readily determine that establishing the elements of the crime required proving — or the witness's admitting — a dishonest act or false statement.

Compare the current FRE 609(a) with the following state rules:

Alaska 609(a)

"(a) General rule. For the purpose of attacking the credibility of a witness, evidence that he has been convicted of a crime is only admissible if the crime involved dishonesty or false statement."

Montana 609

"For the purpose of attacking the credibility of a witness, evidence that the witness has been convicted of a crime is not admissible."

Compare the Federal Rules of Evidence with the following state laws on impeachment:

N.Y. CPLR 4514

"In addition to impeachment in the manner permitted by common law, any party may introduce proof that any witness has made a prior statement inconsistent with his testimony if the statement was made in a writing subscribed by him or was made under oath."

Indiana Code Chapter 34-1-15-1

"When a witness, whether a party to the record or not, is cross examined to lay the foundation for his impeachment by proof of an act or statement inconsistent with his testimony, and is asked if he did not do the act or make the statement, and he answers that he does not recollect having done the act or made the statement, the party thus laying the foundation for impeachment shall have the right to introduce evidence of the act or statement in the same manner as if the witness had answered that he had not done the act or made the statement."

Hawaii Chapter 626 Rule 609.1

"(a) General rule. The credibility of a witness may be attacked by evidence of bias, interest, or motive.

(b) Extrinsic evidence of bias, interest, or motive. Extrinsic evidence of a witness' bias, interest, or motive is not admissible unless, on cross-examination, the matter is brought to the attention of the witness and the witness is afforded an opportunity to explain or deny the matter."

§ 7.03 MIXED PROBLEMS

Problem #7-32: "Betty Sue"

Astrid was charged with counterfeiting. Betty Sue testified as an eyewitness for the prosecution in its case-in-chief.

May the prosecutor ask Betty Sue either of the following questions on direct examination?

1. "Were you convicted of armed robbery in 1990?"

2. "Do you know, Betty Sue, that Astrid was previously convicted of counterfeiting in 1991?"

Which of the following questions are proper impeachment?

3. "Isn't it true, Betty Sue, that you observed Astrid for just under one minute, and not 'around ten minutes' as you just testified?"

4. "You've hated Astrid since she was promoted ahead of you when you worked together at the Department of the Treasury, isn't that right?"

5. "Betty Sue, you've been convicted of shoplifting, correct?"

6. "You've also been convicted of aggravated battery?"

7. "You've also spanked your child?"

8. "In fact, Betty Sue, you have a form of attention deficit disorder, true?"

9. "Betty Sue, didn't you say in your deposition that you weren't sure of the denomination of the bill Astrid used to purchase her groceries, when you just testified that you were positive she used a twenty dollar bill?"

If Astrid testifies that she did not pass a counterfeit bill as charged, can the prosecution, in rebuttal: (1) call Melissa to testify that Astrid is known in the community for being a liar, or (2) call Mistral to testify that Astrid filed a false Sears credit card application?

Problem #7-33: Cliff and Norm

Officer Cliff arrested Norm at Sammy's Pool Hall after Norm battered another patron with a pool cue. At trial, Officer Cliff testifies.

1. Officer Cliff is asked on direct examination whether Norm has a reputation in the community for being violent. Permissible?

2. On cross-examination, Officer Cliff is asked whether he had arrested Norm on two previous occasions. Permissible?

3. If Officer Cliff denies arresting Norm on two other occasions, can a different witness be brought in on rebuttal to testify that she saw Cliff arrest Norm twice before?

4. Can Cliff be asked on cross-examination, "Isn't it true that you were indicted by a grand jury for embezzlement?"

Problem #7-34: Dr. Doctor

Dr. Artis Polaski testified as an expert witness for the plaintiff on the cause of death of a person who died suddenly after returning from a construction job on a Caribbean island.

1. On cross-examination of Dr. Polaski, would it be permissible for the opposing counsel, Sarah, to ask Dr. Polaski, "Your conclusion about the meaning of decedent's symptoms disagrees with Dr. Von Hayes in her treatise, *Tropical Diseases and Their Treatment*, isn't that right?"

2. Also on cross-examination, may Sarah ask Dr. Polaski, "You now testify that you reviewed the records twice prior to reaching your conclusions?" [Yes.] "Yet in your deposition that was taken six months ago, you did not mention that you reviewed any records at all in reaching your conclusion in response to the question, 'What did you do to prepare for reaching a conclusion on the cause of death?' "

3. If Dr. Polaski is asked about and denies having been convicted of filing a false income tax statement, can Sarah offer a certified copy of the conviction in evidence?

Problem #7-35: "A Witness Named Wanda"

The Wankle Co. brought a contract action against Feckless Turbide, Inc. Wanda, a witness to the oral agreement, testified for the plaintiff.

1. On direct examination, Wanda is asked numerous questions. Which, if any, of these questions are permissible?

a. "What occurred at approximately 4 p.m. on January 29th?" [The parties agreed to a restructuring of the debt.]

b. "Did you observe the parties shake hands on the agreement?" [No.]

c. "Why were you there?" [To provide business advice.]

d. "What did Bernie Parmetton, the CEO of Wankle Co., say and do at that time?" [He stormed out of the room.]

e. "Could you repeat for me how the agreement occurred?" [Well, . . .]

2. On cross-examination, counsel asks Wanda numerous questions. Which, if any, of the questions that follow are permissible? Why?

a. "So you were present at the time of the so-called 'agreement'?"

b. "You were not in the room where the alleged handshake occurred during the entire meeting, were you?"

c. "You often dress in outdated fashions, don't you?"

d. "Shantay also was at the meeting, wasn't she?"

Problem #7-36: A Truly Cross-Examination

A gun fight occurred after a dispute at a card game. One of the players was killed. Two people were located as eyewitnesses, fellow card players Kramer and Jerry. Both admitted to the prosecutor that they disliked the police and did not want to testify against their fellow card player, Elaine, who was charged with the crime.

1. Can the prosecutor use leading questions on the direct examination of either Kramer or Jerry? Why?

2. If the prosecution asks Kramer about the evening in question, particularly the incident following the card game that led to the gun fight, can the defense counsel ask about the card game and events that occurred during the game on cross-examination? Why?

3. Is it beyond the scope of the direct examination if, on cross-examination, Kramer is asked whether he had recently been convicted of armed robbery? Why?

4. Is the cross-examination of Kramer or Jerry important to the defense? Why? What might be the objectives of defense counsel in conducting such a cross-examination?

Problem #7-37: The Forgetful Witness

Rohan testified in a land condemnation action for the defense. On direct examination, he is asked where he first heard discussions about the government initiating eminent domain proceedings on the property in question, which was located in a neighborhood of modest means. Rohan responded by saying "I forget."

1. Can counsel ask Rohan to read his notes on the question to the jury?

2. Can Rohan rely on his notes during the testimony? Why?

3. Can counsel suggest to Rohan that "it might have been the International House of Pancakes?"

4. Can counsel show Rohan a note that states "It was IHOP, Mr. Scatter-brained!"? If this method is permissible, why would it not be used?

5. What documents or items may be used to refresh Rohan's memory? Can inadmissible evidence be used to refresh memory? Why?

Problem #7-38: Perjury's Sister

Paulette is prosecuted for perjury. She testifies, claiming that she told the truth when she testified in the previous trial concerning allegations her boyfriend was a major trafficker in narcotics. In rebuttal, can the prosecution call Paulette's estranged brother to testify that Paulette has a reputation in the community for being untruthful? Explain.

§ 7.04 SUMMARY AND REVIEW

1. Compare impeachment evidence and character evidence.

2. How are prior inconsistent statements a form of contradiction?

3. Why is extrinsic impeachment generally more restricted than intrinsic impeachment?

4. Define "bias."

5. What types of crimes may be used to impeach a witness?

6. Why are the permissible forms of impeachment by conviction limited to felonies and crimes of dishonesty or false statement?

7. Why did the FRE adopt a special "prejudice" balancing test for impeachment of criminal defendants with prior convictions?

8. What types of acts are permissible in "prior bad acts" impeachment? Why?

9. What is impeachment by omission?

10. What are the permissible ways to refresh a witness's memory?

You have heard testimony that the day in question was cold, windy, and with above-average precipitation. Do you still maintain it was a nice day?"

Chapter 8

THE COMPETENCY OF WITNESSES [FRE 601–606]

CHAPTER FRAMEWORK: Competency is a prerequisite to witness testimony that requires witnesses to understand what it means to tell the truth. With the presumption of competency in FRE 601, just about all witnesses can testify, with the notable exception of very young children who might not understand what it means to tell the truth. Competency is a separate concept from the credibility of a witness. While competency considerations can bar a witness from testifying, credibility issues involve the weight accorded the testimony by the trier of fact.

WHY ARE THE CONCEPTS IN THIS CHAPTER IMPORTANT? The concepts illustrate a basic prerequisite to witness testimony. Competency concepts provide an initial screening of witnesses to ensure accuracy and confidence in court proceedings — underscoring the importance of truth-telling.

CONNECTIONS: Competency is the first step in witness examination. It also is considered a substantive issue, meaning that when state law supplies the rule of decision in a federal court case pursuant to the *Erie* Doctrine, state law governs competency questions.

CHAPTER OUTLINE:

 I. Who Is Competent to Testify?

   A. General rule: all witnesses competent [FRE 601]

     1. Preference for more, not less, testimony

     2. Preference for and due process requirement of cross-examination — not exclusion — for testing witness

   B. Caveat: federal courts apply state competency rules where state law supplies rule of decision

     1. E.g., State Dead Man's Statutes — prohibit witnesses from testifying about communications or transactions with deceased or insane persons

 II. Requirements for Witness Competency

   A. Understanding what it means to tell the truth

   B. Testimony must be relevant

   C. Generally testimony must be based on personal knowledge [FRE 602]

     1. Exceptions: for expert witness [FRE 703] & admissions by party opponents [FRE 801(d)(2)]

III. Exceptions to Competency

    A. Judges — cannot testify in proceeding they are presiding [FRE 605]

        1. No objection necessary to preserve issue for appeal [FRE 605]

    B. Jurors — cannot testify in trial that they are sitting [FRE 605]

        1. objection is necessary to preserve issue on appeal

    C. Lawyers competent to testify under FRE

        1. Testifying lawyer may be ethically disqualified as counsel [MRPC 3.7]

IV. Special Competency Case

    A. Hypnotically refreshed testimony generally prohibited

        1. Exception if sufficient indicia or reliability

* * * * *

RELEVANT EVIDENCE RULES

Rule 601. Competency to Testify in General

Every person is competent to be a witness unless these rules provide otherwise. But in a civil case, state law governs the witness's competency regarding a claim or defense for which state law supplies the rule of decision.

Rule 602. Need for Personal Knowledge

A witness may testify to a matter only if evidence is introduced sufficient to support a finding that the witness has personal knowledge of the matter. Evidence to prove personal knowledge may consist of the witness's own testimony. This rule does not apply to a witness's expert testimony under Rule 703.

Rule 603. Oath or Affirmation to Testify Truthfully

Before testifying, a witness must give an oath or affirmation to testify truthfully. It must be in a form designed to impress that duty on the witness's conscience.

Rule 604. Interpreter

An interpreter must be qualified and must give an oath or affirmation to make a true translation.

Rule 605. Judge's Competency as a Witness

The presiding judge may not testify as a witness at the trial. A party need not object to preserve the issue.

Rule 606. Juror's Competency as a Witness

(a) At the Trial. A juror may not testify as a witness before the other jurors at the trial. If a juror is called to testify, the court must give a party an opportunity to object outside the jury's presence.

(b) During an Inquiry into the Validity of a Verdict or Indictment.

(1) *Prohibited Testimony or Other Evidence.* During an inquiry into the validity of a verdict or indictment, a juror may not testify about any statement made or incident that occurred during the jury's deliberations; the effect of anything on that juror's or another juror's vote; or any juror's mental processes concerning the verdict or indictment. The court may not receive a juror's affidavit or evidence of a juror's statement on these matters.

(2) *Exceptions.* A juror may testify about whether:

(A) extraneous prejudicial information was improperly brought to the jury's attention;

(B) an outside influence was improperly brought to bear on any juror; or

(C) a mistake was made in entering the verdict on the verdict form.

§ 8.01 COMPETENCY: WHO MAY TESTIFY

[A] Presumption of Competency

All witnesses are presumed to be competent to testify under FRE 601. If a witness is able to tell the truth and provide relevant evidence, the witness can testify.

The FRE 601 presumption of witness competency is not based on a long-standing trial tradition. Historical incompetencies occurred in the common law, as well as by statute. Historically, a person might have been considered incompetent to testify due to a conviction of a felony, a lack of religious beliefs, or mental infirmity. At one time, even witnesses who had a stake in the outcome of a case, such as the parties, were prevented from testifying.

FRE 601 does not always govern competency in federal cases. The FRE defer to state law regarding witness competency, if state law provides the rule of decision in a case. This rule may sound familiar because it is — the provision is identical to the FRE 501 which governs whether state or federal privilege law applies in federal court. *See* FRE 501. *See also* FRE 302, relating to presumptions.

The presumption of competency under FRE 601 is only an initial status; it does not mean that every aspiring witness will be permitted to testify. The presumptively qualified witness must meet the foundational requirement of understanding what it means to tell the truth. FRE 603 reinforces the obligation of witnesses to testify truthfully by requiring an oath to tell the truth or an acknowledgment of a statement designed to impress that duty on the witness's conscience. In addition, the witness must possess some relevant information, and must bypass several carefully delineated exceptions involving testimony by the judge and jurors.

[B] "Dead Man's" Statutes

While states have abolished most incompetencies (e.g., mental infirmity, conviction of a felony) one that has survived to the present day is the so-called "dead man's statute."

"Dead man's statutes" vary in form and substance in those states that have them. Generally, however, such a statute prohibits a claimant from testifying about a communication or transaction with a deceased or insane person in an action brought against that person, that person's estate, or that person's representative. These statutes can be viewed as "anti-gold-digger" rules, because they prevent people from fabricating claims against a now-deceased or insane person (who was or is often quite wealthy). Without the rule, the deceased's estate or insane person would be ill-equipped to refute the alleged communication or transaction.

An example of a "dead man's statute" is found in the Idaho Code.

Idaho Code § 9-202. Who may not testify

The following persons cannot be witnesses:

. . . .

3. Parties or assignors of parties to an action or proceeding, or persons in whose behalf an action or proceeding is prosecuted against an executor or administrator, upon a claim or demand against the estate of a deceased person, as to any communication or agreement, not in writing, occurring before the death of such deceased person.

Practical Tip:

Perserving Testimony. Lawyers should consider the need to preserve testimony in the case of terminally ill or otherwise frail witnesses, for example by videotaping their depositions.

[C] Understanding the Obligation to Be Truthful

The primary foundational requirement for witness competency is that the witness must be able to understand what it means to be truthful. This prerequisite has no bright-line litmus test, perhaps because imposing a bright-line standard would be difficult, if not insuperable. As the Advisory Committee's Note to FRE 601 aptly stated, "No mental or moral qualifications for testifying as a witness are specified. Standards of mental capacity have proved elusive in actual application."

Illustration: Possible Bias

Madeleine Marlin, a former Chief Executive Officer of a large manufacturing firm, dies in a two-car automobile accident on the corner of 14th and Coral Avenues. Her estate is sued for damages by the survivors of the other car. The driver of the other car, Louisa, and her daughter, Carla, age six, wish to testify. Will Louisa and Carla be permitted to testify?

Answer: Both Louisa and Carla likely will be allowed to testify under FRE 601 and under many state rules of evidence as well. The federal rule presumes that both Louisa and Carla are competent to testify, even though both may be biased. If Carla shows that she can understand the truth and provide relevant evidence, her age will not prevent her from testifying.

A "dead man's statute" might apply if state law supplies the rule of decision in the case. Even if such a statute applied, however, the automobile accident would probably not come within the statute's prohibition of testimony about transactions or oral communications. Thus, Carla and Louisa likely would be able to testify.

Practical Tip:

Requirement of Continuing Truthfulness. Lawyers should remind clients and witnesses that the obligation to be truthful applies all the time (e.g., testimony at depositions), that serious consequences flow from untruthfulness (e.g., a charge of perjury), that the lawyer has an ethical obligation to correct untruthful testimony, and that it is ultimately the lawyer's job to deal with unfavorable facts rather than to have others distort the truth.

It is assumed in the FRE that the overwhelming majority of witnesses understand their obligation to testify truthfully. This assumption extends even to convicted perjurers (who will be given an opportunity to incur yet another perjury conviction by taking the witness stand). There is one category where the truthfulness foundation is tested, however, and that is the child witness. An attorney must carefully lay a foundation with child witnesses to establish their understanding of the difference between truth and falsehood.

Illustration: Child Witness

ATTORNEY: Hi, Rebecca. How are you?

A: Fine.

ATTORNEY: Good. I am going to ask you a few questions, Okay?

A: Okay.

ATTORNEY: Can I call you Becca?

A: My Mommy and Daddy do.

ATTORNEY: Becca, how old are you?

A: Four. Last week!

ATTORNEY: Did you have a birthday party on your birthday?

A: Yes. With cake.

ATTORNEY: With whom do you live, Becca?

A: My Mommy and Daddy and Emma.

ATTORNEY: Who is Emma?

A: My sister.

ATTORNEY: Becca, do you know what it means to tell the truth?

A: Yes.

ATTORNEY: What happens when you don't tell the truth?

A: Mommy sends me to timeout.

ATTORNEY: What is that?

A: It is when I am in trouble.

ATTORNEY: What happens during timeout?

A: I stand in a corner. I'm not allowed to talk.

ATTORNEY: Is it fun?

A: Noooo.

ATTORNEY: What happens if you tell the truth?

A: Nothing.

ATTORNEY: No timeout?

A: No.

ATTORNEY: Are you going to tell the truth here today?

A: Yes. (While nodding her head up and down.)

ATTORNEY: Now, remember when there was a fire at your house?

A: Yes. Who was home at the time?

In addition to understanding the obligation of telling the truth, witnesses also must be able to provide relevant testimony. No matter how entertaining or informative irrelevant testimony might be, that testimony will be excluded. Further, even if the testimony is relevant, it generally must be based on personal, first-hand knowledge. *See* FRE 602.

[D]   Requirement of Personal Knowledge

FRE 602 requires all lay witnesses to possess personal knowledge. Without personal knowledge, a lay person likely violates the Rules in at least two ways: (1) the testimony is probably based on hearsay, in which case the original declarants would be the preferable witnesses; and (2) the testimony is probably speculation, which would distract the jury from drawing its own inferences from the admitted evidence.

FRE 602 permits some witnesses to testify without personal knowledge. The most significant example of testimony without personal knowledge involves expert witnesses, who routinely testify based on facts supplied to them either before or during their testimony. *See* FRE 703. Similarly, out-of-court admissions of party opponents (generally offered through the testimony of in-court witnesses) are admissible in evidence even if they were not based on the party's personal knowledge. *See* FRE 801(d)(2).

FRE 602 can be viewed as acting in concert with FRE 701, which describes when lay persons may offer opinions. As FRE 701 explains, a lay witness may offer opinions or inferences if the opinions are "(a) rationally based on the witness's perception; (b) helpful to a clear understanding of the witness's testimony or to determining a fact in issue; and (c) not based on scientific evidence ... or other specialized knowledge...." Thus, the personal knowledge requirement leaves some room for lay witnesses to offer opinions and inferences, but only within narrow guidelines.

Illustration: Requirement of Personal Knowledge

Peter brings suit against his neighbor, Stanley, for civil assault, trespass, and conversion. At trial, Peter calls another neighbor, Howard, to testify. In the course of the direct examination, the following exchange occurs:

PLAINTIFF'S ATTORNEY: Now, Howard, what happened at 6:45 p.m. on January 4th?

A: Stanley walked across the path between his and Peter's house. He was carrying a disgusting dead animal and plopped it down in Peter's backyard. And —

DEFENDANT'S ATTORNEY: Objection. Lack of personal knowledge, Your Honor.

JUDGE: To the bench, counsel.

PLAINTIFF'S ATTORNEY: Your Honor, Howard had seen Peter walk across that path innumerable times on prior occasions, if not this one, and was told by Elma, who always is a reliable source of information for what happens in that part of the neighborhood, that Peter walked across the path on this occasion with the dead animal.

JUDGE: I am going to sustain the objection. Even if Howard had observed Peter traverse the path many times before, he cannot opine that Peter did so on this occasion. If anyone should testify about Peter's alleged trip with the dead animal, it ought to be Elma. Instead, Howard's testimony is hearsay when he offers Elma's statement as his own. There is a great preference for putting Elma on the witness stand to hear about her observations directly. Please continue with the examination. Again, the objection is sustained.

[E] Testimony by Juror, Attorney, or Judge

It is problematic when an attorney in the case, the judge, or one of the jurors is called to testify at trial. This creates at least the appearance of a conflict of interest and possibly an actual conflict that compromises neutrality.

This situation might arise in one of two ways: (1) the judge, a juror, or an attorney is asked to testify about an issue in the case; or (2) one of them is asked to testify about the misconduct of another participant in the trial. An attorney, judge, or juror who is called to testify at trial thereby takes on the additional and possibly conflicting role of a witness. This assumption of the role of witness creates at least an appearance of impropriety and possibly a conflict of interest.

These issues could be addressed under FRE 403, by balancing the risk of unfair prejudice against the probative value of the testimony sought or by a motion for a mistrial. Instead, FRE 605 and 606 deal with some of these issues directly. FRE 605 unequivocally prohibits the presiding judge from testifying in the trial. The judge's impartiality would be completely compromised — in appearance, if not in fact — if the judge took on the role of a witness and testified for one side in a dispute. Also, the mechanics of the judge playing dual roles would be awkward at best. FRE 605 also provides that no objection is needed to "preserve the point" on appeal if a judge testifies; this indicates that such conduct would constitute plain error. *See* FRE 103. The scope of FRE 605 is sufficiently broad to prohibit judicial commentary from the bench that is tantamount to giving testimony. *See United States v. Nickl*, 427 F.3d 1286 (10th Cir. 2005). Judges and their employees, such as law clerks, also violate the rule when commenting about their experiments or visits to locations that concern a case before the judge. *See Kennedy v. Great Atlantic & Pacific Tea Co.*, 551 F.2d 593 (5th Cir. 1977).

FRE 606(a) prohibits jurors from testifying in a case in which they are sitting. It also provides that the party opposing juror testimony must have the opportunity to object outside the presence of the jury in order to preserve the issue for appeal. As with judges, it is extremely rare that jurors will be called to testify in a case in which they are sitting. The jury selection process generally eliminates potential fact witnesses from the jury pool.

FRE 606(b) prohibits juror testimony or affidavits that attack a prior verdict or indictment. It also prohibits a juror from disclosing information concerning the jury's deliberation, including statements about a juror's mental and emotional processes, physical state (e.g., intoxication), votes, and assent or dissent from the final outcome. FRE 606(b)'s prohibition against disclosure should encourage full and frank discussion during jury deliberations, discourage harassment of jurors by unhappy parties, promote verdict finality, and foster public trust in the jury system. *See Virgin Islands v. Gereau*, 523 F.2d 140 (3d Cir. 1975). FRE 606(b) does not preclude juror testimony after a verdict or indictment has been handed down, to the extent that the testimony is offered to prove misconduct or the interjection of extraneous prejudicial information or "outside influence." *See Parker v. Gladden*, 385 U.S. 363 (1966).

Misconduct by jurors and attorneys, as well as by judges, poses a serious threat to the trial process. The legal process is predicated on public acceptance of verdicts as true and just. Particularly in criminal cases, the jury acts on behalf of the community. If misconduct occurs, the public's confidence in the system may be shaken, even damaged irreparably. In a sense, misconduct contaminates the special, prejudice-free environment that the jury system attempts to maintain.

Before a judicial inquiry will be initiated about juror misconduct, the moving party must first make a sufficient showing. *See Hard v. Burlington N. R.R.*, 812 F.2d 482 (9th Cir. 1987). For example, an allegation that a juror performed an experiment regarding the alleged facts of the case was sufficient to justify juror testimony. *See, e.g., In re Beverly Hills Fire Litigation*, 695 F.2d 207 (6th Cir. 1982), *cert. denied*, 461 U.S. 929 (1983) (a juror apparently used his own wiring to conduct an independent experiment in a case concerning a fire that was allegedly caused by faulty wiring). A duty to take juror testimony may arise when the court is informed about evidence obtained by jurors, juror investigations, juror insanity, jurors who have been threatened or bribed, or juror interactions with witnesses or parties. *See* G. Weissenberger and J. Duane, *Federal Rules of Evidence: Rules, Legislative History, Commentary and Authority* (Lexis Pub. Co. 2009).

While the basic rule prohibiting judges from testifying in the trial over which they are presiding is plain on its face, there remain several unanswered questions. It is unclear, for example, whether judges who have been asked to testify in a case or simply have personal knowledge about the events in question, must disqualify themselves from the case even if not actually called to testify. *See* G. Weissenberger and J. Duane, *Federal Rules of Evidence: Rules, Legislative History, Commentary and Authority* (Lexis Pub. Co. 2009). According to the pertinent law, disqualification is warranted when the judge's impartiality in the trial "might reasonably be questioned." 28 U.S.C. § 455. Thus, the appearance of impropriety is crucial to the recusal question. If it appears that judges might be biased, whether they are so in fact, the judges should disqualify themselves.

[F] Hypnotically Refreshed Testimony

A particularly nettlesome competency issue is the admissibility of hypnotically refreshed testimony. Like its counterpart, polygraph evidence, this type of testimony is firmly embedded within the popular culture, but as a matter of evidence law remains highly controversial. In many jurisdictions, hypnotically refreshed testimony is excluded from trial due to its lack of reliability. The exclusion occurs, for example, because hypnotically refreshed testimony often suffers from confabulation (in which the witness fills in and adds, sometimes inaccurately, to the actual recollection of an event) or memory hardening (in which a witness's confidence about the accuracy of recollection increases without justification).

Despite the general exclusion of hypnotically refreshed testimony, several exceptions have been carved out in some jurisdictions, permitting it at trial. If it can be shown that the witness is testifying based on recollections that are independent of the hypnotic inducement, the witness still may be allowed to testify. Also, some jurisdictions admit hypnotically refreshed testimony if it is shown to be sufficiently trustworthy. In these jurisdictions, questions about the accuracy of the testimony bear on the weight accorded the testimony by the trier of fact.

Another exception to the general exclusion of hypnotically refreshed evidence is constitutionally based. This exception, as delineated by the Supreme Court, limits the extent to which hypnotically refreshed testimony by criminal defendants can be excluded from trial. The Due Process Clauses of the Fifth and Fourteenth Amendments, the Compulsory Process Clause of the Sixth Amendment, and the Fifth Amendment's privilege against self-incrimination provide criminal defendants with a qualified constitutional right to present a defense and testify in their own behalf. (*See Rock v. Arkansas*, reprinted in § 8.03[B], *below*.) Because such weighty constitutional rights are implicated, limitations on a criminal defendant's testimony, such as the exclusion of hypnotically refreshed testimony, must not be overbroad or arbitrary.

§ 8.02 COMPETENCY PROBLEMS

Personal Knowledge Requirement Problem

Problem #8-1: Robbin the Hood

Robbin the Hood is prosecuted for bank robbery. At trial, Robbin's wife, Gayle, testifies for the defense. She states that, before Robbin robbed the bank to give to the poor, he was despondent about the state of affairs in this country. The prosecution objects to this testimony, claiming that Gayle lacks personal knowledge about Robbin's state of mind.

1. What ruling and why?

2. Ethics Consideration — Trial Development. During Robbin's trial, he visits his attorney's office, brandishes a gun and exclaims: "I can't take it any longer and I want my wife to get all of my property. Please take care of that and here's the rest of the stolen bank money in my gym bag. I'm going now and finally ending it all!"

(a) Can the lawyer testify about Robin's mental state?

(b) What should the lawyer do regarding the stolen money?

(c) What is the lawyer's obligation to her client regarding his threat to harm himself? Alaska Rules of Prof'l Conduct R. 1.14. *See* MRPC 1.14.

Presumption of Competency Involving Age and Drug Use Problems

Problem #8-2: Say What?

Archie Oakley, age 102, was on his front porch when he observed a purse snatching approximately 20 yards away. While Archie could not positively identify the assailant, he was called to testify by the prosecution to provide other relevant information. Archie concedes that he is deaf in one ear, needs a hearing aid in the other, and has very poor vision. The defendant objects to Archie's testimony, claiming it is extremely unreliable. Is Archie competent to testify?

Problem #8-3: The Habitual Drug Addict

Paul observed an armed robbery in Pacific Heights one foggy Sunday morning. When Paul was called to testify for the prosecution, the defense objected. In an earlier deposition, Paul admitted that he was a heroin addict, and had been one for more than a decade. Should Paul's testimony be permitted?

Obligation of Truthfulness Problem

Problem #8-4: Honest Polly

Polly filed suit in Tax Court. At trial, she refused to swear or affirm on religious grounds. She did however agree to recite a statement that the testimony she was about to give was true and accurate to the best of her knowledge. She also agreed to add to that statement an acknowledgment that she would be subject to penalties for perjury. The Court prohibited her from testifying because of her refusal to swear or affirm. Polly appeals. What result? *See Ferguson v. C.I.R.*, 921 F.2d 588 (5th Cir. 1991).

Child Witnesses Problem

Problem #8-5: Conflicting Answers

Billy, a seven year old boy, was called to testify by the prosecution about a shoplifting he witnessed last year. During voir dire Billy was asked by the trial judge if he knew the difference between telling the truth and telling a lie, to which Billy said he did. Billy was further questioned by defense counsel:

Q: Do you know what a promise is?

A: Yes it when you do not tell another person something you do not want them to know.

Q: Are you sure — that sounds like a secret. Let me ask you again do you know what a promise is?

A: Umm, well a promise is something I guess you make sure you do.

Defense counsel filed a motion to exclude Billy on the grounds that he was incompetent to testify based on Billy's confusion concerning defense counsel's question. The trial judge denied the motion based on Billy's answers and mannerisms which convinced the judge that Billy was competent to testify. The defense appealed the judge's decision saying that Billy was clearly incompetent to testify. What ruling on appeal?

Problem #8-6: Child Abuse

In a prosecution for child abuse, Chirelle, age 4, is called to testify as an eyewitness. Will she be allowed to testify? If she is permitted to testify, what questions would you ask Chirelle to establish that she understands what it means to tell the truth?

Expert Witnesses Problem

Problem #8-7: Malpractice Expert

Andrea sued Dr. Malcovich for medical malpractice in a Minnesota federal court based on diversity of citizenship. A Minnesota state law provides that "experts testifying for plaintiffs in a medical malpractice action in the state must be licensed to practice medicine in the state or a contiguous state." Plaintiff calls Dr. Shira Rogers, a licensed internist/gynecologist in the State of Washington as her expert physician. The defendant objects. What ruling and why?

Judge and Juror Testimony Problems

Problem #8-8: Anyone But You

Judge Liz Wilber lived in a suburban neighborhood outside of Chicago. One wintry Saturday morning while she was walking her dog, Pudge, she witnessed two of her neighbors engaged in a fistfight. The fight ended when one neighbor took out a knife and stabbed the other, resulting in a serious wound. Judge Wilber coincidentally drew the case and presided over the trial.

The defense calls Judge Wilber as a "necessary" witness.

1. Can she testify if she states from the bench that testifying will not impair her impartiality?

2. If no objection is lodged by the opposing counsel, can Judge Wilber then testify?

3. Can the bailiff, who also lives in the neighborhood, testify?

4. Can the court reporter, who is a friend of the defendant, testify as a character witness?

5. Can the defendant's best friend, who was convicted of murder twice and perjury once, testify for the defendant on a minor question of fact?

6. Ethics Consideration. If the defendant's lawyer was the only witness, can opposing counsel have the defendant's lawyer disqualified from the case? Colorado Rules of Prof'l Conduct 3.7. *See* MRPC 3.7.

Problem# 8-9: The Over-Zealous Judge — Surprise Testimony

Defendant, owner of a bar, was charged with selling liquor to minors. At trial the defendant took the stand and testified that he had not sold liquor to minors. The judge asked the defendant several questions while he was on the witness stand:

Q: Didn't you come see me a few weeks ago in my chambers?

Q: And you asked me to let you off? And don't you remember that I told you that if you told the truth I would consider it?

Q: And you told me that you wouldn't tell the truth about it?

Are the judge's questions permissible? *See Terrell v. United States*, 6 F.2d 498 (4th Cir. 1925).

Juror as Witness

Problem #8-10: Jerry the Juror

Jerry, one of 12 jurors in a land condemnation dispute, is called to testify about a witness's credibility. The opponent to the testimony does not object. How should the judge rule?

Problem #8-11: Betty the Doomsday Juror

Betty is called to be a juror in a personal injury case concerning an automobile accident. During voir dire, Betty stated she could be impartial and weigh the evidence fairly. After trial, the jury returned a judgment for the defendant and awarded no damages to the plaintiff. Another juror, Susie, contacted Plaintiff's counsel and reported that Betty constantly noted during jury deliberations that she knew someone who was in a similar accident and, if that person was sued, his life would be finished. Plaintiff's counsel has filed a motion for a new trial based on Susie's statements concerning Betty's comments during jury deliberations. Can Susie's statements about Betty's comments be admitted into evidence to procure a new trial? *See Warger v. Shauers*, 135 S. Ct. 521 (2014).

Problem #8-12 The Googling Juror

Sean Flynn performed a Google search after receiving a juror summons but before voir dire and being seated on the jury. At trial, the judge permitted evidence of prior law suits for the limited purpose of showing the defendant manufacturer had notice of the defect. During jury deliberations and contrary to the trial evidence, five fellow jurors learned of Sean's search that revealed no prior law suits against the defendant. The plaintiff filed a motion for a new trial claiming juror misconduct. May Sean's fellow jurors testify about Sean's statements at the hearing for a new trial? Should the motion be granted?

Competency and Interpreters Problem

Problem #8-13: Iggy the Interpreter

Iggy took the Berlitz School of Languages correspondence course, Interpreting Spanish 101, but flunked out. Even so, Iggy volunteered to act as an interpreter for a Spanish-speaking defendant in an international drug smuggling case. If the prosecution objects, is Iggy still entitled to interpret? Explain.

Prosecutors as Witnesses Problem

Problem #8-14: The Deal

Enos, Nasty, and Usta are members of a radical ecological group that allegedly fire-bombed the office of the Sierra Club. Only Nasty and Usta are charged with the bombing, which killed two people. Enos is called to testify for the prosecution. The defense counsel believes that Enos had been offered a deal by the prosecution in exchange for his testimony, but that he would refuse to acknowledge such a deal at trial. The defense counsel wants to call as a rebuttal witness the assistant prosecutor who the defendant believes offered Enos the deal.

> 1. Can the assistant prosecutor testify? *See United States v. Newman,* 476 F.2d 733 (3d Cir. 1973).

> 2. Ethical Consideration: Nasty and Usta are convicted and sentenced to life in prison. A year after the trial, the prosecutor discovers credible evidence that Nasty and Usta actually had nothing to do with the bombing and that Enos orchestrated and carried out the bombing on his own What are the prosecutor's obligations regarding this new evidence? Idaho Rules of Prof'l Conduct R, 3.8(g) & (h). *See* MRPC 3.8(g) & (h).

Dead Man's Statute Problem

Problem #8-15: Dead Again and Again

Josie agreed in writing to sell Bernard her boat, pending an inspection. The inspection occurred and it was a complete success. Before the completion of the sale, however, Josie died. Bernard then brought suit against Josie's estate based on diversity of citizenship. Bernard sought specific performance of the contract. At trial, Bernard took the witness stand to testify about the terms of the contract. Will he be allowed to testify about the agreement if a "dead man's statute" applies? Explain.

Hypnotically Refreshed Testimony Problem

Problem #8-16: Hypnotized

Lil, the victim of an armed robbery at gunpoint, cannot remember what happened during the robbery no matter how hard she tries to recall the events. After she made numerous unsuccessful attempts to recall the crime, she is hypnotized by a certified police neuropsychologist. After the hypnosis, Lil was able to recall what had occurred during the robbery, even remembering the identity of the perpetrator. Will Lil be allowed to testify at trial?

§ 8.03 CASES AND RULES

[A] United States v. Phibbs

United States Court of Appeals for the Sixth Circuit
999 F.2d 1053 (6th Cir. 1993), cert. denied, 114 S. Ct. 1070 (1994)

RALPH B. GUY, CIRCUIT JUDGE:

Defendants, Raymond Huckelby, Diane Whited, Robert Phibbs, Victor Rojas, and Robert Murr appeal their convictions arising from their participation in a cocaine distribution ring operating in Tennessee and Kentucky. . . .

. . . .

Whited raises the following allegations of error: . . . (5) two key government witnesses should have been declared incompetent to testify. . . .

. . . .

Whited claims that witnesses Jerry Parks and Tommy McKeehan were incompetent to give testimony on grounds of mental incapacity. In the case of Parks, he had previously been found incompetent to stand trial, had a history of auditory delusions, and had spent time in mental health facilities. As for McKeehan, Whited cites an affidavit filed with the district court by his treating psychiatrist that he could not assist his counsel in an upcoming trial because he suffered from "confusion, agitation, paranoia and hallucinations." This affidavit was dated four days prior to McKeehan having entered into a plea agreement with the government. Because of such information, Whited contends that, at the very least, it was error for the court not to conduct a preliminary examination of Parks' and McKeehan's competency as witnesses.

Under Rule 601 of the Federal Rules of Evidence (General Rule of Competency), "[e]very person is competent to be a witness except as otherwise provided in these rules." The Advisory Committee Notes to Rule 601 explain that "[t]his general ground-clearing eliminates all grounds of incompetency not specifically recognized in the rules of this Article." Accordingly, "[n]o mental or moral qualifications for testifying as a witness" are specified. *Id.* This is because "[s]tandards of mental capacity have proved elusive in actual application." *Id.*

Thus, the Federal Rules of Evidence strongly disfavor barring witnesses on competency grounds due to mental incapacity. As we wrote in *United States v. Ramirez*, 871 F.2d 582, 584 (6th Cir.), *cert. denied*, 493 U.S. 841, 110 S. Ct. 127, 107 L. Ed. 2d 88 (1989):

> What must be remembered, and is often confused, is that "competency" is a matter of status not ability. Thus, the only two groups of persons specifically rendered incompetent as witnesses by the Federal Rules of Evidence are judges (Rule 605) and jurors (Rule 606). . . .

The district court did not rule on Parks' competency before he took the stand; later in considering a motion for judgment of acquittal, the court indicated that Parks and McKeehan "were not crazy witnesses." Likewise, it addressed the question of McKeehan's mental capacity during a bench conference held after he had begun to testify. The court stated that it had "observed Mr. McKeehan, and he appears to the Court to be sober, cogent. He appears to the Court to know exactly where he is and what he is doing. . . ."

. . . .

Hence, the district court did not find that Parks and McKeehan were incapable of understanding their oath and obligation to testify truthfully. Nor did the court find, based on its observations, that their mental abilities were so limited that they did not have sufficient capacity to perceive events, to remember them, and to describe them for the benefit of the trier of fact. *See* Fed. R. Evid. 602. The court was not required, as Whited would have it, to conduct a special examination into their competency. If either Parks' or McKeehan's behavior raised concerns stemming from Rule 602 or 603, it could have excluded their testimony (or portions thereof) without any examination whatsoever. Furthermore, the court had the additional authority, pursuant to Rule 403, to exclude their testimony in light of their past or present mental state. The court chose not to take any of these measures in these circumstances. Instead it permitted defense counsel to use the psychiatric records of Parks and McKeehan, as well as other indicia of their mental capacity, to vigorously attack their credibility.

After carefully reviewing the record, we conclude that the district court did not abuse its discretion. . . . As long as a witness appreciates his duty to tell the truth, and is minimally capable of observing, recalling, and communicating events, his testimony should come in for whatever it is worth. It is then up to the opposing party to dispute the witness' powers of apprehension, which well may be impaired by mental illness or other factors. As we are persuaded that Parks and McKeehan were at least minimally capable of offering reliable evidence, the possible weaknesses in their testimony went to its credibility, and so were to be assessed by the jury. . . .

. . . .

[B]   Rock v. Arkansas

United States Supreme Court
483 U.S. 44 (1987)

JUSTICE BLACKMUM delivered the opinion of the Court.

The issue presented in this case is whether Arkansas' evidentiary rule prohibiting the admission of hypnotically refreshed testimony violated the petitioner's constitutional right to testify on her own behalf as a defendant in a criminal case.

Petitioner Vickie Lorene Rock was charged with manslaughter in the death of her husband, Frank Rock, on July 2, 1983. A dispute had been simmering about Frank's wish to move from the couple's small apartment adjacent to Vickie's beauty parlor to a trailer she owned outside town. That night a fight erupted when Frank refused to let petitioner eat some pizza and prevented her from leaving the apartment to get something else to eat. . . . When police arrived on the scene they found Frank on the floor with a bullet wound in his chest. Petitioner urged the officers to help her husband, TR 230, and cried to a sergeant who took her in charge, "please save him" and "don't let him die." . . .

Because petitioner could not remember the precise details of the shooting, her attorney suggested that she submit to hypnosis in order to refresh her memory. Petitioner was hypnotized twice by Doctor Bettye Back, a licensed neuropsychologist with training in the field of hypnosis. . . .

When the prosecutor learned of the hypnosis sessions, he filed a motion to exclude petitioner's testimony. The trial judge held a pretrial hearing on the motion and concluded that no hypnotically refreshed testimony would be admitted. . . . The jury convicted petitioner on the manslaughter charge. . . .

On appeal, the Supreme Court of Arkansas rejected petitioner's claim that the limitations on her testimony violated her right to present her defense. . . . Any "prejudice or deprivation" she suffered "was minimal and resulted from her own actions and not by any erroneous ruling of the court." . . . . We granted certiorari . . . to consider the constitutionality of Arkansas' *per se* rule excluding a criminal defendant's hypnotically refreshed testimony.

Petitioner's claim that her testimony was impermissibly excluded is bottomed on her constitutional right to testify in her own defense. At this point in the development of our adversary system, it cannot be doubted that a defendant in a criminal case has the right to take the witness stand and to testify in his or her own defense. This, of course, is a change from the historic common-law view, which was that all parties to litigation, including criminal defendants, were disqualified from testifying because of their interest in the outcome of the trial. . . .

　. . .

　. . . . The necessary ingredients of the Fourteenth Amendment's guarantee that no one shall be deprived of liberty without due process of law include a right to be heard and to offer testimony:

> "A person's right to reasonable notice of a charge against him, and *an opportunity to be heard in his defense* — a right to his day in court — are basic in our system of jurisprudence; and these rights include, as a minimum, a right to examine the witnesses against him, to offer testimony, and to be represented by counsel." (Emphasis added.) *In re Oliver*, 333 U.S. 257, 273 (1948).

The right to testify is also found in the Compulsory Process Clause of the Sixth Amendment, which grants a defendant the right to call "witness in his favor," a right that is guaranteed in the criminal courts of the States by the Fourteenth Amendment. . . . Logically included in the accused's right to call witnesses whose testimony is "material and favorable to his defense," . . . is a right to testify himself, should he decide it is in his favor to do so. In fact, the most important witness for the defense in many criminal cases is the defendant himself. . . .

. . . .

The Arkansas rule enunciated by the state courts does not allow a trial court to consider whether posthypnosis testimony may be admissible in a particular case; it is a *per se* rule prohibiting the admission at trial of any defendant's hypnotically refreshed testimony on the ground that such testimony is always unreliable. Thus, in Arkansas, an accused's testimony is limited to matters that he or she can prove were remembered before hypnosis. This rule operates to the detriment of any defendant who undergoes hypnosis, without regard to the reasons for it, the circumstances under which it took place, or any independent verification of the information it produced.

In establishing its *per se* rule, the Arkansas Supreme Court simply followed the approach taken by a number of States that have decided that hypnotically enhanced testimony should be excluded at trial on the ground that it tends to be unreliable. Other States that have adopted an exclusionary rule, however, have done so for the testimony of *witnesses*, not for the testimony of a *defendant*. The Arkansas Supreme Court failed to perform the constitutional analysis that is necessary when a defendant's right to testify is at stake.

. . . .

Responses of individuals to hypnosis vary greatly. The popular belief that hypnosis guarantees the accuracy of recall is as yet without established foundation and, in fact, hypnosis often has no effect at all on memory. The most common response to hypnosis, however, appears to be an increase in both correct and incorrect recollections. Three general characteristics of hypnosis may lead to the introduction of inaccurate memories: the subject becomes "suggestible" and may try to please the hypnotist with answers the subject thinks will be met with approval; the subject is likely to "confabulate," that is, to fill in details from the imagination in order to make an answer more coherent and complete; and, the subject experiences "memory hardening," which gives him great confidence in both true and false memories, making effective cross-examination more difficult. . . . Despite the unreliability that hypnosis concededly may introduce, however, the procedure has been credited as instrumental in obtaining investigative leads or identifications that were later confirmed by independent evidence. . . .

. . . .

We are not now prepared to endorse without qualifications the use of hypnosis as an investigative tool; scientific understanding of the phenomenon and of the means to control the effects of hypnosis is still in its infancy. Arkansas, however, has not justified the exclusion of *all* of a defendant's testimony that the defendant is unable to prove to be the product of prehypnosis memory. A State's legitimate interest in barring unreliable evidence does not extend to *per se* exclusions that may be reliable in an individual case. Wholesale inadmissibility of a defendant's testimony is an arbitrary restriction on the right to testify in the absence of clear evidence by the State repudiating the validity of all posthypnosis recollections. . . .

In this case, . . . [t]he tape recordings provided some means to evaluate the hypnosis and the trial judge concluded that Doctor Back did not suggest responses with leading questions. . . . Those circumstances present an argument for admissibility of petitioner's testimony in this particular case, an argument that must be considered by the trial court. Arkansas' *per se* rule excluding all posthypnosis testimony infringes impermissibly on the right of a defendant to testify on his own behalf.

The judgment . . . is vacated, and the case is remanded . . . for further proceedings not inconsistent with this opinion.

[C]   Gardner v. Galetka

United States Court of Appeals for the Tenth Circuit
568 F.3d 862 (10th Cir. 2009)

Ronnie Lee Gardner shot Michael Burdell, an attorney, after being handed a gun when he was being taken from prison to the state district court in Salt Lake City, for a hearing. Burdell had been standing inside the court's archives room. Burdell died and Gardner was convicted of first-degree murder. Between the preliminary hearing and the trial in the case, one of the eyewitnesses, Mr. Macri, underwent hypnosis, without notifying the state. Macri had been standing behind a door in the archives room when Gardner entered. Macri left the room by going around the door. At the hearing, Macri testified that the gun went off at the same time that the door was closing behind him. At trial, and after hypnosis, Macri testified that "simultaneous doesn't quite describe the motion." *Gardner v. Galetka*, 568 F.3d 862, 892 (10th Cir. 2009). Gardner objected to Macri's testimony, claiming that he was prejudiced. Macri's testimony at the hearing, prior to hypnosis, supported Gardner's theory that he shot the gun because he was startled by the door closing. The Tenth Circuit "ha[s] rejected the per se constitutional invalidity of hypnotically-refreshed testimony." *Id.* at 891. Instead, a court must consider " 'whether safeguards have been employed to insure reliability of the testimony to make it admissible.' " *Id.* at 891 (quoting *Robison v. Maynard*, 829 F.2d 1501, 1508 (10th Cir.1987)). Because Macri underwent hypnosis without the state's knowledge, the state was unable to ensure that appropriate safeguards were in place. However, the court determined that the testimony went to a collateral issue because "[i]n both versions . . . the door had already started to close before Mr. Gardner fired the gun, and both supported Mr. Gardner's startle theory . . ." *Id.* at 892.

[D]   Falwell v. Flynt

The Reverend Jerry Falwell brought suit against Larry Flynt and his company, Hustler Magazine, Inc., as a result of an advertisement parody of Reverend Falwell in the magazine. At trial, Larry Flynt's videotaped deposition was admitted in evidence. The defense objected, claiming that Flynt was unable to tell the truth at the time of the deposition because of the effects of medication taken to treat a recently broken leg. The appellate court affirmed the admission of Flynt's deposition, concluding: "The relevant question posed by Flynt's deposition testimony was not one of competency but rather of credibility." *Falwell v. Flynt*, 797 F.2d 1270 (4th Cir. 1986).

[E] Turbyfill v. International Harvester Company

The plaintiff sought damages after being injured on a used car lot. The district court considered whether Michigan's "dead man's statute" applied in a diversity action. The court concluded that in a civil diversity suit, state law governs the competency of witnesses to testify. The court noted:[1]

> It is well established that a federal court must apply the conflict of law rules of the state in which it sits. . . . The conflicts approach in Michigan is to apply Michigan law on procedural questions, including those concerning the admissibility of evidence, even if the substantive law of another jurisdiction provides the rule of decision.

[F] Washington v. Texas

In *Washington v. Texas*, the Supreme Court held that Texas' common-law incompetency provision, which barred accomplices or co-indictees from testifying in favor of each other, violated the Sixth Amendment Compulsory Process Clause, as made applicable to the states through the Fourteenth Amendment. The court stated:[2]

> The right to offer the testimony of witnesses, and to compel their attendance, if necessary, is in plain terms the right to present a defense, the right to present the defendant's version of the facts as well as the prosecution's to the jury so it may decide where the truth lies. Just as an accused has the right to confront the prosecution's witnesses for the purpose of challenging their testimony, he has the right to present his own witnesses to establish a defense. This right is a fundamental element of due process of law.
>
> . . . .
>
> Despite the abolition of the rule generally disqualifying defense witnesses, the common law retained a number of restrictions on witnesses who were physically and mentally capable of testifying. To the extent that they were applicable, they had the same effect of suppressing the truth that the general proscription had had. Defendants and codefendants were among the large class of witnesses disqualified from testifying on the ground of interest. A party to a civil or criminal case was not allowed to testify on his own behalf for fear that he might be tempted to lie. Although originally the disqualification of a co-defendant appears to have been based only on his status as a party to the action, and in some jurisdictions co-indictees were allowed to testify for or against each other if granted separate trials, other jurisdictions came to view that accomplices or co-indictees were incompetent to testify at least in favor of each other even at separate trials, and in spite of statutes making a defendant competent to testify in his own behalf. It was thought that if two persons charged with the same crime were allowed to testify on behalf of each other, "each would try to swear the other out of the charge." This rule, as well

---

[1] Turbyfill v. International Harvester Company, 486 F. Supp. 232 (E.D. Mich. 1980).

[2] Washington v. Texas, 388 U.S. 14 (1967).

as the other disqualifications for interest, rested on the unstated premises that the right to present witnesses was subordinate to the court's interest in preventing perjury, and that erroneous decisions were best avoided by preventing the jury from hearing any testimony that might be perjured, even if it were the only testimony available on a crucial issue.

. . . .

. . . The Framers of the Constitution did not intend to commit the futile act of giving to a defendant the right to secure the attendance of witnesses [through the Compulsory Process Clause] whose testimony he had no right to use.

[G] United States v. Boender

N.D. Illinois
2010 U.S. Dist. LEXIS 32367

ROBERT M. DOW, JR., DISTRICT JUDGE:

On, March 18, 2010, a jury found Defendant guilty of five offenses under the laws of the United States. Of particular pertinence here was the jury's determination that Defendant violated 18 U.S.C. § 666 (federal program bribery) by corruptly giving things of value to former Chicago Alderman Isaac Carothers ("Carothers"). Unsurprisingly, Carothers was mentioned frequently by counsel and by witnesses at trial, though he had pled guilty to various charges prior to trial and was not called as a witness by either side during the trial.

After the jury rendered its verdict and was discharged, the Chicago Sun-Times published an article that included brief comments by two jurors. One juror's comments were anonymously given and have not been singled out by Defendant. The other comments were made by Jennifer Melberg, Juror No. 26. The specific quotations of concern to Defendant were (1) "I was surprised Ald. Carothers wasn't there" and (2) "I thought he would be part of the story because he was part of the story." Def. Reply at 1; see also Natasha Korecki & Art Golab, *Boender Guilty on all Five Counts: 'Difficult Decision' Based on Evidence, Juror Says of Case of Bribing Alderman*, CHI. SUN-TIMES 4 (Mar. 19, 2010).

Defendant filed the instant motion based on Juror No. 26's quotations, as well as the fact that accounts of the proceedings were published and broadcast daily during the trial. Def. Mot. at 1. Defendant's motion seeks an order that would allow his attorneys and investigators to communicate with jurors — not only or even necessarily Juror No. 26, but any juror who proves willing. . . .

. . .

Courts generally are reluctant to pull back the curtain on juror deliberations. . . . "[F]ull and frank discussion in the jury room, jurors' willingness to return an unpopular verdict, and the community's trust in a system that relies on decisions of laypeople would all be undermined by a barrage of postverdict scrutiny of juror conduct." *Id.* The rule against jury testimony in an effort to impeach jury verdicts is well established. . . .

. . .

At common law, however, there were exceptions to the general bar on juror testimony. Thus, although matters intrinsic to jury deliberations almost always were off limits, extraneous influences could be explored. For example, in *Mattox*, the Supreme Court concluded that a defendant was entitled to a new trial where a bailiff made statements regarding the defendant's guilt and the jurors were presented with a newspaper article that similarly opined on the guilt of the defendant. . . .

. . .

Rule 606(b), like the common law rules that it followed, thus draws a distinction between matters intrinsic to juries' decision-making processes and "extraneous influences." *United States v. Paneras*, 222 F.3d 406, 411 (7th Cir. 2000) (collapsing, as many courts have done, the language of the first and second exceptions to Rule 606(b)'s general bar). For example, while a juror is not competent under the Federal Rules of Evidence to testify about a jury-room squabble . . . allegations that a judge had prejudicial conversations with the jury . . . may be examined. . . .

. . .

The issue raised by Defendant's motion, however, is distinct from the intrinsic-extraneous taxonomy of Rule 606(b). The Court agrees with Defendant (Def. Mot. at 1-2) that "[j]uror exposure to press coverage" during trial or deliberations may fall on the admissible side of the Rule 606(b) line. But the question for purposes of deciding the instant motion is whether the quotations in the Chicago Sun-Times story merit further inquiry, including hailing a juror into court for purposes of further investigation. . . .

. . .

In this instance, Defendant contends that juror interviews in this case likely "will yield admissible evidence under Rule 606(b) of the Federal Rule of Evidence." Def. Mot. at 1. He bases the contention on (1) Juror No. 26's statements as reported in the Chicago Sun-Times article and (2) the fact that there was extensive publicity of the proceedings during the trial. The latter basis is infirm and does not require extensive discussion. Therefore, the Court will consider only whether further investigation is warranted based on the Chicago Sun-Times article. Because the showing made by Defendant is "frail and ambiguous" (*King*, 576 F.2d at 438), further inquiry is neither necessary nor appropriate.

. . .

The question remains whether a sufficient showing has been made with respect to Juror No. 26, based on the statements that she reportedly made to the Chicago Sun-Times. . . . The modest expression of juror surprise to which Defendant points simply indicates that the juror anticipated (or perhaps even expected) that an individual who was mentioned frequently during the trial would be called as a witness.

Yet, inquiry into a juror's surprise at the evidence that is presented at trial and her thoughts about the evidence are flatly barred by hundreds of years of common law and the Federal Rules of Evidence, because they relate to juror mental processes. . . .

. . .

In addition, there is no indication from Juror No. 26's statements that she (or any other juror) disregarded the Court's repeated instruction to avoid news coverage of the trial. Rather, the statements suggest that the juror was paying attention to the trial itself, in which Carothers — as well as his house, his zoning efforts on behalf of Defendant, and his acceptance of nearly $40,000 in home improvement work — was in one form or another the subject of testimony by nearly every witness who took the stand. The conclusion that Defendant's motion asks the Court to reach, which is that quotations in the article constitute a "colorable allegation of taint" (*Davis*, 15 F.3d at 1412), simply is not warranted. Any such conclusion would depend on highly aggressive inference-making that the case law counsels against: indeed, the case law teaches that speculative nature of Defendant's showing is fatal to his request. . . .

. . .

Other cases that have raised this issue in a manner that required the district court to conduct an investigation involved far more than intimations. For example, in *United States v. Thomas*, 463 F.2d 1061 (7th Cir. 1972), a juror contacted the defendant's wife claiming that something "very wrong" took place in the jury room. The "very wrong" conduct was that "several jurors had copies of a newspaper article about the case" from the Chicago Tribune. *Id.* at 1062. During deliberations, the juror claimed, those who voted to convict referred repeatedly to the article. *Id.* In overturning the defendant's conviction, the Seventh Circuit held that "the district court, when presented with evidence indicating that a prejudicial news article was actually present in the jury room and, more importantly, that it was in fact used by some jurors to persuade others, was at the very minimum required to investigate further." *Id.* at 1063.

In so ruling, the Seventh Circuit repeated the Supreme Court's admonishment that each case should be considered according to its facts. In *Thomas*, the article in question was "prejudicial on its face." *Thomas*, 463 F.2d at 1064. But here, Defendant is asking the Court both to infer that Juror No. 26 was exposed to news reports and that those (ethereal) news reports were prejudicial. Yet, Defendant has not even come forward with any evidence that there were news reports published during the trial that contained prejudicial information, much less that any juror saw any news reports during the trial, further weakening the already-insufficient basis for conducting further inquiry. . . .

. . .

The Seventh Circuit has stated that "the risk that a juror will be subject to outside forces is a fact of life" (*Davis*, 15 F.3d at 1413), but because Defendant has offered no evidence that juror exposure to "extraneous prejudicial information" was a reality in the life of this case, his motion for permission to communicate with jurors must be denied.

[H]   Rules Comparison

Compare the FRE with the following state rules.

Idaho, Title 9, Section 202 (Supp. 1967).

Who may not testify. The following persons cannot be witnesses:

. . . .

3. Parties or assignors of parties to an action or proceeding, or persons in whose behalf an action or proceeding is prosecuted against an executor or administrator, upon a claim or demand against the estate of a deceased person, as to any communication or agreement, not in writing, occurring before the death of such deceased person.

Texas Rev. Civ. Stat. Art. 3716 (1925).

In actions by or against executors, administrators, or guardians, in which judgment may be rendered for or against them as such, neither party shall be allowed to testify against the others as to any transaction with, or statement by, the testator, intestate or ward, unless called to testify thereto by the opposite party; and the provisions of this article shall extend to and include all actions by or against the heirs or legal representatives of a decedent arising out of any transaction with such decedent.

Georgia Evidence Code Chapter 24-9-7.

(a) The competency of a witness shall be decided by the court. The court shall by examination decide upon the capacity of one alleged to be incompetent from idiocy, lunacy, insanity, drunkenness, or infancy.

(b) If an objection to competency is known, it shall be taken before the witness is examined at all. It may be proved by the witness himself or by other testimony. If proved by other testimony, the witness shall be incompetent to explain it away.

Former Indiana Code Chapter 34-1-14-5.

Except as otherwise provided by statute, the following persons shall not be competent witnesses:

(1) Persons insane at the time they are offered as witnesses, whether they have been so adjudged or not.

(2) Attorneys, as to confidential communications made to them in the course of their professional business, and as to advice given in such cases.

(3) Physicians, as to matter [matters] communicated to them, as such, by patients, in the course of their professional business, or advice given in such cases.

(4) Clergymen, as to confessions or admissions made to them in course of discipline enjoined by their respective churches.

(5) Husband and wife, as to communications made to each other.

§ 8.04   MIXED PROBLEMS

Problem #8-17: "What Shirley Saw"

Shirley Brown, age 4, was the only eyewitness to a homicide that occurred one night at 10 p.m. in the parking lot of the local convenience store, "Burt's Take Out." Shirley's mom had entered the store to get some milk and pay for gas while Shirley sat in the car. Her mother said, "Stay here in the car for a minute, Shirley; I'll be right back."

1. What must occur for Shirley to be competent to testify?

2. Can Shirley's mother, Annie, testify even though she admits to knowing and intensely disliking the defendant?

3. If Shirley's mother also had been an eyewitness, could she still testify if she admitted to being intoxicated at the time of the homicide?

Problem #8-18: The Mugging

Andrew was mugged early one evening after eating at Fat Matt's Ribs. He was too shaken up to identify the perpetrator and had a mental block about the assailant's description for months. The police, through certified hypnotist Dr. Roberto Crizuelo, hypnotized Andrew and obtained a fresh identification of a suspect. The identification resulted in an arrest and trial. Can Andrew testify at trial about the perpetrator's identity? If the defendant had been hypnotized, could the defendant still have testified? Explain.

Problem #8-19: The Dead Man

Jonah died after a protracted battle with cancer. While his will was being probated, a woman who identified herself as "Jonah's friend Mary" claimed that Jonah had promised her $1,000,000 if she provided accounting services for one year. Mary claimed that she had performed her part of this oral bargain, but that Jonah had not performed his.

1. Can Mary collect if she brings an action based on diversity of citizenship in federal court? Why?

2. Ethics Consideration. While Jonah was still alive he told his lawyer that he wanted to thank him for all his legal help by leaving him his car. The lawyer follows Jonah's instructions and drafts his will with a provision giving the car to the lawyer. Has the lawyer violated any ethical rules by doing so? Colorado Rules of Prof'l Conduct R. 1.8 (c). *See* MRPC 1.8 (c).

§ 8.05   RELEVANT ETHICS RULES

Rule 1.14. Client With Impaired Capacity.

(a) When a client's capacity to make adequately considered decisions in connection with a representation is impaired, whether because of minority, mental impairment, or for some other reason, the lawyer shall, as far as reasonably possible, maintain a normal client-lawyer relationship with the client.

(b) When the lawyer reasonably believes that the client has impaired capacity, that the client is at risk of substantial physical, financial, or other harm unless action is taken, and that the client cannot adequately act in the client's own interest, the lawyer may take reasonably necessary protective action, including consulting with individuals or entities that have the ability to take action to protect the client and, in appropriate cases, seeking the appointment of a guardian ad litem, conservator or guardian.

(c) The confidences and secrets of a client with impaired capacity are protected by Rule 1.6. When taking protective action pursuant to paragraph (b), the lawyer is impliedly authorized under Rule 1.6(a) to reveal information about the client, but only to the extent reasonably necessary to protect the client's interests. Alaska Rules of Prof'l Conduct R. 1.14. *See* MRPC 1.14.

Rule 3.7. Lawyer As Witness

(a)   A lawyer shall not act as advocate at a trial in which the lawyer is likely to be a necessary witness unless:

(1)   the testimony relates to an uncontested issue;

(2)   the testimony relates to the nature and value of legal services rendered in the case; or

(3)   disqualification of the lawyer would work substantial hardship on the client.

(b)   A lawyer may act as advocate in a trial in which another lawyer in the lawyer's firm is likely to be called as a witness unless precluded from doing so by Rule 1.7 or Rule 1.9. Colo. Rules of Prof'l Conduct R. 3.7. *See* MRPC 3.7.

Com't [4]: "[P]aragraph (a)(3) recognizes that a balancing is required between the interests of the client and those of the tribunal and the opposing party. Whether the tribunal is likely to be misled or the opposing party is likely to suffer prejudice depends on the nature of the case, the importance and probable tenor of the lawyer's testimony, and the probability that the lawyer's testimony will conflict with that of other witnesses. Even if there is risk of such prejudice, in determining whether the lawyer should be disqualified, due regard must be given to the effect of disqualification on the lawyer's client. It is relevant that one or both parties could reasonably foresee that the lawyer would probably be a witness. The conflict of interest principles stated in Rules 1.7, 1.9 and 1.10 have no application to this aspect of the problem." Colo. Rules of Prof'l Conduct R. 3.7. *See* MRPC 3.7.

Rule 3.8. Special Responsibilities of a Prosecutor

(g) when a prosecutor knows of new, credible material evidence creating a reasonable likelihood that a convicted defendant did not commit an offense of which the defendant was convicted, the prosecutor shall:

   (1) promptly disclose that evidence to an appropriate court or authority, and

   (2) if the conviction was obtained in the prosecutor's jurisdiction,

      (A) promptly disclose that evidence to the defendant unless a court authorizes delay, and

      (B) undertake further investigation, or make reasonable efforts to cause an investigation, to determine whether the defendant was convicted of an offense that the defendant did not commit.

(h) when a prosecutor knows of clear and convincing evidence establishing that a defendant in the prosecutor's jurisdiction was convicted of an offense that the defendant did not commit, the prosecutor shall seek to remedy the conviction. Idaho Rules of Prof'l Conduct R. 3.8 (g). *See* MRPC 1.8.

Com't [9] "A prosecutor's independent judgment, made in good faith, that the new evidence is not of such nature as to trigger the obligations of sections (g) and (h), though subsequently determined to have been erroneous, does not constitute violation of this Rule." Idaho Rules of Prof'l Conduct R. 3.8. *See* MRPC 1.8.

Rule 1.8. Conflict of Interest: Current Clients: Specific Rules

(c) A lawyer shall not solicit any substantial gift from a client, including a testamentary gift, or prepare on behalf of a client an instrument giving the lawyer or a person related to the lawyer any substantial gift unless the lawyer or other recipient of the gift is related to the client. For purposes of this paragraph, related persons include a spouse, child, grandchild, parent, grandparent or other relative or individual with whom the lawyer or the client maintains a close, familial relationship. Colo. Rules of Prof'l Conduct R. 1.8(c). *See* MRPC 1.8(c).

Com't [7] "If effectuation of a substantial gift requires preparing a legal instrument such as a will or conveyance the client should have the detached advice that another lawyer can provide. The sole exception to this Rule is where the client is a relative of the donee." Colo. Rules of Prof'l Conduct R. 1.8(c). *See* MRPC 1.8(c).

§ 8.06 SUMMARY AND REVIEW

1. Compare the competency of a witness to testify with the credibility of witnesses.

2. What are some of the traditional or historical incompetencies?

3. What is a "dead man's statute"?

4. Why did the Supreme Court in *Rock v. Arkansas* overturn Arkansas' per se ban on hypnotically refreshed testimony?

5. Are child witnesses competent to testify? Why?
6. How is competency related to civil procedure?

"Perhaps the witness would like to reconsider his answer to my question."

Chapter 9

OPINIONS AND EXPERT TESTIMONY [FRE 701–706]

CHAPTER FRAMEWORK: There are two types of opinions generally permitted at trial: those from lay witnesses and those from experts. Lay witnesses can express some opinions, but generally the opinions must be rationally based on their perception and helpful to the trier of fact. Experts have much more latitude, but many more prerequisites. There are a variety of touchstones experts must meet in order to testify: (1) experts must be properly qualified as possessing some special knowledge that will (2) assist the trier of fact in doing its job and (3) the scientific, technical, or other basis for their knowledge is reliably based on multiple factors, as is (4) the application of that scientific or technical theory, and (5) the testimony is founded upon only facts and data reasonably relied on by someone in their field. If all of these criteria are met, experts can generally testify. Experts are potent witnesses for several reasons, including their aura of expertise and their ability to testify based on hypothetical questions.

WHY ARE THE CONCEPTS IN THIS CHAPTER IMPORTANT? Opinions are offered in the real world as a natural part of our speech every hour of the day and are common at trial as well. Some lay opinion is allowed based on necessity (almost every assertion is an opinion on some level) and helpfulness to the trier of fact. Expert opinion is significant in a different way. It can help the trier of fact do its job better in understanding the evidence and filling in gaps in knowledge. Also, we are used to expert advice in popular culture, where experts abound. Given the proliferation of experts in every walk of life, and their impact at trial, sifting through the various potential experts to determine who can testify and who cannot is an important function of the judge. In fact, the judicial determination of the admissibility of expert testimony often becomes the center of gravity of a case, where the determination of who can testify and to what often indicates who will likely win or lose and in what way. Thus, the pre-trial determination about expert testimony often triggers settlements of cases.

CONNECTIONS: Lay opinions generally require personal knowledge as described in FRE 602. Thus, the lay opinion rule, FRE 701, builds on the foundation required by FRE 602. FRE 602 exempts expert opinions, however, because experts, upon meeting various requirements, need not have any personal knowledge of an event whatsoever. Admissions of party opponents, moreover, also do not require personal knowledge, thus joining expert opinions in the category of persons and statements freed from the personal knowledge requirement at trial.

CHAPTER OUTLINE:

    I. Lay Witness Opinions [FRE 701]

        A. Requirements: first-hand knowledge and

    B. Testimony must be helpful to trier of fact

    C. Opinion testimony generally prohibited

        1. Exceptions (e.g., speed, time, distance or temperature estimations, a person's appearance or intoxication)

  II. Expert Witnesses [FRE 702]

    A. Opinion testimony permitted even on ultimate issue if:

        1. Subject beyond common knowledge of layman

        2. Helpful to trier of fact and

        3. Witness has expertise

  III. Qualifying Experts [FRE 702] (e.g., profferor bears burden of showing knowledge, training, experience)

  IV. Reliability of Expert Testimony [FRE 702]

    A. Sufficient facts or data

    B. Product of reliable principles and

    C. Principles reliably applied to facts of case

    D. *Daubert* standard — admitting novel scientific testimony

  V. Basis of Expert's Opinion [FRE 703 & 704]

    A. Facts or data reasonably relied on by experts in the field

    B. Testimony re inadmissible facts barred without court's permission

  VI. Expert May Opine on Ultimate Issue in Case [FRE 704]

    A. Exception: no opinion on defendant's mental state

  VII. Expert May State Opinion Without First Disclosing Underlying Facts [FRE 705]

  VIII. Court May Appoint Experts [FRE 706]

* * * * *

RELEVANT EVIDENCE RULES

Rule 701. Opinion Testimony by Lay Witnesses

If a witness is not testifying as an expert, testimony in the form of an opinion is limited to one that is:

(a) rationally based on the witness's perception;

(b) helpful to clearly understanding the witness's testimony or to determining a fact in issue; and

(c) not based on scientific, technical, or other specialized knowledge within the scope of Rule 702.

Rule 702. Testimony by Expert Witnesses

A witness who is qualified as an expert by knowledge, skill, experience, training, or education may testify in the form of an opinion or otherwise if:

(a) the expert's scientific, technical, or other specialized knowledge will help the trier of fact to understand the evidence or to determine a fact in issue;

(b) the testimony is based on sufficient facts or data;

(c) the testimony is the product of reliable principles and methods; and

(d) the expert has reliably applied the principles and methods to the facts of the case.

Rule 703. Bases of an Expert's Opinion Testimony

An expert may base an opinion on facts or data in the case that the expert has been made aware of or personally observed. If experts in the particular field would reasonably rely on those kinds of facts or data in forming an opinion on the subject, they need not be admissible for the opinion to be admitted. But if the facts or data would otherwise be inadmissible, the proponent of the opinion may disclose them to the jury only if their probative value in helping the jury evaluate the opinion substantially outweighs their prejudicial effect.

Rule 704. Opinion on an Ultimate Issue

(a) In General — Not Automatically Objectionable.

An opinion is not objectionable just because it embraces an ultimate issue.

(b) Exception. In a criminal case, an expert witness must not state an opinion about whether the defendant did or did not have a mental state or condition that constitutes an element of the crime charged or of a defense. Those matters are for the trier of fact alone.

Rule 705. Disclosing the Facts or Data Underlying an Expert's Opinion

Unless the court orders otherwise, an expert may state an opinion — and give the reasons for it — without first testifying to the underlying facts or data. But the expert may be required to disclose those facts or data on cross-examination.

Rule 706. Court-Appointed Expert Witnesses

(a) Appointment Process. On a party's motion or on its own, the court may order the parties to show cause why expert witnesses should not be appointed and may ask the parties to submit nominations. The court may appoint any expert that the parties agree on and any of its own choosing. But the court may only appoint someone who consents to act.

(b) Expert's Role. The court must inform the expert of the expert's duties. The court may do so in writing and have a copy filed with the clerk or may do so orally at a conference in which the parties have an opportunity to participate. The expert:

(1) must advise the parties of any findings the expert makes;

(2) may be deposed by any party;

(3) may be called to testify by the court or any party; and

(4) may be cross-examined by any party, including the party that called the expert.

(c) **Compensation.** The expert is entitled to a reasonable compensation, as set by the court. The compensation is payable as follows:

(1) in a criminal case or in a civil case involving just compensation under the Fifth Amendment, from any funds that are provided by law; and

(2) in any other civil case, by the parties in the proportion and at the time that the court directs — and the compensation is then charged like other costs.

(d) **Disclosing the Appointment to the Jury.** The court may authorize disclosure to the jury that the court appointed the expert.

(e) **Parties' Choice of Their Own Experts.** This rule does not limit a party in calling its own experts.

§ 9.01   LAY WITNESS OPINIONS [FRE 701]

The Advisory Committee's Note to FRE 701 explains that lay witnesses must have "first-hand knowledge or observation." Furthermore, lay witness testimony must be "helpful in resolving issues." If a party tries to use a lay witness "to introduce meaningless assertions which amount to little more than choosing up sides, exclusion for lack of helpfulness is called for by the rule."

Lay, or non-expert, witnesses generally are prohibited from offering opinions or drawing conclusions at trial. Instead, lay witnesses are limited to testifying about facts. In essence, lay witnesses may testify only to sensory perceptions — what they saw, heard, smelled, touched, or tasted.

This "facts only" rule serves several different purposes. It is the job of the trier of fact to draw inferences from the evidence presented at trial. If lay witnesses were permitted to draw such inferences, they would be invading the province of the jury. Further, lay witnesses are no better equipped to offer opinions than lay jurors. Thus, lay opinions, if allowed, would waste judicial economy. Also, requiring "facts only" testimony ensures a more accurate reproduction of the event or transaction in question. By minimizing witness interpretation, distortion of the facts likely would be reduced. In addition, lay opinions create a practical difficulty at trial — they are difficult to cross-examine because the premises of the opinion are unknown. Finally, the impact of a lay opinion is often much greater than that of its component parts.

Enforcing the "facts only" rule, however, is not always easy or desirable. It is often difficult to draw a line between facts and opinions — the distinction is generally only a matter of degree and not one of kind. After all, a statement that "the sky is blue" is as much an opinion as it is fact, particularly if "blue" is subject to interpretation. The dividing line between the two often depends on how specific the witness's observation is or how many inferences the witness must draw to yield the observation. Technically, all human assertions require some sort of inference based on perception and, in most cases, memory as well. Thus, perception and memory act as sensory filters that transform sensory observations into opinions.

Also, many witnesses have a natural tendency to speak in terms of opinion; it is linguistically uncomfortable for many people to break down all opinions into facts. A witness may be able to describe some behavior only in terms of opinions, such as testifying that another person was smiling or in love.

Consequently, the FRE permit lay persons to offer certain limited opinions at trial. These opinions must be rationally based on the perception of the witness (i.e., firsthand knowledge) *and* helpful to the trier of fact in understanding the testimony of the witness or in determining a fact in issue. *See* FRE 701.

Lay opinions often are permitted on the following subjects: (1) estimations of speed, distance, or temperature (such as the speed of automobiles or motorcycles); (2) identifications of persons or objects (such as voice or handwriting identification); (3) a person's appearance, including physical characteristics (such as estimating a person's height, age, or weight); (4) the value of one's property or services (such as the value of real estate); (5) odors and their identity (such as smelling smoke); (6) a person's emotional or mental state (such as another person's anger or sadness); and (7) short-hand renditions of fact, comprising sensory impressions commonly recognized in opinion form (such as a person's state of intoxication).

Illustration: Permissible Lay Opinions

Jamie Rockman was an eyewitness to a robbery. In testifying at trial, she stated, "I smelled smoke. So I ran out of my store and saw this guy holding a gun to another man's face. Then the guy took the victim's wallet, and narrowly escaped being hit by a car as he ran across the street. The car skidded what looked like 50 yards down the street at about 30 miles per hour. The guy yelled, 'Hey watch it!' and kept running. Later, I told the police that the guy was approximately five feet, 10 inches tall, and 180 pounds. They played a tape of different people's voices, and I picked the guy's out right away." Are Jamie's opinions admissible?

Answer: Jamie can offer these opinions at trial under FRE 701. Lay opinions about common smells (such as smoke), speed (30 mph), and distance (50 yards down the street) are allowed. Also permitted are estimates of a person's height and weight and identifications of a person's voice. These opinions are within the common experience of lay persons and would assist the jury in either understanding the testimony or a fact in issue.

[1]   When Lay Opinion Helps the Trier of Fact

Lay opinions are often allowed at trial. Sometimes, though, the opinion crosses the line set forth in FRE 701. The following problems help illuminate the lines limiting lay opinion, whether it is the one confining opinions to those that would help the jury or the one prohibiting purportedly lay opinions that are really expert opinions in disguise.

Problem #9-1: Slippery Tiles

Helen slipped and fell on some tiles. George, an eyewitness to Helen's fall, testified at trial, "In my opinion, those tiles were very slippery."

1. Is George's testimony admissible?

2. Assume George had merely said, "Those tiles were definitely slippery!" without adding the words "in my opinion." Would a different conclusion be warranted concerning the admissibility of George's testimony?

Problem #9-2: No Horn

Plaintiff, Betty B., sued defendant, Frances, after a minor car accident. Betty B. claimed that Frances negligently backed her car into Betty's car while both were in a parking lot. Frances denied the charge, and asserted at trial that she honked her horn as she backed up. Betty wishes to testify, "If Frances had honked the horn, I most certainly would have moved my car."

1. Is Betty's testimony admissible?

2. Ethics Consideration. Assume that Betty's contingency fee case against Frances settles. Betty's lawyer deposits the settlement check directly into his personal account. He forgets to notify Betty that the settlement check arrived and waits two weeks before deducting his fees and expenses. He then sends Betty a check for the balance without notifying her of his deductions. Are there any problems with the way Betty's lawyer handled the settlement check? Utah Rules of Prof'l Conduct R. 1.5; Nebraska Rules of Prof'l Conduct R. 1.15. *See* MRPC 1.5; MRPC 1.15.

Problem #9-3: Zoomin'

A small plane crashed onto a busy highway, injuring the passengers of the plane and the occupants of two cars. Anna was an eyewitness. At trial, Anna testified on direct examination:

PLAINTIFF'S ATTORNEY: Anna, in your opinion, how fast was the car traveling when it was hit by the plane?

DEFENDANT'S ATTORNEY: Objection. Improp. Ops / Spec

1. What ruling and why?

PLAINTIFF'S ATTORNEY: Anna, how fast was the plane traveling just before it collided with the car?

DEFENDANT'S ATTORNEY: Objection.

2. What ruling and why?

PLAINTIFF'S ATTORNEY: You have mentioned that there was a smell after the plane crash. What was that smell?

A: It smelled like burning high-grade oil.

DEFENDANT'S ATTORNEY: Objection. Improper opinion. Motion to strike and to instruct the jury to disregard the answer.

3. What ruling and why?

4. Which of the five statements below, if any, are proper lay opinions? Explain your conclusions.

PLAINTIFF'S ATTORNEY: After the plane touched down, you testified that the pilot wobbled out of the craft. Can you describe the pilot?

A: (a) First, I saw him stumble.

A: (b) It smelled like he had been drinking some sort of alcohol.

A: (c) I'd estimate he was about 6'2" and 195 pounds.

A: (d) He looked like he'd been without sleep for a while; he appeared disoriented.

A: (e) By the way he carried himself, it also appeared as if he had a very large ego; I can usually tell these things right off the bat.

(f) Ethics Consideration. The defendant offers to settle the case if the plaintiff's lawyer agrees not to represent any other parties in airplane crash cases involving the defendant. Is this proper? Florida Rules of Prof'l Conduct R. 5.6. *See* MRPC 5.6.

Problem #9-4: The Wink

Detective Kim Gorel was testifying in a homicide trial about her interview with the defendant, Ken. The defense had claimed mistaken identity in its opening statement.

PROSECUTOR: What happened when you were talking with the defendant?

A: The defendant said, "It's a shame that a person was killed," and then he winked at me.

DEFENSE COUNSEL: Objection! Improper opinion.

1. What ruling and why?

PROSECUTOR: What do you mean "he winked"?

A: He raised his left eyebrow and then quickly closed and opened that same eye.

PROSECUTOR: What did you take that to mean?

DEFENSE COUNSEL: Objection. Calls for speculation.

2. What ruling and why?

The prosecution calls a second witness, Al, to testify. It already had been established that a bottle of Kouros cologne was found in the knapsack the defendant was carrying at the time he was arrested.

PROSECUTOR: What did you observe at 9:40 p.m. in the alley adjacent to Johns Street?

A: I saw a man raise up a knife and stab another person. Then he ran quickly by me.

PROSECUTOR: What did you observe when he ran by you?

A: Actually, I was so startled and the shadows were so thick, I did not see his face. But I can tell you this, the guy was wearing Kouros cologne.

DEFENSE COUNSEL: Objection! Improper opinion.

3. How would you rule on this objection if you were the judge?

Problem #9-5: The Peel

Flynn slipped and fell on a banana peel in Kal's General Store. Mintz, testifying as an eyewitness, states, "Yep, Flynn slipped on a banana peel that looked like it had been on the floor for hours. Flynn fell like a sack of bricks."

1. Is Mintz's testimony admissible?

2. What if Joseph had slipped on a different peel in Kal's Store earlier that day and is called to give his opinion about Flynn's fall. Admissible?

3. Ethics Consideration. Outside counsel has regularly represented Kal's General Store for over six years. Kal's owner calls counsel after Flynn files suit. Counsel charges Kal's a reasonable hourly fee but does not tell the store in advance what the fee is and does not provide a written fee agreement. Is this proper? Utah Rules of Prof'l Conduct R. 1.5. *See* MRPC 1.5.

Problem #9-6: Thelma and Louise

In a convenience store robbery gone awry, the perpetrator, Thelma, shot and killed the owner of the store. Thelma is prosecuted for murder. She interposes the insanity defense. In rebuttal, the state calls Louise, a close friend of Thelma's, who had spent several hours with Thelma immediately prior to the robbery attempt. The prosecutor asks Louise for her opinion on whether Thelma appeared sane before the robbery.

1. Is Louise's opinion admissible?

2. Can an eyewitness to the robbery attempt, who had never before met either Thelma or Louise, give her opinion about whether Thelma appeared to be sane at the time of the robbery?

Problem #9-7: I Know It When I See It

Charles Jones' business partner, Paul J., testified about a contract between Charles and a third party: "Now, I'm no handwriting expert, but I've seen Charles sign his name at least 50 times, and the signature on that document is his as sure as I am sitting here."

1. The opponent objects to the testimony, claiming that Paul J. admitted he was not a handwriting expert. What ruling and why?

2. Would the same ruling occur if Paul J. had only observed Charles's signature on ten prior occasions? Why? *See Paccon, Inc. v. United States*, 399 F.2d 162 (Ct. Cl. 1968).

3. Ethics Consideration. Charles Jones filed a motion to disqualify the attorney representing the third party because the attorney had previously represented Jones in his divorce. Should the court grant the motion to disqualify? Arizona Rules of Prof'l Conduct 1.9. *See* MRPC 1.9.

* * * * *

Compare FRE 701 with the following state statute:

Georgia Evidence Code. Chapter 24-9-66.
Market value as opinion evidence; who may testify as to value.

"Direct testimony as to market value is in the nature of opinion evidence. One need not be an expert or dealer in the article in question but may testify as to its value if he has had an opportunity for forming a correct opinion."

§ 9.02   EXPERT WITNESSES [FRE 702–706]

[A]   Introduction

The Advisory Committee's Note to FRE 702 explains that "an intelligent evaluation of facts is often difficult or impossible without the application of some scientific, technical or other specialized knowledge."

Expert evidence is admissible under Rule 702 if "scientific, technical, or other specialized knowledge will assist the trier of fact to understand the evidence or to determine a fact in issue." Fed. R. Evid. 702. The court must determine whether (1) the subject at issue is beyond the common knowledge of the average layman, (2) the witness has sufficient expertise, and (3) the state of the pertinent art or scientific knowledge permits the assertion of a reasonable opinion. . . . An expert may offer an opinion or inference as to the ultimate issue to be decided by the trier of fact.

Maffei v. Northern Ins. Co. of New York, 12 F.3d 892, 897 (9th Cir. 1993).

The Federal Rules of Evidence provide that expert witnesses may give opinion evidence even without hypothetical questions. [If a hypothetical question is used, however, it must not omit a] "material fact essential to the formation of a rational opinion."

Piotrowski v. Southworth Prods. Corp., 15 F.3d 748 (8th Cir. 1994) (quoting in part *Iconco v. Hensen Constr. Co.*, 622 F.2d 1291, 1301 (8th Cir. 1980)).

Trials in the legal system are centered around the introduction of evidence or proof. Often, the jury may not have the necessary knowledge to properly interpret or understand the evidence presented. *See* FRE 702. Expert witnesses are permitted to testify at trial to assist the jury in more accurately assessing the evidence and in determining the relevant facts. In a sense, experts help jurors understand "different realities" as much as they provide jurors with additional information. The experts can be viewed as teachers — and might even have such jobs outside the courtroom.

The increasing complexity of many types of cases, such as patent and commercial litigation actions, and the advances in fact-finding technology, such as DNA testing and computer software, have favored the participation of experts at trial. Their participation has not always been welcomed, however, because of their powers of persuasion and their potential for interfering with or even usurping the trier's function of determining the facts at issue.

Experts differ from lay witnesses at trial in one major respect — experts are routinely permitted to offer their opinions about issues in the case. Experts may even respond to hypothetical questions without possessing any personal knowledge of the facts. Experts provide testimony about premises and assumptions as much as conclusions. How experts and others reached their conclusions is often as important as what these conclusions are. For example, if a medical examiner opines about the cause of death, the support for that conclusion must be articulated and explained. Many experts are called on to present syllogistic reasoning, with major or general premises and minor or case-specific premises leading to their conclusions (e.g., Humans have unique fingerprints. The defendant is human. Thus, the defendant has unique fingerprints which, if found, will reveal where the defendant has been.).

An expert can testify based on three different sources of knowledge: personal observations (such as a treating physician who testifies about an examination of a patient), observations in the courtroom (such as a psychiatric expert who watches an accused testify after the accused has interposed an insanity defense to a criminal charge), and facts made known to the expert at or before trial, such as through hypothetical questions (e.g., "Doctor, assuming the patient has symptoms A, B, and C, what would be your diagnosis of that patient?").

Expert opinions are not without limitation. *See* FRE 702. The opinions must be pertinent to the case, must assist the trier of fact, and must be a product of the witness's expertise. Expert witnesses also must base their testimony on reliable scientific principles. Untested novel scientific analysis can easily mislead the jury and may be excluded as unreliable.

The *Daubert* case, *Daubert v. Merrell Dow Pharmaceuticals, Inc.*, 509 U.S. 579 (1993) (excerpted later in this chapter), created a revolution in how courts admitted expert testimony. *Daubert* held that the Federal Rules superseded the old *Frye* test which asked, "Is the testimony generally accepted in the scientific community?"

Instead of *Frye*'s single factor approach, the *Daubert* Court adopted a multiple-factor test for determining the reliability of scientific expert testimony. To reflect this change, FRE 702 was amended in 2000. The amendment revamped the gatekeeping responsibility of the courts, requiring courts to consider a variety of factors bearing on the reliability of expert testimony. FRE 702's new approach applied to *all* expert testimony, not just testimony based on science. The reliability factors initially described in *Daubert* — whether the technique or theory propounded has been tested, subjected to peer review and publication, has a known rate of error and is generally accepted in the scientific community — have been supplemented by additional factors over time. The Advisory Committee Note to FRE 702 identifies some of these other factors, including whether the technique or theory is part of ongoing research or has been developed for the purposes of testifying, whether the expert has unjustifiably extrapolated an accepted premise to create an improper conclusion, whether the expert has accounted for alternative explanations, whether the expert is being as careful as usual, and whether the overall field of expertise is known to yield reliable results. *See* the 2000 Amendment, FRE 702 Advisory Committee Note.

Daubert's progeny continue to add to the factors to be considered by courts. Predictions of dire consequences resulting from the adoption of the *Daubert* test have not come to pass (such as "too much" or "too little" expert testimony being admitted to trial), and judges have attempted to refine and update their gatekeeping responsibilities under FRE 702.

Background Box: The New Center of Gravity in Civil Cases — The *Daubert* Hearing

The *Daubert* revolution has transformed civil litigation — and to some extent, criminal cases as well — by forcing parties to submit their experts to a *Daubert* review prior to trial. If the expert does not meet the standards, the case is likely irreparably harmed. If the experts do meet the standards, that indicates to the parties what the case is worth and how much it will likely take to settle the case. In any event, the center of gravity of the case has moved to the hearing or argument about the admissibility of the expert witnesses; fewer cases go to trial, if only because of the excessive costs associated with it.

While experts are permitted to testify about the ultimate issues in the case, changes in the FRE prohibit experts from testifying about whether the defendant in a criminal case had the mental state necessary to commit the crime charged. *See* FRE 704(b). This rule was adopted to prevent a battle royale of medical experts arguing about the mental state of a criminal defendant. The provision has been labeled by some as the "Hinckley Rule," because it followed the uproar caused by the verdict in the trial of John Hinckley. Hinckley was charged with the attempted murder of President Ronald Reagan. He was found not guilty by reason of insanity after the introduction of conflicting psychiatric expert testimony under law that was subsequently changed.

Illustrations: Permissible Expert Testimony

1. In a suit for damages resulting from a fire, a veteran fire fighter can testify as an expert on whether the fire was caused by arson.

2. In an employment discrimination suit, a professor of management and marketing can testify as an expert that in light of the latest statistics, plaintiff "was terminated because of his age."

3. In a narcotics prosecution, an experienced Drug Enforcement Administration (DEA) agent can testify as an expert on the purity of heroin commonly sold on the street.

4. In a products liability suit against an automobile manufacturer, an experienced mechanic can testify as an expert about experiments showing that the car's door on the model in question could pop open during a sideswipe accident.

5. In a robbery prosecution, a scientist can testify as an expert that hairs removed from articles used by the robbers were microscopically similar to hair samples taken from the defendants.

6. In a negligence and breach of warranty suit, a pipefitter who is not a metallurgist but who has 33 years of experience can testify as an expert about the quality of pipe hanger construction in helping the jury to resolve the question about how much weight the clamp should have supported. *Cunningham v. Gans*, 507 F.2d 496 (2d Cir. 1974).

Practical Tip:

It is a good idea to contact your expert as soon as possible to maximize the chance of retaining that witness and to ensure sufficient time for expert preparation. Experts may charge clients a premium rate for "last minute" work.

[B] Qualifying the Expert

Experts are defined as those persons with special knowledge, training, experience, or skill who can assist the trier of fact in understanding the evidence or in determining the facts at issue. *See* FRE 702. This expansive definition is based on FRE 702 and is reflected in many state evidence codes as well.

A witness must be shown to be qualified as an expert before he or she will be permitted to testify as an expert. A witness may qualify as an expert by virtue of education, skill, training, experience, or a combination of these factors. Based on this expansive definition of expert, expert witnesses can range from a neurosurgeon testifying about the brain to a farmer testifying about the behavior of cows, or even a burglar testifying about the significance of various burglary tools.

Evidence procedure usually requires counsel to qualify the witness as an expert in a specific field (i.e., not as "a general helpful expert," but, for example, as "an expert in the field of cardiovascular surgery"). The opponent of the witness can accept the witness as an expert, object to the witness as an expert, or ask to conduct a voir dire of the witness about his or her qualifications. The voir dire is a limited cross-examination on qualifications; it does not extend to a far-ranging general impeachment of the witness's credibility.

Illustration: How to Qualify an Expert

In a hearing to determine the competency of the defendant to stand trial, Dr. Susan Trautman Borg is offered as an expert in the psychiatric treatment and diagnosis of mental illness.

PROSECUTOR: Good morning, Dr. Borg. Please state your full name for the record and spell it for the court reporter.

A: Susan Trautman Borg, M.D.

PROSECUTOR: What is your educational background?

A: I received my B.A. and M.D. degrees from Case Western Reserve University. After graduating, I did my internship and residency at Jackson Memorial Hospital in Miami. I had a post-doctoral fellowship in psychiatry at the National Institute of Mental Health in Washington, D.C.

PROSECUTOR: Are you employed?

A: Yes, at the South Allenton State Psychiatric facility.

PROSECUTOR: What is your job at South Allenton State?

A: I am the Director of Psychiatric Services.

PROSECUTOR: How long have you worked there?

A: I have been the Director for seven years. I began at South Allenton as the head resident, spent two years in that position, and then served as Associate Director for three years.

PROSECUTOR: How many patients have you treated for psychiatric illness in those seven years?

A: I'd have to estimate, but I'd say hundreds.

PROSECUTOR: How many patients have you diagnosed as having a mental illness?

A: Based on the Diagnostic and Statistical Manual III-R, which is generally used by psychiatrists and psychologists, I'd say quite a few. Probably several hundred.

PROSECUTOR: What are your job responsibilities?

A: I currently handle a reduced caseload of approximately 10 to 15 patients along with my administrative duties. These duties involve overseeing a department of 20 psychologists and psychiatrists, 10 social workers, and 75 other staff members.

PROSECUTOR: What does Board Certified in psychiatry mean?

A: Board certification exists in various medical specialties. In psychiatry, it means that the psychiatrist has passed an examination designed to ensure an advanced degree of knowledge in that psychiatric field and approved by the American Board of Medical Specialties. To become Board Certified, a person must first become Board Eligible, which requires successfully completing several prerequisites, including an examination. Only a small percentage of psychiatrists are Board Certified.

PROSECUTOR: What is your board status, Doctor?

A: I am Board Certified.

PROSECUTOR: Doctor, to which, if any, professional organizations do you belong?

A: I belong to the American Psychiatric Association, where I am the immediate past president.

PROSECUTOR: Have you published any writings in your field?

A: I have published the paper "Psychotropic Drugs — the Good, the Bad, and the Ugly," in the journal *Nature* in 1991, and have co-authored approximately 50 other pieces in a wide variety of journals. Co-authoring is the general practice of scholars in my medical specialty.

PROSECUTOR: Have you ever testified as an expert in psychiatry?

A: About 150 times, mostly for the prosecution, but sometimes for the defense.

PROSECUTOR: Have you continued your education in psychiatry?

A: Yes. I take three continuing education courses in psychiatry each year, as required, and teach at Allentown University as an adjunct. I also participate in as many educational colloquia as time permits.

PROSECUTOR: Your Honor, I now offer Dr. Borg as an expert in the diagnosis and treatment of mental illness.

[1] Qualifying Experts

The following problems explore the qualifications necessary to testify as an expert.

Problem #9-8: "Will the Real Expert Please Stand Up"

Dr. Will, a chiropractic physician, is asked to testify in a workers' compensation action. Dr. Will is asked to give an opinion about the prognosis regarding defendant's back injury. Which of the following facts are relevant to qualifying Dr. Will as an expert?

1. Dr. Will has worked as a chiropractor for eleven years, seven of those years part time, and has treated 800 patients in that time.

2. Dr. Will has published an article in *The Chiropractic Review*, titled "Neck Pain and What to Do About It."

3. Dr. Will has testified as an expert chiropractor on seventeen different occasions, one time for the defense and sixteen times for the plaintiff.

4. Dr. Will graduated with honors from the Detroit School of Chiropractic Physicians and Surgeons and has taken twenty credits each succeeding year in continuing chiropractic education.

5. Dr. Will received an honorary doctoral degree in biology from Murray State College after serving as fundraising chair for the school for seven consecutive years.

6. Dr. Will has been the chiropractor for Shirley MacLaine and Jack Nicholson, among other famous people.

If Dr. Will is offered as an expert witness and the defense asks to voir dire the witness, will the judge allow it? If so, what kinds of questions should the defense ask Dr. Will?

7. Ethics Consideration. During the voir dire it comes out that Dr. Will is not really a chiropractic physician and that all of his credentials were made up. The attorney who hired Dr. Will as an expert did not look into his background before hiring him. Did the attorney violate any rules of ethics by failing to research Dr. Will's credentials? Arkansas Rules of Prof'l Conduct R. 1.1. *See* MRPC 1.1.

Problem #9-9: Drug Code

In an illegal drug prosecution of Akilah Prescott, Officer Alain testified that he saw Akilah use several specific hand signals to a person on an adjacent street corner, at which time the person went and transferred drugs for money. The prosecution then called Officer Smith-Lawrence, to the stand. The officer, based on his decades of experience as a police officer assigned to the drug unit, testified that the hand signals meant the customer was clean and the sale could proceed as arranged. The defense objected.

1. Is Officer Smith-Lawrence's testimony allowed?

2. *Sharp Eye*. Officer Alain also was asked whether from his post, which was about five houses away from where the defendant was standing, he could tell whether the bulge in Akilah's jacket pocket was caused by a weapon. The

officer was about to answer that, in his expert opinion, he believed it was indeed a gun. Should this testimony be allowed?

Practical Tip:

Expert Preparation. Lawyers should meet with their experts prior to their deposition to review their qualifications and testimony. Experts expect this kind of preparation.

Problem #9-10: "I Can't Get A Reaction"

An action for copyright violation is brought against singer Fred Schmerd for allegedly copying and marketing the Rolling Stones' song, "Satisfaction" as his own. At trial, defendant Schmerd offers his song, "I Can't Get A Reaction," and the expert testimony of Sam Springsteen, a rock 'n' roll artist, to assist the trier of fact in evaluating the supposed similarities between the songs. The plaintiff objects to Springsteen's testimony, claiming he "has no formal education in music." What ruling and why?

[C]   Expert Witnesses and Novel Scientific Evidence

One of the most heavily contested expert testimony issues involves the admissibility of novel scientific evidence. Because scientific evidence has a strong impact on the outcome of a trial, the appropriate standard governing the admissibility of novel scientific evidence has become the subject of fierce debate. The test articulated in *Frye v. United States* (reprinted in § 9.02[F][1], *below*), required novel scientific evidence to be "generally accepted" in the particular scientific field. *Frye* governed in many jurisdictions as a condition of admissibility until the Court, in *Daubert v. Merrell Dow Pharmaceuticals, Inc.* (reprinted in § 9.02[F][3], *below*), held that *Frye* was superseded by the adoption of the FRE.

Even prior to *Daubert*, however, some jurisdictions had already started to replace *Frye* with more flexible approaches. *See Downing v. United States* (reprinted in § 9.02[F][2], *below*). Other jurisdictions following *Frye* limited its application by narrowly defining "novel scientific evidence." A prominent example of this is the *Casey Anthony* case in Florida. She was charged with killing her daughter Caylee in 2008. Prior to trial, her attorneys moved to exclude testimony by one of the state's experts, Dr. Hall, regarding plant and root growth where Caylee's body was found. The state filed a motion to strike the defendant's motion challenging the reliability of the evidence under *Frye*. Judge Perry granted the motion to strike. The judge determined that the expert would be giving opinion testimony and therefore, the testimony is not subject to a *Frye* challenge. In his order, the judge stated:

"Pure opinion" testimony is based solely on the expert's training and experience, personally developed through clinical experience, observation, or research . . . . In arriving at his conclusions, Dr. Hall did not use any scientific tests, principles, procedures, or methodology. He did not read any scientific journals or conduct any experiments. Instead, he relied upon his own analysis of photographs of the plant material at the crime scene. This Court concludes that Dr. Hall will give pure opinion testimony, which is not subject to a *Frye* challenge, so that the state does not have to establish the general acceptance of the opinions to which he will testify. Defense counsel will be able to cross-examine him at trial, and the jury will be entitled to evaluate the weight and credibility to be given to his opinions.

State of Florida v. Casey Marie Anthony, Order Granting Motion to Strike Defendant's Motion to Exclude Unreliable Evidence (Plant or Root Growth), Circuit Court of the Ninth Judicial Circuit in and for Orange County, Florida (Mar. 21, 2011). *See* http://www.ninthcircuit.org/news/High-Profile-Cases/Anthony/Downloads/Order%20Granting%20Motion%20to%20Strike%20Def.%20Motion%20to%20Exclude%20Unreliable%20Evidence%20-%20Plant%20or%20Root%20Growth.pdf.

Problem #9-11: Psychologically Speaking

In a defamation action, the plaintiff offers the testimony of an expert, Dr. Von Freud, who wrote the text, *Psychodynamics of Memory and Perception*. Dr. Von Freud will testify about the inaccuracies of memory and perception. One such problem, according to Von Freud, is the "forgetting curve," which suggests that people forget a greater percentage of information shortly after an event occurs. Another problem is "confabulation," which describes how people add to and alter remembrances as time passes. The defendant objects to Von Freud's proposed testimony. How should the court rule?

Problem #9-12: Malingering M.D.

Dr. Alice Barton-Smith, M.D. is a psychiatrist specializing in malingering (the exaggeration or fabrication of illness or injury for personal gain). In a personal injury case, she is called to testify by the defendant insurance company. Dr. Barton-Smith will testify that, based on her fifteen years of experience in studying malingering, her specific observations of the plaintiff totaling one hour, and her evaluation of the records in this case, the plaintiff was not truthful in her testimony about her whiplash injury. Instead, Dr. Barton-Smith will state that the plaintiff was malingering. Is Dr. Barton-Smith's testimony permissible?

Problem #9-13: My Brand New Miata

Two brand new Miata automobiles collide at the intersection of Fourth and Vine. At trial in a personal injury action arising from the collision, the plaintiff offered a police officer as an expert in accident reconstruction. Several eyewitnesses had previously testified at the trial about the accident.

1. Should the trial court permit the accident reconstruction expert to testify? What factors should the court consider prior to ruling?

2. Ethics Consideration. Prior to trial, defense counsel contacts the police officer who has been designated as an expert in accident reconstruction without the knowledge of the prosecution. Has defense counsel violated any Rules of

Professional Conduct? Delaware Rules of Prof'l Conduct R. 3.4. *See* MRPC 3.4.

Problem #9-14: I've Been Hypnotized

J.B. is charged with killing three young women. At trial, the state offers Dr. Nancy Rourque, a police department neuropsychologist. Dr. Rourque testifies that she hypnotized a witness to the killing. After the hypnosis, the witness was able to remember observing J.B. with one of the victims on the day the victim disappeared. Can Dr. Rourque testify about the hypnosis?

Problem #9-15: Big Tooth

After a particularly gruesome killing, the defendant is arrested and charged with murder. The primary evidence for the prosecution concerns tooth marks found on the victim's shoes. The prosecution intends to show, through the testimony of Dr. Goodenough, a forensic scientist with impeccable credentials, that the tooth marks belonged to the defendant.

1. Which of the following facts would be most likely to render Dr. Goodenough's testimony inadmissible? Explain your answer.

a. Dr. Goodenough was accepted as an expert in forensic science in 458 cases, and he testified for the prosecution in all of them.

b. Dr. Goodenough is being paid $1,000 for his services each day he works for the prosecution (regardless of the outcome of the case).

c. Dr. Goodenough is basing his conclusions in large part on facts not personally known to him (i.e., the doctor is relying on the observations of others).

d. The science of tooth mark analysis is not always accepted in the scientific community as accurate.

2. If Dr. Goodenough is allowed to testify, should he be allowed to describe a test he performed about the tooth mark analysis that formed the basis of his conclusions?

3. If Dr. Goodenough asked your advice on how best to conduct a tooth mark test to maximize its chance for admissibility at trial, what would you tell him?

[D]   Specialized Knowledge and Expertise: Limits on the Subject Matter of Expert Testimony [FRE 702, 704]

While a wide variety of individuals may qualify as experts under the FRE, the nature of expert testimony is not limitless. The following problems illustrate some of the parameters of expert testimony.

[1] When Specialized Knowledge Helps the Trier of Fact

Problem #9-16: Major Photo

The major issue in a murder prosecution was whether the get-away van was in fact the defendant's vehicle. The prosecution offered an expert in photography with extensive experience in a variety of lighting conditions. The photographer will testify about the conditions in which the identification of the van was made. Is this testimony admissible?

Problem #9-17: Expert Damages

In an antitrust action, *Holland v. Biotex, Inc.*, an expert for the plaintiff used regression analysis and the commonly used "yardstick" test to determine damages. The defendant objected to the expert. What ruling and why?

a. Suppose at trial the judge had stated, "Regardless of the testimony's reliability under *Daubert*, I am going to let the plaintiff offer such an expert and then let the defendant rebut with a similar expert. That will keep the playing field even." Permissible?

Problem #9-18: Operation

The sole issue in a medical malpractice case was whether the defendant, Dr. Dent, an emergency room surgeon, was required to operate to save the victim's life or whether there had been a viable alternative treatment. Dr. Scoop, an experienced internist, is called to testify on the defendant's behalf. Dr. Scoop testifies that, in her opinion, "an operation was necessary to save the victim's life."

Is Dr. Scoop's opinion admissible? Does it matter if the opinion concerns the ultimate issue at trial?

Practical Tip: Choosing an Expert:

Select an expert who is an effective communicator — someone who can educate and assist the fact finder in understanding a subject in hope of resolving the case. The expert in this frame of reference is the teacher and the jury her students.

Problem #9-19: Fred Fraud Fred

The defendants, brothers named Fred, were charged with mail fraud, securities fraud, and conspiracy. At trial, the prosecution called a well-known securities analyst to testify about the defendants' conduct. The witness, Rex Limbart, testified that, in his opinion, the actions by the defendants Fred constituted a "clear scheme to defraud others."

1. Is Mr. Limbart's testimony admissible? Why?

2. Ethics Consideration. The brothers want a prominent criminal defense lawyer to represent both of them. Is this a conflict of interest that can be consented to (i.e., if you receive the brothers' informed consent, can you represent them)? Oklahoma Rules of Prof'l Conduct R. 1.7. *See* MRPC 1.7.

Problem #9-20: "Crazy Eddie"

Eddie is charged with the attempted murder of his ex-girlfriend after he sent poisoned candy to her in the mail. At trial, Eddie raises the insanity defense. Dr. Willoughby testifies on Eddie's behalf. He states, "Crazy Eddie is insane, no doubt about it." Is Dr. Willoughby's testimony admissible? Explain.

Problem #9-21: Baseball

James Bell, a promising outfielder for the New Haven Hawks baseball team, signed a multi-year contract with a Japanese major league team. His then-existing New Haven contract allowed both sides to be excused from the contract if "good faith" negotiations did not produce an extended agreement. The Hawks sue, claiming Bell did not act in good faith. At trial, James calls his brother, an expert in negotiations, to testify that "In my opinion, James definitely negotiated in good faith." Is this testimony permissible? Why?

Problem #9-22: This Battery Won't Quit

Bessy's Auto Shop sold large quantities of a battery known as the "No-Kill." Due to a problem with its design, however, the "No-Kill" battery suffered from significant defects. Bessy's brought suit against the manufacturer of the battery, Manny, Inc. At trial, the executive vice president of Bessy's, Marsha Knowles Stanton, is asked to give her opinion on the amount of damages suffered by Bessy's as a result of the defect in the batteries. Can Marsha give her opinion? *See Electro Services, Inc. v. Exide Corp.*, 847 F.2d 1524 (11th Cir. 1988).

Problem #9-23: The Best Defense

Plaintiff filed a civil rights action for damages against the Sheriff's Office, alleging that the Sheriff conducted warrantless searches of his home and office. The plaintiff called famous attorney Matlock Mason to the stand to testify as an expert. Matlock states that the officers' conduct qualifies as a "search," and that the plaintiffs had not legally "consented" to the search. Is Matlock's opinion admissible?

Problem #9-24: Harassment!

In a sexual harassment action, the plaintiff offered the testimony of Dr. Lucy Barnes, an expert psychologist, to describe the profile of a sexual harasser. Dr. Barnes will testify that a sexual harasser is typically married, is the victim's supervisor, and has known the victim for at least six months. Is this testimony admissible?

Problem #9-25: Prof! (a.k.a. "The party as an expert witness")

A university professor sues his employer, claiming age and religious discrimination associated with pay raises. The professor's specialty is statistical data in employment discrimination cases, and he offers himself as an expert witness at trial. Should the court receive such testimony? Why? *See Tagatz v. Marquette Univ.*, 861 F.2d 1040 (7th Cir. 1988).

Problem #9-26: Don't Mess

A prisoner brought a civil rights action based on Title 28, Section 1983 of the United States Code, claiming that prison officials failed to protect him from a knife attack by other inmates in the mess-hall. The plaintiff offers the testimony of an inmate serving a sentence of life imprisonment to testify as an expert on gang violence in prison. Should the inmate be allowed to testify?

Problem # 9-27: The Blind Mule Defense

Sam was arrested at the border in a rental car and charged with the illegal importation of 70,000 methamphetamine pills found in a plastic bag in the gas tank. Sam was also charged with possession with intent to distribute them. The defense called an expert witness to support its theory that the defendant was operating as a "blind mule" for drug distributors. In rebuttal, a government expert testified that in his opinion Sam "realized that he was transporting drugs" given his inconsistent statements and general demeanor before being arrested and the strong odor of gasoline and other masking agents in the car. Sam's counsel objected to the statement that Sam had "realized he was transporting drugs." Is the government's expert testimony admissible?

Problem #9-28: Base Thief

The defendant, Larry, is charged with stealing all of the bases at the local stadium (and not as part of a regularly sanctioned baseball game). At trial, the defendant offers the testimony of a psychiatrist, Dr. Confort, to testify that the defendant could not form the necessary specific intent to steal as required under the law.

    1. Is such expert psychiatric testimony admissible?

    2. Could Dr. Confort testify that the defendant did not know right from wrong at the time he took the bases?

    3. Can Dr. Confort testify as an expert if he was trained as a psychologist and not as a psychiatrist? If he was trained as a social worker?

Problem #9-29: The Law of the Dominica (the issue of foreign law)

Planas, Inc. sued Unesco Shipping for allegedly breaching a contract to import a load of bananas from the Caribbean. At trial, the plaintiff claimed the law of the Dominica applied and asked the court to take judicial notice of it. The court refused to do so. Plaintiff then offered a Dominica law professor to testify about the substance of the pertinent Dominica law. The defendant objects to this testimony. What are the grounds for this objection? What is the proper ruling and why?

limits

[E] The Bases of Expert Testimony [FRE 703, 705]

There are several significant issues relating to the bases of expert opinions. While experts can testify to the basis of their opinions (and often are benefited by explaining how they reached their conclusions) limitations exist. Experts can only rely on the facts or data "reasonably relied on" in their field. FRE 703. Thus, hospital personnel often rely on patients' charts, even though they contain hearsay and other inadmissible evidence. In addition, just because an expert is permitted to rely on inadmissible evidence does not mean that evidence is allowed to be presented to the jury. The 2000 Amendment to FRE 703 effectively closed this "backdoor" way to bring in otherwise inadmissible evidence by requiring that the prejudicial impact of the inadmissible evidence must be substantially outweighed by its probative value for it to be admitted, a very difficult showing to make. FRE 703.

For example, when must an expert disclose the basis of an opinion? What can experts rely on as proper bases for their opinions? These questions will be examined in the following problems.

[1] What Experts Reasonably Rely Upon

Problem #9-30: Where There's Smoke . . .

Plaintiffs filed suit after a fire at the Union Baptist Church killed eight people. At trial, a noted combustion expert, Penny Wilkie, testified about the cause and circumstances of the fire. Dr. Wilkie stated that the fire in the church was "probably caused by a stuffed-up garbage chute." Her testimony was primarily based on the statement of a fireman, John, who reportedly said while fighting the fire, "Hey, there's no smoke coming out of the roof vent next to the garbage chute." John died of smoke inhalation from the fire prior to trial. Can Dr. Wilkie testify if John's statement is inadmissible hearsay?

Practical Tip: Protected Expert Materials:

Experts are routinely requested by the opposing party to bring to their deposition the materials they relied on in forming their opinions. Fed. R. Civ. P. 26(b)(4) (B) protects the expert's draft reports from being turned over to the opposing party.

Problem #9-31: Dr. Heersae

Fran Heersae, M.D., an orthopedist, was called to testify as an expert in a personal injury action regarding damages to the plaintiff, Arlene.

PLAINTIFF'S ATTORNEY: Dr. Heersae, what is your opinion about the extent of the leg injuries suffered by plaintiff Arlene in the accident?

A: In my opinion, plaintiff's injuries are —

DEFENDANT'S ATTORNEY: Objection! Dr. Heersae has not provided the basis for her conclusions, which is required before she can offer her opinion.

1. Is the defense counsel correct? Why or why not?

PLAINTIFF'S ATTORNEY: Doctor, assuming that the plaintiff put ice on the injury within an hour of the accident and was given only two aspirin by the defendant's medical representative and told to "walk it off," in your expert opinion, what impact did this have on the plaintiff's injury?

DEFENDANT'S ATTORNEY: Objection! Calls for speculation.

2. How should plaintiff's counsel respond to this objection?

PLAINTIFF'S ATTORNEY: Doctor, what do you rely on to suggest that the bone is not healing as fast as it should?

A: Well, the duty nurse wrote in the chart on March 23, 25, and 28 that —

DEFENDANT'S ATTORNEY: Objection! Hearsay.

3. How should plaintiff's counsel respond to this objection?

At this point, plaintiff's counsel had no further questions, and the judge turned to Dr. Heersae and asked, "What is the basis, Doctor, of your belief that the plaintiff will have approximately a 20 percent permanent disability in her injured leg?"

4. Is the court permitted to ask such a question?

5. After the cross-examination is concluded, and the plaintiff has rested, the judge desires to call Dr. Hailee Ocala, an orthopedist, to testify. Is this permissible?

§ 9.03   CASES AND RULES

[A]   Frye v. United States

Court of Appeals of District of Columbia
293 F. 1013 (D.C. Cir. 1923)

VAN ORSDEL, ASSOCIATE JUSTICE:

Appellant, defendant below, was convicted of the crime of murder in the second degree, and from the judgment prosecutes this appeal.

A single assignment of error is presented for our consideration. In the course of the trial counsel for defendant offered an expert witness to testify to the result of a deception test made upon defendant. The test is described as the systolic blood pressure deception test. It is asserted that blood pressure is influenced by change in the emotions of the witness, and that the systolic blood pressure rises are bro~

about by nervous impulses sent to the sympathetic branch of the autonomic nervous system. Scientific experiments, it is claimed, have demonstrated that fear, rage, and pain always produce a rise of systolic blood pressure, and that conscious deception or falsehood, concealment of facts, or guilt of crime, accompanied by fear of detection when the person is under examination, raises the systolic blood pressure in a curve, which corresponds exactly to the struggle going on in the subject's mind, between fear and attempted control of that fear, as the examination touches the vital points in respect of which he is attempting to deceive the examiner.

Prior to the trial defendant was subjected to this deception test, and counsel offered the scientist who conducted the test as an expert to testify to the results obtained. The offer was objected to by counsel for the government, and the court sustained the objection. Counsel for defendant then offered to have the proffered witness conduct a test in the presence of the jury. This also was denied.

Counsel for defendant, in their able presentation of the novel question involved, correctly state in their brief that no cases directly in point have been found. The broad ground, however, upon which they plant their case, is succinctly stated in their brief as follows:

> "The rule is that the opinions of experts or skilled witnesses are admissible in evidence in those cases in which the matter of inquiry is such that inexperienced persons are unlikely to prove capable of forming a correct judgment upon it, for the reason that the subject-matter so far partakes of a science, art or trade as to require a previous habit or experience or study in it, in order to acquire a knowledge of it. When the question involved does not lie within the range of common experience or common knowledge, but requires special experience or special knowledge, then the opinions of witnesses skilled in that particular science, art or trade to which the question relates are admissible in evidence."

Numerous cases are cited in support of this rule. Just when a scientific principle or discovery crosses the line between the experimental and demonstrable stages is difficult to define. Somewhere in this twilight zone the evidential force of the principle must be recognized, and while courts will go a long way in admitting expert testimony deduced from a well-recognized scientific principle or discovery, the thing from which the deduction is made must be sufficiently established to have gained general acceptance in the particular field in which it belongs.

We think the systolic blood pressure deception test has not yet gained such standing and scientific recognition among physiological and psychological authorities as would justify the courts in admitting expert testimony deduced from the discovery, development, and experiments thus far made.

The judgment is affirmed.

––––––––––

1. What is meant by "general acceptance" in *Frye*?

2. What is the proper scope of the scientific "field"? Is it a local, regional, national, or international standard?

3. Have rapid advances in technology made *Frye* outdated?

4. Why is the *Frye* test often considered unfriendly to novel scientific evidence?

5. What remains of *Frye* after *Daubert*, below?

[B]   United States v. Downing

Court of Appeals for the Third Circuit
753 F.2d 1224 (3d Cir. 1985)

[The defendant was convicted of mail fraud and other crimes. At trial, the defendant offered an expert psychologist to testify about the unreliability of eyewitness identifications, but the trial court excluded the evidence. On appeal, the Third Circuit Court of Appeals reversed and remanded. The court refused to follow *Frye v. United States*, 293 F. 1013 (D.C. Cir. 1923), and concluded that expert testimony about eyewitness perception meets the helpfulness standard of FRE 702. In rejecting *Frye*, the court reasoned as follows:]

. . . Because the general acceptance standard set out in *Frye* was the dominant view within the federal courts at the time the Federal Rules of Evidence were considered and adopted, one might expect that the rules themselves would make some pronouncement about the continuing vitality of the standard. Neither the text of the Federal Rules of Evidence nor the accompanying notes of the advisory committee, however, explicitly set forth the appropriate standard by which the admissibility of novel scientific evidence is to be established. Although the commentators agree that this legislative silence is significant, they disagree about its meaning. Professors Salzburg and Redden, for example, have stated, "[i]t would be odd if the Advisory Committee and the Congress intended to overrule the vast majority of cases excluding such evidence as lie detectors without explicitly stating so." Salzburg and Redden, [Federal Rules of Evidence Manual] 452 [(3d ed. 1982)].

The opposing view, espoused by Judge Weinstein, Professor Berger, and others, maintains that "[T]he silence of the rule [702] and its drafters should be regarded as tantamount to an abandonment of the general acceptance standard." J. Weinstein and M. Berger, *supra* § 702[03] at 702–16.

Although we believe that "helpfulness" necessarily implies a quantum of reliability beyond that required to meet a standard of bare logical relevance, *see* discussion *infra*, it also seems clear to us that some scientific evidence can assist the trier of fact in reaching an accurate determination of facts in issue even though the principles underlying the evidence have not become "generally accepted" in the field to which they belong. Moreover, we can assume that the drafters of the Federal Rules of Evidence were aware that the *Frye* test was a judicial creation, and we find nothing in the language of the rules to suggest a disapproval of such interstitial judicial rulemaking.

The language of Fed. R. Evid. 702, the spirit of the Federal Rules of Evidence in general, and the experience with the *Frye* test suggest the appropriateness of a more flexible approach to the admissibility of novel scientific evidence. In our view, Rule 702 requires that a district court ruling upon the admission of (novel) scientific evidence, i.e., evidence whose scientific fundaments are not suitable candidates for judicial notice, conduct a preliminary inquiry focusing on (1) the soundness and reliability of the process or technique used in generating the evidence, (2) the possibility that admitting the evidence would overwhelm, confuse, or mislead the jury, and (3) the proffered connection between the scientific research or test result to be presented, and particular disputed factual issues in the case.

Where a form of scientific expertise has no established "track record" in litigation, the court may look to other factors that may bear on the reliability of the evidence.

[C]   Daubert v. Merrell Dow Pharmaceuticals, Inc.

United States Supreme Court
509 U.S. 579 (1993)

JUSTICE BLACKMUN delivered the opinion of the Court.

In this case we are called upon to determine the standard for admitting expert scientific testimony in a federal trial.

I

Petitioners Jason Daubert and Eric Schuller are minor children born with serious birth defects. They and their parents sued respondent in California state court, alleging that the birth defects had been caused by the mothers' ingestion of Bendectin, a prescription anti-nausea drug marketed by respondent. Respondent removed the suits to federal court on diversity grounds.

After extensive discovery, respondent moved for summary judgment, contending that Bendectin does not cause birth defects in humans and that petitioners would be unable to come forward with any admissible evidence that it does. In support of its motion, respondent submitted an affidavit of Steven H. Lamm, physician and epidemiologist, who is a well-credentialed expert on the risks from exposure to various chemical substances. Doctor Lamm stated that he had reviewed all the literature on Bendectin and human birth defects — more than 30 published studies involving over 130,000 patients. No study had found Bendectin to be a human teratogen (i.e., a substance capable of causing malformations in fetuses). On the basis of this review, Doctor Lamm concluded that maternal use of Bendectin during the first trimester of pregnancy has not been shown to be a risk factor for human birth defects.

Petitioners did not (and do not) contest this characterization of the published record regarding Bendectin. Instead, they responded to respondent's motion with the testimony of eight experts of their own, each of whom also possessed impressive credentials. These experts had concluded that Bendectin can cause birth defects. Their conclusions were based upon "in vitro" (test tube) and "in vivo" (live) animal studies that found a link between Bendectin and malformations; pharmacological studies of the chemical structure of Bendectin that purported to show similarities between the structure of the drug and that of other substances known to cause birth defects; and the "reanalysis" of previously published epidemiological (human statistical) studies.

The District Court granted respondent's motion for summary judgment. The court stated that scientific evidence is admissible only if the principle upon which it is based is " 'sufficiently established to have general acceptance in the field to which it belongs.' " (Citations omitted.) The court concluded that petitioners' evidence did not meet this standard. Given the vast body of epidemiological data concerning Bendectin, the court held, expert opinion which is not based on epidemiological evidence is not admissible to establish causation. Thus, the animal-cell studies, live animal studies, and chemical structure analysis on which petitioners had relied could not raise by themselves a reasonably disputable jury issue regarding causation. *Ibid.* Petitioners' epidemiological analysis, based as they were on recalculations of data in previously published studies that had found no causal link between the drug and birth defects, were ruled to be inadmissible because they had not been published or subjected to peer review.

We granted certiorari, 506 U.S. 914 (1992), in light of sharp divisions among the courts regarding the proper standard for the admission of expert testimony.

II

In the 70 years since its formulation in the *Frye* case, the "general acceptance" test has been the dominant standard for determining the admissibility of novel scientific evidence at trial. . . . Although under increasing attack of late, the rule continues to be followed by a majority of courts, including the Ninth Circuit.

The *Frye* test has its origin in a short and citation-free 1923 decision concerning the admissibility of evidence derived from a systolic blood pressure deception test, a crude precursor to the polygraph machine. In what has become a famous (perhaps infamous) passage, the then Court of Appeals for the District of Columbia described the device and its operation and declared:

> "Just when a scientific principle or discovery crosses the line between the experimental and demonstrable stages is difficult to define. Somewhere in this twilight zone the evidential force of the principle must be recognized, and while courts will go a long way in admitting expert testimony deduced from a well-recognized scientific principle or discovery, *the thing from which the deduction is made must be sufficiently established to have gained general acceptance in the particular field in which it belongs.*" 54 App. D.C. at 47, 293 F. at 1014 (emphasis added).

Because the deception test had "not yet gained such standing and scientific recognition among physiological and psychological authorities as would justify the courts in admitting expert testimony deduced from the discovery, development, and experiments thus far made," evidence of its results was ruled inadmissible. *Ibid.*

The merits of the *Frye* test have been much debated, and scholarship on its proper scope and application is legion. Petitioners' primary attack, however, is not on the content but on the continuing authority of the rule. They contend that the *Frye* test was superseded by the adoption of the Federal Rules of Evidence. We agree.

We interpret the legislatively-enacted Federal Rules of Evidence as we would any statute. Rule 402 provides the baseline:

> "All relevant evidence is admissible, except as otherwise provided by the Constitution of the United States, by Act of Congress, by these rules, or by other rules prescribed by the Supreme Court pursuant to statutory authority. Evidence which is not relevant is not admissible."

"Relevant evidence" is defined as that which has "any tendency to make the existence of any fact that is of consequence to the determination of the action more probable or less probable than it would be without the evidence." Rule 401. The rule's basic standard of relevance thus is a liberal one.

Frye, of course, predated the Rules by half a century. In *United States v. Abel*, 469 U.S. 45, 105 S. Ct. 465, 83 L. Ed. 2d 450 (1984), we considered the pertinence of background common law in interpreting the Rules of Evidence. We noted that the Rules occupy the field, but, quoting Professor Cleary, the Reporter, explained that the common law nevertheless could serve as an aid to their application:

> " 'In principle, under the Federal Rules no common law of evidence remains. "All relevant evidence is admissible, except as otherwise provided. . . ." In reality, of course, the body of common law knowledge continues to exist, though in the somewhat altered form of a source of guidance in the exercise of delegated powers.' " *Id.* at 51–52, 105 S. Ct. at 469.

We found the common-law precept at issue in the *Able* case entirely consistent with Rule 402's general requirement of admissibility, and considered it unlikely that the drafters had intended to change the rule. In *Bourjaily v. United States*, 483 U.S. 171, 107 S. Ct. 2775, 97 L. Ed. 2d 144 (1987), on the other hand, the Court was unable to find a particular common-law doctrine in the Rules, and so held it superseded.

Here there is a specific Rule that speaks to the contested issue. Rule 702, governing expert testimony, provides:

> "If scientific, technical, or other specialized knowledge will assist the trier of fact to understand the evidence or to determine a fact in issue, a witness qualified as an expert by knowledge, skill, experience, training, or education, may testify thereto in the form of an opinion or otherwise."

Nothing in the text of this Rule establishes "general acceptance" as an absolute prerequisite to admissibility. Nor does respondent present any clear indication that Rule 702 or the Rules as a whole were intended to incorporate a "general acceptance" standard. The drafting history makes no mention of *Frye*, and a rigid "general acceptance" requirement would be at odds with the "liberal thrust" of the Federal Rules and their "general approach of relaxing traditional barriers to 'opinion' testimony." *Beech Aircraft Corp. v. Rainey*, 488 U.S. at 169, 109 S. Ct. at 450) (citing Rules 701 to 705) . . . . Given the Rules' permissive backdrop and their inclusion of a specific rule on expert testimony that does not mention "general acceptance," the assertion that the Rules somehow assimilated *Frye* is unconvincing. *Frye* made "general acceptance" the exclusive test for admitting expert scientific testimony. That austere standard, absent from and incompatible with the Federal Rules of Evidence, should not be applied in federal trials.

The primary locus of this obligation is Rule 702, which clearly contemplates some degree of regulation of the subjects and theories about which an expert may testify. *"If scientific,* technical or other specialized *knowledge will assist the trier of fact* to understand the evidence or to determine a fact in issue" an expert "may testify *thereto."* The subject of an expert's testimony must be "scientific . . . knowledge." The adjective "scientific" implies a grounding in the methods and procedures of science. Similarly, the word "knowledge" connotes more than the subjective belief or unsupported speculation. The term "applies to any body of known facts or accepted as truths on good grounds." *Webster's Third International Dictionary* 1252 (1986). Of course, it would be unreasonable to conclude that the subject of scientific testimony must be "known" to a certainty; arguably, there are no certainties in science. . . . But, in order to qualify as "scientific knowledge," an inference or assertion must be derived by the scientific method. Proposed testimony must be supported by appropriate validation — i.e., "good grounds," based on what is known. In short, the requirement that an expert's testimony pertain to "scientific knowledge" establishes a standard of evidentiary reliability.

Rule 702 further requires that the evidence or testimony "assist the trier of fact to understand the evidence or to determine a fact in issue." This condition goes primarily to relevance. "Expert testimony which does not relate to any issue in the case is not relevant and, ergo, non-helpful." 3 Weinstein & Berger ¶ 702[02], p. 702–18. . . . Rule 702's "helpfulness" standard requires a valid scientific connection to the pertinent inquiry as a precondition to admissibility.

Faced with a proffer of expert scientific testimony, then, the trial judge must determine at the outset, pursuant to Rule 104(a), whether the expert is proposing to testify to (1) scientific knowledge that (2) will assist the trier of fact to understand or determine a fact in issue. This entails a preliminary assessment of whether the reasoning or methodology underlying the testimony is scientifically valid and of whether that reasoning or methodology properly can be applied to the facts in issue. We are confident that federal judges possess the capacity to undertake this review. Many factors will bear on the inquiry, and we do not presume to set out a definitive checklist or test. But some general observations are appropriate.

Ordinarily, a key question to be answered in determining whether a theory or technique is scientific knowledge that will assist the trier of fact will be whether it can be (and has been) tested. "Scientific methodology today is based on generating hypotheses and testing them to see if they can be falsified; indeed, this methodology is what distinguishes science from other fields of human inquiry." (Citation omitted.)

Another pertinent consideration is whether the theory or technique has been subjected to peer review and publication. Publication (which is but one element of peer review) is not a *sine qua non* of admissibility; it does not necessarily correlate with reliability, . . . and in some instances well-grounded but innovative theories will not have been published. . . . Some propositions, moreover, are too particular, too new, or of too limited interest to be published. But submission to the scrutiny of the scientific community is a component of "good science," in part because it increases the likelihood that substantive flaws in methodology will be detected. . . . The fact of publication (or lack thereof) in a peer-reviewed journal thus will be a relevant, though not dispositive, consideration in assessing the scientific validity of a particular technique or methodology on which an opinion is premised.

Additionally, in the case of a particular scientific technique, the court ordinarily should consider the known or potential rate of error . . . and the existence and maintenance of standards controlling the technique's operation.

Finally, "general acceptance" can yet have a bearing on the inquiry. A "reliability assessment does not require, although it does permit, explicit identification of a relevant scientific community and an express determination of a particular degree of acceptance within that community." (Citation omitted.) Widespread acceptance can be an important factor in ruling particular evidence admissible, and "a known technique that has been able to attract only minimal support within the community," *Downing*, 753 F.2d, at 1238, may properly be viewed with skepticism.

The inquiry envisioned by Rule 702 is, we emphasize, a flexible one. Its over-arching subject is the scientific validity — and thus the evidentiary relevance and reliability — of the principles that underlie a proposed submission. The focus, of course, must be solely on principles and methodology, not on the conclusions that they generate.

III

We conclude by briefly addressing what appear to be two underlying concerns of the parties and *amici* in this case. Respondent expresses apprehension that abandonment of "general acceptance" as the exclusive requirement for admission will result in a "free-for-all" in which befuddled juries are confounded by absurd and irrational pseudoscientific assertions. In this regard respondent seems to us to be overly pessimistic about the capabilities of the jury, and of the adversary system generally. Vigorous cross-examination, presentation of contrary evidence, and careful instruction on the burden of proof are the traditional and appropriate means of attacking shaky but admissible evidence. . . . Additionally, in the event the trial court concludes that the scintilla of evidence presented supporting a position is insufficient to allow a reasonable juror to conclude that the position more likely than not is true, the court remains free to direct a judgment, Fed. Rule Civ. Proc. 50(a), and likewise to grant summary judgment, Fed. Rule Civ. Proc. 56. These conventional devices, rather than wholesale exclusion under an uncompromising "general acceptance" test, are the appropriate safeguards where the basis of scientific testimony meets the standards of Rule 702.

IV

To summarize: "General acceptance" is not a necessary precondition to the admissibility of scientific evidence under the Federal Rules of Evidence, but the Rules of Evidence — especially Rule 702 — do assign to the trial judge the task of ensuring that an expert's testimony both rests on a reliable foundation and is relevant to the task at hand. Pertinent evidence based on scientifically valid principles will satisfy those demands.

The inquiries of the District Court and the Court of Appeals focused almost exclusively on "general acceptance," as gauged by publication and the decisions of other courts. Accordingly, the judgment of the Court of Appeals is vacated and the case is remanded for further proceedings consistent with this opinion. *It is so ordered.*

Background Box:

Daubert essentially asks judges to play amateur scientists. In the role of a gatekeeper, the judge must be able to discern between "junk" science and reliable science — meaning scientific methods trustworthy enough to get before the jury.

[D]　United States v. Rincon

United States Court of Appeals for the Ninth Circuit
28 F.3d 921 (9th Cir. 1994), cert. denied, 115 S. Ct. 605 (1994)

T.G. NELSON, CIRCUIT JUDGE:

I. Overview

Hugo Rincon (Rincon) was convicted on two counts of unarmed bank robbery. On Rincon's first appeal to this court, he contended that the district court erred in refusing to admit expert testimony regarding the reliability of eyewitness identification. We affirmed the district court's exclusion of that expert testimony in *United States v. Rincon (Rincon I)*, 984 F.2d 1003 (9th Cir. 1993). After the Supreme Court's recent decision in *Daubert v. Merrell Dow Pharmaceuticals, Inc.*, 509 U.S. 579, 113 S. Ct. 2786, 125 L. Ed. 2d 469 (1993), regarding the admissibility of expert testimony, the Court remanded this case and asked us to reexamine that issue in light of *Daubert*. We remanded to the district court for reconsideration. The district court upheld its earlier decision to exclude the expert testimony. We affirm.

III. Expert Testimony

We review for abuse of discretion the district court's decision regarding the admissibility of expert testimony on the reliability of eyewitness identifications. . . .

In *Daubert*, the Supreme Court held that Fed.R.Evid. 702 supersedes the general acceptance standard established in *Frye*. 113 S. Ct. at 2793–94. It noted, however, that notwithstanding its holding, the Federal Rules of Evidence still place limits on the admissibility of scientific evidence. *Id.* at 2794–95. "Nor is the trial judge disabled from screening such evidence. To the contrary, under the Rules the trial judge must ensure that any and all scientific testimony or evidence admitted is not only relevant, but reliable." *Id.* at 2795. . . . On remand, the district court excluded the expert testimony on eyewitness identification, ruling that:

1. The proposed testimony invades the province of the jury (i.e., it does not assist the trier of fact);

2. No showing has been made that the testimony relates to an area that is recognized as a science; and

3. The testimony is likely to confuse the jury.

Moreover, the district court stated that "the proposed expert eyewitness identification testimony is being offered by the defense more in the role of an advocate and not as a scientifically valid opinion." We conclude that the district court did not abuse its discretion in excluding Dr. Pezdek's expert testimony because Rincon's proffer failed to satisfy the admissibility standard established in *Daubert.*

A. Scientific Knowledge

"[I]n order to qualify as 'scientific knowledge,' an inference or assertion must be derived by the scientific method. Proposed testimony must be supported by appropriate validation — i.e., 'good grounds,' based on what is known." *Id.* at 2795. . . . *Daubert* set forth several factors which the district court may consider in determining whether a theory or technique constitutes "scientific knowledge," including: (1) whether the theory or technique can be or has been tested; (2) whether the theory or technique has been subjected to peer review and publication; (3) the known or potential rate of error; and (4) the particular degree of acceptance within the scientific community. *Id.* at 2796–97. This list is not exhaustive. Nor did the Court "presume to set out a definitive checklist or test." *Id.* at 2796.

The first inquiry, then, under *Daubert* is whether the proposed testimony of Dr. Pezdek was on a "scientific" subject. On remand, the district court denied Rincon's motion on three grounds, one of which was that "no showing has been made that the testimony relates to an area that is recognized as a science."

In the initial motion, Rincon asserted that Dr. Pezdek held a Ph.D. in psychology from the University of Massachusetts at Amherst, and was a full professor at the Claremont Graduate School of Psychology. She would testify that there are three phases of eyewitness identification: perception and encoding; storage and retention (memory); and retrieval. In turn, the perception and encoding phase are affected by the factors of stress, duration of exposure, cross-racial identification, and availability of facial features (whether or not the face is partially obscured). The storage and retrieval stages are affected by time delay and suggestibility.

However, none of the research was submitted or described so that the district court could determine if the studies were indeed scientific on the basis the Court explained in *Daubert*: "whether the reasoning or methodology underlying the testimony is scientifically valid. . . ." *Daubert*, 13 S. Ct. at 2796.

On remand, Rincon supplemented the record with a copy of an article entitled *The "General Acceptance" of Psychological Research on Eyewitness Testimony.* The article described a survey of sixty-three experts on eyewitness testimony relating to their views of the scientific acceptance of research on a number of topics, including those that Dr. Pezdek would testify to.

However, while the article identified the research on some of the topics, it did not discuss the research in sufficient detail that the district court could determine if the research was scientifically valid. In the argument before the district court, counsel for Rincon told the court that Dr. Pezdek could testify about the studies that had been done on the various topics. However, he again did not offer or describe the studies themselves. The district court's determination that Rincon had not shown the proposed testimony related to a scientific subject is supported by the record.

B. Assist Trier of Fact

Even when a theory or methodology satisfies the "scientific knowledge" requirement, in order to be admissible, expert testimony must also "assist the trier of fact to understand or to determine a fact in issue."

The expert testimony Rincon offered was no doubt relevant to his defense.

In this case, the district court found that Dr. Pezdek's testimony would not assist the trier of fact and that it would likely confuse or mislead the jury. We decline to disturb the district court's ruling.

Even though the factors about which Dr. Pezdek was to testify may have been informative, the district court conveyed that same information by providing a comprehensive jury instruction to guide the jury's deliberations. . . .

The district court gave the jury in this case a comprehensive instruction on eyewitness identifications. The instruction addressed many of the factors about which Dr. Pezdek would have testified. The district court instructed the jury to consider whether: (1) the eyewitness had the capacity and adequate opportunity to observe the offender based upon the length of time for observation as well as the conditions of observation; (2) the identification was the product of the eyewitness's own recollection or was the result of subsequent influence or suggestiveness; (3) the eyewitness has made inconsistent identifications; and (4) the eyewitness was credible. The instruction also pointed out the danger of a show up versus the reliability of a lineup with similar individuals from which the eyewitness must choose. Finally, it permitted the jury to consider, as a factor bearing upon the reliability of the eyewitness testimony, the length of time which may have elapsed between the occurrence of the crime and the eyewitness's identification.

As Rincon's article indicates, "it remains to be seen whether experts can enhance jurors' ability to distinguish accurate from inaccurate eyewitnesses, or whether the dangers of such testimony outweigh its probative value; *e.g.*, whether jurors become not more or less skeptical, but more or less *accurate* in their judgments of eyewitness testimony." In any event, the article is inconclusive as to the effect such evidence has on a jury. Given the powerful nature of expert testimony, coupled with its potential to mislead the jury, we cannot say that the district court erred in concluding that the proffered evidence would not assist the trier of fact and that it was likely to mislead the jury.

Notwithstanding our conclusion, we emphasize that the result we reach in this case is based upon an individualized inquiry, rather that strict application of the past rule concerning expert testimony on the reliability of eyewitness identification. . . . Our conclusion does not preclude the admission of such testimony when the proffering party satisfies the standard established in *Daubert* by showing that the expert opinion is based upon "scientific knowledge" which is both reliable and helpful to the jury in any given case. *See Daubert*, 113 S. Ct. at 2796. District courts must strike the appropriate balance between admitting reliable, helpful expert testimony and excluding misleading or confusing testimony to achieve the flexible approach outlined in *Daubert*. *See id.* at 2798–99. The district court struck such a balance in this case.

V. Conclusion

Rincon has failed to produce sufficient evidence either that the testimony proffered here is based upon "scientific knowledge" or that it would have assisted the trier of fact in this particular case. Accordingly, we conclude that the district court did not abuse its discretion in excluding Dr. Pezdek's testimony.

Affirmed.

[E]   People v. Chambers

Supreme Court of New York, New York County
512 N.Y.S.2d 631 (1987) (Index No. 6394/86)

[Robert Chambers was tried and convicted of murdering Jennifer Levin. He claimed that her death was an accident that occurred during "rough sex." At trial, the prosecutor wished to offer expert testimony about tests performed on the victim's saliva. In support of the expert testimony, the prosecutor argued in its memorandum to the court as follows:]

The defense moved for preclusion of the expert testimony of four witnesses at the upcoming trial of this case, or in the alternative, for "*Frye*" hearings to be conducted to determine the admissibility of the testimony.

Three of the four experts whom the defense moves to preclude have conducted tests and examinations of Jennifer Levin's jacket. Her jacket was recovered at the crime scene. It was found on top of one of her arms as she lay dead in Central Park. It had many blood stains on it. Prior to going to Central Park with this defendant, the jacket was clean. The jacket can be seen in the crime scene photos and Dorian's photos which we can make available to the Court.

The indictment charges intentional murder. If the jacket played a role in causing Jennifer Levin's death, that would be evidence probative of intentional murder. This is especially so in view of the fact that defendant's version of events makes *absolutely* no mention of the blood stained jacket.

The jacket was tested by Dr. Robert Shaler, at that time the Chief of Serology at the New York City Medical Examiner's Office. He was able to determine the blood types of the stains on the jacket. He compared them to Jennifer Levin's blood type and, subsequently, to Robert Chamber's blood type. In this way, as to many of the stains, he can state which stain was from Jennifer Levin's blood and which stain was from Robert Chamber's blood. Dr. Shaler also found amylase stains on the jacket. Amylase is an enzyme found in bodily fluids. It is presumptive of saliva. In order to prove that the amylase was indeed saliva, the jacket was tested by Dr. Michael Woodward of Humagen Inc., Charlottesville, Virginia. He confirmed the presence of saliva on the jacket.

Dr. Peter DeForest, a crime scene reconstruction expert who has testified in court more than eighty times, has analyzed all the physical evidence in this case.

Clearly the blood stained and saliva stained jacket is crucial evidence in this case. Whose blood and saliva it is, how it got on the jacket, and what role the jacket played in causing Jennifer Levin's death are important questions the jury will want answered. The People's expert witnesses help the jury to answer those questions.

The People deny all the allegations contained in the defense brief and consent to a *Frye* hearing as to Dr. Woodward.

As the People made the Court and defense counsel aware before the defense *Frye* motions were served, Dr. Woodward was recently the victim of an accident which required hospitalization and surgery. He lives in Virginia. We have discussed the possibility with the defense of opening and putting on evidence and interrupting the trial for a day or two to conduct a *Frye* hearing as to Dr. Woodward in January when he is able to come to New York. This is an acceptable manner of proceeding for the People.

[Based upon these submissions, the Court ordered a *Frye* hearing. Dr. Woodward was examined by the prosecution and the defense. Following his testimony, the defense argued that the technique he had employed — the use of a monoclonal antibody to identify salivary and pancreatic amylase — was not generally accepted in the scientific community. What follows is a portion of the prosecution and defense arguments.]

Prosecution Argument:

So the only question left then is the second question that is set out on Page Two of their brief.

And that is whether or not the tests used by Dr. Woodward have gained general acceptance through the reliability in the scientific field.

And, specially, Judge, the question is whether or not his use of a monoclonal antibody to specifically identify salivary and pancreatic amylase by the use of his enzyme-capture assay is generally accepted by the members of the scientific field who work with monoclonal antibodies for amylase.

You heard two of the leading experts in the world on this area. You heard Dr. Woodward and Dr. Bruns say variously that monoclonal antibodies have been used to identify closely-related antigens for many years.

You heard that Dr. Woodward has developed his own quality controls.

You heard that he has used monoclonals to identify amylase in blind unknown samples from the F.B.I. and National Cancer Institute.

You heard that Dr. Woodward's work in developing monoclonal antibodies specifically for salivary and pancreatic amylase was peer-reviewed in two stages of his own work, in the development of his monoclonals in order to get funding to begin and then to continue.

There is nothing novel anymore. They told you about using monoclonal antibodies to identify amylase.

Your Honor, without getting into the law, what we have to establish and what I submit we did establish was the reasonable accuracy of this test in the general scientific acceptance of the test.

Every useful development, Judge, must have its first day in court. Court cases are full of conflicting opinions of all kinds of experts.

Please don't let the fact that Dr. Woodward and Dr. Bruns have not testified before make you think that their work is not reliable; to the contrary, they have never been asked to testify before.

They both testified that where monoclonal antibodies were concerned there is no fundamental difference between testing dried stains and liquid serum or saliva.

That's because of the very nature of monoclonal antibody science, how specific they are and how they do not cross-react.

If they want to quibble about how this test was done, they can do so in front of the jury, your Honor, in terms of science and in terms of law.

Defense Argument:

It is not — and I think Mr. Kendris said it and I agree — it is not for the Court to quibble with science. The Court is not a scientist. We're not scientists. And the jury certainly isn't a scientist.

But it is for scientists to quibble with science, to make sure that it's good science.

And the problem in this case is that no one has checked out what they want to testify to. No one has tested it. No one has verified it. No one has published about it. No one has testified about it.

It's the scientists themselves who have not reached a conclusion. They have not even tried to reach a conclusion that what Dr. Woodward testified to is reliable, is scientifically acceptable, and can do what he says it can do, which is that he can perform a test a year later on a dried stain and tell this Court and jury something about what was left on a denim jacket a year ago. Because this is what we're talking about.

He developed his method for it and his monoclonal to tell how much salivary or pancreatic amylase is in human serum, a liquid given to him by a hospital.

Then he has to make a leap. He has to say that the test that's under development to do this from serum can also tell salivary and pancreatic from the dried stain. That's Leap Number One.

Then he has to make another leap. Not only can I tell the salivary and pancreatic in a dried stain today, but I can tell you something about what was there nine months, sixteen months ago. That's Leap Number Two.

And the final leap is that after I made a guess about what was there a year ago, I can tell you where it came from, which is consistent with saliva.

And in each step of the way from the first through the last it is clear from their testimony that there has been no scientific acceptance, testing, or proof that these things are accurate and accepted in the scientific community.

He says that in order to determine that you have to know something about how these enzymes survive drying, you have to know how long they can be on a denim jacket. You throw it around the police station, wherever it was, how they survived. Because he's got to make a conclusion based on what he finds today as to what was there.

And, again, everyone admits there had never been any tests or anyone else, by anyone, not even tests, let alone publishing or testifying on the effect of drying these enzymes.

How do they survive having been dried and sat around for a year?

No one has tested that.

That's the nub of the case. Mr. Kendris can get up and he can tell you I think these witnesses, doctors, they are scientists, the fact is the scientific community hasn't accepted it, and a murder case is not the place to test it out.

[Several days after the motion was argued, the Court ruled in favor of the defense and excluded Dr. Woodward's testimony. No opinion accompanied the ruling. Without Dr. Woodward, Dr. DeForest, the reconstruction expert, also was not able to testify.]

Did the court make the proper decision? Would the court have reached the same conclusion if it had the benefit of the Supreme Court decision in *Daubert*?

[F]   General Electric Co. v. Joiner

United States Supreme Court
522 U.S. 136 (1997)

CHIEF JUSTICE REHNQUIST delivered the opinion of the Court.

We granted certiorari in this case to determine what standard an appellate court should apply in reviewing a trial court's decision to admit or exclude expert testimony under *Daubert v. Merrell Dow Pharmaceuticals, Inc.*, 509 U.S. 579, 113 S. Ct. 2786, 125 L. Ed. 2d 469 (1993). We hold that abuse of discretion is the appropriate standard.

We apply this standard and conclude that the District Court in this case did not abuse its discretion when it excluded certain proffered expert testimony.

[Joiner sued General Electric and others, alleging that he contracted lung cancer as a result of exposure to polychlorinated biphenyls (PCBs) in his work with electrical transformers. The District Court granted summary judgment for petitioners because it excluded the testimony of Joiner's experts, ruling that their testimony about a link between exposure to PCBs and the type of lung cancer he, a smoker, had contracted did not rise above "subjective belief or unsupported speculation." The Court of Appeals for the Eleventh Circuit reversed. 78 F.3d 524 (1996). Holding that, "because the Federal Rules of Evidence governing expert testimony display a preference for admissibility, we apply a particularly stringent standard of review to the trial judge's exclusion of expert testimony," the Court of Appeals held that the District Court had erred in excluding the testimony of Joiner's expert witnesses.]

We granted petitioners' petition for a writ of certiorari, 520 U.S. — (1997), and we now reverse.

II

Petitioners challenge the standard applied by the Court of Appeals in reviewing the District Court's decision to exclude respondent's experts' proffered testimony. They argue that that court should have applied traditional "abuse-of-discretion" review. Respondent agrees that abuse of discretion is the correct standard of review. He contends, however, that the Court of Appeals applied an abuse-of-discretion standard in this case. As he reads it, the phrase "particularly stringent" announced no new standard of review. It was simply an acknowledgement that an appellate court can and will devote more resources to analyzing district court decisions that are dispositive of the entire litigation. All evidentiary decisions are reviewed under an abuse of discretion standard. He argues, however, that it is perfectly reasonable for appellate courts to give particular attention to those decisions that are outcome determinative.

We have held that abuse of discretion is the proper standard of review of a district court's evidentiary rulings. . . . Indeed, our cases on the subject go back as far as *Spring Co. v. Edgar*, 99 U.S. 645, 658 (1879), where we said that "cases arise where it is very much a matter of discretion with the court whether to receive or exclude the evidence; but the appellate court will not reverse in such a case, unless the ruling is manifestly erroneous." The Court of Appeals suggested that *Daubert* somehow altered this general rule in the context of a district court's decision to exclude scientific evidence. But *Daubert* did not address the standard of appellate review for evidentiary rulings at all. It did hold that the "austere" *Frye* standard of "general acceptance" had not been carried over into the Federal Rules of Evidence. But the opinion also said:

> "That the *Frye* test was displaced by the Rules of Evidence does not mean, however, that the Rules themselves place no limits on the admissibility of purportedly scientific evidence. Nor is the trial judge disabled from screening such evidence. To the contrary, under the Rules the trial judge must ensure that any and all scientific testimony or evidence admitted is not only relevant, but reliable." 509 U.S. at 589. (Footnote omitted).

Thus, while the Federal Rules of Evidence allow district courts to admit a somewhat broader range of scientific testimony than would have been admissible under *Frye*, they leave in place the "gatekeeper" role of the trial judge in screening such evidence. A court of appeals applying "abuse-of-discretion" review to such rulings may not categorically distinguish between rulings allowing expert testimony and rulings which disallow it. Compare *Beech Aircraft Corp v. Rainey*, 488 U.S. 153, 172, (1988) (applying abuse-of-discretion review to a lower court's decision to exclude evidence) with *United States v. Abel*, supra at 54, 105 S. Ct. at 470 (applying abuse-of-discretion review to a lower court's decision to admit evidence). We likewise reject respondent's argument that because the granting of summary judgment in this case was "outcome determinative," it should have been subjected to a more searching standard of review. On a motion for summary judgment, disputed issues of fact are resolved against the moving party — here, petitioners. But the question of admissibility of expert testimony is not such an issue of fact, and is reviewable under the abuse of discretion standard.

We hold that the Court of Appeals erred in its review of the exclusion of Joiner's experts' testimony. In applying an overly "stringent" review to that ruling, it failed to give the trial court the deference that is the hallmark of abuse-of-discretion review. . . .

Petitioners contended that the statements of Joiner's experts regarding causation were nothing more than speculation. Petitioners criticized the testimony of the experts in that it was "not supported by epidemiological studies . . . [and was] based exclusively on isolated studies of laboratory animals." . . . Joiner responded by claiming that his experts had identified "relevant animal studies which support their opinions." . . . . He also directed the court's attention to four epidemiological studies on which his experts had relied.

Respondent points to *Daubert*'s language that the "focus, of course, must be solely on principles and methodology, not on the conclusions that they generate." 509 U.S. at 595. He claims that because the District Court's disagreement was with the conclusion that the experts drew from the studies, the District Court committed legal error and was properly reversed by the Court of Appeals. But conclusions and methodology are not entirely distinct from one another. Trained experts commonly extrapolate from existing data. But nothing in either *Daubert* or the Federal Rules of Evidence requires a district court to admit opinion evidence which is connected to existing data only by the ipse dixit of the expert. A court may conclude that there is simply too great an analytical gap between the data and the opinion proffered. See *Turpin v. Merrell Dow Pharmaceuticals, Inc.*, 959 F.2d 1349, 1360 (CA 6), cert. denied, 506 U.S. 826 (1992). That is what the District Court did here, and we hold that it did not abuse its discretion in so doing.

We hold, therefore, that abuse of discretion is the proper standard by which to review a district court's decision to admit or exclude scientific evidence. We further hold that, because it was within the District Court's discretion to conclude that the studies upon which the experts relied were not sufficient, whether individually or in combination, to support their conclusions that Joiner's exposure to PCBs contributed to his cancer, the District Court did not abuse its discretion in excluding their testimony. . . .

. . . We accordingly reverse the judgment of the Court of Appeals and remand this case for proceedings consistent with this opinion. It is so ordered.

[G]   Kumho Tire Co. v. Carmichel

United States Supreme Court
526 U.S. 137 (1999)

JUSTICE BREYER delivered the opinion of the Court.

In *Daubert v. Merrell Dow Pharmaceuticals, Inc.*, 509 U.S. 579 (1993), this Court focused upon the admissibility of scientific expert testimony. It pointed out that such testimony is admissible only if it is both relevant and reliable. And it held that the Federal Rules of Evidence "assign to the trial judge the task of ensuring that an expert's testimony both rests on a reliable foundation and is relevant to the task at hand." *Id.* at 597. The Court also discussed certain more specific factors, such as testing, peer review, error rates, and "acceptability" in the relevant scientific community, some or all of which might prove helpful in determining the reliability of a particular scientific "theory or technique." *Id.* at 593–594.

This case requires us to decide how *Daubert* applies to the testimony of engineers and other experts who are not scientists. We conclude that *Daubert's* general holding — setting forth the trial judge's general "gatekeeping" obligation — applies not only to testimony based on "scientific" knowledge, but also to testimony based on "technical" and "other specialized" knowledge. *See* Fed. Rule Evid. 702. We also conclude that a trial court may consider one or more of the more specific factors that *Daubert* mentioned when doing so will help determine that testimony's reliability. But, as the Court stated in *Daubert*, the test of reliability is "flexible," and *Daubert's* list of specific factors neither necessarily nor exclusively applies to all experts or in every case. Rather, the law grants a district court the same broad latitude when it decides how to determine reliability as it enjoys in respect to its ultimate reliability determination. *See General Electric Co. v. Joiner*, 522 U.S. 136, 143, (1997) (courts of appeals are to apply "abuse of discretion" standard when reviewing district court's reliability determination). Applying these standards, we determine that the District Court's decision in this case — not to admit certain expert testimony — was within its discretion and therefore lawful.

Kumho Tire petitioned for certiorari, asking us to determine whether a trial court "may" consider *Daubert's* specific "factors" when determining the "admissibility of an engineering expert's testimony." Pet. for Cert. i. We granted certiorari in light of uncertainty among the lower courts about whether, or how, *Daubert* applies to expert testimony that might be characterized as based not upon "scientific" knowledge, but rather upon "technical" or "other specialized" knowledge. Fed. Rule Evid. 702; *compare, e.g., Watkins v. Telsmith, Inc.*, 121 F.3d 984, 990–991 (CA5 1997), *with, e.g., Compton v. Subaru of America, Inc.*, 82 F.3d 1513, 1518–1519 (CA10), *cert. denied*, 519 U.S. 1042 (1996).

II

In *Daubert*, this Court held that Federal Rule of Evidence 702 imposes a special obligation upon a trial judge to "ensure that any and all scientific testimony is not only relevant, but reliable." 509 U.S. at 589. The initial question before us is whether this basic gatekeeping obligation applies only to "scientific" testimony or to all expert testimony. We, like the parties, believe that it applies to all expert testimony. *See* Brief for Petitioners 19; Brief for Respondents 17.

For one thing, Rule 702 itself says:

> "If scientific, technical, or other specialized knowledge will assist the trier of fact to understand the evidence or to determine a fact in issue, a witness qualified as an expert by knowledge, skill, experience, training, or education, may testify thereto in the form of an opinion or otherwise."

This language makes no relevant distinction between "scientific" knowledge and "technical" or "other specialized" knowledge. It makes clear that any such knowledge might become the subject of expert testimony. In *Daubert*, the Court specified that it is the Rule's word "knowledge," not the words (like "scientific") that modify that word, that "establishes a standard of evidentiary reliability." 509 U.S. at 589–590. Hence, as a matter of language, the Rule applies its reliability standard to all "scientific," "technical," or "other specialized" matters within its scope. We concede that the Court in *Daubert* referred only to "scientific" knowledge. But as the Court there said, it referred to "scientific" testimony "because that was the nature of the expertise" at issue. *Id.* at 590, n. 8.

Neither is the evidentiary rationale that underlay the Court's basic *Daubert* "gatekeeping" determination limited to "scientific" knowledge. *Daubert* pointed out that Federal Rules 702 and 703 grant expert witnesses testimonial latitude unavailable to other witnesses on the "assumption that the expert's opinion will have a reliable basis in the knowledge and experience of his discipline." Id. at 592 (pointing out that experts may testify to opinions, including those that are not based on firsthand knowledge or observation). The Rules grant that latitude to all experts, not just to "scientific" ones.

Finally, it would prove difficult, if not impossible, for judges to administer evidentiary rules under which a gatekeeping obligation depended upon a distinction between "scientific" knowledge and "technical" or "other specialized" knowledge. There is no clear line that divides the one from the others. Disciplines such as engineering rest upon scientific knowledge. Pure scientific theory itself may depend for its development upon observation and properly engineered machinery. And conceptual efforts to distinguish the two are unlikely to produce clear legal lines capable of application in particular cases.

Neither is there a convincing need to make such distinctions. Experts of all kinds tie observations to conclusions through the use of what Judge Learned Hand called "general truths derived from . . . specialized experience." Hand, Historical and Practical Considerations Regarding Expert Testimony, 15 Harv. L. Rev. 40, 54 (1901). And whether the specific expert testimony focuses upon specialized observations, the specialized translation of those observations into theory, a specialized theory itself, or the application of such a theory in a particular case, the expert's testimony often will rest "upon an experience confessedly foreign in kind to [the jury's] own." *Ibid.* The trial judge's effort to assure that the specialized testimony is reliable and relevant can help the jury evaluate that foreign experience, whether the testimony reflects scientific, technical, or other specialized knowledge.

We conclude that *Daubert's* general principles apply to the expert matters described in Rule 702. The Rule, in respect to all such matters, "establishes a standard of evidentiary reliability." 509 U.S. at 590. It "requires a valid . . . connection to the pertinent inquiry as a precondition to admissibility." Id. at 592. And where such testimony's factual basis, data, principles, methods, or their application are called sufficiently into question, see Part III, infra, the trial judge must determine whether the testimony has "a reliable basis in the knowledge and experience of [the relevant] discipline." 509 U.S. at 592.

The petitioners ask more specifically whether a trial judge determining the "admissibility of an engineering expert's testimony" may consider several more specific factors that *Daubert* said might "bear on" a judge's gate-keeping determination. Brief for Petitioners i. These factors include:

— Whether a "theory or technique . . . can be (and has been) tested";

— Whether it "has been subjected to peer review and publication";

— Whether, in respect to a particular technique, there is a high "known or potential rate of error" and whether there are "standards controlling the technique's operation"; and

— Whether the theory or technique enjoys " 'general acceptance' " within a " 'relevant scientific community.' " 509 U.S. at 592–594, 113 S. Ct. 2786.

Emphasizing the word "may" in the question, we answer that question yes.

Engineering testimony rests upon scientific foundations, the reliability of which will be at issue in some cases. . . . In other cases, the relevant reliability concerns may focus upon personal knowledge or experience. *Daubert* makes clear that the factors it mentions do not constitute a "definitive checklist or test." Id. at 593. And *Daubert* adds that the gatekeeping inquiry must be " 'tied to the facts' " of a particular "case." Id. at 591 (quoting *United States v. Downing*, 753 F.2d 1224, 1242 (CA3 1985)). We agree with the Solicitor General that "the factors identified in *Daubert* may or may not be pertinent in assessing reliability, depending on the nature of the issue, the expert's particular expertise, and the subject of his testimony." The conclusion, in our view, is that we can neither rule out, nor rule in, for all cases and for all time the applicability of the factors mentioned in *Daubert*, nor can we now do so for subsets of cases categorized by category of expert or by kind of evidence. Too much depends upon the particular circumstances of the particular case at issue.

Daubert itself is not to the contrary. It made clear that its list of factors was meant to be helpful, not definitive. Indeed, those factors do not all necessarily apply even in every instance in which the reliability of scientific testimony is challenged. It might not be surprising in a particular case, for example, that a claim made by a scientific witness has never been the subject of peer review, for the particular application at issue may never previously have interested any scientist. Nor, on the other hand, does the presence of *Daubert's* general acceptance factor help show that an expert's testimony is reliable where the discipline itself lacks reliability, as, for example, do theories grounded in any so-called generally accepted principles of astrology or necromancy.

At the same time, and contrary to the Court of Appeals' view, some of *Daubert's* questions can help to evaluate the reliability even of experience-based testimony. In certain cases, it will be appropriate for the trial judge to ask, for example, how often an engineering expert's experience-based methodology has produced erroneous results, or whether such a method is generally accepted in the relevant engineering community. Likewise, it will at times be useful to ask even of a witness whose expertise is based purely on experience, say, a perfume tester able to distinguish among 140 odors at a sniff, whether his preparation is of a kind that others in the field would recognize as acceptable.

We must therefore disagree with the Eleventh Circuit's holding that a trial judge may ask questions of the sort *Daubert* mentioned only where an expert "relies on the application of scientific principles," but not where an expert relies "on skill- or experience-based observation." 131 F.3d at 1435. We do not believe that Rule 702 creates a schematism that segregates expertise by type while mapping certain kinds of questions to certain kinds of experts. Life and the legal cases that it generates are too complex to warrant so definitive a match.

To say this is not to deny the importance of *Daubert's* gatekeeping requirement. The objective of that requirement is to ensure the reliability and relevancy of expert testimony. Rather, we conclude that the trial judge must have considerable leeway in deciding in a particular case how to go about determining whether particular expert testimony is reliable. That is to say, a trial court should consider the specific factors identified in *Daubert* where they are reasonable measures of the reliability of expert testimony.

C

The trial court must have the same kind of latitude in deciding *how* to test an expert's reliability, and to decide whether or when special briefing or other proceedings are needed to investigate reliability, as it enjoys when it decides *whether or not* that expert's relevant testimony is reliable. Our opinion in *Joiner* makes clear that a court of appeals is to apply an abuse-of-discretion standard when it "reviews a trial court's decision to admit or exclude expert testimony." 522 U.S. at 138–39. That standard applies as much to the trial court's decisions about how to determine reliability as to its ultimate conclusion. Otherwise, the trial judge would lack the discretionary authority needed both to avoid unnecessary "reliability" proceedings in ordinary cases where the reliability of an expert's methods is properly taken for granted, and to require appropriate proceedings in the less usual or more complex cases where cause for questioning the expert's reliability arises. Indeed, the Rules seek to avoid "unjustifiable expense and delay" as part of their search for "truth" and the "just determination" of proceedings. Fed. Rule Evid. 102. Thus, whether *Daubert's* specific factors are, or are not, reasonable measures of reliability in a particular case is a matter that the law grants the trial judge broad latitude to determine. *See Joiner, supra,* at 143. And the Eleventh Circuit erred insofar as it held to the contrary.

In sum, Rule 702 grants the district judge the discretionary authority, reviewable for its abuse, to determine reliability in light of the particular facts and circumstances of the particular case. The District Court did not abuse its discretionary authority in this case. Hence, the judgment of the Court of Appeals is

Reversed.

[H]   State v. Kelly

State v. Kelly, 97 N.J. 178, 478 A.2d 364 (1984), examines the propriety of admitting expert testimony on the battered woman syndrome. The court held that such testimony, while based on a novel science, is permissible so long as the underlying science is shown to be sufficiently reliable.

The court first observed that expert testimony on the battered woman syndrome was relevant to show both the honesty of the defendant's fear of serious bodily harm and the reasonableness of that fear. The court further concluded that testimony on the battered woman syndrome would assist the jury in determining facts at issue, stating that the subject of battered woman syndrome was "beyond the ken of the average juror and thus is suitable for explanation through expert testimony."

The court then discussed the requirements for admitting evidence in "a relatively new field of research, such as that of the battered woman syndrome." The court stated that:

> [T]here are three ways a proponent of scientific evidence can prove its general acceptance and thereby its reliability: (1) by expert testimony as to the general acceptance, among those in the profession, of the premises on which the proffered expert witness based his or her analysis; (2) by authoritative scientific and legal writings indicating that the scientific community accepts the premises underlying the proffered testimony; and (3) by judicial opinions that indicate the expert's premises have gained general acceptance.

Based on the record before it, the court found that the battered woman syndrome had a "sufficient scientific basis" to meet the reliability requirements for admission.

1. Did the Court in *Kelly* appear to adopt the *Frye* or *Daubert* tests of admissibility?

2. How significant to the outcome of the case is testimony on the battered woman syndrome?

3. Will the jury be able to accurately assess testimony on the battered woman syndrome?

[I] United States v. Piccinonna

United States Court of Appeals for the Eleventh Circuit
885 F.2d 1529 (11th Cir. 1989)

FAY, CIRCUIT JUDGE.

Julio Piccinonna appeals his conviction on two counts of knowingly making false material statements to a Grand Jury in violation of Title IV of the Organized Crime Control Act of 1970 . . . . Piccinonna argues that the trial judge erred in refusing to admit the testimony of his polygraph expert and the examination results.

I. Background

Julio Piccinonna has been in the waste disposal business in South Florida for over twenty-five years. In 1983, a Grand Jury conducted hearings to investigate antitrust violations in the garbage business. The government believed that South Florida firms in the waste disposal business had agreed not to compete for each other's accounts, and to compensate one another when one firm did not adhere to the agreement and took an account from another firm.

Prior to trial, Piccinonna requested that the Government stipulate to the admission into evidence of the result of a polygraph test which would be administered subsequently. The Government refused to stipulate to the admission of any testimony regarding the polygraph test or its results. Despite the Government's refusal, George B. Slattery, a licensed polygraph examiner, tested Piccinonna on November 25, 1985. Piccinonna asserted that the expert's report left no doubt that he did not lie when he testified before the Grand Jury. . . . On November 27, 1985, Piccinonna filed a motion with the district court requesting a hearing on the admission of the polygraph testimony. On January 6, 1986, the district court held a hearing on the defendant's motions. Due to the per se rule, which holds polygraph evidence inadmissible in this circuit, the trial judge refused to admit the evidence. The judge noted, however, that the Eleventh Circuit may wish to reconsider the issue of the admissibility of polygraph evidence since these tests have become much more widely used, particularly by the Government. . . .

II. The Per Se Rule

In federal courts, the admissibility of expert testimony concerning scientific tests or findings is governed by Rule 702 of the Federal Rules of Evidence. Rule 702 provides:

> If scientific, technical, or other specialized knowledge will assist the trier of fact to understand the evidence or to determine a fact in issue, a witness qualified as an expert by knowledge, skill, experience, training or education, may testify thereto in the form of an opinion or otherwise.

Fed. R. Evid. 702. Under this rule, to admit expert testimony the trial judge must determine that the expert testimony will be relevant and will be helpful to the trier of fact. In addition, courts require the proponent of the testimony to show that the principle or technique is generally accepted in the scientific community.

[W]e believe it is no longer accurate to state categorically that polygraph testing lacks general acceptance for use in all circumstances. For this reason, we find it appropriate to reexamine the per se exclusionary rule and institute a rule more in keeping with the progress made in the polygraph field.

III. Differing Approaches to Polygraph Admissibility

Courts excluding polygraph evidence typically rely on three grounds: 1) the unreliability of the polygraph test, 2) the lack of standardization of polygraph procedure, and 3) undue impact on the jury. Proponents of admitting polygraph evidence have attempted to rebut these concerns. With regard to unreliability, proponents stress the significant advances made in the field of polygraphy. Professor McCormick argues that the fears of unreliability "are not sufficient to warrant a rigid exclusionary rule. A great deal of lay testimony routinely admitted is at least as unreliable and inaccurate, and other forms of scientific evidence involve risks of instrumental or judgmental error." (Citation omitted.) Further, proponents argue that the lack of standardization is being addressed and will progressively be resolved as the polygraph establishes itself as a valid scientific test. . . . Finally, proponents argue that there is no evidence that jurors are unduly influenced by polygraph evidence. . . . In fact, several studies refute the proposition that jurors are likely to give disproportionate weight to polygraph evidence.

In the wake of new empirical evidence and scholarly opinion which have undercut many of the traditional arguments against admission of polygraph evidence, a substantial number of courts have revisited the admissibility question. Three roughly identifiable approaches to the problem have emerged. First, the traditional approach holds polygraph evidence inadmissible when offered by either party, either as substantive evidence or as relating to the credibility of a witness. . . . Second, a significant number of jurisdictions permit the trial court, in its discretion, to receive polygraph evidence if the parties stipulate to the evidence's admissibility before the administration of the test and if certain other conditions are met. Finally, some courts permit the trial judge to admit polygraph evidence even in the absence of a stipulation, but only when special circumstances exist. In these jurisdictions, the issue is within the sound discretion of the trial judge.

The common thread running through the various approaches taken by the courts which have modified the per se rule is a recognition that while wholesale exclusion under Rule 702 is unwarranted, there must be carefully constructed limitations placed upon the use of polygraph evidence in court. Absent a stipulation by the parties, we are unable to locate any case in which a court has allowed polygraph expert testimony offered as substantive proof of the truth or falsity of the statements made during the polygraph examination. The myriad of "special circumstances" and conditions that have been held to constitute appropriate scenarios for use of polygraph evidence are necessarily rough estimates by the courts of when and where the danger of unfair prejudice due to the admission of the evidence is least significant.

IV. Principles for Admissibility

There is no question that in recent years polygraph testing has gained increasingly widespread acceptance as a useful and reliable scientific tool. Because of the advances that have been achieved in the field which have led to the greater use of polygraph examination, coupled with a lack of evidence that juries are unduly swayed by polygraph evidence, we agree with those courts which have found that a per se rule disallowing polygraph evidence is no longer warranted. Of course, polygraphy is a developing and inexact science, and we continue to believe it inappropriate to allow the admission of polygraph evidence in all situations in which more proven types of expert testimony are allowed. However, as Justice Potter Stewart wrote, "any rule that impedes the discovery of truth in a court of law impedes as well the doing of justice." (Citation omitted.) Thus, we believe the best approach in this area is one which balances the need to admit all relevant and reliable evidence against the danger that the admission of the evidence for a given purpose will be unfairly prejudicial. Accordingly we outline two instances where polygraph evidence may be admitted at trial, which we believe achieve the necessary balance.

A. Stipulation

The first rule governing admissibility of polygraph evidence is one easily applied. Polygraph expert testimony will be admissible in this circuit when both parties stipulate in advance as to the circumstances of the test and as to the scope of its admissibility. The stipulation as to circumstances must indicate that the parties agree on material matters such as the manner in which the test is conducted, the nature of the questions asked, and the identity of the examiner administering the test. The stipulation as to scope of admissibility must indicate the purpose or purposes for which the evidence will be introduced. Where the parties agree to both of these conditions in advance of the polygraph test, evidence of the test results is admissible.

B. Impeachment or Corroboration

The second situation in which polygraph evidence may be admitted is when used to impeach or corroborate the testimony of a witness at trial. Admission of polygraph evidence for these purposes is subject to three preliminary conditions. First, the party planning to use the evidence at trial must provide adequate notice to the opposing party that the expert testimony will be offered. Second, polygraph expert testimony by a party will be admissible only if the opposing party was given reasonable opportunity to have [his] own polygraph expert administer a test covering substantially the same questions. Failure to provide adequate notice or reasonable opportunity for the opposing side to administer its own test is proper grounds for exclusion of the evidence.

Finally, whether used to corroborate or impeach, the admissibility of the polygraph administrator's testimony will be governed by the Federal Rules of Evidence for the admissibility of corroboration or impeachment testimony. [E]vidence that a witness passed a polygraph examination, used to corroborate that witness's in-court testimony, would not be admissible under Rule 608 unless or until the credibility of that witness were first attacked. Even where the above three conditions are met, admission of polygraph evidence for impeachment or corroboration purposes is left entirely to the discretion of the trial judge.

Thus under the Federal Rules of Evidence governing the admissibility of expert testimony, the trial court may exclude polygraph expert testimony because 1) the polygraph examiner's qualifications are unacceptable; 2) the test procedure was unfairly prejudicial or the test was poorly administered; or 3) the questions were irrelevant or improper. The trial judge has wide discretion in this area, and rulings on admissibility will not be reversed unless a clear abuse of discretion is shown.

V. Conclusion

We neither expect nor hope that today's holding will be the final word within our circuit on this increasingly important issue. The advent of new and developing technologies calls for flexibility within the legal system so that the ultimate ends of justice may be served. It is unwise to hold fast to a familiar rule when the basis for that rule ceases to be persuasive. We believe that the science of polygraphy has progressed to a level of acceptance sufficient to allow the use of polygraph evidence in limited circumstances where the danger of unfair prejudice is minimized. We proceed with caution in this area because the reliability of polygraph testing remains a subject of intense scholarly debate. As the field of polygraph testing continues to progress, it may become necessary to reexamine the rules regarding the admissibility of polygraph evidence.

The judgment of conviction is *Vacated*

[J]   Rules Comparison

Compare the pertinent FRE 702, 703, 704 and 705, with the following state rules on expert testimony:

Ohio Rule of Evidence 703. Bases of Opinion Testimony by Experts

The facts or data in the particular case upon which an expert bases an opinion or inference may be those perceived by him or admitted in evidence at the hearing.

Delaware Rule of Evidence 705. Disclosure of Facts or Data Underlying Expert Opinion

(a) Disclosure of Facts or Data Underlying Expert Opinion. The expert may testify in terms of opinion or inference, provided he first identifies the facts and data upon which he bases his opinion and his reasons for the opinion, unless the court requires otherwise. The expert may in any event be required to disclose the underlying facts or data on cross-examination.

(b) Objection. An adverse party may object to the testimony of an expert on the ground that he does not have a sufficient basis for expressing an opinion. He may, before the witness gives his opinion, be allowed to conduct a voir dire examination directed to the underlying facts or data on which the opinion is based.

§ 9.04   MIXED PROBLEMS

Problem #9-32: "In My Opinion"

Janie, who is known for her opinions on everything, was an eyewitness to a carjacking in a shopping center parking lot. Two men are charged with the crime and Janie testifies at trial. Which of the following testimony would be proper?

1. Janie: "I'd estimate that the men were both about six feet tall and weighed 175 pounds."

2. Janie: "One of the men, the guy who went to the passenger side of the car, smelled of alcohol."

3. Janie: "That same guy looked quite angry, like he had just stepped on a tack."

4. Janie: "They both looked like vicious killers."

5. Janie: "They drove away at about 80 miles per hour after knocking the driver, who looked like a teenage boy, violently to the ground; those two guys are carjackers as sure as I'm sitting here!"

6. Janie: "After they left, I smelled burnt rubber from the tires. They were obviously in quite a hurry to get away."

Problem #9-33: Daughter of Ms. Jean Dixon

In a murder trial in which the defense is mistaken identity, the defendant calls to the witness stand a psychic, Akilah, who claims she saw a metaphysical image of the murderer and it was not the defendant. Permissible? Why?

Problem #9-34: Sister-in-Law

Andi, a surgeon, is sued for malpractice after a routine gall bladder operation went awry. At trial, Dr. Andi called her sister, Dr. Natsu, an internist, to testify on her behalf. Natsu is asked whether, in her expert opinion, Andi acted with the requisite standard of care during the operation.

1. Is this question permissible? Why?

2. Could Dr. Natsu testify if her opinion was based largely on the hearsay statements of other doctors? Please explain.

Problem #9-35: Cops

Sgt. Darryl Johnson of New York's lower east side has been an undercover police officer attached to the narcotics division for twelve years. During that time, he has participated in several thousand drug arrests, many of which concerned cocaine trafficking. Could Sgt. Johnson properly testify in a cocaine distribution case as an expert? For example, could Johnson testify that the amount of crack cocaine seized from a defendant's residence indicated that the drugs were intended for distribution and not personal use, that drug traffickers regularly take payment in ten or twenty dollar bills, and that scales, razor blades, and cellular phones were commonly part of drug transactions? Please explain.

Problem #9-36: The Legacy of *Daubert*

Explain whether any of the following experts would be allowed to testify under either *Frye* or *Daubert*.

1. DPT. Li, a two-year-old child, died after suffering a brain seizure. The seizure occurred five days after she was given a DPT vaccination (a shot combining vaccines for diphtheria, pertussis (whooping cough), and tetanus). Li's parents brought suit claiming the vaccination caused the seizure. Dr. Randi Palmer, an epidemiologist, testified for the plaintiff. Dr. Palmer said a study indicated that DPT vaccines could cause seizures up to a week after administration. The study covered seven cases of children who had been vaccinated. Dr. Palmer observed that there were 1,182 cases of serious neurological illness in children between the ages of two and three years of age during the previous year. No prior neurological testing had been done on the seven children before they were vaccinated. The results of this study had not been duplicated in any subsequent controlled study. Dr. Palmer further observed that when animals were given pertussis, some developed brain damage. Should Dr. Palmer be permitted to testify? Why?

2. Pest Control. The Smyths filed suit against Ralph's Pest Control because of family health problems they claim were caused by Ralph's commercial termiticide (involving the "tenting" and fumigating of the Smyths' house). The plaintiffs' expert, Dr. Marjorie Palmetto, utilized an experimental test not generally accepted by the scientific community to conclude that, while other potential causes still remained, the Smyths' illnesses could be traced to Ralph's tenting. Should Dr. Palmetto be permitted to testify? Why?

3. Acne 10. Plaintiff, Polly, used a special topical acne medication during pregnancy. After her child was born with birth defects, she and her husband brought suit, claiming that the medication caused the defects. The plaintiffs' expert, Dr. Rhonda Vanderstern, a highly respected dermatologist, testified that, in her expert opinion, the dosage of the medication was sufficient to cause the defects. Dr. Vanderstern based her opinion on a study that had not been subject to peer testing. Dr. Vanderstern could not provide any published material that supported her conclusions. (She did point to several tests administered on animals, however, that generally supported her conclusions.) Should Dr. Vanderstern be permitted to testify? Why?

Problem #9-37: Non-Scientific Expert Testimony — Gangs

Detective was called as an expert witness in a case against an alleged gang member. The defendant in the case was alleged to be a member of a gang that Detective had investigated for 10 years. Over the years, Detective has interviewed thousands of members of the gang and testified in nearly 100 court proceedings related to this particular gang. The Defendant objects to Detective's testimony as an expert witness on the basis that it is unreliable under *Daubert*. What result? *See United States v. Umana*, 2010 U.S. Dist. LEXIS 46910.

Problem #9-38: Another Barry, Baseball & Steroids Moment!

The prosecution alleges that Barry knowingly lied to a grand jury when he denied ever using steroids and is prosecuted for perjury. Dr. Don Drysdale, a government witness and the former longstanding, head of the IAC Olympic Analytical Laboratory, is an anti-doping expert. Dr. Drysdale will testify that Barry's urine sample eight years ago tested positive for: clomiphene, which is a female fertility drug used as a masking agent by some athletes taking steroids; the designer steroid THG; and synthetic testosterone. The defense objects to Dr. Drysdale's testimony on the following grounds: (1) it is irrelevant; (2) the urine analysis is not a proper subject for expert testimony and fails the *Daubert* test; (3) Dr. Drysdale is unreliable because he is a consultant on a book about baseball and illegal drugs; and (4) the testimony's prejudicial value substantially outweighs its probative value. Should the court sustain the defense objection?

§ 9.05   RELEVANT ETHICS RULES

Rule 1.5 Fees

(c) A fee may be contingent on the outcome of the matter for which the service is rendered, except in a matter in which a contingent fee is prohibited by paragraph (d) or other law. A contingent fee agreement shall be in a writing signed by the client and shall state the method by which the fee is to be determined, including the percentage or percentages that shall accrue to the lawyer in the event of settlement, trial or appeal; litigation and other expenses to be deducted from the recovery; and whether such expenses are to be deducted before or after the contingent fee is calculated. The agreement must clearly notify the client of any expenses for which the client will be liable whether or not the client is the prevailing party. Upon conclusion of a contingent fee matter, the lawyer shall provide the client with a written statement stating the outcome of the matter and, if there is a recovery, showing the remittance to the client and the method of its determination.

(d) A lawyer shall not enter into an arrangement for, charge or collect:

(1) any fee in a domestic relations matter, the payment or amount of which is contingent upon the securing of a divorce or upon the amount of alimony or support, or property settlement in lieu thereof; or

(2) a contingent fee for representing a defendant in a criminal case. Utah Rules of Prof'l Conduct R. 1.5. *See* MRPC 1.5.

Rule § 3-501.15 Safekeeping property

(a) A lawyer shall hold property of clients or third persons that is in a lawyer's possession in connection with a representation separate from the lawyer's own property. Funds shall be kept in a separate account maintained in the state where the lawyer's office is situated. Other property shall be identified as such and appropriately safeguarded. Complete records of such account funds and other property shall be kept by the lawyer and shall be preserved for a period of 5 years after termination of the representation.

(b) A lawyer may deposit the lawyer's own funds in a client trust account for the sole purpose of paying bank service charges on that account, but only in an amount necessary for that purpose.

(c) A lawyer shall deposit into a client trust account legal fees and expenses that have been paid in advance, to be withdrawn by the lawyer only as fees are earned or expenses incurred.

(d) Upon receiving funds or other property in which a client or third person has an interest, a lawyer shall promptly notify the client or third person. Except as stated in this rule or otherwise permitted by law or by agreement with the client, a lawyer shall promptly deliver to the client or third person any funds or other property that the client or third person is entitled to receive and, upon request by the client or third person, shall promptly render a full accounting regarding such property.

(e) When in the course of representation a lawyer is in possession of property in which two or more persons (one of whom may be the lawyer) claim interests, the property shall be kept separate by the lawyer until the dispute is resolved. The lawyer shall promptly distribute all portions of the property as to which the interests are not in dispute. Nebraska Rules of Prof'l Conduct R. § 3-501.15. *See* MRPC 1.15.

Rule 4-5.6 Restrictions On Right To Practice

A lawyer shall not participate in offering or making: **(a)** a partnership, shareholders, operating, employment, or other similar type of agreement that restricts the rights of a lawyer to practice after termination of the relationship, except an agreement concerning benefits upon retirement; or **(b)** an agreement in which a restriction on the lawyer's right to practice is part of the settlement of a client controversy. Florida Rules of Prof'l Conduct R. 4-5.6. *See* MRPC 5.6.

ER 1.9 Duties to Former Clients

(a) A lawyer who has formerly represented a client in a matter shall not thereafter represent another person in the same or a substantially related matter in which that person's interests are materially adverse to the interests of the former client unless the former client gives informed consent, confirmed in writing.

(b) A lawyer shall not knowingly represent a person in the same or a substantially related matter in which a firm with which the lawyer formerly was associated had previously represented a client:

(1) whose interests are materially adverse to that person; and

(2) about whom the lawyer had acquired information protected by ERs 1.6 and 1.9(c) that is material to the matter;

unless the former client gives informed consent, confirmed in writing.

(c) A lawyer who has formerly represented a client in a matter shall not thereafter:

(1) use information relating to the representation to the disadvantage of the former client except as these Rules would permit or require with respect to a client, or when the information has become generally known; or

(2) reveal information relating to the representation except as these Rules would permit or require with respect to a client. Arizona Rules of Prof'l Conduct R. 1.9. *See* MRPC 1.9.

Rule 1.1 Competence

A lawyer shall provide competent representation to a client. Competent representation requires the legal knowledge, skill, thoroughness and preparation reasonably necessary for the representation. Arkansas Rules of Prof'l Conduct R.1.1. *See* MRPC 1.1.

Rule 3.4 Fairness to opposing party and counsel

A lawyer shall not:

(a) unlawfully obstruct another party's access to evidence or unlawfully alter, destroy or conceal a document or other material having potential evidentiary value. A lawyer shall not counsel or assist another person to do any such act;

(b) falsify evidence, counsel or assist a witness to testify falsely, or offer an inducement to a witness that is prohibited by law.

(c) knowingly disobey an obligation under the rules of a tribunal, except for an open refusal based on an assertion that no valid obligation exists;

(d) in pretrial procedure, make a frivolous discovery request or fail to make reasonably diligent efforts to comply with a legally proper discovery request by an opposing party;

(e) in trial, allude to any matter that the lawyer does not reasonably believe is relevant or that will not be supported by admissible evidence, assert personal knowledge of facts in issue except when testifying as a witness, or state a personal opinion as to the justness of a cause, the credibility of a witness, the culpability of a civil litigant or the guilt or innocence of an accused; or

(f) request a person other than a client to refrain from voluntarily giving relevant information to another party unless:

(1) the person is a relative or an employee or other agent of a client; and

(2) the lawyer reasonably believes that the person's interests will not be adversely affected by refraining from giving such information. Delaware Rules of Prof'l Conduct R. 3.4. *See* MRPC 3.4.

Rule 1.7 Conflicts of Interest: Current Clients

(a) Except as provided in paragraph (b), a lawyer shall not represent a client if the representation involves a concurrent conflict of interest. A concurrent conflict of interest exists if:

(1) the representation of one client will be directly adverse to another client; or

(2) there is a significant risk that the representation of one or more clients will be materially limited by the lawyer's responsibilities to another client, a former client or a third

person or by a personal interest of the lawyer.

(b) Notwithstanding the existence of a concurrent conflict of interest under paragraph (a) a lawyer may represent a client if:

(1) the lawyer reasonably believes that the lawyer will be able to provide competent and diligent representation to each affected client;

(2) the representation is not prohibited by law;

(3) the representation does not involve the assertion of a claim by one client against another client represented by the lawyer in the same litigation or other proceeding before a tribunal; and

(4) each affected client gives informed consent, confirmed in writing. Oklahoma Rules of Prof'l Conduct R. 1.7. *See* MRPC 1.7.

§ 9.06 SUMMARY AND REVIEW

1. Compare the permissible scope of lay witness testimony with that of experts.

2. What is the difference, if any, between the requirement that expert witnesses be "helpful" to the trier of fact and the requirement that all admissible evidence be relevant?

3. About which of the following subject areas can an expert testify? Explain your conclusion.

    a. The effects on cows of drinking salt water.

    b. The explanation of entries in the books of a bank cashier.

    c. The consequences of using diet pills.

    d. The use of astrology to show the defendant's character.

4. Why are experts allowed to generally testify about the ultimate issue?

5. Why are experts not permitted to testify about whether the mental state or condition of a criminal defendant meets the criminal requirements?

6. Can an expert base his or her opinion on hearsay? Why?

7. When must experts disclose the basis for their opinions?

Chapter 10

HEARSAY [FRE 801–807]

CHAPTER FRAMEWORK: Hearsay analysis yields several types of evidence. The first type includes evidence that does not meet one or more of the hearsay elements. This type of evidence cannot be called hearsay. The second type of evidence is the group of statements that technically meets the hearsay definition, but is considered sufficiently reliable by the framers of the rules to warrant a separate category not deemed hearsay. This category includes special prior statements by a testifying witness and statements by party opponents offered against them. The third type of evidence meets all of the elements and is indeed hearsay. This category of evidence is not excluded under the hearsay rule because the evidence has indicia of reliability and thus is eligible for admissibility as an exception to the hearsay rule. The remaining category of statements constitutes inadmissible hearsay.

WHY ARE THE CONCEPTS IN THIS CHAPTER IMPORTANT? Hearsay often is a focal point in Evidence Law courses, on the bar exam, and in the real world. It teases and taunts law students and attorneys alike with its difficult to comprehend definition and myriad of exceptions. It is consequently worth the time required to better understand the hearsay rules and how to apply them.

CONNECTIONS: *Relevance* determines whether some statements are offered for the truth of the matter asserted or just because the statements have been uttered. Hearsay generally is offered to prove an issue in the case and is a *form of substantive proof.* While hearsay declarants sometimes do not testify, these pseudo-witnesses still present credibility issues and can be *impeached,* almost like testifying witnesses at trial.

CHAPTER OUTLINE

I. Definition of Hearsay [FRE 801]
   A. Elements required
      1. Out-of-court
      2. Statement
      3. By a declarant and
      4. Offered for the truth of the matter asserted
   B. Application of elements
      1. If one element missing, not hearsay
      2. If not hearsay, proponent of the evidence still must meet other foundational requirements (e.g., relevance) to be admissible

II. Statutory Not Hearsay [FRE 801(d)]

   A. Special prior statements of a witness

     1. Prior consistent statements offered to rebut charge of fabrication

     2. Prior inconsistent statements under oath in another proceeding

     3. Prior identification

   B. Opposing party's statements (formerly called admissions of a party opponent)

     1. Elements

     2. Misnomer of term "admission" — inculpatory statements not required; need only statement by party, and statement offered by opposing party.

     3. Five Types — personal and vicarious

       a. Personal *any*

       b. Adoptive *agree to anothers statement*

       c. Authorized *spokesperson*

       d. Agent *unauth. / employers*

       e. Co-conspirator

III. Hearsay, but an Exception to the Basic Rule of Exclusion [FRE 803, 804]

   A. Two types — availability of declarant irrelevant; unavailability required

   B. Availability irrelevant — some indicia of reliability

   C. Unavailability required — means unavailability of testimony, not declarant physically

IV. Hearsay Within Hearsay [FRE 805]

   A. Means multiple layers of hearsay

   B. Each strand of hearsay must be admissible to prevent exclusion

V. Impeachment of Hearsay Declarants [FRE 806]

   A. Permissible

   B. Some limitations

VI. Hearsay Catch-All Exception [FRE 807]

* * * * *

RELEVANT RULES OF EVIDENCE

Rule 801. Definitions That Apply to This Article; Exclusions from Hearsay

(a) Statement. "Statement" means a person's oral assertion, written assertion, or nonverbal conduct, if the person intended it as an assertion.

(b) Declarant. "Declarant" means the person who made the statement.

(c) Hearsay. "Hearsay" means a statement that: **(1)** the declarant does not make while testifying at the current trial or hearing **(2)** a party offers in evidence to prove the truth of the matter asserted in the statement.

(d) Statements That Are Not Hearsay. A statement that meets the following conditions is not hearsay:

(1) *A Declarant-Witness's Prior Statement.* The declarant testifies and is subject to cross-examination about a prior statement, and the statement:

(A) is inconsistent with the declarant's testimony and was given under penalty of perjury at a trial, hearing, or other proceeding or in a deposition;

(B) is consistent with the declarant's testimony and is offered:

(i) to rebut an express or implied charge that the declarant recently fabricated it or acted from a recent improper influence or motive in so testifying; or

(ii) to rehabilitate the declarant's credibility as a witness when attacked on another ground; or

(C) identifies a person as someone the declarant perceived earlier.

(2) *An Opposing Party's Statement.* The statement is offered against an opposing party and:

(A) was made by the party in an individual or representative capacity;

(B) is one the party manifested that it adopted or believed to be true;

(C) was made by a person whom the party authorized to make a statement on the subject;

(D) was made by the party's agent or employee on a matter within the scope of that relationship and while it existed; or

(E) was made by the party's coconspirator during and in furtherance of the conspiracy. The statement must be considered but does not by itself establish the declarant's authority under (C); the existence or scope of the relationship under (D); or the existence of the conspiracy or participation in it under (E).

Rule 802. The Rule Against Hearsay

Hearsay is not admissible unless any of the following provides otherwise:

- a federal statute;
- these rules; or
- other rules prescribed by the Supreme Court.

Rule 803. Exceptions to the Rule Against Hearsay — Regardless of Whether the Declarant Is Available as a Witness

The following are not excluded by the rule against hearsay, regardless of whether the declarant is available as a witness:

(1) *Present Sense Impression.*

A statement describing or explaining an event or condition, made while or immediately after the declarant perceived it.

(2) *Excited Utterance.*

A statement relating to a startling event or condition, made while the declarant was under the stress of excitement that it caused.

(3) *Then-Existing Mental, Emotional, or Physical Condition.*

A statement of the declarant's then-existing state of mind (such as motive, intent, or plan) or emotional, sensory, or physical condition (such as mental feeling, pain, or bodily health), but not including a statement of memory or belief to prove the fact remembered or believed unless it relates to the validity or terms of the declarant's will.

(4) *Statement Made for Medical Diagnosis or Treatment.*

A statement that: **(A)** is made for — and is reasonably pertinent to — medical diagnosis or treatment; and **(B)** describes medical history; past or present symptoms or sensations; their inception; or their general cause.

(5) *Recorded Recollection.*

A record that:

(A) is on a matter the witness once knew about but now cannot recall well enough to testify fully and accurately;

(B) was made or adopted by the witness when the matter was fresh in the witness's memory; and

(C) accurately reflects the witness's knowledge.

If admitted, the record may be read into evidence but may be received as an exhibit only if offered by an adverse party.

(6) *Records of a Regularly Conducted Activity.* A record of an act, event, condition, opinion, or diagnosis if:

(A) the record was made at or near the time by — or from information transmitted by — someone with knowledge;

(B) the record was kept in the course of a regularly conducted activity of a business, organization, occupation, or calling, whether or not for profit;

(C) making the record was a regular practice of that activity;

(D) all these conditions are shown by the testimony of the custodian or another qualified witness, or by a certification that complies with Rule 902(11) or (12) or with a statute permitting certification; and

(E) the opponent does not show that the source of information or the method or circumstances of preparation indicate a lack of trustworthiness.

(7) *Absence of a Record of a Regularly Conducted Activity.* Evidence that a matter is not included in a record described in paragraph (6) if:

(A) the evidence is admitted to prove that the matter did not occur or exist;

(B) a record was regularly kept for a matter of that kind; and

(C) the opponent does not show that the possible source of the information or other circumstances indicate a lack of trustworthiness.

(8) *Public Records.* A record or statement of a public office if:

(A) it sets out:

    (i) the office's activities;

    (ii) a matter observed while under a legal duty to report, but not including, in a criminal case, a matter observed by law-enforcement personnel; or

    (iii) in a civil case or against the government in a criminal case, factual findings from a legally authorized investigation; and

(B) the opponent does not show that the source of information or other circumstances indicate a lack of trustworthiness.

(9) *Public Records of Vital Statistics.* A record of a birth, death, or marriage, if reported to a public office in accordance with a legal duty.

(10) *Absence of a Public Record.* Testimony — or a certification under Rule 902 — that a diligent search failed to disclose a public record or statement if the testimony or certification is admitted to prove that:

(A) the record or statement does not exist; or

(B) a matter did not occur or exist, if a public office regularly kept a record or statement for a matter of that kind.

(11) *Records of Religious Organizations Concerning Personal or Family History.* A statement of birth, legitimacy, ancestry, marriage, divorce, death, relationship by blood or marriage, or similar facts of personal or family history, contained in a regularly kept record of a religious organization.

(12) *Certificates of Marriage, Baptism, and Similar Ceremonies.* A statement of fact contained in a certificate:

(A) made by a person who is authorized by a religious organization or by law to perform the act certified;

(B) attesting that the person performed a marriage or similar ceremony or administered a sacrament; and

(C) purporting to have been issued at the time of the act or within a reasonable time after it.

(13) *Family Records.* A statement of fact about personal or family history contained in a family record, such as a Bible, genealogy, chart, engraving on a ring, inscription on a portrait, or engraving on an urn or burial marker.

(14) *Records of Documents That Affect an Interest in Property.* The record of a document that purports to establish or affect an interest in property if:

(A) the record is admitted to prove the content of the original recorded document, along with its signing and its delivery by each person who purports to have signed it;

(B) the record is kept in a public office; and

(C) a statute authorizes recording documents of that kind in that office.

(15) *Statements in Documents That Affect an Interest in Property.* A statement contained in a document that purports to establish or affect an interest in property if the matter stated was relevant to the document's purpose — unless later dealings with the property are inconsistent with the truth of the statement or the purport of the document.

(16) *Statements in Ancient Documents.* A statement in a document that is at least 20 years old and whose authenticity is established.

(17) *Market Reports and Similar Commercial Publications.* Market quotations, lists, directories, or other compilations that are generally relied on by the public or by persons in particular occupations.

(18) *Statements in Learned Treatises, Periodicals, or Pamphlets.* A statement contained in a treatise, periodical, or pamphlet if:

(A) the statement is called to the attention of an expert witness on cross-examination or relied on by the expert on direct examination; and

(B) the publication is established as a reliable authority by the expert's admission or testimony, by another expert's testimony, or by judicial notice.

If admitted, the statement may be read into evidence but not received as an exhibit.

(19) *Reputation Concerning Personal or Family History.* A reputation among a person's family by blood, adoption, or marriage — or among a person's associates or in the community — concerning the person's birth, adoption, legitimacy, ancestry, marriage, divorce, death, relationship by blood, adoption, or marriage, or similar facts of personal or family history.

(20) *Reputation Concerning Boundaries or General History.* A reputation in a community — arising before the controversy — concerning boundaries of land in the community or customs that affect the land, or concerning general historical events important to that community, state, or nation.

(21) *Reputation Concerning Character.* A reputation among a person's associates or in the community concerning the person's character.

(22) *Judgment of a Previous Conviction.* Evidence of a final judgment of conviction if:

> **(A)** the judgment was entered after a trial or guilty plea, but not a nolo contendere plea;
>
> **(B)** the conviction was for a crime punishable by death or by imprisonment for more than a year;
>
> **(C)** the evidence is admitted to prove any fact essential to the judgment; and
>
> **(D)** when offered by the prosecutor in a criminal case for a purpose other than impeachment, the judgment was against the defendant.

The pendency of an appeal may be shown but does not affect admissibility.

(23) *Judgments Involving Personal, Family, or General History, or a Boundary.* A judgment that is admitted to prove a matter of personal, family, or general history, or boundaries, if the matter:

> **(A)** was essential to the judgment; and
>
> **(B)** could be proved by evidence of reputation.

(24) [*Other Exceptions.*] [Transferred to Rule 807.]

Rule 804. Exceptions to the Rule Against Hearsay — When the Declarant Is Unavailable as a Witness

(a) Criteria for Being Unavailable. A declarant is considered to be unavailable as a witness if the declarant:

> **(1)** is exempted from testifying about the subject matter of the declarant's statement because the court rules that a privilege applies;
>
> **(2)** refuses to testify about the subject matter despite a court order to do so;
>
> **(3)** testifies to not remembering the subject matter;
>
> **(4)** cannot be present or testify at the trial or hearing because of death or a then- existing infirmity, physical illness, or mental illness; or
>
> **(5)** is absent from the trial or hearing and the statement's proponent has not been able, by process or other reasonable means, to procure:

(A) the declarant's attendance, in the case of a hearsay exception under Rule 804(b)(1) or (6); or

(B) the declarant's attendance or testimony, in the case of a hearsay exception under Rule 804(b)(2), (3), or (4).

But this subdivision (a) does not apply if the statement's proponent procured or wrongfully caused the declarant's unavailability as a witness in order to prevent the declarant from attending or testifying.

(b) The Exceptions. The following are not excluded by the rule against hearsay if the declarant is unavailable as a witness:

(1) *Former Testimony.* Testimony that:

(A) was given as a witness at a trial, hearing, or lawful deposition, whether given during the current proceeding or a different one; and

(B) is now offered against a party who had — or, in a civil case, whose predecessor in interest had — an opportunity and similar motive to develop it by direct, cross-, or redirect examination.

(2) *Statement Under the Belief of Imminent Death.* In a prosecution for homicide or in a civil case, a statement that the declarant, while believing the declarant's death to be imminent, made about its cause or circumstances.

(3) *Statement Against Interest.* A statement that

(A) a reasonable person in the declarant's position would have made only if the person believed it to be true because, when made, it was so contrary to the declarant's proprietary or pecuniary interest or had so great a tendency to invalidate the declarant's claim against someone else or to expose the declarant to civil or criminal liability; and

(B) is supported by corroborating circumstances that clearly indicate its trustworthiness, if it is offered in a criminal case as one that tends to expose the declarant to criminal liability.

(4) *Statement of Personal or Family History.* A statement about:

(A) the declarant's own birth, adoption, legitimacy, ancestry, marriage, divorce, relationship by blood, adoption, or marriage, or similar facts of personal or family history, even though the declarant had no way of acquiring personal knowledge about that fact; or

(B) another person concerning any of these facts, as well as death, if the declarant was related to the person by blood, adoption, or marriage or was so intimately associated with the person's family that the declarant's information is likely to be accurate.

(5) *[Other Exceptions.]* [Transferred to Rule 807.]

(6) *Statement Offered Against a Party That Wrongfully Caused the Declarant's Unavailability.* A statement offered against a party that wrongfully caused — or acquiesced in wrongfully causing — the declarant's unavailability as a witness, and did so intending that result.

Rule 805. Hearsay Within Hearsay

Hearsay within hearsay is not excluded by the rule against hearsay if each part of the combined statements conforms with an exception to the rule.

Rule 806. Attacking and Supporting the Declarant's Credibility

When a hearsay statement — or a statement described in Rule 801(d)(2)(C), (D), or (E) — has been admitted in evidence, the declarant's credibility may be attacked, and then supported, by any evidence that would be admissible for those purposes if the declarant had testified as a witness. The court may admit evidence of the declarant's inconsistent statement or conduct, regardless of when it occurred or whether the declarant had an opportunity to explain or deny it. If the party against whom the statement was admitted calls the declarant as a witness, the party may examine the declarant on the statement as if on cross-examination.

Rule 807. Residual Exception

(a) In General. Under the following circumstances, a hearsay statement is not excluded by the rule against hearsay even if the statement is not specifically covered by a hearsay exception in Rule 803 or 804:

(1) the statement has equivalent circumstantial guarantees of trustworthiness;

(2) it is offered as evidence of a material fact;

(3) it is more probative on the point for which it is offered than any other evidence that the proponent can obtain through reasonable efforts; and

(4) admitting it will best serve the purposes of these rules and the interests of justice.

(b) Notice. The statement is admissible only if, before the trial or hearing, the proponent gives an adverse party reasonable notice of the intent to offer the statement and its particulars, including the declarant's name and address, so that the party has a fair opportunity to meet it.

§ 10.01 INTRODUCTION

"The solution evolved by the common law has been a general rule excluding hearsay but subject to numerous exceptions under circumstances supposed to furnish guarantees of trustworthiness." FRE Article VIII, Advisory Committee's Note, "Introductory Note: The Hearsay Problem." This solution, while adopted by the FRE, remains somewhat controversial, given the number and nature of the hearsay exclusions. While alternatives exist — hearsay could have been admitted subject to a judicial determination of reliability and unfair prejudice under FRE 403 — the rationale for a general rule of preference for live testimony was set forth in the Advisory Committee's Note, "Introductory Note: The Hearsay Problem":

> The factors to be considered in evaluating the testimony of a witness are perception, memory and narration . . . [and sometimes sincerity]. . . . In order to encourage the witness to do his best with respect to each of these factors, and to expose any inaccuracies which may enter in, the Anglo-American tradition has evolved three conditions under which witnesses will ideally be required to testify: (1) under oath, (2) in the personal presence of the trier of fact, (3) subject to cross-examination.

These three conditions for witnesses favor face-to-face live testimony. Taking an oath creates the solemnity and formality that fosters truth-telling. The presence of the trier of fact permits the trier to judge the witness's demeanor — are they speaking with authenticity or prevarication? Finally, cross-examination is the way for testimony and its assumptions and context to be tested. Well-crafted cross-examination can expose inconsistencies, gaps, and assumptions of testimony.

Hearsay generally circumvents these three conditions, creating additional questions about a declarant's believability and accuracy. It is not so much that hearsay statements are necessarily false, just that there are often no good ways to assess their truthfulness.

Often, for good reason, the hearsay rule occupies the attention of students and trial lawyers alike. Working to understand the hearsay rules can be a Byzantine experience, akin to a wild roller coaster ride. The basic rule is concisely stated. According to FRE 802, hearsay generally is excluded from evidence. The rationale is straightforward as well — the evidence is not trustworthy. This lack of trustworthiness is not an inherent characteristic of the evidence. Rather, it means the trier of fact is deemed to be unable to properly evaluate and weigh hearsay evidence.

FRE 801 defines hearsay as (1) an out-of-court (2) statement (3) made by a declarant and (4) offered for the truth of the matter asserted. Evidence must meet all of these foundational requirements to be excluded as hearsay. If evidence does not meet even one of these elements, it is not hearsay. That does not mean it is automatically admissible; however; it still must satisfy all of the other requirements of the FRE.

While the hearsay rule is framed as a general prohibition, numerous exceptions exist. The exceptions permit certain types of reliable hearsay statements. There are two types of exceptions: (1) evidence which is labeled "not hearsay" by the Rules (FRE 801(d)), that really are exemptions from the rule's application; and (2) evidence which is labeled "hearsay exception" by the Rules (FRE 803, 804).

FRE 801(d)(1), for example, treats as non-hearsay: (1) special types of prior statements of the witness, such as (a) prior statements under oath which are inconsistent with the witness's testimony at trial; (b) prior statements which are consistent with the witness's testimony at trial offered to rebut a charge of recent fabrication or contrivance; and (c) prior statements of identification; and (2) admissions of a party opponent. Note that the elements of the hearsay rule are still met with these exemptions; there are simply sufficient grounds for avoiding the exclusionary rule.

Hearsay that does not fall within the special prior statements of a witness or admissions categories of FRE 801(d) might still be admissible as a hearsay exception. The numerous exceptions to the hearsay rule can be found in FRE 803 and 804.

Thus, evidence will be excluded as inadmissible hearsay if and only if: (1) the evidence meets all of the hearsay requirements; (2) it is not a special prior statement of the witness or an admission of a party opponent (what the Rules say is "not hearsay"); and (3) it is not within one of the many hearsay exceptions.

§ 10.02 DEFINITION OF HEARSAY [FRE 801]

Unless all of the elements of the hearsay definition are satisfied, the evidence will not be considered hearsay. A brief review of each hearsay element is presented below, followed by problems.

[A] Out-of-Court

If statements are extrajudicial, outside of the current official proceeding, they qualify as "out-of-court." Out-of-court really means the statement is made by the declarant off of the witness stand when not testifying, and does not literally mean outside of the physical courtroom.

Illustration

Horace Debussy Jones testified in a preliminary hearing in an assault and battery prosecution. At trial, the preliminary hearing transcript was offered in evidence and an objection was made based on hearsay. Is the transcript "out-of-court"?

Answer: The transcript is considered to be "out-of-court" for the purposes of the hearsay rule. A proceeding independent of the trial, even one that is part of the same case, is considered to be out-of-court.

[B] Statement

A *statement* is an oral or written assertion or non-verbal conduct intended by the declarant to be a communication to others (i.e., assertive). An assertion generally concerns a fact (e.g., The sun is out; I am sleepy), but can be an opinion as well (e.g., Chocolate ice cream is the best flavor). The key to understanding assertions is that they are intentional or purposeful.

While most statements are communicated to others, they need not in fact be disclosed or communicated. For example, a diary, even though not intended for review by others, may include statements. Words written in the diary that do not have assertive content, however, do not qualify as statements.

It is often difficult to determine when non-verbal conduct constitutes a statement. Non-verbal conduct will constitute a statement only if the primary motive of the actor is to communicate to others. Examples of non-verbal statements include a "thumbs-up" signal, a "wave" goodbye, or a "nod of the head" yes.

Illustration

Nick Santurce told his co-worker, Omar Kal, "I like working in the mill." Minutes later, he hit his thumb with a hammer and yelled, "Ouch!" Are Nick's utterances considered statements?

Answer: Santurce's utterance about working in the mill is a statement because it is assertive. Santurce is communicating an opinion about how he likes his job. His response to being hit with a hammer, however, is probably not a statement. The utterance was not likely an assertion intended to communicate to others, but rather simply an expression of pain.

[C] By a Declarant

A *declarant* is the source of the out-of-court statement. A declarant must be a human being. An animal who "talks" (such as "Mr. Ed," the "talking" horse star of a television series of the same name) does not qualify, nor does a machine such as a radar gun. (If a machine is the source of the assertion, the issue generally concerns the accuracy of that machine. Then, the question becomes one of authentication.)

Usually, the declarant is a different person than the testifying witness. If a witness testifies about her own prior out-of-court statements, however, the witness and the declarant are one and the same person. The witness then wears two hats — the declarant of the out-of-court statement and the in-court witness. Contrary to an oft repeated belief, the prior out-of-court statements of a testifying witness offered for the truth of the matter asserted are technically hearsay. Viewing prior statements of a testifying witness as hearsay is justified as a rule of preference. That is, it is preferable for a witness to testify directly about an event and not through his or her own prior hearsay statements.

Illustration

Alonzo witnessed a motorcycle accident as he sat in his backyard with his wife, Sally. He immediately wrote down what had happened. At trial, one year later, Alonzo testified about the date in question. He ended up reading his notes to the jury since his memory of the event was incomplete. Is there a hearsay declarant in this problem?

Answer: Alonzo is both the testifying witness and the hearsay declarant for the purposes of the hearsay rule. When he read his notes to the jury, he was not testifying based on present memory, but rather to his own out-of-court statement, i.e., the written notes. Thus, he was the hearsay declarant of the notes.

[D] Offered for the Truth of the Matter Asserted

A statement is *offered for the truth of the matter asserted* if it is offered to show that its factual content is true (e.g., the statement "the sky is blue" is asserting that the color of the sky is blue). A statement offered for its truth means that the statement is being used to help prove an element in the case or in a defense. The statement and the element are not necessarily the same, though. In fact, the statement and the element may require several inferences to connect with each other. For example, the statement, "Look, Jim is running away from the police!," may be offered for its truth, that Jim was running away, inferring that he was more likely guilty of the crime with which he was charged.

Statements not offered for the truth of the matter asserted can be relevant and helpful to the trier of fact simply because they have been said, without regard to whether they are true. Statements *not* offered for the truth of the matter asserted vary widely, but often fall into one of several major categories. These include:

1. *State of mind.* Some statements offered to prove either the listener's or the declarant's state of mind are not offered for their content or truth. Statements offered to show the effect on the listener are often relevant whether or not they are true, such as warnings ("Hey, watch out for . . .") or those statements that provide the listener with notice as required by law ("Please be advised that this lawsuit is being filed on . . ."). These statements are not being offered for their truth.

Some statements may be offered to show the *declarant's* state of mind and not their truth. For example, a grandiose or nonsensical assertion by a declarant can be offered to show that the declarant suffers from a psychiatric illness and not for the truth of the statement. The assertion by the declarant, "I am a walrus," for example, could possibly be offered for its truth, that the declarant is a walrus, but is more likely to be used to show that the declarant is suffering from a psychotic delusion.

Illustration

Bobbi started acting strangely one day. She would say, "I am the Queen of England! Obey!" and then she would punch people, sometimes severely. In a subsequent battery trial, she raised the insanity defense. She wishes to offer her statements about being the Queen of England. Are these statements hearsay?

Answer: These statements are not hearsay because they are not offered for the truth of the matter asserted. Bobbi's statements about being the Queen of England are not offered to show that Bobbi is in fact the Queen, which is the truth of the matter asserted. Instead, they are offered to show that Bobbi was suffering from delusions and a psychosis. Since the statements are offered to show declarant-Bobbi's psychotic state of mind and not for their truth, they are not hearsay.

2. *Impeachment.* Prior inconsistent statements of a testifying witness are generally not offered at trial for the truth of the matter asserted, but rather to show that the witness is less credible because he or she has uttered two inconsistent statements. It does not matter whether it is the prior statement or the one uttered at trial which is truthful. The mere fact that a witness has made contradictory statements makes him or her less credible.

Illustration

Jasmine testified at trial that "the crash caused the tire to roll 10 yards away from the car." On cross-examination, she was asked whether she had told her friend Carl prior to trial that "I saw the tire roll 20 yards away from the car as a result of the crash!" Is Jasmine's prior statement offered for the truth of the matter asserted?

Answer: Jasmine's prior statement to Carl is being offered just because it was said, not for its truth about how far away the tire rolled from the car. Jasmine is less believable as a witness if she has uttered contradictory statements. Only if Jasmine's prior inconsistent statement was made under oath in a prior proceeding could it also be admitted for its truth under FRE 801(d)(1)(A).

3. *Res gestae.* Some statements are not offered for the truth, but simply as background evidence to "complete the story" of an incident or event. By completing the story, res gestae evidence helps make sense of other admitted evidence. Such a situation may occur, for example, where only one of the speaker's statements in a conversation is independently admissible. Admitting the other speaker's statements may be necessary to understand the independently admissible statements.

The res gestae exception is rarely used. If large quantities of hearsay were to be admitted as res gestae background evidence, it would swallow up the hearsay rule of exclusion.

Illustration

At trial, the prosecution offered into evidence the contents of a telephone conversation between the defendant, Angela, and her friend, Carol. The prosecution argued that Angela's statements in the conversation were admissions by a party-opponent under FRE 801(d)(2)(A). Are Carol's statements admissible?

Answer: Carol's statements may be admissible as *res gestae* evidence — not for their truth, but to complete the story of the telephone conversation and to make sense of Angela's independently admissible statements.

4. *Operative facts* (also called facts of independent legal significance). Some statements create legal obligations or duties. When this occurs, the statement is not offered for the truth of the matter asserted, but instead is offered to show simply that the statement was made. For example, operative facts include those statements which give rise to a defamation action and those constituting the offer and acceptance of a contract.

Illustration

One night, while playing cards, Suzanne boasted, "I'll give $50 to anyone who can name the capital of Kentucky." Lucille correctly observed that Frankfort was the capital. Is Suzanne's statement offered for its truth or as an operative fact?

Answer: Suzanne's statement is an offer to enter into a unilateral contract and consequently considered an operative fact, one of independent legal significance that lies outside of the hearsay definition. If Suzanne testifies to her prior statement at trial, it is admissible not for its truth, but simply because the words were spoken. Suzanne's offer created a legal obligation.

5. *Verbal acts.* A category of statements related to operative facts is called verbal acts. Verbal acts are the words accompanying an act that help to explain the legal significance of that act. One example would be a statement accompanying a donative

transfer of property, clarifying whether the transfer was an irrevocable gift or merely a loan.

Illustration

Joan celebrated her 60th birthday. At a small party in her honor, her oldest child, Elizabeth, handed her the keys to a brand new pick-up truck and said, "This truck is all yours to use in the summer! Happy Birthday!" Is this statement offered for the truth of the matter asserted?

Answer: Elizabeth's statement would not be admissible for the truth of the matter asserted, but rather as a verbal act, to indicate that the transfer of the truck was a loan and not a gift.

[E] Problems

Problem #10-1: Dognapping!

George A. Barnwell is charged with stealing and then selling neighborhood dogs for considerable profit. Little Sally Ann owned a dog name Fido, who was one of the animals allegedly sold by defendant Barnwell. At Barnwell's trial, which of the following testimony meets the technical definition of hearsay?

1. Sally Ann testified that, when she saw Fido in Barnwell's yard eating a steak, Fido wagged his tail upon seeing her.

2. Sally Ann testified that she said to her friend, Britt, while observing Fido in Barnwell's yard, "Britt, that's my dog!"

3. Sally Ann told the police that the dog she saw in Barnwell's yard was Fido.

4. When Officer Barnaby asked Sally Ann if she was sure it was Fido, Sally Ann scratched her head, looked quizzical, and then nodded her head, yes.

5. Sally Ann testified that the dog she saw in Barnwell's backyard was her very own Fido.

Problem #10-2: Go Ahead, Make My . . .

A civil assault and battery action arose from a dispute between Bernard and Stan about who would mow the strip of grass between their two houses. At trial, the plaintiff, Bernard, calls his friend, Dan, to the witness stand. Dan was questioned by plaintiff's attorney about the altercation.

PLAINTIFF'S ATTORNEY: Dan, please describe what happened between Bernard and Stan.

A: Bernard spoke with me later that same day. He said that his neighbor Stan sucker punched him in the mouth when they were discussing who was responsible for mowing the strip of grass between their houses.

DEFENDANT'S ATTORNEY: Objection! Hearsay.

Is Dan's testimony hearsay? Why?

Problem #10-3: Hoops

Barnaby Jordy, a star basketball player on the Indiana Powerglide hurt his knee during a game. He limped to the sideline, grimacing in pain while clutching his knee. Are Barnaby's actions hearsay? Why?

Problem #10-4: Admitted

The primary issue in the case is whether Jack had a psychiatric illness. Evidence is offered showing that Jack's doctor admitted Jack to the state psychiatric hospital for observation. Is Jack's admission to the hospital hearsay? Why?

Problem #10-5: By the Pale Moonlight

On the issue of the defendant's sanity, the defendant's wife testified that he would regularly bark at the moon, say strange things, and live periodically in a doghouse in the backyard. Is this conduct hearsay? Why?

Problem #10-6: Time of Death

The decedent suffered fatal injuries in an automobile accident. The only issue in a subsequent personal injury action arising from the accident is the time of death. The decedent's estate calls an emergency medical technician to testify that he saw Dr. Marko pull a sheet up over the decedent's head in the emergency room after an examination. Is this conduct hearsay? Why?

Problem #10-7: Nadia II

Nadia agreed to sell her car to Vladimir pending an inspection. The parties signed a written contract. Before it could be executed, however, Nadia died. The inspection revealed that Nadia's car had significant structural defects, and Vladimir refused to purchase it. The representative of Nadia's estate sued for specific performance and damages. As part of Vladimir's case-in-chief, Vladimir intends to testify about the terms of the contract, including the inspection clause. Would Vladimir's testimony be hearsay? (Note: this problem presents a potential "dead man's statute" competency issue as well. *See* Chapter 8.)

Problem #10-8: The Scarlet Letters

The sole issue in an action involving a contested will was the competency of the testator, who had been a wealthy but very eccentric man. The testator left all of his money to his estranged wife in his earlier will, and all of his money to his pet pigeons in his last apparent will and testament. Evidence on the question of the testator's competence included letters written to the testator from business men and women seeking to do business with him. Are these letters hearsay? Why?

Problem #10-9: Big Mouth

Ruanda sued Alice for defamation. Ruanda contended that during a public lecture, Alice had said Ruanda was "more corrupt than Ulysses S. Grant's entire administration, and less trustworthy than Attila the Hun."

At trial, Alice testified on direct examination.

DEFENDANT'S ATTORNEY: What did you say in your speech?

PLAINTIFF'S ATTORNEY: Objection! The question calls for hearsay.

1. Is Alice's speech hearsay?

2. Is Alice's speech admissible? Why?

Problem #10-10: Here Comes the Bride

The primary issue in a case was whether Roy and Kate were legally married. Janet testifies that she attended the wedding and heard both Roy and Kate say to each other "I do," in response to the question "Do you take this person to be your lawfully wedded spouse?"

1. Is Janet's testimony hearsay? Why?

2. If Janet had testified that "two hours after the wedding, Roy and Kate told me they both said 'I do' during the wedding ceremony," would Janet's testimony be hearsay? Why?

3. What if Janet had testified, "I saw the wedding rehearsal and were they nervous! They still said 'I do' in the rehearsal, though, just as they had planned. Actually, it was one of the few times before the divorce I did not see them fighting." Hearsay? Compare your conclusion to answers 1. and 2., above.

Problem #10-11: Cry, Cry, Cry

On the issue of whether John can talk, John offers a statement he made the day before trial to his mother, "I can cry." Is this statement hearsay? Why?

Problem # 10-12: Talk Is Cheap

On the issue of whether John can cry, John offers the same statement that he made to his mother the day before trial, "I can cry." Is this statement hearsay? Why?

Problem #10-13: The Whole Truth

Sarah, age five, claims that she was sexually molested by Ron, a neighbor of her uncle, Harry. Harry took care of Sarah on a regular basis. Sarah could not remember which of Uncle Harry's neighbors molested her, but she did remember some of the contents of the house in which the molestation occurred. Sarah made statements to her mother and the police about various articles in the house. The prosecution offers these statements at trial. Are these statements offered for the truth of the matter asserted? Why? (*See Bridges v. State*, 247 Wis. 350, 19 N.W.2d 529 (1945)).

Problem #10-14: Peach Mint

A well-known bank officer, Kelly, is sued for allegedly converting funds from her former employer, City Bank. At trial, Barry testified for the plaintiff, City Bank. Barry was asked on cross-examination, "Contrary to your statement on direct examination that Kelly had a meeting about the missing funds with other bank officers, didn't you say last week that Kelly did *not* have a meeting about the disappearance of the money with other bank officers?"

Plaintiff's counsel objected to this question, claiming that Barry's prior statement is inadmissible hearsay. What ruling and why?

Problem #10-15: You're Going to Make It After All

Jane, after moving to Minneapolis/St. Paul, takes a ride on her new pair of roller blades. After completing her skate, she put the roller blades outside the front door of her apartment. When she returned for the skates minutes later, they were gone. Tim, standing nearby, said, "Oh, Barney just stopped by and took the skates." Jane sued Barney for conversion. At trial, Jane called Tim to testify on her behalf. When Jane's counsel asked Tim who took the roller blades, he stated, "Why, Alice took them."

1. Can Jane impeach Tim on direct examination with his previous out-of-court statement?

2. Is Tim's prior statement admissible for the truth of the matter asserted? Why?

3. If Jane produces no evidence other than Tim's testimony and a stipulation that Jane's skates were taken without permission, will Jane win at trial? What is the significance of Tim being a "turncoat" witness?

[F]   Cases

[1]   Sir Walter Raleigh's Case

Prior to the adoption of a rule excluding hearsay from trial, Sir Walter Raleigh was prosecuted for conspiracy to overthrow Queen Elizabeth, the Queen of England. A significant part of the case against Raleigh was the hearsay testimony of an alleged co-conspirator, Lord Cobham. Cobham remained in a foreign prison during the trial and did not testify. Cobham's allegations were introduced as hearsay. Part of the trial colloquy was as follows (*see* J.G. Phillimore, *History and Principles of the Law of Evidence*, p. 157 (1850)):

> *Raleigh:* But it is strange to see how you press me still with my Lord Cobham, and yet will not produce him; it is not for gaining of time or prolonging my life that I urge this; he is in the house hard by, and may soon be brought hither; let him be produced, and if he will yet accuse me or avow this confession of his, it shall convict me and ease you of further proof.

> *Lord Cecil:* Sir Walter Raleigh presseth often that my Lord Cobham should be brought face to face; if he ask a thing of grace and favour, they must come

from him only who can give them; but if he ask a matter of law, then, in order that we, who sit here as commissioners, may be satisfied, I desire to hear the opinions of my Lords, the Judges, whether it may be done by law.

The Judges all answered, "that in respect it might be a mean to cover many with treasons, and might be prejudicial to the King, therefore, by the law, it was not sufferable."

Popham, C.J.: There must not such a gap be opened for the destruction of the King as would be if we should grant this; you plead hard for yourself, but the laws plead as hard for the King. Where no circumstances do concur to make a matter probable, then an accuser may be heard; but so many circumstances agreeing and confirming the accusation in this case, the accuser is not to be produced; for, having first confessed against himself voluntarily, and so charged another person, if we shall now hear him again in person, he may, for favour or fear, retract what formerly he hath said, and the jury may, by that means, be inveigled. . . .

Raleigh: I have already often urged the producing of my Lord Cobham, but it is still denied me. I appeal now once more to your Lordships in this: my Lord Cobham is the only one that hath accused me, for all the treasons urged upon me are by reflection from him. It is now clear that he hath since retracted; therefore since his accusation is recalled by himself, let him now by word of mouth convict or condemn me. Campion, the Jesuit, was not denied to have his accusers face to face. And if that be true which hath been some labored all this day, that I have been the setter-on of my Lord Cobham, his instigator, and have *infused* these treasons upon him, as hath been said, then have I been the efficient cause of his destruction; all his honours, houses, lands, and good, and all he hath, are lost by me; against whom, then, should he seek revenge but upon me? and the world knoweth him as revengeful of nature as any man living. Besides, a dying man is ever presumed to speak truth: now Cobham is absolutely in the King's mercy; to excuse me cannot avail him, by accusing me he may hope for favour. It is you, then, Mr. Attorney, that should press his testimony, and I ought to fear his producing, if all that be true which you have alleged.

Lord Henry Howard. Sir Walter, you have heard that it cannot be granted; pray importune us no longer.

Sir Walter Raleigh. Nay, my Lord, it toucheth my life, which I value at as a high a rate as your Lordship does yours.

Lord Cecil. I am afraid my often speaking may give opinion to the hearers that I have delight to hear myself talk. Sir Walter Raleigh has often urged, and still doth urge, the producing of my Lord Cobham, I would know of my Lords the Judges, if it might not stand with the order of our proceedings to take a further time, and know his Majesty's pleasure in that which is desired.

The Judges resolved that the Proceedings must go on and receive an end.

Attorney General: I shall now produce a witness *viva voce.*

[The Attorney General, Lord Coke, the prosecutor in this matter, then offered the testimony of a sailor named *Dyer*, who said,] "Being at Lisbon, there came to me a Portuguese gentleman, who asked me how the King of England did, and whether he was crowned? I answered him, that I hoped our noble king was well, and crowned by this; but the time was not come when I came from the coast of Spain. 'Nay,' said he 'your kind shall never be crowned, for Don Cobham and Don Raleigh will cut his throat before he come to be crowned.' And this, in time, was found to be spoken in mid-July."

Raleigh: This is the saying of some wild Jesuit or beggarly priest; but what proof is it against me?

Attorney General: It must perforce arise out of some preceding intelligence, and shews that your treason had wings.

[Upon the conclusion of the presentation of evidence, Raleigh was found guilty of treason and executed.]

[2]   Zippo Manufacturing Co. v. Rogers Imports, Inc.

United States District Court for the Southern District of New York
216 F. Supp. 670 (S.D.N.Y. 1963)

[The Zippo Manufacturing Company brought suit to prevent other companies from imitating the shape and appearance of Zippo's cigarette lighter. Zippo offered several opinion surveys at trial. In these surveys, the respondents were shown lighters manufactured by Zippo and its competitors, and were asked to identify them. The purpose of these studies was to show that potential customers viewed the products as similar. The court considered whether the studies were hearsay.]

The cases holding that surveys are not hearsay do so on the basis that the surveys are not offered to prove the truth of what respondents said and, therefore, do not fall within the classic definition of hearsay. This approach has been criticized because, it is said, the answers to questions in a survey designed to prove the existence of a specific idea in the public mind are offered to prove the truth of the matter contained in these answers. Under this argument, when a respondent is asked to identify who thinks the lighter is a Zippo, the response is regarded as if he said, "I believe that this unmarked lighter is a Zippo." Since the matter to be proved in a secondary meaning case is respondent's belief that the lighter shown him is a Zippo lighter, a respondent's answer is hearsay in the classic sense. Others have criticized the non-hearsay characterization, regardless of whether surveys are offered to prove the truth of what respondents said because the answers in a survey depend for their probative value on the sincerity of respondents. One of the purposes of the hearsay rule is to subject to cross-examination statements which depend on the declarant's narrative sincerity.

The answer of a respondent that he thinks an unmarked lighter is a Zippo is relevant to the issue of secondary meaning only if, in fact, the respondent really does believe that the unmarked lighter is a Zippo. Under this view, therefore, answers in a survey should be regarded as hearsay.

Regardless of whether the surveys in this case could be admitted under the non-hearsay approach, they are admissible because the answers of respondents are expressions of presently existing state of mind, attitude, or belief. There is a recognized exception to the hearsay rule for such statements, and under it the statements are admissible to prove the truth of the matter contained therein.

[3]   Wright v. Doe D. Tatham

House of Lords
7 AD. & E. 313 (1837)

[This case involved a will contest in which the heir of the testator, Tatham, the testator's cousin, argued that the testator was mentally incompetent to leave property to the testator's steward, a man named George Wright. The steward offered in rebuttal three letters written to the testator, Marsden, while he was alive. The letter writers asked the testator to do business with them, inferring the testator's competence. The heir sought to have the letters excluded as hearsay.]

BOSANQUET, J.:

In support of the affirmative [competence of the testator,] three letters were tendered in evidence.

First, the letters cannot be admissible unless they are relevant to the matter in issue, which matter is the capacity of the testator. The contents of the letters have no direct relation to the testator's state of mind, but may be taken to shew the opinion of the writers that the person addressed was of competent understanding. If the writers of these letters were produced as witnesses and examined upon oath, their opinion would be receivable in evidence, because the grounds of their knowledge and the credibility of their testimony might be ascertained by cross-examination; but I know of no rule by which the opinion, however clearly expressed, of a person, however well informed, is receivable in evidence, unless it be given in the course of legal examination.

That the three letters were each of them written by the persons whose names they bear, and sent, at some time before they were found, to the testator's house, no doubt are facts, and those facts are proved on oath; and the letters are without a doubt admissible on an issue in which the fact of sending such letters by those persons, and within that limit of time, is relevant to the matter in dispute; as, for instance, on a feigned issue to try the question whether such letters were sent to the testator's house, or on any issue in which it is the material question whether such letters or any of them had been sent. Verbal declarations of the same parties are also facts, and in like manner admissible under the same circumstances; and so would letters or declarations to third persons upon the like supposition.

But the question is, whether the contents of these letters are evidence of the fact to be proved upon this issue, — that is, the actual existence of the qualities which the testator is, in those letters, by implication, stated to possess; and those letters may be considered in this respect to be on the same footing as if they had contained a direct and positive statement that he was competent. For this purpose they are mere hearsay evidence, statements of the writers, not on oath, of the truth of the matter in question, with this addition, that they have acted upon the statements on the faith of their being true, by their sending the letters to the testator. That an acting cannot give a sufficient sanction for the truth of the statement is perfectly plain; for it is clear that, if the same statements had been made by parol or in writing to a third person, that would have been insufficient; and this is conceded by the learned counsel for the plaintiff in error. Yet in both cases there has been an acting on the belief of the truth, by making the statement, or writing and sending a letter to a third person; and what difference can it possibly make that this is an acting of the same nature by writing and sending the letter to the testator? It is admitted, and most properly, that you have no right to use in evidence the fact of writing, and sending a letter to a third person containing a statement of competence, on the ground that it affords an inference that such an act would not have been done unless the statement was true, or believed to be true, although such an inference no doubt would be raised in the conduct of the ordinary affairs of life, if the statement were made by a man of veracity. But it cannot be raised in a judicial inquiry; and, if such an argument were admissible, it would lead to the indiscriminate admission of hearsay evidence of all manner of facts.

The conclusion at which I have arrived is, that proof of a particular fact, which is not of itself a matter in issue, but which is relevant only as implying a statement or opinion of a third person on the matter in issue is inadmissible in all cases where such a statement or opinion not on oath would be of itself inadmissible; and, therefore, in this case the letters which are offered only to prove the competence of the testator, that is the truth of the implied statements therein contained, were properly rejected, as the mere statement or opinion of the writer would certainly have been inadmissible.

[4] United States of America, Plaintiff v. Albert Charles Zenni, Jr., Et, Al., Defendants

United States District Court for the Eastern District of Kentucky
492 F. Supp. 464 (E.D. Ky. 1980)

BERTELSMAN, DISTRICT JUDGE.

This prosecution for illegal bookmaking activities presents a classic problem in the law of evidence, namely, whether implied assertions are hearsay. The problem was a controversial one at common law, the discussion of which has filled many pages in the treatises and learned journals. Although the answer to the problem is clear under the Federal Rules of Evidence, there has been little judicial treatment of the matter, and many members of the bar are unfamiliar with the marked departure from the common law the Federal Rules have effected on this issue.

FACTS

The relevant facts are simply stated. While conducting a search of the premises of the defendant, Ruby Humphrey, pursuant to a lawful search warrant which authorized a search for evidence of bookmaking activity, government agents answered the telephone several times. The unknown callers stated directions for the placing of bets on various sporting events. The government proposes to introduce this evidence to show that the callers believed that the premises were used in betting operations. The existence of such belief tends to prove that they were so used. The defendants object on the ground of hearsay.

COMMON LAW BACKGROUND

At common law, the hearsay rule applied "only to evidence of out-of-court statements offered for the purpose of proving that the facts are as asserted in the statement."

On the other hand, not all out-of-court expression is common law hearsay. For instance, an utterance offered to show the publication of a slander, or that a person was given notice of a fact, or orally entered into a contract, is not hearsay.

In the instant case, the utterances of the absent declarants are not offered for the truth of the words, and the mere fact that the words were uttered has no relevance of itself. Rather they are offered to show the declarants' belief in a fact sought to be proved. At common law this situation occupied a controversial no-man's land. It was argued on the one hand that the out-of-court utterance was not hearsay, because the evidence was not offered for any truth stated in it, but for the truth of some other proposition inferred from it. On the other hand, it was also argued that the reasons for excluding hearsay applied, in that the evidence was being offered to show declarant's belief in the implied proposition, and he was not available to be cross-examined. Thus, the latter argument was that there existed strong policy reasons for ruling that such utterances were hearsay.

The classic case, which is discussed in virtually every textbook on evidence, is *Wright v. Tatham*, 7 Adolph. & E. 313, 386, 112 Eng.Rep. 488 (Exch. Ch. 1837), and 5 Cl. & F. 670, 739, 47 Rev. Rep. 136 (H.L. 1838). Described as a "celebrated and hard-fought cause," *Wright v. Tatham* was a will contest, in which the will was sought to be set aside on the grounds of the incompetency of the testator at the time of its execution. The proponents of the will offered to introduce into evidence letters to the testator from certain absent individuals on various business and social matters. The purpose of the offer was to show that the writers of the letters believed the testator was able to make intelligent decisions concerning such matters, and thus was competent.

One of the illustrations advanced in the judicial opinions in *Wright v. Tatham* is perhaps even more famous than the case itself. This is Baron Parke's famous sea captain example. Is it hearsay to offer as proof of the seaworthiness of a vessel that its captain, after thoroughly inspecting it, embarked on an ocean voyage upon it with his family?

The court in *Wright v. Tatham* held that implied assertions of this kind were hearsay. The rationale, as stated by Baron Parke, was as follows:

> "The conclusion at which I have arrived is, that proof of a particular fact which is not of itself a matter in issue, but which is relevant only as implying a statement or opinion of a third person on the matter in issue, is inadmissible in all cases where such a statement or opinion not on oath would be of itself inadmissible; and, therefore, in this case the letters which are offered only to prove the competence of the testator, that is the truth of the implied statements therein contained, were properly rejected, as the mere statement or opinion of the writer would certainly have been inadmissible."

This was the prevailing common law view, where the hearsay issue was recognized. But frequently, it was not recognized. Thus, two federal appellate cases involving facts virtually identical to those in the case at bar did not even discuss the hearsay issue, although the evidence admitted in them would have been objectionable hearsay under the common law view.

THE FEDERAL RULES OF EVIDENCE

The common law rule that implied assertions were subject to hearsay treatment was criticized by respected commentators for several reasons. A leading work on the Federal Rules of Evidence, referring to the hotly debated question whether an implied assertion stands on better ground with respect to the hearsay rule than an express assertion, states:

> "By the time the federal rules were drafted, a number of eminent scholars and revisers had concluded that it does. Two principal arguments were usually expressed for removing implied assertions from the scope of the hearsay rule. First, when a person acts in a way consistent with a belief but without intending by his act to communicate that belief, one of the principal reasons for the hearsay rule to exclude declarations whose veracity cannot be tested by cross-examination does not apply, because the declarant's sincerity is not then involved. In the second place, the underlying belief is in some cases self-verifying:
>
> 'There is frequently a guarantee of the trustworthiness of the inference to be drawn . . . because the actor has based his actions on the correctness of his belief, i.e. his actions speak louder than words.' "

In a frequently cited article the following analysis appears:

> "But ought the hearsay rule be deemed applicable to evidence of conduct? As McCormick has observed, the problem 'has only once received any adequate discussion in any decided case,' *i.e.*, in *Wright v. Tatham*, already referred to. And even in that case the court did not pursue its inquiry beyond the point of concluding that evidence of an 'implied' assertion must necessarily be excluded wherever evidence of an 'express' assertion would be inadmissible. But as has been pointed out more than once (although I find no *judicial* recognition of the

difference), the 'implied' assertion is, from the hearsay standpoint, not nearly as vulnerable as an express assertion of the fact which the evidence is offered to establish.

"This is on the assumption that the conduct was 'nonassertive;' that the passers-by had their umbrellas up for the sake of keeping dry, not for the purpose of telling anyone it was raining; that the truck driver started up for the sake of resuming his journey, not for the purpose of telling anyone that the light had changed; that the vicar wrote the letter to the testator for the purpose of settling the dispute with the latter, rather than with any idea of expressing his opinion of the testator's sanity. And in the typical 'conduct as hearsay' case this assumption will be quite justifiable.

"On this assumption, it is clear that evidence of conduct must be taken as freed from at least one of the hearsay dangers, *i.e.*, mendacity. A man does not lie to himself. Put otherwise, if in doing what he does a man has no intention of asserting the existence or non-existence of a fact, it would appear that the trustworthiness of evidence of this conduct is the same whether he is an egregious liar or a paragon of veracity. Accordingly, the lack of opportunity for cross-examination in relation to his veracity or lack of it, would seem to be of no substantial importance. Accordingly, the usual judicial disposition to equate the 'implied' to the 'express' assertion is very questionable."

The drafters of the Federal Rules agreed with the criticisms of the common law rule that implied assertions should be treated as hearsay and expressly abolished it. They did this by providing that no oral or written expression was to be considered as hearsay, unless it was an "assertion" concerning the matter sought to be proved and that no nonverbal conduct should be considered as hearsay, unless it was intended to be an "assertion" concerning said matter. The relevant provisions are:

Rule 801.

"(a) Statement. A *'statement'* is (1) an oral or written *assertion* or (2) nonverbal conduct of a person, if it is *intended by him as an assertion.*

(c) Hearsay. 'Hearsay' is a *statement*, other than one made by the declarant while testifying at the trial or hearing, offered in evidence to prove the truth of the matter asserted."

Rule 802.

"*Hearsay is not admissible* except as provided by these rules or by other rules prescribed by the Supreme Court pursuant to statutory authority or by Act of Congress." (Emphasis added).

"Assertion" is not defined in the rules, but has the connotation of a forceful or positive declaration.

The Advisory Committee note concerning this problem states:

"The definition of 'statement' assumes importance because the term is used in the definition of hearsay in subdivision (c). *The effect of the definition of 'statement' is to exclude from the operation of the hearsay rule all evidence of conduct, verbal or nonverbal, not intended as an assertion. The key to the definition is that nothing is an assertion unless intended to be one.*

"It can scarcely be doubted that an assertion made in words is intended by the declarant to be an assertion. Hence verbal assertions readily fall into the category of 'statement.' Whether nonverbal conduct should be regarded as a statement for purposes of defining hearsay requires further consideration. Some nonverbal conduct, such as the act of pointing to identify a suspect in a lineup, is clearly the equivalent of words, assertive in nature, and to be regarded as a statement. Other nonverbal conduct, however, may be offered as evidence that the person acted as he did because of his belief in the existence of the condition sought to be proved, from which belief the existence of the condition may be inferred. This sequence is, arguably, in effect an assertion of the existence of the condition and hence properly includable within the hearsay concept. *See* Morgan, "Hearsay Dangers and the Application of the Hearsay Concept," 62 Harv. L. Rev. 177, 214, 217 (1948), and the elaboration in Finman, "Implied Assertions as Hearsay: Some Criticisms of the Uniform Rules of Evidence," 14 Stan. L. Rev. 682 (1962).

Admittedly evidence of this character is untested with respect to the perception, memory, and narration (or their equivalents) of the actor, *but the Advisory Committee is of the view that these dangers are minimal in the absence of an intent to assert and do not justify the loss of the evidence on hearsay grounds.* No class of evidence is free of the possibility of fabrication, but the likelihood is less with nonverbal than with assertive verbal conduct. The situations giving rise to the nonverbal conduct are such as virtually to eliminate questions of sincerity. Motivation, the nature of the conduct, and the presence or absence of reliance will bear heavily upon the weight to be given the evidence. Falknor, "The 'Hear-Say' Rule as a 'See-Do' Rule: Evidence of Conduct," 33 Rocky Mt. L. Rev. 133 (1961). *Similar considerations govern nonassertive verbal conduct and verbal conduct which is assertive but offered as a basis for inferring something other than the matter asserted,* also excluded from the definition of hearsay by the language of subdivision (c)." (Emphasis added).

This court, therefore, holds that, "Subdivision (a)(2) of Rule 801 removes implied assertions from the definition of statement and consequently from the operation of the hearsay rule." Applying the principles discussed above to the case at bar, this court holds that the utterances of the betters telephoning in their bets were nonassertive verbal conduct, offered as relevant for an implied assertion to be inferred from them, namely that bets could be placed at the premises being telephoned. The language is not an assertion on its face, and it is obvious these persons did not intend to make an assertion about the fact sought to be proved or anything else.

As an implied assertion, the proffered evidence is expressly excluded from the operation of the hearsay rule by Rule 801 of the Federal Rules of Evidence, and the objection thereto must be overruled. An order to that effect has previously been entered.

[5]   United States v. Alosa

United States Court of Appeals for the First Circuit
14 F.3d 693 (1st Cir. 1994)

BOUDIN, CIRCUIT JUDGE:

On April 9, 1992, law enforcement agents armed with a search warrant entered the home of Pasquale and Lisa Alosa in Loudon, New Hampshire. The search uncovered substantial amounts of marijuana, marijuana plants, a basement "garden" for growing them, scales, plastic bags, two loaded handguns, and 16 other unloaded firearms. Also found were two different collections of papers which, for simplicity, have been referred to as ledgers. A man named Robb Hamilton was also present on the premises and was later implicated.

Both Alosas and Hamilton were later named in an indictment that . . . charged Pasquale and Lisa in four counts.

[T]he second string to [Pasquale's] bow on appeal is a claim that the court erred in admitting the drug ledgers. One set of papers had been found inside a stove in the kitchen; the other set was in the living room. They contained entries concerning various transactions, including amounts and customer names. The government not only introduced the ledgers but, over objection, offered expert handwriting and print evidence that associated both ledgers in some degree with Lisa and one of them with Hamilton.

Pasquale's brief says that it was error to admit the ledgers because the government failed to offer evidence, independent of the ledgers, to show that they qualified as co-conspirator statements made in furtherance of the conspiracy. Under Fed. R. Evid. 801(d)(2)(E), a statement avoids hearsay objections if the trial judge finds by a preponderance of the evidence that an out-of-court statement was made by a co-conspirator and was made in furtherance of the conspiracy. *See Bourjaily v. United States,* 483 U.S. 171, 107 S. Ct. 2775, 97 L. Ed. 2d 144 (1987). It may lessen the confusion that surrounds drug ledger evidence to point out that what needs to be proved for admissibility depends upon the use to be made of the evidence.

First, if records manifestly are or are shown by other evidence to be drug records, they are admissible "real evidence" tending to make it more likely that a drug business was being conducted, *see United States v. Tejada,* 886 F.2d 483, 487 (1st Cir. 1989), and for this use there is ordinarily no hearsay problem to be overcome. Rather, the records help to show "the character and use of the place where the notebooks were found," *United States v. Wilson,* 532 F.2d 641, 645 (8th Cir. 1976), just like drugs, scales and guns. Here, the nature of the ledgers was indicated not only by the type of entry — which would have been sufficient — but also by expert testimony from a DEA agent who gave his opinion that the records related to drug transactions.[1]

---

[1] (Court's original footnote 3) Using the entries to show the character of the ledgers as drug records does, of course, present some of the risks of hearsay; but under the modern definition of hearsay, such a use does not render the entries hearsay because the entries are not being used to prove the truth of the matter

Second, in this case the ledgers served the further purpose of helping to prove the existence of a conspiracy. Pasquale's own involvement in drugs was established by his pleas and much other evidence, but relatively little direct evidence in his trial showed active participation by Lisa in the business (her own admissions to the police were not made known to Pasquale's jury). Most of the drugs and related items were found either in Pasquale's areas of the house or in common areas. But the ledgers, once they were tied to Lisa by handwriting and print evidence, made the inference of conspiracy easy. Once again this use of the ledgers presented no hearsay problem in this case. The "truth" of individual statements in the ledgers is beside the point; all that matters is that the ledgers are drug records to which Lisa may be linked by other evidence. Nor is there a hearsay problem posed by testimony from a handwriting or print expert that connected Lisa to the ledgers. Thus, for the most important use of the ledgers in this case — to help show more than one participant and thus a conspiracy — there was no need for a preliminary finding of likely conspiracy nor any need to satisfy Rule 801(d)(2)(E).

Third, when it made its proffer in support of the ledgers, the government reserved the right to use the ledgers to show not only the fact of conspiracy but also, by relying on specific entries, the dimensions of the conspiracy. To the extent that the prosecutor wanted to argue that an individual entry was "true" — say, one showing a specific sale of a specific amount to a specific person — then some hearsay exception or exclusion did need to be satisfied. Here, Rule 801(d)(2)(E) was invoked. In admitting the evidence, the district court expressly found by a preponderance of the evidence that the ledgers were made by conspirators in furtherance of the conspiracy.

These findings were amply supported by admissible non-hearsay evidence.[2] Lisa's presence in the home, with a marijuana garden in the cellar and drugs and paraphernalia throughout, was highly suggestive. The notion that "presence" at a crime does not equal guilt is not a ban on common sense inferences: the evidence of pervasive drug production and dealing in Lisa's home was material evidence that made her involvement more plausible. Once she was linked to the drug ledgers — a linkage that also did not happen to depend on hearsay — the trial judge could easily conclude that a conspiracy had been shown and admit the ledgers for the truth of the statements contained within them.

Not only did the evidence of joint drug dealing between husband and wife satisfy Rule 801(d)(2)(E) — which requires only a probability or likelihood of conspiracy — but the evidence amply satisfied the higher standard of proof beyond a reasonable doubt required for conviction.

---

asserted in the entries (e.g., that a specific transaction took place on a particular date). *See* Fed. R. Evid. 801(c) (hearsay is an out of court statement offered "to prove the truth of the matter asserted"); 2 John W. Strong et al., McCormick on Evidence § 250, at 112 (1992) (collecting cases).

[2] (Court's original footnote 4) Actually, Fed. R. Evid. 104(a) permits the judge to consider the hearsay statements for their truth in making the admissibility findings, *see* Bourjaily, 483 U.S. at 178–80, 107 S. Ct. at 2780–81, although this court has recently joined other circuits in holding that there must be some evidence of conspiracy independent of the hearsay statements themselves. . . .

[G] Review Problems

Problem #10-16: Is It Really Hearsay?

State whether the following statements are hearsay. Assume all statements are made out of court unless otherwise indicated. Determine only whether all of the elements of hearsay are met, not whether the item will be admissible.

1. To show that a bird named Crackers is owned by Sounia, Crackers' statements when she is in the same room with Sounia, "That's my Sounia! Caw! That's my Sounia!" *✗ no declarant*

2. On the issue of whether Mary liked Lee, the fact that Mary hugged Lee upon seeing him. *Maybe (motive)*

3. On the issue of whether Mary liked Lee, the fact that Mary chose Lee last for her team in a moot court competition. *✗ statement*

4. On the issue of whether Mary liked Lee, Mary's statement, "I like Lee." *✓*

5. On the question of who robbed the laundromat at gunpoint, witness Paul's deposition statement, "Larry robbed the laundromat." *✓*

6. To prove that Theresa and Sal are married, testimony by Roseanne that they said "I do" when asked by the priest whether they would take each other as lawfully wedded husband and wife. *✗*

7. To prove that Cassandra stabbed her husband DeWayne, the fact that Cassandra was seen fleeing their house at 4:15 p.m., five minutes before the police arrived at the house to investigate loud noises. *✗ conduct*

8. On the issue of whether Beowulf died as a result of the accident, Beowulf's statement immediately after the accident, "The red Jeep Laredo just hit me and knocked me over." *✓*

9. To show that Jeanette committed a murder, the fact that she attempted to poison a prospective witness after she (Jeanette) had been charged with the crime. *✗ (also char. ev.)* *✓*

10. To prove that Percival died of accidental causes, the autopsy report indicating such. *✓*

11. To prove that Steve is Patrick's father, testimony that Steve often referred to Patrick as "my son." *✓*

12. On the issue of whether Riddick had struck Lennox, Riddick's statement, "I boxed his ears but good." *✓*

13. To show that Louis Lightfeather committed the robbery of the convenience store, his written confession. *✓*

14. To show that Belinda went to the store with Aretha, the overheard question, "Why did Belinda go to the store with Aretha?" *✓*

15. To show that the road turns sharply, Otis' statement, "Hey, watch out, that road turns sharply!"

16. To show that the driver of the car was negligent in running off of the road at the turn, Otis' statement, "Hey, watch out, that road turns sharply!"

17. To impeach Grover, a witness in the case, Grover is asked on cross-examination, "Didn't you say at the time of the incident that you were not home at all that night, unlike your testimony today?"

18. On the issue of whether the new model of the four-wheel-drive vehicle, the Laramie Cruiser, was safe, a *Consumer Reports* article declaring it to be "extraordinarily safe."

19. On the issue of whether the accused committed burglary, evidence that the defendant twice attempted to escape the jurisdiction after being arrested for the crime.

20. On the question of whether the Jaguar XJ12 convertible was a gift or loan from Ronald Crump, Crump's statement, "Here are the keys to the Jaguar; you can use it for a year as a birthday present."

21. On the issue of whether a newspaper article had defamed the mayor, a statement by the reporter the day after the article had been published to the effect that "Yeah, I said some not-so-nice things about the mayor in that article."

Problem #10-17: Is It Really Hearsay II?

State whether each of the following statements technically satisfies the requirements of hearsay. Answer each question either "yes," meaning the utterance technically satisfies the hearsay definition, or "no," meaning the utterance is not technically hearsay.

Assume all statements are made out-of-court unless otherwise indicated. (*Note:* This question does *not* ask whether the evidence ultimately will be admissible. Admissibility is predicated on various other requirements as well.)

1. To show that the witness, Darlene, is telling the truth, Darlene testifies on direct, "I said in my deposition last Wednesday, consistent with my testimony here today, that the blue car ran the red light."

2. On the issue of who started a fistfight between Cassidy and the Sundance Kid, a pre-fight statement by Jones to the Sundance Kid, "Hey, Sundance, Cassidy is gunning for you."

3. On the issue of whether there was a breach of contract, Lynn testified at trial that "the contract stated I was to deliver the pork bellies by the 16th."

4. To show that Larry and Claudia were friends, the fact that they talked to each other at a party for several hours.

5. On the issue of whether Arlene committed the crime, her pre-trial claim, "I did not commit this crime."

6. On the issue of whether Joe conspired to commit the crime, Joe signaled "thumbs up" when he was asked to join the conspiracy.

7. On the issue of whether Joe agreed to commit the crime, Joe remained silent when asked by his friend, Rick, "You're not going to chicken out on this job, are you?"

8. On the issue of whether Stevie paid a parking ticket, Stevie possessed a violator's "receipt of payment" issued by the Department of Motor Vehicles.

9. To show that Stevie paid a parking ticket, a photograph of Stevie paying money at the cashier's window of the Department of Motor Vehicles.

10. On the question of whether Sally died in the helicopter crash, Sally's statement made immediately after the crash "Hey, I'm still alive!"

11. On the issue of whether the defendant attempted to bribe a government official named Ted, evidence that the defendant attempted to kill Ted before he could testify against the defendant at trial.

12. On the issue of whether the transfer of Joan's Jaguar automobile to Kim was a gift or a loan, the statement by Joan one hour after the transfer occurred (and offered at trial by Joan), "that was a loan I made to Kim."

13. On the question of whether Amy, the defendant, acted in self-defense in killing Vinnie, the victim, her statement made just prior to the fight in question and offered by her at trial, "I am scared of Vinnie, the victim."

14. On the issue of whether the taxi cab was safe, the fact that the cab driver drove away in the cab after a visual inspection of it.

15. On the issue of whether the defendant, South, is guilty of the crime charged, evidence that South yelled "Over here!" and set a fire at the scene of a gang fight to intentionally direct suspicion to him and away from the youngest members of the gang, East and West.

16. On the issue of whether Ozzie likes Harriet, Ozzie's prior statement, "Harriet has no faults."

17. On the issue of whether Ozzie likes Harriet, Ozzie's statement, "I like Harriet very much."

18. On the issue of whether Ozzie left all of his money to Harriet, Ozzie's statement, "I like Harriet very much."

19. On the issue of whether Sharon had been poisoned, her prior statement, "I've been poisoned!" offered by her at trial.

20. On the issue of whether Sharon acted reasonably in drinking a glass of liquid that contained poison, the statement by her friend just before she drank the liquid, "Watch out for that glass of pink-colored liquid, Sharon, it looks like poison."

21. On the issue of whether his leg hurt, Alan's statement, "My leg is hurting me."

22. On the issue of who shot the sheriff, Eric's statement offered by him, "I did not shoot the sheriff."

23. On the issue of whether Cassandra went to the store on the afternoon in question, Cassandra's statement made that morning, "I'm going to go to the store this afternoon to get some shopping done."

24. On the issue of whether Cassandra went to the store that afternoon, her husband Herman's statement, also made that morning, "Cassandra told me she's going to go to the store this afternoon."

25. To show that the lamp belonged to Rebecca and not to her boyfriend Jordan, Jordan's statement, "This lamp belongs to Rebecca."

26. To further show that the lamp belonged to Rebecca and not Jordan, Jordan's statement, "This is one ugly lamp."

27. On the issue of how Lenny felt about Brian, the fact that Lenny shook hands with Brian upon seeing him.

28. To show that Barnaby committed the crime of mayhem, his unsuccessful attempt to bribe a prospective witness after his arrest.

29. To show that Paolo is not a thief, the fact that he was named chief financial officer by the president of the company.

§ 10.03 STATUTORY NON-HEARSAY [FRE 801(D)]

FRE 801(d) declares that certain out-of-court statements are not hearsay, even though they technically meet all of the hearsay elements. Because of this seeming contradiction, we are labeling this section "statutory" non-hearsay. The important point is not the label, which could also be hearsay "exemptions" or "hearsay but not excluded," but rather that these categories escape the general hearsay exclusionary rule.

These statements include certain prior statements of witnesses and admissions by party opponents. The rationales underlying these exemptions extend beyond the reliability of the statements. Admissions, for example, might not be reliable, but are a product of the adversary system and can be rebutted by parties if they want to attempt to do so. With prior statements of witnesses, by definition, a witness is testifying and subject to cross-examination to flesh out the degree of reliability of the prior statement.

[A] Prior Statements of Witnesses [FRE 801(d)(1)]

The FRE permit prior statements of a testifying witness to be admitted for the truth of the matter asserted in three situations, provided that the witness is subject to cross-examination at trial about the prior statements:

1. *Sworn prior inconsistent statements of witnesses.* Prior inconsistent statements of a witness are admissible for the truth of the matter asserted if they were made under oath and subject to the penalty of perjury at a prior trial, hearing, deposition,

or other qualifying proceeding (such as a grand jury proceeding). Because the prior statement was made under oath, and there is an opportunity at trial to cross-examine the witness on it, sufficient indicia of reliability exist to admit the statement for its truth.

2. *Prior consistent statements of witnesses.* A prior consistent statement of a witness is admissible for the truth of the matter asserted if the statement is offered to rebut a charge of recent contrivance or fabrication. These prior consistent statements, unlike prior inconsistent statements admitted for the truth, need not be made under oath. When not offered pursuant to this provision, prior consistent statements are generally considered cumulative and are excluded as unfairly prejudicial.

3. *Prior identifications by witnesses.* The fact that a witness has made an identification of another person prior to trial may be admitted at trial for the truth of the matter asserted. This situation arises often in criminal cases where the witness has identified the alleged perpetrator of the crime in a line-up, a photo array (a group of photographs), or a "show up" (a specially arranged observation of a defendant shortly after his arrest). The prior identification is closer in time to the event and, consequently, may even be preferable to a subsequent in-court identification at trial.

Illustration

Arnie, an eyewitness, was deposed two weeks prior to a trial for bank robbery. After testifying at trial for the government, he was cross-examined by the defense.

DEFENSE COUNSEL: Arnie, you just stated that the robbery occurred at teller window number two, correct?"

A: Yes, that's right.

DEFENSE COUNSEL: Arnie, didn't you say in your March 4th deposition, referring to page six, line nine, that "the robbery occurred at teller window number three?"

A: That is correct.

Is Arnie's prior deposition statement admissible for the truth of the matter asserted?

Answer: Prior inconsistent statements are generally admissible solely to impeach the credibility of the witness and not for the truth of the matter asserted. Arnie's prior statement, however, was made under oath subject to the penalty of perjury in a proper proceeding under FRE 801(d)(1)(A), a deposition. Further, Arnie could be cross-examined at trial on his prior statement. Therefore, the prior statement will be admitted not only to impeach Arnie, but also for the truth of the matter asserted.

Problem #10-18: "Muck"

In a slip-and-fall case, the plaintiff, Rose, called a witness, Wanda, to testify that moments before the plaintiff slipped in a certain area, the ground was full of mud and "muck." On cross-examination, Wanda was asked if she had stated in a deposition just *nonhearsay* (margin annotation)

three weeks after the accident that the surrounding area "looked damp, but was actually firm and solid."

Is the witness's prior statement admissible? If it is admitted, is it allowed as (1) impeachment? (2) for the truth of the matter asserted? (3) both impeachment and substantive evidence? or (4) neither impeachment nor substantive evidence? Explain your answer.

Problem #10-19: "The Case"

At trial, Lenny is cross-examined about the contents of an attaché case he was carrying two years earlier. Lenny responds to plaintiff's counsel by saying, "The attaché case only contained two pairs of socks and no classified papers."

1. If one month prior to trial, Lenny had made a prior inconsistent statement to a friend, Melissa, about the contents of the case ("the case had two top secret documents," said Lenny), can the statement be offered for the truth of the matter asserted?

2. If Lenny had made the prior statement about the attaché case to the police during an interrogation, would it be admissible for the truth of the matter asserted?

3. If the prior inconsistent statement to the friend in 1. is elicited on cross-examination, can Lenny testify on redirect examination that, "I told my wife, Shari, two years ago that the case contained only two pairs of socks and nothing else"?

Problem #10-20: Bobomeister

Bob testifies in a commercial litigation action about the books kept by the defendant company, Gilko and Associates. On cross-examination, Bob is asked whether the figures he quoted were recently created "due to the potential multi-million dollar judgment in this lawsuit." On re-direct examination, Bob indignantly stated, "Hey, I told my partner more than one year ago, before I had ever heard of this lawsuit, that those were the correct figures."

1. If Bob's statement is objected to as hearsay, what ruling and why?

2. Does it matter whether Bob's prior statement is under oath?

Problem #10-21: The Key to Rebecca

Rebecca gave the cashier a counterfeit $20 bill, prompting the cashier to call the police. When the police arrived, the cashier pointed to Rebecca as the person who handed her the counterfeit bill. Rebecca was arrested and later prosecuted. At trial, the cashier testified that she did not remember what the perpetrator looked like. The cashier then testified about her prior identification of Rebecca. Is the cashier's testimony hearsay? Is it admissible?

Problem #10-22: Blind Man's Bluff

A blind man grabs a person who picked his pocket and holds him. The police arrive and detain the pickpocket. The blind man says, "This guy tried to rob me," patting the pickpocket at his side. At trial, the police officer testifies to the blind man's statement. Is the testimony hearsay? Explain.

Problem #10-23: That's the Man, Officer!

In a robbery trial, an eyewitness, Ethel, testifies that she saw the defendant snatch the victim's purse and quickly exit the mall through the Kmart located on the mall's south side. Ethel added, "I ran up to Officer Thursday. I was out of breath and couldn't speak. Later, he showed me several photographs. I pointed to the photograph of the defendant, indicating that he was the guy who snatched the purse and ran out of the Kmart."

    1. Is Ethel's testimony hearsay? Why?

    2. Ethel wishes to testify that "my best friend, Marv, was standing right next to me when the defendant ran out of the store. Marv also told the police officer after looking at the pictures that the defendant was the fellow who snatched the purse." Is this testimony admissible?

[B] Opposing Party Statements [FRE 801(d)(2)]

To constitute opposing party statements under the restyled FRE, an out-of-court statement must fulfill two requirements. The statement (1) must have been made by or on behalf of a party opponent, and (2) must be offered against that party. By this definition, it becomes clear that the word previously used before the restyling, "admissions" is a misnomer — the opposing party need not admit anything in the statement. Rather, the theory of opposing party statements is that "you made the statement, now you explain it." This signifies that a party will be held responsible for his or her own utterances, whether a fact is "admitted" in the statement or not.

In addition, the rationale underlying admissibility is so strong that a lack of personal knowledge by the declarant is not a bar to admission. Statements by opposing parties are admissible under FRE 801 even if they violate the personal knowledge requirement and the rule prohibiting lay opinions.

There are five different types of opposing party statements recognized by the FRE. A statement is considered part of this category in each of the following situations:

    1. It is the party's own statement. FRE 801(d)(2)(A).

    2. The party adopts or acquiesces in the statement of another person. FRE 801(d)(2)(B).

    3. The party authorizes another person to make statements about a subject. FRE 801(d)(2)(C).

4. The party's agent or servant makes the statement concerning a matter within the scope of the agency or employment, during the existence of the relationship. FRE 801 (d)(2)(D).

5. A co-conspirator of the party makes the statement during and in furtherance of the conspiracy. FRE 801(d)(2)(E).

Illustration

Phil and Mark had a fistfight after Mark called Phil a child. During the fight, Phil broke Mark's nose. Mark filed suit for assault and battery against Phil, and offered Phil's statement made just after the fight, "I only broke Mark's nose after he attacked me; we both completely lost our tempers." Is Phil's statement an admission by a party opponent?

Answer: Phil's statement is an admission by a party opponent under FRE 801(d)(2)(A) because it meets both criteria of the rule: (1) it is a statement of a party opponent (Phil), (2) offered against him. It is not required that the statement "admit" anything, and indeed, Phil's statement contains both inculpatory and exculpatory components.

Problem #10-24: Murder at the Cotton Club

Bella is charged with murdering Dan at the Cotton Club Dance Hall on June 13th at 11 p.m. Bella raises the defense of mistaken identity, alleging that she was out of town during the evening in question. The prosecution offers a witness, William, who states, "Bella told me on the morning of June 13 that she intended to go to the Cotton Club that night." Is Bella's statement hearsay? Explain.

Problem #10-25: Defamation

A disputed issue in a defamation action was whether the statement made by defendant was indeed "about the plaintiff" as required. On cross-examination of the defendant, she virtually conceded that the statement in question concerned the plaintiff.

1. Is the defendant's testimony a binding judicial admission?

2. If the defendant had admitted that the statement concerned the plaintiff in the defendant's answer to the complaint, would the concession be binding? Why?

Problem #10-26: Hot Air

A twin-engine plane flying for Horton Air, a small commuter airline, was forced to make an emergency crash landing after the engines failed. The pilot jumped out unscathed and stated to the press as soon as it arrived, "While I did not see the mechanics work on this plane, this landing was due to the incompetence of the mechanics and not pilot error, I'll tell you that!"

1. If several injured passengers brought suit against the pilot, can the passengers offer the pilot's statements in evidence? Why?

2. Will the answer to 1. hinge on whether the pilot's statement was based on personal knowledge?

3. If Horton Air is also sued, can the pilot's statements be offered against the company? Explain.

Problem #10-27: Hey, Hey, What Do You Say?

Georgie, at his weekly card game, was being teased by the other card players. "Hey, hey, Georgie, I heard you were the person responsible for sticking up the First National Bank last week and escaping with $83,000 in new $50 bills. Is it true, Georgie?" Georgie did not respond, but merely smiled weakly and dealt the cards. Is Georgie's silence hearsay? Explain.

Problem #10-28: You Said What?

At Bilkem, Inc., the press secretary, Jondi Howard, spoke to the media about alleged charges of company pollution. Jondi stated, "In the immediate neighborhood, we only release treated sludge that has been proven safe enough to eat, not that I'd recommend it."

If the neighborhood homeowners association brings suit against Bilkem, Inc., can it offer Jondi's statement? Is the statement hearsay? Why?

Problem #10-29: Liberty

Liberty, an accountant with SBP Proskour Company, a chemical manufacturer, stated at a private dinner party to some friends that "SBP Proskour is really pouring those hazardous chemicals into the river, including dangerous PCBs." In a subsequent lawsuit accusing SBP Proskour of improperly dumping chemicals into the river, one of the friends who heard Liberty's statement at the dinner party is called to testify about the statement for the plaintiffs. Is Liberty's statement hearsay? Explain.

unauthorized

Problem #10-30: "I'm Outta Here."

Jimmy resigned from the Tandy Corp. on March 6th and circulated his resignation letter to his colleagues via e-mail. Jimmy resigned his position as safety director for the new Tandy Chocolate Bar because "while I enjoyed my time here, especially with colleagues, I found my strong interest in safety to differ from the company's." In a subsequent suit against Tandy for tainted chocolate bars, could the plaintiff offer Jimmy's resignation letter as an agency admission? Why or why not?

Problem #10-31: Interstate 95

Suzannah Craft was a driver for Marko Brothers Produce Co. when she collided with another truck. The accident caused damage to both vehicles and spilled the contents of the truck all over the highway. Suzannah called her boss immediately after the accident, and said, in a voice loud enough for many to hear, "I'm sorry Shirley. I think my foot had fallen asleep and I was trying to kick it awake when the accident occurred." Shirley, the boss, responded by saying, "You're fired!"

agency
+ active
employ.

Are Suzannah's statements admissible at trial in a suit brought by the other truck driver against Marko Brothers Produce Co.? Explain.

Problem #10-32: New Deli

The defendants, siblings Renee and Robert Roanoke, are co-owners of the New Downtown Deli. They were recently prosecuted for racketeering and mail fraud. At trial, the prosecution offers a statement made by Renee against both defendants. Renee was overheard saying to Robert three months prior to their arrest that "we really need some Swiss Bank accounts to handle those questionable wire transactions."

What will the prosecution argue in favor of admitting Renee's statement? What ruling and why?

Co-consp.

Problem #10-33: Moe, Larry, and Shirley

Moe, Larry, and Shirley methodically planned a series of bank robberies. Before they were able to carry out their intentions, however, the police learned of the plot and arrested them. During the arrest, Moe blurted out, "Okay, so we were going to rob some banks. You wouldn't have caught us except you got lucky; Larry and Shirley had mapped out ingenious plans."

1. If the prosecution offers Moe's statement to the police against Larry and Shirley at trial, is the statement hearsay? Explain. *no*

2. Is there any change in the admissibility of Moe's statement if the three defendants are charged only with attempted bank robbery, and not conspiracy to rob a bank?

3. Does it matter in answering 1. whether the three defendants are tried jointly or separately?

4. How will the case of *Bruton v. United States*, 391 U.S. 123 (1968), affect the admissibility of Moe's statement? *See* Ch. 11, *The Confrontation Clause.*

Problem #10-34: The Altos

Tommy Alto was the head of a large criminal money laundering and gambling operation. One day, Tommy was informed that his associate's wife was going to tell all. Tommy visited his associate's house for dinner and told the wife that he and Tommy "had to take out a guy who talked too much about the dirty money and gambling; he will not be singing anymore." Tommy's associate is later charged with money laundering, illegal gambling, and murder. Are the statements Tommy made to the associate's wife admissible against the associate?

Problem #10-35: CI (Confidential Informant) New York

In the Bronx, not far from Yankee Stadium, a confidential informant had infiltrated a ring of ticket scalpers. The six ticket scalpers considered the CI one of them and told him everything. The CI relayed the information to the police. In a subsequent trial against the scalpers, could the police officer testify for the prosecution as to what the CI had told him during the conspiracy? Why or why not?

[C]   Cases and Rules

[1]   United States v. Day

United States Court of Appeals for the Sixth Circuit
789 F.2d 1217 (6th Cir. 1986)

[The defendants were convicted of preparing false income tax returns in violation of federal law. The government introduced at trial a prior sworn recorded statement by one of the defendants, Moore, that resulted from an interview with government agents. The statement was offered for the truth of the matter asserted as a prior inconsistent statement of the witness under oath. *See* FRE 801(d)(1)(A).]

The precise qualifying language of [Rule 801(d)(1)(A)] mandates that the declarant's inconsistent statement be given "under oath *subject to the penalty of perjury* at a trial, hearing, or other proceeding or in a deposition." Although [defendant] Moore's statement [offered under 801(d)(1)(A)] was characterized as a sworn statement, the evidence failed to disclose whether Doble [who took the statement] had legal authority to administer an oath that would invoke the penalty of perjury upon a showing that the declarant perjured himself. The proponent of a hearsay statement bears the burden of proving each element of a given hearsay exception. . . . Because the record is devoid of any evidence that Doble had been invested with the legal authority to officially administer an oath that would and could subject Moore to the penalty of perjury at a trial, this court cannot conclude, as a matter of law, that Moore's statement was given under oath and was in fact subject to the penalty of perjury.

The government's position, to be viable, must also qualify the interview conducted by Bright and Doble as an "other proceeding" defined in the above rule. A legislative history of 801(d)(1)(A) discloses that Congress intended to qualify only those prior inconsistent statements that were highly reliable and firmly anchored in the probability of truth as admissible substantive evidence. . . .

Several circuits have already incorporated the congressional intent into decisions that have refused to admit statements given under informal circumstances tantamount to a station house interrogation setting which later prove inconsistent with a declarant's trial testimony and have denied their admissibility as substantive evidence pursuant to 801(d)(1)(A). Mindful of the congressional intent to ensure the reliability and truthfulness of any prior inconsistent statement as a condition of its admissibility as substantive evidence at trial, this court must evaluate the reliability and truthfulness of the Moore statement by examining the totality of the circumstances that pervaded the Moore interview.

Apart from the fatal infirmity of the controversial Moore recording, namely, the complete absence of affirmative proof that it was given under an oath that invoked the penalty of perjury, the statement fails to satisfy the criteria imposed by Congress to qualify it as a prior inconsistent statement given during the course of an "other proceeding" because the circumstances surrounding the recording of the statement militate against reliability and truthfulness.

Initially, it is interesting to note that agents Bright and Doble characterized their meeting with Moore as an interview and not a formal proceeding. Although the statement was purportedly a sworn attestation, the evidence failed to disclose that it was given "under oath subject to the penalty of perjury." Moreover, Moore's motivation, mirrored in the tone and content of the statement, disclaims its reliability and truthfulness.

Moore's statement was patently self-serving, calculated to exculpate himself from criminal activity at the expense of his associates by intentionally diverting attention to and incriminating Day as "a damn crook" and Pack as the architect of the check conversion scheme, both of whom counseled and directed him in his business and financial affairs.

Accordingly, for the reasons articulated herein, this Court concludes that Moore's statement is fatally flawed because it was not given "under an oath subject to the penalty of perjury" and because the statement was given under circumstances more aptly described as a station house interrogation than an "other proceeding" which would, as contemplated by 801(d)(1)(A) of the Federal Rules of Evidence, ensure and inspire the reliability and truthfulness of the statements. To permit it to be considered as substantive evidence by the jury constituted prejudicial error as against all defendants.

[2]   United States v. Flecha

United States Court of Appeals for the Second Circuit
539 F.2d 874 (2d Cir. 1976)

[In *United States v. Flecha*, the defendant was convicted of importing and possessing marijuana with the intent to distribute it, and conspiracy to do the same. On appeal, the defendant objected to the admission of a statement by a codefendant, named Gonzalez.]

After all the defendants had been arrested, the agents found four bales containing 287 pounds of marijuana in the place where they had been dragged by the four who were aboard ship. The captain of the vessel testified that when he came aboard about 1:45 a.m. Suarez failed to inform him of the presence of unauthorized persons on the ship, although it was part of his duty to do so.

Not satisfied with this compelling case, the prosecutor elicited from Agent Cabrera that, as all five defendants were standing in line, he heard Gonzalez say in Spanish, apparently to Flecha:

Why so much excitement? If we are caught, we are caught.

The three lawyers who represented defendants Banguera, Suarez and Pineda-Marin immediately sought an instruction that this was "not binding" on their clients; the court said "Granted." Counsel for Flecha then joined in the application. Judge Weinstein asked Agent Cabrera how far away Flecha was from Gonzalez; Cabrera answered that Flecha was right next to Gonzalez, only six to twelve inches away. The judge then denied Flecha's application.

Although the judge did not articulate his reasons for granting the applications of Banguera, Suarez and Pineda-Marin but denying Flecha's, it is not difficult to reconstruct what his thought process must have been. To state the matter in terms of the later-enacted Federal Rules of Evidence, which in respects here relevant do not differ from the common law, the judge properly concluded that Gonzalez' declaration was not admissible as "a statement by a co-conspirator of a party during the course and in furtherance of the conspiracy," Rule 801(d)(2)(E), since the conspiracy was over and the statement was not in furtherance of it. He must also have concluded that the declaration was not admissible under Rule 803(2), the hearsay exception for "(a) statement relating to a startling event or condition made while the declarant was under the stress of excitement caused by the event or condition." This was probably right since Gonzalez' plea by its own terms indicated a lack of excitement. His allowing Gonzalez' statement to stand against Flecha although not against the three other objectors must thus have rested on a belief that as to Flecha the case fell within Rule 801(d)(2)(B), allowing receipt, as an admission of the party against whom it is offered, of "a statement of which he has manifested his adoption or belief in its truth."

The brief voir dire demonstrates that the judge fell into the error, against which Dean Wigmore so clearly warned, 4 Wigmore, Evidence § 1071, at 102 (Chadbourn rev. 1972), of jumping from the correct proposition that hearing the statement of a third person is a necessary condition for adoption by silence, see e.g., United States v. Moore, 522 F.2d 1068, 1074–76 (9 Cir. 1975), cert. denied, 423 U.S. 1049, 96 S.Ct. 775, 46 L. Ed. 2d 637 (1976), to the incorrect conclusion that it is a sufficient one. After quoting the maxim "silence gives consent," Wigmore explains "that the inference of assent may safely be made only when no other explanation is equally consistent with silence; and there is always another possible explanation namely, ignorance or dissent unless the circumstances are such that a dissent would in ordinary experience have been expressed if the communication had not been correct." (Emphasis supplied.) However, "the force of the brief maxim has always been such that in practice . . . a sort of working rule grew up that whatever was said in a party's presence was receivable against him as an admission, because presumably assented to. This working rule became so firmly entrenched in practice that frequent judicial deliverances became necessary in order to dislodge it; for in this simple and comprehensive form it ignored the inherent qualifications of the principle." (Emphasis in original.) Among the judicial deliverances quoted, it suffices to cite Chief Justice Shaw's statements in Commonwealth v. Kenney, 53 Mass. 235, 237 (1847), that before receiving an admission by silence the court must determine, inter alia "whether he (the party) is in such a situation that he is at liberty to make any reply" and "whether the statement is made under such circumstances, and by such persons, as naturally to call for a reply, if he did not intend to admit it"; and Lord Justice Bowen's more succinct statement in Wiedemann v. Walpole, 2 Q.B. 534, 539 (1891):

Silence is not evidence of an admission, unless there are circumstances which render it more reasonably probable that a man would answer the charge made against him than that he would not.

We find nothing in the Advisory Committee's Note to Rule 801(d)(2)(B) to indicate any intention to depart from these sound principles. To the contrary the Committee noted that difficulties had been raised in criminal cases and that "the inference is a fairly weak one, to begin with."

We find it hard to think of a case where response would have been less expectable than this one. Flecha was under arrest, and although the Government emphasizes that he was not being questioned by the agents, and had not been given Miranda warnings, it is clear that many arrested persons know, without benefit of warnings, that silence is usually golden. Beyond that, what was Flecha to say? If the Spanish verb used by Gonzalez has the same vagueness as "caught," it would have been somewhat risible for Flecha, surrounded by customs agents, to have denied that he had been. Of course, Flecha could have said "Speak for yourself" or something like it, but it was far more natural to say nothing.

There is no force in the Government's argument that Gonzalez' statement "was not admitted for its truth, but rather for what it showed about Gonzalez' and Flecha's state of mind," and thus was not hearsay. Of course, it was not hearsay as to Gonzalez but in order to be relevant against Flecha, it would have to be at least a description by Gonzalez of Flecha's state of mind ("You know you are guilty") and that would be hearsay unless Flecha adopted it by silence. There is equally little force in the Government's claim of inadequacy in the objection of counsel. The judge saw the point perfectly well and thought he had met it when it was established that Gonzalez' statement was made in Flecha's presence. In this he was mistaken, as has been shown.

[3] Mahlandt v. Wild Canid Survival & Research Center

United States Court of Appeals for the Eighth Circuit
588 F.2d 626 (8th Cir. 1978)

The case of *Mahlandt v. Wild Canid Survival & Research Center* arose out of an attack by a domesticated wolf named Sophie on a child. The wolf was in the custody of the defendant corporation at the time of the attack. At trial, the plaintiff offered a note written by an employee of the defendant corporation, Mr. Poos, to a superior. Mr. Poos' note stated, "Owen, would you call me at home, 727-5080? Sophie bit a child that came in our backyard. All has been taken care of. I need to convey what happened to you." In analyzing whether this statement constituted an admission, the Court stated:

So the statement in the note pinned on the door is not hearsay, and is admissible against Mr. Poos. It was his own statement, and as such was clearly different from the reported statement of another. Example, "I was told that. . . ." *See Cedeck v. Hamiltonian Fed. Sav. & L. Ass'n*, 551 F.2d 1136 (8th Cir. 1977). It was also a statement of which he had manifested his adoption or belief in its truth. And the same observations may be made of the statement made later in the day to Mr. Sexton that, "Sophie had bit a child . . . ."

Are these statements admissible against Wild Canid Survival and Research Center, Inc.? They were made by Mr. Poos when he was an agent or servant of the Wild Canid Survival and Research Center, Inc., and they concerned a matter within the scope of his agency, or employment, i. e., his custody of Sophie, and were made during the existence of that relationship.

The court also noted that an admission need not be broadcast to a third party to be admissible (quoting from the Advisory Committee's Note to Proposed Rule 801):

[C]ommunication to an outsider has not generally been thought to be an essential characteristic of an admission. Thus a party's books or records are useable against him, without regard to any intent to disclose to third persons.

[4] Bourjaily v. United States

United States Supreme Court
483 U.S. 171 (1987)

CHIEF JUSTICE REHNQUIST delivered the opinion of the Court:

Federal Rules of Evidence 801(d)(2)(E) provides: "A statement is not hearsay if . . . [t]he statement is offered against a party and is . . . a statement by a coconspirator of a party during the course and in furtherance of the conspiracy." We granted certiorari to answer three questions regarding the admission of statements under Rule 801(d)(2)(E): (1) whether the court must determine by independent evidence that the conspiracy existed and that the defendant and the declarant were members of this conspiracy; (2) the quantum of proof on which such determinations must be based; and (3) whether a court must in each case examine the circumstances of such a statement to determine its reliability. 479 U.S. 881, 107 S. Ct. 268, 93 L. Ed. 2d 246 (1986).

. . . .

Before admitting a co-conspirator's statement over an objection that it does not qualify under Rule 801(d)(2)(E), a court must be satisfied that the statement actually falls within the definition of the Rule. There must be evidence that there was a conspiracy involving the declarant and the nonoffering party, and that the statement was made "during the course and in furtherance of the conspiracy." Federal Rule of Evidence 104(a) provides: "Preliminary questions concerning . . . the admissibility of evidence shall be determined by the court." Petitioner and the Government agree that the existence of a conspiracy and petitioner's involvement in it are preliminary questions of fact that, under Rule 104, must be resolved by the court. The Federal Rules, however, nowhere define the standard of proof the court must observe in resolving these questions.

We are therefore guided by our prior decisions regarding admissibility determinations that hinge on preliminary factual questions. We have traditionally required that these matters be established by a preponderance of proof. Evidence is placed before the jury when it satisfies the technical requirements of the evidentiary Rules, which embody certain legal and policy determinations. The inquiry made by a court concerned with these matters is not whether the proponent of the evidence wins or loses his case on the merits, but whether the evidentiary Rules have been satisfied. Thus, the evidentiary standard is unrelated to the burden of proof on the substantive issues, be it a criminal case . . . or a civil case. The preponderance standard ensures that before admitting evidence, the court will have found it more likely than not that the technical issues and policy concerns addressed by the Federal Rules of Evidence have been afforded due consideration. As in *Lego v. Twomey*, 404 U.S. 477, 488, 92 S. Ct. 619, 626, 30 L. Ed. 2d 618 (1972), we find "nothing to suggest that admissibility rulings have been unreliable or otherwise wanting in quality because not based on some higher standard." We think that our previous decisions in the area resolve the matter. . . . Therefore, we hold that when the preliminary facts relevant to Rule 801(d)(2)(E) are disputed, the offering party must prove them by a preponderance of the evidence.[3]

Petitioner argues that in determining whether a conspiracy exists and whether the defendant was a member of it, the court must look only to independent evidence — that is, evidence other than the statements sought to be admitted.

Petitioner concedes that Rule 104, on its face, appears to allow the court to make the preliminary factual determinations relevant to Rule 801(d)(2)(E) by considering any evidence it wishes, unhindered by considerations of admissibility. Brief for Petitioner 27. That would seem to many to be the end of the matter. Congress has decided that courts may consider hearsay in making these factual determinations. Out-of-court statements made by anyone, including putative co-conspirators, are often hearsay. Even if they are, they may be considered, *Glasser* and the boot-strapping rule notwithstanding. But petitioner nevertheless argues that the bootstrapping rule, as most Courts of Appeals have construed it, survived this apparently unequivocal change in the law unscathed and that Rule 104, as applied to the admission of co-conspirator's statements, does not mean what it says. We disagree.

Petitioner claims that Congress evidenced no intent to disturb the bootstrapping rule, which was embedded in the previous approach, and we should not find that Congress altered the rule without affirmative evidence so indicating. It would be extra-ordinary to require legislative history to *confirm* the plain meaning of Rule 104. The Rule on its face allows the trial judge to consider any evidence whatsoever, bound only by the rules of privilege. We think that the Rule is sufficiently clear that to the extent that it is inconsistent with petitioner's interpretation of *Glasser* and *Nixon*, the Rule prevails. (Footnote omitted.)

Nor do we agree with petitioner that this construction of Rule 104(a) will allow courts to admit hearsay statements without any credible proof of the conspiracy, thus fundamentally changing the nature of the co-conspirator exception. Petitioner starts with the proposition that co-conspirators' out-of-court statements are deemed unreli-

---

[3] (Court's original footnote 1) We intimate no view on the proper standard of proof for questions falling under Federal Rule of Evidence 104(b) (conditional relevancy). We also decline to address the circumstances in which the burden of coming forward to show that the proffered evidence is inadmissible is appropriately placed on the nonoffering party. . . . Finally, we do not express an opinion on the proper order of proof that trial courts should follow in concluding that the preponderance standard has been satisfied in an ongoing trial.

able and are inadmissible, at least until a conspiracy is shown. Since these statements are unreliable, petitioner contends that they should not form any part of the basis for establishing a conspiracy, the very antecedent that renders them admissible.

Petitioner's theory ignores two simple facts of evidentiary life. First, out-of-court statements are only presumed unreliable. The presumption may be rebutted by appropriate proof. . . . Second, individual pieces of evidence, insufficient in themselves to prove a point, may in cumulation prove it. The sum of an evidentiary presentation may well be greater than its constituent parts. Taken together, these two propositions demonstrate that a piece of evidence, unreliable in isolation, may become quite probative when corroborated by other evidence. A per se rule barring consideration of these hearsay statements during preliminary fact finding is not therefore required. Even if out-of-court declarations by co-conspirators are presumptively unreliable, trial courts must be permitted to evaluate these statements for their evidentiary worth as revealed by the particular circumstances of the case. Courts often act as fact finders, and there is no reason to believe that courts are any less able to properly recognize the probative value of evidence in this particular area. The party opposing admission has an adequate incentive to point out the shortcomings in such evidence before the trial court finds the preliminary facts. If the opposing party is unsuccessful in keeping the evidence from the fact finder, he still has the opportunity to attack the probative value of the evidence as it relates to the substantive issue in the case.

We think that there is little doubt that a co-conspirator's statements could themselves be probative of the existence of a conspiracy and the participation of both the defendant and the declarant in the conspiracy. Petitioner's case presents a paradigm. The out-of-court statements of Lonardo indicated that Lonardo was involved in a conspiracy with a "friend." The statements indicated that the friend had agreed with Lonardo to buy a kilogram of cocaine and to distribute it. The statements also revealed that the friend would be at the hotel parking lot, in his car, and would accept the cocaine from Greathouse's car after Greathouse gave Lonardo the keys. Each one of Lonardo's statements may itself be unreliable, but taken as a whole, the entire conversation between Lonardo and Greathouse was corroborated by independent evidence. The friend, who turned out to be petitioner, showed up at the prearranged spot at the prearranged time. He picked up the cocaine, and a significant sum of money was found in his car. On these facts, the trial court concluded, in our view correctly, that the Government had established the existence of a conspiracy and petitioner's participation in it.

[5]   Rules Comparison

Compare FRE 801(d)(1) and (2) with the following state rules:

Arizona Rule of Evidence 801(d)(1)

(d) Statements which are not hearsay. A statement is not hearsay if:

(1) Prior statement by witness. The declarant testifies at the trial or hearing and is subject to cross-examination concerning the statement, and the statement is (A) inconsistent with his testimony, or (B) consistent with his

testimony and is offered to rebut an express or implied charge against him of recent fabrication or improper influence or motive, or (C) one of identification of a person made after perceiving him.

Michigan Rule of Evidence 801(d)(2)

(2) Admission by party-opponent. The statement is offered against a party and is (A) his own statement, in either his individual or a representative capacity, except statements made in connection with a guilty plea to a misdemeanor motor vehicle violation, . . . or (B) a statement of which he has manifested his adoption or belief in its truth, subject to the rule announced in *People v. Bobo*, 390 Mich. 355 (1973), or (C) a statement by a person authorized by him to make a statement concerning the subject, or . . . (E) a statement by a co-conspirator of a party during the course and in furtherance of the conspiracy on independent proof of the conspiracy.

[D] Review Problems

Problem #10-36: Bribery

Mayor Maitland is prosecuted for taking a bribe from several contractors through their attorney, Gabe. At his trial, Maitland testifies he didn't take any bribe and he wasn't even in the same room with Gabe at any time on the evening in question.

1. On cross-examination, can defendant Maitland be asked "Didn't you state in your deposition, 'I was with Gabe only a short time that evening'?" If this question is permissible, will the statement be admissible only to impeach Maitland or for the truth of its contents as well? Why?

2. On cross-examination, counsel implied that Maitland recently manufactured his assertion that he did not spend any time with Gabe that evening. On redirect examination, Maitland was asked, "What, if anything, did you do later that evening after the party?" Maitland answered, "I told my wife that that crook Gabe was at the party and I only yelled hello and exchanged the usual pleasantries briefly from the adjacent room." Is this answer permissible? Why?

3. Maitland is also asked on redirect, "Who, if anyone, was with Gabe?" Maitland answered: "When I saw them, I told my friend Steve, 'Hey, that's my opponent's campaign manager, Ted Souvlos, with Gabe! Strange.'" Admissible? Explain.

Problem #10-37: Dognappers

Midnight Blue, a black labrador retriever, was stolen from his doghouse by several professional dognappers. Two months after the theft, a neighbor, Mr. Rogers, positively identified the dognappers in a lineup. At the dognappers' trial, Mr. Rogers testified for the prosecution. Can he be asked about his identification of the dognappers at the lineup? Explain.

Problem #10-38: Translator

The Arturo Gonzalez Mortgage Broker Company, headquartered in Mexico City, but with branches in New York and San Antonio, was charged with numerous violations of securities regulations. A translator for the president of the company stated at a news conference, "President Gonzalez is confident that the company will be cleared of all charges. He has fired the disloyal member of the board of trustees, Mr. Perdido, who set him up on the financial transactions in question." Are the statements by the translator admissible against the president and the company? Explain.

Problem #10-39: Free Agent

A disputed issue at trial was whether Barry was acting as the agent of employer Giant Bread when there was an accident involving the Giant Bread truck that Barry was driving. The truck barreled into the living room of the MacKenzie family, along with 10,000 loaves of Giant Bread. Luckily, no one was hurt. Several hours after the accident, Barry told the police officer preparing an accident investigation report, "I am the agent of Giant Bread and the accident was all my fault. The bread shifted and I turned around to look. Boom, there I was in their living room. I was much better at my other job." Are Barry's statements admissible against Giant Bread in a subsequent action brought by the MacKenzies against the company? Why?

Problem #10-40: Just a Guess

Margaret was the Chief Operating Officer for Lorton's Limo Service. After being informed that car No. 8 was in an accident for the third time that month, Margaret threw up her hands and exclaimed for everyone in the office to hear, "Car No. 8 is Willie's car, and I'll bet the accident was our fault because he was probably drinking again." Are Margaret's statements admissible at trial in an action against Lorton's Limo Service? Why?

Problem #10-41: Confession

Catarina and Bob made an elaborate plan to kill Catarina's husband, but were caught before they could carry it out. As the police put the handcuffs on them, Bob blurted out, "Dear, I didn't think this plan of ours about your *$#@(% husband had any holes in it; these cops must have been very, very lucky to catch us."

1. Are Bob's statements admissible against Bob in a later trial for conspiracy to commit murder? Why?

2. If Catarina is tried separately, are Bob's statements admissible against Catarina? Explain.

§ 10.04   HEARSAY EXCEPTIONS [FRE 803, 804]

[A]   Introduction

Some out-of-court utterances fall within the definition of hearsay and do not qualify either as a special prior statement of a witness or as a party admission. This type of evidence may still survive a hearsay objection, however, by falling within one of many express exceptions.

Under the FRE, the exceptions are divided into two main groups — those in which the declarant's availability is irrelevant to whether the evidence is admissible (FRE 803), and those in which the declarant must be unavailable to testify (FRE 804).

The exceptions under FRE 803 are predicated on the reliability of the hearsay statements. Hearsay statements are presumed reliable, for example, in situations where there is little opportunity for fabrication (e.g., spontaneous statements) or minimal incentive for fabrication (e.g., statements made for the purpose of medical diagnosis or treatment or statements that are a part of regular business records). Other statements are considered reliable because of the regularity with which they are made and that they are regularly relied on by others to be accurate (e.g., business and public records, market reports).

While reliability also is a linchpin of admissibility under FRE 804, the hearsay exceptions requiring the unavailability of the declarant have the added rationale of necessity — only if the declarant is unavailable and cannot testify about the event will hearsay be permitted as a substitute. This category is narrower than FRE 803, given the preference for live testimony.

Illustration

Desdemona, age 14, was struck by a hit-and-run driver as she walked in her neighborhood. She was uninjured, but very frightened. When her mother arrived home one hour later, Desdemona exclaimed, "Mom, it was a blue pick-up truck that struck me!" At a subsequent trial of the driver, Desdemona's mother intends to testify about Desdemona's statement. Can her mother testify?

Answer: Desdemona's statement about the pick-up truck is technically hearsay. It reflects all of the hearsay elements: It is (1) out-of-court (uttered in Desdemona's house prior to trial); (2) a statement (an assertion that a blue pick-up truck struck her); (3) by a declarant (Desdemona); and (4) offered for the truth of the matter asserted (that a certain blue truck committed the hit-and-run). It is admissible hearsay, however, if the statement falls within a hearsay exception. In this particular instance, Desdemona's statement may qualify as an excited utterance. It was made under the stress of excitement caused by a startling event and the statement related to that event. (*See* FRE 803(2)). If it is an excited utterance, Desdemona's mother can testify to the statement even if Desdemona is present and able to testify, since unavailability of the declarant is not required for the exceptions under FRE 803.

[B]　Problems — Availability of Declarant Immaterial [FRE 803]

[1]　Present Sense Impressions, Excited Utterances, Present State of Mind, Statements Made for Purposes of Medical Diagnosis, and Prior Recollection Recorded

These hearsay exceptions are all grounded in sufficient indicia of reliability to warrant excepting them from the general hearsay exclusion. FRE 803(1), (2), and (3), present sense impressions, excited utterances and state of mind, in particular, share a common thread — they are made spontaneously, without the time for reflection or thought. Further, present sense impressions and state of mind observations also are close in time to the event or activity in question, negating the need to remember. The spontaneity for excited utterances is thought to be the presence of excitement, although this exception has been criticized for the same reason — excitement is thought to foster inaccuracy even though it might be stilling reflection at the same time. The longstanding history of this exception has overcome such objections. Statements made for medical diagnosis or treatment seems to stand out from the others in this group because these statements can be in the past-tense, "backwards looking." Their reliability is ensured by their purpose — to obtain accurate diagnosis and treatment from the information provided by the declarant.

These hearsay exceptions have an added dimension lying outside evidentiary boundaries — the Constitution. Even if statements are admissible under the hearsay rules, their admissibility in a criminal trial against an accused must still comply with the Sixth Amendment Confrontation Clause. While the next chapter will review the Confrontation Clause in depth — particularly since new life has been breathed into it after *Crawford v. Washington*, 541 U.S. 36 (2004) — it is useful to think about whether the evidence is being offered by the government against a criminal defendant, particularly for these exceptions and the business records exceptions.

The scope of these provisions is often ambiguous. For example, how long can excitement from an incident last to support an exception under FRE 803(2)? Also, under FRE 803(3), does a statement about planning on meeting another person come in for only the declarant's intent or both the declarant and the person(s) the declarant aims to meet? These issues are not directly answered by the rules, and require interpretation.

Problem #10-42: Hoops II

Bari is charged with the murder of Kim "Hoops" Henderson. At trial, the prosecution calls Kim's neighbor, Bernie, to testify. Bernie says that, one hour before Kim's disappearance, his 15-year-old son Josh calmly stated, "Pops, there goes Hoops Henderson with her basketball to the park again. She is with Bari." Can Bernie testify about his son Josh's statement? Explain.

Problem #10-43: Demoted

A sales representative for a pharmaceutical firm was demoted for "weak perfor-mance." The rep brought suit, citing stellar company reviews, strong client recom-mendations, and large amounts of business the rep had done on the company's behalf. The firm offered in evidence in-house company memos explaining why the company was demoting the plaintiff, calling the memos present-sense impressions under FRE 803(1). Admissible hearsay? Explain.

Problem #10-44: Arson Redux

A witness for the prosecution in an arson case testifies that as she was watching television, she stated to her husband, "Isaac, it smells like kerosene around here, don't you think?" (The house caught fire moments later.) Is this statement admissible through a hearsay exception? If this statement is excluded from trial, what is the most likely reason why?

Problem #10-45: Slip and Fall

Plaintiff sued defendant Grocery Store. Plaintiff is on the witness stand, testifying on direct examination.

PLAINTIFF'S ATTORNEY: What happened on March 1, 1993, at 3:00 p.m.?

A: I slipped and fell in the defendant's grocery store.

PLAINTIFF'S ATTORNEY: What occurred immediately following your fall?

A: A clerk of some sort rushed up to me and stated, "Hey, that garbage has been on the floor for a couple of hours, let me help you up."

DEFENDANT'S ATTORNEY: Objection. Hearsay.

1. What ruling and why? *overrule*

2. What is the relevance of the Advisory Committee's Note to Federal Rule of Evidence 803(1)? *agency / or 803(2)*

PLAINTIFF'S ATTORNEY: What else, if anything, occurred?

A: I heard a bystander, who I did not know and have not seen since, say, "Look Hernando, that man just slipped and hit his head hard on the floor!"

DEFENDANT'S ATTORNEY: Objection. Hearsay.

3. What ruling and why? *unk.*

PLAINTIFF'S ATTORNEY: How did you feel at approximately 7:00 p.m. that night?

A: I felt achy all over, like my bones were not glued together very well.

DEFENDANT'S ATTORNEY: Objection. Hearsay.

4. What ruling and why?

 x in court

A: I told my wife Susan that my skid-proof shoes did not stop me from falling over backwards on some junk left on the floor of the defendant's grocery store.

DEFENDANT'S ATTORNEY: Objection. Hearsay.

5. What ruling and why?

Problem #10-46: "So How Was YOUR Day?"

During her lunch hour, Amy witnessed a horrific car crash in which several people were seriously injured. Because Amy was shaken up after observing the carnage at close range, she left her investment banking job much earlier than usual. After an hour-long commute home, she still felt agitated. When she walked into the house, her sister, Emma, asked her about her day. Scarcely able to contain herself, Amy said, "I saw a woman and two youngsters practically killed by a guy who ran a red light! He went through the intersection long after the light had turned red. It made me sick."

The people injured in the crash subsequently brought suit and Emma is asked to testify about Amy's statement. Amy is available to testify, but prefers not to recall the incident. Is Emma permitted to testify to Amy's statement? Explain.

Problem #10-47: "No Breaks"

Pamela Plaintiff files suit against Erik Defendant, claiming that Erik negligently caused an automobile accident. Erik took the witness stand on his own behalf. During the course of his testimony, Erik stated, "Just as I was preparing to stop at the red light, I yelled to my wife, Marge, who was in the passenger seat, 'Honey, I have no brakes!'"

Is this statement an admission under FRE 801(d)(2)? Explain.

Problem #10-48: New York State of Mind

Bo is charged with murdering Vince in upstate New York. At trial, William testified for the defense. William stated that during a conversation with Bo one week before Vince mysteriously disappeared, Bo had stated:

1. "I like Vince." *803(3)*

2. "As a matter of fact, Vince was my best friend last year." *803(3)*

3. "I think I'll pay Vince a visit tomorrow to tell him how I feel."

4. "Vince told me, 'Bo, I'm going out of town in a couple of days to go fishing with Fred.'"

Are any of these statements admissible hearsay? Explain.

Problem #10-49: Who Shot J.R.?

Harry Hogan is charged with attempted murder after allegedly shooting and seriously injuring J.R. At trial, a government witness, Landon, testified about the events on the evening of April 26, 1993, when J.R. was shot.

PROSECUTOR: What happened at approximately 7 p.m. on April 26, 1993?

A: (1) J.R. told me he was going to go to Hogan's house that night to drink some beers; (2) J.R. told me he had visited Hogan for the three previous nights as well; (3) J.R. said he's feeling kind of depressed and that his head hurts; (4) J.R. said he had twisted his knee the week before in a touch football game and wanted to know if I had any aspirin or pain reliever to give to him.

DEFENSE COUNSEL: Objection to the entire answer. Motion to strike.

What ruling and why? (Consider each of the four parts of Landon's testimony separately.)

Problem #10-50: Bella with a Twist (a.k.a. Bella II)

Bella is charged with murdering Dan at the Cotton Club Dance Hall on June 13th at 2 a.m. She claims mistaken identity — she was in a different city on the night in question. On rebuttal, the prosecution offers Farquahr to testify, "Dan told me on June 12th that he and Bella were going to meet at the Cotton Club later that evening."

Is Dan's statement admissible hearsay? Explain.

Problem #10-51: Food Poisoning

During the busy afternoon rush hour, Suzy became very sick. She was quickly transported by ambulance to the Healthwise Hospital, located downtown. On the way, Suzy managed to tell the emergency medical technician in the ambulance that "I started feeling dizzy and faint after I had the lobster special at Ernie's Beef and Beer Joint; I'm sure it is food poisoning because Ernie's chefs are careless and do not cook the food as thoroughly as they should."

Suzy subsequently brings suit against Ernie's. She wishes to introduce her prior statements to the emergency medical technician. Which of Suzy's statements, if any, are admissible hearsay?

Problem #10-52: All Within the Family

As the family sat around the dinner table, the father informed the mother that their eight-year-old son "has a bad cold and needs some cold medication." If this statement is offered at trial to prove that the son had a bad cold at that time, should it be admitted? Why?

Problem #10-53: Child Abuse

Little Joey, age 6, complained to his mother one morning about "all of the things the babysitter did to me two days ago." His mom, Rachel, took little Joey to Dr. Susan Barkin, who asked Joey about the incident. Joey described sex acts that the babysitter allegedly performed. Are Joey's statements to Rachel or Dr. Barkin hearsay? Explain.

Problem #10-54: Iggy

Jane is prosecuted for murder after allegedly participating in a drug deal that went sour. At trial, the government informant, Iggy, testified that Jane told him to call a certain telephone number for the drugs. That phone number linked Jane to the victim. Iggy wrote down the phone number two hours after learning about it. At trial, Iggy testified on direct examination:

PROSECUTOR: Iggy, what was the phone number that Jane gave to you?

DEFENSE COUNSEL: Objection. Hearsay.

1. What ruling and why?

A: I don't remember what the phone number was; it has been fourteen months since Jane gave it to me.

PROSECUTOR: Is there anything that might refresh your recollection?

A: Possibly.

> [At this point, the prosecutor asked the clerk to mark for identification purposes the piece of paper on which Iggy wrote down the phone number in question. The prosecutor then showed it to opposing counsel and asked for permission from the judge to approach the witness.]

PROSECUTOR: Iggy, showing you what has been marked as government's Exhibit #8 for identification purposes, would you please read it silently to yourself?

DEFENSE COUNSEL: Objection. Once the witness is unable to remember factual observations under Federal Rule of Evidence 612, counsel cannot pursue the matter further.

2. Is defense counsel correct?

> [The prosecutor continued to question the witness after first taking back into her possession Exhibit #8 for identification purposes.]

PROSECUTOR: Iggy, is your memory now refreshed?

A: Sheesh, I'm afraid not. There is probably nothing that could make me remember what happened fourteen months ago.

PROSECUTOR: Iggy, handing you once again government's Exhibit #8 for identification purposes, do you recognize it?

A: Yes.

PROSECUTOR: What is it?

A: It's the piece of paper with the phone number you just asked me about.

PROSECUTOR: How do you recognize it?

A: I wrote the phone number down; it is my handwriting and I remember writing it.

PROSECUTOR: Is Exhibit #8 for identification purposes in substantially the same condition as it was when you wrote it down?

A: Yes.

PROSECUTOR: I now offer government's Exhibit #8 for identification purposes in evidence, Your Honor.

DEFENSE COUNSEL: Objection. Hearsay.

3. What ruling and why?

PROSECUTOR: Iggy, at what time did you write down the phone number?

A: Oh, about two hours after Jane gave it to me — when it was still pretty fresh in my memory and I knew that what I wrote down was accurate.

PROSECUTOR: I re-offer government's Exhibit #8 for identification purposes in evidence, Your Honor.

4. What ruling and why?

5. If the exhibit is admissible, does the jury get to view it? Why? What's the reasoning behind this part of the rule?

6. Suppose Iggy did not write down the number himself. Instead, if Iggy had looked at a phone number written down by someone else immediately after speaking with Jane and had remarked, "Yeah, that's it, that's the phone number Jane gave to me," would the exhibit still be admissible? Explain.

Problem #10-55: Hurricane

After a hurricane, Stanley's house suffered extensive damage. Stanley promptly made a claim for the damage, including a large amount for ruined personal property. At a trial on the issue of the value of the goods destroyed, Stanley could not remember the amounts he had paid for the goods. Stanley kept a ledger book, however, in which he wrote down precisely what he had paid for each of the goods. He did so because the purchases were then "still fresh in my mind; I had remembered the exact price."

1. Can Stanley's memory be refreshed with the ledger book? Would use of the book to refresh his memory constitute a hearsay violation?

2. Can the ledger book be offered in evidence? (Assume that the book is *not* a business record.) Explain.

[2] Business Records

Business records have a long history of admissibility, with a strong foundation in the common law preceding the FRE. There are two types of records — public and private — and separate exceptions for each. Private records require a person with knowledge to make a regular record about a regular business activity at or near the time of the activity or transaction and, based on a judge's determination, show that the record is trustworthy and kept within a business chain of other employees. Public records by persons acting within their government jobs are presumptively trustworthy because of the need for reliable government records.

The premise for the admissibility of both public and private records, therefore, is their reliability. Here, that reliability is in part derived from the regularity of the records — in being made and in being relied on by others for the smooth operation of the marketplace. The FRE recognize, however, that not all business-related records are indeed reliable. If a private record lacks indicia of reliability because of where it is found, the condition it is in, or whether there is a strong motive for bias by the maker, such as records prepared for litigation, then the court is authorized to exclude it.

In addition, business records can be seen as a pragmatic exception. The disruption to business activities would be significant if live testimony was required by the record-maker every time a business transaction or activity was called into question. Further, few people would remember business activities from years before, let alone the preceding months or weeks, even if transactions or activities were recorded.

Private records are considered first below; then public records. It is useful to compare and contrast the two categories.

Does the following illustration of laying a foundation for business records comport with FRE 803(6)? Explain.

MARYLAND — DISTRICT OF COLUMBIA — VIRGINIA CRIMINAL PRACTICE INSTITUTE TRIAL MANUAL (2-5, 2-9 (1964))

2.02 Introducing Business Records

1. Your Honor, I would like to have this instrument marked as defense Exhibit #1 for identification.

2. State your name.

3. Where do you reside, [Mr./Ms. Witness]?

4. And what is your occupation?

5. Where are you employed?

6. What is the nature of your employer's business?

7. And what is the nature of your work there?

8. Were you so employed there on [date in question]?

9. Now, as the [position title], do you have the responsibility of keeping the records concerning [subject matter]?

10. What is the method utilized for keeping these records?

11. Is this followed with respect to every [entry] [patient, etc.]?

12. I show you defendant's Exhibit #1 for identification, purporting to be [document title], and ask you whether these are the original records which you have kept in your position?

13. Were these records in your custody on [date]?

14. And were they in your custody prior to your bringing them to court this morning?

15. Where were they kept?

16. Were the entries made herein made shortly after the transaction they record?

17. Who provided the information contained therein?

18. Was it his [or her] duty to collect this data and pass it on to you?

19. And were these entries made in the usual and ordinary course of business?

20. To the best of your knowledge, are they true and correct?

Then move to admit defense Exhibit #1 for identification purposes in evidence.

Problem #10-56: Schultz's Security Company

Schultz's Security Company supplied armed security guards to most of the grocery and convenience stores in the city. One night, Smitty, the night watchman at Furnald's Midnight Grocery and an employee of Schultz's Security Company, spotted a prowler trying to break into the back of the store. Smitty immediately sent a message to the company dispatcher via walkie-talkie. The dispatcher relayed the message to the chief of security's secretary. She took notes and gave them to Schultz's secretary to type them up in the form of a report, which is the company's customary practice. After the incident, Smitty examined the scene and took down the statement of the supermarket owner about what had happened, also a company practice. The supermarket owner's statements were incorporated into Smitty's report. The entire record, including the supermarket owner's statements, is offered at a trial involving the attempted break-in.

Is Smitty's report a business record under the FRE? Explain.

Problem #10-57: Square Hip

Hipnote Law School, a private university, sues Jim Square for theft of services after Square enrolled at the law school on fraudulent grounds. To prove the enrollment of Square in the school, Hipnote offers an employee of Student Services as a witness.

PLAINTIFF'S ATTORNEY: Would you state your name for the record?

A: Shira Stone.

PLAINTIFF'S ATTORNEY: Why are you here today, Shira?

A: To testify about the records of Hipnote Law School.

PLAINTIFF'S ATTORNEY: Are you familiar with Hipnote Law School's records?

A: Yes.

PLAINTIFF'S ATTORNEY: How are you familiar with them?

A: I am the Assistant Coordinator at Hipnote's Student Services Office, and although I am not the records custodian, I do work with the records people fairly often.

DEFENDANT'S ATTORNEY: Objection. A records custodian is required to lay the foundation, Your Honor.

1. What ruling and why?

PLAINTIFF'S ATTORNEY: What kind of records are kept at Student Services?

A: We keep records of student registration.

PLAINTIFF'S ATTORNEY: How are such records related to your business at student services?

A: It is a regular activity in our department to keep such records.

PLAINTIFF'S ATTORNEY: [After having the exhibit marked for identification and shown to opposing counsel] I show you, Shira, what has been marked as plaintiff's Exhibit #3 for identification purposes. What is it?

A: It is the registration form of Jim Square.

PLAINTIFF'S ATTORNEY: Who made it?

A: I don't know; it could have been any one of four different student services employees. We all work together in compiling information on the receipt of tuition payments, the pre-registration information, and the registration data, and I'm not sure which one of the others filled this one out.

PLAINTIFF'S ATTORNEY: I now offer plaintiff's Exhibit #3 for identification purposes in evidence.

DEFENDANT'S ATTORNEY: Objection. (1) The witness does not know who made the record and (2) the predicate does not fulfill the requirements of Federal Rule of Evidence 803(6).

2. What ruling and why?

Problem #10-58: Fill 'Er Up

Johnny was a gas station attendant at the local Phipps 46 gasoline station. One evening, at approximately 9:00 p.m., Johnny was robbed by two men wearing masks. It is the policy of Phipps to record criminal activity at the station with particularity in the company logs. In compliance with the company's requirement, Johnny wrote down in the company logs a detailed description of the robbery. Two men were apprehended and charged with the crime. Can either the prosecution or the defendants offer Johnny's entry in the gas station logs as business records? Explain.

Problem #10-59: The Diary

Alan Tomas, a sophomore at the University of North Shebokan, keeps a diary. In the diary, Alan routinely records the bets made by other students with him and the amounts Alan paid out as part of his campus gambling operation. Tomas's gambling ring is discovered and he is dismissed from school. Tomas sued to be reinstated. If the case goes to trial, can the defendant school offer the diary as a business record? Explain.

Problem #10-60: Blood Tests

The Jacksonville Memorial Hospital conducted lab blood tests on Janice Boston, shipping the actual blood work to QTest Labs, located nearby. QTest Labs stamps on all of its test results, "Not to be used in a court of law as part of litigation; for medical purposes only." The test results suggested Boston suffered from diabetes. The treating physician, Dr. Greff, missed the information and Janice nearly died. Totally incapacitated, Janice sued Dr. Greff. (She settled with the hospital.) Janice wishes to offer the lab tests in evidence. Are the tests admissible hearsay?

Problem #10-61: Expert Opinion

A twelve-year-old girl, Sally, was bitten on the hand by defendant's dog and treated for cuts. A week later, the injury worsened, and Sally went to the emergency room of the nearby hospital, St. Marks. Dr. Estelle Benson examined Sally prior to making the following entry in her report: "A twelve-year-old girl, Sally, presented with a swollen hand (evidence of a dog bite), an infection surrounding the bite, and alopecia. Based upon my experience, observations, and tests, it is likely that the dog bite suffered by Sally caused her alopecia." Is this statement a proper part of a business record?

Problem #10-62: Schmydlap v. Off Track Railroad

Plaintiff Schmydlap brings suit against the Off Track Railroad after one of Off Track's trains ran over her foot.

1. At trial, can Off Track offer an accident report prepared by the train's engineer, Casey, now deceased, about the accident? (Note: Accident reports are routinely made by Off Track after every accident.)

2. Schmydlap offers the report of a physician who evaluated Schmydlap's foot injuries for the purpose of testifying at trial. Is the report admissible? Explain.

3. Plaintiff offers a hospital report prepared by the emergency room of Community General Hospital, which diagnosed plaintiff as suffering from severe shock as well as a foot injury. Is the report hearsay? Is it admissible?

4. Plaintiff offers the rainfall records of the National Weather Bureau. The records indicate that it was a bright sunny day without any precipitation at the time of the accident. Are these records admissible?

5. The engineer of the train, Casey, was given a Breathalyzer test immediately following the accident. Prior to offering the Breathalyzer results at trial,

plaintiff offers a Breathalyzer decal, certifying that the machine was tested as required by law and found to be accurate. The decal also states the machine was calibrated at the required times. Is this decal admissible?

6. Plaintiff offers the report of a latent fingerprint examination that concluded that the engineer's fingerprints were on a bottle of whiskey found underneath the engineer's seat on the train. Is the report admissible?

7. Plaintiff offers the results of an Interstate Commerce Commission (ICC) report containing conclusions that the engineer was at fault in the accident. Is the ICC report admissible?

8. A State Highway Patrol Officer, Ann Sitosky, prepared an accident report on a two-car crash that occurred during rush hour. The officer included the statement of a bystander, who said, "I can't believe the lady in the Buick made a left turn after the light had turned red!" In a subsequent personal injury action, can the report, including the bystander's statement, be introduced into evidence? (Assume no state accident report privilege applies.)

Problem #10-63: Six-Mile-Island

Several employees injured in an accident at a nuclear power plant bring suit against the power plant company. At trial, the plaintiffs offer the report prepared by an investigator of the Occupation, Safety, and Health Administration (OSHA) of the federal government. After numerous interviews with those persons involved with the nuclear plant and several trips to the accident site, the investigator concluded that the accident was caused by the negligence of the defendant company.

1. Is this report admissible in the suit brought by the employees?

2. Would a birth certificate of a person injured in an accident be admissible?

3. Would the OSHA report or birth certificate be admissible if offered by the government in a parallel criminal action against several power plant employees? Explain.

Problem #10-64: Chemist

Becca is a chemist for the police department. Her job calls for her to test substances to determine whether they are illegal narcotics. After every test, she writes up a copious and detailed report of her findings. Becca usually testifies at trial about these conclusions. On one occasion, however, she was sick with the flu and unable to attend the trial. Can the prosecution use her report to prove that the substance in question was an illegal narcotic? Explain.

Problem #10-65: More Records

Which of the following would be admissible as business records? Explain your answer.

1. A Merrill Lynch credit report.

2. An IBM executive's daily appointment register.

3. Letters sent by a Ralston-Purina executive to business associates.

4. A bank teller's list of serial numbers of the currency the teller disbursed on a particular day.

5. A grocery list kept by the same bank teller, maintained on a weekly basis.

6. The notes taken by a *Wall Street Journal* reporter for a story.

7. The occasional notes taken by a radio talk show host.

8. An invoice received by a customer of Auto King for four new tires purchased by the customer. Is the "lack of trustworthiness" clause in FRE 803(8) intended to apply to only section (c) of 803(8) or to sections (a) and (b) as well?

[3] Other Hearsay Exceptions

Some of the hearsay exceptions covered below are not as widely used as the ones previously covered, such as business records. These exceptions are important, nonetheless, and all have particular indicia of reliability that allow for their avoidance of hearsay exclusion. Several of the exceptions appear to be related to each other, either for their authoritativeness, their form, or other basis.

Problem #10-66: Bonfire and Vanity

Slooter, a stockbroker, was sued by a client, Roy. Roy claimed that Slooter, despite being asked to do so, failed to purchase 1,000 shares of Bonfire and Vanity, Inc., a new scientific beauty research firm. To prove damages, Roy offers a copy of the *New York Times* financial page on the day in question, listing the opening and closing prices of Bonfire and Vanity.

1. Is this newspaper listing admissible hearsay?

2. Roy also offers a copy of the New York City phone directory to show that the phone number Slooter is alleged to have dialed was the number of a rival brokerage house. Is the phone directory admissible hearsay?

Problem #10-67: Now That's a Knife

In a personal injury action for medical malpractice, Dr. Mia Surgeon is the defendant. An important issue is whether Dr. Surgeon used the correct surgical equipment. The defense offered an expert, Dr. Susan Slandon, who testified that Surgeon used the appropriate equipment to perform the operation. On cross-examination, the opposing counsel wishes to question the witness about a passage from an authoritative treatise, *Jacobellis' Medical Guide*. The book indicates that the defendant selected improper equipment for the plaintiff's operation. Is this evidence hearsay? Explain.

Problem #10-68: Forgery

In a forgery prosecution of Danny Defendant, Danny offers a character witness, Meryl. Meryl testifies that Danny's reputation in the community is one of truthfulness and veracity. The prosecution objects, claiming that the evidence about Danny's reputation in the community is inadmissible hearsay. Do you agree?

Problem #10-69: Billionaire's Landing

Jim Lucasey, a billionaire of large physical proportions, dies of a heart attack. He leaves half of his estate to his wife, Eloise, and the other half to charitable organizations. In a subsequent proceeding, a woman named Jane Barnes steps forward, claiming to be his wife. Jane offers a marriage certificate in evidence in support of her claim.

1. Is this certificate hearsay? Is it admissible hearsay?

2. Later in the same hearing, a question arises as to whether Lucasey owned a particular piece of property located in Southern Illinois. Jane offers in evidence a deed to that property in Lucasey's name. Is the deed admissible?

3. In a surprising twist, a man shows up at the hearing claiming to be Jim Lucasey's long-lost son, Fred, from a prior marriage. The claim appears to be supported by an old family Bible. Fred's name had been written in it as one of the children of Jim and Suzannah Lucasey, Jim's first wife, who died suddenly at the age of 28. Is this Bible admissible hearsay?

4. As a result of Fred's appearance, a question arose as to precisely when Jim's last wife, Eloise Lucasey, died. A witness at trial testifies that Eloise Lucasey's tombstone states that she died on March 4, 1961. Is this statement hearsay? Is it admissible hearsay?

[C]   Hearsay Exceptions — Declarant Must Be Unavailable [FRE 804]

[1]   Introduction

Certain types of hearsay statements are admissible only if the declarant is unavailable to testify. These hearsay statements include former testimony, dying declarations (statements made under the belief of impending death), statements against the declarant's interest, and statements of personal or family history. This type of hearsay possesses indicia of reliability, but is not considered as reliable as the exceptions listed in FRE 803. This conclusion is reflected in FRE 804, which authorizes the exceptions only if the declarant is not available to testify. In such cases, these hearsay statements are admissible because they are necessary for a full and fair review of the facts at trial.

While necessity is a factor weighing in favor of inclusion of these statements, the "unavailability" hearsay exceptions also are based on guarantees of trustworthiness. For example, former testimony is not as valuable as "live" in-court testimony, but is still trustworthy because it was closer in time to the event in question, given under oath, and subject to examination by a party with a similar motive. A statement against interest is trustworthy because it is against the declarant's interest at the time the statement is made, and a person would not be expected to make such a potentially damaging statement if it were not true. "Dying declarations" are reliable because people are not expected to be duplicitous about the cause of their own apparent impending death, particularly if they are religious-minded. (The validity of the dying declaration rationale, however, has been the subject of considerable debate.)

[2] Requirement of Unavailability [FRE 804(a)]

Under FRE 804, a prerequisite to admissibility is the unavailability of the declarant. "Unavailability" does not so much refer to the physical unavailability of the person, but rather to the unavailability of the declarant's testimony. This means that a declarant can sometimes be unavailable even when physically present in court and testifying. A testifying witness will be unavailable, for example, if she has suffered from amnesia or a stroke and has no current memory of the event in question, or if he has become mentally ill and is unable to provide relevant evidence as a witness.

Illustration

Murray is indicted on charges of embezzling government funds. His wife, Leslie, is called to testify at trial for the government. She refuses to testify, invoking the adverse spousal testimony privilege. The prosecution then seeks to offer Leslie's preliminary hearing transcript as "former testimony." Is Leslie unavailable for the purposes of FRE 804(a)?

Answer: Invoking a claim of privilege renders a witness unavailable for the purposes of FRE 804(a) (*See* FRE 804(a)(1); FRE 804(a), Advisory Committee's Note). Thus, the prosecution has satisfied the threshold requirement that the witness is unavailable to testify. To admit the preliminary hearing transcript, the prosecution must show that the evidence meets the former testimony requirements and does not violate any of the other evidentiary exclusionary rules (e.g., the transcript must be authenticated and must not be unfairly prejudicial or subject to the rule excluding hearsay).

Problem #10-70: I'm a Toys R Them Kid

In a civil assault and battery action, Schmerd was called as the central eyewitness for the defense. At trial, Schmerd was asked to state his name for the record. He responded by singing the "I'm a Toys R Them Kid" theme song. It was soon discovered that Schmerd had been in and out of psychiatric hospitals for years. Y(M.I.)

1. Is Schmerd considered "unavailable to testify"? Explain.

2. Now assume that Schmerd instead had full mental capacity. If the defendant had given Schmerd an all-expenses-paid trip to Mexico to "avoid the stresses of having to testify at trial" and Schmerd was out of the jurisdiction at the time of trial, would he have been considered unavailable to testify?

N, no good faith

[3]   Former Testimony [FRE 804(b)(1)]

The prior testimony of an unavailable witness is not excluded as hearsay under FRE 804(b)(1), so long as several foundational requirements are met. The prior testimony must have been given under oath in a proceeding, such as in a deposition. The proceeding requirement is not expressly defined and depends on the totality of the circumstances. The more formality associated with the event, the more likely it will be considered a proceeding. In addition, the rule requires that the same party against whom the former testimony is now offered (or, in a civil case, the same party or a predecessor in interest), must have had an opportunity to examine the declarant in the prior proceeding. While such an examination often would be on cross-examination, it can be during other types of examination. To ensure fairness, the party against whom the testimony is now offered must have a similar motive to develop the testimony in both the earlier and current proceedings.

Illustration

Craig testified for the defendant in a civil forfeiture trial. The verdict was reversed on appeal and the case was retried by the same parties. Craig is deceased at the time of the retrial. If the defendant offers Craig's testimony from the first trial in evidence, will it be admissible as former testimony?

Answer: Craig's testimony in the first trial is precisely the kind of testimony admissible as former testimony under FRE 804(b)(1). It is testimony given by Craig in a prior proceeding between the same parties. The plaintiff in the earlier proceeding had an opportunity and similar motive to develop Craig's testimony on cross-examination. Consequently, the requirements of FRE 804(b)(1) are met.

Problem #10-71: Doctor Hooligan

During an investigation of Dr. Hooligan for the illegal distribution of steroids, an important government witness, Wayne, testified before the grand jury. Prior to trial, Wayne died. Can the government use Wayne's sworn grand jury testimony against Dr. Hooligan in a subsequent prosecution? Explain. x dying dec. b/c ③

Problem #10-72: Joseph Isuzu

The primary witness for the government in a homicide prosecution, Joseph Isuzu, tells a completely different story on the witness stand than he did in a sworn deposition immediately after the killing.

1. Is the deposition former testimony under FRE 804?

2. Instead of changing his story on the witness stand, suppose Joseph was simply unable to remember the events in question, saying, "I've had some serious memory problems recently; I've forgotten what happened." Can Joseph be impeached with the deposition as a prior inconsistent statement?

3. Can the deposition be admitted as former testimony on behalf of the government?

4. Would the deposition be admissible as former testimony if the defense, during the deposition, had declined to cross-examine Joseph?

Problem #10-73: Grand Jury

The government's confidential informant, Karen, testified before the grand jury, implicating the defendant in a conspiracy to unlawfully import firearms. Prior to trial, Karen is murdered.

> 1. Can the prosecution offer Karen's grand jury testimony in the defendant's subsequent conspiracy trial?

> 2. Assume the same facts as above, except that the confidential informant testified before the grand jury under a grant of immunity and was considered to be an "almost comically unreliable character." Is the grand jury testimony admissible if offered by the defense?

Problem #10-74: Peter v. Dieter

There was an auto accident in which one car was driven by Peter and the other by Dieter. George was a guest in Peter's car at the time of the accident, and Wendy the Witness observed the accident. Peter sues Dieter (*Peter v. Dieter*) and Wendy testifies at trial on Peter's behalf. In a later proceeding, George the Guest sues Dieter (*George v. Dieter*). Wendy the Witness has since moved far away and is unavailable to testify, so George offers Wendy's testimony from the first trial (*Peter v. Dieter*). Dieter objects. What ruling and why? Fred Defendant is tried on a felony charge of arson (*United States v. Fred*). Wilma the Witness testifies for the prosecution. In a subsequent case, Fred sues Goodhands Insurance Company to recover the losses caused by the fire (*Fred v. Goodhands Insurance Company*). Goodhands Insurance Company proves Wilma's death and offers a transcript of Wilma's former testimony in the arson trial. Fred objects. What ruling and why?

Problem #10-75: Conspiracy, Privilege, and Hearsay

The defendant, Wayne, is charged with conspiracy to distribute narcotics. Wayne offers the testimony of a co-conspirator, who promptly invokes his privilege against self-incrimination. The defendant then offers the testimony of the co-conspirator during his guilty plea proceeding. Is this testimony admissible under FRE 804(b)(1)?

[4] Dying Declarations [FRE 804(b)(2)]

So-called "dying declarations," statements made under the belief of impending death, are admitted on the premise that assertions about the circumstances of a person's impending death by a person who is knowingly dying possess sufficient indicia of reliability. That is, it is believed that a person who is dying will likely speak the truth about the circumstances of a perceived impending death. For statements to be admitted in evidence, though, the declarant need not ultimately die; the declarant need only believe at the time of the statement that he or she is dying. The declarant's belief can be determined by the circumstances, such as what others are telling the declarant, the declarant's own statements or the declarant's awareness of a deteriorating physical condition. The statements, however, must concern the cause or circumstances of the supposed impending death and not other areas of the declarant's life that might need closure. Even if this foundation is met, the statements are only admissible in homicide or civil cases.

Illustration

Alan was the victim of a gunshot wound after he investigated a noise near the rear door of his house. When his friend, Felicia, ran over to Alan after hearing the gunshot, Alan stated, "Felicia! I'm dying! George, the curious fellow from 14th Street, shot me. Goodbye." Alan then died. George is tried for murdering Alan. Can Felicia testify about Alan's statement for the prosecution?

Answer: Felicia can testify about Alan's statement. Although Alan's statement is hearsay, it is admissible as a dying declaration. Alan is dead and, therefore, unavailable to testify. Alan's statement was made while he believed he was going to die, and was about the cause or circumstances of his death. Thus, the requirements of FRE 804(b)(2) have been met. Furthermore, Alan's statement is offered in a prosecution for homicide, satisfying the "type of case" limitation of FRE 804(b)(2).

Problem #10-76: Next Time I'll Have Tea

Mrs. Halyard became violently ill after having her morning coffee. Later that afternoon, as she lay sick in her bed, she said to her maid, "It was my husband who poisoned me." Mrs. Halyard thereafter lapsed into a coma. One week later, without regaining consciousness, she died. If Mrs. Halyard's husband is prosecuted for murder, can the prosecution offer in evidence Mrs. Halyard's statement to the maid? Why?

Problem #10-77: I Wuz Robbed!

As Joan Plunkett lay dying of gunshot wounds after a robbery of her purse, she gasped, "I know my time is almost up, thanks to that gunshot wound. I want you to know that it was Pete Pardo who robbed me!" Joan then lapsed into a coma. The prosecution offers Joan's statement against Pete Pardo in his subsequent trial for robbery. Is Joan's statement admissible if offered by the prosecution? Explain.

Problem #10-78: Dr. Dr.

Wanda returns home only to find her husband Harry shot in the shoulder. Harry said, "Honey, I've been shot! Call Dr. Feelgood right away to fix me up. By the way, John Smith shot me." Harry then dies. In a subsequent prosecution of John Smith for murder, does the hearsay exception for dying declarations apply to Harry's statements to Wanda? Explain.

Problem #10-79: The X-Terminator

As Salvatore Bernstein knowingly lay dying, he stated, "It was Jackson the exterminator who shot me." Sal miraculously recovered and he brought suit against Jackson for his injuries. Can Sal offer his prior statement at trial? Why?

Problem #10-80: Mystery Death

Doug Defendant is charged with conspiracy to illegally influence the operations of an Employee Benefit Plan. A government witness states in his testimony to the grand jury, "I know he's going to kill me for saying this, but it was the defendant who tried to heist millions from the Employee Benefit Plan." The witness is later mysteriously killed. Can the government offer the witness's grand jury testimony at trial? Explain.

[5]   Statements Against Interest [FRE 804(b)(3)]

Statements against interest are different than admissions by a party opponent in at least three significant respects: (1) statements against interest require the declarant to be unavailable to testify — party admissions do not; (2) statements against interest do not have to have been made by parties or their agents — party admissions must have been; and (3) statements against interest must have been against the declarant's pecuniary, proprietary, civil, or penal interest at the time of utterance — no such limitation applies to party admissions.

Illustration

Gordon Pizatta, a well-known tax attorney, spoke at a tax seminar to several hundred attorneys. In his speech, Gordon admitted to conspiring with a large accounting firm to unlawfully understate the taxes of several Fortune 500 companies. Gordon later died of a heart attack while at a New York Rangers hockey game. In a subsequent suit by the Internal Revenue Service against the Fortune 500 companies whose incomes were understated, can Gordon's speech be offered as a statement against interest?

Answer: Gordon's statement likely would qualify as a statement against interest. As a result of his death, Gordon is unavailable to testify. At the time he made the statement, the utterance was certainly against his interest in avoiding civil liability (he exposed himself to liability for the underpayments), as well as his penal interest (he could be criminally charged for his conduct). A reasonable person in Gordon's position would not have made such a statement during a speech unless it were true.

Problem #10-81: I Own the Bank

George Watts tells the 4-H Club during a speech, "I own the Watts Savings and Loan Company." At the time he made the statement, Watts Savings and Loan was considered one of the most robust banks in the country. Two years later, everything unraveled for Mr. Watts and his bank, and Watts was charged with various counts of misconduct pertaining to the bank. In a subsequent civil suit against several of Mr. Watts's partners, Watts becomes unavailable to testify. The plaintiffs want to use Watts' statement conceding ownership. Is Watts's statement admissible as a statement against interest? Explain.

Problem #10-82: (Not) My Car, (Not) My Bridge

Ricky, who often suffered from delusions of grandeur, took some out-of-town visitors on a tour of his hometown, San Francisco. As they neared the Golden Gate

Bridge, Ricky exclaimed:

1. "Hey, that's the Golden Gate Bridge; I must confess I don't own it."

2. "While I'm at it, let me confess that I don't own this Jaguar convertible I'm driving, either; I just lease it."

Is either of Ricky's assertions a declaration against interest? Explain.

Problem #10-83: The Monastery

Katie Von Riggin, a billionaire, discovers Buddhism. She denounces her worldly possessions and boards a flight to Tibet, where she plans to spend the rest of her natural life in a monastery. As the plane takes off, she exclaims, "I must set the record straight before I begin my new life; I did pay Lurch to kill my poor departed husband and his lover."

Is this statement admissible if offered by the prosecution in Lurch's subsequent trial for murdering Katie's husband?

Problem #10-84: The Greatest

Harry was boasting one day in prison, "I'm the greatest killer of 'em all; no one can touch me, I float so fast. Why, I'm the one who killed that Jones fellow. Hah! They're prosecuting that poor goat, Spellman; what a joke." At Spellman's trial, Spellman wishes to offer Harry's statement after demonstrating that Harry is unavailable to testify.

Is Harry's statement admissible? What is the relevance of *Chambers v. Mississippi*, 410 U.S. 284 (1973)?

Problem #10-85: Larry Lives!

On a special edition of "Larry Lives!" (a popular television talk show), the famous guest is Fred Famous, known for being hip and cool. In a startling admission, Famous concedes, "Yes, it is true I had an affair with Cher's hairdresser's cousin, who is 35 years my senior. I also would act uncool by watching *Brady Bunch* reruns when I was with her because she thought it was sexy. I'm quite embarrassed to tell you these things, I must say." If Fred becomes unavailable to testify about these statements in a later trial, are the statements admissible as declarations against interest? Explain.

Problem #10-86: Whiny

Willie Whiny was asked whether he shot and injured his co-worker, Charley. Willie responded by stating, "Sure I shot the #$@@#!#%$%!$P*!$# guy! He was beating me up with a tire iron!" Assume that Willie is unavailable to testify. Is this statement a statement against interest? Is it self-serving or disserving? Should the court admit the whole statement, just the disserving part, or none of it?

Problem #10-87: Wally the Weasel

The defendant, Isaac, is charged with the possession with intent to distribute cocaine. Wally the Weasel, who had just pled guilty to 98 counts on a criminal indictment, told authorities that he would be able to help them because he had personal information that the defendant was, in fact, guilty. Soon thereafter, Wally disappears.

1. Are Wally's statements admissible against the defendant at trial?

2. If Isaac testifies that while in prison he was told by Willie, a fellow inmate, "Too bad you're going down for the count; I was the one who was going to sell all the coke to the government informant." Is Willie's statement admissible?

[6] Personal or Family History [FRE 804(b)(4)]

A special hearsay exception exists for statements concerning important personal or family milestones such as birth, adoption, marriage, divorce, ancestry, and the like.

Problem #10-88: Happy Birthday

Sharlene sought payment from her insurance company relating to her sister's death. At trial, Sharlene's counsel, Steven, asked her on direct examination, "What did your sister say was her date of birth?" The defense counsel, Lee, objected, stating, "That would be speculation, Your Honor. Her sister had no personal knowledge of her date of birth. Furthermore, it would be hearsay."

How would you respond if you were Sharlene's counsel?

[D] Attacking and Supporting the Credibility of the Declarant

Under FRE 806, a declarant's credibility can be attacked and supported almost as if the person had testified. Since declarants are effectively pseudo-witnesses, they are testifying without taking the witness stand — the weight of their testimony must be assessed by the jury through the usual methods of impeachment, despite the lack of opportunity to actually cross-examine the declarant.

Problem #10-89: "Yeah, he was there"

An issue at trial was whether the defendant was in the crowd of a free rock concert in downtown Greensboro. James was overheard at the concert saying, "Hey look, there goes the defendant, leaving the concert. He's almost jogging. Hmmm." If this statement is admitted under FRE 803(1), Present Sense Impression, can Sharon be offered by the defense to testify, "James has a reputation in the community for being untruthful. In fact, I saw him lie on his driver's license exam last year." Explain.

[E] Residual Exception

In 1997, the FRE were amended to combine the two residual hearsay clauses, 803(24) and 804(b)(5), into one rule. *See* Advisory Committee Note to FRE 807. Substantively, nothing was changed.

Problem #10-90: Old News

After its place of worship collapsed, the Church of Nazareth brought suit against the Smallstate Insurance Company seeking payment on an insurance policy. The insurance company claimed that the collapse resulted from noncompensable structural damage due to a fire 30 years earlier. The plaintiff Church claimed the collapse was caused by a lightning strike the day before. At trial, the plaintiff Church offered a 30-year-old newspaper article written and published at the time of the fire. The article indicated that the fire occurred behind the Church, without damaging the building.

Assume that the newspaper article is not an ancient document. Is the article admissible? On what grounds?

[F] Cases and Rules

[1] Miller v. Keating

United States Court of Appeals for the Third Circuit
754 F.2d 507 (3d Cir. 1885)

In *Miller v. Keating*, a statement made by an unknown declarant was offered at trial, which concerned an automobile accident. There was no evidence at trial showing that the declarant actually had personal knowledge of what had occurred or that the declarant was excited when he spoke. The Third Circuit Court of Appeals held that the statement was properly excluded.

> The district court admitted into evidence a statement, made by an unidentified declarant at the scene of an automobile accident, amounting to an accusation that the accident was the fault of plaintiff Carol Miller. The district judge admitted the statement as *"res gestae,"* without making reference to any of the hearsay exceptions in Fed.R.Evid. 803, or any findings of fact on the issue of admissibility. Fed.R.Evid. 104(a). We conclude that the district judge erred.

> On January 18, 1982, Carol Miller was driving her white Ford LTD east on U.S. Route 22, a limited access highway, near Easton, Pennsylvania. She carried a passenger named Annette Vay. It is undisputed that Miller and Vay were traveling behind a UPS truck and that both vehicles switched into the lefthand lane to avoid a stalled vehicle in the righthand lane near the 25th Street exit ramp. It is also undisputed that, soon thereafter, the Miller car was struck from behind by defendant Texaco's tractor-trailer driven by co-defendant Lawrence Keating. The force of the collision propelled the Miller car first into the side of a car stopped in the righthand lane and then into the rear of the UPS truck. Mrs. Miller sustained serious injuries in the collision. The driver of the car stopped in the righthand lane was Kenneth Parris. His wife, Elfriede Parris, was a passenger.

> Let us first dispose of the possibility that the admission of the unidentified declarant's statement was harmless error. The trial judge has aided us by his

opinion denying a new trial. As he put it, "if the evidentiary ruling was wrong, it would require a new trial because the admission of the declarant's statement cannot be classified as harmless error." App. at 363. We agree. The statement supports the defendants' claim that Mrs. Miller was to blame for the accident and contradicts sworn eyewitness testimony that the Miller car was stopped for several seconds before the Texaco truck hit it.

The first of these expresses the familiar principle that a witness may not testify about a subject without personal knowledge. Fed. R. Evid. 602. This rule applies with equal force to hearsay statements. *Kornicki v. Calmar Steamship Corporation*, 460 F.2d 1134, 1138 (3d Cir. 1972). To be admissible, the declarant of an excited utterance must personally observe the startling event. *McLaughlin v. Vinzant*, 522 F.2d 448, 451 (1st Cir. 1975). The burden of establishing perception rests with the proponent of the evidence. *David v. Pueblo Supermarkets of St. Thomas, Inc.*, 740 F.2d 230, 235 (3d Cir. 1984). As in all questions of admissibility, the resolution of any dispute of fact necessary to the question is confided to the trial judge to be decided by a preponderance of the evidence. And while the trial judge is not confined to legally admissible evidence in making the determination, Fed. R. Evid. 104(a), still he must make the findings necessary to support admissibility.

Direct proof of perception, or proof that forecloses all speculation is not required. On the other hand, circumstantial evidence of the declarant's personal perception must not be so scanty as to forfeit the "guarantees of trustworthiness" which form the hallmark of all exceptions to the hearsay rule.

[2]   United States v. Iron Shell

United States Court of Appeals for the Eighth Circuit
633 F.2d 77 (8th Cir. 1980)

In United States v. Iron Shell, the defendant was prosecuted for assault with intent to commit rape. The victim spoke to a police officer about an hour after the assault. The statements were admitted at trial under the excited utterance exception to the hearsay rule. On appeal, the Eighth Circuit Court of Appeals concluded that it was not an abuse of the trial court's discretion to admit statements made as much as 75 minutes after the fact as excited utterances. The Court of Appeals also noted that the Confrontation Clause was not violated by such hearsay statements; the statements had "sufficient reliability in order to provide the trier of fact a satisfactory basis for evaluating the truth of the prior statements."

[3]   Mutual Life Insurance Co. v. Hillmon

United States Supreme Court
145 U.S. 285 (1892)

Mr. Justice Gray delivered the opinion of the Court:

[Court's statement of facts] On July 13, 1880, Sallie E. Hillmon, a citizen of Kansas, brought an action against the Mutual Life Insurance Company, a corporation of New York, on a policy of insurance, dated December 10, 1878, on the life of her husband, John W. Hillmon, in the sum of $10,000.

[T]he declaration alleged that Hillmon died on March 17, 1879, during the continuance of the policy, but that the defendant, though duly notified of the fact, had refused to pay the amount of the policy, or any part thereof; and the answer denied the death of Hillmon [and claimed that plaintiff] falsely pretended and represented that Hillmon was dead, and that a dead body which they had procured was his, whereas in reality he was alive and in hiding.

At the trial the plaintiff introduced evidence tending to show that on or about March 5, 1879, Hillmon and Brown left Wichita in the State of Kansas, and traveled together through Southern Kansas in search of a site for a cattle ranch; that on the night of March 18, while they were in camp at a place called Crooked Creek, Hillmon was killed by the accidental discharge of a gun; that Brown at once notified persons living in the neighborhood; and that the body was thereupon taken to a neighboring town, where, after an inquest, it was buried.

The defendants introduced evidence tending to show that the body found in the camp at Crooked Creek on the night of March 18 was not the body of Hillmon, but was the body of one Frederick Adolph Walters. Upon the question whose body this was, there was much conflicting evidence, including photographs and descriptions of the corpse, and of the marks and scars upon it, and testimony to its likeness to Hillmon and to Walters.

The defendants introduced testimony that Walters left his home at Fort Madison in the State of Iowa in March, 1878, and was afterwards in Kansas in 1878, and in January and February, 1879; that during that time his family frequently received letters from him, the last of which was written from Wichita; and that he had not been heard from since March 1879. The defendants also offered the following evidence:

Elizabeth Rieffenach testified that she was a sister of Frederick Adolph Walters, and lived at Fort Madison; and thereupon, as shown by the bill of exceptions, the following proceedings took place:

"Witness further testified that she had received a letter written from Wichita, Kansas about the 4th or 5th day of March 1879, by her brother Frederick Adolph; that the letter was dated at Wichita, and was in the handwriting of her brother; that she had searched for the letter, but could not find the same, it being lost; that she remembered and could state the contents of the letter."

"Thereupon the defendants' counsel asked the questions: 'State the contents of that letter.' To which the plaintiff objected, on the ground that the same is incompetent, irrelevant, and hearsay. The objection was sustained, and the defendants duly excepted. The following is the letter as stated by witness:

"Wichita, Kansas,

March 4th or 5th or 3d or 4th — I don't know — 1879.

Dear sister and all: I now in my usual style drop you a few lines to let you know that I expect to leave Wichita on or about March the 5th, with a certain Mr. Hillmon, a sheep trader, for Colorado or parts unknown to me. I expect to see the country now. News are of no interest to you, as you are not acquainted here. I will close with compliments to all inquiring friends. Love to all.

"I am truly your brother,

Fred. Adolph Walters."

The evidence that Walters was at Wichita on or before March 5, and had not been heard from since, together with the evidence to identify as his the body found at Crooked Creek on March 18, tended to show that he went from Wichita to Crooked Creek between those dates. Evidence that just before March 5 he had the intention of leaving Wichita with Hillmon would tend to . . . show that he went from Wichita to Crooked Creek with Hillmon. Letters from him to his family and his betrothed were the natural, if not the only attainable, evidence of his intention.

The existence of a particular intention in a certain person at a certain time being a material fact to be proved, evidence that he expressed that intention at that time is as direct evidence of the fact, as his own testimony that he then had that intention would be. After his death there can hardly be any other way of proving it; and while he is still alive, his own memory of his state of mind at a former time is no more likely to be clear and true than a bystander's recollection of what he then said, and is less trustworthy than letters written by him at the very time and under circumstances precluding suspicion of misrepresentation.

The letters in question were competent, not as narratives of facts communicated to the writer by others, nor yet as proof that he actually went away from Wichita, but as evidence that, shortly before the time when other evidence tended to show that he went away, he had the intention of going, and of going with Hillmon, which made it more probable both that he did go and that he went with Hillmon, than if there had been no proof of such intention. In view of the mass of conflicting testimony introduced upon the question whether it was the body of Walters that was found in Hillmon's camp, this evidence might properly influence the jury in determining that question.

The rule applicable to this case has been thus stated by this court: "Wherever the bodily or mental feelings of an individual are material to be proved, the usual expressions of such feelings are original and competent evidence. Those expressions are the natural reflexes of what it might be impossible to show by other testimony. If there be such other testimony, this may be necessary to set the facts thus developed in their true light, and to find them their proper effect. As independent explanatory or corroborative evidence, it is often indispensable to the due administration of justice.

Such declarations are regarded as verbal acts, and are as competent as any other testimony, when relevant to the issue. Their truth or falsity is an inquiry for the jury." *Insurance Co. v. Mosley*, 8 Wall. 397, 404, 405.

Upon principle and authority, therefore, we are of opinion that the two letters were competent evidence of the intention of Walters at the time of writing them, which was material fact bearing upon the question in controversy; and that for the exclusion of these letters, as well as for the undue restriction of the defendants' challenges, the verdicts must be set aside, and a new trial had.

---

1. What is the basis for the rule in *Hillmon*?

2. Was the letter from Walters to his sister admissible to show both Walters's and Hillmon's intent, or just Walters's? If you were the judge, how would you rule on such an issue?

[4] Shepard v. United States

United States Supreme Court
290 U.S. 96 (1933)

Mr. Justice Cardozo delivered the opinion of the Court.

The petitioner, Charles A. Shepard, a major in the medical corps of the United States army, has been convicted of the murder of his wife, Zenana Shepard, at Fort Riley, Kansas, a United States military reservation. The jury having qualified their verdict by adding thereto the words "without capital punishment" (18 U.S.C. § 567), the defendant was sentenced to imprisonment for life. The judgment of the United States District Court has been affirmed by the Circuit Court of Appeals for the Tenth Circuit, one of the judges of that court dissenting. 62 F. (2d) 683; 64 F. (2d) 641. A writ of certiorari brings the case here.

The crime is charged to have been committed by poisoning the victim with bichloride of mercury. The defendant was in love with another woman, and wished to make her his wife. There is circumstantial evidence to sustain a finding by the jury that to win himself his freedom he turned to poison and murder. Even so, guilt was contested and conflicting inferences are possible. The defendant asks us to hold that by the acceptance of incompetent evidence the scales were weighted to his prejudice and in the end to his undoing.

The evidence complained of was offered by the Government in rebuttal when the trial was nearly over. On May 22, 1929, there was a conversation in the absence of the defendant between Mrs. Shepard, then ill in bed, and Clara Brown, her nurse. The patient asked the nurse to go to the closet in the defendant's room and bring a bottle of whisky that would be found upon a shelf. When the bottle was produced, she said that this was the liquor she had taken just before collapsing. She asked whether enough was left to make a test for the presence of poison, insisting that the smell and taste were strange. And then she added the words "Dr. Shepard has poisoned me."

The admission of this declaration, if erroneous, was more than unsubstantial error. As to that the parties are agreed. The voice of the dead wife was heard in accusation of her husband, and the accusation was accepted as evidence of guilt. If the evidence was incompetent, the verdict may not stand.

Upon the hearing in this court the Government finds its main prop in the position that what was said by Mrs. Shepard was admissible as a dying declaration. This is manifestly the theory upon which it was offered and received. The prop, however, is a broken reed. To make out a dying declaration the declarant must have spoken without hope of recovery and in the shadow of impending death. The record furnishes no proof of that indispensable condition. So, indeed, it was ruled by all the judges of the court below, though the majority held the view that the testimony was competent for quite another purpose, which will be considered later on.

We have said that the declarant was not shown to have spoken without hope of recovery and in the shadow of impending death. Her illness began on May 20. She was found in a state of collapse, delirious, in pain, the pupils of her eyes dilated, and the retina suffused with blood. The conversation with the nurse occurred two days later. At that time her mind had cleared up, and her speech was rational and orderly. There was as yet no thought by any of her physicians that she was dangerously ill, still less that her case was hopeless. To all seeming she had greatly improved, and was moving forward to recovery. There had been no diagnosis of poison as the cause of her distress. Not till about a week afterwards was there a relapse, accompanied by an infection of the mouth, renewed congestion of the eyes, and later hemorrhages of the bowels. Death followed on June 15.

Nothing in the condition of the patient on May 22 gives fair support of the conclusion that hope had then been lost. She may have thought she was going to die and have said so to her nurse, but this was consistent with hope, which could not have been put aside without more to quench it. Indeed, a fortnight later, she said to one of her physicians, though her condition was then grave, "You will get me well, won't you?" Fear or even belief that illness will end in death will not avail of itself to make a dying declaration. There must be "a settled hopeless expectation" (Willes, J. in *Reg.* v. *Peel*, 2 F. & F. 21, 22) that death is near at hand, and what is said must have been spoken in the hush of its impending presence[citations omitted] Despair of recovery may indeed be gathered from the circumstances if the facts support the inference. *Carver v. United States, supra;* Wigmore, Evidence, § 1442. There is no unyielding ritual of words to be spoken by the dying. Despair may even be gathered though the period of survival outruns the bounds of expectation. Wigmore, § 1441. What is decisive is the state of mind. Even so, the state of mind must be exhibited in the evidence, not left to conjecture. The patient must have spoken with the consciousness of a swift and certain doom.

What was said by this patient was not spoken in that mood. There was no warning to her in the circumstances that her words would be repeated and accepted as those of a dying wife, charging murder to her husband, and charging it deliberately and solemnly as a fact within her knowledge. To the focus of that responsibility her mind was never brought. She spoke as one ill, giving voice to the beliefs and perhaps the conjectures of the moment. The liquor was to be tested, to see whether her beliefs were sound. She did not speak as one dying, announcing to the survivors a definite conviction, a legacy of knowledge on which the world might act when she had gone. . . .

[I]n suits upon insurance policies, declarations by an insured that he intends to go upon a journey with another, may be evidence of a state of mind lending probability to the conclusion that the purpose was fulfilled. *Mutual Life Ins. v. Hillmon, supra.* The ruling in that case marks the high water line beyond which courts have been unwilling to go. It has developed a substantial body of criticism and commentary. Declarations of intention, casting light upon the future, have been sharply distinguished from declarations of memory, pointing backwards to the past. There would be an end, or nearly that, to the rule against hearsay if the distinction were ignored.

The testimony now questioned faced backward and not forward. This at least it did in its most obvious implications. What is even more important, it spoke to a past act, and more than that, to an act by some one not the speaker. Another tendency, if it had any, was a filament too fine to be disentangled by a jury.

Reversed.

---

1. How is this case different from *Hillmon?*

2. What would Mrs. Shepard have had to say to satisfy a hearsay exception?

[5] United States v. Pheaster

United States Court of Appeals for the Ninth Circuit
544 F.2d 353 (9th Cir. 1976)

The issue in *United States v. Pheaster* was whether a statement of intent to do something with another person is admissible to show both the intent of the declarant and the other person or only the intent of the declarant. The Ninth Circuit Court of Appeals stated that:

> When hearsay evidence concerns the declarant's statement of his intention to do something with another person, the *Hillmon* Doctrine requires that the trier of fact infer from the state of mind of the declarant the probability of a particular act not only by the declarant but also by the other person.

The Court of Appeals noted that the California Supreme Court, in *People v. Alcalde,* 24 Cal. 2d 177, 148 P.2d 627 (1944), agreed with this expansive interpretation of the *Hillmon* Doctrine. It also discussed the apparent conflict between the Advisory Committee's Note and the Notes of the House Committee on the Judiciary. The House Committee on the Judiciary stated that (House Report No. 93-650, note to paragraph (3), 28 U.S.C.A. at 579):

> The committee intends that the rule be construed to limit the doctrine of *Mutual Life Insurance Co. v. Hillmon* [citation omitted] so as to render statements of intent by a declarant admissible only to prove his future conduct, not the future conduct of another person.

The Court of Appeals concluded, however, that "although the matter is certainly not free from doubt, we read the note of the Advisory Committee as presuming that the *Hillmon* Doctrine would be incorporated in full force, including necessarily the application in *Hillmon* itself."

Which reading of the *Hillmon* rule is preferable, the narrow or the expansive view? Explain your answer.

[6]   Palmer v. Hoffman

United States Supreme Court
318 U.S. 109 (1943)

MR. JUSTICE DOUGLAS delivered the opinion of the Court:

This case arose out of a grade crossing accident which occurred in Massachusetts. Diversity of citizenship brought it to the federal District Court in New York. . . .

The accident occurred on the night of December 25, 1940. On December 27, 1940, the engineer of the train, who died before the trial, made a statement at a freight office of petitioners where he was interviewed by an assistant superintendent of the road and by a representative of the Massachusetts Public Utilities Commission. *See* Mass. Gen. L. (1932) c. 159, § 29. This statement was offered in evidence by petitioners under the Act of June 20, 1936, 49 Stat. 1561, 28 U.S.C. § 695.[4] They offered to prove (in the language of the Act) that the statement was signed in the regular course of business, it being the regular course of such business to make such a statement. Respondent's objection to its introduction was sustained.

We agree with the majority view below that it was properly excluded.

We may assume that if the statement was made "in the regular course" of business, it would satisfy the other provisions of the Act. But we do not think that it was made "in the regular course" of business within the meaning of the Act. The business of the petitioners is the railroad business. That business like other enterprises entails the keeping of numerous books and records essential to its conduct or useful in its efficient operation. Though such books and records were considered reliable and trustworthy for major decisions in the industrial and business world, their use in litigation was greatly circumscribed or hedged about by the hearsay rule — restrictions which greatly increased the time and cost of making the proof where those who made the records were numerous. 5 Wigmore, Evidence (3d ed., 1940) § 1530. It was that

---

[4] (Court's original footnote 1) "In any court of the United States and in any court established by Act of Congress, any writing or record, whether in the form of an entry in a book or otherwise, made as a memorandum or record of any act, transaction, occurrence, or event, shall be admissible as evidence of said act, transaction, occurrence, or event, if it shall appear that it was made in the regular course of any business, and that it was the regular course of such business to make such memorandum or record at the time of such act, transaction, occurrence, or event or within a reasonable time thereafter. All other circumstances of the making of such writing or record, including lack of personal knowledge by the entrant to maker, may be shown to affect its weight, but they shall not affect its admissibility. The term 'business' shall include business, profession, occupation, and calling of every kind."

problem which started the movement towards adoption of legislation embodying the principles of the present Act. . . . And the legislative history of the Act indicates the same purpose.

In short, it is manifest that in this case those reports are not for the systematic conduct of the enterprise as a railroad business. Unlike payrolls, accounts receivable, accounts payable, bills of lading and the like, these reports are calculated for use essentially in the court, not in the business. Their primary utility is in litigating, not in railroading.

It is, of course, not for us to take these reports out of the Act if Congress has put them in. But there is nothing in the background of the law on which this Act was built or in its legislative history which suggests for a moment that the business of preparing cases for trial should be included. In this connection it should be noted that the Act of May 6, 1910, 36 Stat. § 350, 45 U.S.C. § 38, requires officers of common carriers by rail to make under oath monthly reports of railroad accidents to the Interstate Commerce Commission, setting forth the nature and causes of the accidents and the circumstances connected therewith. And the same Act (45 U.S.C. § 40) gives the Commission authority to investigate and to make reports upon such accidents. It is provided, however, that "Neither the report required by section 38 of this title nor any report of the investigation provided for in section 40 of this title nor any part thereof shall be admitted as evidence or used for any purpose in any suit or action for damages growing out of any matter mentioned in said report or investigation." 45 U.S.C. § 41. A similar provision (36 Stat. 916, 54 Stat. 148, 45 U.S.C. § 33) bars the use in litigation of reports concerning accidents resulting from the failure of a locomotive boiler or its appurtenances. 45 U.S.C. §§ 32, 33. That legislation reveals an explicit Congressional policy to rule out reports of accidents which certainly have as great a claim to objectivity as the statement sought to be admitted in the present case. We can hardly suppose that Congress modified or qualified by implication these long standing statutes when it permitted records made "in the regular course" of business to be introduced. Nor can we assume that Congress having expressly prohibited the use of the company's reports on its accidents impliedly altered that policy when it came to reports by its employees to their superiors. The inference is wholly the other way.

The several hundred years of history behind the Act . . . indicate the nature of the reforms which it was designed to effect. It should of course be liberally interpreted so as to do away with the anachronistic rules which gave rise to its need and at which it was aimed. But "regular course" of business must find its meaning in the inherent nature of the business in question and in the methods systematically employed for the conduct of the business as a business.

Affirmed.

[7] Beech Aircraft Corp. v. Rainey

United States Supreme Court
488 U.S. 153 (1988)

Justice Brennan delivered the opinion of the Court:

In this action we address a longstanding conflict among the Federal Courts of Appeals over whether Federal Rule of Evidence 803(8)(C), which provides an exception to the hearsay rule for public investigatory reports containing "factual findings," extends to conclusions and opinions contained in such reports. We also consider whether, on the facts of this litigation, the trial court abused its discretion in refusing to admit, on cross-examination, testimony intended to provide a more complete picture of a document about which the witness had testified on direct.

This litigation stems from the crash of a Navy training aircraft at Middleton Field, Alabama, on July 13, 1982, which took the lives of both pilots on board, Lieutenant Commander Barbara Ann Rainey and Ensign Donald Bruce Knowlton.

At trial, the only seriously disputed question was whether pilot error or equipment malfunction had caused the crash. Both sides relied primarily on expert testimony. One piece of evidence presented by the defense was an investigative report prepared by Lieutenant Commander William Morgan on order of the training squadron's commanding officer and pursuant to authority granted in the Manual of the Judge Advocate General. This "JAG" Report, completed during the six weeks following the accident, was organized into sections labeled "finding of fact," "opinions," and "recommendations," and was supported by some 60 attachments. The "finding of facts" included statements like the following:

> "13. At approximately 1020, while turning crosswind, without proper interval, 3E955 crashed, immediately caught fire and burned.

> "27. At the time of impact, the engine of 3E955 was operating but was operating at reduced power."

Controversy over what "public records and reports" are made not excludable by Rule 803(8)(C) has divided the federal courts from the beginning. In the present litigation, the Court of Appeals followed the "narrow" interpretation of *Smith v. Ithaca Corp., supra,* 612 F.2d at 220–223, which held that the term "factual findings" did not encompass "opinions" or "conclusions." Courts of appeal other than those of the Fifth and Eleventh Circuits, however, have generally adopted a broader interpretation. For example, the Court of Appeals for the Sixth Circuit, in *Baker v. Elcona Homes Corp.,* 588 F.2d 551, 557–558 (1978), *cert. denied,* 441 U.S. 933 (1979), held that "factual findings admissible under Rule 803(8)(C) may be those which are made by the preparer of the report from disputed evidence. . . ." The other courts of appeals that have squarely confronted the issue have also adopted the broader interpretation. We agree and hold that factually based conclusions or opinions are not on that account excluded from the scope of Rule 803(8)(C).

Because the Federal Rules of Evidence are a legislative enactment, we turn to the "traditional tools of statutory construction," *INS v. Cardoza-Fonseca*, 480 U.S. 421, 446 (1987), in order to construe their provisions. We begin with the language of the Rule itself. Proponents of the narrow view have generally relied heavily on a perceived dichotomy between "fact" and "opinion" in arguing for the limited scope of the phrase "factual findings." *Smith v. Ithaca Corp., supra* contrasted the term "factual findings" in Rule 803(8)(C) with the language of Rule 803(6) (records of regularly conducted activity), which expressly refers to "opinions" and "diagnoses." "Factual findings" the court opined, must be something other than opinions. *Smith, supra* at 221–22.

For several reasons, we do not agree. In the first place, it is not apparent that the term "factual findings" should be read to mean simply "facts" (as opposed to "opinions" or "conclusions"). A common definition of "finding of fact" is, for example, "[a] conclusion by way of reasonable inference from the evidence." *Black's Law Dictionary* 569 (5th ed. 1979). To say the least, the language of the Rule does not compel us to reject the interpretation that "factual findings" includes conclusions or opinions that flow from a factual investigation. Second, we note that, contrary to what is often assumed, the language of the Rule does not state that "factual findings" are admissible, but that "reports . . . setting forth . . . factual findings [are]."

The Advisory Committee's comments are notable, first, in that they contain no mention of any dichotomy between statements of "fact" and "opinions" or "conclusions." What was on the Committee's mind was simply whether what it called "evaluative reports" should be admissible. Illustrating the previous division among the courts on this subject, the Committee cited numerous cases in which the admissibility of such reports had been both sustained and denied. It also took note of various federal statutes that made certain kinds of evaluative reports admissible in evidence. What is striking about all of these examples is that these were *reports that stated conclusions.* . . . The Committee's concern was clearly whether reports of this kind should be admissible. Nowhere in its comments is there the slightest indication that it even considered the solution of admitting only "factual" statements from such reports. Rather the Committee referred throughout to "reports," without such differentiation regarding the statements they contained. What the Committee referred to in the Rule's language as "reports . . . setting forth . . . factual findings" is surely nothing more or less than what in its commentary it called "evaluative reports." Its solution as to their admissibility is clearly stated in the final paragraph of its report on this Rule. That solution consists of two principles: First, the "rule . . . assumes admissibility in the first instance. . . ." Second, it provides "ample provision for escape if sufficient negative factors are present."

That "provision for escape" is contained in the final clause of the Rule: evaluative reports are admissible "unless the sources of information or other circumstances indicate lack of trustworthiness." This trustworthiness inquiry — and not an arbitrary distinction between "fact" and "opinion" — was the Committee's primary safeguard against the admission of unreliable evidence, and it is important to note that it applies to all elements of the report. Thus, a trial judge has the discretion, and indeed the obligation, to exclude an entire report or portion thereof — whether narrow "factual" statements or broader "conclusions" — that she determined to be untrustworthy. Moreover, safeguards built in to other portions of the Federal Rules, such as those dealing with relevance and prejudice, provide the court with additional means of scrutinizing and, where appropriate, excluding evaluative reports or portions of them. And of course it goes without saying that the admission of a report containing "conclusions" is subject to the ultimate safeguard — the opponent's right to present evidence tending to contradict or diminish the weight of those conclusions.

Our conclusion that neither the language of the Rule nor the intent of its framers calls for a distinction between "fact" and "opinion" is strengthened by the analytical difficulty of drawing such a line.

We hold, therefore, that portions of investigatory reports otherwise admissible under Rule 803(8)(C) are not inadmissible merely because they state a conclusion or opinion. As long as the conclusion is based on a factual investigation and satisfies the Rule's trustworthiness requirement, it should be admissible along with other portions of the report. As the trial judge in this action determined that certain of the JAG Report's conclusions were trustworthy, he rightly allowed them to be admitted into evidence. We therefore reverse the judgment of the Court of Appeals in respect of the Rule 803(8)(C) issue

---

1. What are the "tools of statutory construction" used by the Court in *Rainey*?

2. Create an argument that is contrary to the Supreme Court's opinion.

[8]   Dallas County v. Commercial Union Assurance Co.

United States Court of Appeals for the Fifth Circuit
286 F.2d 388 (5th Cir. 1961)

WISDOM, CIRCUIT JUDGE:

[This case was decided prior to the adoption of the Federal Rules of Evidence. It provides a seminal example of how hearsay evidence may still be admissible even though the evidence does not fall within an express exception to the hearsay rule.]

Dallas County sued its insurance company for damage to the local courthouse. The damage resulted from the collapse of the courthouse clock tower on July 7, 1957. The issue at trial was whether the collapse of the tower was attributable to a compensable lightning strike, which occurred only days before the collapse, or, as the defendant insurance companies claimed, to noncompensable structural defects.]

On a bright sunny morning, July 7, 1957, the clock tower of the Dallas County Courthouse at Selma, Alabama, commenced to lean, made loud cracking and popping noises, then fell, and telescoped into the courtroom. Fortunately, the collapse of the tower took place on a Sunday morning; no one was injured, but damage to the courthouse exceeded $100,000. An examination of the tower debris showed the presence of charcoal and charred timbers. The State Toxicologist, called in by Dallas County, reported the char was evidence that lightning struck the courthouse. Later, several residents of Selma reported that a bolt of lightning struck the courthouse on July 2, 1957. On this information, Dallas County concluded that a lightning bolt had hit the building causing the collapse of the clock tower five days later. Dallas County carried insurance for loss to its courthouse caused by fire or lightning. The insurance engineers and investigators found that the courthouse collapsed of its own weight. They reported that the courthouse had not been struck by lightning; that lightning could not have caused the collapse of the tower; that the collapse of the tower was caused by structural weaknesses attributable to a faulty design, poor construction, gradual deterioration of the structure, and overloading brought about by remodeling and recent installation of an air condition system, part of which was constructed over the courtroom trusses. In their opinion, the char was the result of a fire in the courthouse tower and roof that must have occurred many, many years before July 7, 1957. The insurers denied liability.

[The plaintiff offered testimony that some charred timber had been discovered in the courthouse after the collapse, supporting the inference that the lightning strike had caused the fall. In reply, the defendants offered a fifty-eight year old newspaper account from the June 9, 1901, *Selma Morning Times*, describing a fire in the courthouse tower. If such a fire had occurred, that would explain the presence of charred timber found in the clock tower.]

This appeal presents a single question — the admissibility in evidence of a newspaper to show that the Dallas County Courthouse in Selma, Alabama was damaged by fire in 1901. We hold that the newspaper was admissible, and affirm the judgment below.

During the trial the defendants introduced a copy of the *Morning Times* of Selma for June 9, 1901. This issue carried an unsigned article describing a fire that occurred at two in the morning of June 9, 1901, while the courtroom was still under construction. The article stated, in part: "The unfinished dome of the County's new courthouse was in flames at the top, and soon fell in. The fire was soon under control and the main building was saved. . . ." The insurers do not contend that the collapse of the tower resulted from unsound charred timbers used in the repair of the building after the fire; they offered the newspaper account to show there had been a fire long before 1957 that would account for charred timber in the clock tower. . . .

The plaintiff objected that the newspaper article was hearsay; that it was not a business record nor an ancient document, nor was it admissible under any recognized exception to the hearsay doctrine. The trial judge admitted the newspaper as part of the records of the *Selma Times-Journal.*

In the Anglo-American adversary system of law, courts usually will not admit evidence unless its accuracy and trustworthiness may be tested by cross-examination. Here, therefore, the plaintiff argues that the newspaper should not be admitted: "You cannot cross-examine a newspaper."

There is no procedural canon against the exercise of common sense in deciding the admissibility of hearsay evidence. Taking a common sense view of this case, it is inconceivable to us that a newspaper reporter in a small town would report there was a fire in the dome of the new courthouse — if there had been no fire. He is without motive to falsify.

We hold, that in matters of local interest, when the fact in question is of such a public nature it would be generally known throughout the community, and when the questioned fact occurred so long ago the testimony of an eyewitness would probably be less trustworthy than a contemporary newspaper account, a federal court, under Rule 43(a), may relax the exclusionary rules to the extent of admitting the newspaper article in evidence. We do not characterize this newspaper as a "business record," nor as an "ancient document," nor as any other readily identifiable and happily tagged species of hearsay exception. It is admissible because it is necessary and trustworthy, relevant and material, and its admission is within the trial judge's exercise of discretion in holding the hearing within reasonable bounds. Judgment is affirmed.

[9]   United States v. Salerno

United States Supreme Court
505 U.S. 317 (1992)

JUSTICE THOMAS delivered the opinion of the Court:

Federal Rule of Evidence 804(b)(1) states an exception to the hearsay rule that allows a court, in certain circumstances, to admit the former testimony of an unavailable witness. We must decide in this case whether the Rule permits a criminal defendant to introduce the grand jury testimony of a witness who asserts the Fifth Amendment privilege at trial.

The seven respondents, Anthony Salerno, Vincent DiNapoli, Louis DiNapoli, Nicholas Auletta, Edward Halloran, Alvin O. Chattin, and Aniello Migliore, allegedly took part in the activities of a criminal organization known as the Genovese Family of La Cosa Nostra (Family) in New York City.

According to the indictment and evidence later admitted at trial, the Family used its influence over labor unions and its control over the supply of concrete to rig bidding on large construction projects in Manhattan. The Family purportedly allocated contracts for these projects among a so-called "Club" of six concrete companies in exchange for a share of the proceeds.

Much of the case concerned the affairs of the Cedar Park Concrete Construction Corporation (Cedar Park). Two of the owners of the firm, Frederick DeMatteis and Pasquale Bruno, testified before the grand jury under a grant of immunity. In response to questions by the United States, they repeatedly stated that neither they nor Cedar Park had participated in the Club. At trial, however, the United States attempted to show that Cedar Park, in fact, had belonged to the Club by calling two contractors who had taken part in the scheme and by presenting intercepted conversations among the respondents.

To counter the United States evidence, the respondents subpoenaed DeMatteis and Bruno as witnesses in the hope that they would provide the same exculpatory testimony that they had presented to the grand jury. When both witnesses invoked their Fifth Amendment privilege against self-incrimination and refused to testify, the respondents asked the District Court to admit the transcripts of their grand jury testimony. Although this testimony constituted hearsay, see Rule 801(c), the respondents argued that it fell within the hearsay exception in Rule 804(b)(1) for former testimony of unavailable witnesses.

The District Court refused to admit the grand jury testimony.

The United States Court of Appeals for the Second Circuit reversed, holding that the District Court had erred in excluding DeMatteis and Bruno's grand jury testimony.

We must decide whether the Court of Appeals properly interpreted Rule 804(b)(1) in this case.

The parties agree that DeMatteis and Bruno were "unavailable" to the defense as witnesses, provided that they properly invoked the Fifth Amendment privilege and refused to testify. *See* Rule 804(a)(1). They also agree that DeMatteis and Bruno's grand jury testimony constituted "testimony given as . . . witness[es] at another hearing." They disagree, however, about whether the "similar motive" requirement in the final clause of Rule 804(b)(1) should have prevented admission of the testimony in this case.

Nothing in the language of Rule 804(b)(1) suggests that a court may admit former testimony absent satisfaction of each of the Rule's elements. The United States thus asserts that, unless it had a "similar motive," we must conclude that the District Court properly excluded DeMatteis and Bruno's testimony as hearsay. The respondents, in contrast, urge us not to read Rule 804(b)(1) in a "slavishly literal fashion." Brief for Respondents at 31. They contend that "adversarial fairness" prevents the United States from relying on the similar motive requirement in this case. We agree with the United States.

When Congress enacted the prohibition against admission of hearsay in Rule 802, it placed 24 exceptions in Rule 803 and 5 additional exceptions in Rule 804. Congress thus presumably made a careful judgment as to what hearsay may come into evidence and what may not. To respect its determination, we must enforce the words that it enacted. The respondents, as a result, had no right to introduce DeMatteis and Bruno's former testimony under Rule 804(b)(1) without showing a "similar motive." This Court cannot alter evidentiary rules merely because litigants might prefer different rules in a particular class of cases.

We . . . fail to see how we may create an exception to Rule 804(b)(1). . . . In this case, the language of Rule 804(b)(1) does not support the respondents. Indeed, the respondents specifically ask us to ignore it.

[The Supreme Court decided to remand the case. It instructed the lower court to further consider whether the United States had a similar motive to examine the witness in the grand jury proceeding as it had at trial. The Supreme Court concluded that the court of appeals erred in not addressing this question.]

[10]   United States v. MacDonald

United States Court of Appeals for the Fourth Circuit
688 F.2d 224 (4th Cir. 1982)

[The defendant, a Green Beret doctor, was convicted of murdering his wife and children. He claimed at trial that the killings were committed by a band of marauding hippies. The Fourth Circuit Court of Appeals considered the admissibility of certain statements at trial.]

Since the commission of the crimes in February 1970, MacDonald has maintained that he and his family all were victims of a bizarre cult attack. He claims that the perpetrators included three men and a woman wearing a floppy hat, having blond hair, and wearing boots. The woman, he says, was Helena Stoeckley. [Stoeckley's statements, some of which admitted to participating in the killings, were offered by defendant but excluded by the trial court. Stoeckley was considered unavailable for trial, and the issue on appeal was whether her statements fell within the declarations against interest provision of the Federal Rules of Evidence, 804(b)(3).]

Thus, as applied to criminal matters, three requisites must be met prior to reception of the hearsay testimony [under Rule 804(b)(3)]. First, the declarant must be unavailable. Second, from the perspective of the average, reasonable person, the statement must have been truly adverse to the declarant's penal interest, considering when it was made. *Cf. United States v. Evans*, 635 F.2d 1124 (4th Cir. 1980), *cert. denied*, 452 U.S. 943, 101 S. Ct. 3090, 69 L. Ed. 2d 958 (1981) (suggesting that statement is not against penal interest where declarant made statements which appeared to subject himself to criminal liability but which actually would constitute defense to more serious crime). Finally, corroborating circumstances must clearly establish the trustworthiness of the statement.

We have no difficulty in agreeing with appellant that declarant Stoeckley was unavailable and that her statements, if true, clearly would be against her penal interest. The question remains, however, whether the "corroborating circumstances clearly indicate the trustworthiness of the statement[s]."

At bottom, the sticking point here, as recognized by the district court, is the fundamental problem of trustworthiness. While MacDonald is able to point to a number of corroborating circumstances, he does not demonstrate, finally, that they make Stoeckley's alleged declaration trustworthy. Her apparent longstanding drug habit made her an inherently unreliable witness. Moreover, her vacillation about whether or not she remembered anything at all about the night of the crime lends force to the view that everything she has said and done in this regard was a product of her drug addiction. Given the declarant's "pathetic" appearance, our conviction is that the district court was not in error in adjudging that defendant failed to carry his burden under Rule 804(b)(3).

[11]   Horne v. Owens-Corning Fiberglas Corp.

United States Court of Appeals for the Fourth Circuit
4 F.3d 276 (4th Cir. 1993)

ERVIN, CHIEF JUDGE:

Linda P. Horne, together with her husband Benny Gerald Horne, initiated this products liability action against Owens-Corning Fiberglas Corporation ("Owens-Corning") and numerous other asbestos manufacturers, alleging that Benny Horne's exposure to insulation manufactured by Owens-Corning and containing asbestos caused him to contract lung cancer. After Benny Horne's death, Linda Horne ("Horne") proceeded with the action as executrix of his estate. At the close of the trial, the jury returned a verdict form finding Owens-Corning negligent, Benny Horne contributorily negligent, and Owens-Corning not willfully and wantonly negligent. Based on these findings, Horne could not recover. Horne now appeals the district court's admission of various pieces of evidence and the format of the jury verdict form. After reviewing these issues, we find Horne's appeal to be without merit and, accordingly, affirm. . . .

Owens-Corning introduced, and the district court admitted, portions of the February 11, 1981, and March 27, 1981 depositions of Mr. W.G. Hazard, a former industrial hygienist for the Owens-Illinois Company, Owens-Corning's predecessor in ownership of Kaylo. The district court admitted the Hazard depositions pursuant to Rule 804(b)(1) of the Federal Rules of Evidence. Rule 804(b)(1) provides:

> "(b) Hearsay exceptions. The following are not excluded by the hearsay rule if the declarant is unavailable as a witness:
>
> (1) Former testimony. Testimony given as a witness . . . in a deposition taken in compliance with law in the course of the same or another proceeding, if the party against whom the testimony is now offered, or, in a civil action or proceeding, a predecessor in interest, had an opportunity and similar motive to develop the testimony by direct, cross, or redirect examination."

Fed. R. Evid. 804(b)(1). The Notes of the Advisory Committee following the rule raise the question "whether strict identity, or privity, should continue as a requirement with respect to the party against whom offered." *Id.* advisory committee notes. The notes suggest that "the rule departs to the extent of allowing substitution of one with the right and opportunity to develop the testimony with similar motive and interest." *Id.*

When reviewing the admissibility of evidence pursuant to Rule 804(b)(1), we have focused on the similarity of motives between the predecessor in interest and the one against whom the deposition is now offered to determine the scope of Rule 804(b)(1). In a situation in which the motives differ, the testimony may not be introduced. Our decision in Lohrmann v. Pittsburgh Corning Corp. demonstrates this limit to admissibility. *See Lohrmann,* 782 F.2d at 1160–61. In *Lohrmann* the prior action from which the deposition derived involved claims based on the hazardous effects upon the health of plant workers exposed to raw asbestos. *Id.* at 1161. The *Lohrmann* plaintiff sought to introduce the deposition against Pittsburgh Corning Corp., a manufacturer of asbestos not involved in the earlier litigation. *Id.* at 1160. The *Lohrmann* plaintiff was not a plant worker, but a pipe-fitter, who from time to time worked in close proximity to insulators and others using products containing processed asbestos. *Id.* at 1161. Cross-examination in the deposition would not have brought out the distinction between employees exposed to raw asbestos and those exposed to asbestos by-products and dust. *Id.* Therefore, we affirmed the district court's determination that the deposition did not present a similar opportunity and motive to develop testimony and should not be admitted against Pittsburgh Corning Corp. in the subsequent litigation. *Id.*

Horne challenges the admission of the Hazard depositions on two grounds. First, she claims that the court failed to determine the witness's unavailability. Second, she claims that the participants in the deposition did not share similar motives to develop testimony as she, preventing the testimony from being introduced against her now.

In this case the district court made the following findings regarding witness availability:

> *The Court:* Is he dead now?
>
> *Mr. Modesitt:* I am under the belief that he is dead. He is unavailable at any rate, but I think he's dead.
>
> *The Court:* How do you know he is unavailable? Well, I will be here about 8:15 and we will take this and anything else up that you have at that time.
>
> *Recess.*

Upon resuming proceedings the next day, neither party nor the court revisited the availability issue, and Horne did not renew her objection. Despite the absence of a finding as to availability, we see no merit in Horne's challenge on this basis. The record indicates that Owens-Corning represented that Hazard was dead, and Horne did not, nor does she now, contest the fact. Without some evidence of Hazard's availability, we cannot conclude that the district court's failure to make findings specifically as to unavailability represents an abuse of discretion. The court's admission of the Hazard deposition pursuant to Rule 804(b)(1) implicitly incorporates a finding of unavailability absent the introduction of evidence to the contrary.

As a second ground for challenging the Hazard depositions, Horne suggests that the claimants in the other asbestos litigation for which Hazard gave his depositions were not predecessors in interest to Horne. Horne's contention is based on a misapprehension of the law, not on valid distinctions between the litigants. Rather than pointing to factual and legal differences in the proceedings, such as those detailed in *Lohrmann*, Horne contends that the other claimants are not predecessors in interest because they have no relationship to Horne. Horne's argument relies on the need for some showing of privity. The *Lohrmann* holding makes clear that privity is not the gravamen of the analysis. Instead, the party against whom the deposition is offered must point up distinctions in her case not evident in the earlier litigation that would preclude similar motives of witness examination.

Horne offers no such distinctions; therefore, the district court's introduction of the deposition excerpts does not represent an abuse of discretion.

[12]   Williamson v. United States

United States Supreme Court
512 U.S. 594 (1994)

JUSTICE O'CONNOR delivered the opinion of the Court, except as to Part II-C:

In this case we clarify the scope of the hearsay exception for statements against penal interest. Fed. Rule Evid. 804(b)(3).

A deputy sheriff stopped the rental car driven by Reginald Harris for weaving on the highway. Harris consented to a search of the car, which revealed 19 kilograms of cocaine in two suitcases in the trunk. Harris was promptly arrested.

Shortly after Harris' arrest, Special Agent Donald Walton of the Drug Enforcement Administration (DEA) interviewed him by telephone. During that conversation, Harris said that he got the cocaine from an unidentified Cuban in Fort Lauderdale; that the cocaine belonged to petitioner Williamson; and that it was to be delivered that night to a particular dumpster. Williamson was also connected to Harris by physical evidence. The luggage bore the initials of Williamson's sister, Williamson was listed as an additional driver on the car rental agreement, and an envelope addressed to Williamson and a receipt with Williamson's girlfriend's address were found in the glove compartment.

Several hours later, Agent Walton spoke to Harris in person. During that interview, Harris said he had rented the car a few days earlier and had driven it to Fort Lauderdale to meet Williamson. According to Harris, he had gotten the cocaine from a Cuban who was Williamson's acquaintance, and the Cuban had put the cocaine in the car with a note telling Harris how to deliver the drugs. Harris repeated that he had been instructed to leave the drugs in a certain dumpster, to return in his car, and to leave without waiting for anyone to pick up the drugs.

Agent Walton then took steps to arrange a controlled delivery of the cocaine. But as Walton was preparing to leave the interview room, Harris "got out of [his] chair . . . and . . . took a half step toward [Walton] . . . and . . . said, . . . 'I can't let you do that,' threw his hands up and said 'that's not true, I can't let you go up there for no reason.'" App.40. Harris told Walton he had lied about the Cuban, the note, and the dumpster. The real story, Harris said, was that he was transporting the cocaine to Atlanta for Williamson, and that Williamson was traveling in front of him in another rental car. Harris added that after his car was stopped, Williamson turned around and drove past the location of the stop, where he could see Harris' car with its trunk open. *Ibid.* Because Williamson had apparently seen the police searching the car, Harris explained that it would be impossible to make a controlled delivery. *Id.* at 41.

Harris told Walton that he had lied about the source of the drugs because he was afraid of Williamson. *Id.* at 61, 68; see also *id.*, at 30–31. Though Harris freely implicated himself, he did not want his story to be recorded, and he refused to sign a written version of the statement. *Id.* at 24–25. Walton testified that he had promised to report any cooperation by Harris to the Assistant United States Attorney. Walton said Harris was not promised any reward or other benefit for cooperating. *Id.* at 25–26.

Williamson was eventually convicted of possessing cocaine with intent to distribute, conspiring to possess cocaine with intent to distribute, and traveling interstate to promote the distribution of cocaine, 21 U.S.C. §§ 841(a)(1), 846; 18 U.S.C. § 1952. When called to testify at Williamson's trial, Harris refused, even though the prosecution gave him use immunity and the court ordered him to testify and eventually held him in contempt. The District Court then ruled that, under Rule 804(b)(3), Agent Walton could relate what Harris had said to him. . . . The Court of Appeals for the Eleventh Circuit affirmed without opinion.

The hearsay rule, Fed. Rule Evid. 802, is premised on the theory that out-of-court statements are subject to particular hazards. The declarant might be lying; he might have misperceived the events which he relates; he might have faulty memory; his words might be misunderstood or taken out of context by the listener. And the ways in which these dangers are minimized for in-court statements — the oath, the witness' awareness of the gravity of the proceedings, the jury's ability to observe the witness' demeanor, and, most importantly, the right of the opponent to cross-examine — are generally absent for things said out of court.

Nonetheless, the Federal Rules of Evidence also recognize that some kinds of out-of-court statements are less subject to these hearsay dangers, and therefore except them from the general rule that hearsay is inadmissible. One such category covers statements that are against the declarant's interest:

> "statement[s] which at the time of [their] making . . . so far tended to subject the declarant to . . . criminal liability . . . that a reasonable person in the declarant's position would not have made the statement[s] unless believing [them] to be true." Fed. Rule Evid. 804(b)(3).

To decide whether Harris' confession is made admissible by Rule 804(b)(3), we must first determine what the Rule means by "statement," which Federal Rule of Evidence 801(a)(1) defines as "an oral or written assertion." One possible meaning, "a report or narrative," Webster's Third New International Dictionary 2229, defn. 2(a) (1961), connotes an extended declaration. Under this reading, Harris' entire confession — even if it contains both self-inculpatory and non-self-inculpatory parts — would be admissible so long as in the aggregate the confession sufficiently inculpates him. Another meaning of "statement," "a single declaration or remark," *ibid.*, defn. 2(b), would make Rule 804(b)(3) cover only those declarations or remarks within the confession that are individually self-inculpatory.

Although the text of the Rule does not directly resolve the matter, the principle behind the Rule, so far as it is discernible from the text, points clearly to the narrower reading. Rule 804(b)(3) is founded on the commonsense notion that reasonable people who are not especially honest tend not to make self-inculpatory statements unless they believe them to be true. This notion simply does not extend to the broader definition of "statement." The fact that a person is making a broadly self-inculpatory confession does not make more credible the confession's non-self-inculpatory parts. One of the most effective ways to lie is to mix falsehood with truth, especially truth that seems particularly persuasive because of its self-inculpatory nature.

In this respect, it is telling that the non-self-inculpatory things Harris said in his first settlement actually proved to be false, as Harris himself admitted during the second interrogation. And when part of the confession is actually self-exculpatory, the generalization on which Rule 804(b)(3) is founded becomes even less applicable. Self-exculpatory statements are exactly the ones which people are most likely to make even when they are false; and mere proximity to other, self-inculpatory, statements does not increase the plausibility of the self-exculpatory statements.

Nothing in the text of Rule 804(B)(3) or the general theory of the hearsay Rules suggests that admissibility should turn on whether a statement is collateral to a self-inculpatory statement. The fact that a statement is self-inculpatory does make it more reliable; but the fact that a statement is collateral to a self-inculpatory statement says nothing at all about the collateral statement's reliability. We see no reason why collateral statements, even ones that are neutral as to interest, *post*, at 2443–44, should be treated any differently from other hearsay statements that are generally excluded.

In our view, the most faithful reading of Rule 804(b)(3) is that it does not allow admission of non-self-inculpatory statements, even if they are made with a broader narrative that is generally self-inculpatory. The district court may not just assume for purposes of Rule 804(b)(3) that a statement is self-inculpatory because it is part of a fuller confession, and this is especially true when the statement implicates someone else. "[T]he arrest statements of a codefendant have traditionally been viewed with special suspicion. Due to his strong motivation to implicate the defendant and to exonerate himself, a codefendant's statements about what the defendant said or did are less credible than ordinary hearsay evidence."

JUSTICE KENNEDY suggests that the Advisory Committee's Notes to Rules 804(b)(3) should be read as endorsing the position we reject — that an entire narrative, including non-self-inculpatory parts (but excluding the clearly self-serving parts, *post*, at 11), may be admissible if it is in the aggregate self-inculpatory. *See post*, at 2442. The Notes read, in relevant part:

> " "[T]he third-party confession . . . may include statements implicating [the accused], and under the general theory of declarations against interest they would be admissible as related statements . . . by no means is it required that all statements implicating another person be excluded from the category of declarations against interest. Whether a statement is in fact against interest must be determined from the circumstances of each case. Thus a statement admitting guilt and implicating another person, made while in custody, may well be motivated by a desire to curry favor with the authorities and hence fail to qualify as against interest. . . . On the other hand, the same words spoken under different circumstances, *e.g.*, to an acquaintance, would have no difficulty in qualifying. . . . The balancing of self-serving against dissenting *[sic]* aspects of a declaration is discussed in McCormick § 256." 28 U.S.C.App., p. 790."

This language, however, is not particularly clear, and some of it — especially the

Advisory Committee's endorsement of the position taken by Dean McCormick's treatise — points the other way:

> "A certain latitude as to contextual statements, neutral as to interest, giving meaning to the declaration against interest seems defensible, but bringing in self-serving statements contextually seems questionable. . . . Admitting the deserving parts of the declaration, and excluding the self-serving parts . . . seems the most realistic method of adjusting admissibility to trustworthiness, where the serving and deserving parts can be severed." *See* C. McCormick, *Law of Evidence* § 256, pp. 551–553 (1954). (Footnotes omitted.)

Without deciding exactly how much weight to give the Notes in this particular situation, we conclude that the policy expressed in the statutory text points clearly enough in one direction that it outweighs whatever force the Notes may have.

[W]hether a statement is self-inculpatory or not can only be determined by viewing it in context. Even statements that are on their face neutral may actually be against the declarant's interest. "I hid the gun in Joe's apartment" may not be a confession of a crime; but if it is likely to help the police find the murder weapon, then it is certainly self-inculpatory. "Sam and I went to Joe's house" might be against the declarant's interest if a reasonable person in the declarant's shoes would realize that being linked to Joe and Sam would implicate the declarant in Joe and Sam's conspiracy.

In this case, however, we cannot conclude that all that Harris said was properly admitted. Some of Harris' confession would clearly have been admissible under Rule 804(b)(3); for instance, when he said he knew there was cocaine in the suitcase, he essentially forfeited his only possible defense to a charge of cocaine possession, lack of knowledge. But other parts of his confession, especially the parts that implicated Williamson, did little to subject Harris himself to criminal liability.

Nothing in the record shows that the District Court or the Court of Appeals inquired whether each of the statements in Harris' confession was truly self-inculpatory. As we explained above, this can be a fact-intensive inquiry, which would require careful examination of all the circumstances surrounding the criminal activity involved; we therefore remand to the Court of Appeals to conduct this inquiry in the first instance.

The judgment of the Court of Appeals is vacated, and the case is remanded for further proceedings consistent with this opinion.

So ordered.

JUSTICE KENNEDY, with whom THE CHIEF JUSTICE and JUSTICE THOMAS join, concurring in the judgment:

The Court resolves the issue, as I understand its opinion, by adopting the extreme position that no collateral statements are admissible under Rule 804(b)(3). *See ante*, at 2435 (adopting "narrower reading" that "Rule 804(b)(3) cover[s] only those declarations or remarks within the confession that are individually self-inculpatory"); (GINSBURG, J., concurring in part and concurring in judgment); but cf., (SCALIA, J., concurring). The Court reaches that conclusion by relying on the "principle behind the Rule" that reasonable people do not make statements against their interest unless they are telling the truth, and reasons that this policy "expressed in the statutory text," "simply does not extend" to collateral statements. Though conceding that Congress can "make statements admissible based on their proximity to self-inculpatory statements," the Court says that it cannot "lightly assume that the ambiguous language means anything so inconsistent with the Rule's underlying theory."

With respect, I must disagree with this analysis. All agree that the justification for admission of hearsay statements against interest was, as it still is, that reasonable people do not make those statements unless believing them to be true, but that has not resolved the long-running debate over the admissibility of collateral statements, as to which there is no clear consensus in the authorities. Indeed, to the extent the authorities come close to any consensus, they support admission of some collateral statements. *See supra*, at 2440–41. Given that the underlying principle for the hearsay exception has not resolved the debate over collateral statements one way or the other, I submit that we should not assume that the text of Rule 804(b)(3), which is silent about collateral statements, in fact incorporates one of the competing positions. The Rule's silence no more incorporates Jefferson's position respecting collateral statements than it does McCormick's or Wigmore's.

First, the Advisory Committee's Note establishes that some collateral statements are admissible. In fact, it refers in specific terms to the issue we here confront: "[o]rdinarily the third-party confession is thought of in terms of exculpating the accused, but this is by no means always or necessarily the case: it may include statements implicating him, and under the general theory of declarations against interest they would be admissible as related statements." 28 U.S.C. App., p. 790. This language seems a forthright statement that collateral statements are admissible under Rule 804(b)(3).

Absent contrary indications, we can presume that Congress intended the principles and terms used in the Federal Rules of Evidence to be applied as they were at common law. *See Daubert v. Merrell Dow Pharmaceuticals, Inc.*, 509 U.S. —, —, 113 S. Ct. 2786, 2793–2794, 125 L. Ed. 2d 469 (1993); *see also Midlantic Nat. Bank v. New Jersey Dept. of Environmental Protection*, 474 U.S. 494, 501, 106 S. Ct. 755, 759–760, 88 L. Ed. 2d 859 (1986) ("if Congress intends for legislation to change the interpretation of a judicially created concept, it makes that intent specific"). Application of that principle indicates that collateral statements should be admissible. . . . Indeed, the Advisory Committee Note itself, in stating that collateral statements would be admissible, referred to the "general theory" that related statements are admissible, an indication of the state of the law at the time the rule was enacted. Rule 804(b)(3) does not address the issue, but Congress legislated against the common law background allowing admission of some collateral statements, and I would not assume that Congress gave the common law rule silent burial in Rule 804(b)(3).

[13] Rules Comparison

Several states have adopted hearsay exceptions for statements by child victims of sexual or physical abuse. The FRE do not have a comparable exception. Should the FRE adopt a similar provision? Are such statements sufficiently reliable? Review the pertinent Delaware hearsay exception:

Delaware, Title 11, § 3513. Hearsay exception for child victim's out-of-court statement of abuse

(a) An out-of-court statement made by a child under 11 years of age at the time of the proceeding concerning an act that is a material element of the offense relating to sexual abuse, or physical abuse . . . that is not otherwise admissible in evidence is admissible in any judicial proceeding if the requirement of subsections (b)–(f) of this section are met.

(b) An out-of-court statement may be admitted as provided in subsection (a) of this section if:

(1) The child is present and his or her testimony touches upon the event and is subject to cross-examination rendering such prior statement admissible under § 3507 of this title; or

(2)a. The child is found by the court to be unavailable to testify on any of these grounds:

1. The child's death;

2. The child's absence from the jurisdiction;

3. The child's total failure of memory;

4. The child's persistent refusal to testify despite judicial requests to do so;

5. The child's physical or mental disability;

6. The existence of a privilege involving the child;

7. The child's incompetency, including the child's inability to communicate about the offense because of fear or a similar reason;

8. Substantial likelihood that the child would suffer severe emotional trauma from testifying at the proceeding or by means of a videotaped deposition or closed-circuit television; and

b. The child's out-of-court statement is shown to possess particularized guarantees of trustworthiness.

(c) A finding of unavailability under subsection (b)(2)a.8. of this section must be supported by expert testimony.

(d) The proponent of the statement must inform the adverse party of the proponent's intention to offer the statement and the content of the statement sufficiently in advance of the proceeding to provide the adverse party with a fair opportunity to prepare a response to the statement before the proceeding at which it is offered.

[G] Review Problems

Problem #10-91: "Missing . . ."

Shawna went to a party one chilly January night to take a break from entering data on her computer. The last time anyone saw her was when she left the party, apparently alone. Peter is charged with Shawna's murder. Which of the following testimony is admissible hearsay?

1. Susan: I heard Shawna say at the party: "I'm just going to go to the liquor store with Peter; I'll be back."

2. Susan: I told Shawna, "Is that a gun Peter is showing Diane over there? It looks like a Smith and Wesson."

3. Susan: Peter said as he left the party that he was going to go home to sleep because he was feeling very tired.

4. Susan: Shawna knew that I was doing my neurology residency, and she asked me what to do about some dizzy spells she had been having.

Problem #10-92: Sheperd's Pie

Several hours after eating some sheperd's pie, Mrs. Connolly shrieked, "My hands are tingling; that snake Mr. Connolly must have poisoned me!" Mrs. Connolly then collapsed and died. Mr. Connolly was charged with her murder. Are Mrs. Connolly's statements admissible at trial? Why?

Problem #10-93: Records

In a prom-night accident, a joy-riding, intoxicated high school senior named Royce drives at high speed into a group of freshmen and sophomores gathered at a street corner near the high school. Miraculously, no one is killed. Several serious injuries, however, occur. In a subsequent trial brought by the parents of the injured bystanders, which records are admissible hearsay?

1. The hospital records reflecting the injuries of the bystanders.

2. The repair records of the car that crashed as regularly maintained by Briarcliff Service Station and Auto Repair.

3. The notes taken by one of the parents detailing the torturous recovery of one of the victims.

4. The records of the weather bureau for that day regarding rain and time of sunset.

5. The police report providing a description of the accident and its cause.

Problem #10-94: "I Swear to Tell . . ."

A witness, Arton Serma, testified at a congressional oversight hearing on subcontracting irregularities in the Army and then promptly disappeared. In a subsequent criminal trial brought against one of the subcontractors, can the defendant offer the videotape of Arton's testimony against the prosecution? Why?

Problem #10-95: The Fugitive

A significant issue in a probate proceeding was whether a fugitive, Frank, who was wanted in the death of his wife, was still alive. Two months earlier, Arturo knowingly lay dying at the hands of an intruder. He blurted out, "Jermaine killed Frank last month!" Arturo then died. Are these statements admissible at trial? Why?

Problem #10-96: Dead Overdrive

Joel's best friend Pasquale was charged with improperly charging for "overdrive" on various model cars when the "overdrive" was merely decorative. When Joel was asked why he did not come to his friend's defense, Joel stated, "Because they would've found out that I knew more about those charges than Pasquale did." If Joel suffers a stroke and is unable to testify, can Pasquale offer Joel's statement at his trial on fraud charges?

Problem #10-97: Grand Jury II

A witness, Davey, testified before the grand jury investigating claims of child abuse at a day-care center. Prior to the trial, Davey suffers an incapacitating stroke. Can Davey's grand jury testimony be offered at trial? By the prosecution? By the defendant? Why?

§ 10.05   MISCELLANEOUS HEARSAY ISSUES [FRE 805, 806]

Problem #10-98: Chicken at Rest

Howard and Carol were at their favorite chicken fast-food restaurant when Howard began to choke on a piece of boneless chicken. Howard was rushed to the hospital, where a fragment of a hair brush was extracted from his stomach. Officer Dudley's report contained the following notation: "It was reported to me by the store manager, Alec David Black, that the assistant manager, Michael Lucas, said that an employee, Gail Marsden, had lost her hair brush earlier that same day at the restaurant."

Is this report, with the above notation, admissible at trial?

Problem #10-99: You Dirty Rat!

Janni, an eyewitness, testifies for the defendant, Lenny, in a robbery trial. Janni states that she heard a bystander, Deborah, exclaim at the time of the robbery, "Look! There goes Lenny with the purse down the alley!" The hearsay statement of Deborah was admitted as an excited utterance after some discussion at sidebar.

The prosecution subsequently offers evidence that Deborah has been convicted of burglary twice and shoplifting once. Are Deborah's prior convictions admissible?

Problem #10-100: Katie and the Videotape

Katie was interviewing an eyewitness, Ed, in a highly publicized criminal case involving a professional baseball manager and several politicians for her morning television show, *Yesterday & Today*. The interview was taped. That same day, Katie taped a deposition given by the same witness, as part of her ongoing story. The next day, Ed disappeared, never to be seen or heard from again. Can either of Katie's videotapes be admitted in the criminal trial?

§ 10.06 SUMMARY AND REVIEW

1. What does "offered for the truth of the matter asserted" mean?

2. When is evidence *not* offered for the truth of the matter asserted?

3. When is non-verbal conduct hearsay?

4. Are assertions such as those in *Wright v. Doe D. Tatham* hearsay under the FRE? Explain.

5. When are prior statements of a witness not hearsay, despite being offered for the truth of the matter asserted?

6. What are admissions by a party opponent?

7. Compare admissions with implied admissions.

8. Does the rule excluding lay opinion testimony apply to admissions? Explain.

9. What are the prerequisites of co-conspirator admissions? What is the quantum of proof required for the admission of co-conspirator statements?

10. What is the rationale underlying the spontaneous statement, excited utterance, and state of mind exceptions to the hearsay rule?

11. Compare and contrast the business records exception (FRE 803(6)), with the public records exception, (FRE 803(8)). What differences are there, if any?

12. Is testimony of a witness before a grand jury "former testimony" under FRE 804(b)(1)? Why?

13. What are the limitations of the "dying declaration" exception to the hearsay rule?

14. Why did the FRE abandon the requirement that declarations against interest must be against either the speaker's pecuniary or proprietary interest?

Problem #10-101: Jones v. State University

J.D. Jones was fired from his job at State University. The dismissal letter stated that he was a drunkard on the job, which caused him to be unable to fulfill his responsibilities and duties. Jones brought suit against the University, claiming defamation.

A former co-worker, Alice, will testify. State whether (1) Alice's testimony is hearsay, and if it is, (2) whether it is admissible. In addition, state (3) which party likely will offer the testimony. Alice's testimony is as follows:

1. "Jones is 46 years old and has two relatives living in the Akron area, near where we work."

2. "All of us at work think that Jones is the nicest guy, and that he does not have a major alcohol problem."

3. "I heard in the lunch room at work that he had fallen down eight times last week, and that his breath was real bad; you know, it smelled like alcohol."

4. "I saw him work every day of each semester, and he seemed to be fine. I could not tell if he was intoxicated."

5. "I saw him stumble at times, but Jones said that he had a hip problem that caused him trouble when he walked."

6. "Here's the University memorandum that says, 'Dear Mr. Jones; We must unfortunately release you from your employment. You have been a drunkard on the job, causing you to be unable to fulfill your responsibilities and duties.'"

7. "I saw Jones at the Salty Dog Bar and Grill quaffing two lite beers last Wednesday at lunch."

8. "When Jones was handed the memorandum, I heard Sally, the assistant registrar, exclaim, 'He's fainting. Catch him!'"

9. "Last week Sally said that she was going to meet Jones at the Salty Dog after work to have a couple of beers."

10. "I heard Jones tell the nurse that his hip hurt badly, so much so that he was having trouble sleeping and walking, and that he needed some medication to ease the pain. He also told the nurse that the University was trying to run him out of school on some trumped-up alcohol charge and he had to work harder as a result."

11. "I have here a memorandum from University Security, stating, 'The subject, J.D. Jones, has been investigated on suspicion of narcotics use. We conclude that he is not a drug addict. We believe, however, that he has experimented with marijuana. We further conclude that he is an alcoholic.'"

12. "After work one day we were all standing around, teasing each other. Another employee, I forget who, said to Jones, 'So, is it true that you are best friends with Jack Daniels? Is it?' Jones just blushed, sort of smiled, and did not say anything."

Chapter 11

THE CONFRONTATION CLAUSE

CHAPTER FRAMEWORK: The Confrontation Clause protects criminal defendants by affording them the opportunity to confront the witnesses against them at trial. The Clause is not interpreted literally and is given its interpretive meaning by judges, mostly the justices of the Supreme Court. The Clause protects the accused in federal courts directly through the Sixth Amendment and in state courts indirectly from the Sixth Amendment through the Fourteenth Amendment's due process clause.

There are two strands of Confrontation Clause analysis: (1) the use of unconfronted hearsay in criminal cases; and (2) the use of substitutes for face-to-face confrontation between witness and accused, generally arising with child witnesses.

In the use of hearsay, the new Confrontation Clause analysis after the seminal case of *Crawford v. Washington*, 541 U.S. 36 (2004), at a minimum applies the Clause to all "testimonial" statements offered against the accused. If testimonial statements are offered, the accused generally must have had the opportunity to cross-examine a currently unavailable declarant.

WHY ARE THE CONCEPTS IN THIS CHAPTER IMPORTANT? The Confrontation Clause offers an intersection between a statutory code (the FRE) and the Constitution. This window into constitutional analysis has increasing importance after the *Crawford* decision.

CONNECTIONS: The Confrontation Clause analysis is very much a part of hearsay analysis and can arise in sexual assault or domestic violence cases or any other case where 911 calls or police interviews play a role in a criminal investigation. The Clause also connects to constitutional interpretation.

CHAPTER OUTLINE:

    I. The Right to Confrontation of Witnesses Under the Sixth Amendment

        A. When does the clause apply?

            1. Applies directly to the federal government and to the states through the Fourteenth Amendment's Due Process Clause and the Incorporation Doctrine

            2. The Clause applies to testimonial statements

                a. And only testimonial statements

                b. Means? A declarant can reasonably expect the statements to be used in a subsequent criminal trial.

                    i. Can be formal statements, like affidavits.

       ii. Can be informal statements, during informal interrogation, as well.

       iii. Meets a primary purpose of establishing facts for possible use in a later proceeding, not to meet an on-going emergency.

       iv. Context-based analysis is used; many factors are considered.

   3. Testimonial statements are excluded from a criminal trial against a defendant if the defendant did not have a prior opportunity to examine the declarant about the statements.

      a. A substitute for the actual declarant is insufficient.

      b. Only the opportunity, not the actual examination, is required.

      c. The opponent of the statement must not have had the prior opportunity to direct or cross-examine the declarant.

  B. Applying the Confrontation Clause — three-step analytical framework

   1. Is the statement testimonial?

   2. Is the statement offered at a trial against an accused?

   3. Was there a prior opportunity for examination of the declarant by the accused?

II. Waiver of Rights

  A. Express

  B. Implied — e.g., forfeiture by wrongdoing

III. Confrontation, *Crawford*, and its Progeny

  A. The Basic Rule:

    Crawford v. Washington, 541 U.S. 36 (2003)

  B. What Is a Testimonial Statement?

    Hammon v. Indiana; Davis v. Washington, 547 U.S. 813 (2006)

    Michigan v. Bryant, 131 S. Ct. 1143 (2011)

    Ohio v. Clark, ___U.S. ___, 135 S. Ct. 2173 (2015)

  C. Experts and Confrontation

    Melendez-Diaz v. Massachusetts, 129 S. Ct. 2527 (2009)

    Bullcoming v. New Mexico, 131 S. Ct. 2705 (2011)

    Williams v. Illinois, 567 U.S. ___, 132 S. Ct. 2221 (2012)

  D. Waiver of Confrontation Rights

    Giles v. California, 554 U.S. 353 (2008)

  E. Child Witnesses and Face-to-Face Confrontation

    Maryland v. Craig, 497 U.S. 836 (1990)

§ 11.01   INTRODUCTION

The Sixth Amendment to the United States Constitution states, "In all criminal prosecutions, the accused shall enjoy the right . . . to be confronted with the witnesses against him."

THE EXCLUSION OF HEARSAY AND THE CONFRONTATION CLAUSE

Over the past several decades, two distinctive threads of Confrontation Clause analysis developed. One thread involved the potential exclusion of hearsay statements offered by the prosecution against defendants in criminal cases. Another thread involved the use of a surrogate form of confrontation, other than face-to-face observation, mostly in cases involving child witnesses. The hearsay statement thread was wrested from its moorings in *Crawford v. Washington*, 541 U.S. 36 (2004). In that case, Justice Scalia shuffled the entire analysis of when and how the Clause applied. In effect, *Crawford* rearranged the constitutional firmament into two categories: testimonial hearsay; and everything else.

The traditional approach applied to all hearsay. As advanced in *Ohio v. Roberts*, 448 U.S. 56 (1980), if the hearsay was within a "firmly rooted" exception, it was considered to have presumptive reliability. That analysis no longer governs.

Crawford v. Washington and Hearsay

Crawford v. Washington, 541 U.S. 36 (2004) creates a new structure for Confrontation Clause analysis. Lynchpins, or important components, now include whether the hearsay declarant is unavailable to testify and whether the nature of the hearsay statement is considered testimonial. Thus, the duality of analysis focuses on the declarant and the nature of the statement, much like FRE 804. Further, subsequent cases have carved out an exception to Confrontation requirements, when the testimonial statements were not made with the primary purpose or understanding that the statements would be used later in a criminal investigation. *Davis v. Washington*, 547 U.S. 813 (2006); *Hammon v. Indiana*, 546 U.S. 1213 (2006). One significant tributary of this exception involves statements made for the primary purpose of resolving an ongoing emergency. See *Michigan v. Bryant*, 562 U.S. 344 (2011).

Unavailability

Crawford directs courts to assess whether the declarant is available to testify. If not, it imposes a requirement that the opponent must have had an opportunity to examine the declarant about the statement. The requirement of an opportunity means the opponent has a strategic choice — to examine or not — that need not be utilized.

Testimonial Hearsay

The new approach requires a determination of whether the hearsay is testimonial. No matter how firmly rooted, testimonial statements are only admissible if the defendant had a prior opportunity to cross-examine the now unavailable declarant.

Testimonial statements include affidavits, statements that are the product of custodial interrogation by police, depositions, courtroom testimony, and "statements that were made under circumstances which would lead an objective witness reasonably to believe that the statement would be available for use at a later trial." *Crawford*, 541 U.S. at 52 (Scalia, J.)

Questions remain. After *Crawford*, what does "testimonial" really mean? As the cases show, the contours of the term testimonial are still being drawn.

Example #1

Rae Wiggins, known widely as Rae Carruth, was an NFL wide receiver for the Carolina Panthers who was convicted of conspiracy to kill his pregnant girlfriend. At the time of Cherica Adams's death, she was driving her car with Carruth in another car, driving in front of her. Apparently, Carruth slowed his car down and a third car drove up alongside Adams's car and someone inside that car shot her. Adams then called 911 and provided information about the attack, including Carruth's participation. Adams made additional statements at the scene and at the hospital to a police officer, Officer Grant. Adams also wrote notes about the incident for a nurse at the hospital, Nurse Willard, before she lapsed into a coma.

This case raises several Confrontation Clause issues. First, did the Clause apply to the 911 call? The statement made to the officer at the hospital? The handwritten notes made for the nurse? The answer lies first in whether these would be considered testimonial statements, a critical assessment for determining whether the Confrontation Clause even applies. The Supreme Court explains the scope of the meaning of the word "testimonial" in a series of cases. The primary purpose in uttering the statements matters. Was it to meet and stop an on-going emergency? Or were the statements offered for crime interdiction purposes (i.e., testimonial)? If the statements were testimonial in nature, then the prosecution can offer them against the accused at trial only if the accused was first afforded the opportunity for prior confrontation. This is not an absolute requirement, because an accused can waive his rights and forfeit them by wrongdoing. In this case, there are many relevant questions. Were Adams's statements testimonial? If yes, there was no prior opportunity for confrontation and consequently they generally should be excluded. But the statements might still not be excluded here if the forfeiture by wrongdoing exception applies. So the confrontation analysis has several steps, each of which is nuanced and contextual, requiring the application of a rule and consideration of the particular facts.

[Note that even if the confrontation analysis ends without excluding the statements, the statements might still be excluded as unreliable hearsay. Thus, a hearsay analysis must still take place.]

Illustration

Eaney, Meany, and Miney Moe were arrested for conspiracy to import cocaine. At their arrest, Eaney blurted out, "Hah! You did not catch us with any drugs; we were too quick for you coppers!" The three defendants were tried jointly and Eaney's statement was offered against him at trial. (The statement would not constitute a co-conspirator admission because it was not made in furtherance of the conspiracy.) If

Eaney decided not to testify, would a limiting instruction, telling the jury that the statement is admitted solely as an admission against Eaney and not against the other defendants, overcome any Confrontation Clause objections?

Answer: If Eaney's statement is admitted against him in his joint trial with Meany and Miney, the Confrontation Clause rights of Meany and Miney would be violated. A limiting instruction, informing the jury that it should disregard the statement against Meany and Miney, without Eaney testifying and being subject to cross-examination, fails to sufficiently minimize the prejudicial impact of the statement (*see Bruton v. United States*, 391 U.S. 123 (1968) *infra*). Note also that Eaney's statement likely is not "testimonial" under *Crawford* and consequently would not violate *Crawford's* cross-examination mandate. If it was considered to be testimonial, unavailability and a prior opportunity to cross-examine likely would be required.

§ 11.02   *CRAWFORD* AND ITS PROGENY

[A]   The Basic Rule

Crawford v. Washington
541 U.S. 36 (2004)

JUSTICE SCALIA delivered the opinion of the Court.

Petitioner Michael Crawford stabbed a man who allegedly tried to rape his wife, Sylvia. At his trial, the State played for the jury Sylvia's tape-recorded statement to the police describing the stabbing, even though he had no opportunity for cross-examination. The Washington Supreme Court upheld petitioner's conviction after determining that Sylvia's statement was reliable. The question presented is whether this procedure complied with the Sixth Amendment's guarantee that, "in all criminal prosecutions, the accused shall enjoy the right . . . to be confronted with the witnesses against him."

I

On August 5, 1999, Kenneth Lee was stabbed at his apartment. Police arrested petitioner later that night. After giving petitioner and his wife *Miranda* warnings, detectives interrogated each of them twice. Petitioner eventually confessed that he and Sylvia had gone in search of Lee because he was upset over an earlier incident in which Lee had tried to rape her. The two had found Lee at his apartment, and a fight ensued in which Lee was stabbed in the torso and petitioner's hand was cut.

Petitioner gave the following account of the fight:

"Q. Okay. Did you ever see anything in [Lee's] hands?

"A. I think so, but I'm not positive.

"Q. Okay, when you think so, what do you mean by that?

"A. I couda swore I seen him goin' for somethin' before, right before everything happened. He was like reachin', fiddlin' around down here and stuff . . . and I just . . . I don't know, I think, this is just a possibility, but I think, I think that he pulled somethin' out and I grabbed for it and that's how I got cut . . . but I'm not positive. I, I, my mind goes blank when things like this happen. I mean, I just, I remember things wrong, I remember things that just doesn't, don't make sense to me later."

Sylvia generally corroborated petitioner's story about the events leading up to the fight, but her account of the fight itself was arguably different — particularly with respect to whether Lee had drawn a weapon before petitioner assaulted him:

"Q. Did Kenny do anything to fight back from this assault?

"A. (pausing) I know he reached into his pocket . . . or somethin' . . . I don't know what.

"Q. After he was stabbed?

"A. He saw Michael coming up. He lifted his hand . . . his chest open, he might [have] went to go strike his hand out or something and then (inaudible).

"Q. Okay, you, you gotta speak up.

"A. Okay, he lifted his hand over his head maybe to strike Michael's hand down or something and then he put his hands in his . . . put his right hand in his right pocket . . . took a step back . . . Michael proceeded to stab him . . . then his hands were like . . . how do you explain this . . . open arms . . with his hands open and he fell down . . . and we ran (describing subject holding hands open, palms toward assailant).

"Q. Okay, when he's standing there with his open hands, you're talking about Kenny, correct?

"A. Yeah, after, after the fact, yes.

"Q. Did you see anything in his hands at that point?

"A. (pausing) um um (no)."

The State charged petitioner with assault and attempted murder. At trial, he claimed self-defense. Sylvia did not testify because of the state marital privilege, which generally bars a spouse from testifying without the other spouse's consent. In Washington, this privilege does not extend to a spouse's out-of-court statements admissible under a hearsay exception, so the State sought to introduce Sylvia's tape-recorded statements to the police as evidence that the stabbing was not in self-defense. Noting that Sylvia had admitted she led petitioner to Lee's apartment and thus had facilitated the assault, the State invoked the hearsay exception for statements against penal interest.

Petitioner countered that, state law notwithstanding, admitting the evidence would violate his federal constitutional right to be "confronted with the witnesses against him." According to our description of that right in *Ohio v. Roberts*, 448 U.S. 56 (1980), it does not bar admission of an unavailable witness's statement against a criminal defendant if the statement bears "adequate 'indicia of reliability.' " To meet that test, evidence must either fall within a "firmly rooted hearsay exception" or bear "particularized guarantees of trustworthiness." The trial court here admitted the statement on the latter ground, offering several reasons why it was trustworthy: Sylvia was not shifting blame but rather corroborating her husband's story that he acted in self-defense or "justified reprisal"; she had direct knowledge as an eyewitness; she was describing recent events; and she was being questioned by a "neutral" law enforcement officer. The prosecution played the tape for the jury and relied on it in closing, arguing that it was "damning evidence" that "completely refutes [petitioner's] claim of self-defense." The jury convicted petitioner of assault.

We granted certiorari to determine whether the State's use of Sylvia's statement violated the Confrontation Clause.

II

The Constitution's text does not alone resolve this case. One could plausibly read "witnesses against" a defendant to mean those who actually testify at trial, those whose statements are offered at trial, or something in-between. We must therefore turn to the historical background of the Clause to understand its meaning.

The right to confront one's accusers is a concept that dates back to Roman times. The founding generation's immediate source of the concept, however, was the common law. English common law has long differed from continental civil law in regard to the manner in which witnesses give testimony in criminal trials. The common-law tradition is one of live testimony in court subject to adversarial testing, while the civil law condones examination in private by judicial officers. See 3 W. Blackstone, *Commentaries on the Laws of England* 373–374 (1768).

Nonetheless, England at times adopted elements of the civil-law practice. Justices of the peace or other officials examined suspects and witnesses before trial. These examinations were sometimes read in court in lieu of live testimony, a practice that "occasioned frequent demands by the prisoner to have his 'accusers,' i.e., the witnesses against him, brought before him face to face." 1 J. Stephen, *History of the Criminal Law of England* 326 (1883). In some cases, these demands were refused. See 9 W. Holdsworth, History of English Law 216–217, 228 (3d ed. 1944).

The most notorious instances of civil-law examination occurred in the great political trials of the 16th and 17th centuries. One such was the 1603 trial of Sir Walter Raleigh for treason. Lord Cobham, Raleigh's alleged accomplice, had implicated him in an examination before the Privy Council and in a letter. At Raleigh's trial, these were read to the jury. Raleigh argued that Cobham had lied to save himself: "Cobham is absolutely in the king's mercy; to excuse me cannot avail him; by accusing me he may hope for favour." D. Jardine, *Criminal Trials* 435 (1832). Suspecting that Cobham would recant, Raleigh demanded that the judges call him to appear, arguing that "[t]he Proof of the Common Law is by witness and jury: let Cobham be here, let him speak it. Call my accuser before my face . . . ." 2 How St. Tr., at 15–16. The judges refused, *id.*, at 24, and, despite Raleigh's protestations that he was being tried "by the Spanish Inquisition," *id.*, at 15, the jury convicted, and Raleigh was sentenced to death.

One of Raleigh's trial judges later lamented that "the justice of England has never been so degraded and injured as by the condemnation of Sir Walter Raleigh.'" 1 Jardine, *supra*, at 520. Through a series of statutory and judicial reforms, English law developed a right of confrontation that limited these abuses.

Controversial examination practices were also used in the Colonies. Early in the 18th century, for example, the Virginia Council protested against the Governor for having "privately issued several commissions to examine witnesses against particular men *ex parte*," complaining that "the person accused is not admitted to be confronted with, or defend himself against his defamers." *A Memorial Concerning the Maladministrations of His Excellency Francis Nicholson*, reprinted in 9 English Historical Documents 253, 257 (D. Douglas ed. 1955).

Many declarations of rights adopted around the time of the Revolution guaranteed a right of confrontation. The proposed Federal Constitution, however, did not. The First Congress responded by including the Confrontation Clause in the proposal that became the Sixth Amendment.

Early state decisions shed light upon the original understanding of the common-law right. *State v. Webb*, 2 N.C. 103 (1794) (*per curiam*), decided a mere three years after the adoption of the Sixth Amendment, held that depositions could be read against an accused only if they were taken in his presence. Rejecting a broader reading of the English authorities, the court held: "It is a rule of the common law, founded on natural justice, that no man shall be prejudiced by evidence which he had not the liberty to cross examine." *Id.*

III

This history supports two inferences about the meaning of the Sixth Amendment.

First, the principal evil at which the Confrontation Clause was directed was the civil-law mode of criminal procedure, and particularly its use of *ex parte* examinations as evidence against the accused. It was these practices that the Crown deployed in notorious treason cases like Raleigh's; that the Marian statutes invited; that English law's assertion of a right to confrontation was meant to prohibit; and that the founding-era rhetoric decried. The Sixth Amendment must be interpreted with this focus in mind.

Accordingly, we once again reject the view that the Confrontation Clause applies of its own force only to in-court testimony, and that its application to out-of-court statements introduced at trial depends upon "the law of Evidence for the time being." 3 Wigmore § 1397. Leaving the regulation of out-of-court statements to the law of evidence would render the Confrontation Clause powerless to prevent even the most flagrant inquisitorial practices. Raleigh was, after all, perfectly free to confront those who read Cobham's confession in court.

This focus also suggests that not all hearsay implicates the Sixth Amendment's core concerns. An off-hand, overheard remark might be unreliable evidence and thus a good candidate for exclusion under hearsay rules, but it bears little resemblance to the civil-law abuses the Confrontation Clause targeted. On the other hand, *ex parte* examinations might sometimes be admissible under modern hearsay rules, but the Framers certainly would not have condoned them.

The text of the Confrontation Clause reflects this focus. It applies to "witnesses" against the accused — in other words, those who "bear testimony." 1 N. Webster, *An American Dictionary of the English Language* (1828). "Testimony," in turn, is typically "[a] solemn declaration or affirmation made for the purpose of establishing or proving some fact." *Ibid.* An accuser who makes a formal statement to government officers bears testimony in a sense that a person who makes a casual remark to an acquaintance does not. The constitutional text, like the history underlying the common-law right on confrontation, thus reflects an especially acute concern with a specific type of out-of-court statement.

Various formulations of this core class of "testimonial" statements exist: "ex parte in-court testimony or its functional equivalent — that is, material such as affidavits, custodial examinations, prior testimony that the defendant was unable to cross-examine, or similar pretrial statements that declarants would reasonably expect to be used prosecutorially," . . . "extrajudicial statements . . . contained in formalized testimonial materials, such as affidavits, depositions, prior testimony, or confession," . . . "statements that were made under circumstances which would lead an objective witness reasonably to believe that the statement would be available for use at a later trial" . . . . These formulations all share a common nucleus and then define the Clause's coverage at various levels of abstraction around it. Regardless of the precise articulation, some statements qualify under any definition — for example, *ex parte* testimony at a preliminary hearing.

Statements taken by police officers in the course of interrogations are also testimonial under even a narrow standard.

In sum, even if the Sixth Amendment is not solely concerned with testimonial hearsay, that is its primary object, and interrogations by law enforcement officers fall squarely within that class. (Footnote 4: We use the term "interrogation" in its colloquial, rather than any technical legal, sense.

The historical record also supports a second proposition: that the Framers would not have allowed admission of testimonial statements of a witness who did not appear at trial unless he was unavailable to testify, and the defendant had had a prior opportunity for cross-examination. The text of the Sixth Amendment does not suggest any open-ended exceptions from the confrontation requirement to be developed by the courts. Rather, the "right . . . to be confronted with the witnesses against him" is most naturally read as a reference to the right on confrontation at common law, admitting only those exceptions established at the time of the founding. As the English authorities above reveal, the common law in 1791 conditioned admissibility of an absent witness's examination on unavailability and a prior opportunity to cross-examine. The Sixth Amendment therefore incorporates those limitations.

IV

Our case law has been largely consistent with these two principles. Our leading early decision, for example, involved a deceased witness's prior trial testimony. *Mattox v. United States*, 156 U.S. 237 (1895). In allowing the statement to be admitted, we relied on the fact that the defendant had had, at the first trial, an adequate opportunity to confront the witness: "The substance of the constitutional protection is preserved to the prisoner in the advantage he has once had of seeing the witness face to face, and of subjecting him to the ordeal of a cross-examination. This, the law says, he shall under no circumstances be deprived of." *Id.*

Even our recent cases, in their outcomes, hew closely to the traditional line. *Ohio v. Roberts* admitted testimony from a preliminary hearing at which the defendant had examined the witness. *Lilly v. Virginia* excluded testimonial statements that the defendant had had no opportunity to test by cross-examination. And *Bourjaily v. United States* admitted statements made unwittingly to an FBI informant after applying a more general test that did not make prior cross-examination an indispensable requirement.

Our cases have thus remained faithful to the Framers' understanding: Testimonial statements of witnesses absent from trial have been admitted only where the declarant is unavailable, and only where the defendant has had a prior opportunity to cross-examine.

V

Although the results of our decisions have generally been faithful to the original meaning of the Confrontation Clause, the same cannot be said of our rationales. *Roberts* conditions the admissibility of all hearsay evidence on whether it falls under a "firmly rooted hearsay exception;" or bears "particularized guarantees of trustworthiness." This test departs from the historical principles identified above in two respects. First, it is too broad: It applies the same mode of analysis whether or not the hearsay consists of *ex parte* testimony. This often results in close constitutional scrutiny in cases that are far removed from the core concerns of the Clause. At the same time, however, the test is too narrow: It admits statements that *do* consist of *ex parte* testimony upon a mere finding of reliability. This malleable standard often fails to protect against paradigmatic confrontation violations.

Members of this Court and academics have suggested that we revise our doctrine to reflect more accurately the original understanding of the Clause. They offer two proposals: First, that we apply the Confrontation Clause only to testimonial statements, leaving the remainder to regulation by hearsay law — thus eliminating the overbreadth referred to above. Second, that we impose an absolute bar to statements that are testimonial, absent a prior opportunity to cross-examine — thus eliminating the excessive narrowness referred to above.

In *White* we considered the first proposal and rejected it. Although our analysis in this case casts doubt on that holding, we need not definitely resolve whether it survives our decision today, because Sylvia Crawford's statement is testimonial under any definition. This case does, however, squarely implicate the second proposal.

Where testimonial statements are involved, we do not think the Framers meant to leave the Sixth Amendment's protection to the vagaries of the rules of evidence, much less to amorphous notions of "reliability." Certainly none of the authorities discussed above acknowledges any general reliability exception to the common-law rule. Admitting statements deemed reliable by a judge is fundamentally at odds with the right of confrontation. To be sure, the Clause's ultimate goal is to ensure reliability of evidence, but it is a procedural rather than a substantive guarantee. It commands, not that evidence be reliable, but that reliability be assessed in a particular manner: by testing in the crucible of cross-examination. The Clause thus reflects a judgment, not only about the desirability of reliable evidence (a point on which there could be little dissent), but about how reliability can best be determined.

The *Roberts* test allows a jury to hear evidence, untested by the adversary process, based on a mere judicial determination of reliability. It thus replaces the constitutionally prescribed method of assessing reliability with a wholly foreign one.

The Raleigh trial itself involved the very sorts of reliability determinations that *Roberts* authorizes. In the face of Raleigh's repeated demands for confrontation, the prosecution responded with many of the arguments a court applying *Roberts* might invoke today: that Cobham's statements were self-inculpatory, that they were not made in the heat of passion, and that they were not "extracted from [him] upon any hopes or promise of Pardon." It is not plausible that the Framers' only objection to the trial was that Raleigh's judges did not properly weigh these factors before sentencing him to death. Rather, the problem was that the judges refused to allow Raleigh to confront Cobham in court, where he could cross-examine him and try to expose his accusation as a lie.

Dispensing with confrontation because testimony is obviously reliable is akin to dispensing with jury trial because a defendant is obviously guilty. This is not what the Sixth Amendment prescribes.

The legacy of *Roberts* in other courts vindicates the Framers' wisdom in rejecting a general reliability exception. The framework is so unpredictable that it fails to provide meaningful protection from even core confrontation violations.

Reliability is an amorphous, if not entirely subjective, concept. There are countless factors bearing on whether a statement is reliable; the nine-factor balancing test applied by the Court of Appeals below is representative. Whether a statement is deemed reliable depends heavily on which factors the judge considers and how much weight he accords each of them. Some courts wind up attaching the same significance to opposite facts. For example, the Colorado Supreme Court held a statement more reliable because its inculpation of the defendant was "detailed," while the Fourth Circuit found a statement more reliable because the portion implicating another was "fleeting."

The unpardonable vice of the Roberts test, however, is not its unpredictability, but its demonstrated capacity to admit core testimonial statements that the Confrontation Clause plainly meant to exclude. Despite the plurality's speculation in *Lilly* that it was "highly unlikely" that accomplice confessions implicating the accused could survive *Roberts*, courts continue routinely to admit them.

To add insult to injury, some of the courts that admit untested testimonial statements find reliability in the very factors that *make* the statements testimonial. As noted earlier, one court relied on the fact that the witness's statement was made to police while in custody on pending charges — the theory being that this made the statement more clearly against penal interest and thus more reliable. Other courts routinely rely on the fact that a prior statement is given under oath in judicial proceedings. That inculpating statements are given in a testimonial setting is not an antidote to the confrontation problem, but rather the trigger that makes the Clause's demands most urgent.

Roberts' failings were on full display in the proceedings below. Sylvia Crawford made her statement while in police custody, herself a potential suspect in the case. Indeed, she had been told that whether she would be released "depended on how the investigation continues."

Each of the courts also made assumptions that cross-examination might well have undermined. The trial court, for example, stated that Sylvia Crawford's statement was reliable because she was an eyewitness with direct knowledge of the events. But Sylvia at one point told the police that she had "shut [her] eyes and . . . didn't really watch" part of the fight, and that she was "in shock." The trial court also buttressed its reliability finding by claiming that Sylvia was "being questioned by law enforcement, and, thus, the [questioner] is . . . neutral to her and not someone who would be inclined to advance her interests and shade her version of the truth unfavorably toward the defendant." The Framers would be astounded to learn that *ex parte* testimony could be admitted against a criminal defendant because it was elicited by "neutral" government officers. But even if the court's assessment of the officer's motives was accurate, it says nothing about Sylvia's perception of her situation. Only cross-examination could reveal that.

The State Supreme Court gave dispositive weight to the interlocking nature of the two statements — that they were both ambiguous as to when and whether Lee had a weapon. The court's claim that the two statements were *equally* ambiguous is hard to accept.

The prosecutor obviously did not share the court's view that Sylvia's statement was ambiguous — he called it "damning evidence" that "completely refutes [petitioner's] claim of self-defense." We have no way of knowing whether the jury agreed with the prosecutor or the court. Far from obviating the need for cross-examination, the "interlocking" ambiguity of the two statements made it all the more imperative that they be tested to tease out the truth.

We readily concede that we could resolve this case by simply reweighing the "reliability factors" under *Roberts* and finding that Sylvia Crawford's statement falls short. But we view this as one of those rare cases in which the result below is so improbable that it reveals a fundamental failure on our part to interpret the Constitution in a way that secures its intended constraint on judicial discretion.

* * *

Where nontestimonial hearsay is at issue, it is wholly consistent with the Framer's design to afford the States flexibility in their development of hearsay law — as does *Roberts,* and as would an approach that exempted such statements from Confrontation Clause scrutiny altogether. Where testimonial evidence is at issue, however, the Sixth

Amendment demands what the common law required: unavailability and a prior opportunity for cross-examination. We leave for another day any effort to spell out a comprehensive definition of "testimonial." Whatever else the term covers, it applies at a minimum to prior testimony at a preliminary hearing, before a grand jury, or at a former trial; and to police interrogations. These are the modern practices with closest kinship to the abuses at which the Confrontation Clause was directed.

In this case, the State admitted Sylvia's testimonial statement against petitioner, despite the fact that he had no opportunity to cross-examine her. That alone is sufficient to make out a violation of the Sixth Amendment. *Roberts* notwithstanding, we decline to mine the record in search of indicia of reliability. Where testimonial statements are at issue, the only indicium of reliability sufficient to satisfy constitutional demands is the one the Constitution actually prescribes: confrontation.

The judgment of the Washington Supreme Court is reversed, and the case is remanded for further proceedings not inconsistent with this opinion. It is so ordered.

Chief Justice Rehnquist, with whom Justice O'Connor joins, concurring in the judgment.

I dissent from the Court's decision to overrule *Ohio v. Roberts*. I believe that the Court's adoption of a new interpretation of the Confrontation Clause is not backed by sufficiently persuasive reasoning to overrule long-established precedent. Its decision casts a mantle of uncertainty over future criminal trials in both federal and state courts, and is by no means necessary to decide the present case.

The Court's distinction between testimonial and nontestimonial statements, contrary to its claim, is no better rooted in history than our current doctrine. Under the common law, although the courts were far from consistent, out-of-court statements made by someone other than the accused and not taken under oath, unlike *ex parte* depositions or affidavits, were generally not considered substantive evidence upon which a conviction could be based. Testimonial statements such as accusatory statements to police officers likely would have been disapproved of in the 18th century, not necessarily because they resembled *ex parte* affidavits or depositions as the Court reasons, but more likely than not because they were not made under oath. Without an oath, one usually did not get to the second step of whether confrontation was required.

Thus, while I agree that the Framers were mainly concerned about sworn affidavits and depositions, it does not follow that they were similarly concerned about the Court's broader category of testimonial statements. As far as I can tell, unsworn testimonial statements were treated no differently at common law than were nontestimonial statements, and it seems to me any classification of statements as testimonial beyond that of sworn affidavits and depositions will be somewhat arbitrary, merely a proxy for what the Framers might have intended had such evidence been liberally admitted as substantive evidence like it is today.

I therefore see no reason why the distinction the Court draws is preferable to our precedent. Starting with Chief Justice Marshall's interpretation as a Circuit Justice in 1807, 16 years after the ratification of the Sixth Amendment, *United States v. Burr*, we have never drawn a distinction between testimonial and nontestimonial statements.

And for that matter, neither has any other court of which I am aware. I see little value in trading our precedent for an imprecise approximation at this late date.

In choosing the path it does, the Court of course overrules *Ohio v. Roberts*, a case decided nearly a quarter of a century ago, *Stare decisis* is not an inexorable command in the area of constitutional law, but by and large, it "is the preferred course because it promotes the evenhanded, predictable, and consistent development of legal principles, fosters reliance on judicial decisions, and contributes to the actual and perceived integrity of the judicial process." The Court grandly declares that 'we leave for another day any effort to spell out a comprehensive definition of "testimonial.'" But the thousands of federal prosecutors and the tens of thousands of state prosecutors need answers as to what beyond the specific kinds of "testimony" the Court lists is covered by the new rule. They need them now, not months or years from now. Rules of criminal evidence are applied every day in courts throughout the country, and parties should not be left in the dark in this manner.

To its credit, the Court's analysis of "testimony" excludes at least some hearsay exceptions, such as business records and official records. To hold otherwise would require numerous additional witnesses without any apparent gain in the truth-seeking process. Likewise to the Court's credit is its implicit recognition that the mistaken application of its new rule by courts which guess wrong as to the scope of the rule is subject to harmless-error analysis.

But these are palliatives to what I believe is a mistaken change of course. It is a change of course not in the least necessary to reverse the judgment of the Supreme Court of Washington in this case. The result the Court reaches follows inexorably from *Roberts* and its progeny without any need for overruling that line of cases. No re-weighing of the "reliability factors," which is hypothesized by the Court is required to reverse the judgment here. A citation to *Idaho v. Wright* would suffice. For the reasons stated, I believe that this would be a far preferable course for the Court to take here.

[B] What Is a "Testimonial Statement?"

[1] Distinguishing Testimonial Statements From Statements Made for the Primary Purpose of Resolving an On-Going Emergency

Hammon v. Indiana; Davis v. Washington
547 U.S. 813 (2006)

JUSTICE SCALIA delivered the opinion of the Court.

These cases require us to determine when statements made to law enforcement personnel during a 911 call or at a crime scene are "testimonial" and thus subject to the requirements of the Sixth Amendment's Confrontation Clause.

I

A

The relevant statements in *Davis v. Washington*, No. 05–5224, were made to a 911 emergency operator on February 1, 2001. In the ensuing conversation, the operator ascertained that [the 911 caller] McCottry was involved in a domestic disturbance with her former boyfriend Adrian Davis, the petitioner in this case:

"911 Operator: Hello.

"Complainant: Hello.

"911 Operator: What's going on?

"Complainant: He's here jumpin' on me again.

"911 Operator: Okay. Listen to me carefully. Are you in a house or an apartment?

"Complainant: I'm in a house.

"911 Operator: Are there any weapons?

"Complainant: No. He's usin' his fists.

"911 Operator: Okay. Has he been drinking?

"Complainant: No.

"911 Operator: Okay, sweetie. I've got help started. Stay on the line with me, okay?

"Complainant: I'm on the line.

"911 Operator: Listen to me carefully. Do you know his last name?

"Complainant: It's Davis.

"911 Operator: Davis? Okay, what's his first name?

"Complainant: Adrian

"911 Operator: What is it?

"Complainant: Adrian.

"911 Operator: Adrian?

"Complainant: Yeah.

"911 Operator: Okay. What's his middle initial?

"Complainant: Martell. He's runnin' now." App. in No. 05–5224, pp. 8–9.

. . . McCottry described the context of the assault, after which the operator told her that the police were on their way. . . .

The police arrived within four minutes of the 911 call and observed McCottry's shaken state, the "fresh injuries on her forearm and her face," and her "frantic efforts to gather her belongings and her children so that they could leave the residence." 154 Wash.2d 291, 296, 111 P.3d 844, 847 (2005) (en banc).

The State charged Davis with felony violation of a domestic no-contact order. "The State's only witnesses were the two police officers who responded to the 911 call. Both officers testified that McCottry exhibited injuries that appeared to be recent, but neither officer could testify as to the cause of the injuries." McCottry presumably could have testified as to whether Davis was her assailant, but she did not appear. Over Davis's objection, based on the Confrontation Clause of the Sixth Amendment, the trial court admitted the recording of her exchange with the 911 operator, and the jury convicted him. The Washington Court of Appeals affirmed. The Supreme Court of Washington, with one dissenting justice, also affirmed, concluding that the portion of the 911 conversation in which McCottry identified Davis was not testimonial, and that if other portions of the conversation were testimonial, admitting them was harmless beyond a reasonable doubt. 154 Wash.2d, at 305, 111 P.3d, at 851. We granted certiorari.

B

In *Hammon v. Indiana*, No. 05–5705, police responded late on the night of February 26, 2003, to a "reported domestic disturbance" at the home of Hershel and Amy Hammon. 829 N.E.2d 444, 446 (Ind. 2005). They found Amy alone on the front porch, appearing " 'somewhat frightened,' " but she told them that " 'nothing was the matter,' ". She gave them permission to enter the house, where an officer saw "a gas heating unit in the corner of the living room" that had "flames coming out of the . . . partial glass front. Hershel, meanwhile, was in the kitchen. He told the police "that he and his wife had 'been in an argument' but 'everything was fine now' and the argument 'never became physical.' ". By this point Amy had come back inside . . . . After hearing Amy's account, the officer "had her fill out and sign a battery affidavit." Amy handwrote the following: "Broke our Furnace & shoved me down on the floor into the broken glass. Hit me in the chest and threw me down. Broke our lamps & phone. Tore up my van where I couldn't leave the house. Attacked my daughter."

The State charged Hershel with domestic battery and with violating his probation. Amy was subpoenaed, but she did not appear at his subsequent bench trial. The State called the officer who had questioned Amy, and asked him to recount what Amy told him and to authenticate the affidavit. Hershel's counsel repeatedly objected to the admission of this evidence. Nonetheless, the trial court admitted the affidavit as a "present sense impression," and Amy's statements as "excited utterances" that "are expressly permitted in these kinds of cases even if the declarant is not available to testify," The officer thus testified that Amy

> "informed me that she and Hershel had been in an argument. That he became irrate [sic] over the fact of their daughter going to a boyfriend's house. The argument became . . . physical after being verbal.

"She informed me Mr. Hammon had pushed her onto the ground, had shoved her head into the broken glass of the heater and that he had punched her in the chest twice I believe." [App. in No. 05-5705], at 17–18.

The trial judge found Hershel guilty on both charges, *id.*, and the Indiana Court of Appeals affirmed in relevant part. The Indiana Supreme Court also affirmed, concluding that Amy's statement was admissible for state-law purposes as an excited utterance, that "a 'testimonial' statement is one given or taken in significant part for purposes of preserving it for potential future use in legal proceedings," where "the motivations of the questioner and declarant are the central concerns," and that Amy's oral statement was not "testimonial" under these standards. It also concluded that, although the affidavit was testimonial and thus wrongly admitted, it was harmless beyond a reasonable doubt, largely because the trial was to the bench. We granted certiorari.

II

The Confrontation Clause of the Sixth Amendment provides: "In all criminal prosecutions, the accused shall enjoy the right . . . to be confronted with the witnesses against him." In [2004], we held that this provision bars "admission of testimonial statements of a witness who did not appear at trial unless he was unavailable to testify, and the defendant had had a prior opportunity for cross-examination." A critical portion of this holding, and the portion central to resolution of the two cases now before us, is the phrase "testimonial statements." Only statements of this sort cause the declarant to be a "witness" within the meaning of the Confrontation Clause. It is the testimonial character of the statement that separates it from other hearsay that, while subject to traditional limitations upon hearsay evidence, is not subject to the Confrontation Clause.

Our opinion in *Crawford* set forth "[v]arious formulations" of the core class of " 'testimonial' " statements, but found it unnecessary to endorse any of them, because "some statements qualify under any definition" Among those, we said, were "[s]tatements taken by police officers in the course of interrogations,. Questioning that generated the deponent's statement in *Crawford* — which was made and recorded while she was in police custody, after having been given Miranda warnings as a possible suspect herself — "qualifies under any conceivable definition" of an " 'interrogation,' " We therefore did not define that term, except to say that "[w]e use [it] . . . in its colloquial, rather than any technical legal, sense," and that "one can imagine various definitions . . . , and we need not select among them in this case." The character of the statements in the present cases is not as clear, and these cases require us to determine more precisely which police interrogations produce testimony.

Without attempting to produce an exhaustive classification of all conceivable statements — or even all conceivable statements in response to police interrogation — as either testimonial or nontestimonial, it suffices to decide the present cases to hold as follows: Statements are nontestimonial when made in the course of police interrogation under circumstances objectively indicating that the primary purpose of the interrogation is to enable police assistance to meet an ongoing emergency. They are testimonial when the circumstances objectively indicate that there is no such ongoing emergency, and that the primary purpose of the interrogation is to establish or prove past events potentially relevant to later criminal prosecution.

III

In Crawford, it sufficed for resolution of the case before us to determine that "even if the Sixth Amendment is not solely concerned with testimonial hearsay, that is its primary object, and interrogations by law enforcement officers fall squarely within that class." *Id.*, at 53. Moreover, as we have just described, the facts of that case spared us the need to define what we meant by "interrogations." The *Davis* case today does not permit us this luxury of indecision. The inquiries of a police operator in the course of a 911 call are an interrogation in one sense, but not in a sense that "qualifies under any conceivable definition." We must decide, therefore, whether the Confrontation Clause applies only to testimonial hearsay; and, if so, whether the recording of a 911 call qualifies.

The answer to the first question was suggested in Crawford, even if not explicitly held:

> "The text of the Confrontation Clause reflects this focus [on testimonial hearsay]. It applies to 'witnesses' against the accused — in other words, those who 'bear testimony.' 1 N. Webster, An American Dictionary of the English Language (1828). 'Testimony,' in turn, is typically 'a solemn declaration or affirmation made for the purpose of establishing or proving some fact.' An accuser who makes a formal statement to government officers bears testimony in a sense that a person who makes a casual remark to an acquaintance does not." 541 U.S., at 51.

A limitation so clearly reflected in the text of the constitutional provision must fairly be said to mark out not merely its "core," but its perimeter.

We are not aware of any early American case invoking the Confrontation Clause or the common-law right to confrontation that did not clearly involve testimony as thus defined. Well into the 20th century, our own Confrontation Clause jurisprudence was carefully applied only in the testimonial context. See, *e.g.*, *Reynolds v. United States*, 98 U.S. 145, 158 (1879) (testimony at prior trial was subject to the Confrontation Clause, but petitioner had forfeited that right by procuring witness's absence).

Even our later cases, conforming to the reasoning of *Ohio v. Roberts*, 448 U.S. 56 (1980), never in practice dispensed with the Confrontation Clause requirements of unavailability and prior cross-examination in cases that involved testimonial hearsay, see *Crawford*, 541 U.S., at 57–59 (citing cases), with one arguable exception, see *id.*, at 58, n. 8, (discussing *White v. Illinois*, 502 U.S. 346). Where our cases did dispense with those requirements — even under the *Roberts* approach — the statements at issue were clearly nontestimonial. See, *e.g.*, *Bourjaily v. United States*, 483 U.S. 171, 181–184 (1987) (statements made unwittingly to a Government informant); *Dutton v. Evans*, 400 U.S. 74, 87–89 (1970) (plurality opinion) (statements from one prisoner to another).

Most of the American cases applying the Confrontation Clause or its state constitutional or common-law counterparts involved testimonial statements of the most formal sort — sworn testimony in prior judicial proceedings or formal depositions under oath — which invites the argument that the scope of the Clause is limited to that very formal category. But the English cases that were the progenitors of the Confrontation Clause did not limit the exclusionary rule to prior court testimony and formal depositions, see *Crawford, supra*, at 52, and n. 3. In any event, we do not think it conceivable that the protections of the Confrontation Clause can readily be evaded by having a note-taking policeman *recite* the unsworn hearsay testimony of the declarant, instead of having the declarant sign a deposition. Indeed, if there is one point for which no case — English or early American, state or federal — can be cited, that is it.

The question before us in *Davis*, then, is whether, objectively considered, the interrogation that took place in the course of the 911 call produced testimonial statements. When we said in *Crawford, supra*, at 53, that "interrogations by law enforcement officers fall squarely within [the] class" of testimonial hearsay, we had immediately in mind (for that was the case before us) interrogations solely directed at establishing the facts of a past crime, in order to identify (or provide evidence to convict) the perpetrator. The product of such interrogation, whether reduced to a writing signed by the declarant or embedded in the memory (and perhaps notes) of the interrogating officer, is testimonial. It is, in the terms of the 1828 American dictionary quoted in *Crawford*, " '[a] solemn declaration or affirmation made for the purpose of establishing or proving some fact.' " (The solemnity of even an oral declaration of relevant past fact to an investigating officer is well enough established by the severe consequences that can attend a deliberate falsehood.). A 911 call, on the other hand, and at least the initial interrogation conducted in connection with a 911 call, is ordinarily not designed primarily to "establis[h] or prov[e]" some past fact, but to describe current circumstances requiring police assistance.

The difference between the interrogation in *Davis* and the one in *Crawford* is apparent on the face of things. In *Davis*, McCottry was speaking about events *as they were actually happening*, rather than "describ [ing] past events," *Lilly v. Virginia*, 527 U.S. 116 (1999) (plurality opinion). Sylvia Crawford's interrogation, on the other hand, took place hours after the events she described had occurred. Moreover, any reasonable listener would recognize that McCottry (unlike Sylvia Crawford) was facing an ongoing emergency. Although one *might* call 911 to provide a narrative report of a crime absent any imminent danger, McCottry's call was plainly a call for help against bona fide physical threat. Third, the nature of what was asked and answered in *Davis*, again viewed objectively, was such that the elicited statements were necessary to be able to *resolve* the present emergency, rather than simply to learn (as in *Crawford*) what had happened in the past. That is true even of the operator's effort to establish the identity of the assailant, so that the dispatched officers might know whether they would be encountering a violent felon. See, *e.g., Hiibel v. Sixth Judicial Dist. Court of Nev, Humboldt Cty.*, 542 U.S. 177, 186 (2004). And finally, the difference in the level of formality between the two interviews is striking. Crawford was responding calmly, at the station house, to a series of questions, with the officer-interrogator taping and making notes of her answers; McCottry's frantic answers were provided over the phone, in an environment that was not tranquil, or even (as far as any reasonable 911 operator could make out) safe.

We conclude from all this that the circumstances of McCottry's interrogation objectively indicate its primary purpose was to enable police assistance to meet an ongoing emergency. She simply was not acting as a *witness;* she was not *testifying.* What she said was not "a weaker substitute for live testimony" at trial, *United States v. Inadi,* 475 U.S. 387, 394 (1986), like Lord Cobham's statements in *Raleigh's Case,* 2 How. St. Tr. 1 (1603), or Jane Dingler's *ex parte* statements against her husband in *King v. Dingler,* 2 Leach 561, 168 Eng. Rep. 383 (1791), or Sylvia Crawford's statement in *Crawford.* In each of those cases, the *ex parte* actors and the evidentiary products of the *ex parte* communication aligned perfectly with their courtroom analogues. McCottry's emergency statement does not. No "witness" goes into court to proclaim an emergency and seek help.

Davis seeks to cast McCottry in the unlikely role of a witness by pointing to English cases. None of them involves statements made during an ongoing emergency. In *King v. Brasier,* 1 Leach 199, 168 Eng. Rep. 202 (1779), for example, a young rape victim, "immediately on her coming home, told all the circumstances of the injury" to her mother. *Id.,* at 200, 168 Eng. Rep., at 202. The case would be helpful to Davis if the relevant statement had been the girl's screams for aid as she was being chased by her assailant. But by the time the victim got home, her story was an account of past events.

This is not to say that a conversation which begins as an interrogation to determine the need for emergency assistance cannot, as the Indiana Supreme Court put it, "evolve into testimonial statements," 829 N.E.2d, at 457, once that purpose has been achieved. In this case, for example, after the operator gained the information needed to address the exigency of the moment, the emergency appears to have ended (when Davis drove away from the premises). The operator then told McCottry to be quiet, and proceeded to pose a battery of questions. It could readily be maintained that, from that point on, McCottry's statements were testimonial, not unlike the "structured police questioning" that occurred in *Crawford.* This presents no great problem. Just as, for Fifth Amendment purposes, "police officers can and will distinguish almost instinctively between questions necessary to secure their own safety or the safety of the public and questions designed solely to elicit testimonial evidence from a suspect," *New York v. Quarles,* 467 U.S. 649, 658–659 (1984), trial courts will recognize the point at which, for Sixth Amendment purposes, statements in response to interrogations become testimonial. Through *in limine* procedure, they should redact or exclude the portions of any statement that have become testimonial, as they do, for example, with unduly prejudicial portions of otherwise admissible evidence. Davis's jury did not hear the *complete* 911 call, although it may well have heard some testimonial portions. We were asked to classify only McCottry's early statements identifying Davis as her assailant, and we agree with the Washington Supreme Court that they were not testimonial. That court also concluded that, even if later parts of the call were testimonial, their admission was harmless beyond a reasonable doubt. Davis does not challenge that holding, and we therefore assume it to be correct.

Determining the testimonial or nontestimonial character of the statements that were the product of the interrogation in *Hammon* is a much easier task, since they were not much different from the statements we found to be testimonial in *Crawford.*

It is entirely clear from the circumstances that the interrogation was part of an investigation into possibly criminal past conduct — as, indeed, the testifying officer expressly acknowledged, There was no emergency in progress; the interrogating officer testified that he had heard no arguments or crashing and saw no one throw or break anything, *id.*, at 25. When the officer questioned Amy for the second time, and elicited the challenged statements, he was not seeking to determine (as in *Davis*) "what is happening," but rather "what happened." Objectively viewed, the primary, if not indeed the sole, purpose of the interrogation was to investigate a possible crime — which is, of course, precisely what the officer *should* have done.

It is true that the *Crawford* interrogation was more formal. It followed a *Miranda* warning, was tape-recorded, and took place at the station house. While these features certainly strengthened the statements' testimonial aspect — made it more objectively apparent, that is, that the purpose of the exercise was to nail down the truth about past criminal events — none was essential to the point. It was formal enough that Amy's interrogation was conducted in a separate room, away from her husband (who tried to intervene), with the officer receiving her replies for use in his "investigat[ion]." What we called the "striking resemblance" of the *Crawford* statement to civil-law *ex parte* examinations, 541 U.S., at 52, is shared by Amy's statement here. Both declarants were actively separated from the defendant — officers forcibly prevented Hershel from participating in the interrogation. Both statements deliberately recounted, in response to police questioning, how potentially criminal past events began and progressed. And both took place some time after the events described were over. Such statements under official interrogation are an obvious substitute for live testimony, because they do precisely *what a witness does* on direct examination; they are inherently testimonial. Although we necessarily reject the Indiana Supreme Court's implication that virtually any "initial inquiries" at the crime scene will not be testimonial, we do not hold the opposite — that *no* questions at the scene will yield nontestimonial answers. We have already observed of domestic disputes that "[o]fficers called to investigate . . . need to know whom they are dealing with in order to assess the situation, the threat to their own safety, and possible danger to the potential victim." *Hiibel*, 542 U.S., at 186. Such exigencies may *often* mean that "initial inquiries" produce nontestimonial statements. But in cases like this one, where Amy's statements were neither a cry for help nor the provision of information enabling officers immediately to end a threatening situation, the fact that they were given at an alleged crime scene and were "initial inquiries" is immaterial.

IV

Respondents in both cases, joined by a number of their *amici*, contend that the nature of the offenses charged in these two cases — domestic violence — requires greater flexibility in the use of testimonial evidence. This particular type of crime is notoriously susceptible to intimidation or coercion of the victim to ensure that she does not testify at trial. When this occurs, the Confrontation Clause gives the criminal a windfall. We may not, however, vitiate constitutional guarantees when they have the effect of allowing the guilty to go free. Cf. *Kyllo v. United States*, 533 U.S. 27 (2001) (suppressing evidence from an illegal search). But when defendants seek to undermine the judicial process by procuring or coercing silence from witnesses and victims, the

Sixth Amendment does not require courts to acquiesce. While defendants have no duty to assist the State in proving their guilt, they *do* have the duty to refrain from acting in ways that destroy the integrity of the criminal-trial system. We reiterate what we said in *Crawford:* that "the rule of forfeiture by wrongdoing . . . extinguishes confrontation claims on essentially equitable grounds." 541 U.S., at 62. That is, one who obtains the absence of a witness by wrongdoing forfeits the constitutional right to confrontation.

We have determined that, absent a finding of forfeiture by wrongdoing, the Sixth Amendment operates to exclude Amy Hammon's affidavit. The Indiana courts may (if they are asked) determine on remand whether such a claim of forfeiture is properly raised and, if so, whether it is meritorious.

*   *   *

We affirm the judgment of the Supreme Court of Washington. We reverse the judgment of the Supreme Court of Indiana, and remand the case to that court for proceedings not inconsistent with this opinion.

It is so ordered.

JUSTICE THOMAS, concurring in the judgment in part and dissenting in part.

In *Crawford v. Washington*, 541 U.S. 36 (2004), we abandoned the general reliability inquiry we had long employed to judge the admissibility of hearsay evidence under the Confrontation Clause, describing that inquiry as *"inherently*, and therefore *permanently*, unpredictable." Today, a mere two years after the Court decided *Crawford*, it adopts an equally unpredictable test, under which district courts are charged with divining the "primary purpose" of police interrogations. Besides being difficult for courts to apply, this test characterizes as "testimonial," and therefore inadmissible, evidence that bears little resemblance to what we have recognized as the evidence targeted by the Confrontation Clause. Because neither of the cases before the Court today would implicate the Confrontation Clause under an appropriately targeted standard, I concur only in the judgment in *Davis v. Washington*, and dissent from the Court's resolution of *Hammon v. Indiana*.

Neither the 911 call at issue in *Davis* nor the police questioning at issue in *Hammon* is testimonial under the appropriate framework. Neither the call nor the questioning is itself a formalized dialogue. Nor do any circumstances surrounding the taking of the statements render those statements sufficiently formal to resemble the Marian examinations; the statements were neither Mirandized nor custodial, nor accompanied by any similar indicia of formality. Finally, there is no suggestion that the prosecution attempted to offer the women's hearsay evidence at trial in order to evade confrontation. See 829 N.E.2d 444, 447 (Ind.2005) (prosecution subpoenaed Amy Hammon to testify, but she was not present); 154 Wash.2d 291, 296, 111 P.3d 844, 847 (2005) (en banc) (State was unable to locate Michelle McCottry at the time of trial). Accordingly, the statements at issue in both cases are nontestimonial and admissible under the Confrontation Clause.

Because the standard adopted by the Court today is neither workable nor a targeted attempt to reach the abuses forbidden by the Clause, I concur only in the judgment in *Davis v. Washington*, No. 05–5224, and respectfully dissent from the Court's resolution of *Hammon v. Indiana.*

[2] Further Distinguishing Testimonial Statements From Statements Made for the Primary Purpose of Resolving an On-Going Emergency

The Supreme Court has devoted a significant amount of attention to the question of where the line falls dividing statements about what happened at an event and therefore are generally a violation of the Confrontation Clause and those statements whose primary purpose is to assist in resolving an on-going emergency. This issue is especially acute when the police are dealing with open crimes of violence, as the next case shows.

Michigan v. Bryant
131 S. Ct. 1143 (2011)

Justice Sotomayor delivered the opinion of the Court.

At respondent Richard Bryant's trial, the court admitted statements that the victim, Anthony Covington, made to police officers who discovered him mortally wounded in a gas station parking lot. A jury convicted Bryant of, *inter alia*, second-degree murder. On appeal, the Supreme Court of Michigan held that the Sixth Amendment's Confrontation Clause . . . rendered Covington's statements inadmissible testimonial hearsay, and the court reversed Bryant's conviction. We granted the State's petition for a writ of certiorari . . . . We hold that the circumstances of the interaction between Covington and the police objectively indicate that the "primary purpose of the interrogation" was "to enable police assistance to meet an ongoing emergency." Therefore, Covington's identification and description of the shooter and the location of the shooting were not testimonial statements, and their admission at Bryant's trial did not violate the Confrontation Clause. We vacate the judgment of the Supreme Court of Michigan and remand.

The Confrontation Clause of the Sixth Amendment states: "In all criminal prosecutions, the accused shall enjoy the right . . . to be confronted with the witnesses against him." The Fourteenth Amendment renders the Clause binding on the States. *Pointer v. Texas*, 380 U.S. 400, 403 (1965). In *Ohio v. Roberts*, 448 U.S. 56, 66 (1980), we explained that the confrontation right does not bar admission of statements of an unavailable witness if the statements "bea[r] adequate 'indicia of reliability.' " We held that reliability can be established if "the evidence falls within a firmly rooted hearsay exception," or if it does not fall within such an exception, then if it bears "particularized guarantees of trustworthiness."

Nearly a quarter century later, we decided *Crawford v. Washington*, 541 U.S. 36. [We overruled] *Ohio v. Roberts.*

Crawford examined the common-law history of the confrontation right and explained that "the principal evil at which the Confrontation Clause was directed was the civil-law mode of criminal procedure, and particularly its use of *ex parte* examinations as evidence against the accused." . . . . We defined "testimony" as " '[a] solemn declaration or affirmation made for the purpose of establishing or proving some fact.'. We noted that "[a]n accuser who makes a formal statement to government officers bears testimony in a sense that a person who makes a casual remark to an acquaintance does not." We therefore limited the Confrontation Clause's reach to testimonial statements and held that in order for testimonial evidence to be admissible, the Sixth Amendment "demands what the common law required: unavailability and a prior opportunity for cross-examination."

In 2006, the Court in *Davis v. Washington* and *Hammon v. Indiana*, took a further step to "determine more precisely which police interrogations produce testimony" and therefore implicate a Confrontation Clause bar. We explained that when *Crawford* said that " 'interrogations by law enforcement officers fall squarely within [the] class' of testimonial hearsay, we had immediately in mind (for that was the case before us) interrogations solely directed at establishing the facts of a past crime, in order to identify (or provide evidence to convict) the perpetrator.

We thus made clear in *Davis* that not all those questioned by the police are witnesses and not all "interrogations by law enforcement officers," are subject to the Confrontation Clause.

When, as in *Davis*, the primary purpose of an interrogation is to respond to an "ongoing emergency," its purpose is not to create a record for trial and thus is not within the scope of the Clause. But there may be *other* circumstances, aside from ongoing emergencies, when a statement is not procured with a primary purpose of creating an out-of-court substitute for trial testimony. In making the primary purpose determination, standard rules of hearsay, designed to identify some statements as reliable, will be relevant. Where no such primary purpose exists, the admissibility of a statement is the concern of state and federal rules of evidence, not the Confrontation Clause.

Deciding this case also requires further explanation of the "ongoing emergency" circumstance addressed in *Davis*. Because *Davis* and *Hammon* arose in the domestic violence context, that was the situation "we had immediately in mind (for that was the case before us)." We now face a new context: a nondomestic dispute, involving a victim found in a public location, suffering from a fatal gunshot wound, and a perpetrator whose location was unknown at the time the police located the victim.

To determine whether the "primary purpose" of an interrogation is "to enable police assistance to meet an ongoing emergency," *Davis*, 547 U.S., at 822, which would render the resulting statements nontestimonial, we objectively evaluate the circumstances in which the encounter occurs and the statements and actions of the parties.

An objective analysis of the circumstances of an encounter and the statements and actions of the parties to it provides the most accurate assessment of the "primary purpose of the interrogation." The circumstances in which an encounter occurs — *e.g.*, at or near the scene of the crime versus at a police station, during an ongoing emergency or afterwards — are clearly matters of objective fact. The statements and actions of the parties must also be objectively evaluated. That is, the relevant inquiry is not the subjective or actual purpose of the individuals involved in a particular encounter, but rather the purpose that reasonable participants would have had, as ascertained from the individuals' statements and actions and the circumstances in which the encounter occurred.

As our recent Confrontation Clause cases have explained, the existence of an "ongoing emergency" at the time of an encounter between an individual and the police is among the most important circumstances informing the "primary purpose" of an interrogation. The existence of an ongoing emergency is relevant to determining the primary purpose of the interrogation because an emergency focuses the participants on something other than "prov[ing] past events potentially relevant to later criminal prosecution." Rather, it focuses them on "end[ing] a threatening situation."

Finally, [as] *Davis* made clear, whether an ongoing emergency exists is simply one factor — albeit an important factor — that informs the ultimate inquiry regarding the "primary purpose" of an interrogation. Another factor the Michigan Supreme Court did not sufficiently account for is the importance of *informality* in an encounter between a victim and police. Formality is not the sole touchstone of our primary purpose inquiry because, although formality suggests the absence of an emergency and therefore an increased likelihood that the purpose of the interrogation is to "establish or prove past events potentially relevant to later criminal prosecution," informality does not necessarily indicate the presence of an emergency or the lack of testimonial intent. The court below, however, too readily dismissed the informality of the circumstances in this case in a single brief footnote and in fact seems to have suggested that the encounter in this case was formal. As we explain further below, the questioning in this case occurred in an exposed, public area, prior to the arrival of emergency medical services, and in a disorganized fashion. All of those facts make this case distinguishable from the formal station-house interrogation in *Crawford*.

In addition to the circumstances in which an encounter occurs, the statements and actions of both the declarant and interrogators provide objective evidence of the primary purpose of the interrogation.

Davis requires a combined inquiry that accounts for both the declarant and the interrogator. In many instances, the primary purpose of the interrogation will be most accurately ascertained by looking to the contents of both the questions and the answers. To give an extreme example, if the police say to a victim, "Tell us who did this to you so that we can arrest and prosecute them," the victim's response that "Rick did it," appears purely accusatory because by virtue of the phrasing of the question, the victim necessarily has prosecution in mind when she answers.

The combined approach also ameliorates problems that could arise from looking solely to one participant. Predominant among these is the problem of mixed motives on the part of both interrogators and declarants. Police officers in our society function as both first responders and criminal investigators. Their dual responsibilities may mean that they act with different motives simultaneously or in quick succession. See *New York v. Quarles*, 467 U.S. 649, 656 (1984).

As we suggested in *Davis*, when a court must determine whether the Confrontation

Clause bars the admission of a statement at trial, it should determine the "primary purpose of the interrogation" by objectively evaluating the statements and actions of the parties to the encounter, in light of the circumstances in which the interrogation occurs. As the context of this case brings into sharp relief, the existence and duration of an emergency depend on the type and scope of danger posed to the victim, the police, and the public.

We first examine the circumstances in which the interrogation occurred. The parties disagree over whether there was an emergency when the police arrived at the gas station.

The record reveals little about the motive for the shooting. What Covington did tell the officers was that he fled Bryant's back porch, indicating that he perceived an ongoing threat. The police did not know, and Covington did not tell them, whether the threat was limited to him. The potential scope of the dispute and therefore the emergency in this case thus stretches more broadly than those at issue in *Davis* and *Hammon* and encompasses a threat potentially to the police and the public.

This is also the first of our post-*Crawford* Confrontation Clause cases to involve a gun. The physical separation that was sufficient to end the emergency in *Hammon* was not necessarily sufficient to end the threat in this case; Covington was shot through the back door of Bryant's house. Bryant's argument that there was no ongoing emergency because "[n]o shots were being fired," surely construes ongoing emergency too narrowly.

At bottom, there was an ongoing emergency here where an armed shooter, whose motive for and location after the shooting were unknown, had mortally wounded Covington within a few blocks and a few minutes of the location where the police found Covington.

For their part, the police responded to a call that a man had been shot. As discussed above, they did not know why, where, or when the shooting had occurred. Nor did they know the location of the shooter or anything else about the circumstances in which the crime occurred. The questions they asked — "what had happened, who had shot him, and where the shooting occurred," — were the exact type of questions necessary to allow the police to " 'assess the situation, the threat to their own safety, and possible danger to the potential victim' " and to the public, including to allow them to ascertain "whether they would be encountering a violent felon,". In other words, they solicited the information necessary to enable them "to meet an ongoing emergency exception."

Nothing in Covington's responses indicated to the police that, contrary to their expectation upon responding to a call reporting a shooting, there was no emergency or that a prior emergency had ended. Covington did indicate that he had been shot at another location about 25 minutes earlier, but he did not know the location of the shooter at the time the police arrived and, as far as we can tell from the record, he gave no indication that the shooter, having shot at him twice, would be satisfied that Covington was only wounded. In fact, Covington did not indicate any possible motive for the shooting, and thereby gave no reason to think that the shooter would not shoot again if he arrived on the scene. As we noted in *Davis*, "initial inquiries" may "*often* . . . produce nontestimonial statements. The initial inquiries in this case resulted in the type of nontestimonial statements we contemplated in *Davis*.

Finally, we consider the informality of the situation and the interrogation. This situation is more similar, though not identical, to the informal, harried 911 call in *Davis* than to the structured, station-house interview in *Crawford*. As the officers' trial testimony reflects, the situation was fluid and somewhat confused: the officers arrived at different times; apparently each, upon arrival, asked Covington "what happened?"; and, contrary to the dissent's portrayal, (opinion of SCALIA, J.), they did not conduct a structured interrogation. The informality suggests that the interrogators' primary purpose was simply to address what they perceived to be an ongoing emergency, and the circumstances lacked any formality that would have alerted Covington to or focused him on the possible future prosecutorial use of his statements.

Because the circumstances of the encounter as well as the statements and actions of Covington and the police objectively indicate that the "primary purpose of the interrogation" was "to enable police assistance to meet an ongoing emergency," Covington's identification and description of the shooter and the location of the shooting were not testimonial hearsay. The Confrontation Clause did not bar their admission at Bryant's trial.

For the foregoing reasons, we hold that Covington's statements were not testimonial and that their admission at Bryant's trial did not violate the Confrontation Clause. We leave for the Michigan courts to decide on remand whether the statements' admission was otherwise permitted by state hearsay rules. The judgment of the Supreme Court of Michigan is vacated, and the case is remanded for further proceedings not inconsistent with this opinion.

It is so ordered.

JUSTICE KAGAN took no part in the consideration or decision of this case.

JUSTICE THOMAS, concurring in the judgment.

I agree with the Court that the admission of Covington's out-of-court statements did not violate the Confrontation Clause, but I reach this conclusion because Covington's questioning by police lacked sufficient formality and solemnity for his statements to be considered "testimonial."

In determining whether Covington's statements to police implicate the Confrontation Clause, the Court evaluates the " 'primary purpose' " of the interrogation. The majority's analysis which relies on, what the police knew when they arrived at the scene, the specific questions they asked, the particular information Covington conveyed, the weapon involved, and Covington's medical condition illustrates the uncertainty that this test creates for law enforcement and the lower courts. I have criticized the primary-purpose test as "an exercise in fiction" that is "disconnected from history" and "yields no predictable results."

Rather than attempting to reconstruct the "primary purpose" of the participants, I would consider the extent to which the interrogation resembles those historical practices that the Confrontation Clause addressed. This interrogation bears little if any resemblance to the historical practices that the Confrontation Clause aimed to eliminate. Covington thus did not "bea[r] testimony" against Bryant, and the introduction of his statements at trial did not implicate the Confrontation Clause. I concur in the judgment.

JUSTICE SCALIA, dissenting.

Today's tale — a story of five officers conducting successive examinations of a dying man with the primary purpose, not of obtaining and preserving his testimony regarding his killer, but of protecting him, them, and others from a murderer somewhere on the loose — is so transparently false that professing to believe it demeans this institution. But reaching a patently incorrect conclusion on the facts is a relatively benign judicial mischief; it affects, after all, only the case at hand. In its vain attempt to make the incredible plausible, however — or perhaps as an intended second goal — today's opinion distorts our Confrontation Clause jurisprudence and leaves it in a shambles. Instead of clarifying the law, the Court makes itself the obfuscator of last resort. Because I continue to adhere to the Confrontation Clause that the People adopted, as described in Crawford v. Washington, I dissent.

In *Crawford*, we held that this provision guarantees a defendant his common-law right to confront those "who 'bear testimony' " against him. A witness must deliver his testimony against the defendant in person, or the prosecution must prove that the witness is unavailable to appear at trial and that the defendant has had a prior opportunity for cross-examination.

A statement is testimonial "when the circumstances objectively indicate . . . that the primary purpose of the interrogation is to establish or prove past events potentially relevant to later criminal prosecution."

Crawford and *Davis* did not address whose perspective matters — the declarant's, the interrogator's, or both — when assessing "the primary purpose of [an] interrogation."

A declarant-focused inquiry is also the only inquiry that would work in every fact pattern implicating the Confrontation Clause. The Clause applies to volunteered testimony as well as statements solicited through police interrogation. An inquiry into an officer's purposes would make no sense when a declarant blurts out "Rick shot me" as soon as the officer arrives on the scene. I see no reason to adopt a different test — one that accounts for an officer's intent — when the officer asks "what happened" before the declarant makes his accusation. (This does not mean the interrogator is irrelevant. The identity of an interrogator, and the content and tenor of his questions, can bear upon whether a declarant intends to make a solemn statement, and envisions its use at a criminal trial. But none of this means that the interrogator's purpose matters.)

Looking to the declarant's purpose (as we should), this is an absurdly easy case. Roughly 25 minutes after Anthony Covington had been shot, Detroit police responded to a 911 call reporting that a gunshot victim had appeared at a neighborhood gas station. They quickly arrived at the scene, and in less than 10 minutes five different Detroit police officers questioned Covington about the shooting. Each asked him a similar battery of questions: "what happened" and when, "who shot the victim," and "where" did the shooting take place. After Covington would answer, they would ask follow-up questions, such as "how tall is" the shooter. The battery relented when the paramedics arrived and began tending to Covington's wounds.

From Covington's perspective, his statements had little value except to ensure the arrest and eventual prosecution of Richard Bryant. He knew the "threatening situation" had ended six blocks away and 25 minutes earlier when he fled from Bryant's back porch. Even if Bryant had pursued him (unlikely), and after seeing that Covington had ended up at the gas station was unable to confront him there before the police arrived (doubly unlikely), it was entirely beyond imagination that Bryant would again open fire while Covington was surrounded by five armed police officers. And Covington knew the shooting was the work of a drug dealer, not a spree killer who might randomly threaten others.

Covington's knowledge that he had nothing to fear differs significantly from Michelle McCottry's state of mind during her "frantic" statements to a 911 operator at issue in *Davis*. Her "call was plainly a call for help against a bona fide physical threat" describing "events *as they were actually happening*." She did not have the luxuries of police protection and of time and space separating her from immediate danger that Covington enjoyed when he made his statements.

The Court's distorted view creates an expansive exception to the Confrontation Clause for violent crimes. Because Bryant posed a continuing threat to public safety in the Court's imagination, the emergency persisted for confrontation purposes at least until the police learned his "motive for and location after the shooting." It may have persisted in this case until the police "secured the scene of the shooting" two-and-a-half hours later.

But today's decision is not only a gross distortion of the facts. It is a gross distortion of the law — a revisionist narrative in which reliability continues to guide our Confrontation Clause jurisprudence, at least where emergencies and faux emergencies are concerned.

According to today's opinion, the *Davis* inquiry into whether a declarant spoke to end an ongoing emergency or rather to "prove past events potentially relevant to later criminal prosecution," is *not* aimed at answering whether the declarant acted as a witness. Instead, the *Davis* inquiry probes the *reliability* of a declarant's statements, "[i]mplicit[ly]" importing the excited-utterances hearsay exception into the Constitution. A statement during an ongoing emergency is sufficiently reliable, the Court says, "because the prospect of fabrication . . . is presumably significantly diminished," so it "does not [need] to be subject to the crucible of cross-examination."

The Court recedes from *Crawford* in a second significant way. It requires judges to conduct "open-ended balancing tests" and "amorphous, if not entirely subjective," inquiries into the totality of the circumstances bearing upon reliability. Where the prosecution cries "emergency," the admissibility of a statement now turns on "a highly context-dependent inquiry," into the type of weapon the defendant wielded, the type of crime the defendant committed, the medical condition of the declarant, if the declarant is injured, whether paramedics have arrived on the scene, whether the encounter takes place in an "exposed public area," whether the encounter appears disorganized, whether the declarant is capable of forming a purpose, whether the police have secured the scene of the crime, the formality of the statement, and finally, whether the statement strikes us as reliable. This is no better than the nine-factor balancing test we rejected in *Crawford*.

JUSTICE GINSBURG dissenting.

I would add, however, this observation. In *Crawford v. Washington*, this Court noted that, in the law we inherited from England, there was a well-established exception to the confrontation requirement: The cloak protecting the accused against admission of out-of-court testimonial statements was removed for dying declarations. This historic exception, we recalled in *Giles v. California*, applied to statements made by a person about to die and aware that death was imminent. Were the issue properly tendered here, I would take up the question whether the exception for dying declarations survives our recent Confrontation Clause decisions. The Michigan Supreme Court, however, held, as a matter of state law, that the prosecutor had abandoned the issue. The matter, therefore, is not one the Court can address in this case.

[3]   Statement About Child Abuse to Person Other Than Police Officer

In a decision involving a child abuse case, the question revolved around whether a statement made to persons other than police officers could be testimonial for the purposes of the Clause. This had been an unanswered question since *Crawford*.

Ohio v. Clark
576 U.S. __, 135 S. Ct. 2173 (2015)

JUSTICE ALITO delivered the opinion of the Court.

Darius Clark sent his girlfriend hundreds of miles away to engage in prostitution and agreed to care for her two young children while she was out of town. A day later, teachers discovered red marks on her 3-year-old son, and the boy identified Clark as his abuser. The question in this case is whether the Sixth Amendment's Confrontation Clause prohibited prosecutors from introducing those statements when the child was not available to be cross-examined. Because neither the child nor his teachers had the primary purpose of assisting in Clark's prosecution, the child's statements do not implicate the Confrontation Clause and therefore were admissible at trial.

The Sixth Amendment's Confrontation Clause, which is binding on the States through the Fourteenth Amendment, provides: "In all criminal prosecutions, the accused shall enjoy the right . . . to be confronted with the witnesses against him."

In *Crawford v. Washington*, 541 U.S. 36 (2004), we explained that "witnesses," under the Confrontation Clause, are those "who bear testimony," and we defined "testimony" as "a solemn declaration or affirmation made for the purpose of establishing or proving some fact." *Id.*, at 51 But our decision in *Crawford* did not offer an exhaustive definition of "testimonial" statements. Our more recent cases have labored to flesh out what it means for a statement to be "testimonial." In *Davis v. Washington* and *Hammon v. Indiana*, 547 U.S. 813 (2006), which we decided together, we dealt with statements given to law enforcement officers by the victims of domestic abuse. The victim in *Davis* made statements to a 911 emergency operator during and shortly after her boyfriend's violent attack. In *Hammon*, the victim, after being isolated from her abusive husband, made statements to police that were memorialized in a " 'battery affidavit.' " *Id.*, at 820.

We held that the statements in *Hammon* were testimonial, while the statements in *Davis* were not. Announcing what has come to be known as the "primary purpose" test, we explained: "Statements are nontestimonial when made in the course of police interrogation under circumstances objectively indicating that the primary purpose of the interrogation is to enable police assistance to meet an ongoing emergency. They are testimonial when the circumstances objectively indicate that there is no such ongoing emergency, and that the primary purpose of the interrogation is to establish or prove past events potentially relevant to later criminal prosecution." *Id.*, at 822. Because the cases involved statements to law enforcement officers, we reserved the question whether similar statements to individuals other than law enforcement officers would raise similar issues under the Confrontation Clause. *See id.*, at 823, n. 2.

In *Michigan v. Bryant*, 562 U.S. 344 (2011), we further expounded on the primary purpose test. The inquiry, we emphasized, must consider "all of the relevant circumstances." *Id.*, at 369. And we reiterated our view in *Davis* that, when "the primary purpose of an interrogation is to respond to an 'ongoing emergency,' its purpose is not to create a record for trial and thus is not within the scope of the [Confrontation] Clause." 562 U.S., at 358. At the same time, we noted that "there may be other circumstances, aside from ongoing emergencies, when a statement is not procured with a primary purpose of creating an out-of-court substitute for trial testimony." *Ibid.*

One additional factor is "the informality of the situation and the interrogation." *Id.*, at 377. A "formal station-house interrogation," like the questioning in *Crawford*, is more likely to provoke testimonial statements, while less formal questioning is less likely to reflect a primary purpose aimed at obtaining testimonial evidence against the accused. *Id.*, at 366, 377. And in determining whether a statement is testimonial, "standard rules of hearsay, designed to identify some statements as reliable, will be relevant." *Id.*, at 358–359. In the end, the question is whether, in light of all the circumstances, viewed objectively, the "primary purpose" of the conversation was to "creat[e] an out-of-court substitute for trial testimony." *Id.*, at 358. Applying these principles in *Bryant*, we held that the statements made by a dying victim about his assailant were not testimonial because the circumstances objectively indicated that the conversation was primarily aimed at quelling an ongoing emergency, not establishing evidence for the prosecution. Because the relevant statements were made to law enforcement officers, we again declined to decide whether the same analysis applies to statements made to individuals other than the police.

Thus, under our precedents, a statement cannot fall within the Confrontation Clause unless its primary purpose was testimonial. "Where no such primary purpose exists, the admissibility of a statement is the concern of state and federal rules of evidence, not the Confrontation Clause." *Id.*, at 359.

In this case, we consider statements made to preschool teachers, not the police. We are therefore presented with the question we have repeatedly reserved: whether statements to persons other than law enforcement officers are subject to the Confrontation Clause. Because at least some statements to individuals who are not law enforcement officers could conceivably raise confrontation concerns, we decline to adopt a categorical rule excluding them from the Sixth Amendment's reach. Nevertheless, such statements are much less likely to be testimonial than statements to law enforcement officers. And considering all the relevant circumstances here, L.P.'s statements clearly were not made with the primary purpose of creating evidence for Clark's prosecution. Thus, their introduction at trial did not violate the Confrontation Clause.

Clark's efforts to avoid this conclusion are all off-base. He emphasizes Ohio's mandatory reporting obligations, in an attempt to equate L.P.'s teachers with the police and their caring questions with official interrogations. But the comparison is inapt. The teachers' pressing concern was to protect L.P. and remove him from harm's way.

It is irrelevant that the teachers' questions and their duty to report the matter had the natural tendency to result in Clark's prosecution. The statements at issue in Davis and Bryant supported the defendants' convictions, and the police always have an obligation to ask questions to resolve ongoing emergencies. Yet, we held in those cases that the Confrontation Clause did not prohibit introduction of the statements because they were not primarily intended to be testimonial.

We reverse the judgment of the Supreme Court of Ohio and remand the case for further proceedings not inconsistent with this opinion.

It is so ordered.

§ 11.03 PROBLEMS

Problem #11-1: Conspiracy Theorists

Bob, Carol, Ted, and Alice are involved in a conspiracy to defraud investors in a pyramid scheme. Many of the statements they made to each other during the conspiracy were secretly taped. At a subsequent trial, the prosecutor attempts to offer these statements as admissions. The defendants object, claiming the statements violate their Confrontation Clause rights. How should a judge rule? Why?

Problem #11-2: A Voluntary Interview

Arlo was asked to come to the police station to offer what he saw and heard after a violent crime took place in the house next door the night before. Arlo engaged in a conversation with the police, who noted they might use this information in a later trial. If Arlo leaves the jurisdiction and cannot be found, can his statements be used in a subsequent trial charging Arlo's roommate with the violent crime?

Problem #11-3: State Law vs. the Confrontation Clause

North Dakota enacts a law that states, "Any out-of-court statements deemed to be testimonial by the court are admissible, subject to the accused having a right to subpoena the declarant to testify at trial. Otherwise, without a subpoena, no such testimony by the declarant is required." Does the North Dakota law protect the defendant's rights under the Confrontation Clause by providing an opportunity to subpoena a witness to cross-examine him or her? Why or why not?

Problem #11-4: Autopsy Report

In a murder trial, the prosecution offered the autopsy report of the medical examiner, stating that the deceased died from gunshot wounds to the side and back of his head. The medical examiner did not testify. Are autopsy reports testimonial?

Problem #11-5: Rape Crisis Center

Aimee A. was raped and went immediately to the Rape Crisis Center, where she was treated. Aimee was given a consent form for a forensic examination, which she signed. Aimee gave a statement to the treating nurse-practitioner and was examined with a police officer present. Is Aimee's statement to the treating nurse testimonial? If an "objective witness" standard is used, does that weigh in favor of or against the statement being considered testimonial?

Problem #11-6: Miami CI (Confidential Informant)

A confidential informant on a big narcotics bust in South Beach, Miami, was given helpful information from a declarant who did not know the recipient was operating as a confidential informant. The confidential informant wishes to testify at trial about the information. Does this violate the defendant's Confrontation Clause rights? Why or why not?

Problem #11-7: Miami CI Continued

Suppose the informant in problem #11-6 did not testify, but told a police officer everything the CI (confidential informant) knew about the defendant. Can a police officer offer the CI's first-hand observations of the defendant and his drug operation without violating *Crawford*? Why or why not?

Problem #11-8: Elderly Eyewitness

Eddie Elkhorn was an eyewitness to a robbery of a convenience store in Tampa, Florida. Elkhorn, age 81, was on vacation in Tampa and was about to return home to his house in western Australia. To preserve his testimony, Elkhorn gave an oral statement to the police. Although he could not identify the perpetrator, Elkhorn corroborated several important background facts. He started suffering health problems upon returning home. Are Elkhorn's statements testimonial? Does the prosecutor have to pay for Eddie to return to testify if the prosecution wants to use his statement? Should a balancing test be used?

Problem #11-9: Eaney, Meany, and Miney Revisited

Eaney, Meany, and Miney were released from prison. They returned to the illegal business of importing narcotics and were caught a second time. Wiretaps revealed Eaney declaring, "Way to go, Meany and Miney! This plan to bring in cocaine will work this time." The three brothers were tried separately. The prosecution offered Eaney's statement against Meany as an admission of a co-conspirator. The arresting officer, who overheard the wiretap, testified regarding the statement. Meany objected, claiming that there was no showing by the prosecution that the declarant, Eaney, was unavailable to testify or available for cross-examination.

> 1. Must the prosecutor show that Eaney was unavailable to testify in order to comply with the Confrontation Clause?

> 2. What if Eaney had said to the police upon being apprehended, "So we did it; you can't pin it on us." Could the prosecution offer this statement against Eaney in his joint trial with Meany and Miney?

Problem #11-10: Formerly Funny

Jose Funny was indicted for masterminding a car theft ring. In the preliminary hearing, Tabitha testified about the car theft operation. At trial, Tabitha failed to appear despite a subpoena instructing her to do so. If the prosecution offers Tabitha's preliminary hearing transcript in evidence as former testimony at trial, will the transcript meet the requirements of the Confrontation Clause?

§ 11.04 EXPERTS AND CONFRONTATION

[A] Melendez-Diaz v. Massachusetts

United States Supreme Court
129 S. Ct. 2527 (2009)

JUSTICE SCALIA delivered the opinion of the Court.

The Massachusetts courts in this case admitted into evidence affidavits reporting the results of forensic analysis which showed that material seized by the police and connected to the defendant was cocaine. The question presented is whether those affidavits are "testimonial," rendering the affiants "witnesses" subject to the defendant's right of confrontation under the Sixth Amendment.

I

In 2001, Boston police officers [arrested several men in a drug sting,] one of whom was petitioner Luis Melendez-Diaz. The officers placed all three men in a police cruiser.

During the short drive to the police station, the officers observed their passengers fidgeting and making furtive movements in the back of the car. After depositing the men at the station, they searched the police cruiser and found a plastic bag containing 19 smaller plastic bags hidden in the partition between the front and back seats. They submitted the seized evidence to a state laboratory required by law to conduct chemical analysis upon police request.

Melendez-Diaz was charged with distributing cocaine and with trafficking in cocaine in an amount between 14 and 28 grams. At trial, the prosecution placed into evidence the bags seized from Wright and from the police cruiser. It also submitted three "certificates of analysis" showing the results of the forensic analysis performed on the seized substances. The certificates reported the weight of the seized bags and stated that the bags "[h]a[ve] been examined with the following results: The substance was found to contain: Cocaine." The certificates were sworn to before a notary public by analysts at the State Laboratory Institute of the Massachusetts Department of Public Health, as required under Massachusetts law. Mass. Gen. Laws, ch. 111, § 13.

Petitioner objected to the admission of the certificates, asserting that our Confrontation Clause decision in required the analysts to testify in person. The objection was overruled, and the certificates were admitted pursuant to state law as "prima facie evidence of the composition, quality, and the net weight of the narcotic . . . analyzed." The jury found Melendez-Diaz guilty. He appealed, contending, among other things, that admission of the certificates violated his Sixth Amendment right to be confronted with the witnesses against him . . . . We granted certiorari.

II

The Sixth Amendment to the United States Constitution, made applicable to the States via the Fourteenth Amendment, (1965), provides that "[i]n all criminal prosecutions, the accused shall enjoy the right . . . to be confronted with the witnesses against him." In *Crawford*, after reviewing the Clause's historical underpinnings, we held that it guarantees a defendant's right to confront those "who 'bear testimony'" against him. A witness's testimony against a defendant is thus inadmissible unless the witness appears at trial or, if the witness is unavailable, the defendant had a prior opportunity for cross-examination.

Our opinion described the class of testimonial statements covered by the Confrontation Clause as follows:

> "Various formulations of this core class of testimonial statements exist: *ex parte* in-court testimony or its functional equivalent-that is, material such as affidavits, custodial examinations, prior testimony that the defendant was unable to cross-examine, or similar pretrial statements that declarants would reasonably expect to be used prosecutorially; extrajudicial statements . . . contained in formalized testimonial materials, such as affidavits, depositions, prior testimony, or confessions; statements that were made under circumstances which would lead an objective witness reasonably to believe that the statement would be available for use at a later trial."

There is little doubt that the documents at issue in this case fall within the "core class of testimonial statements" thus described. Our description of that category mentions affidavits twice. See also (1992) (THOMAS, J., concurring in part and concurring in judgment) ("[T]he Confrontation Clause is implicated by extrajudicial statements only insofar as they are contained in formalized testimonial materials, such as affidavits, depositions, prior testimony, or confessions"). The documents at issue here, while denominated by Massachusetts law "certificates," are quite plainly affidavits: "declaration [s] of facts written down and sworn to by the declarant before an officer authorized to administer oaths." Black's Law Dictionary 62 (8th ed.2004). They are incontrovertibly a " 'solemn declaration or affirmation made for the purpose of establishing or proving some fact.' " *Crawford, supra,* at 51. The fact in question is that the substance found in the possession of Melendez-Diaz and his codefendants was, as the prosecution claimed, cocaine-the precise testimony the analysts would be expected to provide if called at trial. The "certificates" are functionally identical to live, in-court testimony, doing "precisely what a witness does on direct examination." *Davis v. Washington,* 547 U.S. 813, 830 (2006).

Here, moreover, not only were the affidavits " 'made under circumstances which would lead an objective witness reasonably to believe that the statement would be available for use at a later trial,' " but under Massachusetts law the *sole purpose* of the affidavits was to provide "prima facie evidence of the composition, quality, and the net weight" of the analyzed substance, Mass. Gen. Laws, ch. 111, § 13. We can safely assume that the analysts were aware of the affidavits' evidentiary purpose, since that purpose-as stated in the relevant state-law provision-was reprinted on the affidavits themselves.

In short, under our decision in *Crawford* the analysts' affidavits were testimonial statements, and the analysts were "witnesses" for purposes of the Sixth Amendment. Absent a showing that the analysts were unavailable to testify at trial *and* that petitioner had a prior opportunity to cross-examine them, petitioner was entitled to " 'be confronted with' " the analysts at trial.

III

Respondent and the dissent advance a potpourri of analytic arguments in an effort to avoid this rather straightforward application of our holding in *Crawford.* Before addressing them, however, we must assure the reader of the falsity of the dissent's opening alarm that we are "sweep[ing] away an accepted rule governing the admission of scientific evidence" that has been "established for at least 90 years" and "extends across at least 35 States and six Federal Courts of Appeals."

The vast majority of the state-court cases the dissent cites in support of this claim come not from the last 90 years, but from the last 30, and not surprisingly nearly all of them rely on our decision in *Ohio v. Roberts,* 448 U.S. 56 (1980), or its since-rejected theory that unconfronted testimony was admissible as long as it bore indicia of reliability, As for the six Federal Courts of Appeals cases cited by the dissent, five of them postdated and expressly relied on *Roberts.*

A review of cases that predate the *Roberts* era yields a mixed picture. As the dissent notes, three state supreme court decisions from the early 20th century denied confrontation with respect to certificates of analysis regarding a substance's alcohol content. But other state courts in the same era reached the opposite conclusion. this much is entirely clear: In faithfully applying *Crawford* to the facts of this case, we are not overruling 90 years of settled jurisprudence. It is the dissent that seeks to overturn precedent by resurrecting *Roberts* a mere five years after it was rejected in *Crawford*.

We turn now to the various legal arguments raised by respondent and the dissent.

Respondent first argues that the analysts are not subject to confrontation because they are not "accusatory" witnesses, in that they do not directly accuse petitioner of wrongdoing; rather, their testimony is inculpatory only when taken together with other evidence linking petitioner to the contraband. This finds no support in the text of the Sixth Amendment or in our case law.

The Sixth Amendment guarantees a defendant the right "to be confronted with the witnesses *against him*." (Emphasis added.) To the extent the analysts were witnesses (a question resolved above), they certainly provided testimony *against* petitioner, proving one fact necessary for his conviction-that the substance he possessed was cocaine. The contrast between the text of the Confrontation Clause and the text of the adjacent Compulsory Process Clause confirms this analysis. While the Confrontation Clause guarantees a defendant the right to be confronted with the witnesses "against him," the Compulsory Process Clause guarantees a defendant the right to call witnesses "in his favor." U.S. Const., Amdt.6. The text of the Amendment contemplates two classes of witnesses-those against the defendant and those in his favor. The prosecution *must* produce the former; the defendant *may* call the latter. Contrary to respondent's assertion, there is not a third category of witnesses, helpful to the prosecution, but somehow immune from confrontation.

The dissent first contends that a "conventional witness recalls events observed in the past, while an analyst's report contains near-contemporaneous observations of the test." It is doubtful that the analyst's reports in this case could be characterized as reporting "near-contemporaneous observations"; the affidavits were completed almost a week after the tests were performed. (the tests were performed on November 28, 2001, and the affidavits sworn on December 4, 2001). But regardless, the dissent misunderstands the role that "near-contemporaneity" has played in our case law. The dissent notes that that factor was given "substantial weight" in *Davis*, but in fact that decision *disproves* the dissent's position. There the Court considered the admissibility of statements made to police officers responding to a report of a domestic disturbance. By the time officers arrived the assault had ended, but the victim's statements-written and oral-were sufficiently close in time to the alleged assault that the trial court admitted her affidavit as a "present sense impression." *Davis*, 547 U.S., at 820. Though the witness's statements in *Davis* were "near-contemporaneous" to the events she reported, we nevertheless held that they could *not* be admitted absent an opportunity to confront the witness.

A second reason the dissent contends that the analysts are not "conventional witnesses" (and thus not subject to confrontation) is that they "observe[d] neither the crime nor any human action related to it." The dissent provides no authority for this particular limitation of the type of witnesses subject to confrontation. Nor is it conceivable that all witnesses who fit this description would be outside the scope of the Confrontation Clause. For example, is a police officer's investigative report describing the crime scene admissible absent an opportunity to examine the officer? The dissent's novel exception from coverage of the Confrontation Clause would exempt all expert witnesses-a hardly "unconventional" class of witnesses.

A third respect in which the dissent asserts that the analysts are not "conventional" witnesses and thus not subject to confrontation is that their statements were not provided in response to interrogation. As we have explained, "[t]he Framers were no more willing to exempt from cross-examination volunteered testimony or answers to open-ended questions than they were to exempt answers to detailed interrogation." *Davis.* Respondent and the dissent cite no authority, and we are aware of none, holding that a person who volunteers his testimony is any less a " 'witness against' the defendant," than one who is responding to interrogation. In any event, the analysts' affidavits in this case *were* presented in response to a police request. See Mass. Gen. Laws, ch. 111, §§ 12–13. If an affidavit submitted in response to a police officer's request to "write down what happened" suffices to trigger the Sixth Amendment's protection (as it apparently does, see *Davis*, 547 U.S., at 819–820 (Thomas, J., concurring in judgment in part and dissenting in part)), then the analysts' testimony should be subject to confrontation as well.

Respondent and the dissent may be right that there are other ways-and in some cases better ways-to challenge or verify the results of a forensic test. But the Constitution guarantees one way: confrontation. We do not have license to suspend the Confrontation Clause when a preferable trial strategy is available.

Nor is it evident that what respondent calls "neutral scientific testing" is as neutral or as reliable as respondent suggests. Forensic evidence is not uniquely immune from the risk of manipulation. According to a recent study conducted under the auspices of the National Academy of Sciences, "[t]he majority of [laboratories producing forensic evidence] are administered by law enforcement agencies, such as police departments, where the laboratory administrator reports to the head of the agency." National Research Council of the National Academies, Strengthening Forensic Science in the United States: A Path Forward 6-1 (Prepublication Copy Feb. 2009) (hereinafter National Academy Report). And "[b]ecause forensic scientists often are driven in their work by a need to answer a particular question related to the issues of a particular case, they sometimes face pressure to sacrifice appropriate methodology for the sake of expediency." *Id.*, at S-17. A forensic analyst responding to a request from a law enforcement official may feel pressure-or have an incentive-to alter the evidence in a manner favorable to the prosecution.

Confrontation is one means of assuring accurate forensic analysis. While it is true, as the dissent notes, that an honest analyst will not alter his testimony when forced to confront the defendant, the same cannot be said of the fraudulent analyst. This case is illustrative. The affidavits submitted by the analysts contained only the bare-bones statement that "[t]he substance was found to contain: Cocaine." At the time of trial, petitioner did not know what tests the analysts performed, whether those tests were routine, and whether interpreting their results required the exercise of judgment or the use of skills that the analysts may not have possessed. While we still do not know the precise tests used by the analysts, we are told that the laboratories use "methodology recommended by the Scientific Working Group for the Analysis of

Seized Drugs." At least some of that methodology requires the exercise of judgment and presents a risk of error that might be explored on cross-examination. See 2 P. Giannelli & E. Imwinkelried, Scientific Evidence § 23.03[c] (4th ed. 2007) (identifying four "critical errors" that analysts may commit in interpreting the results of the commonly used gas chromatography/mass spectrometry analysis).

The same is true of many of the other types of forensic evidence commonly used in criminal prosecutions. "[T]here is wide variability across forensic science disciplines with regard to techniques, methodologies, reliability, types and numbers of potential errors, research, general acceptability, and published material." National Academy Report S-5.

Respondent argues that the analysts' affidavits are admissible without confrontation because they are "akin to the types of official and business records admissible at common law." But the affidavits do not qualify as traditional official or business records, and even if they did, their authors would be subject to confrontation nonetheless.

Documents kept in the regular course of business may ordinarily be admitted at trial despite their hearsay status. See Fed. Rule Evid. 803(6). But that is not the case if the regularly conducted business activity is the production of evidence for use at trial. Our decision in *Palmer v. Hoffman*, 318 U.S. 109, (1943), made that distinction clear. There we held that an accident report provided by an employee of a railroad company did not qualify as a business record because, although kept in the regular course of the railroad's operations, it was "calculated for use essentially in the court, not in the business." The analysts' certificates-like police reports generated by law enforcement officials-do not qualify as business or public records for precisely the same reason. See Rule 803(8) (defining public records as "excluding, however, in criminal cases matters observed by police officers and other law enforcement personnel").

Respondent seeks to rebut this limitation by noting that at common law the results of a coroner's inquest were admissible without an opportunity for confrontation. But as we have previously noted, whatever the status of coroner's reports at common law in England, they were not accorded any special status in American practice. See *Crawford*, 541 U.S., at 47, n. 2. . . .

Respondent asserts that we should find no Confrontation Clause violation in this case because petitioner had the ability to subpoena the analysts. But that power-whether pursuant to state law or the Compulsory Process Clause-is no substitute for the right of confrontation. Unlike the Confrontation Clause, those provisions are of no use to the defendant when the witness is unavailable or simply refuses to appear. See, e.g., *Davis*, 547 U.S., at 820 ("[The witness] was subpoenaed, but she did not appear at . . . trial"). Converting the prosecution's duty under the Confrontation Clause into the defendant's privilege under state law or the Compulsory Process Clause shifts the consequences of adverse-witness no-shows from the State to the accused. More fundamentally, the Confrontation Clause imposes a burden on the prosecution to present its witnesses, not on the defendant to bring those adverse witnesses into court. Its value to the defendant is not replaced by a system in which the prosecution presents its evidence via *ex parte* affidavits and waits for the defendant to subpoena the affiants if he chooses.

Finally, respondent asks us to relax the requirements of the Confrontation Clause to accommodate the " 'necessities of trial and the adversary process.' " It is not clear whence we would derive the authority to do so . . . .

Perhaps the best indication that the sky will not fall after today's decision is that it has not done so already. Many States have already adopted the constitutional rule we announce today,11 while many others permit the defendant to assert (or forfeit by silence) his Confrontation Clause right after receiving notice of the prosecution's intent to use a forensic analyst's report. Despite these widespread practices, there is no evidence that the criminal justice system has ground to a halt in the States that, one way or another, empower a defendant to insist upon the analyst's appearance at trial. Indeed, in Massachusetts itself, a defendant may subpoena the analyst to appear at trial, and yet there is no indication that obstructionist defendants are abusing the privilege.

*   *   *

This case involves little more than the application of our holding in *Crawford v. Washington*. The Sixth Amendment does not permit the prosecution to prove its case via *ex parte* out-of-court affidavits, and the admission of such evidence against Melendez-Diaz was error. We therefore reverse the judgment of the Appeals Court of Massachusetts and remand the case for further proceedings not inconsistent with this opinion.

It is so ordered.

JUSTICE THOMAS, concurring.

I write separately to note that I continue to adhere to my position that "the Confrontation Clause is implicated by extrajudicial statements only insofar as they are contained in formalized testimonial materials, such as affidavits, depositions, prior testimony, or confessions." *White v. Illinois*, 502 U.S. 346, 365 (1992). I join the Court's opinion in this case because the documents at issue in this case "are quite plainly affidavits." As such, they "fall within the core class of testimonial statements" governed by the Confrontation Clause.

JUSTICE KENNEDY, with whom the CHIEF JUSTICE, JUSTICE BREYER, and JUSTICE ALITO join, dissenting.

The Court sweeps away an accepted rule governing the admission of scientific evidence. Until today, scientific analysis could be introduced into evidence without testimony from the "analyst" who produced it. This rule has been established for at least 90 years. It extends across at least 35 States and six Federal Courts of Appeals. Yet the Court undoes it based on two recent opinions that say nothing about forensic analysts: *Crawford v. Washington* (2004) and *Davis v. Washington* (2006).

It is remarkable that the Court so confidently disregards a century of jurisprudence. We learn now that we have misinterpreted the Confrontation Clause-hardly an arcane or seldom-used provision of the Constitution-for the first 218 years of its existence. The immediate systemic concern is that the Court makes no attempt to acknowledge the real differences between laboratory analysts who perform scientific tests and other, more conventional witnesses-"witnesses" being the word the Framers used in the Confrontation Clause.

Crawford and *Davis* dealt with ordinary witnesses-women who had seen, and in two cases been the victim of, the crime in question. Those cases stand for the proposition that formal statements made by a conventional witness-one who has personal knowledge of some aspect of the defendant's guilt-may not be admitted without the witness appearing at trial to meet the accused face to face. But *Crawford* and *Davis* do not say-indeed, could not have said, because the facts were not before the Court-that anyone who makes a testimonial statement is a witness for purposes of the Confrontation Clause, even when that person has, in fact, witnessed nothing to give them personal knowledge of the defendant's guilt.

Because *Crawford* and *Davis* concerned typical witnesses, the Court should have done the sensible thing and limited its holding to witnesses as so defined. Indeed, as Justice THOMAS warned in his opinion in *Davis*, the Court's approach has become "disconnected from history and unnecessary to prevent abuse." 547 U.S., at 838 The Court's reliance on the word "testimonial" is of little help, of course, for that word does not appear in the text of the Clause.

The Court dictates to the States, as a matter of constitutional law, an as-yet-undefined set of rules governing what kinds of evidence may be admitted without in-court testimony. Indeed, under today's opinion the States bear an even more onerous burden than they did before *Crawford*. Then, the States at least had the guidance of the hearsay rule and could rest assured that "where the evidence f[ell] within a firmly rooted hearsay exception," the Confrontation Clause did not bar its admission. *Ohio v. Roberts*, 448 U.S. 56, 66 (1980) (overruled by *Crawford*). Now, without guidance from any established body of law, the States can only guess what future rules this Court will distill from the sparse constitutional text. See, *e.g., Mendez, Crawford v. Washington*: A Critique, 57 Stan. L.Rev. 569, 586–593 (2004) (discussing unanswered questions regarding testimonial statements).

The Court's opinion suggests this will be a body of formalistic and wooden rules, divorced from precedent, common sense, and the underlying purpose of the Clause. Its ruling has vast potential to disrupt criminal procedures that already give ample protections against the misuse of scientific evidence. For these reasons, as more fully explained below, the Court's opinion elicits my respectful dissent.

I

The Court says that, before the results of a scientific test may be introduced into evidence, the defendant has the right to confront the "analyst." *Ante*, at 2531 – 2532. One must assume that this term, though it appears nowhere in the Confrontation Clause, nevertheless has some constitutional substance that now must be elaborated in future cases. There is no accepted definition of analyst, and there is no established precedent to define that term.

Consider how many people play a role in a routine test for the presence of illegal drugs. One person prepares a sample of the drug, places it in a testing machine, and retrieves the machine's printout-often, a graph showing the frequencies of radiation absorbed by the sample or the masses of the sample's molecular fragments. See 2 P. Giannelli & E. Imwinkelried, Scientific Evidence § 23.03 (4th ed. 2007) (describing common methods of identifying drugs, including infrared spectrophotometry, nuclear magnetic resonance, gas chromatography, and mass spectrometry). A second person interprets the graph the machine prints out-perhaps by comparing that printout with published, standardized graphs of known drugs. Meanwhile, a third person-perhaps an independent contractor-has calibrated the machine and, having done so, has certified that the machine is in good working order. Finally, a fourth person-perhaps the laboratory's director-certifies that his subordinates followed established procedures.

It is not at all evident which of these four persons is the analyst to be confronted under the rule the Court announces today. If all are witnesses who must appear for in-court confrontation, then the Court has, for all practical purposes, forbidden the use of scientific tests in criminal trials. As discussed further below, requiring even one of these individuals to testify threatens to disrupt if not end many prosecutions where guilt is clear but a newly found formalism now holds sway. . . . . Today's decision demonstrates that even in the narrow category of scientific tests that identify a drug, the Court cannot define with any clarity who the analyst is. Outside this narrow category, the range of other scientific tests that may be affected by the Court's new confrontation right is staggering.

[For example,] the defense has the right to call its own witnesses to show that the chain of custody is not secure. But that does not mean it can demand that, in the prosecution's case in chief, each person who is in the chain of custody-and who had an undoubted opportunity to taint or tamper with the evidence-must be called by the prosecution under the Confrontation Clause. And the same is true with lab technicians.

The Confrontation Clause is simply not needed for these matters. Where, as here, the defendant does not even dispute the accuracy of the analyst's work, confrontation adds nothing.

For the sake of these negligible benefits, the Court threatens to disrupt forensic investigations across the country and to put prosecutions nationwide at risk of dismissal based on erratic, all-too-frequent instances when a particular laboratory technician, now invested by the Court's new constitutional designation as the analyst, simply does not or cannot appear.

The Court's holding is a windfall to defendants, one that is unjustified by any demonstrated deficiency in trials, any well-understood historical requirement, or any established constitutional precedent. [Consequently, I respectfully dissent.]

[B]   Bullcoming v. New Mexico

United States Supreme Court
131 S. Ct. 2705 (2011)

JUSTICE GINSBURG delivered the opinion of the Court except as to Part IV and footnote 6. JUSTICE SCALIA joined that opinion in full, JUSTICES SOTOMAYOR and KAGAN joined as to all but Part IV and JUSTICE THOMAS joined as to all but Part IV and footnote 6. JUSTICE SOTOMAYOR filed an opinion concurring in part. JUSTICE KENNEDY filed a dissenting opinion, in which CHIEF JUSTICE ROBERTS and JUSTICES BREYER and ALITO.

In *Melendez-Diaz v. Massachusetts*, 557 U.S. ___ (2009), this Court held that a forensic laboratory report stating that a suspect substance was cocaine ranked as testimonial for purposes of the Sixth Amendment's Confrontation Clause. The report had been created specifically to serve as evidence in a criminal proceeding. Absent stipulation, the Court ruled, the prosecution may not introduce such a report without offering a live witness competent to testify to the truth of the statements made in the report.

In the case before us, petitioner Donald Bullcoming was arrested on charges of driving while intoxicated (DWI). Principal evidence against Bullcoming was a forensic laboratory report certifying that Bullcoming's blood-alcohol concentration was well above the threshold for aggravated DWI. At trial, the prosecution did not call as a witness the analyst who signed the certification. Instead, the State called another analyst who was familiar with the laboratory's testing procedures, but had neither participated in nor observed the test on Bullcoming's blood sample. The New Mexico Supreme Court determined that, although the blood-alcohol analysis was "testimonial," the Confrontation Clause did not require the certifying analyst's in-court testimony. Instead, New Mexico's high court held, live testimony of another analyst satisfied the constitutional requirements.

The question presented is whether the Confrontation Clause permits the prosecution to introduce a forensic laboratory report containing a testimonial certification — made for the purpose of proving a particular fact — through the in-court testimony of a scientist who did not sign the certification or perform or observe the test reported in the certification. We hold that surrogate testimony of that order does not meet the constitutional requirement. The accused's right is to be confronted with the analyst who made the certification, unless that analyst is unavailable at trial, and the accused had an opportunity, pretrial, to cross-examine that particular scientist.

The State and its *amici* urge that unbending application of the Confrontation Clause to forensic evidence would impose an undue burden on the prosecution. This argument, also advanced in the dissent, largely repeats a refrain rehearsed and rejected in *Melendez-Diaz*. The constitutional requirement, we reiterate, "may not [be] disregard[ed] . . . at our convenience . . . ."

*   *   *

For the reasons stated, the judgment of the New Mexico Supreme Court is reversed, and the case is remanded for further proceedings not inconsistent with this opinion.

It is so ordered.

JUSTICE KENNEDY, with whom the CHIEF JUSTICE, JUSTICE BREYER, and JUSTICE ALITO join, dissenting.

[In] *Melendez-Diaz v. Massachusetts*, 557 U.S. ___ (2009), [the Court] held [a] report inadmissible because no one was present at trial to testify to its contents. Whether or not one agrees with the reasoning and the result in *Melendez-Diaz*, the Court today takes the new and serious misstep of extending that holding to instances like this one. Here a knowledgeable representative of the laboratory was present to testify and to explain the lab's processes and the details of the report; but because he was not the analyst who filled out part of the form and transcribed onto it the test result from a machine printout, the Court finds a confrontation violation. Some of the principal objections to the Court's underlying theory have been set out earlier and need not be repeated here. (KENNEDY, J., dissenting). Additional reasons, applicable to the extension of that doctrine and to the new ruling in this case, are now explained in support of this respectful dissent.

Before today, the Court had not held that the Confrontation Clause bars admission of scientific findings when an employee of the testing laboratory authenticates the findings, testifies to the laboratory's methods and practices, and is cross-examined at trial. Far from replacing live testimony with "systematic" and "extrajudicial" examinations, *Davis v. Washington*, 547 U.S. 813, 835, 836 (2006) (THOMAS, J., concurring in judgment in part and dissenting in part), these procedures are fully consistent with the Confrontation Clause and with well-established principles for ensuring that criminal trials are conducted in full accord with requirements of fairness and reliability and with the confrontation guarantee. They do not "resemble Marian proceedings." *Id.* at 837.

The procedures followed here, but now invalidated by the Court, make live testimony rather than the "solemnity" of a document the primary reason to credit the laboratory's scientific results. Unlike *Melendez-Diaz*, where the jury was asked to credit a laboratory's findings based solely on documents that were "quite plainly affidavits," here the signature, heading, or legend on the document were routine authentication elements for a report that would be assessed and explained by in-court testimony subject to full cross-examination. The only sworn statement at issue was that of the witness who was present and who testified.

Crawford itself does not compel today's conclusion. It is true, as Crawford confirmed, that the Confrontation Clause seeks in part to bar the government from replicating trial procedures outside of public view. *See* 541 U.S., at 50; [*Michigan v.*] *Bryant, Crawford* explained that the basic purpose of the Clause was to address the sort of abuses exemplified at the notorious treason trial of Sir Walter Raleigh.

A rule that bars testimony of that sort, however, provides neither cause nor necessity to impose a constitutional bar on the admission of impartial lab reports like the instant one, reports prepared by experienced technicians in laboratories that follow professional norms and scientific protocols.

In the meantime, New Mexico's experience exemplifies the problems ahead. From 2008 to 2010, subpoenas requiring New Mexico analysts to testify in impaired-driving cases rose 71%, to 1,600 — or 8 or 9 every workday. New Mexico Scientific Laboratory Brief 2. In a State that is the Nation's fifth largest by area and that employs just 10 total analysts, each analyst in blood alcohol cases recently received 200 subpoenas per year, The analysts now must travel great distances on most working days. The result has been, in the laboratory's words, "chaotic." *Id.*, at 5. And if the defense raises an objection and the analyst is tied up in another court proceeding; or on leave; or absent; or delayed in transit; or no longer employed; or ill; or no longer living, the defense gets a windfall. As a result, good defense attorneys will object in ever-greater numbers to a prosecution failure or inability to produce laboratory analysts at trial. The concomitant increases in subpoenas will further impede the state laboratory's ability to keep pace with its obligations. Scarce state resources could be committed to other urgent needs in the criminal justice system.

* * *

Seven years after its initiation, it bears remembering that the *Crawford* approach was not preordained. This Court's missteps have produced an interpretation of the word "witness" at odds with its meaning elsewhere in the Constitution, including elsewhere in the Sixth Amendment, see Amar, *Sixth Amendment First Principles*, 84 Geo. L.J. 641, 647, 691–696 (1996), and at odds with the sound administration of justice. It is time to return to solid ground. A proper place to begin that return is to decline to extend *Melendez-Diaz* to bar the reliable, commonsense evidentiary framework the State sought to follow in this case.

[C]　Williams v. Illinois

United States Supreme Court
567 U.S. __, 132 S. Ct. 2221 (2012)

JUSTICE ALITO announced the judgment of the Court and delivered an opinion, in which THE CHIEF JUSTICE, JUSTICE KENNEDY, and JUSTICE BREYER join.

In this case, we decide whether *Crawford v. Washington*, 541 U.S. 36 (2004), precludes an expert witness from testifying in a manner that has long been allowed under the law of evidence. Specifically, does *Crawford* bar an expert from expressing an opinion based on facts about a case that have been made known to the expert but about which the expert is not competent to testify? We also decide whether *Crawford* substantially impedes the ability of prosecutors to introduce DNA evidence and thus may effectively relegate the prosecution in some cases to reliance on older, less reliable forms of proof.

In petitioner's bench trial for rape, the prosecution called an expert who testified that a DNA profile produced by an outside laboratory, Cellmark, matched a profile produced by the state police lab using a sample of petitioner's blood. On direct examination, the expert testified that Cellmark was an accredited laboratory and that Cellmark provided the police with a DNA profile. The expert also explained the notations on documents admitted as business records, stating that, according to the records, vaginal swabs taken from the victim were sent to and received back from Cellmark. The expert made no other statement that was offered for the purpose of identifying the sample of biological material used in deriving the profile or for the purpose of establishing how Cellmark handled or tested the sample. Nor did the expert vouch for the accuracy of the profile that Cellmark produced.

[Despite Petitioner's claim to the contrary,] we now conclude that this form of expert testimony does not violate the Confrontation Clause because that provision has no application to out-of-court statements that are not offered to prove the truth of the matter asserted. When an expert testifies for the prosecution in a criminal case, the defendant has the opportunity to cross-examine the expert about any statements that are offered for their truth. Out-of-court statements that are related by the expert solely for the purpose of explaining the assumptions on which that opinion rests are not offered for their truth and thus fall outside the scope of the Confrontation Clause. Applying this rule to the present case, we conclude that the expert's testimony did not violate the Sixth Amendment.

As a second, independent basis for our decision, we also conclude that even if the report produced by Cellmark had been admitted into evidence, there would have been no Confrontation Clause violation. The Cellmark report is very different from the sort of extrajudicial statements, such as affidavits, depositions, prior testimony, and confessions that the Confrontation Clause was originally understood to reach. The report was produced before any suspect was identified. The report was sought not for the purpose of obtaining evidence to be used against petitioner, who was not even under suspicion at the time, but for the purpose of finding a rapist who was on the loose. And the profile that Cellmark provided was not inherently inculpatory. On the contrary, a DNA profile is evidence that tends to exculpate all but one of the more than 7 billion people in the world today.

[In this case, a young woman, L.J., had been raped in Chicago, Illinois, in 2000. Various DNA testing occurred, and a perpetrator was identified and prosecuted. At a later bench trial, various experts testified about their DNA analysis. A forensic specialist, Sandra Lambatos, also testified. Lambatos testified that she had compared samples tested by others, a practice she said was "commonly accepted" when it came to "one DNA expert relying on records from another DNA expert." One of the samples was prepared by Cellmark Diagnostics Laboratory, an "accredited crime lab." Lambatos then testified that as a result of the comparison, the defendant could not be excluded as a perpetrator.]

The trial court found petitioner guilty of the charges against him. [The state appeals court and Illinois Supreme Court affirmed the decision.]

The Confrontation Clause of the Sixth Amendment provides that, "[i]n all criminal prosecutions, the accused shall enjoy the right " to be confronted with the witnesses against him." [Our decision in 2004 in] *Crawford* has resulted in a steady stream of new cases in this Court. Two of these decisions involved scientific reports. In *Melendez-*

Diaz, the defendant was arrested and charged with distributing and trafficking in cocaine. The trial court . . . admitted into evidence three "certificates of analysis" from the state forensic laboratory stating that the bags [contained cocaine].

The Court held that the admission of these certificates, which were executed under oath before a notary, violated the Sixth Amendment. They were "'quite plainly affidavits,'" *id.* at 330 (Thomas, J., concurring), used to prove the truth of the matter they asserted. In *Bullcoming*, we held that another scientific report could not be used as substantive evidence against the defendant unless the analyst who prepared and certified the report was subject to confrontation. The Court stated simply: "The accused's right is to be confronted with the analyst who made the certification."

In concurrence, Justice Sotomayor highlighted the importance of the fact that the forensic report had been admitted into evidence for the purpose of proving the truth of the matter it asserted. "We would face a different question," she observed, "if asked to determine the constitutionality of allowing an expert witness to discuss others' testimonial statements if the testimonial statements were not themselves admitted as evidence." We now confront that question.

It has long been accepted that an expert witness may voice an opinion based on facts concerning the events at issue in a particular case even if the expert lacks firsthand knowledge of those facts. At common law, courts developed two ways to deal with this situation. An expert could rely on facts that had already been established in the record. But because it was not always possible to proceed in this manner, and because record evidence was often disputed, courts developed the alternative practice of allowing an expert to testify in the form of a "hypothetical question." Under this approach, the expert would be asked to assume the truth of certain factual predicates, and was then asked to offer an opinion based on those assumptions.

There is a long tradition of the use of hypothetical questions in American courts. Modern rules of evidence continue to permit experts to express opinions based on facts about which they lack personal knowledge, but these rules dispense with the need for hypothetical questions. Under both the Illinois and the Federal Rules of Evidence, an expert may base an opinion on facts that are "made known to the expert at or before the hearing," but such reliance does not constitute admissible evidence of this underlying information. Fed. R. Evid. 703.

This feature of Illinois and federal law is important because *Crawford*, while departing from prior Confrontation Clause precedent in other respects, took pains to reaffirm the proposition that the Confrontation Clause "does not bar the use of testimonial statements for purposes other than establishing the truth of the matter asserted." 541 U.S. at 59–60, n. 9 (citing *Tennessee v. Street*, 471 U.S. 409).

The principal argument advanced to show a Confrontation Clause violation concerns the phrase that Lambatos used when she referred to the DNA profile that the ISP lab received from Cellmark.

In the view of the dissent, the following is the critical portion of Lambatos' testimony, with the particular words that the dissent finds objectionable italicized:

"Q Was there a computer match generated of the male DNA profile *found in semen from the vaginal swabs of [L.J.]* to a male DNA profile that had been identified as having originated from Sandy Williams?

"A Yes, there was." *Post*, at 7 (opinion of Kagan J.)

According to the dissent, the italicized phrase violated petitioner's confrontation right because Lambatos lacked personal knowledge that the profile produced by Cellmark was based on the vaginal swabs taken from the victim, L.J. As the dissent acknowledges, there would have been "nothing wrong with Lambatos's testifying that two DNA profiles — the one shown in the Cellmark report and the one derived from Williams's blood — matched each other; that was a straightforward application of Lambatos's expertise." *Post*, at 12. Thus, if Lambatos' testimony had been slightly modified as follows, the dissent would see no problem.

"Q Was there a computer match generated of the male DNA profile *produced by Cellmark* ~~found in semen from the vaginal swabs of [L.J.]~~ to a male DNA profile that had been identified as having originated from Sandy Williams?

"A Yes, there was."

The defect in this argument is that under Illinois law (like federal law) it is clear that the putatively offending phrase in Lambatos' testimony was not admissible for the purpose of proving the truth of the matter asserted — *i.e.*, that the matching DNA profile was "found in semen from the vaginal swabs." There is no reason to think that the trier of fact took Lambatos' answer as substantive evidence to establish where the DNA profiles came from.

The dissent's argument would have force if petitioner had elected to have a jury trial. In that event, there would have been a danger of the jury's taking Lambatos' testimony as proof that the Cellmark profile was derived from the sample obtained from the victim's vaginal swabs. Absent an evaluation of the risk of juror confusion and careful jury instructions, the testimony could not have gone to the jury.

This case, however, involves *a bench trial* and we must assume that the trial judge understood that the portion of Lambatos' testimony to which the dissent objects was not admissible to prove the truth of the matter asserted. The dissent, on the other hand, reaches the truly remarkable conclusion that the wording of Lambatos' testimony confused the trial judge. This argument reflects a profound lack of respect for the acumen of the trial judge.

[W]e conclude that petitioner's Sixth Amendment confrontation right was not violated. Even if the Cellmark report had been introduced for its truth, we would nevertheless conclude that there was no Confrontation Clause violation.

The abuses that the Court has identified as prompting the adoption of the Confrontation Clause shared the following two characteristics: (a) they involved out-of-court statements having the primary purpose of accusing a targeted individual of engaging in criminal conduct and (b) they involved formalized statements such as affidavits, depositions, prior testimony, or confessions. The Cellmark report is very different. It plainly was not prepared for the primary purpose of accusing a targeted individual. In identifying the primary purpose of an out-of-court statement, we apply an objective test. *Bryant.* We look for the primary purpose that a reasonable person would have ascribed to the statement, taking into account all of the surrounding circumstances. Here, the primary purpose of the Cellmark report, viewed objectively, was not to accuse petitioner or to create evidence for use at trial. When the ISP lab sent the sample to Cellmark, its primary purpose was to catch a dangerous rapist who was still at large, not to obtain evidence for use against petitioner, who was neither in custody nor under suspicion at that time. Under these circumstances, there was no "prospect of fabrication" and no incentive to produce anything other than a scientifically sound and reliable profile.

It is also significant that in many labs, numerous technicians work on each DNA profile. ("[A]pproximately 10 Cellmark analysts were involved in the laboratory work in this case"). When the work of a lab is divided up in such a way, it is likely that the sole purpose of each technician is simply to perform his or her task in accordance with accepted procedures. For the two independent reasons explained above, we conclude that there was no Confrontation Clause violation in this case. Accordingly, the judgment of the Supreme Court of Illinois is *Affirmed.*

JUSTICE THOMAS, concurring in the judgment.

I agree with the plurality that the disclosure of Cellmark's out-of-court statements through the expert testimony of Sandra Lambatos did not violate the Confrontation Clause. I reach this conclusion, however, solely because Cellmark's statements lacked the requisite "formality and solemnity" to be considered "'testimonial'" for purposes of the Confrontation Clause. *See Michigan v. Bryant* (Thomas, J., concurring in judgment).

JUSTICE KAGAN, with whom JUSTICE SCALIA, JUSTICE GINSBURG, and JUSTICE SOTOMAYOR join, dissenting.

Some years ago, the State of California prosecuted a man named John Kocak for rape. At a preliminary hearing, the State presented testimony from an analyst at the Cellmark Diagnostics Laboratory — the same facility used to generate DNA evidence in this case. The analyst had extracted DNA from a bloody sweatshirt found at the crime scene and then compared it to two control samples — one from Kocak and one from the victim. The analyst's report identified a single match: As she explained on direct examination, the DNA found on the sweatshirt belonged to Kocak. But after undergoing cross-examination, the analyst realized she had made a mortifying error. She took the stand again, but this time to admit that the report listed the victim's control sample as coming from Kocak, and Kocak's as coming from the victim. So the DNA on the sweatshirt matched not Kocak, but the victim herself. ("I'm a little hysterical right now, but I think . . . the two names should be switched"). In trying Kocak, the State would have to look elsewhere for its evidence.

Our Constitution contains a mechanism for catching such errors — the Sixth Amendment's Confrontation Clause. That Clause, and the Court's recent cases interpreting it, require that testimony against a criminal defendant be subject to cross-examination. And that command applies with full force to forensic evidence of the kind involved in both the Kocak case and this one. In two decisions issued in the last three years, this Court held that if a prosecutor wants to introduce the results of forensic testing into evidence, he must afford the defendant an opportunity to cross-examine an analyst responsible for the test.

Under our Confrontation Clause precedents, this is an open-and-shut case. The State of Illinois prosecuted Sandy Williams for rape based in part on a DNA profile created in Cellmark's laboratory. Yet the State did not give Williams a chance to question the analyst who produced that evidence. Instead, the prosecution introduced the results of Cellmark's testing through an expert witness who had no idea how they were generated.

The Court today disagrees, though it cannot settle on a reason why. Justice Alito, joined by three other Justices, advances two theories — that the expert's summary of the Cellmark report was not offered for its truth, and that the report is not the kind of statement triggering the Confrontation Clause's protection. In the pages that follow, I call Justice Alito's opinion "the plurality," because that is the conventional term for it. But in all except its disposition, his opinion is a dissent: Five Justices specifically reject every aspect of its reasoning and every paragraph of its explication. (Thomas, J., concurring in judgment) ("I share the dissent's view of the plurality's flawed analysis"). Justice Thomas, for his part, contends that the Cellmark report is nontestimonial on a different rationale. But no other Justice joins his opinion or subscribes to the test he offers.

That creates five votes to approve the admission of the Cellmark report, but not a single good explanation. The plurality's first rationale endorses a prosecutorial dodge; its second relies on distinguishing indistinguishable forensic reports. I would choose another path — to adhere to the simple rule established in our decisions, for the good reasons we have previously given. Because defendants like Williams have a constitutional right to confront the witnesses against them, I respectfully dissent from the Court's fractured decision.

"[W]hen the State elected to introduce" the substance of Cellmark's report into evidence, the analyst who generated that report "became a witness" whom Williams "had the right to confront." *Bullcoming*, 564 U.S., at ___ . As we stated just last year, "Our precedent[s] cannot sensibly be read any other way." *Id.*

Real-World Scenario: Senior Citizen — Not the Typical "Early Bird" Special

Two elderly women in their mid-70s were convicted of murder in California for killing two elderly men six years apart to collect life insurance proceeds. The women lived in Los Angeles and were listed as beneficiaries on several life insurance policies taken out on the men. The modus operandi for the killings was the automobile. The woman ran the men over with their cars and then collected more than one-half of a million dollars in insurance proceeds.

> At trial, the prosecution alleged that at least one of the men was drugged beforehand. A laboratory director testified for the prosecution. The director stated that the blood analysis reflected in reports from experts showed that one of the men had a drug in his blood that caused drowsiness. The director did not perform the tests in the reports. Did the laboratory director's testimony violate the accused's Confrontation Clause rights?

What does *Williams v. Illinois*, 567 U.S. __, 132 S. Ct. 2221 (2012), mean for expert testimony? There are at least a dozen cases pending before the Court seeking clarification of *Williams*, a case that exemplifies the difficulties of creating coherence from a multiplicity of doctrinal rationales. The splintered Court, with a 4-1-4 plurality, left many questions about the admissibility of experts testifying to statements by non-testifying persons and left lower courts grasping for a predictable pronouncement to follow. While there is a rule courts follow for plurality decisions — *e.g.*, "[w]hen a fragmented Court decides a case and no single rationale explaining the result enjoys the assent of five Justices, the holding of the Court may be viewed as the position taken by those members who concurred in the judgments on the narrowest grounds," *Marks v. United States*, 430 U.S. 188, 193 (1977) — no such clear lowest common denominator is apparent in *Williams*. What statements are admissible, and under what rationale, is still open to debate.

§ 11.05 MORE PROBLEMS

Problem #11-11: Baby Jessica

Jessica, age 5, tells her mother that "the man next door did stuff to me before." Jessica's mother then took her to a child psychologist, Dr. Thomas, who interviewed and examined Jessica. If a neighbor, John Barton, is subsequently charged with various crimes of child sexual abuse against Jessica, can Jessica's mother and Dr. Thomas testify about Jessica's statements to them? If Jessica testifies, can she do so outside the physical presence of the defendant?

Problem #11-12: Ready and Available

Margot is an eyewitness to a stabbing outside of a New Mexico tavern, La Bonita. At the time of the stabbing, Margot exclaimed, "Look, Ricardo just stabbed Pepe after Pepe punched him!" Ricardo is prosecuted for the stabbing. Margot is available to testify, but prefers not to do so. Can someone who heard Margot's statement testify to it without violating Ricardo's Confrontation Clause rights? Explain.

Problem #11-13: "I Confess"

Nick confesses to the ATM robbery and shooting of a doctor coming off of a late shift at the Graddy Hospital. Nick stated, "Barnes and I thought we would just get some easy money; no one was supposed to get hurt, honest."

Nick and Barnes are jointly tried in state court for the robbery and shooting. Nick's confession is offered by the prosecution against Nick alone. The prosecutor informs the judge that she would not oppose the judge giving the jury a limiting instruction on the evidence. The limiting instruction would inform the jury that the confession is being admitted solely against Nick and should not be used at all against Barnes. (Nick chooses not to testify.) Is this approach permissible?

Problem #11-14: Jogger

Carrie was brutally beaten during her afternoon jog. The police arrived at the scene soon thereafter.

(a) Immediately after the beating, Carrie was interviewed at the scene by police officers and provided some descriptive information about the assailants, who were still at large.

(b) Approximately one week after the beating, Carrie left the hospital and identified Barnett as her attacker in a line-up at the police station (where Barnett was one of six persons in the line-up). Barnett is tried for the beating almost two years after it occurred. If Carrie can no longer identify Barnett as her attacker, will the admission of the line-up identification violate Barnett's Confrontation Clause rights? Explain.

§ 11.06   WAIVER OF CONFRONTATION RIGHTS

Giles v. California
554 U.S. 353 (2008)

In *Giles*, the Supreme Court decided the standard governing when the Confrontation right would be forfeited by wrongdoing. Giles was convicted of murder after the trial court permitted prosecutors to introduce hearsay statements made by the victim to a police officer who was responding to a domestic violence alert. At issue before the Supreme Court was whether the unconfronted testimony of the victim was properly admitted under the forfeiture exception. The Court considered whether the forfeiture exception applied only when there was an intentional act designed to prevent the witness from testifying or if it also applied when an intentional criminal act had the unintended consequence of preventing witness testimony. Led again by Justice Scalia, the Supreme Court adopted the former approach because it was established at the founding of the Amendment that there must be conduct *designed* to prevent subsequent testimony. As applied to Giles, the intentionality of the criminal act does not suffice to show there was a design to prevent testimony at a subsequent time. Because the intent of the defendant was not considered in determining whether there was such a design, whether intent existed was a matter to be considered by the court below on remand. The Court stated:

> The terms used to define the scope of the forfeiture rule suggest that the exception applied only when the defendant engaged in conduct *designed* to prevent the witness from testifying. The rule required the witness to have been "kept back" or "detained" by "means or procurement" of the defendant. Although there are definitions of "procure" and "procurement" that would merely require that a defendant have caused the witness's absence, other definitions would limit the causality to one that was *designed* to bring about

the result "procured." See 2 N. Webster, An American Dictionary of the English Language (1828) (defining "procure" as "to *contrive* and effect" (emphasis added)); *ibid.* (defining "procure" as "to get; to gain; to obtain; as by request, loan, effort, labor or purchase"); 12 Oxford English Dictionary 559 (2d ed. 1989) (def. I(3)) (defining "procure" as "[t]o contrive or devise with care (an action or proceeding); to endeavour to cause or bring about (mostly something evil) *to* or *for* a person"). Similarly, while the term "means" could sweep in all cases in which a defendant caused a witness to fail to appear, it can also connote that a defendant forfeits confrontation rights when he uses an intermediary for the purpose of making a witness absent. See 9 *id.*, at 516 ("[A] person who intercedes for another or uses influence in order to bring about a desired result"); N. Webster, An American Dictionary of the English Language 822 (1869) ("That through which, or by the help of which, an end is attained").

Cases and treatises of the time indicate that a purpose-based definition of these terms governed.

The state courts in this case did not consider the intent of the defendant because they found that irrelevant to application of the forfeiture doctrine. This view of the law was error, but the court is free to consider evidence of the defendant's intent on remand.

§ 11.07   PRONG #2 OF CONFRONTATION CLAUSE ANALYSIS: FACE-TO-FACE CONFRONTATION FOR SEXUAL ASSAULT OR CHILD ABUSE WITNESSES

Maryland v. Craig illustrates the child abuse and sexual assault strand of confrontation analysis.

Maryland v. Craig
497 U.S. 836 (1990)

Justice O'Connor delivered the opinion of the Court.

This case requires us to decide whether the Confrontation Clause of the Sixth Amendment categorically prohibits a child witness in a child abuse case from testifying against a defendant at trial, outside the defendant's physical presence, by one-way closed circuit television.

The Confrontation Clause of the Sixth Amendment, made applicable to the States through the Fourteenth Amendment, provides: "In all criminal prosecutions, the accused shall enjoy the right . . . to be confronted with the witnesses against him."

We observed in *Coy v. Iowa* that "the Confrontation Clause guarantees the defendant a face-to-face meeting with witnesses appearing before the trier of fact."

We have never held, however, that the Confrontation Clause guarantees criminal defendants the *absolute* right to a face-to-face meeting with witnesses against them at trial. Indeed, in *Coy v. Iowa*, we expressly "le[ft] for another day . . . the question whether any exceptions exist" to the "irreducible literal meaning of the Clause: 'a right to *meet face to face* all those who appear and give evidence *at trial.*'" . . . The procedure challenged in *Coy* involved the placement of a screen that prevented two child witnesses in a child abuse case from seeing the defendant as they testified at trial. . . . In holding that the use of this procedure violated the defendant's right to confront witnesses against him, we suggested that any exception to the right "would surely be allowed only when necessary to further an important public policy" — i.e., only upon a showing of something more than the generalized, "legislatively imposed presumption of trauma" underlying the statute at issue in that case. . . . We concluded that "[s]ince there ha[d] been no individualized findings that these particular witnesses needed special protection, the judgment [in the case before us] could not be sustained by any conceivable exception." . . . Because the trial court in this case made individualized findings that each of the child witnesses needed special protection, this case requires us to decide the question reserved in *Coy.*

The central concern of the Confrontation Clause is to ensure the reliability of the evidence against a criminal defendant by subjecting it to rigorous testing in the context of an adversary proceeding before the trier of fact. The word "confront," after all, also means a clashing of forces or ideas, thus carrying with it the notion of adversariness.

The combined effect of these elements of confrontation — physical presence, oath, cross-examination, and observation of demeanor by the trier of fact — serves the purposes of the Confrontation Clause by ensuring that evidence admitted against an accused is reliable and subject to the rigorous adversarial testing that is the norm of Anglo-American criminal proceedings.

Although face-to-face confrontation forms "the core of the values furthered by the Confrontation Clause," . . . we have nevertheless recognized that it is not the *sine qua non* of the confrontation right.

For this reason, we have never insisted on an actual face-to-face encounter at trial in *every* instance in which testimony is admitted against a defendant. Instead, we have repeatedly held that the Clause permits, where necessary, the admission of certain hearsay statements against a defendant despite the defendant's inability to confront the declarant at trial.

In sum, our precedents establish that "the Confrontation Clause reflects a *preference* for face-to-face confrontation at trial," a preference that "must occasionally give way to considerations of public policy and the necessities of the case." Thus, though we reaffirm the importance of face-to-face confrontation with witnesses appearing at trial, we cannot say that such confrontation is an indispensable element of the Sixth Amendment's guarantee of the right to confront one's accusers.

Maryland's statutory procedure, when invoked, prevents a child witness from seeing the defendant as he or she testifies against the defendant at trial. We find it significant, however, that Maryland's procedure preserves all of the other elements of the confrontation right: The child witness must be competent to testify and must testify under oath; the defendant retains full opportunity for contemporaneous cross-examination; and the judge, jury, and defendant are able to view (albeit by video monitor) the demeanor (and body) of the witness as he or she testifies. Although we are mindful of the many subtle effects face-to-face confrontation may have on an adversary criminal proceeding, the presence of these other elements of confrontation — oath, cross-examination, and observation of the witness' demeanor — adequately ensures that the testimony is both reliable and subject to rigorous adversarial testing in a manner functionally equivalent to that accorded life, in-person testimony. . . . We are therefore confident that use of the one-way closed circuit television procedure, where necessary to further an important state interest, does not impinge upon the truth-seeking or symbolic purposes of the Confrontation Clause.

We have of course recognized that a State's interest in "the protection of minor victims of sex crimes from further trauma and embarrassment" is a "compelling" one. . . . "[W]e have sustained legislation aimed at protecting the physical and emotional well-being of youth even when the laws have operated in the sensitive area of constitutionally protected rights." *Ferber, supra,* at 757.

We likewise conclude today that a State's interest in the physical and psychological well-being of child abuse victims may be sufficiently important to outweigh, at least in some cases, a defendant's right to face his or her accusers in court. That a significant majority of States has enacted statutes to protect child witnesses from the trauma of giving testimony in child abuse cases attests to the widespread belief in the importance of such a public policy. . . . Thirty-seven States, for example, permit the use of videotaped testimony of sexually abused children; 24 States have authorized the use of one-way closed circuit television testimony in child abuse cases; and 8 States authorize the use of a two-way system in which the child-witness is permitted to see the courtroom and the defendant on a video monitor and in which the jury and judge is permitted to view the child during the testimony.

Accordingly, we hold that, if the State makes an adequate showing of necessity, the state interest in protecting child witnesses from the trauma of testifying in a child abuse case is sufficiently important to justify the use of a special procedure that permits a child witness in such cases to testify at trial against a defendant in the absence of face-to-face confrontation with the defendant.

Problem #11-15: Baby Jessica's Twin Sister

Jessica's twin sister was allegedly sexually abused by her stepfather. In the stepfather's criminal trial on charges of child molestation, can the prosecution offer the sister's videotaped deposition instead of her live testimony? Explain.

§ 11.08 SUMMARY AND REVIEW

1. If hearsay evidence is offered at trial, when is a showing of witness unavailability required to comply with the Confrontation Clause?

2. What does the "testimonial statement" requirement of *Crawford* mean?

3. When is a 911 emergency call recording subject to the Confrontation Clause?

4. How does *Bryant* define "primary purpose of the interrogation?"

5. Are the Supreme Court's decisions in the area of child sexual abuse cases consistent with the words and intent of the Confrontation Clause? Explain.

Chapter 12

PRIVILEGES [FRE 501]

CHAPTER FRAMEWORK: Privileges exclude otherwise relevant evidence from trial because of more important public policies. These policies often revolve around confidential relationships, like attorney-client, psychotherapist-patient, and clergy-penitent. Other policies include the protection of individual freedoms from the government, such as the Fifth Amendment privilege against self-incrimination. Still other policies arise from the need to promote effective law enforcement that results in a privilege for the identity of informants.

Privileges are not absolute and have exceptions. Exceptions include the express waiver by the holder (e.g., the holder intentionally breaches confidentiality by informing a third party), implied waivers due to the conduct of the holder (e.g., the holder raises an insanity defense at trial and thereby waives the psychotherapist-patient privilege), and conflicting policies (e.g., the duty to warn others of impending harm arises if a psychotherapist is informed of such harm in a psychotherapy session).

Under the FRE, the privilege rule, FRE 501, is the only rule that generally directs courts to use the federal common law. All other evidence rules are codified in the FRE. The common law tradition has some advantages, though, fostering flexibility and responsiveness to societal change.

Federal court cases based on the diversity of citizenship sometimes raise special evidentiary issues. Federal court cases based on diversity of citizenship involve the application of some state rules of evidence. These rules are part of the substantive law being applied to a case, not its procedural guidelines. The application of state substantive laws in federal court makes sense when one sees that diversity of citizenship jurisdiction essentially permits state court cases to be tried in federal court so that one of the parties do not have a "home" advantage. One such area of the FRE considered to be substantive is the law of privilege. Consequently, in diversity actions, state privilege law will be applied, not the federal common law.

WHY ARE THE CONCEPTS IN THIS CHAPTER IMPORTANT? Privileges reveal the tension between public policy values and the need to admit helpful relevant evidence at trial to promote accurate fact-finding. Privilege law also illuminates how rules based on public policy can shift with societal changes.

CONNECTIONS: Privileges connect to the quasi-privileges of the 400 Series, including subsequent remedial measures, settlement offers, plea bargaining, liability insurance, and sexual assault cases. The privilege rule also raises questions about the differences between relying on common law rules and statutes, particularly their respective interpretation and mechanisms for change.

CHAPTER OUTLINE:

   I. Privileges

       A. Protect evidence from disclosure

       B. Evidence protected even if relevant

           1. Public policy concerns outweigh need for disclosure

  II. Sources

       A. Common law

           1. E.g., Attorney-client privilege

       B. Statutes

           1. E.g., Physician-patient privilege

       C. Constitution

           1. E.g., Fifth Amendment privilege against self-incrimination

 III. Operation

       A. Motion in limine to exclude

       B. Timely objection at trial

       C. Privilege may be waived if no objection or motion in limine

 IV. Principles Behind Privileges

       A. Recognized relationship

       B. Confidential communication

       C. Holder may assert privilege

       D. If waived, no protection

       E. Exception may operate to remove protection

           1. E.g., Crime-fraud exception

   V. Specific Examples

       A. Husband-wife privileges

           1. Adverse spousal testimony

           2. Confidential communications

       B. Attorney-client privilege

 VI. Other Privileges

       A. Work product

       B. Psychotherapist-patient

       C. Physician-patient

       D. Fifth Amendment privilege against self-incrimination

       E. Governmental privileges

* * * * *

RELEVANT EVIDENCE RULES

Rule 501. Privilege in General

The common law — as interpreted by United States courts in the light of reason and experience — governs a claim of privilege unless any of the following provides otherwise:

- the United States Constitution;

- a federal statute; or

- rules prescribed by the Supreme Court.

But in a civil case, state law governs privilege regarding a claim or defense for which state law supplies the rule of decision.

Rule 502. Attorney-Client Privilege and Work Product; Limitations on Waiver

The following provisions apply, in the circumstances set out, to disclosure of a communication or information covered by the attorney-client privilege or work-product protection.

- **(a)** **Disclosure Made in a Federal Proceeding or to a Federal Office or Agency; Scope of a Waiver.** When the disclosure is made in a federal proceeding or to a federal office or agency and waives the attorney-client privilege or work-product protection, the waiver extends to an undisclosed communication or information in a federal or state proceeding only if:

  - **(1)** the waiver is intentional;

  - **(2)** the disclosed and undisclosed communications or information concern the same subject matter; and

  - **(3)** they ought in fairness to be considered together.

- **(b)** **Inadvertent Disclosure.** When made in a federal proceeding or to a federal office or agency, the disclosure does not operate as a waiver in a federal or state proceeding if:

  - **(1)** the disclosure is inadvertent;

  - **(2)** the holder of the privilege or protection took reasonable steps to prevent disclosure; and

  - **(3)** the holder promptly took reasonable steps to rectify the error, including (if applicable) following Federal Rule of Civil Procedure 26(b)(5)(B).

- **(c)** **Disclosure Made in a State Proceeding.** When the disclosure is made in a state proceeding and is not the subject of a state-court order concerning waiver, the disclosure does not operate as a waiver in a federal proceeding if the disclosure:

  - **(1)** would not be a waiver under this rule if it had been made in a federal proceeding; or

  - **(2)** is not a waiver under the law of the state where the disclosure occurred.

(d) **Controlling Effect of a Court Order.** A federal court may order that the privilege or protection is not waived by disclosure connected with the litigation pending before the court — in which event the disclosure is also not a waiver in any other federal or state proceeding.

(e) **Controlling Effect of a Party Agreement.** An agreement on the effect of disclosure in a federal proceeding is binding only on the parties to the agreement, unless it is incorporated into a court order.

(f) **Controlling Effect of this Rule.** Notwithstanding Rules 101 and 1101, this rule applies to state proceedings and to federal court-annexed and federal court-mandated arbitration proceedings, in the circumstances set out in the rule. And notwithstanding Rule 501, this rule applies even if state law provides the rule of decision.

(g) **Definitions.** In this rule:

  (1) "attorney-client privilege" means the protection that applicable law provides for confidential attorney-client communications; and

  (2) "work-product protection" means the protection that applicable law provides for tangible material (or its intangible equivalent) prepared in anticipation of litigation or for trial.

§ 12.01 RELEVANT FRE: ENACTED AND PROPOSED (BUT REJECTED) RULES

ENACTED FRE

In 1972, the Supreme Court proposed thirteen specific FRE concerning various privileges. However, they were rejected by Congress, which adopted only FRE 501 which was amended in 2011. The Senate Committee on the Judiciary explained that "a federally developed common law based on modern reason and experience shall apply except where the State nature of the issues renders deference to State privilege law the wiser course, as in the usual diversity case." FRE 501, Report of Senate Committee on the Judiciary.

In 2008, Congress enacted FRE 502 to "resolve[] some longstanding disputes in the courts about the effect of certain disclosures of communications or information protected by the attorney-client privilege or as work product." FRE 502 also addressed concerns about litigation costs "necessary to protect against [the] waiver of [the] attorney-client privilege or [the] work product [doctrine]." The fear is that "any disclosure (however innocent or minimal) will operate as a subject matter waiver of all protected . . . information." FRE 502, Advisory Committee.

Rule 501. General Rule.
*** [*See* **text of FRE 501 following the outline at the beginning of this chapter**]

Rule 502. Attorney-Client Privilege and Work Product; Limitations on Waiver.
*** [*See* **text of FRE 502 following the outline at beginning of this chapter**]

Rule 1101. Applicability of Rules.

> **(c) Rule of Privilege.** The rules on privilege apply to all stages of a case or proceeding.

PROPOSED (BUT REJECTED) FRE

Proposed Rule 502. Required Reports Privileged By Statute. [Not Enacted]

A person, corporation, association, or other organization or entity, either public or private, making a return or report required by law to be made has a privilege to refuse to disclose and to prevent any other person from disclosing the return or report, if the law requiring it to be made so provides. A public officer or agency to whom a return or report is required by law to be made has a privilege to refuse to disclose the return or report if the law requiring it to be made so provides. No privilege exists under this rule in actions involving perjury, false statements, fraud in the return or report, or other failure to comply with the law in question.

Proposed Rule 503. Lawyer-Client Privilege. [Not Enacted]

(a) Definitions. As used in this rule:

> **(1)** A "client" is a person, public officer, or corporation, association, or other organization or entity, either public or private, who is rendered professional legal services by a lawyer, or who consults a lawyer with a view to obtaining professional legal services from him.

> **(2)** A "lawyer" is a person authorized, or reasonably believed by the client to be authorized, to practice law in any state or nation.

> **(3)** A "representative of the lawyer" is one employed to assist the lawyer in the rendition of professional legal services.

> **(4)** A communication is "confidential" if not intended to be disclosed to third persons other than those to whom disclosure is in furtherance of the rendition of professional legal services to the client or those reasonably necessary for the transmission of the communication.

(b) General rule of privilege. A client has a privilege to refuse to disclose and to prevent any other person from disclosing confidential communications made for the purpose of facilitating the rendition of professional legal services to the client, (1) between himself or his representative and his lawyer or his lawyer's representative, or (2) between his lawyer and the lawyer's representative, or (3) by him or his lawyer to a lawyer representing another in a matter of common interest, or (4) between representatives of the client or between the client and a representative of the client, or (5) between lawyers representing the client.

(c) Who may claim the privilege. The privilege may be claimed by the client, his guardian or conservator, the personal representative of a deceased client, or the successor, trustee, or similar representative of a corporation, association, or other organization, whether or not in existence. The person who was the lawyer at the time of the communication may claim the privilege but only on behalf of the client . . .

(d) Exceptions. There is no privilege under this rule:

(1) Furtherance of crime or fraud. If the services of the lawyer were sought or obtained to enable or aid anyone to commit or plan to commit what the client knew or reasonably should have known to be a crime or fraud; or

(2) Claimants through same deceased client. As to a communication relevant to an issue between parties who claim through the same deceased client, regardless of whether the claims are by testate or intestate succession or by inter vivos transaction; or

(3) Breach of duty by lawyer or client. As to a communication relevant to an issue of breach of duty by the lawyer to his client or by the client to his lawyer; or

(4) Document attested by lawyer. As to a communication relevant to an issue concerning an attested document to which the lawyer is an attesting witness; or

(5) Joint clients. As to a communication relevant to a matter of common interest between two or more clients if the communication was made by any of them to a lawyer retained or consulted in common, when offered in an action between any of the clients.

Proposed Rule 504. Psychotherapist-Patient Privilege. [Not Enacted]

(a) Definitions.

(1) A "patient" is a person who consults or is examined or interviewed by a psychotherapist.

(2) A "psychotherapist" is (A) a person authorized to practice medicine in any state or nation, or reasonably believed by the patient so to be, while engaged in the diagnosis or treatment of a mental or emotional condition, including drug addiction, or (B) a person licensed or certified as a psychologist under the laws of any state or nation, while similarly engaged.

(3) A communication is "confidential" if not intended to be disclosed to third persons other than those present to further the interest of the patient in the consultation, examination, or interview, or persons reasonably necessary for the transmission of the communication, or persons who are participating in the diagnosis and treatment under the direction of the psychotherapist, including members of the patient's family.

(b) General rule of privilege. A patient has a privilege to refuse to disclose and to prevent any other person from disclosing confidential communications, made for the purposes of diagnosis or treatment of his mental or emotional condition, including drug addiction, among himself, his psychotherapist, or persons who are participating in the diagnosis or treatment under the direction of the psychotherapist, including members of the patient's family.

(c) Who may claim the privilege. The privilege may be claimed by the patient, by his guardian or conservator, or by the personal representative of a deceased patient. . . .

(d) Exceptions.

(1) Proceedings for hospitalization. There is no privilege under this rule for communications relevant to an issue in proceedings to hospitalize the patient for mental illness, if the psychotherapist in the course of diagnosis or treatment has determined that the patient is in need of hospitalization.

(2) Examination by order of judge. If the judge orders an examination of the mental or emotional condition of the patient, communications made in the course thereof are not privileged . . . .

(3) Condition an element of claim or defense. There is no privilege under this rule as to communications relevant to an issue of the mental or emotional condition of the patient in any proceeding in which he relies upon the condition as an element of his claim or defense, or, after the patient's death, in any proceeding in which any party relies upon the condition as an element of his claim or defense.

Proposed Rule 505. Husband-Wife. [Not Enacted]

(a) General rule of privilege. An accused in a criminal proceeding has a privilege to prevent his spouse from testifying against him.

(b) Who may claim the privilege. The privilege may be claimed by the accused or by the spouse on his behalf. The authority of the spouse to do so is presumed in the absence of evidence to the contrary.

(c) Exceptions. There is no privilege under this rule (1) in proceedings in which one spouse is charged with a crime against the person or property of the other or of a child of either, or with a crime against the person or property of a third person committed in the course of committing a crime against the other, or (2) as to matters occurring prior to the marriage, or (3) in proceedings in which a spouse is charged with importing an alien for prostitution or other immoral purposes . . . .

Proposed Rule 506. Communications to Clergymen. [Not Enacted]

(a) **Definitions.** As used in this rule:

(1) A "clergyman" is a minister, priest, rabbi, or other similar function-ary of a religious organization, or an individual reasonably believed so to be by the person consulting him.

(2) A communication is "confidential" if made privately and not intended for further disclosure except to other persons present in furtherance of the purpose of the communication.

(b) **General rule of privilege.** A person has a privilege to refuse to disclose and to prevent another from disclosing a confidential communication by the person to a clergyman in his professional character as spiritual advisor.

(c) **Who may claim the privilege.** The privilege may be claimed by the person, by his guardian or conservator, or by his personal representative if he is deceased. The clergyman may claim the privilege on behalf of the person
. . . .

Proposed Rule 507. Political Vote. [Not Enacted]

Every person has a privilege to refuse to disclose the tenor of his vote at a political election conducted by secret ballot unless the vote was cast illegally.

Proposed Rule 508. Trade Secrets. [Not Enacted]

A person has a privilege, which may be claimed by him or his agent or employee, to refuse to disclose and to prevent other persons from disclosing a trade secret owned by him, if the allowance of the privilege will not tend to conceal fraud or otherwise work injustice. When disclosure is directed, the judge shall take such protective measure as the interests of the holder of the privilege and of the parties and the furtherance of justice **may require.**

Proposed Rule 509. Secrets of State and Other Official Information. [Not En-acted]

(a) **Definitions**

(1) **Secret of state.** A "secret of state" is a governmental secret relating to the national defense or the international relations of the United States.

(2) **Official information.** "Official information" is information within the custody or control of a department or agency of the government the disclosure of which is shown to be contrary to the public interest . . .

(b) **General rule of privilege.** The government has a privilege to refuse to give evidence and to prevent any person from giving evidence upon a showing of reasonable likelihood of danger that the evidence will disclose a secret of state or official information, as defined in this rule.

Proposed Rule 510. Identity of Informer. [Not enacted]

(a) **Rule of privilege.** The government or a state or subdivision thereof has a privilege to refuse to disclose the identity of a person who has furnished information relating to or assisting in an investigation of a possible violation of law to a law enforcement officer or member of a legislative committee or its staff conducting an investigation.

(b) **Who may claim.** The privilege may be claimed by an appropriate representative of the government, regardless of whether the information was furnished to an officer of the government . . . except that in a criminal case the privilege shall not be allowed if the government objects.

(c) **Exceptions.**

(1) **Voluntary disclosure; informer a witness.** No privilege exists under this rule if the identity of the informer or his interest in the subject matter of his communication has been disclosed to those who would have cause to resent the communication . . . or if the informer appears as a witness for the government.

(2) **Testimony on merits.** If it appears from the evidence in the case or from other showing by a party that an informer may be able to give testimony necessary to a fair determination of the issue of guilt or innocence in a criminal case or of a material issue on the merits in a civil case . . . the judge shall give the government an opportunity to show in camera facts relevant to determining whether the informer can, in fact, supply that testimony . . .

(3) **Legality of obtaining evidence.** If information from an informer is relied upon to establish the legality of the means by which evidence was obtained and the judge is not satisfied that the information was received from an informer reasonably believed to be reliable or credible, he may require the identity of the informer to be disclosed . . .

Proposed Rule 511. Waiver of Privilege by Voluntary Disclosure. [Not Enacted]

A person upon whom these rules confer a privilege against disclosure of the confidential matter or communication waives the privilege if he or his predecessor while holder of the privilege voluntarily discloses or consents to disclosure of any significant part of the matter or communication. This rule does not apply if the disclosure is itself a privileged communication.

§ 12.02   INTRODUCTION TO PRIVILEGES

Privileges are founded on a "public good transcending the normally predominant principle of utilizing all rational means for ascertaining [the] truth." *Elkins v. United States*, 364 U.S. 206 (1960) (Frankfurter, J., dissenting).

[A] The Definition of Privileged Evidence

A privilege permits the non-disclosure of information. It can be framed as both a right and a power — a right to refuse the dissemination of information and the power to control that information, even after one's death. In effect, a privilege wraps potential evidence in a "cone of silence," much like the shield used to ensure private communications in a popular television show of the 1970s, *Get Smart*.

Privileges may operate both inside and outside of the courtroom. A privilege may be invoked in response to pretrial discovery requests, coerced interrogation, or an attempt to compel testimony. Thus, a deponent in a pretrial deposition may assert one privilege, a person being interrogated by the police may claim another privilege, and a person's estate may advance still another privilege on the decedent's behalf.

Significantly, a privilege operates regardless of the relevance or the importance of the evidence. Even if the evidence is crucial to the outcome of a case or is as important to an entire community as the location of a murder victim's body, the privilege rules maintain the "cone of silence." This limitation on the search for truth is deemed warranted because of public policy considerations, which are believed to outweigh the need for the evidence at trial. In effect, privileges advance certain values thought to outweigh the value of a fair and accurate trial process. These values, such as the ability to speak in confidence to an attorney, therapist, spouse, or priest, are essential to core relationships that should not be compromised.

As illustrated by the rejection of specific codified privileges by the drafters of the FRE, the decision as to what values to recognize through the law of privileges is a difficult one. Why, for example, should a patient's discussions with a psychotherapist be protected, but not an alleged sexual assault victim's conversation with a licensed sexual assault counselor? Why should the spousal relationship be protected by two privileges, the confidential communications and adverse testimony privileges, when there is absolutely no protection for conversations between parent and child? Much of the demarcation between what is privileged and what is not owes its existence to the historical development of the law. The fact that some privileges, such as attorney-client and husband-wife, are historically embedded in the common law has not stopped the debate. Some observers have argued that the relationship between parent and child, for example, is as central and needs as much fostering as spousal and attorney-client relationships.

The exclusion of useful evidence based on privilege is unusual but not unique. The law of privilege parallels the rules relating to several other evidentiary exclusions, including "relevant but inadmissible" evidence such as subsequent remedial measures, offers to compromise (and completed compromises), offers to pay medical expenses, and plea negotiations. *See* FRE 407–410. Those exclusions are sometimes labeled "quasi-privileges," and also are based — at least in part — on public policy considerations designed to encourage certain conduct by the parties.

[B] Federal and State Privileges

Privileges operate in both federal and state courts. The type of evidence that is considered privileged may vary from state to state, from federal to state court, and within the same court over time. Whether a privilege is located in federal or state court, it generally operates in the same way — to exclude evidence.

Significantly, state privilege rules sometimes operate in federal court proceedings, effectively replacing the federal common law. Under FRE 501, state privileges apply when state law provides the rule of decision in a civil action or proceeding, which most often occurs in cases in which federal jurisdiction is based on the diversity of citizenship. *See Erie R. Co. v. Tompkins*, 304 U.S. 64 (1938).

[C] Sources of Privilege

Privileges are created by courts through the common law, by legislatures through statutory enactments, and by the Constitution. All three sources of privilege may be invoked at a single trial or hearing. An example of a privilege firmly entrenched in the common law is the attorney-client privilege, which protects confidential communications between a lawyer and her client. An example of a privilege essentially constructed by statute is the physician-patient privilege. A prime example of a constitutional privilege is the Fifth Amendment privilege against self-incrimination.

While privileges used to be created primarily through the common law, the law of privilege in most states is currently based on statute. The codifications of privileges often reflect the established common law, such as the attorney-client privilege. Sometimes, states have expanded the number of privileges through statutory enactments, adding such privileges as an accident report privilege, an accountant-client privilege, a sexual assault counselor-victim privilege, and a domestic violence counselor-victim privilege. Some of these privileges are designed to encourage the flow of information for public policy reasons. One apt illustration is the accident report privilege, which requires a person who has been in an automobile accident to make a statement to a police officer writing a report about the accident, while "immunizing" that statement from disclosure.

The third source of privilege, the United States Constitution, contains some important express and implied privileges. The Fifth Amendment, as noted above, contains the privilege against self-incrimination. This privilege, often described as "taking the Fifth," is an important protection against coerced testimony. *See, e.g., United States v. Hubbell*, 167 F.3d 552 (D.C. Cir. 1999). Another important constitutional privilege is executive privilege, the implied privilege derived from the principle of the separation of powers. This privilege protects the interests of the United States government by exempting some presidential communications from disclosure in a trial or hearing. *See United States v. Nixon*, 418 U.S. 683 (1974) (holding there was a constitutional basis for the executive privilege but that it was only a qualified privilege, depending on the subject matter, and approving an *in camera* balancing of the need for the evidence in a criminal case and the governmental interest in confidentiality).

Illustration: Watergate

In the early 1970s, the Committee to Reelect the President (C.R.E.E.P.) engaged in various surveillance and spying activities against political opponents. This group, whose mission was to reelect President Richard M. Nixon, burglarized the office of Daniel Ellsberg's psychiatrist, hoping to find incriminating information. (Ellsberg had leaked "The Pentagon Papers," government documents concerning the Vietnam War, to the *New York Times*.) The burglary, at an apartment complex called The Watergate, led to news reports about a cover-up of the relationship between the burglars and C.R.E.E.P. The authors of most of the news reports were two reporters for the *Washington Post*, Robert Woodward and Carl Bernstein. The reporters refused to disclose their sources, particularly the main one, whom they called "Deep Throat." What is the basis for their refusal?

Answer: The basis for refusing to disclose sources, even in the face of a subpoena, is often called "the newsperson's privilege" or "journalist's privilege," and is traced to the First Amendment of the Constitution. The freedom of the press has been interpreted to include a qualified privilege for journalists that allows them to refuse to disclose their sources. The privilege is qualified, however, and not absolute. A judge might find the privilege outweighed by a particular interest in national security. Over the years, many reporters have voiced a preference for jail to disclosure, warning that forced disclosure would negatively impact the freedom of sources to provide information.

An additional illustration of the scope of the constitutionally-based executive privilege resulted from the investigation of President William Jefferson Clinton and others in his administration by special prosecutor Kenneth Starr. In one case, a question arose as to whether Secret Service agents assigned to guard the president in the White House could invoke executive privilege. The Court of Appeals held that there was no such ancillary privilege and that the agents would have to disclose what they saw and heard. Thus, Secret Service agents could be called to testify before a grand jury about the president. *See In re Sealed Case*, 148 F.3d 1073 (D.C. Cir. 1998), *cert. denied*, 525 U.S. 990 (1998).

[D] The Operation of Privileges

Privileges do not operate automatically. A privilege will operate only upon a timely refusal to disclose information or to testify, usually occurring through an objection at trial or a motion in limine (in advance). Without such action by counsel, an otherwise valid privilege may be waived. Waiver is a complicated concept. It can occur by implication as well as by express statement. An implied waiver might occur under widely disparate circumstances, such as if a party reveals confidential communications to a third party, raises a claim at trial that creates a need for the privileged information, (e.g., the insanity defense), or, at least under the common law, has privileged information intercepted by an eavesdropper.

Even if counsel objects to disclosure, the objection must be timely. Once a timely objection is made, the court usually considers the merits of the claim *in camera*, outside the hearing of the jury. The need for secrecy is clear. Once jurors have heard evidence, it is extremely difficult for them to "unhear" it. It is up to the court to determine whether the testimony is or is not privileged under the rules.

Not all privileges exclude evidence in the same way. Some privileges extend only to confidential communications, such as the clergy-penitent privilege. For privileges based on communications, the witness must still testify and provide all relevant, non-privileged information. The witness may refuse to answer all questions whose answer comes within the domain of the privilege.

In contrast to the communication-based privileges, the adverse testimonial privilege permits a spouse who is a witness to completely refuse to testify against the other. It does not matter whether the testimony sought from the witness-spouse is privileged or not. As a matter of public policy, the sanctity of the marital relationship warrants that a spouse not be placed in the unseemly position of being coerced to testify against the other and undermine the relationship.

Privilege Assertion Problems

Problem #12-1: Privilege Logs

In keeping with jurisdiction practice, the court asked the parties to file privilege logs by a certain time regarding allegedly privileged information. The defense submitted some privilege claims, but forgot to include Dr. Permbutton, who had testified in a previous trial on similar, but not identical, issues. At trial, the opposing counsel called Dr. Permbutton to testify. The defense objected, claiming privilege. Who wins? *See GFI, Inc., v. Franklin Corp.*, 265 F.3d 1268 (Fed. Cir. 2001).

Practical Tip:

Privilege Logs. Create a privilege log — a list (or electronic folder) of important communications that you feel are privileged from disclosure — at the start of representation. Courts generally require a pre-trial log of documents that are claimed to be privileged. *See 8 Fed. Prac. & Proc. Civ.* § 2016.1 (3d ed.) *Privileged Matter — Assertion of Privilege.*

Problem #12-2: Cinderella Boat Company

The Cinderella Boat Company, which specializes in boat rentals in Fort Myers, Florida, regularly conducts internal investigations and makes confidential incident reports relating to all problems occurring with one of its boats. On January 4th, a rental boat caught fire while in an inland canal, injuring the captain and two passengers. After its investigation, the Company created a confidential file explaining what went wrong and how it was going to prevent similar occurrences in the future. In subsequent litigation brought by the injured passengers in federal court against the Cinderella Company, the plaintiffs seek the disclosure of the file through discovery. Is disclosure permissible?

[E] Confidential Communication Privileges

Generally confidential communication privileges, such as the attorney-client and the clergy-penitent, are based on the following principles:

- There is generally a special legally recognized *relationship* between the holder of the privilege and the person being consulted (e.g., the husband-wife, the attorney-client, and the priest-penitent relationships).

- There is a *communication* — written, oral, or nonverbal — between the holder and the person consulted.

- The communication is confidential.

- The *holder* of the privilege, generally the client, patient, or supplicant, can assert it, or the person consulted may assert it on the holder's behalf.

- The privilege does not operate if it has been expressly or impliedly *waived*.

- An *exception* to the privilege, such as using the privilege to commit a future crime, removes its protective cloak.

As noted above, not every important relationship is protected under the confidential communications privileges. While some relationships, such as marriage, are given extensive protection by allowing the spouses to refuse to testify at all, even to things other than confidential communications, other relationships, such as that of parent and child, receive no protection. *See In re Grand Jury*, 103 F.3d 1140 (3d Cir. 1997). "Although legal academicians appear to favor adoption of a parent-child testimonial privilege, no federal Court of Appeals and no state Supreme Court has recognized such a privilege." *Id.* at 1145 n.6.

[F] Public Policy-Based Privileges Generally

Many states create privileges based on public policy. These states want to encourage certain types of behavior and conclude that, without the privilege, the desired behavior will not be advanced. One example of a privilege generated by public policy is the privilege for domestic violence victims and counselors, which applies to confidential communications between the two for the purpose of counseling. Several states have made such communications privileged to promote the disclosure and free flow of information. Another example of a public-policy privilege is the journalist privilege. *See Mary-Rose Papandrea, Citizen Journalism and the Reporter's Privilege*, 91 Minn. L. Rev. 515, 535 (2007) (reporting that 32 states and the District of Columbia statutorily recognize some sort of reporter's privilege to increase the flow of information to benefit society); *McKevitt v. Pallasch*, 339 F.3d 530 (7th Cir. 2003) (finding a large number of federal courts surprisingly recognize a reporter's privilege even though the Supreme Court declined to adopt such a privilege rooted in the First Amendment in *Branzburg v. Hayes*, 408 U.S. 665 (1972)).

§ 12.03   THE FEDERAL RULES OF EVIDENCE APPROACH TO PRIVILEGE

Privileges in federal court are generally derived from the federal common law, with one glaring exception. When the state law supplies the rule of decision, such as in cases based on the diversity of citizenship, the pertinent state privilege law applies. *See Erie R. Co. v. Tompkins*, 304 U.S. 64 (1938). In this regard, privilege rules are considered "substantive" law and not simply "procedural rules relating to trial governance." The Senate Committee charged with reviewing the proposed rules concluded that federal "common law based on modern reason and experience shall apply, except where the State nature of the issues renders deference to State privilege law the wiser course, as in the usual diversity case." (FRE 501, Report of Senate Committee on the Judiciary.)

It is at first glance perplexing why Congress decided to retain the traditional but evolving common law instead of enacting specific privilege rules, especially in light of the fairly specific codification in the other areas of the FRE. Privileges, in particular, provided Congress with a controversial and difficult subject, one firmly rooted in public policy. If any evidence area generated sparks of excitement in the general public as well as with trial lawyers and legal scholars, this was it. The controversial nature of the subject and thorniness of negotiating a consensus on what to include in the realm of exclusions provide some insight into why Congress might have decided to leave this area virtually untouched.

The drafters of the FRE had suggested adopting thirteen distinct privilege rules (*see* § 12.01). The proposed rules included a wide variety of privileges, many of which had been well established in federal and state common law. Instead of adopting any or all of these specific privileges, the authors of the FRE chose to adopt a single governing rule on privilege. FRE 501 perpetuates the use of the privileges previously recognized in the federal common law. Interestingly, the rejected privileges have been treated differently by the courts. In some cases, the courts have turned to the proposed rules for assistance in determining the parameters of federal common law privilege. *E.g., United States v. McPartlin*, 595 F.2d 1321 (7th Cir. 1979). In other cases, the courts have not given the proposals any weight at all. *E.g., United States v. Bizzard*, 674 F.2d 1382 (11th Cir. 1982).

It has been widely debated as to whether this approach to privileges was appropriate. On the one hand, a single general rule casting a backward glance to established precedent incorporates the wisdom of the federal judiciary, which is already responsible for applying the doctrine of privilege, while also permitting flexibility and responsiveness to changing times. On the other hand, the domain of privilege is the one area where regulators failed to codify bright-line rules and where historical precedent trumps modern ideas about what should be privileged, such as by denying protection to statements by victims of sexual abuse or domestic violence.

§ 12.04   SOME SPECIFIC PRIVILEGES

[A]   The Husband-Wife Privileges: Adverse Spousal Testimony and Confidential Communications

Two well-recognized privileges in both federal and state law concern the husband and wife. Each privilege has markedly different characteristics and must be distinguished from the other one. The important distinctions include what triggers the privileges, their scope of application, the types of cases in which they apply, and who holds the privilege.

[1]   The Adverse Spousal Testimony Privilege

The adverse spousal testimony privilege is triggered at the time a spouse is called to testify against his or her spouse. As the word "spouse" suggests, there must be a valid marriage at the time of trial. This marriage requirement is met even if the spouses were separated at the time of trial, depending on the length and nature of the separation. The privilege applies to common law marriages where recognized by states and does not apply to sham marriages.

If the privilege is triggered, the husband and wife are afforded considerable protection. The adverse spousal testimony privilege allows the accused's spouse to choose not to take the witness stand and testify.

While the scope of the adverse spousal privilege is broad, covering both confidential and non-confidential communications and testimony of any sort, the privilege is only available in criminal cases. A spouse may assert the privilege at any stage of a criminal proceeding, including a grand jury investigation.

Also, the privilege is only held by the testifying spouse, and not the defendant spouse. This means that if the witness spouse wishes to testify, the defendant spouse cannot prevent it.

The privilege was not always held by the testifying spouse. Under earlier federal common law, it was the defendant spouse who held the key to opposing spousal testimony. This earlier rule was abandoned in *Trammel v. United States*, 445 U.S. 40(1980), in which the Supreme Court held that the prevailing rule, enunciated in *Hawkins v. United States*, 358 U.S. 74 (1958), should be changed. *Hawkins* had perpetuated the common law rule, which barred testimony by one spouse against the other unless both consented. The court in *Trammel* found that the justification for the *Hawkins* rule no longer existed, and overruled it. The Court stated:

> Our consideration of the foundations for the privilege and its history satisfy us that "reason and experience" no longer justify so sweeping a rule as that found acceptable by the Court in *Hawkins*. Accordingly, we conclude that the existing rule should be modified so that the witness spouse alone has a privilege to refuse to testify adversely; the witness may be neither compelled to testify nor foreclosed from testifying. This modification — vesting the privilege in the witness spouse — furthers the important public interest in marital harmony without unduly burdening legitimate law enforcement needs.

What the justices appear to be saying here is that if a spouse wishes to testify against his or her spouse, the public policy of saving the marriage is not worth much, if anything at all. (One can only imagine the conversation at the breakfast table the day after one spouse voluntarily testifies against the other spouse.)

[2]　The Confidential Communications Privilege

The confidential communications privilege also is triggered by a valid marriage, but the marriage need only have existed at the time of the communication. Thus, a communication that occurred years prior to a trial still might be privileged, so long as it was made during the marriage, even if the husband and wife had long since been divorced by the time of trial.

The scope of the confidential communications privilege is narrower than that of the adverse spousal testimony privilege. The confidential communications privilege merely prohibits the disclosure by the spouse-witness of any confidential communications with the other spouse occurring during the marriage. This means that a spouse still can be called to the witness stand and asked to testify about observations concerning the other spouse or non-confidential communications with the spouse.

The confidential communications privilege may apply in both criminal and civil cases, and either spouse may assert the privilege. Thus, a spouse-defendant can prevent an adverse spouse-witness from testifying about confidential communications, subject to several important exceptions. These exceptions include proceedings in which one spouse has been charged with crimes against the other spouse or against one of the spouse's children.

Husband-Wife Privilege Problems

Problem #12-3: Bonnie and Clyde Scenarios

1. Bonnie and Clyde lived together for two years. During that time, Clyde told Bonnie that he robbed banks for a living. The two subsequently were married. Clyde was then charged with several bank robberies. Is Clyde's statement to Bonnie privileged?

2. The prosecution calls Bonnie to testify that Clyde was wearing a red sweater and matching suede shoes on the day of one of the robberies.

a. Can Clyde prevent Bonnie from testifying to those facts if the husband-wife confidential communications privilege applies?

b. Can Clyde prevent Bonnie from testifying to those facts if the adverse spousal testimony privilege applies?

3. Clyde tells his secretary to take down the following letter, to be delivered to Bonnie: "Bonnie, meet me at the southeast corner of the bank right before closing time. Bring all of the 'stuff' for the bank; you know what I mean. Love and Kisses, Clyde." The government wishes to introduce this letter at the bank robbery trial in which Clyde is the defendant. Is this letter admissible? Explain.

4. Bonnie dies of a chronic illness during the trial. Does Bonnie's death terminate the husband-wife confidential communications privilege?

5. Based on bruises found on Bonnie, Clyde also is charged with aggravated battery, a felony. At trial, Bonnie is called to testify by the prosecution. Can Clyde assert one of the marital privileges? Can Bonnie claim privilege and refuse to testify?

6. Suppose that after Clyde's death, Clyde's estate is sued by a third party claiming that Clyde had robbed the third party, buried the jewelry that he had taken, and informed Bonnie of the location of the jewelry before he had died. If Bonnie was indeed told by Clyde that he had stolen the jewelry and had buried it in a certain place, must Bonnie disclose this information at trial?

Problem #12-4: Privilege Exception — the Miscreant Spouse

A husband informed his wife that he had hid a laptop from the police during an investigation of their home. The wife subsequently informed her husband that she had turned over the laptop to the police. The husband stated: "You screwed up everything; I'm going to lose my job and go to jail. I should have shot you." The husband is charged with pornography offenses involving his daughter. At trial, the prosecutor offered these statements, and the husband objected invoking the marital communications privilege. How should the court rule? *See United States v. Breton*, 740 F.3d 1 (1st Cir. 2014).

[B] The Attorney-Client Privilege

[1] Elements of Privilege

The most widely known privilege is the attorney-client privilege. This privilege extends to confidential communications between the attorney and client. To protect the attorney-client relationship, even introductory confidential conversations are protected, as are communications with necessary parties present, such as a paralegal or a client's translator. *See United States v. Ackert*, 169 F.3d 136, 139–40 (2d Cir. 1999) (noting an exception to the waiver of the attorney-client privilege where a third party is required to communicate information between the attorney and client to assist in rendering legal advice).

Practical Tip:

Discuss Privilege with Client. Inform clients at the initial interview about the significance and scope of the attorney-client privilege, including the need to exclude unnecessary third parties from attorney-client communications to protect the privilege.

What is not protected, however, is material evidence. If a client gives the attorney potential evidence to hold or control, that evidence is not imbued with the attorney-client privilege. In *State ex rel. Sowers v. Olwell*, 64 Wash. 2d 828, 394 P.2d 681 (1964), an attorney was served with a subpoena asking him to produce "all knives in [his] possession and under [his] control relating to Henry LeRoy Gray, Gloria Pugh or John W. Warren." The attorney refused to comply, asserting the attorney-client privilege on behalf of his client. The Supreme Court of Washington held that the attorney's refusal was improper, stating:

> Here we must consider the balancing process between the attorney/client privilege and the public interest in criminal investigation. We are in agreement that the attorney/client privilege is applicable to the knife held by appellant, but do not agree that the privilege warrants the attorney, as an officer of the court, from withholding it after being properly requested to produce the same. The attorney should not be a depository for criminal evidence (such as a knife, other weapons, stolen property, etc.), which in itself has little, if any, material value for the purposes of aiding counsel in the preparation of the defense of his client's case.

Background Box: Asserting Privileges:

A good-faith claim of the attorney client privilege constitutes a valid defense to a finding of contempt. *See Waste Management of Washington v. Kattler*, 776 F.3d 336 (5th Cir. 2015) (rejecting a contempt finding against a lawyer who refused to turn over an iPod claiming it was protected by the attorney-client privilege and following *Maness v. Meyers*, 419 U.S. 449 (1975), which recognized that ordering a party to reveal information could cause irreparable injury because an appellate court cannot undo what has been done to the attorney-client privilege and the attorney-work-product doctrine)).

Attorney-Client Privilege Problems

Problem #12-5: Free Toaster Oven

Amy worries that she may have committed a crime, so she seeks legal advice. After going food shopping, she stops and speaks to a person named Mazzen, who is seated in a booth outside of the supermarket. The booth is decorated with a large sign stating, "Lawyer — reasonable fees. First consultation free." Amy discusses her situation with Mazzen, but decides not to hire him.

1. If Amy is later charged with a crime concerning the same situation she discussed with Mazzen, can the prosecutor call Mazzen to testify about what Amy told him? What is the significance of Amy's decision not to hire Mazzen?

2. If it turns out that Mazzen had passed the bar examination, but had never completed his bar application and thus was not a qualified lawyer at the time he offered his advice, can he be now called to testify?

3. If, during the same conversation, Amy sought business advice from Mazzen (who had an M.B.A. as well as a law degree) about a particular real estate investment that was quite successful, would the conversation be privileged?

4. If Amy's brother, Lenny, says to Amy, "Don't worry, I'll pay for your attorney," and as a result, Amy hires Mazzen, is there still an attorney-client relationship between Amy and Mazzen? Or is the relationship between Lenny and Mazzen? *See, e.g., United States v. Edwards*, 39 F. Supp. 2d 716 (M.D. La. 1999).

5. Suppose Amy hires Mazzen and there is immediate friction between them. After just one month of representation, Amy fired Mazzen, but not before providing him with incriminating information that could easily lead to her criminal conviction. Two months later, Amy is charged with a crime, and Mazzen is called to testify by the prosecution. Mazzen would love nothing better than to tell everyone what Amy had told him. Can Mazzen disclose all? Does it matter whether Amy had given Mazzen specific instructions regarding any subsequent disclosure of their conversations?

Problem #12-6: No Name

A defense lawyer, Paula, is subpoenaed by a grand jury investigating a stabbing leading to a person's death.

1. Paula is asked about a knife allegedly given to Paula by her client. If, in fact, her client did give her a knife, can Paula refuse to acknowledge or disclose information about the knife? Does Paula have to turn the knife over to the prosecution?

2. Paula is asked by the grand jury about the name of the person who is paying her attorney's fees and the amount of those fees. Paula refuses to answer, claiming that the answer is privileged information. Is it? *See Baird v. Koerner*, 279 F.2d 623 (9th Cir. 1960).

3. The prosecutor issues a subpoena for Paula's personal notes about the case. Must she disclose them?

4. Assuming that the name of Paula's client is disclosed, can her client be subpoenaed to provide a handwriting sample?

5. Can Paula's client be required to provide a hair sample, to determine if hairs found at the crime scene match those of her client?

6. Paula's client asks Paula how best to lie before the grand jury. Does the attorney-client privilege apply?

Problem #12-7: The Client

While meeting in private with Cassandra, the attorney for his paper company, Ned informs her that he has extorted money from several public officials. He provides Cassandra with specific information about the acts of extortion.

1. Does the attorney-client privilege apply to the conversation between Cassandra and Ned? Explain. What should Cassandra do upon hearing this information? Would it make any difference if the conversation took place in the middle of a crowded "happy hour" party? Explain.

2. Can Cassandra waive the attorney-client privilege without the approval of Ned? Why?

3. If Ned asks Cassandra's help in extricating himself from his "very last" extortion against the new mayor, is the conversation privileged? Why?

4. **Ethics Consideration.** Cassandra is licensed to practice law in New Jersey, where the headquarters of the paper company is located. Ned, the owner of the paper company, is being charged in Delaware. May Cassandra represent Ned in Delaware without violating any rules of professional conduct? *See* Delaware Rules of Prof'l Conduct R. 5.5. MRPC 5.5.

Problem #12-8: Time of Counsel?

During discovery in a torts action, the defendant asked plaintiff about the exact time plaintiff had retained counsel (i.e., "When did you retain counsel?"). Plaintiff objected, claiming the attorney-client privilege.

1. Who wins?

2. During the plaintiff's deposition, the defendant also asked her several questions about her trial consultant, Professor Garp, a non-testifying consulting expert in trial strategy and deposition preparation. The questions included the following. On how many occasions did you meet with Professor Garp? Did Professor Garp provide you with guidance in your conduct as a witness? Did you rehearse any of your prospective testimony in the presence of Professor Garp? In the course of preparing for this deposition . . . did anyone provide you with materials to review? The plaintiff's lawyer objected, citing the work-product doctrine. What result?

Problem #12-9: Threats

In a criminal proceeding, the accused was convicted on all four counts of felony indictment. Later, when the accused met privately with his attorney, he said, "And one other thing, my friend, I invoke my attorney-client privilege to tell you that if these convictions are not reversed and reversed soon, you will not be walking around plying your merry trade." Counsel, shortly thereafter, reveals these statements to the court. Permissible?

Problem #12-10: Send It to the Accountant

In a corporate breach of contract claim, an accountant was asked by the attorney for the defendant company to compute different views of tax consequences of several prior sales. These views were not related to strategy in the breach of contract claim, but could be useful to the company for financial reasons. The plaintiff asks for the resulting documents prepared by the accountant in discovery. Are these documents privileged?

[2] The Attorney-Client Privilege and the Corporate (Entity) Client

At common law, the paradigm for the attorney-client privilege involved a lawyer offering advice to an individual person. Lawyers also advise all kinds of entities, such as corporations, partnerships, and unincorporated associations, and they can assert the attorney-client privilege. As businesses and corporations started to consult regularly with attorneys, the problem of the scope of the attorney-client privilege arose — who in a corporation possessed the privilege? The early law granted a privilege only to the "control group" in a corporation — those persons who had controlling power over the corporation.

The traditional rule proved to be less than satisfactory, however, given modern business practices. Often, many members of a corporation outside of the control group consulted attorneys on legal matters for the company. These consultations were awkward at best, given their potential risk of disclosure. Much of the difficulty was rectified in the case of *Upjohn v. United States*, 449 U.S. 383 (1981). *Upjohn* addressed the issue of the scope of the attorney-client privilege in the corporate setting. The Supreme Court adopted a more flexible test instead of the bright-line control group requirement. The Court stated:

> The narrow scope given the attorney client privilege [in the control group test] not only makes it difficult for corporate attorneys to formulate sound advice when their client is faced with a specific legal problem but also threatens to limit the valuable efforts of corporate counsel to ensure their client's compliance with the law. . . . The very terms of the [control group] test adopted by the court below suggest the unpredictability of its application. The test restricts the availability of the privilege to those officers who play a "substantial role" in deciding and directing a corporation's legal response.

In light of this position, the Supreme Court held that middle-level and lower-level employees also could claim the attorney-client privilege, so long as they were acting in the course of their duties on a subject relevant to the corporation. *See also Harper & Row Publishers, Inc. v. Decker*, 423 F.2d 487, 491–92 (7th Cir. 1970).

Problem #12-11: I.B.S.

The I.B.S. Corporation consults with its attorney, Bingem, Dingem, and Wingem, about pending litigation against the company. A technician employed by I.B.S. is subpoenaed to provide information about his communications with the attorneys for I.B.S. Can the technician assert the attorney-client privilege?

Problem #12-12: L.A. Cooke

A company named L.A. Cooke is charged with fraudulently violating securities laws relating to a stock redemption. Can the shareholders obtain the communications between the corporation's managers and its attorneys relating to the stock repudiation? *See Ward v. Succession of Freeman*, 854 F.2d 780 (5th Cir. 1988).

Problem #12-13 Who's the Client — the CEO or the Entity?

A grand jury issues a subpoena for the Zen Company's documents, including emails, during the past year. Zen's CEO consults with its outside corporate counsel, Attorney Jones, about subpoena compliance. Because of that consultation and unbeknownst to Jones, the CEO determines that the government is interested in several emails and she does not prevent their deletion. The government learns of the CEO's inaction and charges her with obstruction of justice. The grand jury then subpoenas Jones to disclose the contents of his consultation with the CEO concerning the original subpoena for Zen's documents. Zen's CEO objects and claims the attorney-client privilege prevents Jones' disclosure.

1. What result?

2. Assume the government argues that the crime-fraud exception to the privilege applies, warranting disclosure of the contents of the consultation. What kind of evidentiary showing must the government make before the court will review privileged communications to determine whether the exception applies?

3. Assume the Zen company terminates the CEO and decides that the better strategy is to cooperate with the government and waives the attorney-client privilege. The former CEO objects to disclosing the substance of her consultation with Jones. Although Zen retained and paid Jones, the CEO claims the company cannot waive the privilege because Jones represented her individually and not Zen. What result?

Problem #12-14: Internal Investigations by In-house Counsel & Others

The Zippy Company employs Olivia as in-house counsel. She believes some of Zippy's financial resources are being diverted for illegal activity. Olivia recommends to the CEO that Zippy's legal department conduct an internal investigation of possible financial wrongdoing without first conferring with Zippy's outside counsel.

1. Can Olivia claim the attorney-client privilege covers her interviews with Zippy employees about the investigation without first consulting with outside counsel?

2. Olivia directs non-attorneys to help with the internal investigation by interviewing some employees. Can Olivia claim the attorney-client privilege covers these communications with non-attorneys?

3. Does the attorney-client privilege cover employee interviews who were not first informed that the purpose was to assist Zippy in obtaining legal advice?

Practical Tip:

State privilege law applies in a federal case where state law provides the basis for deciding the case. *See DiBella v. Hopkins*, 403 F.3d 102, 120 (2d Cir. 2005).

[3]   Limitations on Waiver of the Attorney-Client and Work Product

FRE 502 has two purposes. First, it resolves judicial "disputes in the courts about the effect of certain disclosures of communications or information protected by the attorney-client privilege or as work product." *See* FRE 502 Advisory Committee Note. Litigators fear that any disclosure of communications or information — no matter how minimal or inadvertent — will constitute a waiver of all protected communications or information concerning the subject matter in the disclosures. The concern about subject matter waiver generates considerable litigation expense as parties review documents to protect against any inadvertent disclosure of privileged matter. The advent of electronically stored information has significantly increased this expense. FRE 502's second purpose is to reduce the increasingly burdensome litigation expense associated with privilege document review by establishing clear rules for avoiding subject matter waiver.

Subsection (a) of FRE 502 governs disclosures in federal proceedings and limits the waiver of the attorney-client and work-product privileges to only the information or communications disclosed if the waiver is unintentional. Intentional waivers in federal proceedings permit the opposing party to obtain additional undisclosed information if the subject matter of the disclosed and undisclosed communications is the same and fairness dictates that they ought to be considered together.

Subsection (b) provides that communications or information that are inadvertently disclosed in a federal proceeding will not operate as a waiver in any federal or state proceeding provided: "the holder [of the privilege or protection] took reasonable steps to prevent disclosure and also promptly took reasonable steps to rectify the error." *See* FRE 502. Advisory Committee Note. "Depending on the circumstances, a party that uses advanced analytical software applications and linguistic tools in screening for privilege and work product may be found to have taken 'reasonable steps' to prevent inadvertent disclosure." *Id.*

FRE 502(c) requires the disclosing party to assert the attorney-client or work-product privileges as soon as possible after learning of the inadvertent disclosure. The party should notify, preferably in writing, the recipient of the assertion. *See* Fed. R. Civ. Proc. 26(b)(5)(B). The disclosing party should also request the return of any inadvertently disclosed information and, possibly seek a protective order to prevent its further use or dissemination. *See Multiquip, Inc. v. Water Management Systems LLC*, EJL-REB, 2009 WL 4261214 at 5* (D. Idaho 2009). W. Grimm, Lisa Yurwit Bergstrom & Matthew P. Kraeuter, *Federal Rule of Evidence 502: Has It Lived Up to Its Potential*, 17 Rich. J. L. & Tech. 8, 45–54 (2011).

The two remaining subsections, 502(d) and (e), facilitate discovery in important ways. FRE 502(d) authorizes federal courts to issue orders precluding a waiver of the attorney-client and work-product privileges in the instant case or any subsequent federal or state proceedings. FRE 502(e) permits litigants to agree to limit the waiver of privileges. These private agreements may be incorporated into a court order.

[C]　Other Privileges

There are several other well-established privileges, including the "work product" privilege, the psychotherapist-patient privilege, and the clergy-penitent privilege. These privileges will be discussed below.

[1]　"Work Product" Privilege

The so-called "work product" privilege is really an appendage of litigation. It prevents the discovery of mental impressions, conclusions, opinions, or legal theories of attorneys (or representatives of those attorneys) involved in, or preparing for, litigation. *See* Fed. R. Civ. P. 26(b)(3); *Hickman v. Taylor*, 329 U.S. 495 (1947). This protection of litigation strategy allows attorneys to try their own cases, and permits some secrecy in how evidence is offered, approached, and evaluated by the parties. Significantly, the work-product privilege applies only to materials that are "otherwise discoverable." Thus, if materials are protected by another privilege, such as the attorney-client privilege, the issue of work-product protection need never arise. *See, e.g., Miller v. Federal Express Corp.*, 186 F.R.D. 376 (W.D. Tenn. 1999).

Privileged Documents — The Work-Product Privilege

Problem #12-15: Of Napkins, Notes, and Work Product

After an automobile accident at 8 p.m. on January 12, 2007, on College Avenue between Paula and Donna, the two drivers exchanged phone numbers and talked. Donna said to Paula, "I don't think we need to make a federal case out of this. I don't remember everything that happened. I never saw you coming! But at least we both seem to be okay. Since your car sustained what looks like a direct hit and has lots of damage and my car has minimal damage, I'll pay you $15,000. That should cover everything. Does that sound fair?" Paula then said to Donna, "Look, I understand and that's fine with me, I think. I am late for an important appointment." Donna said, "Sure thing." The next day, Donna contacted her attorney, Alicia, and told her the whole story. Alicia immediately called a friend, an expert in accident reconstruction, Rolle, and had a meeting during which they discussed who was at fault and even toured the scene and looked at Donna's car. Alicia wrote on a napkin to emphasize for Rolle two things: important facts, and likely arguments at trial. The attorney then took notes about their meeting and asked to be given the digital photos taken by Donna's friend Sue at the scene shortly after the accident.

Donna sent the check within two weeks and did not hear anything about the accident for five months. After five months, she received the check back in the mail uncashed and a letter from Paula's attorney. The letter stated Paula was filing suit and seeking $250,000 for damages to Paula's car, loss of future earnings, and debilitating back pain.

In discovery, Paula requested:

(1) the notes taken by Donna's attorney in her meeting with Rolle the expert;

(2) the napkin on which the attorney wrote down information for Rolle; and

(3) the digital photos taken by Sue at the scene, because the photos might offer helpful information for the defense.

    1. Should these requests be granted?

    2. Assume Rolle testified at trial. The plaintiff wanted to use the substance of the napkin in cross-examination. Permitted?

Problem #12-16: The Union

James was the president of the largest union in New York City. During a difficult period in which the union threatened to strike, James met with several union representatives about their strategy regarding a potential strike. Before a strike could occur, the employer sued the union in federal court, claiming that it had violated several federal labor laws. James met with the union's lawyer, Emily, who wrote down her thoughts about the situation, including the strategies and tactics that were legally available. During pre-trial discovery, the employer sought disclosure of the meeting James had with his representatives and of Emily's notes of her meeting with James.

What must be disclosed, if anything?

[2] Psychotherapist-Patient Privilege

A psychotherapist-patient privilege is recognized under the common law of many states and now under the federal common law. *See Jaffee v. Redmond,* 518 U.S. 1, (1996). In *Jaffee,* a police officer who killed a man while on duty was sued for violating that person's civil rights. The defendant officer received counseling following the incident from a licensed clinical social worker. The plaintiff sought the disclosure of the substance of that counseling, and the therapist was ordered to do so by the judge. The defendant and therapist refused, claiming it was protected by a psychotherapist-patient privilege. The Supreme Court agreed, finding that, given the states' enthusiastic endorsement of the privilege, the federal law should reflect the same. The Court found that the privilege extended not only to psychiatrists and psychologists, but also to licensed clinical social workers who are administering psychotherapy.

Significantly, the privilege only extends to confidential communications during the course of diagnosis or treatment of the patient. Statements made outside of diagnosis or treatment, such as those involving business matters or other unrelated subjects, are not privileged. Further, the privilege, like others, may be expressly or impliedly waived. An implied waiver may occur when litigants place their mental state at issue or sue the professional, necessitating the use of the psychotherapy records. In *Jaffee,* the officer refused to expressly waive the privilege and did not impliedly waive the privilege by asserting an insanity defense.

Illustration: Insanity Defense

Mark David Chapman shot and killed John Lennon, the former Beatle, outside of Lennon's apartment building in New York City in 1980. Chapman pled guilty to the crime, although he could have sought a trial. If Chapman had asked for a trial and raised an insanity defense, his prior visits to a psychotherapist would have been subject to discovery by the prosecution because his assertion of insanity created an implied waiver of his psychotherapist-patient privilege — under either New York or federal law.

Problem # 2-17: Crazy for You

Alex is charged with murder. Alex has been in therapy for nine years to treat his excessive and repetitive outburst of anger against others.

1. If Alex raises an insanity defense at trial, can the prosecution call Alex's therapist, Marcy, to the witness stand to testify about what Alex told her in their therapy sessions? Why?

2. Ethics Consideration. Attorney Jones represents Alex. Alex instructs the therapist to tell Jones what Alex said during his last therapy sessions. While this information was not disclosed to Jones by Alex, and therefore would not be protected by attorney-client privilege, would it nevertheless be protected by the ethical duty of confidentiality? See Maryland Rules of Prof'l Conduct R. 1.6; MRPC 1.6.

Problem #12-18: Bundy

The defendant, Bundy, is charged with a series of rapes. The prosecution attempts to discover what Bundy told his psychiatrists prior to the date charges were filed.

1. Are the conversations between Bundy and his psychiatrists privileged?

2. Would the conversations be privileged if the secretary of one of the psychotherapists was privy to the conversations?

Problem #12-19: Still Crazy, After All These . . .

Paul, the defendant, objects to the admission of statements he made to his physician, Dr. Simon, claiming that he believed Dr. Simon was a psychotherapist. At a sidebar, the plaintiff's attorney makes the following proffer:

PLAINTIFF'S ATTORNEY: Your Honor, the evidence will show Dr. Simon has been a practicing podiatrist for twenty-one years and planned on doing bunion surgery on the defendant. Paul knew Dr. Simon was a podiatrist and not a psychotherapist. Paul's statements to Dr. Simon are not part of the psychotherapist-patient relationship.

DEFENDANT'S ATTORNEY: Your Honor, with all due respect, Dr. Simon discussed James Redfield's book, *The Tenth Insight*, with Paul, as well as the Dali Lama's book, *The Art of Happiness*. Everybody knows those books are within the realm of psychology.

How should the judge rule? *See Henry v. Kernan*, 177 F.3d 1152, 1159 (9th Cir. 1999).

[3]   Physician-Patient Privilege

Under the federal common law, there was no privilege to avoid disclosure of confidential information shared in a physician-patient relationship. A majority of state jurisdictions have altered this rule, however, protecting confidential communications between a physician and her patient. *See, e.g.*, N.Y. Rev. Stat. 1828, 406 (pt. 3, ch. 7, Tit. 3, Art. 9, Section 73). Some of these states provide only limited protection to the doctor-patient relationship, requiring the disclosure of information under a court subpoena or extending protection only during the course of litigation. (*See, e.g.*, Florida Evidence Code, FL Stat., Chapter 90, *et seq.*)

Like the attorney-client and similar confidential communications privileges, the doctor-patient privilege, where recognized, is generally held by the patient. The privilege does not include the fact that the doctor has treated the patient or peripheral facts about the treatment such as how many times treatment has occurred. Also, the privilege may be abrogated for equally important public policy purposes, such as the disclosure of the existence of communicable or deadly disease, like tuberculosis or AIDS. On the other hand, if the privilege attaches, it generally prevails even after the patient has died.

Problem #12-20: Booth

J.W. Booth woke up his family physician, claiming he was shot while hunting in Washington, D.C. The doctor examined the wound and saw that Booth was losing blood. Booth was taken to the doctor's adjoining office, where the doctor treated Booth. Booth then hurried away, despite remaining in a medically unstable condition.

If the treatment occurred in a state where the physician-patient privilege is recognized, and the state law supplies the rule of decision in a case where Booth's injury and its cause are relevant, can the doctor be required to testify about both the treatment he provided Booth and about the statements made by Booth to him?

Problem: #12-21: Booth II

Suppose that, in the previous problem, Booth's brother, Bob Booth, helped to carry Booth to the doctor's office and assisted during the treatment. Can Booth's brother be required to testify about what he saw and heard in the doctor's office?

[4]   The Fifth Amendment Privilege Against Self-Incrimination

While it is amorphous in scope and heavily litigated, the Fifth Amendment privilege against self-incrimination is quickly defined. It prohibits any compelled testimony that is self-incriminatory. *See, e.g., United States v. Hubbell*, 167 F.3d 552 (D.C. Cir. 1999). The privilege protects against incrimination that would result from compelled testimony — e.g., not from independent, preexisting documents — and it must be "substantial and real." *Id.* Thus, the modern interpretation is not tied so much to privacy, which focuses on the freedom from government snooping, as it is to autonomy and the freedom from governmental compulsion. *Id.* at 572. It is not a violation of the privilege to compel a defendant to provide a hair sample, voice print, or even blood, for example, while it is a violation to force communications that implicate the defendant in a crime, such as confessions.

Problem #12-22: Lowering the Bar

Lynn filed a bar complaint against her attorney, Sam, complaining that he acted unethically in disclosing certain confidential information she gave him in the course of their attorney-client relationship to an opposing party in litigation. The Bar Disciplinary Commission wrote to Sam, asking for his understanding of the facts. Sam claimed that his Fifth Amendment right against self-incrimination protected him from providing any information. Is Sam correct?

Problem #12-23: Illegal Gambling

To stop the proliferation of unlawful gambling in the United States, Congress enacts a law requiring "all proceeds from gambling, legal or otherwise, to be declared as income for tax purposes." Is this law constitutional? Why?

Problem #12-24: Father and Son

John Sr. tells John Jr., "Look, I want you to keep a secret. Just between us, I cheated a bit on my taxes to help the family through hard times. Now the Internal Revenue Service is after me. Even if what I did was criminal, I never wanted to hurt you, got that? One more thing, try to minimize the expenses at college this semester; this fight is going to be a costly one."

If John Sr. is charged with tax evasion, can the prosecution call John Jr. as a witness to testify to the above conversation? Must John Jr. testify? What would you argue on John Sr.'s behalf?

Problem #12-25: Deep Throat

The identity of Deep Throat, the mysterious informant in the Watergate scandal who supposedly leaked information to the journalists, Woodward and Bernstein, becomes an issue in a subsequent trial. The media defendant in the trial subpoenas Woodward and Bernstein. Can the reporters refuse to disclose the name of their informant? *See United States v. Caporale*, 806 F.2d 1487 (11th Cir. 1986). Does it matter whether it is a criminal or civil case?

Problem #12-26: Confession

Joanne is charged with kidnapping. The prosecution attempts to introduce inculpatory statements Joanne made to her priest during a confession immediately prior to the kidnapping.

Are the statements Joanne made to her priest admissible? If Joanne had mentioned the substance of the confession to her mother, can the priest be subpoenaed to testify?

§ 12.05 CASES AND RULES

[A] Upjohn Co. v. United States

United States Supreme Court
449 U.S. 383 (1981)

JUSTICE REHNQUIST delivered the opinion of the Court:

We granted certiorari in this case to address important questions concerning the scope of the attorney-client privilege in the corporate context and the applicability of the work-product doctrine in proceedings to enforce tax summonses. 445 U.S. 925 . . . . With respect to the privilege question the parties and various *amici* have described our task as one of choosing between two "tests" which have gained adherents in the courts of appeals. We are acutely aware, however, that we sit to decide concrete cases and not abstract propositions of law. We decline to lay down a broad rule or series of rules to govern all conceivable future questions in this area, even were we able to do so. We can and do, however, conclude that the attorney-client privilege protects the communications involved in this case from compelled disclosure and that the work-product doctrine does apply in tax summons enforcement proceedings.

Petitioner Upjohn Co. manufactures and sells pharmaceuticals here and abroad. In January 1976 independent accountants conducting an audit of one of Upjohn's foreign subsidiaries discovered that the subsidiary made payments to or for the benefit of foreign government officials in order to secure government business. The accountants [] so informed petitioner, Mr. Gerard Thomas, Upjohn's Vice President, Secretary, and General Counsel. . . . It was decided that the company would conduct an internal investigation of what were termed "questionable payments." As part of this investigation the attorneys prepared a letter containing a questionnaire which was sent to "All Foreign General and Area Managers" over the Chairman's signature. . . . Managers were instructed to treat the investigation as "highly confidential" and not to discuss it with anyone other than Upjohn employees who might be helpful in providing the requested information. Responses were to be sent directly to Thomas. Thomas and outside counsel also interviewed the recipients of the questionnaire and some 33 other Upjohn officers or employees as part of the investigation.

On November 23, 1976, the [Internal Revenue] Service issued a summons . . . demanding production of:

> "All files relative to the investigation conducted under the supervision of Gerard Thomas to identify payments to employees of foreign governments. . . ."The records should include but not be limited to written questionnaires sent to managers of the Upjohn Company's foreign affiliates, and memorandums or notes of the interviews conducted . . . with officers and employees of the Upjohn Company and its subsidiaries." . . .

The company declined to produce the documents specified on the grounds that they were protected from disclosure by the attorney-client privilege.

Federal Rule of Evidence 501 provides that "the privilege of a witness . . . shall be governed by the principles of the common law as they may be interpreted by the courts of the United States in light of reason and experience." The attorney-client privilege is the oldest of the privileges for confidential communications known to the common law. Its purpose is to encourage full and frank communication between attorneys and their clients and thereby promote broader public interests in the observance of law and administration of justice. The privilege recognizes that sound legal advice or advocacy serves public ends and that such advice or advocacy depends upon the lawyer's being fully informed by the client. As we stated last Term in *Trammel v. United States*, 445 U.S. 40, 51 . . . (1980): "The lawyer-client privilege rests on the need for the advocate and counselor to know all that relates to the client's reasons for seeking representation if the professional mission is to be carried out." And in *Fisher v. United States*, 425 U.S. 391, 403 . . . (1976), we recognized the purpose of the privilege to be "to encourage clients to make full disclosure to their attorneys." . . . Admittedly complications in the application of the privilege arise when the client is a corporation, which in theory is an artificial creature of the law, and not an individual; but this Court has assumed that the privilege applies when the client is a corporation.

The Court of Appeals, however, considered the application of the privilege in the corporate context to present a "different problem," since the client was an inanimate entity and "only the senior management, guiding and integrating the several operations, . . . can be said to possess an identity analogous to the corporation as a whole." 600 F.2d at 1226. The first case to articulate the so-called "control group test" adopted by the court below . . . reflected a similar approach:

> "[T]he most satisfactory solution . . . is that if the employee making the communication, of whatever rank he may be, is in a position to control or even to take a substantial part in a decision about any action which the corporation may take upon the advice of the attorney, . . . then, in effect, *he is (or personifies) the corporation* when he makes his disclosure to the lawyer and the privilege would apply." (Emphasis supplied.)

Such a view, we think, overlooks the fact that the privilege exists to protect not only the giving of professional advice to those who can act on it but also the giving of information to the lawyer to enable him to give sound and informed advice.

. . . Middle-level — and indeed lower-level — employees can, by actions within the scope of their employment, embroil the corporation in serious legal difficulties, and it is only natural that these employees would have the relevant information needed by corporate counsel if he is adequately to advise the client with respect to such actual or potential difficulties.

The control group test adopted by the court below thus frustrates the very purpose of the privilege by discouraging the communication of relevant information by employees of the client to attorneys seeking to render legal advice to the client corporation. The attorney's advice will also frequently be more significant to noncontrol group members than to those who officially sanction the advice, and the control group test makes it more difficult to convey full and frank legal advice to the employees who will put into effect the client corporation's policy.

The narrow scope given the attorney-client privilege by the court below not only makes it difficult for corporate attorneys to formulate sound advice when their client is faced with a specific legal problem but also threatens to limit the valuable efforts of corporate counsel to ensure their client's compliance with the law. In light of the vast and complicated array of regulatory legislation confronting the modern corporation, corporations, unlike most individuals, "constantly go to lawyers to find out how to obey the law," Burnham, *The Attorney-Client Privilege in the Corporate Arena*, 24 Bus. Law. 901, 913 (1969), particularly since compliance with the law in this area is hardly an instinctive matter. . . . The test adopted by the court below is difficult to apply in practice, though no abstractly formulated and unvarying "test" will necessarily enable courts to decide questions such as this with mathematical precision. But if the purpose of the attorney-client privilege is to be served, the attorney and client must be able to predict with some degree of certainty whether particular discussions will be protected. An uncertain privilege, or one which purports to be certain but results in widely varying applications by the courts, is little better than no privilege at all. The very terms of the test adopted by the court below suggest the unpredictability of its application. The test restricts the availability of the privilege to those officers who play a "substantial role" in deciding and directing a corporation's legal response. Disparate decisions in cases applying this test illustrate its unpredictability.

The communications at issue were made by Upjohn employees to counsel for Upjohn acting as such, at the direction of the corporate superiors in order to secure legal advice from counsel. . . . The communications concerned matters within the scope of the employees' corporate duties, and the employees themselves were sufficiently aware that they were being questioned in order that the corporation could obtain legal advice. . . . Pursuant to explicit instructions from the Chairman of the Board, the communications were considered "highly confidential" when made . . . and have been kept confidential by the company. Consistent with the underlying purposes of the attorney-client privilege, these communications must be protected against compelled disclosure.

[W]e conclude that the narrow "control group test" . . . cannot, consistent with "the principles of common law as . . . interpreted . . . in light of reason and experience," Fed. Rule Evid. 501, govern the development of the law in this area.

[B]   Nix v. Whiteside

United States Supreme Court
475 U.S. 157 (1986)

CHIEF JUSTICE BURGER delivered the opinion of the Court:

We granted certiorari to decide whether the Sixth Amendment right of a criminal defendant to assistance of counsel is violated when an attorney refuses to cooperate with the defendant in presenting perjured testimony at his trial.

I

Whiteside was convicted of second-degree murder by a jury verdict which was affirmed by the Iowa courts. The killing took place on February 8, 1977, in Cedar Rapids, Iowa. Whiteside and two others went to one Calvin Love's apartment late that night, seeking marihuana. Love was in bed when Whiteside and his companions arrived; an argument between Whiteside and Love over the marihuana ensued. At one point, Love directed his girlfriend to get his "piece," and at another point got up, then returned to his bed. According to Whiteside's testimony, Love then started to reach under his pillow and moved toward Whiteside. Whiteside stabbed Love in the chest, inflicting a fatal wound.

Whiteside was charged with murder, and when counsel was appointed he objected to the lawyer initially appointed, claiming that he felt uncomfortable with a lawyer who had formerly been a prosecutor. Gary L. Robinson was then appointed and immediately began an investigation. Whiteside gave him a statement that he had stabbed Love as the latter "was pulling a pistol from underneath the pillow on the bed." Upon questioning by Robinson, however, Whiteside indicated that he had not actually seen a gun, but that he was convinced that Love had a gun. . . .

. . . About a week before trial, during preparation for direct examination, Whiteside for the first time told Robinson and his associate Donna Paulsen that he had seen something "metallic" in Love's hand. When asked about this, Whiteside responded:

"[I]n Howard Cook's case there was a gun. If I don't say I saw a gun, I'm dead."

Robinson told Whiteside that such testimony would be perjury and repeated that it was not necessary to prove that a gun was available but only that Whiteside reasonably believed that he was in danger. On Whiteside's insisting that he would testify that he saw "something metallic" Robinson told him, according to Robinson's testimony:

"[W]e could not allow him to [testify falsely] because that would be perjury, and as officers of the court we would be suborning perjury if we allowed him to do it; . . . I advised him that if he did do that it would be my duty to advise the Court of what he was doing and that I felt he was committing perjury; also, that I probably would be allowed to attempt to impeach that particular testimony." App. to Pet. for Cert. A-85.

Robinson also indicated he would seek to withdraw from the representation if Whiteside insisted on committing perjury. (Footnote omitted.)

Whiteside testified in his own defense at trial and stated that he "knew" that Love had a gun and that he believed Love was reaching for a gun and he had acted swiftly in self-defense. On cross-examination, he admitted that he had not actually seen a gun in Love's hand. . . . .

II

The right of an accused to testify in his defense is of relatively recent origin. Until the latter part of the preceding century, criminal defendants in this country, as at common law, were considered to be disqualified from giving sworn testimony at their own trial by reason of their interest as a party to the case.

By the end of the 19th century, however, the disqualification was finally abolished by statute in most states and in the federal courts.

In *Strickland v. Washington*, we held that to obtain relief by way of federal habeas corpus on a claim of a deprivation of effective assistance of counsel under the Sixth Amendment, the movant must establish both serious attorney error and prejudice. To show such error, it must be established that the assistance rendered by counsel was constitutionally deficient in that "counsel made errors so serious that counsel was not functioning as 'counsel' guaranteed the defendant by the Sixth Amendment."

In *Strickland*, we recognized counsel's duty of loyalty and his "overarching duty to advocate the defendant's cause." *Ibid.* Plainly, that duty is limited to legitimate, lawful conduct compatible with the very nature of a trial as a search for truth. Although counsel must take all reasonable lawful means to attain the objectives of the client, counsel is precluded from taking steps or in any way assisting the client in presenting false evidence or otherwise violating the law. This principle has consistently been recognized in most unequivocal terms by expositors of the norms of professional conduct since the first Canons of Professional Ethics were adopted by the American Bar Association in 1908. . . .

These principles have been carried through to contemporary codifications of an attorney's professional responsibility. Disciplinary Rule 7-102 of the Model Code of Professional Responsibility (1980), entitled "Representing a Client Within the Bounds of the Law," provides:

"(A) In his representation of a client, a lawyer shall not:

"(4) Knowingly use perjured testimony or false evidence.

"(7) Counsel or assist his client in conduct that the lawyer knows to be illegal or fraudulent."

This provision has been adopted by Iowa, and is binding on all lawyers who appear in its courts. *See* Iowa Code of Professional Responsibility for Lawyers (1985). The more recent Model Rules of Professional Conduct (1983) similarly admonish attorneys to obey all laws in the course of representing a client.

It is universally agreed that at a minimum the attorney's first duty when confronted with a proposal for perjurious testimony is to attempt to dissuade the client from the unlawful course of conduct.

The commentary thus also suggests that an attorney's revelation of his client's perjury to the court is a professionally responsible and acceptable response to the conduct of a client who has actually given perjured testimony.

On this record, the accused enjoyed continued representation within the bounds of reasonable professional conduct, and did in fact exercise his right to testify; at most he was denied the right to have the assistance of counsel in the presentation of false testimony. . . . A defendant who informed his counsel that he was arranging to bribe or threaten witnesses or members of the jury would have no "right" to insist on counsel's assistance or silence. Counsel would not be limited to advising against that conduct. An attorney's duty of confidentiality, which totally covers the client's admission of guilt, does not extend to a client's announced plans to engage in future criminal conduct. . . . In short, the responsibility of an ethical lawyer, as an officer of the court and a key component of a system of justice, dedicated to a search for truth, is essentially the same whether the client announces an intention to bribe or threaten witnesses or jurors or to commit or procure perjury. No system of justice worthy of the name can tolerate a lesser standard.

We hold that, as a matter of law, counsel's conduct complained of here cannot establish the prejudice required for relief under the second strand of the *Strickland* inquiry.

Whiteside's attorney treated Whiteside's proposed perjury in accord with professional standards, and since Whiteside's truthful testimony could not have prejudiced the result of his trial, the Court of Appeals was in error to direct the issuance of a writ of habeas corpus and must be reversed.

[C]   Jaffee v. Redmond

United States Supreme Court
518 U.S. 1 (1996)

JUSTICE STEVENS:

After a traumatic incident in which she shot and killed a man, a police officer received extensive counseling from a licensed clinical social worker. The question we address is whether statements the officer made to her therapist during the counseling sessions are protected from compelled disclosure in a federal civil action brought by the family of the deceased. Stated otherwise, the question is whether it is appropriate for federal courts to recognize a "psychotherapist privilege" under Rule 501 of the Federal Rules of Evidence.

On June 27, 1991, Redmond was the first officer to respond to a "fight in progress" call at an apartment complex. . . . [During the fracas], Redmond drew her service revolver. Two other men then burst out of the building, one, Ricky Allen, chasing the other. . . . Redmond shot Allen when she believed he was about to stab the man he was chasing.

I

Petitioner [administrator of the estate of Ricky Allen] filed suit in Federal District Court alleging that [police officer] Redmond had violated Allen's constitutional rights by using excessive force during the encounter at the apartment complex. . . .

[A]fter the shooting[,] Redmond had participated in about 50 counseling sessions with Karen Beyer, a clinical social worker. . . . Petitioner sought access to Beyer's notes concerning the sessions for use in cross-examining Redmond. Respondents vigorously resisted . . . [and refused to comply with the district judge's] order to disclose the contents of Beyer's notes.

II

. . . "[T]he common law is not immutable but flexible, and by its own principles adapts itself to varying conditions." *Funk v. United States*, 290 U.S. 371, 383 . . . (1933). . . . .

III

Like the spousal and attorney-client privileges, the psychotherapist-patient privilege is "rooted in the imperative need for confidence and trust." [*Trammel v. United States*, 445 U.S. 40, 51 (1980).] . . . . Because of the sensitive nature of the problems for which individuals consult psychotherapists, disclosure of confidential communications made during counseling sessions may cause embarrassment or disgrace.

The psychotherapist privilege serves the public interest by facilitating the provision of appropriate treatment for individuals suffering the effects of a mental or emotional problem. . . .

That it is appropriate for the federal courts to recognize a psychotherapist privilege under Rule 501 is confirmed by the fact that all 50 States and the District of Columbia have enacted into law some form of psychotherapist privilege.

V

The conversations between Officer Redmond and Karen Beyer and the notes taken during their counseling sessions are protected from compelled disclosure under Rule 501 of the Federal Rules of Evidence.

The judgment of the Court of Appeals is affirmed.

[D] Trammel v. United States

In *Trammel v. United States*, 445 U.S. 40 (1980), the Supreme Court reconsidered the rule concerning the adverse spousal testimony privilege. The prevailing rule had been enunciated in *Hawkins v. United States*, 358 U.S. 74 (1958), which perpetuated the common law rule. The common law permitted the privilege to be asserted by either the non-testifying or the testifying spouse. The Court in *Trammel* found that the justification for the *Hawkins* rule no longer existed, and overruled it. The Court stated:

> Our consideration of the foundations for the privilege and its history satisfy us that "reason and experience" no longer justify so sweeping a rule as that found acceptable by the Court in *Hawkins*. Accordingly, we conclude that the existing rule should be modified so that the witness spouse alone has a privilege to refuse to testify adversely; the witness may be neither compelled to testify nor foreclosed from testifying. This modification — vesting the

privilege in the witness spouse — furthers the important public interest in marital harmony without unduly burdening legitimate law enforcement needs.

1. Which rule is more realistic, the one announced in *Hawkins* or its replacement in *Trammel*?

2. If no adverse spousal testimony privilege existed, would coerced testimony by one spouse against the other irretrievably harm a marriage?

[E]   State ex rel. Sowers v. Olwell

The case of *State ex rel. Sowers v. Olwell*, 394 P.2d 681 (1964), addresses the question of whether the attorney-client privilege protects material evidence of a crime given to an attorney by his or her client. The Supreme Court of Washington answered this question in the negative, although it also concluded that an attorney cannot be forced to divulge information communicated within the attorney-client relationship. Counsel was served with a subpoena asking him to produce "all knives in [his] possession and under [his] control relating to Henry LeRoy Gray, Gloria Pugh or John W. Warren." The attorney refused to comply, asserting the attorney-client privilege on behalf of his client. The Supreme Court of Washington held that the attorney's refusal was not entirely proper. The Court stated:

> Here we must consider the balancing process between the attorney-client privilege and the public interest in criminal investigation. We are in agreement that the attorney/client privilege is applicable to the knife held by appellant, but do not agree that the privilege warrants the attorney, as an officer of the court, from withholding it after being properly requested to produce the same. The attorney should not be a depository for criminal evidence (such as a knife, other weapons, stolen property, etc.), which in itself has little, if any, material value for the purposes of aiding counsel in the preparation of the defense of his client's case. Such evidence given the attorney during legal consultation for information purposes and used by the attorney in preparing the defense of his client's case, whether or not the case ever goes to trial, could clearly be withheld for a reasonable period of time. It follows that the attorney, after a reasonable period, should, as an officer of the court, on his own motion, turn the same over to the prosecution.

[F]   Schipp v. General Motors Corporation

United States District Court for the
Eastern District Of Arkansas
457 F. Supp. 2d 917 (E.D. Ark. 2006)

General Motors issued three subpoenas duces tecum to obtain documents prepared by Ann Kennedy's insurance carrier during the investigation of the accident at issue in this action. Specifically, GM sought to discover a recorded statement of Kennedy taken on July 26, 2002; a summary of that recorded statement prepared on July 27, 2002; an investigation report of the insurance adjuster prepared on August 13, 2002; and witness statements obtained by Kennedy's insurance carrier. Kennedy has objected.

GM has moved to compel. GM asks for an award of the reasonable expenses incurred in making this motion, including reasonable attorney's fees, pursuant to Rule 37(a)(4) of the Federal Rules of Civil Procedure.

Kennedy gave a statement to her insurer on July 26, 2002, two days after the accident. She argues that this statement is protected by the attorney-client privilege. In diversity cases, federal courts follow state law on questions of privilege. . . . Arkansas has not ruled on whether a communication between an insurer and its insured may be protected by the attorney-client privilege. Many states [–] and what appears to be a majority [–] have held, depending on varying factors, that such a communication may be protected by the privilege.

The courts have looked at a number of factors to determine whether a statement given by an insured to his insurer is privileged. Those factors include: 1) whether the insurance contract obligates the insurance company to defend claims, 2) whether the relationship between the insurer and the attorney exists at the time of the communication between the insurer and the insured, 3) whether the insurer is advised of the confidential information at the direction of an attorney, and 4) whether the communication is made for the dominant purpose of litigation . . .

A number of jurisdictions have held that statements between an insured and insurer are not privileged.

Although the Supreme Court of Arkansas has not decided this issue, its decisions make clear two relevant aspects of the attorney-client privilege in Arkansas. First, "[t]he burden of showing that a privilege applies is upon the party asserting it." . . . . Thus, the burden is on Kennedy to show that her statement is privileged. Second, "[t]he purpose of the attorney-client privilege is to promote 'full and frank communication' between attorneys and clients, and that, in turn, promotes the observance of law and administration of justice." . . . . It should be noted that other states have cited the same purpose in recognizing a statement between an insured and an insurer as protected by the attorney-client privilege.

In *Courteau*, a hospital's insurance carrier hired an attorney to investigate the circumstances surrounding a potential claim. . . . The attorney then "immediately requested statements from employees involved who were potential defendants." . . . . The Supreme Court of Arkansas held that the hospital employees and physicians were "clients" of the hospital's attorney, and the communications between them were therefore privileged in spite of the fact that some of those communications were "relayed through corporate channels."

Perhaps more illuminating is *Holt*, where an automobile accident caused five deaths, the insurance carrier hired attorneys to represent the insured, and the attorneys in turn hired an expert to prepare an accident reconstruction report. . . . A prosecuting attorney then issued a subpoena duces tecum to the accident reconstructionist to obtain a complete copy of the report. . . . The court held, however, that the report, as well as all communications between the attorneys, the reconstructionist, and the insured, were "protected by attorney-client privilege." In reaching its conclusion, the court applied Arkansas Rule of Evidence 502, which states in pertinent part:

(2) A representative of the client is *one having authority to obtain professional legal services*, or to act on advice rendered pursuant thereto, on behalf of the client.

(b) General Rule of Privilege. A client has a privilege to refuse to disclose and to prevent any other person from disclosing confidential communications made for the purpose of facilitating the rendition of professional legal services to the client (1) *between himself* or his representative *and* his lawyer or *his lawyer's representative*, (2) between his lawyer and the lawyer's representative, [or] (4) between representatives of the client or *between the client and a representative of the client*

Although the matter is not free from doubt, this Court believes that on the facts of this case the Supreme Court of Arkansas would find that Kennedy's recorded statement to her insurer is protected by the attorney-client privilege. It should have been obvious when Kennedy gave her recorded statement that claims would be made against her and that she would call upon her insurer to defend those claims. Although the policy is not in the record, the Court assumes that it is a standard automobile liability policy pursuant to which the insurer selects and compensates defense counsel and pursuant to which the insured must cooperate with the insurer. Kennedy was entitled to expect that her insurance carrier would engage a lawyer to represent her, which means that she was entitled to view her insurer as her representative for purposes of obtaining legal services. Kennedy's statement to her insurer was a step in the process of obtaining legal representation pursuant to the insurance contract. GM's motion compelling discovery of Kennedy's recorded statement is denied.

GM also seeks to discover other insurance claims files, including the summary of Kennedy's recorded statement prepared on July 27, 2002, and the investigation report of the insurance adjuster, prepared on August 13, 2002. Kennedy asserts that these files are work product prepared in anticipation of litigation and therefore protected from discovery. *See* Fed. R. Civ. Pro. 26(b)(3). "The work product privilege operates to ensure that an opponent cannot secure materials that an adversary has prepared in anticipation of litigation." In a diversity case, the Court applies federal law to resolve work product claims. The Eighth Circuit has ruled that "the party seeking protection must show the materials were prepared in anticipation of litigation, i.e., because of the prospect of litigation," *id.*, as "the work product rule does not come into play merely because there is a remote prospect of future litigation."

GM argues that "unless and until an insurance company can demonstrate that it reasonably considered a claim to be more likely than not headed for litigation, the natural inference is that the documents in its claims file that predate this realization were prepared in the ordinary course of business . . . ." *S.D. Warren Co. v. Eastern Elec. Corp.*, 201 F.R.D. 280, 285 (D. Me. 2001). Here, it was obvious on the night of the accident that claims would be asserted against Kennedy. It is undisputed that Kennedy's vehicle crossed the median of an interstate highway and crashed into oncoming traffic. As a result, one person was killed and two others were injured. A reasonable person would expect litigation to ensue. Documents prepared afterwards would have been created in anticipation of litigation. Those documents are therefore protected by the work-product doctrine.

Documents covered by the work-product doctrine can nevertheless be discovered if a party shows a "substantial need" of the documents and an inability to obtain a substantial equivalent of the documents or information without "undue hardship." . . . . However, a "party . . . does not demonstrate substantial need when it merely seeks corroborative evidence." . . . GM has had the opportunity to depose each eye witness of the accident, including Ann Kennedy, in addition to any person with knowledge of the accident. GM's desire to obtain "immediate factual observations unmarred by the passage of time" does not rise to the level of substantial need imposed by Rule 26. In short, documents prepared by Kennedy's insurer, on the facts of this case, are protected by the work-product doctrine because they were prepared in anticipation of litigation and because GM has failed to demonstrate a substantial need for them.

GM's motion to compel production of Kennedy's statement is denied. GM's motion to compel production of the insurer's claim file is denied except as to verbatim statements of persons other than Kennedy. Kennedy must produce all verbatim, non-party witness statements within five business days after entry of this Order. GM's request to be reimbursed for the reasonable expenses in making this motion, including reasonable attorneys' fees, is denied. . . .

[G] Rules Comparison

Georgia Chapter 24-9-21. Confidentiality of Certain Communications.

There are certain admissions and communications excluded on grounds of public policy. Among these are:

(1) Communications between husband and wife;

(2) Communications between attorney and client;

(3) Communications among grand jurors;

(4) Secrets of state; and

(5) Communications between psychiatrist and patient.

Florida Statute § 90.5035. Sexual Assault Counselor-Victim Privilege.

(1) For purposes of this section:

(a) a "rape crisis center" is any public or private agency that offers assistance to victims of sexual assault or sexual battery and their families.

(b) a "sexual counselor" is any employee of a rape crisis center whose primary purpose is the rendering of advice, counseling, or assistance to victims of sexual assault or sexual battery.

(2) A victim has a privilege to refuse to disclose and to prevent any other person from disclosing, a confidential communication made by the victim to a sexual assault counselor or any record made in the course of advising,

counseling, or assisting the victim. Such confidential communication or record may be disclosed only with the prior written consent of the victim. This privilege includes any advice given by the sexual assault counselor in the course of that relationship.

Florida Statute § 90.5055. Accountant-Client Privilege.

(2) A client has a privilege to refuse to disclose, and to prevent any other person from disclosing, the contents of confidential communications with an accountant when such other person learned of the communications because they were made in the rendition of accounting services to the client. This privilege includes other confidential information obtained by the accountant from the client for the purpose of rendering accounting advice.

Nebraska § 27-504. Physician-Patient Privilege.

(2) A patient has a privilege to refuse to disclose and to prevent any other person from disclosing confidential communications made for the purposes of diagnosis or treatment of his or her physical, mental, or emotional condition among himself or herself, his or her physician, or persons who are participating in the diagnosis or treatment under the direction of the physician, including members of the patient's family.

Hawaii Rule 506. Communications to Clergyman.

(a) **Definitions.** As used in this rule:

(1) A "clergyman" is a minister, priest, rabbi, Christian Science practitioner, or other similar functionary of a religious organization, or an individual reasonably believed so to be by the person consulting him.

(2) A communication is "confidential" if made privately and not intended for further disclosure except to other persons present in furtherance of the purpose of the communication.

(b) **General rule of privilege.** A person has a privilege to refuse to disclose and to prevent another from disclosing a confidential communication by the person to a clergyman in his professional character as spiritual advisor.

New Jersey § 2A:84A-21. Newspaperman's Privilege.

Subject to Rule 37, a person engaged on, engaged in, connected with, or employed by a news media for the purpose of gathering, procuring, transmitting, compiling, editing or disseminating news for the general public or on whose behalf news is so gathered, procured, transmitted, compiled, edited or disseminated has a privilege to refuse to disclose, in any legal or quasi-legal proceeding or before any investigative body, including, but not limited to, any court, grand jury, petit jury, administrative agency, the Legislature or legislative committee, or elsewhere:

a. The source, author, means, agency or person from or through whom any information was procured, obtained, supplied, furnished, gathered, transmitted, compiled, edited, disseminated, or delivered; and

b. Any news or information obtained in the course of pursuing his professional activities whether or not it is disseminated."

(1) Communications between husband and wife;

(2) Communications between attorney and client;

(3) Communications among grand jurors;

(4) Secrets of state; and

(5) Communications between psychiatrist and patient.

Florida Statute § 90.5035. Sexual Assault Counselor-Victim Privilege.

(1) For purposes of this section:

(a) a "rape crisis center" is any public or private agency that offers assistance to victims of sexual assault or sexual battery and their families.

(b) a "sexual counselor" is any employee of a rape crisis center whose primary purpose is the rendering of advice, counseling, or assistance to victims of sexual assault or sexual battery.

(2) A victim has a privilege to refuse to disclose and to prevent any other person from disclosing, a confidential communication made by the victim to a sexual assault counselor or any record made in the course of advising, counseling, or assisting the victim. Such confidential communication or record may be disclosed only with the prior written consent of the victim. This privilege includes any advice given by the sexual assault counselor in the course of that relationship.

Florida Statute § 90.5055. Accountant-Client Privilege.

(2) A client has a privilege to refuse to disclose, and to prevent any other person from disclosing, the contents of confidential communications with an accountant when such other person learned of the communications because they were made in the rendition of accounting services to the client. This privilege includes other confidential information obtained by the accountant from the client for the purpose of rendering accounting advice.

Nebraska § 27-504. Physician-Patient Privilege.

(2) A patient has a privilege to refuse to disclose and to prevent any other person from disclosing confidential communications made for the purposes of diagnosis or treatment of his or her physical, mental, or emotional condition among himself or herself, his or her physician, or persons who are participat-

ing in the diagnosis or treatment under the direction of the physician, including members of the patient's family.

Hawaii Rule 506. Communications to Clergyman.

(a) Definitions. As used in this rule:

(1) A "clergyman" is a minister, priest, rabbi, Christian Science practitioner, or other similar functionary of a religious organization, or an individual reasonably believed so to be by the person consulting him.

(2) A communication is "confidential" if made privately and not intended for further disclosure except to other persons present in furtherance of the purpose of the communication.

(b) General rule of privilege. A person has a privilege to refuse to disclose and to prevent another from disclosing a confidential communication by the person to a clergyman in his professional character as spiritual advisor.

New Jersey § 2A:84A-21. Newspaperman's Privilege.

Subject to Rule 37, a person engaged on, engaged in, connected with, or employed by a news media for the purpose of gathering, procuring, transmitting, compiling, editing or disseminating news for the general public or on whose behalf news is so gathered, procured, transmitted, compiled, edited or disseminated has a privilege to refuse to disclose, in any legal or quasi-legal proceeding or before any investigative body, including, but not limited to, any court, grand jury, petit jury, administrative agency, the Legislature or legislative committee, or elsewhere:

a. The source, author, means, agency or person from or through whom any information was procured, obtained, supplied, furnished, gathered, transmitted, compiled, edited, disseminated, or delivered; and

b. Any news or information obtained in the course of pursuing his professional activities whether or not it is disseminated.

Wisconsin Chapter 905.16. Communications to Veteran Mentors.

(2) General Rule of Privilege. A veteran or member has a privilege to refuse to disclose and to prevent another from disclosing confidential communication made by the veteran or member to a veteran mentor while the veteran mentor is acting within the scope of his or her duties under the veterans mentoring program.

(4) Exception. There is no privilege under this section as to the following:

(a) A communication that indicates that the veteran or member plans or threatens to commit a crime or to seriously harm himself or herself.

(b) A communication that the veteran or member has agreed in writing to allow to be disclosed as condition of his or her participation in the veterans mentoring program.

§ 12.06 MIXED PROBLEMS

Problem #12-27: "Til Death do Us Part . . ."

Elouisa and Louis, who lived together but were not married, decided to commit a series of crimes as they traveled across the Midwest. They planned on stealing a car and then robbing the local savings and loan in Cisco, Texas. The car theft and bank robbery were successful, but Elouisa and Louis were captured when they took a hostage as they fled the bank.

1. If Louis alone is charged with the crimes of car theft, robbery, and kidnapping because of Elouisa's failing health, can Elouisa be called to testify about what Louis told her in planning the car theft and bank robbery? Could she testify to what she saw during the robbery? Why?

2. If Louis and Elouisa had been engaged when the crimes were being planned and committed, and had married just prior to trial, would the marital communications privilege apply? Why? Who holds that privilege?

3. If the nuptials between Louis and Elouisa occurred just prior to trial, would the spousal incapacity privilege apply? Why? Would Elouisa be able to testify at all? Who holds that privilege?

4. If Louis and Elouisa had been married during the planning and commission of the crimes, but had divorced prior to trial, would the marital communications privilege still apply during trial? Would the spousal incapacity privilege apply? Explain.

Problem #12-28: Attorney-Client Privilege

Andy Attorney represented Jane after she was charged with removing her children from the state in violation of a court order regarding custody. At trial, an e-mail conversation between Attorney and Jane was introduced. Attorney objected that part of the e-mail conversation was missing but did not object that the e-mail was protected by the attorney-client privilege. The e-mail was admitted into evidence. Attorney filed a motion asking the court to investigate how the State came into possession of the e-mail and who altered it. Jane was acquitted. Attorney filed a motion, claiming that the state violated the attorney-client privilege. What result? *See O'Brien v. Superior Court*, 939 A.2d 1223 (Conn. App. 2008). *See also* Connecticut Rules of Prof'l Conduct R. 3.1; MRPC 3.1.

Problem #12-29: Work-Product Waiver

Harold Kearns was an attorney for, and friend of, the late Hannah Smythe, a famous model. Kearns sued the O'Toole Law Firm for slander and invasion of privacy. Kearns sought the disclosure of various documents through discovery. The firm claimed the work-product privilege prevented disclosure of certain of the requested documents that were based on investigations by Sal Slick. These investigations were performed on behalf of their client Virginia Smythe, Hannah's mother. The documents were prepared in anticipation of litigation. Slick and another investigator, Sarah Slye, made statements on the Internet and disclosed information to an author who was writing book about Hannah. May the O'Toole law firm refuse to disclose the documents on the basis of the work-product privilege? *See Stern v. O'Quinn*, 253 F.R.D. 663 (S.D. Fla. 2008).

Problem #12-30: Inadvertent Email Disclosure

The defendant moved to claw back a mistakenly disclosed email that was allegedly privileged because it involved an employee response to in-house counsel regarding the location of certain documents. The email was drafted prior to the suit and the subject line read "Some Information for Patent Infringement Case." The defendant learned of the email disclosure when the plaintiff attached it as an exhibit to a motion. The defendant immediately informed the plaintiff that the email constituted privileged information and asked for its return, the destruction of all copies, and that it be stricken from the plaintiff's motion. The defendant had produced more than a million documents during discovery and used advanced software to screen for privileged material. Somehow this one email was misplaced in a "prescreened folder" without ever having been screened.

1. In-house counsel does not directly use the email's factual information about the physical location of documents to advise the defendant. Does the attorney-client privilege prevent the disclosure of the email?

2. The defendant claims the work-product doctrine protects the email from disclosure. Does the work-product doctrine protect the email from disclosure? Does it make a difference whether the email is only factual work-product or mental process work-product?

3. Assuming the email is protected from disclosure by the work-product doctrine, did the defendant's disclosure waive the protection?

§ 12.07 RELEVANT ETHICS RULES

Rule 5.5 Unauthorized practice of law; multijurisdictional practice of law

(a) A lawyer shall not practice law in a jurisdiction in violation of the regulation of the legal profession in that jurisdiction, or assist another in doing so.

(b) A lawyer who is not admitted to practice in this jurisdiction shall not:

(1) except as authorized by these Rules or other law, establish an office or other systematic and continuous presence in this jurisdiction for the practice of law; or

(2) hold out to the public or otherwise represent that the lawyer is admitted to practice law in this jurisdiction.

(c) A lawyer admitted in another United States jurisdiction or in a foreign jurisdiction, and not disbarred or suspended from practice in any jurisdiction, may provide legal services on a temporary basis in this jurisdiction that:

(1) are undertaken in association with a lawyer who is admitted to practice in this jurisdiction and who actively participates in the matter;

(2) are in or reasonably related to a pending or potential proceeding before a tribunal in this or another jurisdiction, if the lawyer, or a person the lawyer is assisting, is authorized by law or order to appear in such proceeding or reasonably expects to be so authorized;

(3) are in or reasonably related to a pending or potential arbitration, mediation, or other alternative dispute resolution proceeding in this or another jurisdiction, if the services arise out of or are reasonably related to the lawyer's practice in a jurisdiction in which the lawyer is admitted to practice and are not services for which the forum requires pro hac vice admission; or

(4) are not within paragraphs (c)(2) or (c)(3) and arise out of or are reasonably related to the lawyer's practice in a jurisdiction in which the lawyer is admitted to practice.

(d) A lawyer admitted in another United States jurisdiction, or in a foreign jurisdiction, and not disbarred or suspended from practice in any jurisdiction, may provide legal services in this jurisdiction that:

(1) are provided to the lawyer's employer or its organizational affiliates after compliance with Supreme Court Rule 55.1(a)(1) and are not services for which the forum requires pro hac vice admission; or

(2) are services that the lawyer is authorized to provide by federal law or other law of this jurisdiction. Del. Rules of Prof'l Conduct R. 5.5. *See* MRPC 5.5.

Rule 1.6 Confidentiality of Information

(a) A lawyer shall not reveal information relating to representation of a client unless the client gives informed consent, the disclosure is impliedly authorized in order to carry out the representation, or the disclosure is permitted by paragraph (b).

(b) A lawyer may reveal information relating to the representation of a client to the extent the lawyer reasonably believes necessary:

(1) to prevent reasonably certain death or substantial bodily harm;

(2) to prevent the client from committing a crime or fraud that is reasonably certain to result in substantial injury to the financial interests or property of another and in furtherance of which the client has used or is using the lawyer's services;

(3) to prevent, mitigate, or rectify substantial injury to the financial interests or property of another that is reasonably certain to result or has resulted from the client's commission of a crime or fraud in furtherance of which the client has used the lawyer's services;

(4) to secure legal advice about the lawyer's compliance with these Rules, a court order or other law;

(5)   to establish a claim or defense on behalf of the lawyer in a controversy between the lawyer and the client, to establish a defense to a criminal charge, civil claim, or disciplinary complaint against the lawyer based upon conduct in which the client was involved or to respond to allegations in any proceeding concerning the lawyer's representation of the client; or

(6)   to comply with these Rules, a court order or other law. Md. Lawyer's R. Prof'l Conduct 1.6. *See* MRPC 1.6.

Rule 3.1 Meritorious Claims and Contentions

A lawyer shall not bring or defend a proceeding, or assert or controvert an issue therein, unless there is a basis in law and fact for doing so that is not frivolous, which includes a good faith argument for an extension, modification or reversal of existing law. A lawyer for the defendant in a criminal proceeding, or the respondent in a proceeding that could result in incarceration, may nevertheless so defend the proceeding as to require that every element of the case be established. Conn. Rules of Prof'l Conduct R. 3.1. *See* MRPC 3.1.

§ 12.08   SUMMARY AND REVIEW

1.   How many privileges do the Federal Rules of Evidence expressly recognize?

2.   How many marital privileges exist? Why?

3.   Who should own or hold the adverse spousal privilege, the accused or the spouse who is called to testify? Why?

4.   What are the various sources of federal privileges?

5.   When does state privilege law apply in federal court?

6.   Why have a privilege for the political vote?

7.   Why have a privilege for the identity of an informer?

8.   How can a privilege be waived?

9.   Why don't the states and federal common law recognize a parent-child privilege?

Chapter 13

AUTHENTICATION, IDENTIFICA~~~~~
BEST EVIDENCE RULE

CHAPTER FRAMEWORK: Authentication and i~~~~~ation create a special application of relevancy — whether evidence being admitted or offered at trial is what it purports to be. The chain of inferences used for authentication, like those used for basic relevance, are needed once again.

While authentication has broad applicability, the best evidence rule has narrow applicability. It only applies when proving an important writing in a case or a witness is testifying from a writing and not memory of the actual events.

WHY ARE THE CONCEPTS IN THIS CHAPTER IMPORTANT? Authentication is an important procedural device that is integral to admitting evidence at trial. It is useful to understand the best evidence rule to appreciate fully its limited applicability.

CONNECTIONS: Authentication connects to relevance and trial skills (e.g., laying a foundation). The best evidence rule also connects to the use of policy — preventing fraud — and whether the rule appropriately advances that policy in the electronic era.

CHAPTER OUTLINE:

Common exception — duplicates

   2. Other exceptions —

      a. original lost or destroyed

      b. original not obtainable or in possession of opponent

      c. writing concerns a collateral matter

  D. Why the term, BE is a misnomer?

     1. BE Rule does not require the strongest evidence to prove a point, the rule only prefers the original "writing" and often allows substitutes for the original

* * * * *

RELEVANT EVIDENCE RULES

Rule 901. Authenticating or Identifying Evidence

(a) In General. To satisfy the requirement of authenticating or identifying an item of evidence, the proponent must produce evidence sufficient to support a finding that the item is what the proponent claims it is.

(b) Examples. The following are examples only — not a complete list — of evidence that satisfies the requirement:

(1) Testimony of a Witness with Knowledge. Testimony that an item is what it is claimed to be.

(2) Nonexpert Opinion About Handwriting. A nonexpert's opinion that handwriting is genuine, based on a familiarity with it that was not acquired for the current litigation.

(3) Comparison by an Expert Witness or the Trier of Fact. A comparison with an authenticated specimen by an expert witness or the trier of fact.

(4) Distinctive Characteristics and the Like. The appearance, contents, substance, internal patterns, or other distinctive characteristics of the item, taken together with all the circumstances.

(5) Opinion About a Voice. An opinion identifying a person's voice — whether heard firsthand or through mechanical or electronic transmission or recording — based on hearing the voice at any time under circumstances that connect it with the alleged speaker.

(6) Evidence About a Telephone Conversation. For a telephone conversation, evidence that a call was made to the number assigned at the time to:

(A) a particular person, if circumstances, including self-identification, show that the person answering was the one called; or

(B) a particular business, if the call was made to a business and the call related to business reasonably transacted over the telephone.

(7) Evidence About Public Records. Evidence that:

(A) a document was recorded or filed in a public office as authorized by law; or

(B) a purported public record or statement is from the office where items of this kind are kept.

(8) Evidence About Ancient Documents or Data Compilations. For a document or data compilation, evidence that it:

(A) is in a condition that creates no suspicion about its authenticity;

(B) was in a place where, if authentic, it would likely be; and

(C) is at least 20 years old when offered.

(9) Evidence About a Process or System. Evidence describing a process or system and showing that it produces an accurate result.

(10) Methods Provided by a Statute or Rule. Any method of authentication or identification allowed by a federal statute or a rule prescribed by the Supreme Court.

Rule 902. Evidence That Is Self-Authenticating

The following items of evidence are self-authenticating; they require no extrinsic evidence of authenticity in order to be admitted:

(1) Domestic Public Documents That Are Sealed and Signed. A document that bears:

(A) a seal purporting to be that of the United States; any state, district, commonwealth, territory, or insular possession of the United States; the former Panama Canal Zone; the Trust Territory of the Pacific Islands; a political subdivision of any of these entities; or a department, agency, or officer of any entity named above; and

(B) a signature purporting to be an execution or attestation.

(2) Domestic Public Documents That Are Not Sealed but Are Signed and Certified. A document that bears no seal if:

(A) it bears the signature of an officer or employee of an entity named in Rule 902(1)(A); and

(B) another public officer who has a seal and official duties within that same entity certifies under seal — or its equivalent — that the signer has the official capacity and that the signature is genuine.

(3) Foreign Public Documents. A document that purports to be signed or attested by a person who is authorized by a foreign country's law to do so. The document must be accompanied by a final certification that certifies the genuineness of the signature and official position of the signer or attester — or of any foreign official whose certificate of genuineness relates to the signature or attestation or is in a chain of certificates of genuineness relating to the signature or attestation. The certification may be made by a secretary of a United States embassy or legation; by a consul general, vice consul, or consular agent of the United States; or by a diplomatic or consular official of the foreign country assigned or accredited to the United States. If all parties have been given a reasonable opportunity to investigate the document's authenticity and accuracy, the court may, for good cause, either:

(A) order that it be treated as presumptively authentic without final certification.

(B) allow it to be evidenced by an attested summary with or without final certification.

(4) Certified Copies of Public Records. A copy of an official record — or a copy of a document that was recorded or filed in a public office as authorized by law — if the copy is certified as correct by:

(A) the custodian or another person authorized to make the certification; or

(B) a certificate that complies with Rule 902(1), (2), or (3), a federal statute, or a rule prescribed by the Supreme Court.

(5) Official Publications. A book, pamphlet, or other publication purporting to be issued by a public authority.

(6) Newspapers and Periodicals. Printed material purporting to be a newspaper or periodical.

(7) Trade Inscriptions and the Like. An inscription, sign, tag, or label purporting to have been affixed in the course of business and indicating origin, ownership, or control.

(8) Acknowledged Documents. A document accompanied by a certificate of acknowledgment that is lawfully executed by a notary public or another officer who is authorized to take acknowledgments.

(9) Commercial Paper and Related Documents. Commercial paper, a signature on it, and related documents, to the extent allowed by general commercial law.

(10) Presumptions Under a Federal Statute. A signature, document, or anything else that a federal statute declares to be presumptively or prima facie genuine or authentic.

(11) Certified Domestic Records of a Regularly Conducted Activity. The original or a copy of a domestic record that meets the requirements of Rule 803(6)(A)–(C), as shown by a certification of the custodian or another qualified person that complies with a federal statute or a rule prescribed by the Supreme Court. Before the trial or hearing, the proponent must give an adverse party reasonable written notice of the intent to offer the record — and must make the record and certification available for inspection — so that the party has a fair opportunity to challenge them.

(12) Certified Foreign Records of a Regularly Conducted Activity. In a civil case, the original or a copy of a foreign record that meets the requirements of Rule 902(11), modified as follows: the certification, rather than complying with a federal statute or Supreme Court rule, must be signed in a manner that, if falsely made, would subject the maker to a criminal penalty in the country where the certification is signed. The proponent must also meet the notice requirements of Rule 902(11).

Rule 903. Subscribing Witness's Testimony

A subscribing witness's testimony is necessary to authenticate a writing only if required by the law of the jurisdiction that governs its validity.

Rule 1001. Definitions That Apply to This Article

In this article:

(a) A "writing" consists of letters, words, numbers, or their equivalent set down in any form.

(b) A "recording" consists of letters, words, numbers, or their equivalent recorded in any manner.

(c) A "photograph" means a photographic image or its equivalent stored in any form.

(d) An "original" of a writing or recording means the writing or recording itself or any counterpart intended to have the same effect by the person who executed or issued it. For electronically stored information, "original" means any printout — or other output readable by sight — if it accurately reflects the information. An "original" of a photograph includes the negative or a print from it.

(e) A "duplicate" means a counterpart produced by a mechanical, photographic, chemical, electronic, or other equivalent process or technique that accurately reproduces the original.

Rule 1002. Requirement of the Original

An original writing, recording, or photograph is required in order to prove its content unless these rules or a federal statute provides otherwise.

Rule 1003. Admissibility of Duplicates

A duplicate is admissible to the same extent as the original unless a genuine question is raised about the original's authenticity or the circumstances make it unfair to admit the duplicate.

Rule 1004. Admissibility of Other Evidence of Content

An original is not required and other evidence of the content of a writing, recording, or photograph is admissible if:

(a) all the originals are lost or destroyed, and not by the proponent acting in bad faith;

(b) an original cannot be obtained by any available judicial process;

(c) the party against whom the original would be offered had control of the original; was at that time put on notice, by pleadings or otherwise, that the original would be a subject of proof at the trial or hearing; and fails to produce it at the trial or hearing; or

(d) the writing, recording, or photograph is not closely related to a controlling issue.

Rule 1005. Copies of Public Records to Prove Content

The proponent may use a copy to prove the content of an official record — or of a document that was recorded or filed in a public office as authorized by law — if these conditions are met: the record or document is otherwise admissible; and the copy is certified as correct in accordance with Rule 902(4) or is testified to be correct by a witness who has compared it with the original. If no such copy can be obtained by reasonable diligence, then the proponent may use other evidence to prove the content.

Rule 1006. Summaries to Prove Content

The proponent may use a summary, chart, or calculation to prove the content of voluminous writings, recordings, or photographs that cannot be conveniently examined in court. The proponent must make the originals or duplicates available for examination or copying, or both, by other parties at a reasonable time and place. And the court may order the proponent to produce them in court.

Rule 1007. Testimony or Statement of a Party to Prove Content

The proponent may prove the content of a writing, recording, or photograph by the testimony, deposition, or written statement of the party against whom the evidence is offered. The proponent need not account for the original.

Rule 1008. Functions of the Court and Jury

Ordinarily, the court determines whether the proponent has fulfilled the factual conditions for admitting other evidence of the content of a writing, recording, or photograph under Rule 1004 or 1005. But in a jury trial, the jury determines — in accordance with Rule 104(b) — any issue about whether:

(a) an asserted writing, recording, or photograph ever existed;

(b) another one produced at the trial or hearing is the original; or

(c) other evidence of content accurately reflects the content.

* * * * *

§ 13.01   AUTHENTICATION AND IDENTIFICATION

[A]   Requirement of Authentication

"The requirement of authentication or identification as a condition precedent to admissibility is satisfied by evidence sufficient to support a finding that the matter in question is what its proponent claims." FRE 901(a).

"Authentication and identification represent a special aspect of relevancy. . . . Wigmore describes the need for authentication as 'an inherent logical necessity.' " Advisory Committee Note, FRE 901.

In a sense, all evidence admitted at trial must first be authenticated, including witnesses, and not just because of the express rule on authentication, FRE 901. Authentication involves laying a foundation showing that evidence is relevant and, at least to a certain extent, reliable — that the evidence is what it purports to be. Authentication, therefore, can be viewed as a special type of foundational relevancy requirement that applies to a wide variety of evidence. It also addresses another type of relevancy problem. If the evidence is not authentic, it likely will be irrelevant or misleading in the attempt to prove the case. For example, a knife produced at trial will be helpful only if it is relevant to resolving the issues in the case (e.g., it is the knife used in the killing at issue or it is sufficiently similar to the alleged knife to be used for demonstrative purposes). Similarly, a photograph must be a fair and accurate representation of whatever it depicts or else it will be misleading. Even witnesses must be authentic, meaning helpful to resolving the issues in the case, or else they will serve to waste judicial economy and distract jurors from their fact-finding responsibilities.

The FRE on the subject, 901, 902, and 903, focus on specific authentication problems. The major issue at trial is determining what method will be sufficient to authenticate each kind of evidence. FRE 901 provides some assistance in this endeavor. It lists some methods of authentication that are used in common situations. For example, FRE 901 discusses ways to authenticate voices, handwriting, and telephone conversations. *See* FRE 901(b).

FRE 902 provides help with a different issue: forms of evidence that everyone knows are authentic, but will require considerable expenditures of time and effort to formally lay the foundation. In these instances, the rule spares a party the trouble of formally offering evidence (and minimizes the disruption to those who would otherwise be asked to testify to lay the foundation) by creating a category of "self-authenticating" evidence. This does not mean that the evidence itself does the actual authenticating. Instead, like judicially noticed evidence, this category of evidence simply bypasses the formalities of laying the foundation. Other objections to the admissibility of evidence can still be raised, just not one based on the lack of foundation.

The category of self-authenticating evidence includes, for example, certified copies of public records such as convictions of crimes, newspapers, periodicals, trade inscriptions, and commercial paper. *See* FRE 902.

[B]   Procedures for Authentication

The authentication and introduction of evidence generally proceed in the following fashion. After evidence is marked, identified, and shown to opposing counsel, there are three traditional questions to ask the witness who is authenticating it:

1. Do you recognize prosecution/plaintiff/defendant's Exhibit #1 for identification purposes?

2. What is Exhibit #1 for identification purposes?

3. How do you recognize it?

These three questions form the basic core of laying a foundation. Additional questions are sometimes required. Real or documentary evidence can be modified or altered. For example, a shotgun can be sawed off, a document can be erased or changed, and metal can rust or erode. Consequently, a fourth question is usually required to ensure that the real or documentary evidence has not been changed in such a way as to make it unfairly prejudicial.

4. Witness, is Exhibit #1 for identification purposes in substantially the same condition as it was when you last saw it on June 5th of this year?

An additional requirement may arise for evidence that is susceptible to changes in its condition between the time the evidence is gathered and the time it is presented in court. In such cases, authentication is not complete with the asking of the four "magic" questions — a "chain of custody" for the evidence must be shown as well. A chain of custody traces custody of the evidence from its source, such as the crime scene in a criminal case or the accident scene in a personal injury action, all the way to the courtroom, and shows that no alteration or tampering has occurred. For example, narcotics or an ordinary kitchen knife must be traced to the crime scene to ensure that the evidence has not been tampered with or altered. The chain-of-custody requirement helps ensure that evidence is what it purports to be.

A chain of custody is not always necessary. An item that is unique and therefore readily identifiable does not require such a foundation. To illustrate, a specially designed pearl-handled, neon green knife with the word "Mom" inlaid in jade on the handle likely will be considered unique, which would abrogate the need to establish a chain of custody. Further, non-unique real evidence sometimes can be made unique. A plain, ordinary knife, for example, will become unique if a witness's initials and the date of recovery are etched into its handle.

For representative evidence, such as photographs, the inquiry focuses not on the likelihood of alteration, but on the accuracy of the evidence. Photographs may distort and not simply reproduce pertinent information. A photograph of an intersection on a bright, sunny day may be substantially different from a photograph of the same intersection during stormy conditions, which may have prevailed at the time in question. Further, the physical characteristics of an intersection can change dramatically over time. Thus, a fourth question is required to authenticate representative evidence.

5. Is Exhibit #1 for identification purposes a fair and accurate representation of what it depicts as of a particular time and date (i.e., when the incident in question occurred)?

If evidence is authenticated, it may then be offered by a party "into evidence" at any time during the party's case. The offer need not occur when the authenticating witness is on the witness stand, although that is the most common and most appropriate time. Offering the evidence while the witness is on the stand affords the party the opportunity to repair any problems that might arise with the offer. The court will usually ask for objections prior to admitting the evidence. It also may permit a brief voir dire by the opposing party concerning authentication. When a party conducts a voir dire on an exhibit, it is essentially a miniature cross-examination restricted to the question of whether a proper foundation has been laid for admissibility.

If evidence is admitted, it is the offering party's responsibility to request that it be "published" (i.e., shown) to the jury. Generally, the court will allow admitted evidence to be published to the jury, subject to exceptions such as easily lost or fragile items. When publication is occurring, the questioning of a witness usually ceases.

As noted above, some evidence is self-authenticating. *See* FRE 902, Advisory Committee's Note. Self-authenticating evidence, such as domestic public documents, both under seal and not under seal, official publications, newspapers and periodicals, and trade inscriptions, among other evidence also can be published to the jury.

[C] Problems

Problem #13-1: Yeah, That's the Ticket

In a complex commercial litigation case, the plaintiff offers various items in evidence. What would the plaintiff have to do, if anything, to authenticate the following evidence? Explain.

1. A telephone conversation.

2. A business associate's handwriting.

3. A *Newsweek* magazine. 902

4. A Diet Coke label.

5. A photograph of the defendant.

6. A blueprint of a house.

Problem #13-2: Authenticate This . . .

After picking up his daughter from school in their green Town & Country van, Jean turned onto busy Commercial Boulevard. When he looked down to put the Raffi tape into the cassette player, he drifted into the left lane of the road. The driver in the left lane, Dirk, was speeding and not paying attention. In the ensuing crash, Dirk broke his leg, but everyone else was fine. Jean was sued by Dirk. In this lawsuit, how would you authenticate the following:

1. A photograph of the scene of the auto accident.

2. The statement of a bystander, who happened to be a C.P.A.

3. The report of the emergency room physician after treating Dirk.

4. The police officer's accident report.

5. A can of Budweiser beer recovered from the backseat of Dirk's car.

Problem #13-3: Not So Sweet

Rick and Associates, an advertising firm, sued Sarah's Pastries for breach of contract. Rick claimed that Sarah owed him $4,000 for their performance under an agreement to create an advertising campaign. Rick's associate, Pam, had agreed on Rick's behalf to create a print advertising campaign for Sarah's cooking store in several newspapers and trade publications. Sarah's associate, Ben and Pam had signed the agreement after three telephone calls between them. Further, Ben sent back the agreement with a separate piece of paper indicating that Sarah always reserved the right to review any advertising proposal "to her personal satisfaction." Three advertisements were created and run in the various papers after Pam had sent them to Ben via Bay State Messenger Service. Rick requested payment from Sarah, and had not heard any reply after four days.

You represent Sarah's Pastries at trial.

1. What evidence would you offer on Sarah's behalf? How will you authenticate that evidence?

2. What evidence will Rick offer? How will you oppose that evidence?

Problem #13-4: Who Said That?

Tylie Gooding was an executive at Ortuna Web Systems, a business-to-business e-commerce company. During a highly contentious meeting, she observed a heated argument between Paul, the Chief Executive Officer, and Lisette, the Chief Financial Officer. Lisette ended up suing Paul and the company, claiming she had been fired at the meeting. Paul rebutted her claims by alleging that Lisette had quit during the meeting. Tylie is questioned at trial:

PLAINTIFF'S ATTORNEY: Tylie, what did you see at the meeting that occurred in the company boardroom at 3:00 p.m. on the 4th?

A: I saw a ferocious argument between Paul and Lisette over the company's direction. It was a real power struggle that I thought would come to blows.

PLAINTIFF'S ATTORNEY: Tylie, what if anything did you hear while you were at that meeting?

A: Bits and pieces of things. I heard Lisette say something like "we used to make money the old-fashioned way, by earning it," or something like that.

PLAINTIFF'S ATTORNEY: I show you what has been marked Plaintiff's Exhibit A for identification purposes. Do you recognize it?

A: It is a cassette tape.

PLAINTIFF'S ATTORNEY: How do you recognize it?

A: I've seen cassettes before; own a lot, for that matter. I believe I have heard this one as well.

PLAINTIFF'S ATTORNEY: (playing it outside of the hearing of the jury) Do you recognize the contents of this cassette tape?

A: Parts.

PLAINTIFF'S ATTORNEY: How do you recognize parts?

A: I was at the meeting and caught a lot of what they were saying.

PLAINTIFF'S ATTORNEY: Your Honor, I offer in evidence Plaintiff's Exhibit A for Identification Purposes.

JUDGE: Any objections?

DEFENDANT'S ATTORNEY: May I voir dire on the exhibit, Your Honor?

JUDGE: Certainly.

DEFENDANT'S ATTORNEY: Now, you did not record this audiotape, did you, Tylie?

A: No, sir.

DEFENDANT'S ATTORNEY: You don't remember all of what was said, only parts, right?

A: True, but large parts of it.

DEFENDANT'S ATTORNEY: You don't know who handled this tape prior to it appearing in court or whether it has been the subject of tampering?

A: True.

DEFENDANT'S ATTORNEY: I object, Your Honor, to the admission of the tape. There may be a break in the chain of custody and Tylie cannot recollect all of the conversation.

If you are the judge, how would you rule on the admissibility of the audiotape? *See United States v. Brown*, 136 F.3d 1176 (7th Cir. 1998).

Problem #13-5: The Piece of Paper

The defendant, Mary Lou's Books, Inc., allegedly failed to fulfill payment on several promissory notes. The plaintiff, Rasheed, of Rasheed's Book Supplies, testifies in an action for nonpayment about the notes. Rasheed's counsel wishes to introduce the notes in evidence. What must counsel do to authenticate the notes? Explain.

Problem #13-6: He Just Wrote Me a . . .

After Troy's death, his brother Roy brought an action to probate a letter from Troy as the will. The letter stated, "I devise to you, Roy, this 4th day of January in the year 2001, my entire antique car collection worth approximately $1 million." What must Roy show to properly authenticate the letter? Explain.

Problem #13-7: The Chase

Bennard was pulled over by the police on a routine traffic stop. Before the police officer could walk to Bennard's car, he sped away, initiating a high-speed chase. Several people were injured when Bennard crashed his car while traveling at excessive speed. At trial, the prosecution offers an audiotape of the police pursuit, including the voice of the pursuing officers describing what was occurring. If the prosecution offers the affidavit of the police officer speaking on the tape and corroborating eyewitness statements, should a court consider the tape as authenticated?

a. Must a chain of custody be established for the audio tape?

b. Could a lay witness's familiarity with the voices on the tape suffice to lay a foundation?

Problem #13-8: It Is Your Fingerprint, Not Mine

At trial in a case involving the armed robbery of a store, the prosecution offered a gun that was found in the store after the robbery. A fingerprint found on the gun allegedly belonged to the defendant. Defendant claimed it was the police officer's fingerprint, not his. At trial, the prosecution offered a certified copy of a state fingerprint report showing it was the defendant's fingerprint — and the defendant's alone — that was found on the weapon. Should the court admit the copy without a witness to lay a foundation?

Problem #13-9: The Mall

Li Sing was injured at the In Town Shopping Mall when a display fell on her. Li sued the Mall for damages. At trial, Li wanted to introduce a photograph of the area in which the display was maintained. What must counsel do to lay a foundation for the photograph of the display? Please demonstrate what Li must do to lay the proper foundation.

§ 13.02   THE BEST EVIDENCE RULE

[A]   Production of Original Document

"In an earlier day, when discovery and other related procedures were strictly limited, the misleading[ly] named 'best evidence rule' afforded substantial guarantees against inaccuracies and fraud by its insistence upon production of original documents." FRE 1001, Advisory Committee's Note.

The "best evidence rule" imposes a special type of authentication requirement, which is why it is grouped with authentication in this chapter. As the Advisory Committee noted above, this type of evidence — writings — can be quite suspect, given its susceptibility to fraud and distortion. Consequently, the FRE, continuing the tradition of the common law, sought to minimize potential problems by requiring the originals of writings that play a significant role at trial.

The best evidence rule often plays a secondary role in law school evidence courses and even in actual trials. However, objections based on the best evidence rule can cause quite a stir, if only because there are many attorneys and judges who fail to grasp its intricacies. Because of its mystique, the rule often provides a formidable objection, much more formidable than the situation warrants.

As noted above, the so-called "best evidence rule" is actually a misnomer. While appearing to require the "best evidence," the rule really has a much more circumscribed application. It is more accurately described as "the original writings rule" or, as it is sometimes called, the "original documents" rule. The rule applies only when proving the contents of a writing that is related to an issue in a case. For example, the rule would apply to the written contract in a breach of contract action or to a motion picture in an obscenity action. The rule would not apply to an eyewitness to an automobile accident who took notes about the accident but left them at home, since the testimony is being offered to prove the circumstances of the accident, not the contents of the witness's notes.

Even in situations where the rule applies, it is perforated with exceptions. For example, a duplicate generally will suffice instead of the original (*see* FRE 1003), and summaries may be permitted in place of voluminous writings (*see* FRE 1006). While the best evidence rule may have limited applicability and is "fraught with exceptions," there is good reason for it. One apt illustration of its value can be found in *Seiler v. Lucasfilm*, 808 F.2d 1316 (9th Cir. 1986), *cert. denied*, 484 U.S. 826 (1987). In *Seiler*, a graphic artist alleged that filmmaker George Lucas and others infringed the copyright on creatures he had created, called "Garthian Striders." Plaintiff contended that Lucas had used similar creatures, which he called "Imperial Walkers," in the science fiction film, *The Empire Strikes Back*. At trial, the plaintiff intended to offer blow-ups of the Garthian Striders. After a pre-trial evidentiary hearing on the matter, the trial court held that the best evidence rule prevented the plaintiff from offering the blow-ups, and granted summary judgment for the defendants.

The trial court's ruling was based on the fact that the plaintiff could not produce the original drawings of the Garthian Striders, or in the alternative, any evidence of their existence prior to 1980, when *The Empire Strikes Back* was released. Because of the danger of fraud, secondary evidence was excluded.

On appeal, the Ninth Circuit affirmed. The Court stated, "We hold that Seiler's drawings were 'writings' within the meaning of [the best evidence rule]; . . . The contents of Seiler's work are at issue. . . . Since the contents are material and must be proved, Seiler must either produce the original or show that it is unavailable through no fault of his own. . . . This he could not do." 808 F.2d at 1318–1319. In fact, the Ninth Circuit noted that this case supported the very reason for the best evidence rule. Seiler's evidence consisted of reconstructions that apparently were made after the film was released, without any proof that his creations existed prior to the film. The text of this opinion is reprinted in § 13.04.

The best evidence rule applies only to "writings," "recordings," and "photographs," which can include documents, X-rays, motion pictures, and videotapes. *See* FRE 1001(1), (2), 1002. Sometimes, what constitutes a "writing" for the purposes of the rule is unclear. In *United States v. Duffy*, 454 F.2d 809 (5th Cir. 1972), for example, the defendant was convicted of transporting a stolen motor vehicle in interstate commerce. The car contained a suitcase that included a white shirt that had a laundry label reading, "D-U-F." The government offered testimony about the shirt at trial without producing it. In a decision handed down prior to the adoption of the FRE, the Fifth Circuit affirmed the trial court's decision to permit the testimony. The Court of Appeals stated:

> The [best evidence rule] is not, by its terms or because of the policies underlying it, applicable to the instant case. The shirt with a laundry mark would not, under ordinary understanding, be considered a writing, and would not, therefore, be covered by the best evidence rule. When the disputed evidence, such as the shirt in this case, is an object bearing a mark or inscription, and is therefore a chattel and a writing, the trial judge has discretion to treat the evidence as a chattel or as a writing. . . . The shirt was collateral evidence of the crime. Furthermore, it was only one piece of evidence in a substantial case against Duffy. *Id.* at 812.

Under the best evidence rule, disputes about whether a writing ever existed, whether a different writing is the original, or whether other evidence correctly reflects the writing's contents are considered questions of fact to be determined by the trier of fact. FRE 1008. These are not questions of conditional relevance to be determined by the court pursuant to FRE 104(b).

Illustration

Princess Genevieve files an invasion of privacy action against *The Daily Star Mail* tabloid for publishing a photograph of her at a secluded Caribbean hideaway with her new boyfriend, Count Zigfried von Jonk. Does the best evidence rule apply to the production of the photograph at trial?

Answer: The best evidence rule likely applies to the photograph. The photograph is not collateral to the case, but rather is the basis of the cause of action. A photograph also is considered to be a writing pursuant to FRE 1001. Thus, *The Daily Star Mail* must produce the original photograph unless one of the numerous statutory exceptions governs.

[B] Exceptions to Requirement of Original

The flexibility of the "original writing" rule is a prevailing characteristic. As the Advisory Committee stated, "[b]asically the rule requiring the production of the original as proof of contents has developed as a rule of preference: if failure to produce the original is satisfactorily explained, secondary evidence is admissible." FRE 1004, Advisory Committee's Note. This rationale is based on common sense. If a writing is at issue, the writing should be produced for a first-hand review. Production of the writing should not be required, however, if it would not be helpful to resolving the issues of the trial or would involve considerable extra time and expense.

Even when the rule applies, the non-production of the original writing is allowed when:

• A duplicate is offered in lieu of the original. A "duplicate" is a counterpart produced from the original by a technique, such as photography or re-recording, that accurately reproduces the original. *See* FRE 1001(e). A duplicate is allowed in all situations when proving the contents of a writing, except: (1) when there exists a genuine question as to the authenticity of the original writing, such as a dispute over which of the parties possesses the real contract in question; or (2) when the admission of a duplicate would be unfair under the particular circumstances. *See* FRE 1003.

• The original has been lost or destroyed in the absence of bad faith. *See* FRE 1004(a).

• The original is not obtainable by any available judicial process. For example, it is locked away in a safe in a foreign country and cannot be retrieved. *See* FRE 1004(b).

• The original is in the possession of the opposing party. This exception prevents the rule from being used as both a sword and a shield, which would occur if a party possessing the original asks that the opposing party be penalized for not producing the original. *See* FRE 1004(c).

• The writing whose contents are in question is collateral to the issues at trial. *See* FRE 1004(d).

Other limitations on the requirement of providing the original are as follows:

• Copies of public records are permitted to promote judicial economy and avoid "serious inconvenience." *See* FRE 1005, Advisory Committee's Note.

• Summaries of voluminous writings are allowed to promote judicial economy. *See* FRE 1006.

• The testimony, deposition, or written admission of a party opponent about the contents of the writing may be used as proof of the contents without the production of the original. *See* FRE 1007.

[C] Problems

Problem #13-10: Hagar

Harold Hagar was hired to build a porch on Paulette Pogo's house. Hagar claimed he was not paid for the job after completing it, so he brought suit. At trial, the only issue was whether Hagar completed the work. Hagar testified in his case-in-chief.

PLAINTIFF'S ATTORNEY: Hagar, are you employed?

A: Yes, I am a licensed building contractor.

DEFENDANT'S ATTORNEY: Objection. Since Hagar is testifying about a written license, he is violating the best evidence rule.

1. Is the defense counsel correct? Why?

PLAINTIFF'S ATTORNEY: Who did the work on the infrastructure of the deck?

A: Johnny Red Walker.

DEFENDANT'S ATTORNEY: Objection. Johnny Red Walker is the best witness to testify about who did the work on the deck. This testimony violates the best evidence rule.

2. Is the defense counsel correct? Why?

PLAINTIFF'S ATTORNEY: What was your role in the project?

A: I supervised construction and kept copious records on a daily basis of who did what.

DEFENDANT'S ATTORNEY: Objection. Again, Your Honor, Hagar's testimony is in violation of the best evidence rule. Hagar must bring in the records and then properly authenticate them as business records.

3. Is the defense counsel correct? Why?

Problem #13-11: Sweet Suit

The plaintiff, Ethel, sued the defendant, Rose, for breach of contract involving the sale of chocolate bars on March 12th. The sole issue at trial was whether the number of bars stated in the contract was 3,800 or 38,000. The defendant offers a duplicate of the contract at trial.

Will a duplicate suffice? Explain.

Problem #13-12: More Breach

In the same breach of contract action as in the previous problem, the defendant Rose contends that the original contract was washed away in a huge rainstorm that destroyed her office. She only managed to save a copy of it.

Will the defendant be able to offer a copy of the contract in lieu of the original? Explain.

Problem #13-13: Meet the Jetsons

Plaintiff, the Jetson Motor Credit Company, sued the defendant for allegedly failing to make a $5,500 payment on defendant's new Astro electric car. At trial, the defendant, Elroy, offers a duplicate of his payment receipt.

Will the duplicate receipt violate the best evidence rule? Explain.

Problem #13-14: Elroy Was Here

Elroy subsequently brings suit for an alleged overpayment to Jetson. Jetson defends by claiming that no overpayment occurred and that he had a receipt to prove it. At trial, Jetson forgets to bring in the receipt, but still testifies about the payment. Elroy objects to the testimony, claiming that testimony about the payment without the receipt violates the best evidence rule.

How should the judge rule on this question?

Problem #13-15: All Business

To prove that a famous person had been present on the San Diego boat, *All Business*, the plaintiff offers the duplicate of a photograph taken of the famous individual on the boat.

Is the duplicate admissible? Why?

Problem #13-16: I Confess!

Defendant Magoo is charged with a crime. After orally confessing to the police, the defendant signs a verbatim written version of his confession. At trial, the police forget to bring the written confession, but attempt to testify about the oral confession anyway.

May a police officer who heard the confession testify to it? Why?

Problem #13-17: Dat's Da Guy

Hillerich is charged with bank robbery of the National Bank. Bradley, the teller who was robbed, testifies for the prosecution. He is shown a copy of a photograph of the robbery taken by the bank surveillance camera. Bradley then is asked to verify the people and their locations depicted in the photograph. Bradley also indicates that the photograph shows the robber carrying a gun in his belt. (Bradley does not independently remember seeing the gun on the assailant during the robbery because of Bradley's fear at the time.)

1. Does this testimony violate the best evidence rule? Why?

2. What significance is there, if any, that the defendant contests the authenticity of the photograph?

Problem #13-18: Roll the Videotape, Please

Barnaby sues NBS Television for distributing a videotape in which NBS made allegedly libelous statements about him. At trial, Barnaby testifies about the tape, but does not bring it with him.

1. Does Barnaby's testimony violate the best evidence rule? Explain.

2. If Barnaby brings a copy of the videotape, does this satisfy the best evidence rule? Explain.

3. The president of NBS was overheard two weeks prior to trial at a cocktail party saying, "Our employee said in that videotape that Barnaby was a slippery snake — so what?" Does Barnaby still have to offer the original videotape?

4. If Barnaby has accidentally destroyed the videotape, what recourse does he have, if any, at trial?

Problem #13-19: Damages

In a workers' compensation action, the primary issue at trial was the plaintiff's earning capacity. Plaintiff testified on direct examination.

PLAINTIFF'S ATTORNEY: How much did you earn in 1992?

A: I earned the amount of —

DEFENDANT'S ATTORNEY: Objection. This testimony violates the best evidence rule, Your Honor.

1. Why does the defense counsel claim that this testimony violates the best evidence rule?

2. What ruling and why?

Problem #13-20: Speaking Spanish.

In a drug prosecution, the prosecution submitted English language translations of Spanish audiotapes involving discussions between an undercover officer and the defendant.

1. Does the best evidence rule apply if no other evidence of the conversations is offered?

2. Do the translations violate the best evidence rule?

§ 13.03   CASES

[A]   Seiler v. Lucasfilm

United States Court of Appeals for the Ninth Circuit
808 F.2d 1316 (9th Cir. 1987)

FARRIS, CIRCUIT JUDGE:

Lee Seiler, a graphic artist and creator of science fiction creatures, alleged copyright infringement by George Lucas and others who created and produced the science fiction movie *The Empire Strikes Back*. Seiler claimed that creatures known as "Imperial Walkers" which appeared in *The Empire Strikes Back* infringed Seiler's copyright on his own creatures called "Garthian Striders." *The Empire Strikes Back* appeared in 1980; Seiler did not obtain his copyright until 1981.

Because Seiler wished to show blown-up comparisons of his creatures and Lucas' Imperial Walkers to the jury at opening statement, the district judge held a pre-trial evidentiary hearing. At the hearing, Seiler could produce no originals of his Garthian Striders nor any documentary evidence that they existed before *The Empire Strikes Back* appeared in 1980. The district judge, applying the best evidence rule, found that Seiler had lost or destroyed the originals in bad faith under Fed.R.Evid. 1004(1) and denied admissibility of any secondary evidence, even the copies that Seiler had deposited with the Copyright Office. With no admissible evidence, Seiler then lost at summary judgment.

Facts

Seiler contends that he created and published in 1976 and 1977 science fiction creatures called Garthian Striders. In 1980, George Lucas released *The Empire Strikes Back*, a motion picture that contains a battle sequence depicting giant machines called Imperial Walkers. In 1981 Seiler obtained a copyright on his Striders, depositing with the Copyright Office "reconstructions" of the originals as they had appeared in 1976 and 1977.

Seiler contends that Lucas' Walkers were copied from Seiler's Striders which were allegedly published in 1976 and 1977. Lucas responds that Seiler did not obtain his copyright until one year after the release of *The Empire Strikes Back* and that Seiler can produce no documents that antedate *The Empire Strikes Back*.

Because Seiler proposed to exhibit his Striders in a blow-up comparison to Lucas' Walkers at opening statement, the district judge held an evidentiary hearing on the admissibility of the "reconstructions" of Seiler's Striders. Applying the "best evidence rule," Fed. R. Evid. 1001–1008, the district court found at the end of a seven-day hearing that Seiler lost or destroyed the originals in bad faith under Rule 1004(1) and that consequently no secondary evidence, such as the post-Empire Strikes Back reconstructions, was admissible. In its opinion the court found specifically that **Seiler** testified falsely, purposefully destroyed or withheld in bad faith the originals, and fabricated and misrepresented the nature of his reconstructions. The district court granted summary judgment to Lucas after the evidentiary hearing.

On appeal, Seiler contends 1) that the best evidence rule does not apply to his works, [and] 2) that if the best evidence rule does apply, Rule 1008 requires a jury determination of the existence and authenticity of his originals. . . .

Discussion

1. Application of the best evidence rule

The best evidence rule embodied in Rules 1001–1008 represented a codification of longstanding common law doctrine. Dating back to 1700, the rule requires not, as its common name implies, the best evidence in every case but rather the production of an original document instead of a copy. Many commentators refer to the rule not as the best evidence rule but as the original document rule.

Rule 1002 states: "To prove the content of a writing, recording, or photograph, the original writing, recording, or photograph is required, except as otherwise provided in these rules or by Act of Congress." Writings and recordings are defined in Rule 1001 as "letters, words, or numbers, or their equivalent, set down by handwriting, typewriting, printing, photostating, photographing, magnetic impulse, mechanical or electronic recording, or other form of data compilation."

The Advisory Committee Note supplies the following gloss:

> Traditionally the rule requiring the original centered upon accumulations of data and expressions affecting legal relations set forth in words and figures. This meant that the rule was one essentially related to writings. Present day techniques have expanded methods of storing data, yet the essential form which the information ultimately assumes for usable purposes is words and figures. Hence the considerations underlying the rule dictate its expansion to include computers, photographic systems, and other modern developments.

Some treatises, whose approach seems more historical than rigorously analytic, opine without support from any cases that the rule is limited to words and figures. 5 *Weinstein's Evidence* (1983), ¶ 1001(1) [01] at 1001–11; 5 Louisell & Mueller, § 550 at 285.

We hold that Seiler's drawings were "writings" within the meaning of Rule 1001(1); they consist not of "letters, words, or numbers" but of "their equivalent." To hold otherwise would frustrate the policies underlying the rule and introduce undesirable inconsistencies into the application of the rule.

In the days before liberal rules of discovery and modern techniques of electronic copying, the rule guarded against incomplete or fraudulent proof. By requiring the possessor of the original to produce it, the rule prevented the introduction of altered copies and the withholding of originals. The purpose of the rule was thus long thought to be one of fraud prevention, but Wigmore pointed out that the rule operated even in cases where fraud was not at issue, such as where secondary evidence is not admitted even though its proponent acts in utmost good faith. Wigmore also noted that if prevention of fraud were the foundation of the rule, it should apply to objects as well as writings, which it does not. 4 Wigmore, *Evidence* § 1180 (Chadbourn rev. 1972).

The modern justification for the rule has expanded from prevention of fraud to a recognition that writings occupy a central position in the law. When the contents of a writing are at issue, oral testimony as to the terms of the writing is subject to a greater risk of error than oral testimony as to events or other situations. The human memory is not often capable of reciting the precise terms of a writing, and when the terms are in dispute only the writing itself, or a true copy, provides reliable evidence. To summarize then, we observe that the importance of the precise terms of writings in the world of legal relations, the fallibility of the human memory as reliable evidence of the terms, and the hazards of inaccurate or incomplete duplication are the concerns addressed by the best evidence rule. . . .

Viewing the dispute in the context of the concerns underlying the best evidence rule, we conclude that the rule applies. McCormick summarizes the rule as follows:

"[I]n proving the terms of a writing, where the terms are material, the original writing must be produced unless it is shown to be unavailable for some reason other than the serious fault of the proponent."

McCormick on Evidence § 230, at 704.

The contents of Seiler's work are at issue. There can be no proof of "substantial similarity" and thus of copyright infringement unless Seiler's works are juxtaposed with Lucas' and their contents compared. Since the contents are material and must be proved, Seiler must either produce the original or show that it is unavailable through no fault of his own. Rule 1004(1). This he could not do.

The facts of this case implicate the very concerns that justify the best evidence rule. Seiler alleges infringement by *The Empire Strikes Back*, but he can produce no documentary evidence of any originals existing before the release of the movie. His secondary evidence does not consist of true copies or exact duplicates but of "reconstructions" made after *The Empire Strikes Back*. In short, Seiler claims that the movie infringed his originals, yet he has no proof of those originals.

The dangers of fraud in this situation are clear. The rule would ensure that proof of the infringement claim consists of the works alleged to be infringed. Otherwise, "reconstructions" which might have no resemblance to the purported original would suffice as proof for infringement of the original. Furthermore, application of the rule here defers to the rule's special concern for the contents of writings. Seiler's claim depends on the content of the originals, and the rule would exclude reconstituted proof of the originals' content. Under the circumstances here, no "reconstruction" can substitute for the original.

Seiler argues that the best evidence rule does not apply to his work, in that it is artwork rather than "writings, recordings, or photographs." He contends that the rule both historically and currently embraces only words or numbers. Neither party has referred us to cases which discuss the applicability of the rule to drawings.

To recognize Seiler's works as writings does not, as Seiler argues, run counter to the rule's preoccupation with the centrality of the written word in the world of legal relations. Just as a contract objectively manifests the subjective intent of the makers, so Seiler's drawings are objective manifestations of the creative mind. The copyright laws give legal protection to the objective manifestations of an artist's ideas, just as the law of contract protects through its multifarious principles the meeting of minds evidenced in the contract. Comparing Seiler's drawings with Lucas' drawings is no different in principle than evaluating a contract and the intent behind it. Seiler's "reconstructions" are "writings" that affect legal relations; their copyrightability attests to that.

A creative literary work, which is artwork, and a photograph whose contents are sought to be proved, as in copyright, defamation, or invasion of privacy, are both covered by the best evidence rule. *See* McCormick, § 232 at 706 n. 9; Advisory Committee's Note to Rule 1002; 5 Louisell & Mueller, § 550 at 285 n. 27. We would be inconsistent to apply the rule to artwork which is literary or photographic but not to artwork of other forms. Furthermore, blueprints, engineering drawings, architectural designs may all lack words or numbers yet still be capable of copyright and susceptible to fraudulent alteration. In short, Seiler's argument would have us restrict the definitions of Rule 1001(1) to "words" and "numbers" but ignore "or their equivalent." We will not do so in the circumstances of this case.

Our holding is also supported by the policy served by the best evidence rule in protecting against faulty memory. Seiler's reconstructions were made four to seven years after the alleged originals; his memory as to specifications and dimensions may have dimmed significantly. Furthermore, reconstructions made after the release of the Empire Strikes Back may be tainted, even if unintentionally, by exposure to the movie. Our holding guards against these problems.

2. Rule 1008.

As we hold that the district court correctly concluded that the best evidence rule applies to Seiler's drawings, Seiler was required to produce his original drawings unless excused by the exceptions set forth in Rule 1004. The pertinent subsection is 1004(1), which provides:

> The original is not required, and other evidence of the contents of a writing, recording, or photograph is admissible if —

> (1) Originals lost or destroyed. All originals are lost or have been destroyed, unless the proponent lost or destroyed them in bad faith . . .

In the instant case, prior to opening statement, Seiler indicated that he planned to show to the jury reconstructions of his "Garthian Striders" during the opening statement. The trial judge would not allow items to be shown to the jury until they were admitted in evidence. Seiler's counsel reiterated that he needed to show the reconstructions to the jury during his opening statement. Hence, the court excused the jury and held a seven-day hearing on their admissibility. At the conclusion of the hearing, the trial judge found that the reconstructions were inadmissible under the best evidence rule as the originals were lost or destroyed in bad faith. This finding is amply supported by the record.

Seiler argues on appeal that regardless of Rule 1004(1), Rule 1008 requires a trial because a key issue would be whether the reconstructions correctly reflect the content of the originals. Rule 1008 provides:

> When the admissibility of other evidence of contents of writings, recordings, or photographs under these rules depends upon the fulfillment of a condition of fact, the question whether the condition has been fulfilled is ordinarily for the court to determine in accordance with the provisions of rule 104. However, when an issue is raised (a) whether the asserted writing ever existed, or (b) whether another writing, recording, or photograph produced at the trial is the original, or (c) whether other evidence of contents correctly reflects the contents, the issue is for the trier of facts to determine as in the case of other issues of fact.

Seiler's position confuses admissibility of the reconstructions with the weight, if any, the trier of fact should give them, after the judge has ruled that they are admissible.

Rule 1008 states, in essence, that when the *admissibility* of evidence other than the original depends upon the fulfillment of a condition of fact, the trial judge generally makes the determination of that condition of fact. The notes of the Advisory Committee are consistent with this interpretation in stating: "Most preliminary questions of fact in connection with applying the rule preferring the original as evidence of contents are for the judge . . . [t]hus the question of . . . fulfillment of other conditions specified in Rule 1004 . . . is for the judge." In the instant case, the condition of fact which Seiler needed to prove was that the originals were not lost or destroyed in bad faith. Had he been able to prove this, his reconstructions would have been admissible and then their accuracy would have been a question for the jury. In sum, since admissibility of the reconstructions was dependent upon a finding that the originals were not lost or destroyed in bad faith, the trial judge properly held the hearing to determine their admissibility.

Affirmed.

[B]　United States v. Duffy

United States Court of Appeals for the Fifth Circuit
454 F.2d 809 (5th Cir. 1972)

WISDOM, CIRCUIT JUDGE:

The defendant-appellant James H. Duffy was convicted by a jury of transporting a motor vehicle in interstate commerce from Florida to California knowing it to have been stolen in violation of 18 U.S.C. § 2312. He was sentenced to imprisonment for a term of two years and six months. On this appeal, Duffy complains of error in the admission of certain evidence and of prejudice resulting from members of the jury having been present during a sentencing in an unrelated case. We affirm.

. . . .

Both the local police officers and the F.B.I. agent testified that the trunk of the stolen car contained two suitcases. Found inside one of the suitcases, according to the witnesses, was a white shirt imprinted with a laundry mark reading "D-U-F." The defendant objected to the admission of testimony about the shirt and asked that the Government be required to produce the shirt. The trial judge overruled the objection and admitted the testimony. This ruling is assigned as error.

The appellant argues that the admission of the testimony violated the best evidence rule. According to his conception of the "Rule," the Government should have been required to produce the shirt itself rather than testimony about the shirt. This contention misses the import of the best evidence rule. The "Rule," as it exists today, may be stated as follows:

> [I]n proving the terms of a *writing*, where such terms are material, the original writing must be produced, unless it is shown to be unavailable for some reason other than the serious fault of the proponent. (Emphasis supplied.)

Although the phrase "best evidence rule" is frequently used in general terms, the "rule" itself is applicable only to the proof of the contents of a writing. . . .

The "Rule" is not, by its terms or because of the policies underlying it, applicable to the instant case. The shirt with a laundry mark would not, under ordinary understanding, be considered a writing and would not, therefore, be covered by the best evidence rule. . . . Because the writing involved in this case was simple, the inscription "D-U-F," there was little danger that the witness would inaccurately remember the terms of the "writing." Also the terms of the "writing" were by no means central or critical to the case against Duffy. The crime charged was not possession of a certain article, where the failure to produce the article might prejudice the defense. The shirt was collateral evidence of the crime. Furthermore, it was only one piece of evidence in a substantial case against Duffy.

§ 13.04 SUMMARY AND REVIEW

1. What kinds of evidence must be authenticated? Why?

2. What is the difference between the authentication of real evidence and the authentication of representative evidence?

3. Why is some evidence self-authenticating?

4. Why is the term "best evidence" rule a misnomer?

5. Describe two situations in which the best evidence rule applies.

6. Name three substitutes that may be offered in lieu of the original writing even when the best evidence rule applies.

Problem #13-21: Money-Back Guarantee

Hassan brought suit against a furniture store, alleging that he had canceled his purchase pursuant to the store's "money-back guarantee." Hassan testified at a trial that he had also requested a refund by mail within the 90-day refund window permitted by the store.

1. To assist with his testimony, Hassan created a worksheet reviewing the timing and description of the events in question. Is the worksheet the best evidence of Hassan's testimony? Does the original writings rule apply?

2. If Hassan wrote down the time and date of the mailing in his records but did not bring the records to court, is the original writings rule violated?

3. To show that the letter was received, Hassan was given a return receipt from the post office. If Hassan testifies about the receipt without bringing it to court, does that violate the original writings rule? Why?

Chapter 14

PROOF ISSUES: THE ALLOCATION O JUDICIAL NOTICE, AND PRESUMPTI(301, 302]

CHAPTER FRAMEWORK: This chapter considers proof issues, namely, when there is too much or too little proof, as well as which party has the burden of providing the proof to win.

WHY ARE THE CONCEPTS IN THIS CHAPTER IMPORTANT? These issues are part of the procedural "rules of trial," and illuminate how to negotiate proof issues.

CONNECTIONS: These procedural mechanisms help frame proof questions at trial and connect to the judge's, jury's and attorneys' roles.

CHAPTER OUTLINE:

    I. Proof Issues

        A. Allocation of proof questions

            1. Types of burdens of proof

                a. Burden of going forward

                b. Burden of persuasion

            2. What quantity of proof is required?

            3. Who wins if there is a "tie"?

        B. Judicial notice

        C. Presumptions

* * * *

RELEVANT EVIDENCE RULES

Rule 201. Judicial Notice of Adjudicative Facts

    (a) Scope. This rule governs judicial notice of an adjudicative fact only, not a legislative fact.

    (b) Kinds of Facts That May Be Judicially Noticed. The court may judicially notice a fact that is not subject to reasonable dispute because it:

        (1) is generally known within the trial court's territorial jurisdiction; or

2) can be accurately and readily determined from sources whose accuracy cannot reasonably be questioned.

(c) Taking Notice. The court:

(1) may take judicial notice on its own; or

(2) must take judicial notice if a party requests it and the court is supplied with the necessary information.

(d) Timing. The court may take judicial notice at any stage of the proceeding.

(e) Opportunity to Be Heard. On timely request, a party is entitled to be heard on the propriety of taking judicial notice and the nature of the fact to be noticed. If the court takes judicial notice before notifying a party, the party, on request, is still entitled to be heard.

(f) Instructing the Jury. In a civil case, the court must instruct the jury to accept the noticed fact as conclusive. In a criminal case, the court must instruct the jury that it may or may not accept the noticed fact as conclusive.

Rule 301. Presumptions in Civil Cases Generally

In a civil case, unless a federal statute or these rules provide otherwise, the party against whom a presumption is directed has the burden of producing evidence to rebut the presumption. But this rule does not shift the burden of persuasion, which remains on the party who had it originally.

Rule 302. Applying State Law to Presumptions in Civil Cases

In a civil case, state law governs the effect of a presumption regarding a claim or defense for which state law supplies the rule of decision.

* * * * *

§ 14.01 INTRODUCTION

Who must prove what often determines which of the parties will win a lawsuit. This initial question is described as the allocation of proof. The allocation decision includes which elements the parties must prove and by what quantum of proof.

The term "burden of proof" has different meanings. The initial burden is often described as the "burden of going forward" or the "production burden." This burden requires a party to offer sufficient evidence so that a reasonable juror could find for the party producing the evidence. The judge, not the jury, decides whether the initial production burden has been met. If this burden is met, enough evidence has been presented to create a jury issue on the element in question. If this burden is not met, then there is insufficient evidence to create a jury question — i.e., a reasonable dispute — about the issue. A directed verdict in a civil case, or a motion for judgment of acquittal by a criminal defendant, may follow.

The heavier or more substantial burden of proof is called the burden of persuasion. This requires the party holding the burden to persuade the trier of fact that the elements of the cause of action, claim, or defense exist. The standard or amount of persuasion required to win depends on the nature of the case. In a criminal case, the burden of persuasion is proof beyond a reasonable doubt. In a civil case, it is proof either by clear and convincing evidence or by a preponderance of the evidence.

While one party usually has both the burden of production and the burden of persuasion on an issue, there are times when these burdens are separated and assigned to different parties. When a separation occurs, one of the parties must first meet the burden of production. If this occurs, the burden shifts to the opposing party, who must then satisfy either a burden of production or a burden of persuasion. Shifting burdens in this manner usually plays an integral role in presumptions.

Special types of proof problems may arise at trial. At times, there is so much available proof of a fact that to require a party to produce such proof would waste judicial resources. In other situations, the opposite problem arises — there is such a shortage of proof of a fact that the party who is assigned the burden is virtually assured of losing on the issue. This lack of proof may be beyond the party's control.

When there is an overabundance of available proof, the mechanism of judicial notice may be used to promote trial efficiency. When there is too little proof available to the party holding the burden, the presumption mechanism may be used to "smoke out" proof and promote a fairer result.

§ 14.02   THE ALLOCATION OF PROOF

The allocation of proof between the parties is not based on a random distribution but rather on various underlying policies. The following excerpt from a law review article by Professor Edward Cleary thoughtfully sets forth the policies that assist in deciding who has to prove what in a lawsuit.

PRESUMING AND PLEADING: AN ESSAY ON JURISTIC IMMATURITY

12 Stan. L. Rev. 5 (1959)[1]

By Edward W. Cleary

The Substantive Law

Since all are agreed that procedure exists only for the purpose of putting the substantive law effectively to work, a preliminary look at the nature of substantive law, as viewed procedurally, is appropriate.

Every dog, said the common law, is entitled to one bite. This result was reached from reasoning that man's best friend was not in general dangerous, and hence the owner should not be liable when the dog departed from his normally peaceable pursuits and inflicted injury. Liability should follow only when the owner had reason to know of the dangerous proclivities of his dog, and the one bite afforded notice of

---

[1] Copyright © 1959 by the Stanford Law Review. Reprinted with permission.

those proclivities. So the formula for holding a dog owner liable at common law is: + *ownership* + *notice of dangerous character* + *biting.*

This rule of law becomes monotonous to postmen. Hence the postmen cause to be introduced in the legislature a bill making owners of dogs absolutely liable, *i.e.,* eliminating notice from the formula for liability. At the hearing on the bill, however, the dog lovers appear and, while admitting the justness of the postmen's complaint, point out that a dog ought at least to be entitled to defend himself against human aggression. Then the home owners' lobby points out the usefulness of dogs in guarding premises against prowlers. Balancing these factors, there emerges a statute making dog owners liable for bites inflicted except upon persons tormenting the dog or unlawfully on the owner's premises. The formula for liability now becomes: + *ownership* + *biting - being tormented - unlawful presence on the premises.*

So in any given situation, the law recognizes certain elements as material to the case, and the presence or absence of each of them is properly to be considered in deciding the case. Or, to rephrase in somewhat more involved language, rules of substantive law are "statements of the specific factual conditions upon which specific legal consequences depend. . . . Rules of substantive law are conditional imperatives, having the form: *If* such and such *and* so and so, *etc.* is the case, *and unless* such and such *or unless* so and so, *etc.* is the case, *then* the defendant is liable. . . ." Now obviously the weighing and balancing required to determine what elements ought to be considered material cannot be accomplished by any of the methodologies of procedure. The result is purely a matter of substantive law, to be decided according to those imponderables which travel under the name of jurisprudence.

This view of the substantive law may seem unduly Euclidean, yet some system of analysis and classification is necessary if the law is to possess a measure of continuity and to be accessible and usable.

Prima Facie Case and Defense

Under our adversary method of litigation a trial is essentially not an inquest or investigation but rather a demonstration conducted by the parties.

Since plaintiff is the party seeking to disturb the existing situation by inducing the court to take some measure in his favor, it seems reasonable to require him to demonstrate his right to relief. How extensive must this demonstration be? Should it include every substantive element, which either by its existence or nonexistence may condition his right to relief? If the answer is "yes," then plaintiff under our dog statute would be required to demonstrate each of the elements in the formula: + *ownership* + *biting - tormented - illegal presence on the premises.*

In the ordinary dog case this would not be unduly burdensome, but if the suit is on a contract and we require plaintiff to establish the existence or nonexistence, as may be appropriate, of every concept treated in Corbin and Williston, then the responsibility of plaintiff becomes burdensome indeed and the lawsuit itself may include a large amount of unnecessary territory. Actually, of course, the responsibility for dealing with every element is not placed on plaintiff. Instead we settle for a "prima facie case" or "cause of action," consisting of certain selected elements which are regarded as sufficient to entitle plaintiff to recover, *if* he proves them and *unless* defendant in turn establishes other elements which would offset them. Thus in a simple contract case, by establishing + *offer* + *acceptance* + *consideration* + *breach*, plaintiff is entitled to recover, unless defendant establishes *accord and satisfaction or* + *failure of consideration or* + *illegality or* - *capacity to contract*, and so on.

Observe that the plus and minus signs change, in accord with proper mathematical rules, when we shift elements to the defendant's side of the equation as "defenses." For example, if plaintiff were required to deal with capacity to contract, it would become + *capacity to contract* as a part of his case, rather than the - *capacity to contract* of defendant's case.

Defenses, too, may be prima facie only and subject to being offset by further matters produced by plaintiff, as in the case of the defense of release, offset by the further fact of fraud in the inducement for the release. The entire process is the familiar confessing and avoiding of the common law.

Allocating the Elements

The next step to be taken is the determination whether a particular material element is a part of plaintiff's prima facie case or a defense. Or, referring back to the statement that rules of substantive law are "conditional imperatives, having the form: *If* such and such *and* so and so, *etc.*, is the case . . . *then* the defendant is liable," should the element in question be listed as an *if* or as an *unless*?

In some types of situations, the test has been purely mechanical, with the mechanics in turn likely to be accidental and casual. Thus, in causes of action based on statute, if an exception appears in the enacting clause, *i.e.*, the clause creating the right of action, then the party relying on the statute must show that the case is not within the exception; otherwise the responsibility for bringing the case within an exception falls upon the opposite party. The principle is widely recognized, but the vagaries of statutory draftsmanship detract largely from its certainty of application. Returning to our dogs, two statutes will serve as illustrations.

> "If any dog shall do any damage to either the body or property of any person, the owner . . . shall be liable for such damage, unless such damage shall have been occasioned to the body or property of a person who, at the time such damage was sustained, was committing a trespass or other tort, or was teasing, tormenting or abusing such dog." MASS. ANN. LAWS ch. 140 § 155 (1950).

> "Every person owning or harboring a dog shall be liable to the party injured for all damages done by such dog; but no recovery shall be had for personal injuries to any person when they [sic] are upon the premises of the owner of the dog after night, or upon the owner's premises engaged in some unlawful act in the day time." KY. LAWS 1906, ch. 10, at 25, KY. STATS. 1936 § 68a-5.

The Massachusetts statute was construed as imposing on a two and one quarter year old plaintiff the burden of establishing that he was not teasing, tormenting or abusing the dog, while under the Kentucky statute a plaintiff was held to have stated a prima facie case by alleging only that he was bitten by a dog owned by defendant, leaving questions of presence on the premises at night or unlawful activities in the day time to be brought in as defenses. The difference in result can scarcely be regarded as calculated but is typical. Unfortunately, the statute which states in so many words the procedural effects of its terms is a rarity.

Exceptions in contracts receive similar treatment. If the words of promising are broad, followed by exceptions, the general disposition is to place on defendant the responsibility of invoking the exception. Of course, many of the cases involve insurance policies, with all that implies. In *Munro Brice & Co. v. War Risks Ass'n*, during World War I, one underwriter insured plaintiffs' ship against loss due to hostilities and another underwriter insured it against perils of the sea except consequences of hostilities. The ship was lost, and plaintiffs sued on both policies. The King's Bench Division held that as regards the first policy plaintiffs must show the loss to have been due to hostilities, but that under the second policy merely establishing the loss was sufficient, leaving it to the underwriter to bring in loss by hostilities as a defense. Since evidence of the cause of loss was wholly lacking, the loss fell on the second underwriter.

Julius Stone commented as follows:

> Every qualification of a class can equally be stated without any changes of meaning as an exception to a class not so qualified. Thus the proposition "All animals have four legs except gorillas," and the proposition "all animals which are not gorillas have four legs," are, so far as their meanings are concerned, identical. . . .

> If the distinction becomes an element of the rule and an exception to it does not represent any distinction in meaning, it may still remain a valid distinction for legal purposes. In that case, however, it must turn upon something other than the meaning of the propositions involved. It may turn, for instance, merely upon their relative form or order.

So in a few kinds of cases the answer to the question of allocation is found in the structure of a statute or contract, perhaps with some tenuous reference to intent, either of the legislature or of the contracting parties. But what of the great bulk of the cases, involving neither exception in a statute nor limitation upon words of promising? What general considerations should govern the allocation of responsibility for the elements of the case between the parties?

Precedent may settle the manner in a particular jurisdiction, but precedent as such does nothing for the inquiring mind. Thayer was of the view that questions of allocation were to be referred to the principles of pleading, or perhaps to analysis of the substantive law, and "one has no right to look to the law of evidence for a solution of such questions as these. . . ." Books about pleading, however, have not been numerous in recent years, except for the local practice works; and aside from a brief but provocative treatment by Judge Clark they offer slight assistance. The substantive law texts, when they deal with the matter at all, tend to describe results rather than reasons.

Despite Thayer's strictures, his descendants in the field of writing about evidence, by assuming to deal with problems of burden of proof as an aspect of law of evidence, have found themselves inevitably enmeshed in the problems of allocation and have contributed most of the literature on the subject, although in an introductory and incidental fashion.

Before trying to establish some bench marks for allocation, let us note, though only for the purpose of rejecting them, two which are sometimes suggested. (a) That the burden is on the party having the affirmative; or, conversely stated, that a party is not required to prove a negative. This is no more than a play on words, since practically any proposition may be stated in either affirmative or negative form. Thus a plaintiff's exercise of ordinary care equals absence of contributory negligence, in the minority jurisdictions which place this element in plaintiff's case. In any event, the proposition seems simply not to be so. (b) That the burden is on the party to whose case the element is essential. This does no more than restate the question.

Actually the reported decisions involving problems of allocation rarely contain any satisfying disclosure of the *ratio decidendi.* Implicit, however, seem to be considerations of policy, fairness and probability. None affords a complete working rule. Much overlap is apparent, as sound policy implies not too great a departure from fairness, and probability may constitute an aspect of both policy and fairness. But despite the vagueness of their generality, it is possible to pour enough content into these concepts to give them some real meaning.

(1) *Policy.* As Judge Clark remarks, "One who must bear the risk of getting the matter properly set before the court, if it is to be considered at all, has to that extent the dice loaded against him." While policy more obviously predominates at the stage of determining what elements are material, its influence may nevertheless extend into the state of allocating those elements by way of favoring one or the other party to a particular kind of litigation. Thus a court which is willing to permit a recovery for negligence may still choose to exercise restraints by imposing on plaintiff the burden of freedom from contributory negligence, as a theoretical, though perhaps not a practical, handicap. Or the bringing of actions for defamation may in some measure be discouraged by allocating untruth to plaintiff as an element of his prima facie case, rather than by treating truth as an affirmative defense. And it must be apparent that a complete lack of proof as to a particular element moves allocation out of the class of a mere handicap and makes it decisive as to the element, and perhaps as to the case itself. In *Summers v. Tice,* plaintiff was hunting with two defendants and was shot in the eye when both fired simultaneously at the same bird. The court placed on each defendant the burden of proving that his shot did not cause the injury. To discharge this burden was impossible, since each gun was loaded with identical shot. In *Munro, Brice & Co. v. War Risks Ass'n,*, the absence of proof of the cause of the ship's loss meant that the party on whom that burden was cast lost the case. In these cases the admonition of Julius Stone is particularly apt: "the Courts should not essay the impossible task of making the bricks of judge-made law without handling the straw of policy."

(2) *Fairness.* The nature of a particular element may indicate that evidence relating to it lies more within the control of one party, which suggests the fairness of allocating that element to him. Examples are payment, discharge in bankruptcy, and license, all of which are commonly treated as affirmative defenses. However, caution in making

any extensive generalization is indicated by the classification of contributory negligence, illegality, and failure of consideration also as affirmative defenses, despite the fact that knowledge more probably lies with plaintiff. Certainly in the usual tort cases, knowledge of his own wrongdoing rests more intimately in defendant, though the accepted general pattern imposes this burden on plaintiff.

(3) *Probability.* A further factor which seems to enter into many decisions as to allocation is a judicial, *i.e.*, wholly nonstatistical, estimate of the probabilities of the situation, with the burden being put on the party who will be benefited by a departure from the supposed norm.

The probabilities may relate to the type of situation out of which the litigation arises or they may relate to the type of litigation itself. The standards are quite different and may produce differences in result. To illustrate: If it be assumed that most people pay their bills, the probabilities are that any bill selected at random has been paid; therefore, a plaintiff suing to collect a bill would be responsible for nonpayment as an element of his prima facie case. If, however, attention is limited to bills upon which suit is brought, a contrary conclusion is reached. Plaintiffs are not prone to sue for paid bills, and the probabilities are that the bill is unpaid. Hence payment would be an affirmative defense. Or again, "guest" statutes prohibit nonpaying passengers from recovering for the negligence of the driver. If most passengers are nonpaying, then the element of compensation for the ride would belong in the prima facie case of the passenger-plaintiff. If, however, most passengers in the litigated cases ride for compensation, then absence of compensation would be an affirmative defense. In the payment-of-a-bill situation the probabilities are estimated with regard to the litigated situation, payment being regarded generally as an affirmative defense, while in the guest situation they are estimated with regard to such situations generally and not limited to those which are litigated, status as a non-guest being part of plaintiff's prima facie case. No reason for the shift is apparent, and it may be unconscious. The litigated cases would seem to furnish the more appropriate basis for estimating probabilities.

Matters occurring after the accrual of the plaintiff's right are almost always placed in the category of affirmative defenses. Examples are payment, release, accord and satisfaction, discharge in bankruptcy, and limitations. A plausible explanation is that a condition once established is likely to continue; hence the burden ought to fall on the party benefited by a change.

In the cases of complete absence of proof, a proper application of the probability factor is calculated to produce a minimum of unjust results, and the same is true, though less impressively, even if proof is available.

1. Are the rationales for allocating the elements in crimes, civil actions, and their defenses readily observable in existing laws? Provide illustrations.

2. Which allocation rationale makes the most sense? Which rationale makes the least sense?

Problem #14-1: Desert Island

A pleasure boat went on a three-hour cruise. The weather started getting rough and the tiny ship was eventually shipwrecked. The seven survivors decided that they should create a tribal criminal code for their new community, including a provision defining the crime of robbery. The first problem was deciding which of the following elements should be proven by the prosecution and which by the defense: (1) larceny; (2) by force or fear from a person or that person's presence; (3) duress; (4) sanity; (5) lack of permission; and (6) intoxication.

> 1. Which of these six elements should be proven by the prosecution? Which should be proven by the defense? Explain why you allocated certain elements to the prosecution and certain elements to the defense.

> 2. The survivors also decided to prohibit "harassment." What should the elements of this offense include? Who should prove what?

§ 14.03   JUDICIAL NOTICE [FRE 201]

[A]   Introduction

As the Advisory Committee's Note to FRE 201 explains:

> The usual method of establishing adjudicative facts is through the introduction of evidence, ordinarily consisting of the testimony of witnesses. If particular facts are outside the area of reasonable controversy, this process is dispensed with as unnecessary. A high degree of indisputability is the essential prerequisite.

The judicial notice mechanism may be triggered when the fact to be proven is either so "well known within the jurisdiction" of the trial court or so "capable of accurate and ready determination" by reliance on unimpeachable sources that it is not subject to reasonable dispute. FRE 201. Requiring proof in such situations would waste time and risk improper alternative evaluations by the trier of fact. Consequently, these types of facts are properly subject to judicial notice and admitted in evidence without proof.

FRE 201 distinguishes between legislative and adjudicative facts, permitting judicial notice only of the latter. Adjudicative facts are specific to the parties to the lawsuit. Legislative facts "are those which have relevance to legal reasoning and the law-making process." FRE 201, Advisory Committee's Note. Thus, legislative facts deal with policies that are much broader than the particular case.

Illustrations: Adjudicative Facts

1. That Nationalist Movement rallies were quite often loud and attracted noisy counter-demonstrations. *See Nationalist Movement v. City of Cumming*, 913 F.2d 885 (11th Cir.), *vacated and reh'g granted and vacated*, 921 F.2d 1125 (11th Cir. 1990), *cert. denied*, 111 S. Ct. 767 (1991).

2. That the State of New York has no legal firearms manufacturer within the state. *See United States v. Ramirez*, 910 F.2d 1069 (2d Cir.), *cert. denied*, 498 U. S. 990 (1990).

3. That a person had been convicted of murder (in lieu of a certified copy of the conviction). *See Kowalski v. Gagne*, 914 F.2d 299 (1st Cir. 1990).

4. That the average walking speed of a human being is two to three miles per hour. *See Holst v. United States*, 755 F. Supp. 260 (E.D. Mo. 1991).

5. That 940 St. Nicholas Avenue is in the Borough of Manhattan. *See United States v. Spagnuolo*, 168 F.2d 768 (2d Cir.), *cert. denied*, 335 U.S. 824 (1948).

6. That heroin is a narcotic. *See United States v. Marizal*, 421 F.2d 836 (5th Cir. 1970).

7. That certain DNA profiling procedures are used. *See United States v. Jakobetz*, 955 F.2d 786 (2d Cir.), *cert. denied*, 506 U.S. 834 (1992).

Illustrations: Judicial Notice

1. At issue in a case is whether the National Zoo is located in Washington, D.C. Should the District Court take judicial notice of where the National Zoo is located?

Answer: Judicial notice of the location of the National Zoo is appropriate. Its location is both generally known within the court's jurisdiction and capable of accurate and ready determination, to the extent that the fact is not subject to reasonable dispute. *See* FRE 201(b).

2. In the same case, the court considered whether a particular motion was untimely. Can the court take judicial notice of the fact that during the Christmas-New Year's holiday season, the U.S. mail is used with greater frequency and is generally slower than at other times of the year?

Answer: Judicial notice of the frequency and timeliness of the mail during the Christmas-New Year's holiday season is appropriate as well. This is an adjudicative fact relating to the particular case at hand. This fact also is not subject to reasonable dispute. It is capable of accurate and ready determination through statistics about U.S. mail delivery during the Christmas season. Requiring proof of this fact would be time-consuming and of little value.

[B] Problems

Problem #14-2: "Yes!"

In a case involving the Chicago Bulls, the judge is asked to take judicial notice of the fact that Michael Jordan was voted the "most valuable player" for the 1991–1992 National Basketball Association season. Should the court take judicial notice of this fact? Why?

Problem #14-3: Divorce!

In a divorce action, the petitioner asks the court to take judicial notice that adversarial testimony of parents in the presence of young children is bad policy and would destroy the family unit. Should the court take judicial notice?

Problem #14-4: Trespass

Dave is sued for trespassing on another person's property. At issue in the case is whether it was still light out at the time Dave allegedly trespassed. Dave asked the court to take judicial notice that it was dark out at the time he allegedly entered the property. Should the court take judicial notice?

Problem #14-5: Desegregation!

In a desegregation suit brought in Los Angeles, California, the plaintiff asked the court to take judicial notice of the Supreme Court decision in *Brown v. Board of Education*, 347 U.S. 483 (1954). Should the district court take judicial notice?

Problem #14-6: "We The People"

An issue in a recent lawsuit concerned the exact dates of the Constitutional Convention.

   1. Can the court take judicial notice that the Constitutional Convention took place from May 25 through September 17, 1787?

   2. Would it be appropriate to take judicial notice of the fact that there was a rule of secrecy requiring the framers to close the windows during their discussions?

   3. Can the court take judicial notice of the fact that Rhode Island was the only state that did not attend the convention?

Problem #14-7: Boiling Point

The plaintiff alleges that the defendant threw boiling water at her. Plaintiff asks the court to take judicial notice that water boils at 212 degrees Fahrenheit. Is judicial notice proper?

Problem #14-8: Sweet Moosic

A rock band brings suit for copyright infringement. To show the amount of damages, it uses the record sales of another similar folk-rock band, the Karaoke Kings. The judge happens to be very familiar with the band, even though most people in that jurisdiction have never heard of such a group. Should the judge take judicial notice that the Karaoke Kings band plays music similar to that of the plaintiffs?

Problem #14-9: Admiral T

Davey Jones brings an admiralty suit against June Locker as a result of a boating accident that occurred in the Atlantic Ocean approximately ten miles off of the Maryland coast. Jones asks the court to take judicial notice of maritime law. Should the court take judicial notice?

Problem #14-10: More JN

A federal district court should take judicial notice of which of the following? Explain your answers.

1. A standard chemical dictionary in a case involving some of the chemicals listed.

2. A death certificate on record in the appropriate bureau of records.

3. In a case involving the National Hockey League, the fact that ice hockey is a very rough and physical contact sport.

4. In a case involving a bank loan, the prevailing interest rates at the time the loan was made.

5. In a lawsuit involving the length of time it took to receive a particular letter, the fact that it takes mail from Baltimore to Puerto Rico at least four days to arrive at its destination.

6. The fact that United States geological survey maps show there were numerous geological breaks across the Spokane River in 1911.

7. The contents of a municipal ordinance.

8. In an asbestosis action, the proposition that exposure to asbestos causes cancer.

Problem #14-11: Judicially Noticed

1. In a breach of contract action brought by Rose Hosiery Mills, Inc. against Burlington Hosiery Mills, Inc., can the court take judicial notice that socks and sweaters are usually prepared through a process involving knitting?

2. In an action involving the redistricting of certain voting districts in Kentucky, the judge wishes to take judicial notice of the location of the state capitol. One of the parties, an out-of-state attorney, says "We do not object to the court taking judicial notice of the state capitol. Is it pronounced 'Louie'ville or 'Low-e'ville, Your Honor?" The judge replied, "It is pronounced 'Frankfort' counsel, and I will take judicial notice." Is judicial notice proper? Explain.

3. If the redistricting case was appealed, could the appellate court take judicial notice as to the location of certain towns in Kentucky? Why?

4. In a robbery trial, the court took judicial notice of the effect of a certain anesthetic in ruling that the defendant's confession was involuntary. The judge relied solely on his own experience with this anesthetic. Was the judge's decision proper?

Problem #14-12: What Flavor Would You Like?

Sims became sick after eating a pink-colored ice cream called "Power Rangers Redux" at the local ice cream store. At a subsequent trial, the court took judicial notice that the color of ice cream reflects its flavor. Was this action appropriate?

a. Suppose the judge in the same case noted that he had used the road in front of the ice cream store on many occasions and that he would take judicial notice of the fact that the road was "heavily traveled." Allowed?

[C] Rules Comparison

Compare FRE 201 to the following state rule.

Kansas Statutes Annotated § 60-409 (1983). Facts Which Must or May Be Judicially Noticed

(a) Judicial notice shall be taken without request by a party, of the common law, constitutions and public statutes in force in every state, territory and jurisdiction of the United States, and of such specific facts and propositions of generalized knowledge as are so universally known that they cannot reasonably be the subject of dispute.

(b) Judicial notice may be taken without request by a party, of (1) private acts and resolutions of the Congress of the United States and of the legislature of this state, and duly enacted ordinances and duly published regulations of governmental subdivisions or agencies of this state, and (2) the laws of foreign countries and (3) such facts as are so generally known or of such common notoriety within the territorial jurisdiction of the court that they cannot reasonably be the subject of dispute, and (4) specific facts and propositions of generalized knowledge which are capable of immediate and accurate determination by resort to easily accessible sources of indisputable accuracy.

(c) Judicial notice shall be taken of each matter specified in subsection (b) of this section if a party requests it and (1) furnishes the judge sufficient information to enable him or her properly to comply with the request and (2) has given each adverse party such notice as the judge may require to enable the adverse party to prepare to meet the request.

§ 14.04 PRESUMPTIONS [FRE 301, 302]

[A] Introduction

Presumptions are not themselves evidence; instead, they are ways of dealing with evidence. As Congress has explained, FRE 301 "provides that a presumption shifts to the party against whom it is directed the burden of going forward with evidence to meet or rebut the presumption, but it does not shift to that party the burden of persuasion on the existence of the presumed fact."

Presumptions are evidentiary mechanisms that operate in both civil and criminal cases, although their primary operation is in the civil arena. In criminal cases, constitutional due process requirements limit their function.

There are essentially three general types of presumptions: rebuttable, conclusive, and permissive. Each type operates in a different manner. A true presumption, however, is rebuttable.

Presumptions are created for various reasons, including the following:

1. For social policy reasons (e.g., a child of a married woman is presumed to be legitimate).

2. To "smoke out" evidence (e.g., a bailee is presumed to be negligent if goods were damaged or lost while in his possession).

3. To resolve an impasse in proof (e.g., a violent death is presumed to be accidental and not suicide).

Illustrations: Common Presumptions

1. A letter properly addressed, stamped, and mailed is presumed to have been received.

2. Public officers are presumed to do their duty.

3. A person missing for seven years is presumed to be dead.

4. A child born to a married woman is presumed to be the child of the woman's husband.

5. When a will is made but lost, it is presumed to be revoked.

6. Children under the age of seven are presumed to be incapable of committing a felony.

7. An IRS assessment is presumed to be correct.

8. A bailee who damages or loses goods in her possession is presumed to be negligent.

9. If a violation of the Constitution is shown, irreparable harm is presumed. *See Kaiser v. County of Sacramento*, 780 F. Supp. 1309 (E.D. Cal. 1991).

10. In determining the cause of a death, it is presumed not to be a suicide. *See Duncan v. American Home Assurance Co.*, 747 F. Supp. 1418 (M.D. Ala. 1990).

11. Evidence in a party's possession that is not produced is presumed to be unfavorable to that party. *See In re Richard Buick*, 126 B.R. 840 (E.D. Pa. 1991).

[B]   Rebuttable Presumptions in Civil Cases

Rebuttable presumptions are utilized most often when the party charged with the burden of proving a material fact is unable to do so due to a lack of evidence. The presumption permits the party to prove a substitute fact, often called the basic fact. If the basic fact is shown, the material fact, often called the presumed fact, is considered to exist. The basic fact may be probative of the presumed fact; for example, a letter that has been properly mailed is generally presumed to have been received. However, the basic fact is often insufficient by itself to sustain a finding of the presumed fact.

The amount of assistance given to a party by a rebuttable presumption varies. Rebuttable presumptions generally operate at one of two levels of strength. The stronger version shifts to the opposing party both the burden of production and the burden of persuasion; the weaker version shifts only the burden of production. The weaker version has the virtue of smoking out evidence in the possession of the opposing party, but has been criticized as being too easy to rebut. The stronger version, while more difficult to refute, has been attacked as having too great an impact on the case.

FRE 301 adopts only the weaker version of rebuttable presumptions. Under the weaker version, if the party originally holding the burden of proof offers sufficient evidence of the basic fact, the production burden shifts to the opposing party. The opposing party must then produce sufficient evidence for a reasonable juror to find that the presumed fact does not exist. Whether the party has offered sufficient evidence for a reasonable juror to conclude that the presumed fact does not exist is decided by the court.

If the judge concludes that the opposing party's production burden has been met, the presumption disappears and drops out of the case. The jury is not instructed on the presumption; instead the jury is told that the party originally charged with the burden must persuade it that the presumed fact exists. (In a now disfavored approach used in a minority of jurisdictions, the presumption remains in the case and is treated as evidence.)

If the opposing party cannot meet its burden of production, the presumption stays in the case. The jury is then instructed that if it finds the basic fact by the applicable standard of proof (generally by a preponderance of the evidence in a civil case), it must then find that the presumed fact exists as well.

[C]   Conclusive and Permissive Presumptions in Civil Cases

Presumptions are not always rebuttable. Irrebuttable or conclusive presumptions cannot be rebutted no matter what evidence is offered to the contrary. These are not true presumptions, but rather rules of law disguised as presumptions.

Some presumptions are neither rebuttable nor conclusive, but rather permissive. A permissive presumption simply indicates to the jury that it *may* draw a certain inference from another fact, but that it need not do so. The permissive presumption also is not a true presumption, since the court's instruction simply suggests an inference to the jury, but does not require that the inference be drawn.

Illustrations: Presumptions — Civil Cases

1. Reggie T. Schrader, age 42, disappeared one sunny June day so suddenly it was almost as if he had never existed. He left behind his wife, Kelly, and three children. For Kelly to recover the proceeds of Reggie's life insurance policy, she must prove that Reggie is dead. Many inferences can be drawn from Reggie's disappearance, however. Reggie may have suffered from amnesia and lost his memory, as well as his way home. He also may have intentionally fled his home for a variety of reasons and escaped to another location. Further, he

might have been abducted. Finally, his disappearance may indicate that he was dead. In light of these inferences, will Kelly win her suit to recover on the insurance policy?

Answer: If no presumption existed, Kelly would lose the proceeding because she could not prove that Reggie was dead; too many inferences can be drawn from Reggie's disappearance. A presumption might help to avoid such a result, however, by smoking out any evidence in the possession of the defendant insurance company. Under FRE 301, the presumption would operate by permitting Kelly to show the existence of another fact, called the basic fact, which may be probative of (but likely not dispositive of) the presumed fact. Kelly could instead show that her husband was known to be missing for a certain length of time, such as seven years, and, therefore, was presumed to be dead. Since a true presumption is rebuttable, however, the insurance company would have the opportunity to show that the inference of death is incorrect. The insurance company could force the presumption out of the case if it meets its production burden by offering evidence sufficient for a reasonable juror to believe that Reggie was still alive. Whether the insurance company has met its production burden will be determined by the court.

2. Plaintiff Zina sued defendant Nancy for failure to deliver a shipment of scrap metal as agreed. As part of her case, Zina must prove that Nancy received advance notice of the shipping date. Zina stated that she had mailed the letter as required, but did not know if Nancy had received it. Nancy does not offer any evidence on whether she received notice. Who will win on this issue?

Answer: If no presumption exists, Zina will be unable to carry her burden of showing that notice has been received and Nancy will win. If a presumption exists that a letter properly mailed has been received, however, Zina might win. If Zina proves the basic fact, that the letter was properly mailed, then the burden of production on the issue would shift to Nancy. Nancy would have to rebut the presumed fact, that the letter was received. One of two things will occur. If Nancy rebuts the presumed fact, by offering sufficient evidence to find that the letter was *not* received, the presumption will drop out of the case as if it never existed. If Nancy cannot rebut the presumed fact by producing sufficient evidence of its nonexistence, the presumption will stay in the case. Consequently, the jury will be instructed that if it finds that the letter was properly mailed, it then *must* find that the letter was received.

[D]   Presumptions in Criminal Prosecutions

Presumptions are permitted in criminal cases as well as in civil cases. Due to the nature of criminal cases, however, special restrictions apply. Criminal presumptions may not compromise the requirement that each element of the crime must be proven by the prosecution beyond a reasonable doubt. *See In re Winship*, 397 U.S. 358, 90 S. Ct. 1068, 25 L. Ed. 2d 368 (1970). This constitutional limitation precludes shifting the burden of proof of any element of the crime to the accused. Thus, criminal presumptions may only exist in the "permissive" or inference form.

If a criminal permissive presumption operates, additional limitations apply. The basic fact in a criminal presumption must be rationally connected to the presumed fact to satisfy constitutional due process requirements. Does "rationally connected" mean that the presumed fact must "more likely than not" follow from the basic fact, or must the presumed fact flow from the basic fact "beyond a reasonable doubt"? In *County Court of Ulster County v. Allen* (*see* § 14.04[F][3]), the Court held that a "permissive" criminal presumption is valid only if the presumed fact flows more likely than not from the basic fact. In effect, the presumed fact must flow by a preponderance of the evidence from the basic fact.

Illustration: Permissive Presumption — Criminal Case

Billy Bonanza is charged with knowingly operating an illegal still, a misdemeanor. Billy claimed that he had no knowledge of the still. Under the applicable law, a defendant is presumed to have knowledge of a still if the defendant is present on the still grounds. At trial, the judge solicits the views of the attorneys on the appropriate instruction the jury should receive on the question of knowledge. The prosecution earlier showed that the defendant was arrested on the grounds of the still. What is the proper instruction?

Answer: In a criminal case such as this, the judge may instruct the jury that it *may* find that the defendant knew of the still as a result of his presence on the grounds. This is a permissive instruction since the jury is instructed that it *may* find the presumed fact, not that the jury *must* find it. Even a permissive instruction will be improper, however, if the presumed fact (knowledge of the still) fails to flow from the basic fact (presence on the still grounds) more likely than not. Here, it appears probable that a close physical proximity to the still more likely than not indicates an awareness of it.

[E] Problems

Problem #14-13: The Check's in the Mail

The major issue in an action for the payment of insurance proceeds is whether the plaintiff, Kevin, notified the defendant, Lindsey, of Kevin's intention to renew his insurance by a certain date. Kevin claimed that he mailed the letter more than a week in advance of the time limit. The defendant company claimed that it did not receive notice.

1. What is the most logical way to decide this issue?

2. What are the alternatives?

3. What presumption would you suggest to facilitate an equitable resolution of this case? Explain.

Problem #14-14: Where There's a Will . . .

Real estate magnate Jonas Parchment died, leaving behind two football teams, six houses, and $10,000,000 in cash. Jonas made two wills during his lifetime. The first will left all of his money to the Salvation Army. The second will left his entire estate to his eleven children, to be divided up equally.

1. If the second will had a large "X" drawn through it, and a presumption exists that a will that is made but mutilated is presumed revoked, what would have to be shown for the Salvation Army to recover the entire estate? Assume that the FRE apply.

2. What would the children have to do to rebut such a presumption?

3. What is the basic fact in this presumption?

4. What is the presumed fact?

5. Would the answer to any of the above questions change if the "shifting burden of persuasion" theory governed?

Problem #14-15: Paternity

In a paternity action in Nashville, Tennessee, the wife, Mia, claims her estranged husband, Barry, is the father of her newborn child.

1. If it is presumed in that jurisdiction that a child born to a married woman is the child of the married woman's husband, and it operates as a rebuttable presumption similar to FRE 301, what is the effect of such a presumption?

2. What would Mia have to show to trigger the presumption?

3. What would Barry have to show to rebut the presumption?

4. Apply the shifting burden of persuasion approach to this problem. Would the result change?

Problem #14-16: Will I?

Blanca was an eccentric millionaire who was known to have kept her last will and testament in her refrigerator. After she died, a thorough search of the refrigerator turned up some mustard and spoiled milk, but not her last known will and testament. In Blanca's jurisdiction, a presumption exists that a will properly made and then lost is presumed revoked. An earlier will left all of Blanca's money to research on the improvement of Oreo cookies.

1. If her son claims that the "refrigerator will," which left all of Blanca's money to him, still governs, who will win, the son or the Oreo Cookie Research Institute?

2. If the son could produce some evidence showing that the "refrigerator will" was in fact buried in the back yard, would the outcome of the case change?

Problem #14-17: Rambo Jr.

Rambo Jr. gets restless one day and decides to blow up several buildings and destroy an entire department store. After Rambo goes on his crime spree, he is charged with various counts of destruction of property, criminal trespass, and aggravated battery for the bodily injuries that occurred.

1. Rambo Jr. is six years of age. If a rebuttable presumption exists that a child under the age of seven is presumed to be incapable of committing a felony, what would the state have to show to overcome this presumption?

2. What is the difference in the amount of evidence the state must show if this presumption shifts the burden of persuasion as well as the burden of production?

3. What must the state show to overcome the presumption if it is considered to be conclusive?

4. How should the court instruct the jury if this presumption is considered to be permissive?

Problem #14-18: Drugs

An Oklahoma statute provides that anyone found in a hotel room is presumed to constructively possess illegal narcotics recovered from an open area in that room. Joey was found in a Tulsa hotel room in which two marijuana cigarettes were recovered from an ashtray in the open area of the room. Three friends were in the room with him. Joey was arrested and charged with the unlawful possession of marijuana.

Joey objects to the statute. He claims that he was just stopping by to chat with some friends after purchasing some trinkets for his two-year-old daughter.

1. How should the judge instruct the jury on the presumption?

2. What effect would Joey's testimony about the purpose of his visit to the hotel room have on the presumption?

3. Is this presumption constitutional? Explain.

Problem #14-19: Insanity

The defendant is charged with murder. Under the applicable law, a defendant is presumed to be sane unless he satisfies a burden of production showing that he is insane. If defendant meets this production burden, the government must then prove the defendant is sane beyond a reasonable doubt.

1. How much evidence must the defendant offer to overcome this presumption?

2. Does this presumption shift the burden of persuasion or only the burden of production?

3. If the prosecution fails to meet its burden of persuasion, what is the resulting verdict?

[In 1982, John Hinckley was prosecuted in Washington, D.C., for attempting to murder then-President Ronald Reagan. A statutory scheme similar to the one above existed. The applicable law presumed that a defendant was sane. If the presumption of sanity was rebutted by the defendant, however, the government was then required to prove that the defendant was sane beyond a reasonable doubt. In the Hinckley case, the defendant offered expert testimony on his lack of sanity. Consequently, the government had the burden of proving Hinckley sane beyond a reasonable doubt. The government was unable to meet this difficult, if not insuperable, burden of proof. Ironically, the effect of the statutory scheme was that John Hinckley was never affirmatively found to be insane at the time he shot President Ronald Reagan; the jury's verdict simply indicates that the government did not meet its burden of proving him sane beyond a reasonable doubt.]

Problem #14-20: Lexcedes

James left his new Lexcedes, the result of a joint venture between several car companies, in Sam's Parking Lot. (Sam's motto was: "We take care of your car the way we take care of our own." Sam's employees, however, all drove "junkers" that were left over from a demolition derby.) When James returned for his car, there was a big crater in the trunk and its sides were bashed in. When James asked the attendant what had happened to his car, the attendant said, "I don't know; it sure looks the same as when you brought it in."

James sued Sam's Parking Lot. Suppose that a presumption exists that goods damaged or lost by a bailee while the goods are in the bailee's possession are presumed to have been the result of the bailee's negligence. Also, assume the FRE apply.

1. What will James have to prove to trigger the presumption?

2. If the presumption applies, will James win?

3. If no presumption exists, will James win?

Problem #14-21: Credit Card Balance

Ginny mailed a payment to her credit card company paying off a huge balance. The credit card company claimed it never received the payment and promptly sued for damages, including a substantial late fee. Ginny offered evidence at trial that she had properly addressed the envelope, placed a stamp on it, and mailed it. A presumption exists that "a letter properly addressed, stamped and mailed is presumed to have been received."

1. Does the presumption apply in this case? How should the judge instruct the jury if the company offers no evidence on the issue?

2. What if the company testifies that it did not receive the letter? How should the judge now instruct the jury on this issue?

3. What if the company had stated that it had no knowledge of whether it had received payment because its records were missing, but that Ginny had failed to properly mail the letter because she did not place a stamp on the envelope? How should the judge now instruct the jury on this question?

Problem #14-22: A Question of Criminal Law

Suzanne is charged with the possession of a firearm after being arrested in a hotel room with four other people. Suzanne was a guest of one of the other occupants, Jimi. The room was not registered in her name. The firearm was found in an unlocked drawer of the nightstand. At trial, the prosecutor asked the judge to instruct the jury on the presumption in the jurisdiction that "a person found in a hotel room containing a firearm is presumed to constructively possess that firearm." Should the judge instruct the jury on this presumption? If so, how?

Problem #14-23: On a Roll

A car parked on a steep hill crashed into a car at the bottom of the hill after its parking brake gave out. The owner of the demolished car, Taylor, sued Emma, who was found holding the keys to the runaway car. In the jurisdiction a presumption existed that "ownership of an automobile is presumed from the possession of the automobile's ignition key."

    1. If FRE 301 applies, how would defendant Emma "burst the bubble" of the presumption at trial?

    2. If this presumption had shifted the burden of persuasion, what would be required for Emma to overcome the presumption?

[F]   Cases and Rules

[1] *Vlandis v. Kline*

Connecticut law provided that a state university student who is unmarried and has resided outside the state in the year preceding school attendance would be presumptively and irrebuttably classified as a non-resident for tuition purposes. In *Vlandis v. Kline*, 412 U.S. 441 (1973), the Supreme Court held that this statute violated the due process clause of the Fourteenth Amendment because it "operates to deny a fair opportunity to rebut it" (quoting *Heiner v. Donnan*, 285 U.S. 312, 329 (1932)). The Court concluded that this particular presumption "provides no opportunity for students who applied from out of state to demonstrate that they have become bona fide Connecticut residents." The Court noted that less restrictive alternatives were available to Connecticut to ensure that the state met its legitimate objectives.

[2] Sandstrom v. Montana

United States Supreme Court
442 U.S. 510 (1979)

MR. JUSTICE BRENNAN delivered the opinion of the Court.

The question presented is whether, in a case in which intent is an element of the crime charged, the jury instruction, "the law presumes that a person intends the ordinary consequences of his voluntary acts," violates the Fourteenth Amendment's requirement that the State prove every element of a criminal offense beyond a reasonable doubt.

On November 22, 1976, 18-year-old David Sandstrom confessed to the slaying of Annie Jessen. Based upon the confession and corroborating evidence, petitioner was charged on December 2 with "deliberate homicide," Mont. Code Ann. § 45-5-102 (1978), in that he "purposely or knowingly caused the death of Annie Jessen." App. 34. At trial, Sandstrom's attorney informed the jury that, although his client admitted killing Jessen, he did not do so "purposely or knowingly," and was therefore not guilty of "deliberate homicide" but of a lesser crime. *Id.*, at 6–8. . . .

The prosecution requested the trial judge to instruct the jury that "[t]he law presumes that a person intends the ordinary consequences of his voluntary acts." Counsel objected, arguing that "the instruction has the effect of shifting the burden of proof on the issue of" purpose or knowledge to the defense, and that "that is impermissible under the Federal Constitution, due process of law." . . .

. . . .

. . . We granted certiorari, 439 U.S. 1067 (1979), to decide the important question of the instruction's constitutionality. We reverse.

II

The threshold inquiry in ascertaining the constitutional analysis applicable to this kind of jury instruction is to determine the nature of the presumption it describes. *See Ulster County Court v. Allen, ante,* at 157–163. That determination requires careful attention to the words actually spoken to the jury, see *ante,* at 157–159, n. 16, for whether a defendant has been accorded his constitutional rights depends upon the way in which a reasonable juror could have interpreted the instruction.

Respondent argues, first, that the instruction merely described a permissive inference — that is, it allowed but did not require the jury to draw conclusions about defendant's intent from his actions — and that such inferences are constitutional. Brief for Respondent 3, 15. These arguments need not detain us long, for even respondent admits that "It's possible" that the jury believed they were required to apply the presumption. Tr. of Oral Arg. 18. Sandstrom's jurors were told that "[t]he law presumes that a person intends the ordinary consequences of his voluntary acts." They were not told that they had a choice, or that they might infer that conclusion; they were told only that the law presumed it. It is clear that a reasonable juror could easily have viewed such an instruction as mandatory. . . .

. . . .

. . . Petitioner's jury was told that "*[t]he law presumes* that a person intends the ordinary consequences of his voluntary acts." They were not told that the presumption could be rebutted, as the Montana Supreme Court held, by the defendant's simple presentation of "some" evidence; nor even that it could be rebutted at all. Given the common definition of "presume" as "to suppose without proof," *Webster's New Collegiate Dictionary* 911 (1974), and given the lack of qualifying instructions as to the legal effect of the presumption, we cannot discount the possibility that the jury may have interpreted the instruction in either of two more stringent ways.

First, a reasonable jury could well have interpreted the presumption as "conclusive," that is, not technically as a presumption at all, but rather as an irrebuttable direction by the court to find intent once convinced of the facts triggering the presumption. Alternatively, the jury may have interpreted the instruction as a direction to find intent upon proof of the defendant's voluntary actions (and their "ordinary" consequences), unless *the defendant* proved the contrary by some quantum of proof which may well have been considerably greater than "some" evidence — thus effectively shifting the burden of persuasion on the element of intent. . . .

We do not reject the possibility that some jurors may have interpreted the challenged instruction as permissive, or, if mandatory, as requiring only that the defendant come forward with "some" evidence in rebuttal. However, the fact that a reasonable juror could have given the presumption conclusive or persuasion-shifting effect means that we cannot discount the possibility that Sandstrom's jurors actually did proceed upon one or the other of these latter interpretations. And that means that unless these kinds of presumptions are constitutional, the instruction cannot be judged valid. . . .

. . . .

. . . [A] conclusive presumption in this case would "conflict with the overriding presumption of innocence with which the law endows the accused and which extends to every element of the crime," and would "invade [the] fact finding function" which in a criminal case the law assigns solely to the jury. The instruction announced to David Sandstrom's jury may well have had exactly these consequences. Upon finding proof of one element of the crime (causing death), and of facts insufficient to establish the second (the voluntariness and "ordinary consequences" of defendant's action), Sandstrom's jurors could reasonably have concluded that they were directed to find against defendant on the element of intent. The State was thus not forced to prove "beyond a reasonable doubt . . . every fact necessary to constitute the crime . . . charged," 397 U.S., at 364, and defendant was deprived of his constitutional rights as explicated in *Winship*.

A presumption which, although not conclusive, had the effect of shifting the burden of persuasion to the defendant, would have suffered from similar infirmities. If Sandstrom's jury interpreted the presumption in that manner, it could have concluded that upon proof by the State of the slaying, and of additional facts not themselves establishing the element of intent, the burden was shifted to the defendant to prove that he lacked the requisite mental state. . . .

Because David Sandstrom's jury may have interpreted the judge's instruction as constituting either a burden-shifting presumption like that in *Mullaney*, or a conclusive presumption like those in *Morissette* and *United States Gypsum Co.*, and because either interpretation would have deprived defendant of his right to the due process of law, we hold the instruction given in this case unconstitutional. . . .

[3]   County Court of Ulster County v. Allen

United States Supreme Court
442 U.S. 140 (1979)

MR. JUSTICE STEVENS delivered the opinion of the Court.

A New York statute provides that, with certain exceptions, the presence of a firearm in an automobile is presumptive evidence of its illegal possession by all persons then occupying the vehicle. The United States Court of Appeals for the Second Circuit held that respondents may challenge the constitutionality of this statute in a federal habeas corpus proceeding and that the statute is "unconstitutional on its face." 568 F.2d 998, 1009. We granted certiorari to review these holdings and also to consider whether the statute is constitutional in its application to respondents. 439 U.S. 815.

Four persons, three adult males (respondents) and a 16-year-old girl (Jane Doe, who is not a respondent here), were jointly tried on charges that they possessed two loaded handguns, a loaded machinegun, and over a pound of heroin found in a Chevrolet in which they were riding when it was stopped for speeding on the New York Thruway shortly after noon on March 28, 1973. The two large-caliber handguns, which together with their ammunition weighed approximately six pounds, were seen through the window of the car by the investigating police officer. They were positioned crosswise in an open handbag on either the front floor or the front seat of the car on the passenger side where Jane Doe was sitting. Jane Doe admitted that the handbag was hers. The machinegun and the heroin were discovered in the trunk after the police pried it open. . . .

Counsel for all four defendants objected to the introduction into evidence of the two handguns, the machinegun, and the drugs, arguing that the State had not adequately demonstrated a connection between their clients and the contraband. The trial court overruled the objection, relying on the presumption of possession created by the New York statute. . . .

At the close of the trial, the judge instructed the jurors that they were entitled to infer possession from the defendants' presence in the car. He did not make any reference to the "upon the person" exception in his explanation of the statutory presumption, nor did any of the defendants object to this omission or request alternative or additional instructions on the subject.

Defendants filed a post-trial motion in which they challenged the constitutionality of the New York statute as applied in this case. The challenge was made in support of their argument that the evidence, apart from the presumption, was insufficient to sustain the convictions. The motion was denied, *Id.*, at 775–776, and the convictions were affirmed by the Appellate Division without opinion. . . .

The New York Court of Appeals also affirmed. . . .

Respondents filed a petition for a writ of habeas corpus in the United States District Court for the Southern District of New York contending that they were denied due process of law by the application of the statutory presumption of possession. The

District Court issued the writ, holding that respondents had not "deliberately bypassed" their federal claim by their actions at trial and that the mere presence of two guns in a woman's handbag in a car could not reasonably give rise to the inference that they were in the possession of three other persons in the case. App. to Pet. for Cert. 33a–36a.

The Court of Appeals for the Second Circuit affirmed, but for different reasons. . . . [T]he majority of the court, without deciding whether the presumption was constitutional as applied in this case, concluded that the statute is unconstitutional on its face because the "presumption obviously sweeps within its compass (1) many occupants who may not know they are riding with a gun (which may be out of their sight), and (2) many who may be aware of the presence of the gun but not permitted access to it." . . .

The petition for a writ of certiorari presented three questions: (1) whether the District Court had jurisdiction to entertain respondents' claim that the presumption is unconstitutional; (2) whether it was proper for the Court of Appeals to decide the facial constitutionality issue; and (3) whether the application of the presumption in this case is unconstitutional. We answer the first question in the affirmative, the second two in the negative. We accordingly reverse. . . .

In this case, the Court of Appeals undertook the task of deciding the constitutionality of the New York statute "on its face." Its conclusion that the statutory presumption was arbitrary rested entirely on its view of the fairness of applying the presumption in hypothetical situations — situations, indeed, in which it is improbable that a jury would return a conviction, or that a prosecution would ever be instituted. We must accordingly inquire whether these respondents had standing to advance the arguments that the Court of Appeals considered decisive. An analysis of our prior cases indicates that the answer to this inquiry depends on the type of presumption that is involved in the case.

Inferences and presumptions are a staple of our adversary system of fact finding. It is often necessary for the trier of fact to determine the existence of an element of the crime — that is, an "ultimate" or "elemental" fact — from the existence of one or more "evidentiary" or "basic" facts. . . . The value of these evidentiary devices, and their validity under the Due Process Clause, vary from case to case, however, depending on the strength of the connection between the particular basic and elemental facts involved and on the degree to which the device curtails the fact finder's freedom to assess the evidence independently. Nonetheless, in criminal cases, the ultimate test of any device's constitutional validity in a given case remains constant: the device must not undermine the fact finder's responsibility at trial, based on evidence adduced by the State to find ultimate facts beyond a reasonable doubt. . . .

The most common evidentiary device is the entirely permissive inference or presumption, which allows — but does not require — the trier of fact to infer the elemental fact from proof by the prosecutor of the basic one and which places no burden of any kind on the defendant. . . . In that situation the basic fact may constitute prima facie evidence of the elemental fact. . . . When reviewing this type of device, the Court has required the party challenging it to demonstrate its invalidity as applied to him. . . . Because this permissive presumption leaves the trier of fact free to credit or reject the inference and does not shift the burden of proof, it affects the application of the "beyond a reasonable doubt" standard only if, under the facts of the case, there is no rational way the trier could make the connection permitted by the inference. For only in that situation is there any risk that an explanation of the permissible inference to a jury, or its use by a jury, has caused the presumptively rational fact finder to make an erroneous factual determination.

A mandatory presumption is a far more troublesome evidentiary device. For it may affect not only the strength of the "no reasonable doubt" burden but also the placement of that burden; it tells the trier that he or they *must* find the elemental fact upon proof of the basic fact, at least unless the defendant has come forward with some evidence to rebut the presumed connection between the two facts. . . . In this situation, the Court has generally examined the presumption on its face to determine the extent to which the basic and elemental facts coincide. . . . To the extent that the trier of fact is forced to abide by the presumption, and may not reject it based on an independent evaluation of the particular facts presented by the State, the analysis of the presumption's constitutional validity is logically divorced from those facts and based on the presumption's accuracy in the run of cases. It is for this reason that the Court has held it irrelevant in analyzing a mandatory presumption, but not in analyzing a purely permissive one, that there is ample evidence in the record other than the presumption to support a conviction. . . .

Without determining whether the presumption in this case was mandatory, the Court of Appeals analyzed it on its face as if it were. In fact, it was not, as the New York Court of Appeals had earlier pointed out. 40 N.Y.2d, at 510–511, 354 N.E.2d, at 840.

The trial judge's instructions make it clear that the presumption was merely a part of the prosecution's case,[2] that it gave rise to a permissive inference available only in certain circumstances, rather than a mandatory conclusion of possession, and that it could be ignored by the jury even if there was no affirmative proof offered by defendants in rebuttal.[3] The judge explained that possession could be actual or

---

[2] (Court's original footnote 19) "It is your duty to consider all the testimony in this case, to weigh it carefully and to test the credit to be given to a witness by his apparent intention to speak the truth and by the accuracy of his memory to reconcile, if possible, conflicting statements as to material facts and in such ways to try and get at the truth and to reach a verdict upon the evidence." Tr. 739–740.

"To establish the unlawful possession of the weapons, again the People relied upon the presumption and, in addition thereto, the testimony of Anderson and Lemmons who testified in this case-in-chief." *Id.*, at 744.

"Accordingly, you would be warranted in returning a verdict of guilt against the defendants or defendant if you find the defendants or defendant was in possession of a machine gun and the other weapons and that the fact of possession was proven to you by the People beyond a reasonable doubt, and an element of such proof is the reasonable presumption of illegal possession of a machine gun or the presumption of illegal possession of firearms, as I have just before explained to you." Id., at 746.

[3] (Court's original footnote 20) "Our Penal Law also provides that the presence in an automobile of any machine gun or of any handgun or firearm which is loaded is presumptive evidence of their unlawful possession."

"In other words, these presumptions or this latter presumption upon proof of the presence of the machine gun and the hand weapons, you may infer and draw a conclusion that such prohibited weapon was possessed by each of the defendants who occupied the automobile at the time when such instruments were found. The presumption or presumptions is effective only so long as there is no substantial evidence contradicting the

constructive, but that constructive possession could not exist without the intent and ability to exercise control or dominion over the weapons. He also carefully instructed the jury that there is a mandatory presumption of innocence in favor of the defendants that controls unless it, as the exclusive trier of fact, is satisfied beyond a reasonable doubt that the defendants possessed the handguns in the manner described by the judge. In short, the instructions plainly directed the jury to consider all the circumstances tending to support or contradict the inference that all four of the occupants of the car had possession of the two loaded handguns and to decide the matter for itself without regard to how much evidence the defendants introduced.

Our cases considering the validity of permissive statutory presumptions such as the one involved here have rested on an evaluation of the presumption as applied to the record before the Court. None suggests that a court should pass on the constitutionality of this kind of statute "on its face." It was error for the Court of Appeals to make such a determination in this case.

III

As applied to the facts of this case, the presumption of possession is entirely rational. Notwithstanding the Court of Appeals' analysis, respondents were not "hitchhikers or other casual passengers," and the guns were neither "a few inches in length" nor "out of [respondents'] sight." The argument against possession by any of the respondents was predicated solely on the fact that the guns were in Jane Doe's pocketbook. But several circumstances — which, not surprisingly, her counsel repeatedly emphasized in his questions and his argument . . . made it highly improbably that she was the sole custodian of those weapons.

Even if it was reasonable to conclude that she had placed the guns in her purse before the car was stopped by police, the facts strongly suggest that Jane Doe was not the only person able to exercise dominion over them. The two guns were too large to be concealed in her handbag. The bag was consequently open, and part of one of the guns was in plain view, within easy access of the driver of the car and even, perhaps, of the other two respondents who were riding in the rear seat.

Moreover, it is highly improbable that the loaded guns belonged to Jane Doe or that she was solely responsible for their being in her purse. As a 16-year-old girl in the company of three adult men she was the least likely of the four to be carrying one, let alone two, heavy handguns. It is far more probable that she relied on the pocketknife found in her brassiere for any necessary self-protection. Under these circumstances, it was not unreasonable for her counsel to argue and for the jury to infer that when the car was halted for speeding, the other passengers in the car anticipated the risk of a search and attempted to conceal their weapons in a pocketbook in the front seat. The

---

conclusion flowing from the presumption, and the presumption is said to disappear when such contradictory evidence is adduced." *Id.*, at 743.

"The presumption or presumptions which I discussed with the jury relative to the drugs or weapons in this case need not be rebutted by affirmative proof or affirmative evidence but may be rebutted by any evidence or lack of evidence in the case." *Id.*, at 760.

inference is surely more likely than the notion that these weapons were the sole property of the 16-year-old girl.

Under these circumstances, the jury would have been entirely reasonable in rejecting the suggestion — which, incidentally, defense counsel did not even advance in their closing arguments to the jury — that the handguns were in the sole possession of Jane Doe. Assuming that the jury did reject it, the case is tantamount to one in which the guns were lying on the floor or the seat of the car in the plain view of the three other occupants of the automobile. In such a case, it is surely rational to infer that each of the respondents was fully aware of the presence of the guns and had both the ability and the intent to exercise dominion and control over the weapons. The application of the statutory presumption in this case therefore comports with the standard laid down in *Tot v. United States*, 319 U.S., at 467, and restated in *Leary v. United States*, 395 U.S., at 36. For there is a "rational connection" between the basic facts that the prosecution proved and the ultimate fact presumed, and the latter is "more likely than not to flow from" the former.

Respondents argue, however, that the validity of the New York presumption must be judged by a "reasonable doubt" test rather than the "more likely than not" standard employed in *Leary*. Under the more stringent test, it is argued that a statutory presumption must be rejected unless the evidence necessary to invoke the inference is sufficient for a rational jury to find the inferred fact beyond a reasonable doubt. *See Barnes v. United States*, 412 U.S., at 842–843. Respondents' argument again overlooks the distinction between a permissive presumption on which the prosecution is entitled to rely as one not necessarily sufficient part of its proof and a mandatory presumption which the jury must accept even if it is the sole evidence of an element of the offense.

In the latter situation, since the prosecution bears the burden of establishing guilt, it may not rest its case entirely on a presumption unless the fact proved is sufficient to support the inference of guilt beyond a reasonable doubt. But in the former situation, the prosecution may rely on all of the evidence in the record to meet the reasonable-doubt standard. There is no more reason to require a permissive statutory presumption to meet a reasonable-doubt standard before it may be permitted to play any part in a trial than there is to require that degree of probative force for other relevant evidence before it may be admitted. As long as it is clear that the presumption is not the sole and sufficient basis for a finding of guilt, it need only satisfy the test described in *Leary*.

The permissive presumption, as used in this case, satisfied the *Leary* test. And, as already noted, the New York Court of Appeals has concluded that the record as a whole was sufficient to establish guilt beyond a reasonable doubt.

The judgment is reversed.

[4] Rules Comparison

Florida Statutes § 90.302. Classification of Rebuttable Presumptions

Every rebuttable presumption is either:

(1) A presumption affecting the burden of producing evidence and requiring the trier of fact to assume the existence of presumed fact, unless credible evidence sufficient to sustain a finding of the nonexistence of the presumed fact is introduced, in which event, the existence or nonexistence of the presumed fact shall be determined from the evidence without regard to the presumption; or

(2) A presumption affecting the burden of proof that imposes upon the party against whom it operates the burden of proof concerning the nonexistence of the presumed fact.

Wisconsin Statutes Annotated § 903.03. Presumptions in Criminal Cases

(1) Scope. Except as otherwise provided by statute, in criminal cases, presumptions against an accused, recognized at common law or created by statute, including statutory provisions that certain facts are prima facie evidence of other facts or of guilt, are governed by this rule.

(2) Submission to jury. The judge is not authorized to direct the jury to find a presumed fact against the accused. When the presumed fact establishes guilt or is an element of the offense or negatives a defense, the judge may submit the question of guilt or of the existence of the presumed fact to the jury, if, but only if, a reasonable juror on the evidence as a whole, including the evidence of the basic facts, could find guilt or the presumed fact beyond a reasonable doubt. When the presumed fact has a lesser effect, its existence may be submitted to the jury if the basic facts are supported by substantial evidence, or are otherwise established, unless the evidence as a whole negatives the existence of the presumed fact.

§ 14.05 SUMMARY AND REVIEW

1. Who allocates the burdens of proof and what are the bases on which the allocation is performed?
2. Why is judicial notice used at trial instead of the usual proof procedures?
3. Why is a presumption used at trial instead of the usual proof procedures?
4. What is the difference between a rebuttable presumption and a permissive presumption?
5. Explain the differences between a basic fact and a presumed fact.
6. What are the different types of rebuttable presumptions?
7. What are the limitations on presumptions in criminal cases?

Chapter 15

REVIEW PROBLEMS

§ 15.01 MOCK TRIAL

UNITED STATES v. O'RUBEN

This review problem is presented in the form of a mock trial. It can be acted out by the participants as a trial simulation or used as a longer and more comprehensive review problem. The case involves the robbery of a convenience store, with a sole eye-witness for the prosecution, the store clerk, and the accused for the defense. The sworn statements of the store clerk, Sally Smith, and the defendant, Rick O'Ruben, provide the basis for each witness's testimony. The problem is designed as a comprehensive review of evidence law, touching on many subject areas of the course. Unlike previous problems, where the subject matter is expressly labeled, this review is intended to promote issue-spotting skills and the formulation of trial strategies, as well as legal analysis of specific evidence questions.

The Prosecution's Case

    1. The robbery note.

    2. The gun.

    3. A note written by Sally after the robbery containing the purported getaway car's license plate number.

    4. The testimony of Sally Smith. [This testimony will be consistent with Sally Smith's statement below.]

    5. The sworn statement of Sally Smith:

The following is the true signed and sworn statement of Sally Smith, made within one month of the alleged robbery.

    My name is Sally Smith. I am 29 years old and I had been working on the night shift at Magruder's Convenience Store on Main Street for the past six months. I was let go from Magruder's last Thursday for allegedly taking money from the cash register. They can't prove it, however, and that's because I did not do it. It was the other clerk who did it.

I left college in my junior year and have had a few problems with the law. I was convicted of possessing cocaine, seven years ago; and of the unlawful possession of a firearm, a felony, twelve years ago. I had the gun for protection. The cocaine was my friend's, who was a passenger in my car when I was stopped for a left turn without putting on my blinker. I also was cited for underage drinking at a college concert, with a bunch of my friends.

I am now working as a receptionist in The Body Boutique, a hair and nail salon. I've been there for a week or so, and I like it a lot. I also am taking some on-line courses at the state university and plan on getting my college degree soon.

On the first Wednesday in January of this year I was working the night shift at Magruder's. Magruder's is like any other convenience store — big on the beer, potato chips, muffins, and things like that. There is only one entrance into the store, and the clerk's counter is about ten yards or so from the front entrance. There are six aisles perpendicular to my counter, and mirrors near the ceiling so I can see the entire store. There is a surveillance camera as well, but it wasn't working on January 6th. The lighting is pretty good, since the whole store has fluorescent lights.

I started that evening around 8:00 p.m. It was pretty quiet that night, only about fifteen customers each hour. I even had time to do inventory work. At 9:00 p.m., I was the only person in the store. When this guy walked into the store, he seemed nervous; he looked around some. He then came right up to me at the checkout counter, and put this note on the counter that said, "Your money or your life." I told my sister last week that when he first walked in, he seemed like a nice enough guy at first glance, not the monster he turned out to be.

Anyway, he really was a creep. I guess I was going too slow for him because he hit me on the shoulder real hard with his fist and said, "Faster, faster, sister, I mean it!" I thought I saw a gun in his hand, but I wasn't sure. After I gave him all of the money in the register, he started humming a song; I think it was Springsteen's "Tunnel of Love" or something like that. He then walked quickly out of the store. The whole thing lasted no more than five or so minutes. I felt nauseous, and my knees buckled, but I took a deep breath and ran after him. I saw him get in his car and drive away. I wrote down his license plate number, but I can't remember what I wrote down — I was very nervous at the time. In looking at what I wrote, it says "license plate number: DDP 514."

I then ran back into the store and called the police. I told them a guy had just robbed me. They asked me some things about what he looked like. I told them he was about 5 feet, 10 inches tall and 165 pounds, white male, beard, shoulder-length dark hair, with fingerless black gloves and an earring in his right ear. I told them the robbery probably took a couple of minutes.

Several days after the robbery, the police showed me some photographs of people. I looked over all of them and pointed out the person who I thought was the robber. As sure as I am sitting here, it was that guy, Rick O'Ruben. I had never seen him before, although I did see someone who looked just like him in the nearby supermarket about two months prior to the robbery.

This was one of the scariest things to ever happen to me. I will remember the robber's face as long as I live. I don't ever want to get robbed again; it still causes me nightmares.

As I ran out after the robber, I saw a gun lying on the floor just inside the store entrance. The robber must have dropped it. I had never seen the gun before. I picked up the gun carefully, put my initials on the barrel along with the date, and turned it over to the police, as well as the robbery note and the paper on which I wrote down the license plate number. I put my initials and the date on the robbery note as well.

I swear that this statement is true and accurate to the best of my knowledge.

Signed,

Sally Smith

The Defense Case

1. One of the defendant's blue fingerless gloves.

2. A letter from Rick O'Ruben's friend, Tim, a sailor in the Navy, which reads, "I look forward to playing tennis with you each Wednesday in January, at 8:00 p.m. at Holiday Park. Your Friend, Tim." The letter was dated December 1.

3. The testimony of Rick O'Ruben. [This testimony will be consistent with Rick O'Ruben's statement, below.]

4. The statement of Rick O'Ruben:

The following is the signed and sworn statement of the defendant, Rick O'Ruben, taken on January 30th of the same year.

My name is Rick O'Ruben. I am 27 years old and I live on Talbot Street, right off of Main Street. I shop in the stores, restaurants, and bars in the area, including the Magruder's they say had been robbed. I think Magruder's is overpriced, so I don't go there often.

I am a white male, approximately 6 feet, one inch tall, 190 pounds, with dark shoulder-length hair, no beard or mustache, and an earring in my left ear. I have attended the local community college for one semester and am a licensed automobile mechanic. I work at the Shell station over on 17th Street and own many blue fingerless gloves, which I often wear at work to protect my hands.

I have had a few problems with the law. Seven years ago, I was convicted as an adult of a felony robbery of a Magruder's convenience store. I admit to committing that crime, but not to this one! I was just a kid then and did not know better. I was found guilty of misdemeanor shoplifting three years ago; of a heroin sale as a juvenile; and aggravated mayhem, a felony, two years ago. The mayhem conviction resulted from a bar fight where I was just defending myself.

I've had some tough times. I've been arrested three times for fighting, and two times for vandalism, but they couldn't make any of the charges stick.

On that first Wednesday in January, I was playing tennis at Holiday Park from 8:00 to 9:00 p.m. with my buddy, Tim Lovell, who's in the Navy and presently at sea in the Indian Ocean. Every time Tim is in town, we play tennis on Wednesday evenings in Holiday Park, unless it rains. I don't have a reserved court, but it is not too difficult to get a court at that time. Tim and I are pretty even, although he almost always wins. Actually, that Wednesday night I recall beating him.

When the police arrested me at the Shell Station where I work, I didn't say anything to them. I am innocent though. I have done some bad things in the past, but there is one thing I did not do — and that's rob the Magruder's like they claim.

I have a wife and a four-year-old child named Sherri. I am trying to save some money so Sherri can go to a good school. My wife Becky used to be a bookkeeper, but had to quit because she has bad migraine headaches and has to lie down a lot. I wouldn't do anything to jeopardize my relationship with either of them. That is why I often work overtime at the Shell station. I want us to be able to afford a decent car. Right now I'm driving a junker with the license plate number, "PDD 514."

I was in the Magruder's once or twice in the month prior to that Wednesday to buy some beer and chips. It's on my way home from work.

I owned a gun at one time, just like the handgun they told me they found at Magruder's. My gun was stolen from my car about two months ago along with some other stuff. I used it for protection; I often have to drive through some bad neighborhoods.

I swear the aforementioned is true and accurate to the best of my knowledge.

Signed,

Rick O'Ruben

Stipulations [Agreements by the parties]

1. The government tested the gun and the counter area for fingerprints. Four prints were found on the gun. One matched the defendant, two were of unknown persons, and one was too smudged to make an identification.

2. The alleged robbery note was smudged, preventing any dispositive comparison with the defendant's handwriting. A handwriting expert was consulted who was only able to say that the writing on the note appeared to be "similar" to the defendant's handwriting.

3. The statements of Sally Smith and Rick O'Ruben were taken in depositions. After each deposition, the person making the statement was given an opportunity to review it for any inaccuracies. Each deponent signed the deposition as a true and accurate statement of the facts.

4. The defendant was given his *Miranda* warnings upon his arrest.

5. The defendant is being charged with one count of armed robbery. The judge will instruct the jury on the lesser included charge of robbery as well.

6. The letter from Tim Lovell is authentic.

Brief Jury Instructions

"Members of the jury, the defendant, Rick O'Ruben, stands charged by information of armed robbery, alleged to have been committed in the Magruder's convenience store on January 6th of this year at approximately 9:00 p.m. The defendant has pleaded not guilty.

A defendant is presumed to be innocent until each and every element of the case is proven by the prosecution beyond a reasonable doubt. That means a doubt for which you can give a reason. If a reasonable doubt as to one or more of the elements of the crime charged exists in your mind, you must find the defendant not guilty.

In the present case, the defendant is charged with armed robbery. Robbery is the trespassory taking and carrying away of money or other personal property that may be the subject of a larceny from the person or custody of another person and, in the course of the taking, there is the use of force, violence, assault, or putting in fear.

If, in the course of committing the robbery, the offender possesses a firearm or other deadly weapon, then the robbery is considered to be an armed robbery.

An act shall be deemed "in the course of committing the robbery" if it occurs in an attempt to commit robbery or in flight after the attempt or commission.

If, based on the evidence presented at trial, you find beyond and to the exclusion of every reasonable doubt that on the 6th day of January, the defendant, Rick O'Ruben, did rob the Magruder's store, then you must find the defendant guilty as charged.

Please select a jury foreperson when you first begin to deliberate. You will be permitted to take with you all of the admitted evidence, a verdict form, and a copy of the charging document, the information, which is not evidence. You may now go to the jury room to deliberate."

Assignment

1. Prepare closing arguments for the prosecution and for the defense. (a) What is the theory of each case? (b) How would you argue witness credibility? (c) What is the most significant evidence for each side?

2. (a) Which evidence offered by the prosecution likely will be admitted? (b) Which evidence likely will not be admitted? Explain, describing the likely objections to each piece of evidence and the probable rulings on those objections.

3. (a) Which evidence offered by the defense likely will be admitted? (b) Which evidence likely will not be admitted? Explain, describing the likely objections to each piece of evidence and the probable rulings on those objections.

4. Prepare direct and cross-examinations of Sally Smith and Rick O'Ruben. Do your examinations comply with the applicable rules of evidence?

§ 15.02 PROBLEMS

Problem #15-1: Crash Davis

An automobile accident occurred between cars driven by Davis and Lenny during a busy rush hour one morning. Neither driver was seriously injured. As they waited for the police to arrive, Lenny muttered just within Davis's hearing, "You're going to pay for this!" In response, Davis said to Lenny, "Look, I must admit, I'm not really sure what happened here because I was daydreaming, but it may well be I'm at fault and I did not look where I was going. I'll pay your medical expenses; actually, my insurance company will pay, if you agree not to sue me." Lenny does not accept Davis's proposal and brings suit against Davis.

1. Are Davis's statements to Lenny admissible in a subsequent trial? Explain.

2. If Davis takes the witness stand at trial and states, "I was driving with my full attention on the road when that guy, Lenny, went right through a red light," can Davis's previous statements at the scene be offered to impeach him? Why?

Problem #15-2: Benni and Hannah

Benni and Hannah owned a 1987 Shakami Truck. After they had owned it for three months, the vehicle rolled over, injuring both owners. The car was being properly and non-negligently driven when it crashed. Benni and Hannah brought suit against Shakami, Inc., on a strict products liability theory. The plaintiffs would like to introduce the following evidence at their trial. Will the evidence be admitted? Explain.

1. A *Consumer Reports* magazine article published after the crash claiming that the Shakami truck is not safe, particularly with respect to its susceptibility to rollover.

2. A modification made by Shakami in 1989 that minimizes the potential for roll-over.

Problem #15-3: United States v. Bowie

The defendant, state court judge Allen Bowie, is alleged to have conspired with a friend, Johnny Bart. The object of the conspiracy was to trade a lenient sentence in a serious criminal case for money. The government attempted to catch the judge and his friend by having a retired agent pose as a representative of the soon-to-be sentenced criminal defendant. As a signal that the judge would participate in the conspiracy, he was to have breakfast at the famous Grand Hotel on June 1, 2013. The judge appeared at the hotel as expected.

The government's case is based on the judge's appearance at the hotel, on taped conversations between Bart and the judge that appear to be in some sort of mysterious code, and on the judge's behavior in the criminal case. The judge's defense is that his appearance at the hotel was a coincidence — he often ate there — and that his conversations with Bart were not in code, but merely two friends chatting. Bart is maintaining his silence and refuses to testify for the government. Note that the cases against Bart and the judge are severed for trial.

Decide which of the following potential items of evidence will be admissible:

1. An FBI report, stating that an anonymous source indicated "the judge is willing to trade his office for money."

2. The FBI called the defendant at his hotel in Washington, D.C., for questioning after Bart was arrested. The defendant did not return the call, but instead checked out of the hotel and flew back to his home jurisdiction that same day (two days prior to his scheduled departure).

3. The FBI overheard Bart say to an unidentified third party: "I'm going to meet with the judge tonight; I'll tell him that I've made contact with the pilgrims."

4. The FBI had evidence that the judge was involved in two previous bribery schemes in 2009. No charges were ever filed.

5. The defendant's law clerk wrote a memorandum to the judge stating, "I'm working as fast as I can on this sentencing, Your Honor; I worked the past twelve hours on it and have pushed all other work aside as per your order." (The memorandum was brought to court and testified to by an FBI agent; the clerk was not called as a witness.)

6. A former business associate of Bart claims his reputation in the community is that of a liar.

7. A photograph of the Grand Hotel's restaurant.

8. A photograph of Bart.

9. A diagram of the Grand Hotel's restaurant.

10. The primary FBI witness was convicted of shoplifting three years earlier.

11. The fact that the undercover FBI agent in the case hated judges.

Problem #15-4: Not Again!

The defendant Loni is charged with shoplifting. Upon being apprehended by the store manager, Diane, the manager exclaimed, "I can't believe you just put those cosmetics in your pocket, Ma'am. That is at least the third time this past month you have done something similar to that!" At trial, the prosecution wishes to offer the testimony of the assistant manager, who heard Diane's statement. Is Diane's statement admissible? Explain.

Problem #15-5: One Tough Hombre

In the early morning hours of June 1, 2013, Jorge Gonzales, a longshoreman, was struck on the back of the head with what appeared to be a large baseball bat as he left the Facade 3000 nightclub. There were no eyewitnesses. Jorge suffered head injuries from the blow and a fractured wrist as a result of his fall. Another longshoreman with whom Gonzales had worked, Robert Epstein, is charged with attempted murder. Which of the following evidence is admissible at a subsequent trial? Explain your answers.

Prosecution Evidence

1. Doug King, Jorge's friend, will testify that:

a. He was with Gonzales at Facade 3000 on the evening of May 31 and the morning of June 1, 2013.

b. He saw Epstein leave the disco furtively, like a guilty man, at approximately 1:00 a.m.

c. He heard a sound, saw Gonzales fall to the ground "like a lump of coal," and saw someone large, "like another longshoreman," running away. "It sounded just like Epstein," said King.

d. King and Epstein had a fistfight in May of 2007. Charges were brought against Epstein, but were later dropped.

e. King was drinking Coca-Cola on May 31st, with nothing added.

f. "Epstein is a real violent person — real dangerous to others if you know what I mean. He'll steal you blind, too."

2. On cross-examination, King is asked the following questions. Which of the questions, if any, are permissible?

a. "Weren't you indicted for tax evasion in 2010?"

b. (1) "You were convicted of grand theft auto in 2011, right?" (2) "You were convicted of aggravated assault in 2009?" and (3) "You were adjudicated a juvenile delinquent for murder in 2014?"

c. "You stated in a deposition taken after the incident: 'I left the nightclub with Gonzales and the next thing I knew, Gonzales was lying unconscious on the ground. I don't remember anything else, except for a watch and a baseball bat lying on the ground nearby. The watch, by the way, was later shown to be Epstein's.' "

d. "You hate Epstein as a result of your prior fight with him, correct?"

e. "Two waitresses each served you a rum and Coke mixed drink that night, didn't they?"

f. "Epstein stole a pen from you several years earlier, correct?"

3. Dr. Dent, an expert witness, will testify for the prosecution.

a. Dent is offered as an expert on cause of death, medical diagnosis, and treatment. He states that he has been a pediatric surgeon for five years. Prior to that, he was an emergency room physician for eight years.

b. In Dr. Dent's opinion, the head injuries suffered by Gonzales were a result of being forcefully struck with a blunt object by a large man. Such a blow could easily have killed Gonzales.

c. Dent also believes that, given Epstein's psychological profile as a borderline sociopathic personality (a mental illness, but not a psychosis), Epstein "beyond a doubt" hit Gonzales, and had the "legal intent" to kill him.

Defense Evidence

1. The defendant, Epstein, will testify on direct examination as follows:

a. "I was in the Facade nightclub on the night of May 31st. I left around 11:30 p.m. Earlier in the evening, a customer I did not know challenged me to a fight. I didn't want to fight; I never do. So I walked away as I always do when challenged to a fight, which seems to be about every time I go to a nightclub."

b. "I lost my watch somewhere inside of the disco."

c. "I go to Facade often, and always leave at 11:30 p.m."

d. "I do not remember seeing Jorge at the disco."

2. On cross-examination, Epstein is asked the following questions. Which, if any, are permissible?

a. "Weren't you convicted of aggravated assault of your girlfriend in June of 2011?"

b. "You were convicted of disorderly conduct in 2007 and 2008, right?"

c. "Mr. Epstein, you wrote on a job application that you were certified as a longshoreman in 1991 when, in fact, you had been certified in 1999?"

d. "You stated to a friend prior to trial, 'I'd gone to the club that night and left around 2:00 a.m. because it was boring.' "

Problem #15-6: Transcript

The defendant is charged with selling stolen watches on the streets of San Antonio. At trial, the prosecution offers the testimony of Sam Spark, private eye, who will testify on direct examination as follows:

[State the most likely basis for each of the objections and the likely ruling by the court.]

PROSECUTOR: What happened on June 10, 2013, at approximately 3:00 p.m.?

A: The defendant walked up to me and said, "I will sell you this Cartier watch cheap; today only, $100. What do you say?"

1. What objection should defense counsel make to Sam's answer, and what is the likely ruling?

PROSECUTOR: What occurred after he made you that offer?

A: A police car arrived with its siren blaring and the defendant ran away.

2. What objection should defense counsel make to Sam's answer, and what is the likely ruling?

PROSECUTOR: Where did he go?

A: I'm not sure; I guess he hopped the fence and ran to the porch where he couldn't be found.

3. What objection should defense counsel make to Sam's answer, and what is the likely ruling?

PROSECUTOR: Did you ever see him again?

4. What objection should defense counsel make to this question, and what is the likely ruling?

A: Yeah. I saw him come around the other side of the building, and I pointed to the guy and said, "Look, officer, there is the guy who tried to sell me the watch! That's him."

5. What objection should defense counsel make to Sam's answer, and what is the likely ruling?

PROSECUTOR: After pointing at him, what did you do?

A: I backed away a couple of feet because the defendant looked like he was going to have a fit; I could see "guilty" written all over his face.

6. What objection should defense counsel make to Sam's answer, and what is the likely ruling?

On cross-examination, Sam testifies as follows:

DEFENSE COUNSEL: Last week, during a job interview, you told the owner of the Blue Parrot restaurant that you had prior experience working in restaurants, when you had none, isn't that right?

7. What objection should the prosecutor make to this question, and what is the likely ruling?

A: Well, uh, yes.

DEFENSE COUNSEL: You were convicted in 2010 of the possession of cocaine, weren't you?

8. What objection should the prosecutor make to this question, and what is the likely ruling?

A: Yes. That is correct.

DEFENSE COUNSEL: You have a pending charge against you for the misdemeanor, destruction of property, isn't that right?

9. What objection should the prosecutor make to this question, and what is the likely ruling?

A: Yes.

DEFENSE COUNSEL: You have 30% hearing loss in your right ear, correct?

10. What objection should the prosecutor make to this question, and what is the likely ruling?

A: Yes.

DEFENSE COUNSEL: The defendant's brother beat you up in a fight two years ago, right?

11. What objection should the prosecutor make to this question, and what is the likely ruling?

A: No, it was about even.

DEFENSE COUNSEL: You don't leave tips any time you eat at restaurants, do you?

12. What objection should the prosecutor make to this question, and what is the likely ruling?

A: No sir; I don't believe in it.

Problem #15-7: "The Sheriff"

Which of the following evidence is admissible, if any? Explain your answers.

1. Sheriff Sal, of a small Midwestern town, is sued for negligently running over and injuring the plaintiff, Penny, at a busy intersection. The defendant sheriff testifies on his own behalf. The sheriff states, "Why I told my deputy, Martin, soon after the accident that a woman darted out into the intersection quite suddenly, before I had a chance to hit the brakes."

2. The defendant, Sal, calls his friend, Marcy, to the witness stand to testify that Sal has a reputation for peacefulness in the community.

3. The plaintiff, Penny, then calls Wally Witness in her rebuttal case to testify that Sheriff Sal once had another person fraudulently take a history exam for him in college.

4. The plaintiff also calls Shirley in her rebuttal case to testify that Sheriff Sal has a reputation in the community for being a violent person.

5. After losing the above negligence action, a distraught Sheriff Sal drives home. His mind wanders and he is involved in a serious accident. The sheriff panics and leaves the scene to drive home. He lies down to take a nap. When he awakens, he reads a note left him by his wife: "I'm taking the car to the shop to fix the dents caused by the 'seagull.' No one will ever know what really happened. Love, W." The sheriff is subsequently charged with "reckless driving" and "leaving the scene of the accident." The prosecution offers the note against the sheriff.

Appendix

FEDERAL RULES OF EVIDENCE

Effective July 1, 1975, as amended to December 1, 2015, absent Congressional action

ARTICLE I.   GENERAL PROVISIONS

Rule 101.   Scope; Definitions

(a)   **Scope.** These rules apply to proceedings in United States courts. The specific courts and proceedings to which the rules apply, along with exceptions, are set out in Rule 1101.

(b)   **Definitions.** In these rules:

(1) "civil case" means a civil action or proceeding;

(2) "criminal case" includes a criminal proceeding;

(3) "public office" includes a public agency;

(4) "record" includes a memorandum, report, or data compilation;

(5) a "rule prescribed by the Supreme Court" means a rule adopted by the Supreme Court under statutory authority; and

(6) a reference to any kind of written material or any other medium includes electronically stored information.

(Amended, eff 10-1-87; 11-1-88; 12-1-93; 12-1-11)

Rule 102.   Purpose

These rules should be construed so as to administer every proceeding fairly, eliminate unjustifiable expense and delay, and promote the development of evidence law, to the end of ascertaining the truth and securing a just determination.

(Amended, eff 12-1-11)

Rule 103.   Rulings on Evidence

(a)   **Preserving a Claim of Error.** A party may claim error in a ruling to admit or exclude evidence only if the error affects a substantial right of the party and:

(1) if the ruling admits evidence, a party, on the record:

(A) timely objects or moves to strike; and

(B) states the specific ground, unless it was apparent from the context; or

(2) if the ruling excludes evidence, a party informs the court of its substance by an offer of proof, unless the substance was apparent from the context.

(b)   **Not Needing to Renew an Objection or Offer of Proof.** Once the court rules definitively on the record — either before or at trial — a party need not renew an objection or offer of proof to preserve a claim of error for appeal.

(c)   **Court's Statement About the Ruling; Directing an Offer of Proof.** The court may make any statement about the character or form of the evidence, the objection made, and the ruling. The court may direct that an offer of proof be made in question-and-answer form.

(d)   **Preventing the Jury from Hearing Inadmissible Evidence.** To the extent practicable, the court must conduct a jury trial so that inadmissible evidence is not suggested to the jury by any means.

(e)　Taking Notice of Plain Error. A court may take notice of a plain error affecting a substantial right, even if the claim of error was not properly preserved.

(Amended, eff 12-1-00; 12-1-11)

Rule 104.　Preliminary Questions

(a)　In General. The court must decide any preliminary question about whether a witness is qualified, a privilege exists, or evidence is admissible. In so deciding, the court is not bound by evidence rules, except those on privilege.

(b)　Relevance That Depends on a Fact. When the relevance of evidence depends on whether a fact exists, proof must be introduced sufficient to support a finding that the fact does exist. The court may admit the proposed evidence on the condition that the proof be introduced later.

(c)　Conducting a Hearing So That the Jury Cannot Hear It. The court must conduct any hearing on a preliminary question so that the jury cannot hear it if:

　　(1) the hearing involves the admissibility of a confession;

　　(2) a defendant in a criminal case is a witness and so requests; or

　　(3) justice so requires.

(d)　Cross-Examining a Defendant in a Criminal Case. By testifying on a preliminary question, a defendant in a criminal case does not become subject to cross-examination on other issues in the case.

(e)　Evidence Relevant to Weight and Credibility. This rule does not limit a party's right to introduce before the jury evidence that is relevant to the weight or credibility of other evidence.

(Amended, eff 10-1-87; 12-1-11)

Rule 105.　Limiting Evidence That Is Not Admissible Against Other Parties or for Other Purposes

If the court admits evidence that is admissible against a party or for a purpose — but not against another party or for another purpose — the court, on timely request, must restrict the evidence to its proper scope and instruct the jury accordingly.

(Amended, eff 12-1-11)

Rule 106.　Remainder of or Related Writings or Recorded Statements

If a party introduces all or part of a writing or recorded statement, an adverse party may require the introduction, at that time, of any other part — or any other writing or recorded statement — that in fairness ought to be considered at the same time.

(Amended, eff 10-1-87; 12-1-11)

ARTICLE II. JUDICIAL NOTICE

Rule 201. Judicial Notice of Adjudicative Facts

(a) Scope. This rule governs judicial notice of an adjudicative fact only, not a legislative fact.

(b) Kinds of Facts That May Be Judicially Noticed. The court may judicially notice a fact that is not subject to reasonable dispute because it:

(1) is generally known within the trial court's territorial jurisdiction; or

(2) can be accurately and readily determined from sources whose accuracy cannot reasonably be questioned.

(c) Taking Notice. The court:

(1) may take judicial notice on its own; or

(2) must take judicial notice if a party requests it and the court is supplied with the necessary information.

(d) Timing. The court may take judicial notice at any stage of the proceeding.

(e) Opportunity to Be Heard. On timely request, a party is entitled to be heard on the propriety of taking judicial notice and the nature of the fact to be noticed. If the court takes judicial notice before notifying a party, the party, on request, is still entitled to be heard.

(f) Instructing the Jury. In a civil case, the court must instruct the jury to accept the noticed fact as conclusive. In a criminal case, the court must instruct the jury that it may or may not accept the noticed fact as conclusive.

(Amended, eff 12-1-11)

ARTICLE III. PRESUMPTIONS IN CIVIL CASES

Rule 301. Presumptions in Civil Cases Generally

In a civil case, unless a federal statute or these rules provide otherwise, the party against whom a presumption is directed has the burden of producing evidence to rebut the presumption. But this rule does not shift the burden of persuasion, which remains on the party who had it originally.

(Amended, eff 12-1-11)

Rule 302. Applying State Law to Presumptions in Civil Cases

In a civil case, state law governs the effect of a presumption regarding a claim or defense for which state law supplies the rule of decision.

(Amended, eff 12-1-11)

ARTICLE IV. RELEVANCE AND ITS LIMITS

Rule 401. Test for Relevant Evidence

Evidence is relevant if:

(a) it has any tendency to make a fact more or less probable than it would be without the evidence; and

(b) the fact is of consequence in determining the action.

(Amended, eff 12-1-11)

Rule 402.   General Admissibility of Relevant Evidence

Relevant evidence is admissible unless any of the following provides otherwise:

- the United States Constitution;
- a federal statute;
- these rules; or
- other rules prescribed by the Supreme Court.

Irrelevant evidence is not admissible.

(Amended, eff 12-1-11)

Rule 403.   Excluding Relevant Evidence for Prejudice, Confusion, Waste of Time, or Other Reasons

The court may exclude relevant evidence if its probative value is substantially outweighed by a danger of one or more of the following: unfair prejudice, confusing the issues, misleading the jury, undue delay, wasting time, or needlessly presenting cumulative evidence.

(Amended, eff 12-1-11)

Rule 404.   Character Evidence; Crimes or Other Acts

(a)   Character Evidence.

(1) *Prohibited Uses.* Evidence of a person's character or character trait is not admissible to prove that on a particular occasion the person acted in accordance with the character or trait.

(2) *Exceptions for a Defendant or Victim in a Criminal Case.* The following exceptions apply in a criminal case:

(A) a defendant may offer evidence of the defendant's pertinent trait, and if the evidence is admitted, the prosecutor may offer evidence to rebut it;

(B) subject to the limitations in Rule 412, a defendant may offer evidence of an alleged victim's pertinent trait, and if the evidence is admitted, the prosecutor may:

(i) offer evidence to rebut it; and

(ii) offer evidence of the defendant's same trait; and

(C) in a homicide case, the prosecutor may offer evidence of the alleged victim's trait of peacefulness to rebut evidence that the victim was the first aggressor.

(3) *Exceptions for a Witness.* Evidence of a witness's character may be admitted under Rules 607, 608, and 609.

(b)   Crimes, Wrongs, or Other Acts.

(1) *Prohibited Uses.* Evidence of a crime, wrong, or other act is not admissible to prove a person's character in order to show that on a particular occasion the person acted in accordance with the character.

(2) *Permitted Uses; Notice in a Criminal Case.* This evidence may be admissible for another purpose, such as proving motive, opportunity, intent, preparation, plan, knowledge, identity, absence of mistake, or lack of accident. On request by a defendant in a criminal case, the prosecutor must:

(A) provide reasonable notice of the general nature of any such evidence that the prosecutor intends to offer at trial; and

(B) do so before trial — or during trial if the court, for good cause, excuses lack of pretrial notice.

(Amended, eff 10-1-87; 12-1-91; 12-1-00; 12-1-06; 12-1-11)

Rule 405. Methods of Proving Character

(a) By Reputation or Opinion. When evidence of a person's character or character trait is admissible, it may be proved by testimony about the person's reputation or by testimony in the form of an opinion. On cross-examination of the character witness, the court may allow an inquiry into relevant specific instances of the person's conduct.

(b) By Specific Instances of Conduct. When a person's character or character trait is an essential element of a charge, claim, or defense, the character or trait may also be proved by relevant specific instances of the person's conduct.

(Amended, eff 10-1-87; 12-1-11)

Rule 406. Habit; Routine Practice

Evidence of a person's habit or an organization's routine practice may be admitted to prove that on a particular occasion the person or organization acted in accordance with the habit or routine practice. The court may admit this evidence regardless of whether it is corroborated or whether there was an eyewitness.

(Amended, eff 12-1-11)

Rule 407. Subsequent Remedial Measures

When measures are taken that would have made an earlier injury or harm less likely to occur, evidence of the subsequent measures is not admissible to prove:

- negligence;
- culpable conduct;
- a defect in a product or its design; or
- a need for a warning or instruction.

But the court may admit this evidence for another purpose, such as impeachment or — if disputed — proving ownership, control, or the feasibility of precautionary measures.

(Amended, eff 12-1-97; 12-1-11)

Rule 408.   Compromise Offers and Negotiations

(a)   **Prohibited Uses.** Evidence of the following is not admissible — on behalf of any party — either to prove or disprove the validity or amount of a disputed claim or to impeach by a prior inconsistent statement or a contradiction:

(1) furnishing, promising, or offering — or accepting, promising to accept, or offering to accept — a valuable consideration in compromising or attempting to compromise the claim; and

(2) conduct or a statement made during compromise negotiations about the claim — except when offered in a criminal case and when the negotiations related to a claim by a public office in the exercise of its regulatory, investigative, or enforcement authority.

(b)   **Exceptions.** The court may admit this evidence for another purpose, such as proving a witness's bias or prejudice, negating a contention of undue delay, or proving an effort to obstruct a criminal investigation or prosecution.

(Amended, eff 12-1-06; 12-1-11)

Rule 409.   Offers to Pay Medical and Similar Expenses

Evidence of furnishing, promising to pay, or offering to pay medical, hospital, or similar expenses resulting from an injury is not admissible to prove liability for the injury.

(Amended, eff 12-1-11)

Rule 410.   Pleas, Plea Discussions, and Related Statements

(a)   **Prohibited Uses.** In a civil or criminal case, evidence of the following is not admissible against the defendant who made the plea or participated in the plea discussions:

(1) a guilty plea that was later withdrawn;

(2) a nolo contendere plea;

(3) a statement made during a proceeding on either of those pleas under Federal Rule of Criminal Procedure 11 or a comparable state procedure; or

(4) a statement made during plea discussions with an attorney for the prosecuting authority if the discussions did not result in a guilty plea or they resulted in a later-withdrawn guilty plea.

(b)   **Exceptions.** The court may admit a statement described in Rule 410(a)(3) or (4):

(1) in any proceeding in which another statement made during the same plea or plea discussions has been introduced, if in fairness the statements ought to be considered together; or

(2) in a criminal proceeding for perjury or false statement, if the defendant made the statement under oath, on the record, and with counsel present.

(Amended, 12-12-75; 4-30-79, eff 12-1-80; 12-1-11)

Rule 411.   Liability Insurance

Evidence that a person was or was not insured against liability is not admissible to prove whether the person acted negligently or otherwise wrongfully. But the court may admit this evidence for another purpose, such as proving a witness's bias or prejudice or proving agency, ownership, or control.

(Amended, eff 10-1-87; 12-1-11)

Rule 412.   Sex-Offense Cases: The Victim's Sexual Behavior or Predisposition

(a)   **Prohibited Uses.** The following evidence is not admissible in a civil or criminal proceeding involving alleged sexual misconduct:

(1) evidence offered to prove that a victim engaged in other sexual behavior; or

(2) evidence offered to prove a victim's sexual predisposition.

(b)   **Exceptions.**

(1)   *Criminal Cases.* The court may admit the following evidence in a criminal case:

(A) evidence of specific instances of a victim's sexual behavior, if offered to prove that someone other than the defendant was the source of semen, injury, or other physical evidence;

(B) evidence of specific instances of a victim's sexual behavior with respect to the person accused of the sexual misconduct, if offered by the defendant to prove consent or if offered by the prosecutor; and

(C) evidence whose exclusion would violate the defendant's constitutional rights.

(2)   *Civil Cases.* In a civil case, the court may admit evidence offered to prove a victim's sexual behavior or sexual predisposition if its probative value substantially outweighs the danger of harm to any victim and of unfair prejudice to any party. The court may admit evidence of a victim's reputation only if the victim has placed it in controversy.

(c)   **Procedure to Determine Admissibility.**

(1)   *Motion.* If a party intends to offer evidence under Rule 412(b), the party must:

(A) file a motion that specifically describes the evidence and states the purpose for which it is to be offered;

(B) do so at least 14 days before trial unless the court, for good cause, sets a different time;

(C) serve the motion on all parties; and

(D) notify the victim or, when appropriate, the victim's guardian or representative.

(2)   *Hearing.* Before admitting evidence under this rule, the court must conduct an in camera hearing and give the victim and parties a right to attend and be heard.

Unless the court orders otherwise, the motion, related materials, and the record of the hearing must be and remain sealed.

(d) Definition of "Victim." In this rule, "victim" includes an alleged victim.

(Effective 10-28-78; amended, eff 11-18-88; 12-1-94; 12-1-11)

Rule 413. Similar Crimes in Sexual-Assault Cases

(a) Permitted Uses. In a criminal case in which a defendant is accused of a sexual assault, the court may admit evidence that the defendant committed any other sexual assault. The evidence may be considered on any matter to which it is relevant.

(b) Disclosure to the Defendant. If the prosecutor intends to offer this evidence, the prosecutor must disclose it to the defendant, including witnesses' statements or a summary of the expected testimony. The prosecutor must do so at least 15 days before trial or at a later time that the court allows for good cause.

(c) Effect on Other Rules. This rule does not limit the admission or consideration of evidence under any other rule.

(d) Definition of "Sexual Assault." In this rule and Rule 415, "sexual assault" means a crime under federal law or under state law (as "state" is defined in 18 U.S.C. § 513) involving:

(1) any conduct prohibited by 18 U.S.C. chapter 109A;

(2) contact, without consent, between any part of the defendant's body — or an object — and another person's genitals or anus;

(3) contact, without consent, between the defendant's genitals or anus and any part of another person's body;

(4) deriving sexual pleasure or gratification from inflicting death, bodily injury, or physical pain on another person; or

(5) an attempt or conspiracy to engage in conduct described in subparagraphs (1)–(4).

(Effective 7-9-95; amended, eff 12-1-11)

Rule 414. Similar Crimes in Child-Molestation Cases

(a) Permitted Uses. In a criminal case in which a defendant is accused of child molestation, the court may admit evidence that the defendant committed any other child molestation. The evidence may be considered on any matter to which it is relevant.

(b) Disclosure to the Defendant. If the prosecutor intends to offer this evidence, the prosecutor must disclose it to the defendant, including witnesses' statements or a summary of the expected testimony. The prosecutor must do so at least 15 days before trial or at a later time that the court allows for good cause.

(c) Effect on Other Rules. This rule does not limit the admission or consideration of evidence under any other rule.

(d) Definition of "Child" and "Child Molestation." In this rule and Rule 415:

(1) "child" means a person below the age of 14; and

(2) "child molestation" means a crime under federal law or under state law (as "state" is defined in 18 U.S.C. § 513) involving:

(A) any conduct prohibited by 18 U.S.C. chapter 109A and committed with a child;

(B) any conduct prohibited by 18 U.S.C. chapter 110;

(C) contact between any part of the defendant's body — or an object — and a child's genitals or anus;

(D) contact between the defendant's genitals or anus and any part of a child's body;

(E) deriving sexual pleasure or gratification from inflicting death, bodily injury, or physical pain on a child; or

(F) an attempt or conspiracy to engage in conduct described in subparagraphs (A)–(E).

(Effective 7-9-95; amended, eff 12-1-11)

Rule 415. Similar Acts in Civil Cases Involving Sexual Assault or Child Molestation

(a)   Permitted Uses. In a civil case involving a claim for relief based on a party's alleged sexual assault or child molestation, the court may admit evidence that the party committed any other sexual assault or child molestation. The evidence may be considered as provided in Rules 413 and 414.

(b)   Disclosure to the Opponent. If a party intends to offer this evidence, the party must disclose it to the party against whom it will be offered, including witnesses' statements or a summary of the expected testimony. The party must do so at least 15 days before trial or at a later time that the court allows for good cause.

(c)   Effect on Other Rules. This rule does not limit the admission or consideration of evidence under any other rule.

(Effective 7-9-95; amended, eff 12-1-11)

ARTICLE V.   PRIVILEGES

Rule 501.   Privilege in General

The common law — as interpreted by United States courts in the light of reason and experience — governs a claim of privilege unless any of the following provides otherwise:

- the United States Constitution;
- a federal statute; or
- rules prescribed by the Supreme Court.

But in a civil case, state law governs privilege regarding a claim or defense for which state law supplies the rule of decision.

(Amended, eff 12-1-11)

Rule 502.   Attorney-Client Privilege and Work Product; Limitations on Waiver

The following provisions apply, in the circumstances set out, to disclosure of a communication or information covered by the attorney-client privilege or work-product protection.

(a)   Disclosure Made in a Federal Proceeding or to a Federal Office or Agency; Scope of a Waiver. When the disclosure is made in a federal proceeding or to a federal office or agency and waives the attorney-client privilege or work-product protection, the waiver extends to an undisclosed communication or information in a federal or state proceeding only if:

(1) the waiver is intentional;

(2) the disclosed and undisclosed communications or information concern the same subject matter; and

(3) they ought in fairness to be considered together.

(b)   Inadvertent Disclosure. When made in a federal proceeding or to a federal office or agency, the disclosure does not operate as a waiver in a federal or state proceeding if:

(1) the disclosure is inadvertent;

(2) the holder of the privilege or protection took reasonable steps to prevent disclosure; and

(3) the holder promptly took reasonable steps to rectify the error, including (if applicable) following Federal Rule of Civil Procedure 26(b)(5)(B).

(c)   Disclosure Made in a State Proceeding. When the disclosure is made in a state proceeding and is not the subject of a state-court order concerning waiver, the disclosure does not operate as a waiver in a federal proceeding if the disclosure:

(1) would not be a waiver under this rule if it had been made in a federal proceeding; or

(2) is not a waiver under the law of the state where the disclosure occurred.

(d)   Controlling Effect of a Court Order. A federal court may order that the privilege or protection is not waived by disclosure connected with the litigation pending before the court — in which event the disclosure is also not a waiver in any other federal or state proceeding.

(e)   Controlling Effect of a Party Agreement. An agreement on the effect of disclosure in a federal proceeding is binding only on the parties to the agreement, unless it is incorporated into a court order.

(f)   Controlling Effect of this Rule. Notwithstanding Rules 101 and 1101, this rule applies to state proceedings and to federal court-annexed and federal court-mandated arbitration proceedings, in the circumstances set out in the rule. And notwithstanding Rule 501, this rule applies even if state law provides the rule of decision.

(g) Definitions. In this rule:

(1) "attorney-client privilege" means the protection that applicable law provides for confidential attorney-client communications; and

(2) "work-product protection" means the protection that applicable law provides for tangible material (or its intangible equivalent) prepared in anticipation of litigation or for trial.

(Effective 12-19-2008; amended, eff 12-1-11)

ARTICLE VI. WITNESSES

Rule 601. Competency to Testify in General

Every person is competent to be a witness unless these rules provide otherwise. But in a civil case, state law governs the witness's competency regarding a claim or defense for which state law supplies the rule of decision.

(Amended, eff 12-1-11)

Rule 602. Need for Personal Knowledge

A witness may testify to a matter only if evidence is introduced sufficient to support a finding that the witness has personal knowledge of the matter. Evidence to prove personal knowledge may consist of the witness's own testimony. This rule does not apply to a witness's expert testimony under Rule 703.

(Amended, eff 10-1-87; 11-1-88; 12-1-11)

Rule 603. Oath or Affirmation to Testify Truthfully

Before testifying, a witness must give an oath or affirmation to testify truthfully. It must be in a form designed to impress that duty on the witness's conscience.

(Amended, eff 10-1-87; 12-1-11)

Rule 604. Interpreter

An interpreter must be qualified and must give an oath or affirmation to make a true translation.

(Amended, eff 10-1-87; 12-1-11)

Rule 605. Judge's Competency as a Witness

The presiding judge may not testify as a witness at the trial. A party need not object to preserve the issue.

(Amended, eff 12-1-11)

Rule 606. Juror's Competency as a Witness

(a) **At the Trial.** A juror may not testify as a witness before the other jurors at the trial. If a juror is called to testify, the court must give a party an opportunity to object outside the jury's presence.

(b) **During an Inquiry into the Validity of a Verdict or Indictment.**

(1) *Prohibited Testimony or Other Evidence.* During an inquiry into the validity of a verdict or indictment, a juror may not testify about any statement made or incident that occurred during the jury's deliberations; the effect of anything on that juror's or another juror's vote; or any juror's mental processes concerning the verdict or indictment. The court may not receive a juror's affidavit or evidence of a juror's statement on these matters.

(2) *Exceptions.* A juror may testify about whether:

(A) extraneous prejudicial information was improperly brought to the jury's attention;

(B) an outside influence was improperly brought to bear on any juror; or

(C) a mistake was made in entering the verdict on the verdict form.

(Amended, eff 10-1-87; 11-1-88; 12-1-03; 12-1-11)

Rule 607. Who May Impeach a Witness

Any party, including the party that called the witness, may attack the witness's credibility.

(Amended, eff 10-1-87; 12-1-11)

Rule 608. A Witness's Character for Truthfulness or Untruthfulness

(a) **Reputation or Opinion Evidence.** A witness's credibility may be attacked or supported by testimony about the witness's reputation for having a character for truthfulness or untruthfulness, or by testimony in the form of an opinion about that character. But evidence of truthful character is admissible only after the witness's character for truthfulness has been attacked.

(b) **Specific Instances of Conduct.** Except for a criminal conviction under Rule 609, extrinsic evidence is not admissible to prove specific instances of a witness's conduct in order to attack or support the witness's character for truthfulness. But the court may, on cross-examination, allow them to be inquired into if they are probative of the character for truthfulness or untruthfulness of:

(1) the witness; or

(2) another witness whose character the witness being cross-examined has testified about.

By testifying on another matter, a witness does not waive any privilege against self-incrimination for testimony that relates only to the witness's character for truthfulness.

(Amended, eff 10-1-87; 11-1-88; 12-1-03; 12-1-11)

Rule 609. Impeachment by Evidence of a Criminal Conviction

(a) **In General.** The following rules apply to attacking a witness's character for truthfulness by evidence of a criminal conviction:

(1) for a crime that, in the convicting jurisdiction, was punishable by death or by imprisonment for more than one year, the evidence:

(**A**) must be admitted, subject to Rule 403, in a civil case or in a criminal case in which the witness is not a defendant; and

(**B**) must be admitted in a criminal case in which the witness is a defendant, if the probative value of the evidence outweighs its prejudicial effect to that defendant; and

(2) for any crime regardless of the punishment, the evidence must be admitted if the court can readily determine that establishing the elements of the crime required proving — or the witness's admitting — a dishonest act or false statement.

(**b**) **Limit on Using the Evidence After 10 Years.** This subdivision (b) applies if more than 10 years have passed since the witness's conviction or release from confinement for it, whichever is later. Evidence of the conviction is admissible only if:

(1) its probative value, supported by specific facts and circumstances, substantially outweighs its prejudicial effect; and

(2) the proponent gives an adverse party reasonable written notice of the intent to use it so that the party has a fair opportunity to contest its use.

(**c**) **Effect of a Pardon, Annulment, or Certificate of Rehabilitation.** Evidence of a conviction is not admissible if:

(1) the conviction has been the subject of a pardon, annulment, certificate of rehabilitation, or other equivalent procedure based on a finding that the person has been rehabilitated, and the person has not been convicted of a later crime punishable by death or by imprisonment for more than one year; or

(2) the conviction has been the subject of a pardon, annulment, or other equivalent procedure based on a finding of innocence.

(**d**) **Juvenile Adjudications.** Evidence of a juvenile adjudication is admissible under this rule only if:

(1) it is offered in a criminal case;

(2) the adjudication was of a witness other than the defendant;

(3) an adult's conviction for that offense would be admissible to attack the adult's credibility; and

(4) admitting the evidence is necessary to fairly determine guilt or innocence.

(**e**) **Pendency of an Appeal.** A conviction that satisfies this rule is admissible even if an appeal is pending. Evidence of the pendency is also admissible.

(Amended, eff 10-1-87; 12-1-90; 12-1-06; 12-1-11)

Rule 610.   Religious Beliefs or Opinions

Evidence of a witness's religious beliefs or opinions is not admissible to attack or support the witness's credibility.

(Amended, eff 10-1-87; 12-1-11)

Rule 611.   Mode and Order of Examining Witnesses and Presenting Evidence

(a) Control by the Court; Purposes. The court should exercise reasonable control over the mode and order of examining witnesses and presenting evidence so as to:

(1) make those procedures effective for determining the truth;

(2) avoid wasting time; and

(3) protect witnesses from harassment or undue embarrassment.

(b) Scope of Cross-Examination. Cross-examination should not go beyond the subject matter of the direct examination and matters affecting the witness's credibility. The court may allow inquiry into additional matters as if on direct examination.

(c) Leading Questions. Leading questions should not be used on direct examination except as necessary to develop the witness's testimony. Ordinarily, the court should allow leading questions:

(1) on cross-examination; and

(2) when a party calls a hostile witness, an adverse party, or a witness identified with an adverse party.

(Amended, eff 10-1-87; 12-1-11)

Rule 612. Writing Used to Refresh a Witness's Memory

(a) Scope. This rule gives an adverse party certain options when a witness uses a writing to refresh memory:

(1) while testifying; or

(2) before testifying, if the court decides that justice requires the party to have those options.

(b) Adverse Party's Options; Deleting Unrelated Matter. Unless 18 U.S.C. § 3500 provides otherwise in a criminal case, an adverse party is entitled to have the writing produced at the hearing, to inspect it, to cross-examine the witness about it, and to introduce in evidence any portion that relates to the witness's testimony. If the producing party claims that the writing includes unrelated matter, the court must examine the writing in camera, delete any unrelated portion, and order that the rest be delivered to the adverse party. Any portion deleted over objection must be preserved for the record.

(c) Failure to Produce or Deliver the Writing. If a writing is not produced or is not delivered as ordered, the court may issue any appropriate order. But if the prosecution does not comply in a criminal case, the court must strike the witness's testimony or — if justice so requires — declare a mistrial.

(Amended, eff 10-1-87; 12-1-11)

Rule 613. Witness's Prior Statement

(a) Showing or Disclosing the Statement During Examination. When examining a witness about the witness's prior statement, a party need not show it or disclose its contents to the witness. But the party must, on request, show it or disclose its contents to an adverse party's attorney.

(b) **Extrinsic Evidence of a Prior Inconsistent Statement.** Extrinsic evidence of a witness's prior inconsistent statement is admissible only if the witness is given an opportunity to explain or deny the statement and an adverse party is given an opportunity to examine the witness about it, or if justice so requires. This subdivision (b) does not apply to an opposing party's statement under Rule 801(d)(2).

(Amended, eff 10-1-87; 11-1-88; 12-1-11)

Rule 614. Court's Calling or Examining a Witness

(a) **Calling.** The court may call a witness on its own or at a party's request. Each party is entitled to cross-examine the witness.

(b) **Examining.** The court may examine a witness regardless of who calls the witness.

(c) **Objections.** A party may object to the court's calling or examining a witness either at that time or at the next opportunity when the jury is not present.

(Amended, eff 12-1-11)

Rule 615. Excluding Witnesses

At a party's request, the court must order witnesses excluded so that they cannot hear other witnesses' testimony. Or the court may do so on its own. But this rule does not authorize excluding:

(a) a party who is a natural person;

(b) an officer or employee of a party that is not a natural person, after being designated as the party's representative by its attorney;

(c) a person whose presence a party shows to be essential to presenting the party's claim or defense; or

(d) a person authorized by statute to be present.

(Amended, eff 10-1-87; 11-1-88; 11-18-88; 12-1-98; 12-1-11)

ARTICLE VII. OPINIONS AND EXPERT TESTIMONY

Rule 701. Opinion Testimony by Lay Witnesses

If a witness is not testifying as an expert, testimony in the form of an opinion is limited to one that is:

(a) rationally based on the witness's perception;

(b) helpful to clearly understanding the witness's testimony or to determining a fact in issue; and

(c) not based on scientific, technical, or other specialized knowledge within the scope of Rule 702.

(Amended, eff 10-1-87; 12-1-00; 12-1-11)

Rule 702. Testimony by Expert Witnesses

A witness who is qualified as an expert by knowledge, skill, experience, training, or education may testify in the form of an opinion or otherwise if:

   (a) the expert's scientific, technical, or other specialized knowledge will help the trier of fact to understand the evidence or to determine a fact in issue;

   (b) the testimony is based on sufficient facts or data;

   (c) the testimony is the product of reliable principles and methods; and

   (d) the expert has reliably applied the principles and methods to the facts of the case.

(Amended, eff 12-1-00; 12-1-11)

Rule 703.   Bases of an Expert's Opinion Testimony

An expert may base an opinion on facts or data in the case that the expert has been made aware of or personally observed. If experts in the particular field would reasonably rely on those kinds of facts or data in forming an opinion on the subject, they need not be admissible for the opinion to be admitted. But if the facts or data would otherwise be inadmissible, the proponent of the opinion may disclose them to the jury only if their probative value in helping the jury evaluate the opinion substantially outweighs their prejudicial effect.

(Amended, eff 10-1-87; 12-1-00; 12-1-11)

Rule 704.   Opinion on an Ultimate Issue

   (a)   In General — Not Automatically Objectionable. An opinion is not objectionable just because it embraces an ultimate issue.

   (b)   Exception. In a criminal case, an expert witness must not state an opinion about whether the defendant did or did not have a mental state or condition that constitutes an element of the crime charged or of a defense. Those matters are for the trier of fact alone.

(Amended, eff 10-12-84; 12-1-11)

Rule 705.   Disclosing the Facts or Data Underlying an Expert's Opinion

Unless the court orders otherwise, an expert may state an opinion — and give the reasons for it — without first testifying to the underlying facts or data. But the expert may be required to disclose those facts or data on cross-examination.

(Amended, eff 10-1-87; 12-1-93; 12-1-11)

Rule 706.   Court-Appointed Expert Witnesses

   (a)   Appointment Process. On a party's motion or on its own, the court may order the parties to show cause why expert witnesses should not be appointed and may ask the parties to submit nominations. The court may appoint any expert that the parties agree on and any of its own choosing. But the court may only appoint someone who consents to act.

   (b)   Expert's Role. The court must inform the expert of the expert's duties. The court may do so in writing and have a copy filed with the clerk or may do so orally at a conference in which the parties have an opportunity to participate. The expert:

(1) must advise the parties of any findings the expert makes;

(2) may be deposed by any party;

(3) may be called to testify by the court or any party; and

(4) may be cross-examined by any party, including the party that called the expert.

(c) **Compensation.** The expert is entitled to a reasonable compensation, as set by the court. The compensation is payable as follows:

(1) in a criminal case or in a civil case involving just compensation under the Fifth Amendment, from any funds that are provided by law; and

(2) in any other civil case, by the parties in the proportion and at the time that the court directs — and the compensation is then charged like other costs.

(d) **Disclosing the Appointment to the Jury.** The court may authorize disclosure to the jury that the court appointed the expert.

(e) **Parties' Choice of Their Own Experts.** This rule does not limit a party in calling its own experts.

(Amended, eff 10-1-87; 12-1-11)

ARTICLE VIII. HEARSAY

Rule 801. Definitions That Apply to This Article; Exclusions from Hearsay

(a) **Statement.** "Statement" means a person's oral assertion, written assertion, or nonverbal conduct, if the person intended it as an assertion.

(b) **Declarant.** "Declarant" means the person who made the statement.

(c) **Hearsay.** "Hearsay" means a statement that:

(1) the declarant does not make while testifying at the current trial or hearing; and

(2) a party offers in evidence to prove the truth of the matter asserted in the statement.

(d) **Statements That Are Not Hearsay.** A statement that meets the following conditions is not hearsay:

(1) *A Declarant-Witness's Prior Statement.* The declarant testifies and is subject to cross-examination about a prior statement, and the statement:

(A) is inconsistent with the declarant's testimony and was given under penalty of perjury at a trial, hearing, or other proceeding or in a deposition;

(B) is consistent with the declarant's testimony and is offered:

(i) to rebut an express or implied charge that the declarant recently fabricated it or acted from a recent improper influence or motive in so testifying; or

(ii) to rehabilitate the declarant's credibility as a witness when attacked on another ground; or

(C) identifies a person as someone the declarant perceived earlier.

(2) ***An Opposing Party's Statement.*** The statement is offered against an opposing party and:

(A) was made by the party in an individual or representative capacity;

(B) is one the party manifested that it adopted or believed to be true;

(C) was made by a person whom the party authorized to make a statement on the subject;

(D) was made by the party's agent or employee on a matter within the scope of that relationship and while it existed; or

(E) was made by the party's coconspirator during and in furtherance of the conspiracy.

The statement must be considered but does not by itself establish the declarant's authority under (C); the existence or scope of the relationship under (D); or the existence of the conspiracy or participation in it under (E).

(Amended, eff 10-31-75; 10-1-87; 12-1-97; 12-1-11; 12-11-14)

Rule 802.   The Rule Against Hearsay

Hearsay is not admissible unless any of the following provides otherwise:

- a federal statute;
- these rules; or
- other rules prescribed by the Supreme Court.

(Amended, eff 12-1-11)

Rule 803.   Exceptions to the Rule Against Hearsay — Regardless of Whether the Declarant Is Available as a Witness

The following are not excluded by the rule against hearsay, regardless of whether the declarant is available as a witness:

(1) ***Present Sense Impression.*** A statement describing or explaining an event or condition, made while or immediately after the declarant perceived it.

(2) ***Excited Utterance.*** A statement relating to a startling event or condition, made while the declarant was under the stress of excitement that it caused.

(3) ***Then-Existing Mental, Emotional, or Physical Condition.*** A statement of the declarant's then-existing state of mind (such as motive, intent, or plan) or emotional, sensory, or physical condition (such as mental feeling, pain, or bodily health), but not including a statement of memory or belief to prove the fact remembered or believed unless it relates to the validity or terms of the declarant's will.

(4) ***Statement Made for Medical Diagnosis or Treatment.*** A statement that:

(A) is made for — and is reasonably pertinent to — medical diagnosis or treatment; and

(B) describes medical history; past or present symptoms or sensations; their inception; or their general cause.

(5) *Recorded Recollection.* A record that:

(A) is on a matter the witness once knew about but now cannot recall well enough to testify fully and accurately;

(B) was made or adopted by the witness when the matter was fresh in the witness's memory; and

(C) accurately reflects the witness's knowledge.

If admitted, the record may be read into evidence but may be received as an exhibit only if offered by an adverse party.

(6) *Records of a Regularly Conducted Activity.* A record of an act, event, condition, opinion, or diagnosis if:

(A) the record was made at or near the time by — or from information transmitted by — someone with knowledge;

(B) the record was kept in the course of a regularly conducted activity of a business, organization, occupation, or calling, whether or not for profit;

(C) making the record was a regular practice of that activity;

(D) all these conditions are shown by the testimony of the custodian or another qualified witness, or by a certification that complies with Rule 902(11) or (12) or with a statute permitting certification; and

(E) the opponent does not show that the source of information or the method or circumstances of preparation indicate a lack of trustworthiness.

(7) *Absence of a Record of a Regularly Conducted Activity.* Evidence that a matter is not included in a record described in paragraph (6) if:

(A) the evidence is admitted to prove that the matter did not occur or exist;

(B) a record was regularly kept for a matter of that kind; and

(C) the opponent does not show that the possible source of the information or other circumstances indicate a lack of trustworthiness.

(8) *Public Records.* A record or statement of a public office if:

(A) it sets out:

(i) the office's activities;

(ii) a matter observed while under a legal duty to report, but not including, in a criminal case, a matter observed by law-enforcement personnel; or

(iii) in a civil case or against the government in a criminal case, factual findings from a legally authorized investigation; and

(B) the opponent does not show that the source of information or other circumstances indicate a lack of trustworthiness.

(9) *Public Records of Vital Statistics.* A record of a birth, death, or marriage,

if reported to a public office in accordance with a legal duty.

(10) ***Absence of a Public Record.*** Testimony — or a certification under Rule 902 — that a diligent search failed to disclose a public record or statement if:

(A) the testimony or certification is admitted to prove that

(i) the record or statement does not exist; or

(ii) a matter did not occur or exist, if a public office regularly kept a record or statement for a matter of that kind; and

(B) in a criminal case, a prosecutor who intends to offer a certification provides written notice of that intent at least 14 days before trial, and the defendant does not object in writing within 7 days of receiving the notice—unless the court sets a different time for the notice or the objection.

(11) ***Records of Religious Organizations Concerning Personal or Family History.*** A statement of birth, legitimacy, ancestry, marriage, divorce, death, relationship by blood or marriage, or similar facts of personal or family history, contained in a regularly kept record of a religious organization.

(12) ***Certificates of Marriage, Baptism, and Similar Ceremonies.*** A statement of fact contained in a certificate:

(A) made by a person who is authorized by a religious organization or by law to perform the act certified;

(B) attesting that the person performed a marriage or similar ceremony or administered a sacrament; and

(C) purporting to have been issued at the time of the act or within a reasonable time after it.

(13) ***Family Records.*** A statement of fact about personal or family history contained in a family record, such as a Bible, genealogy, chart, engraving on a ring, inscription on a portrait, or engraving on an urn or burial marker.

(14) ***Records of Documents That Affect an Interest in Property.*** The record of a document that purports to establish or affect an interest in property if:

(A) the record is admitted to prove the content of the original recorded document, along with its signing and its delivery by each person who purports to have signed it;

(B) the record is kept in a public office; and

(C) a statute authorizes recording documents of that kind in that office.

(15) ***Statements in Documents That Affect an Interest in Property.*** A statement contained in a document that purports to establish or affect an interest in property if the matter stated was relevant to the document's purpose — unless later dealings with the property are inconsistent with the truth of the statement or the purport of the document.

(16) ***Statements in Ancient Documents.*** A statement in a document that is at least 20 years old and whose authenticity is established.

(17) Market Reports and Similar Commercial Publications. Market quotations, lists, directories, or other compilations that are generally relied on by the public or by persons in particular occupations.

(18) Statements in Learned Treatises, Periodicals, or Pamphlets. A statement contained in a treatise, periodical, or pamphlet if:

(A) the statement is called to the attention of an expert witness on cross-examination or relied on by the expert on direct examination; and

(B) the publication is established as a reliable authority by the expert's admission or testimony, by another expert's testimony, or by judicial notice.

If admitted, the statement may be read into evidence but not received as an exhibit.

(19) Reputation Concerning Personal or Family History. A reputation among a person's family by blood, adoption, or marriage — or among a person's associates or in the community — concerning the person's birth, adoption, legitimacy, ancestry, marriage, divorce, death, relationship by blood, adoption, or marriage, or similar facts of personal or family history.

(20) Reputation Concerning Boundaries or General History. A reputation in a community — arising before the controversy — concerning boundaries of land in the community or customs that affect the land, or concerning general historical events important to that community, state, or nation.

(21) Reputation Concerning Character. A reputation among a person's associates or in the community concerning the person's character.

(22) Judgment of a Previous Conviction. Evidence of a final judgment of conviction if:

(A) the judgment was entered after a trial or guilty plea, but not a nolo contendere plea;

(B) the conviction was for a crime punishable by death or by imprisonment for more than a year;

(C) the evidence is admitted to prove any fact essential to the judgment; and

(D) when offered by the prosecutor in a criminal case for a purpose other than impeachment, the judgment was against the defendant.

The pendency of an appeal may be shown but does not affect admissibility.

(23) Judgments Involving Personal, Family, or General History, or a Boundary. A judgment that is admitted to prove a matter of personal, family, or general history, or boundaries, if the matter:

(A) was essential to the judgment; and

(B) could be proved by evidence of reputation.

(24) [Other Exceptions.] [Transferred to Rule 807]

(Amended, eff 12-12-75; 10-1-87; 12-1-97; 12-1-00; 12-1-11; 12-1-14)

Rule 804.   Exceptions to the Rule Against Hearsay — When the Declarant Is Unavailable as a Witness

(a)   **Criteria for Being Unavailable.** A declarant is considered to be unavailable as a witness if the declarant:

(1)   is exempted from testifying about the subject matter of the declarant's statement because the court rules that a privilege applies;

(2)   refuses to testify about the subject matter despite a court order to do so;

(3)   testifies to not remembering the subject matter;

(4)   cannot be present or testify at the trial or hearing because of death or a then-existing infirmity, physical illness, or mental illness; or

(5)   is absent from the trial or hearing and the statement's proponent has not been able, by process or other reasonable means, to procure:

(A)   the declarant's attendance, in the case of a hearsay exception under Rule 804(b)(1) or (6); or

(B)   the declarant's attendance or testimony, in the case of a hearsay exception under Rule 804(b)(2), (3), or (4).

But this subdivision (a) does not apply if the statement's proponent procured or wrongfully caused the declarant's unavailability as a witness in order to prevent the declarant from attending or testifying.

(b)   **The Exceptions.** The following are not excluded by the rule against hearsay if the declarant is unavailable as a witness:

(1)   *Former Testimony.* Testimony that:

(A)   was given as a witness at a trial, hearing, or lawful deposition, whether given during the current proceeding or a different one; and

(B)   is now offered against a party who had — or, in a civil case, whose predecessor in interest had — an opportunity and similar motive to develop it by direct, cross-, or redirect examination.

(2)   *Statement Under the Belief of Imminent Death.* In a prosecution for homicide or in a civil case, a statement that the declarant, while believing the declarant's death to be imminent, made about its cause or circumstances.

(3)   *Statement Against Interest.* A statement that:

(A)   a reasonable person in the declarant's position would have made only if the person believed it to be true because, when made, it was so contrary to the declarant's proprietary or pecuniary interest or had so great a tendency to invalidate the declarant's claim against someone else or to expose the declarant to civil or criminal liability; and

(B)   is supported by corroborating circumstances that clearly indicate its trustworthiness, if it is offered in a criminal case as one that tends to expose the declarant to criminal liability.

(4)   *Statement of Personal or Family History.* A statement about:

(A) the declarant's own birth, adoption, legitimacy, ancestry, marriage, divorce, relationship by blood, adoption, or marriage, or similar facts of personal or family history, even though the declarant had no way of acquiring personal knowledge about that fact; or

(B) another person concerning any of these facts, as well as death, if the declarant was related to the person by blood, adoption, or marriage or was so intimately associated with the person's family that the declarant's information is likely to be accurate.

(5) *[Other Exceptions.]* [Transferred to Rule 807.]

(6) ***Statement Offered Against a Party That Wrongfully Caused the Declarant's Unavailability.*** A statement offered against a party that wrongfully caused — or acquiesced in wrongfully causing — the declarant's unavailability as a witness, and did so intending that result.

(Amended, eff 12-12-75; 10-1-87; 11-18-88; 12-1-97; 12-1-10; 12-1-11)

Rule 805. Hearsay Within Hearsay

Hearsay within hearsay is not excluded by the rule against hearsay if each part of the combined statements conforms with an exception to the rule.

(Amended, eff 12-1-11)

Rule 806. Attacking and Supporting the Declarant's Credibility

When a hearsay statement — or a statement described in Rule 801(d)(2)(C), (D), or (E) — has been admitted in evidence, the declarant's credibility may be attacked, and then supported, by any evidence that would be admissible for those purposes if the declarant had testified as a witness. The court may admit evidence of the declarant's inconsistent statement or conduct, regardless of when it occurred or whether the declarant had an opportunity to explain or deny it. If the party against whom the statement was admitted calls the declarant as a witness, the party may examine the declarant on the statement as if on cross-examination.

(Amended, eff 10-1-87; 12-1-97; 12-1-11)

Rule 807. Residual Exception

(a) In General. Under the following circumstances, a hearsay statement is not excluded by the rule against hearsay even if the statement is not specifically covered by a hearsay exception in Rule 803 or 804:

(1) the statement has equivalent circumstantial guarantees of trustworthiness;

(2) it is offered as evidence of a material fact;

(3) it is more probative on the point for which it is offered than any other evidence that the proponent can obtain through reasonable efforts; and

(4) admitting it will best serve the purposes of these rules and the interests of justice.

(b) Notice. The statement is admissible only if, before the trial or hearing, the proponent gives an adverse party reasonable notice of the intent to offer the statement and its particulars, including the declarant's name and address, so that the party has a fair opportunity to meet it.

(Effective 12-1-97; amended, eff 12-1-11)

ARTICLE IX.　AUTHENTICATION AND IDENTIFICATION

Rule 901.　Authenticating or Identifying Evidence

(a)　In General. To satisfy the requirement of authenticating or identifying an item of evidence, the proponent must produce evidence sufficient to support a finding that the item is what the proponent claims it is.

(b)　Examples. The following are examples only — not a complete list — of evidence that satisfies the requirement:

(1)　*Testimony of a Witness with Knowledge.* Testimony that an item is what it is claimed to be.

(2)　*Nonexpert Opinion About Handwriting.* A nonexpert's opinion that handwriting is genuine, based on a familiarity with it that was not acquired for the current litigation.

(3)　*Comparison by an Expert Witness or the Trier of Fact.* A comparison with an authenticated specimen by an expert witness or the trier of fact.

(4)　*Distinctive Characteristics and the Like.* The appearance, contents, substance, internal patterns, or other distinctive characteristics of the item, taken together with all the circumstances.

(5)　*Opinion About a Voice.* An opinion identifying a person's voice — whether heard firsthand or through mechanical or electronic transmission or recording — based on hearing the voice at any time under circumstances that connect it with the alleged speaker.

(6)　*Evidence About a Telephone Conversation.* For a telephone conversation, evidence that a call was made to the number assigned at the time to:

(A)　a particular person, if circumstances, including self-identification, show that the person answering was the one called; or

(B)　a particular business, if the call was made to a business and the call related to business reasonably transacted over the telephone.

(7)　*Evidence About Public Records.* Evidence that:

(A)　a document was recorded or filed in a public office as authorized by law; or

(B)　a purported public record or statement is from the office where items of this kind are kept.

(8)　*Evidence About Ancient Documents or Data Compilations.* For a document or data compilation, evidence that it:

(A)　is in a condition that creates no suspicion about its authenticity;

(B)　was in a place where, if authentic, it would likely be; and

(C) is at least 20 years old when offered.

(9) *Evidence About a Process or System.* Evidence describing a process or system and showing that it produces an accurate result.

(10) *Methods Provided by a Statute or Rule.* Any method of authentication or identification allowed by a federal statute or a rule prescribed by the Supreme Court. (Amended, eff 12-1-11)

Rule 902. Evidence That Is Self- Authenticating

The following items of evidence are self-authenticating; they require no extrinsic evidence of authenticity in order to be admitted:

(1) *Domestic Public Documents That Are Sealed and Signed.* A document that bears:

(A) a seal purporting to be that of the United States; any state, district, commonwealth, territory, or insular possession of the United States; the former Panama Canal Zone; the Trust Territory of the Pacific Islands; a political subdivision of any of these entities; or a department, agency, or officer of any entity named above; and

(B) a signature purporting to be an execution or attestation.

(2) *Domestic Public Documents That Are Not Sealed but Are Signed and Certified.* A document that bears no seal if:

(A) it bears the signature of an officer or employee of an entity named in Rule 902(1)(A); and

(B) another public officer who has a seal and official duties within that same entity certifies under seal — or its equivalent — that the signer has the official capacity and that the signature is genuine.

(3) *Foreign Public Documents.* A document that purports to be signed or attested by a person who is authorized by a foreign country's law to do so. The document must be accompanied by a final certification that certifies the genuineness of the signature and official position of the signer or attester — or of any foreign official whose certificate of genuineness relates to the signature or attestation or is in a chain of certificates of genuineness relating to the signature or attestation. The certification may be made by a secretary of a United States embassy or legation; by a consul general, vice consul, or consular agent of the United States; or by a diplomatic or consular official of the foreign country assigned or accredited to the United States. If all parties have been given a reasonable opportunity to investigate the document's authenticity and accuracy, the court may, for good cause, either:

(A) order that it be treated as presumptively authentic without final certification; or

(B) allow it to be evidenced by an attested summary with or without final certification.

(4) *Certified Copies of Public Records.* A copy of an official record — or a copy of a document that was recorded or filed in a public office as authorized by law — if the copy is certified as correct by:

(A) the custodian or another person authorized to make the certification; or

(B) a certificate that complies with Rule 902(1), (2), or (3), a federal statute, or a rule prescribed by the Supreme Court.

(5) *Official Publications.* A book, pamphlet, or other publication purporting to be issued by a public authority.

(6) *Newspapers and Periodicals.* Printed material purporting to be a newspaper or periodical.

(7) *Trade Inscriptions and the Like.* An inscription, sign, tag, or label purporting to have been affixed in the course of business and indicating origin, ownership, or control.

(8) *Acknowledged Documents.* A document accompanied by a certificate of acknowledgment that is lawfully executed by a notary public or another officer who is authorized to take acknowledgments.

(9) *Commercial Paper and Related Documents.* Commercial paper, a signature on it, and related documents, to the extent allowed by general commercial law.

(10) *Presumptions Under a Federal Statute.* A signature, document, or anything else that a federal statute declares to be presumptively or prima facie genuine or authentic.

(11) *Certified Domestic Records of a Regularly Conducted Activity.* The original or a copy of a domestic record that meets the requirements of Rule 803(6)(A)-(C), as shown by a certification of the custodian or another qualified person that complies with a federal statute or a rule prescribed by the Supreme Court. Before the trial or hearing, the proponent must give an adverse party reasonable written notice of the intent to offer the record — and must make the record and certification available for inspection — so that the party has a fair opportunity to challenge them.

(12) *Certified Foreign Records of a Regularly Conducted Activity.* In a civil case, the original or a copy of a foreign record that meets the requirements of Rule 902(11), modified as follows: the certification, rather than complying with a federal statute or Supreme Court rule, must be signed in a manner that, if falsely made, would subject the maker to a criminal penalty in the country where the certification is signed. The proponent must also meet the notice requirements of Rule 902(11).

(Amended effective 10-1-87; 11-1-88; 12-1-00; 12-1-11)

Rule 903. Subscribing Witness's Testimony

A subscribing witness's testimony is necessary to authenticate a writing only if required by the law of the jurisdiction that governs its validity.

(Amended eff 12-1-11)

ARTICLE X.   CONTENTS OF WRITINGS, RECORDINGS, AND PHOTOGRAPHS

Rule 1001. Definitions That Apply to This Article

In this article:

(a) A "writing" consists of letters, words, numbers, or their equivalent set down in any form.

(b) A "recording" consists of letters, words, numbers, or their equivalent recorded in any manner.

(c) A "photograph" means a photographic image or its equivalent stored in any form.

(d) An "original" of a writing or recording means the writing or recording itself or any counterpart intended to have the same effect by the person who executed or issued it. For electronically stored information, "original" means any printout — or other output readable by sight — if it accurately reflects the information. An "original" of a photograph includes the negative or a print from it.

(e) A "duplicate" means a counterpart produced by a mechanical, photographic, chemical, electronic, or other equivalent process or technique that accurately reproduces the original.

(Amended eff 12-1-11)

Rule 1002. Requirement of the Original

An original writing, recording, or photograph is required in order to prove its content unless these rules or a federal statute provides otherwise.

(Amended eff 12-1-11)

Rule 1003. Admissibility of Duplicates

A duplicate is admissible to the same extent as the original unless a genuine question is raised about the original's authenticity or the circumstances make it unfair to admit the duplicate.

(Amended eff 12-1-11)

Rule 1004. Admissibility of Other Evidence of Content

An original is not required and other evidence of the content of a writing, recording, or photograph is admissible if:

(a) all the originals are lost or destroyed, and not by the proponent acting in bad faith;

(b)   an original cannot be obtained by any available judicial process;

(c) the party against whom the original would be offered had control of the original; was at that time put on notice, by pleadings or otherwise, that the original would be a subject of proof at the trial or hearing; and fails to produce it at the trial or hearing; or

(d) the writing, recording, or photograph is not closely related to a controlling issue.

(Amended, eff 10-1-87; 12-1-11)

Rule 1005. Copies of Public Records to Prove Content

The proponent may use a copy to prove the content of an official record — or of a document that was recorded or filed in a public office as authorized by law — if these conditions are met: the record or document is otherwise admissible; and the copy is certified as correct in accordance with Rule 902(4) or is testified to be correct by a witness who has compared it with the original. If no such copy can be obtained by reasonable diligence, then the proponent may use other evidence to prove the content.

(Amended, eff 12-1-11)

Rule 1006.   Summaries to Prove Content

The proponent may use a summary, chart, or calculation to prove the content of voluminous writings, recordings, or photographs that cannot be conveniently examined in court. The proponent must make the originals or duplicates available for examination or copying, or both, by other parties at a reasonable time and place. And the court may order the proponent to produce them in court.

(Amended, eff 12-1-11)

Rule 1007.   Testimony or Statement of a Party to Prove Content

The proponent may prove the content of a writing, recording, or photograph by the testimony, deposition, or written statement of the party against whom the evidence is offered. The proponent need not account for the original.

(Amended, eff 10-1-87; 12-1-11)

Rule 1008.   Functions of the Court and Jury

Ordinarily, the court determines whether the proponent has fulfilled the factual conditions for admitting other evidence of the content of a writing, recording, or photograph under Rule 1004 or 1005. But in a jury trial, the jury determines — in accordance with Rule 104(b) — any issue about whether:

(a) an asserted writing, recording, or photograph ever existed;

(b) another one produced at the trial or hearing is the original; or

(c) other evidence of content accurately reflects the content.

(Amended, eff 12-1-11)

ARTICLE XI.   MISCELLANEOUS RULES

Rule 1101.   Applicability of the Rules

(a) **To Courts and Judges.** These rules apply to proceedings before:

- United States district courts;
- United States bankruptcy and magistrate judges;
- United States courts of appeals;
- the United States Court of Federal Claims; and
- the district courts of Guam, the Virgin Islands, and the Northern Mariana Islands.

(b) **To Cases and Proceedings.** These rules apply in:

- civil cases and proceedings, including bankruptcy, admiralty and maritime cases;

- criminal cases and proceedings; and

- contempt proceedings, except those in which the court may act summarily.

(c) Rules on Privilege. The rules on privilege apply to all stages of a case or proceeding.

(d) Exceptions. These rules — except for those on privilege — do not apply to the following:

(1) the court's determination, under Rule 104(a), on a preliminary question of a fact governing admissibility;

(2) grand-jury proceedings; and

(3) miscellaneous proceedings such as:

- extradition or rendition;

- issuing an arrest warrant, criminal summons, or search warrant;

- a preliminary examination in a criminal case;

- sentencing;

- granting or revoking probation or supervised release; and

- considering whether to release on bail or otherwise.

(e) Other Statutes and Rules. A federal statute or a rule prescribed by the Supreme Court may provide for admitting or excluding evidence independently from these rules.

(Amended, eff 12-12-75; 10-1-79; 10-1-82; 10-1-87; 11-1-88; 11-18-88; 12-1-93; 12-1-11)

Rule 1102. Amendments

These rules may be amended as provided in 28 U.S.C. § 2072.

(Amended, eff 12-1-91; 12-1-11)

Rule 1103. Title

These rules may be cited as the Federal Rules of Evidence.

(Amended, eff 12-1-11)

INDEX

[References are to sections.]

[References are to sections.]

CONFRONTATION CLAUSE—Cont.
Experts and confrontation, cases on—Cont.
  Williams v. Illinois . . . 11.04[C]
Face-to-face confrontation
  Child abuse witnesses . . . 11.07
  Sexual assault . . . 11.07
Problems, sample . . . 11.03; 11.05
Testimonial statements
  Generally . . . 11.02[B]
  Child abuse statements to non-police officer
    . . . 11.02[B][3]
  On-going emergency statements distinguished from
    . . . 11.02[B][1], [B][2]
Waiver of confrontation rights . . . 11.06

CRIMINAL CASE
Guilt in, probability evidence of . . . 4.02

D

DEAD MAN'S STATUTES
Generally . . . 8.01[B]

DECLARANT
Availability of declarant immaterial (See HEARSAY
  [FRE 801–807], subhead: Declarant, availability of
  immaterial)
Credibility, attacking and supporting . . . 10.04[D]
Hearsay by, definition of . . . 10.02[C]
Unavailability (See HEARSAY [FRE 801–807], sub-
  head: Unavailability a must, declarant's [FRE 804])

DIRECT EVIDENCE
Type of evidence, as . . . 1.05[B]

E

EVIDENCE (GENERALLY)
Generally . . . 1.07
Action, in . . . 1.03
Best evidence rule (See BEST EVIDENCE RULE)
Character (See CHARACTER EVIDENCE [FRE
  404–406])
Circumstantial evidence . . . 1.05[B]
Criminal case, probability evidence of guilt in
  . . . 4.02
Direct evidence . . . 1.05[B]
Excessive violence . . . 4.03
Federal rules . . . 12.03
Habit (See HABIT EVIDENCE [FRE 404–406])
Identifying relevant evidence
  Constructing inference chains . . . 3.02[C][1]
  Relevance and irrelevance, identifying line between
    . . . 3.02[C][2]
Meanings of
  Generally . . . 1.01
  Elaborating on . . . 1.04
Novel scientific evidence and expert witnesses
  . . . 9.02[C]
Privileged, definition of . . . 12.02[A]
Problems, sample . . . 1.06
Real evidence . . . 1.05[A]

EVIDENCE (GENERALLY)—Cont.
Relevant evidence, exclusions of (See RELEVANT
  EVIDENCE, EXCLUSIONS OF [FRE 407–415])
Representative evidence . . . 1.05[A]
Rules of (See RULES OF EVIDENCE)
Scientific evidence . . . 4.04
Testimonial evidence . . . 1.05[A]
Types of
  Direct and circumstantial evidence . . . 1.05[B]
  Real, representative, or testimonial evidence
    . . . 1.05[A]
Unfairly prejudicial (See UNFAIRLY PREJUDICIAL
  EVIDENCE [FRE 403])
Uses of . . . 1.01

EXAMINATION OF WITNESSES [FRE 607–615]
Generally . . . 7.01[A]; 7.04
Principles . . . 7.01[B]
Problems, sample . . . 7.03
Refreshing witness's memory . . . 7.01[F]
Stages of witness testimony . . . 7.01[D]
Testimonial objections . . . 7.01[E]
Viva voce, testimony . . . 7.01[C]
Witnesses . . . 7.01[C]

EXCESSIVE VIOLENCE
Evidence of . . . 4.03

EXPERT WITNESSES [FRE 702–706]
Generally . . . 9.02[A]
Bases of expert testimony
  Generally . . . 9.02[E]
  Reliance by experts, reasonable . . . 9.02[E][1]
Knowledge and expertise, specialized
  Generally . . . 9.02[D]
  Trier of fact, helping . . . 9.02[D][1]
Limits on subject matter of expert testimony [FRE
  702, 704]
  Generally . . . 9.02[D]
  Trier of fact, helping . . . 9.02[D][1]
Novel scientific evidence and . . . 9.02[C]
Qualifying experts . . . 9.02[B], [B][1]

EXTRINSIC IMPEACHMENT
Generally . . . 7.02[C]

F

FEDERAL RULES OF EVIDENCE
Privileges, approach to . . . 12.03

G

GUILTY PLEA [FRE 408–10]
Relevant evidence, exclusions of . . . 6.03

H

HABIT EVIDENCE [FRE 404–406]
Generally . . . 5.10; 5.12
Ethics rules . . . 5.11

[References are to sections.]

[References are to sections.]

[References are to sections.]

[References are to sections.]